TEXAS

HOME
COOKING

Happy Birthday '97

Love Dad

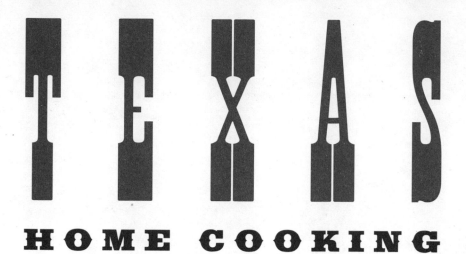

HOME COOKING

Cheryl Alters Jamison
and Bill Jamison

Illustrations by Paul Hoffman

HARVARD COMMON PRESS
Boston, Massachusetts

THE HARVARD COMMON PRESS
535 Albany Street
Boston, Massachusetts 02118

Printed in the United States of America

Library of Congress Cataloging-in-Publication Data

Jamison, Cheryl Alters.
    Texas home cooking / Cheryl Alters Jamison and Bill Jamison.
        p.   cm.
    Includes index.
    ISBN 1-55832-058-X (cloth). -- ISBN 1-55832-059-8 (paper).
    1. Cookery, American--Southwestern style. 2. Cookery--Texas.
I. Jamison, Bill. II. Title.
TX715.2.S69J36 1993
641.59764--dc20   93-29035

Special bulk-order discounts are available on this and other Harvard
Common Press books. Companies and organizations may purchase
books for premiums or for resale, or may arrange a custom edition,
by contacting the Marketing Director at the address above.

Cover design by Kathleen Herlihy-Paoli
Cover illustrations by Andrea Wisnewski
Text design by Bonni Leon
Interior illustrations by Paul Hoffman

10   9   8   7   6   5

For Heather, David, Colby, Tatia, and Britton,
a new generation of Texas cooks and eaters,
and Austin, Krista, B. J., Erik, and Kyle,
the next generation.

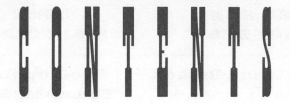

CONTENTS

What We've Got Cooking

"The very fact that I was in Texas for the sole purpose of eating contradicted my blind but resolute conviction that most food down there was, at best, some form of fodder consumed by asbestos-palated goat-ropers for no other reason than to sustain human life. . . . Well, to suggest that I now champion the cause of Texas cookery is a triumph of understatement—not to mention an admission of acute guilt and embarrassment. . . . I need no more convincing that the regional dishes of Texas are not only some of the most inspired in the nation but also some of the most delicious."

James Villas, **American Taste**

*V*illas is an unusual fellow, an eater with an open palate. Most of us would rather wrestle a rattlesnake than give up our food biases. This is particularly true when we're talking about Texas, a place where, as everyone knows, it's better to be bowlegged than subtle or fussy.

If you hear the words *Texas* and *cuisine* used in the same sentence in culinary circles, it's probably the punch line of a joke about Paris, Texas. Even many Texans aren't aware of their state's amazing food heritage and the real potentials of its home cooking. In a land of bull-riding cowboys, high-kicking cheerleaders, and bank-bamboozling millionaires, it's easy to conclude that what you trot out to the table is less pertinent than J. R. Ewing's virtues.

We're here to show you different. Texas has more to boast about in the kitchen, contrary to common belief, than in the boardroom, bedroom, or back room. When the traditional dishes of the state are fixed right, they're as full of flavor as foie gras and as hearty as a honky-tonk angel. We're going to treat you to some meals that'll make you—like James Villas, *Town and Country* editor—pull up a table in the amen corner of Lone Star cooking.

Down-Home Food for Contemporary Cooks

A century ago, in 1893, Alice O'Grady brought European refinement to Texas cooking. That was the year she opened the Argyle Hotel in San Antonio, the only place in the bumptious frontier state where ladies and gentlemen could count on proper manners and silverware. In her elegant restaurant, the Irish-born Miss O'Grady served a range of Continental delicacies plus mashed potatoes dyed pink, cakes with elaborate spun-sugar icing, and congealed salads with pastel-tinted cabbage garnishes.

Texas never quite ceases to be Texas, however gussied up it gets. This is particularly true of the food heritage, which has shown the same kind of staying power as a straight flush. Texans, along with everyone else, have grown more cosmopolitan over the past one hundred years but they have never spurned their roots. Like Alice O'Grady, they have simply incorporated new influences into old food traditions, blending with the contemporary world instead of bowing to it. The result at its best, as we feature it here, is down-home fare with flair, more complex and robust than in the past though true to its original inspiration. We don't dye our mashed potatoes, but they'll tickle you pink if you remember mashed potatoes as bland.

Even with our stress on depth and breadth of flavors, our focus remains real home cooking, not just hearty and familiar but also easy to prepare. We respect professional restaurant chefs and their cookbooks—and we're happy to apply their ideas and techniques when appropriate—but our recipes don't require a Star Wars kitchen, a staff of twenty, or a week of advance planning. Although we pursue and attain a good measure of the rich, multidimensional qualities we admire in fine restaurants, we don't do demi-glaces.

We also don't do hospital vittles. We take health considerations seriously, and usually manage to cut heavy or rich ingredients without sacrificing flavor, but if that doesn't work we don't compromise goodness. Our own approach is to eat less rather than decimate a beloved dish. Besides, plenty of our country favorites in the cookbook are already as light and wholesome as any health food—just more wonderfully savory. We frequently make a low-calorie, low-fat, and mighty tasty meal out of several of our "Supper and Side Dishes" served together.

Texas Home Cooking celebrates down-home American eats. The lineage is purely Lone Star in some cases, and much broader in others. Both sorts of dishes make up a delightful culinary legacy that's still as lively as a fiddle tune and as lingering as a slow dance at the prom.

Six Flags and a Dozen Flavors

Texas schools really hammer at the hard facts in history. There's no way you'll graduate from a Texas high school without knowing that the state was a part of six countries at different times. Except for the Republic of Texas, you don't have to name the nations, just count the flags.

Much more important, it seems to us, is the number of cultures that have contributed to the Texas heritage, a figure far higher than six. To begin appreciating the depth and diversity of the state's traditional cooking you need to tally the sources—national, ethnic, and social. Even if we ignore important groups of nineteenth-century settlers that had little lasting influence on the food—French, Italian, and Japanese, among others—the list of peoples who made a difference is impressive. You have to look seriously at Mexicans, Upper South frontiersmen, plantation Southerners, Africans, New Orleans Creoles, Cajuns, Czechs, Germans, and cowboys of all hues.

By the nineteenth century, each group established a culinary legacy that not only has survived to the present, but also at some point passed into general acceptance. Today it's easy to imagine a Texan of any background having a Czech kolache for breakfast, a Mexican enchilada for lunch, and for dinner, a Cajun étouffée washed down with a Bavarian beer and finished off with a Southern pie. With the possible exception of New Orleans, no place in the country has benefited so much from such an extraordinary mingling of food cultures. This culinary diversity is a side of Texas many people don't know, and one that we'll explore in the recipe chapters through hundreds of anecdotes, tall tales, blatant lies, and plain truths.

Fun Food

We'll also tell stories about a more playful side of Texas eats, about delightfully outlandish people, unbelievable places, loony dishes, and crazy cook-offs. You won't hear Texans talk about the state's "cuisine," because that would make the food sound stuffy and boring. Texans want to have fun cooking and they want to have fun eating, ambitions they realize with rare zeal and zaniness.

We hope to convey that enthusiasm in the pages ahead. *Texas Home Cooking* is downright serious about enjoying food, about relishing it as an adventure, a sensuous thrill. That we can turn eating into a frolic is, after all, one of the main ways humans differ from other animals. Let's make the most of it, Texas style, and set our lips to rejoicing.

Old Truths for
New Times

*K*nowledge can be a troublesome thing—hard to obtain and slippery to hold, but quick to kick you in the head when you turn your back. That's what has happened with traditional home cooking in Texas and the rest of the United States. Our grandparents, and their grandparents before them, figured out a lot of ways to achieve peak food flavor with the ingredients and implements at hand. Acquired over generations, that knowledge disappeared as quickly as a pecan pie at Thanksgiving after Americans learned new truths in recent decades about convenience foods, fast cooking methods, international cuisines, and healthy eating.

Then comes the kick. Our interest in freshness results in a rediscovery of regional cooking. Increased global awareness reawakens a sense of self and revives appreciation for local seasonings. The monotony of fast and frozen food makes us yearn for the taste of a down-home meal and the creativity of the kitchen. Grandmother's ghost moves into the microwave.

Now, to get that old flavor we want, we have to relearn or at least remember the old truths of down-home cooking, the how-tos and why-fors of cast iron, the stockpot, and buttermilk. Throughout the recipe chapters, we give scores of "Technique Tips" about specific dishes, but before you put anything on the stove you need to review some general principles that apply broadly to the style of cooking. These are hoary homilies rather than fresh facts, though a teaspoon of this home-kitchen savvy may contain more real flavor than a cup of culinary-academy skill.

Buoyed by Buttermilk

Some Americans look at buttermilk as an heirloom oddity, but in Texas it's still an important ingredient in traditional cooking, a vital agent for flavoring, baking, and marinating. Adding vinegar or lemon juice to regular milk, as many books suggest, makes a poor substitute.

Originally buttermilk was a by-product of butter. The churning motion made the butterfat separate from the whole milk and solidify. The remaining liquid, slightly tart, was called the buttermilk. Today's commercial buttermilk is made by adding a special bacterial culture to low-fat or non-fat milk so that it thickens and develops a tangy taste.

Years ago resourceful cooks found that buttermilk added moistness and a rich aroma to baked goods, and also promoted even, golden browning. Before the days of baking powder, when baking soda was the predominant leavening, an acid was required to release the carbon dioxide that forced the dough or batter to rise. Buttermilk provided the catalyst for the reaction, and still does in many Texas favorites, including buttermilk biscuits and German chocolate cake.

Buttermilk is also a miracle marinade. It enhances a range of fried dishes, including chicken-fried steak, contributing both flavor and moisture to the succulence sought beneath the crust. Used with game, buttermilk breaks down tough tissues, neutralizes gaminess, and again adds moistness to what is often lean, dry meat.

The Spice of Life

Traditional Texas cooking relies on a broad range of seasonings, many of them associated in the past exclusively with one ethnic tradition. Over time most of these spices, sauces, and other flavoring agents drifted loose from their roots and began livening up other local culinary styles. As our recipes demonstrate, you find a distinctive blend of seasonings in Texas food today, producing dishes that are more assertive and multidimensional than the same dish was a generation ago or similar dishes are now in other parts of the country.

CHILES AND CHILI POWDER

Chile and chili are such hot topics in Texas that even the spelling is a hell-raising issue. Following the generally accepted custom, we use the *e* on the end in referring to the capsicum plant and its pods and the *i* in talking about the official state dish of Texas, chili con carne, and related products. In recent years some Lone Star aficionados have staged a mock war with New Mexico, claiming that even their neighbors' famous capsicums should be spelled with an *i*, but the clamor is more of a marketing gambit than a language lecture.

Spanish and Mexican settlers taught other Texans the love of chiles as far back as the last century. The fruit remains a primary element of Tex-Mex cooking, and is certainly the core of chili, but chile also finds its way into almost every kind of cooking in the state. Today Texas farmers grow about 120 varieties of chile, which range from mild to fiery and come fresh, dried, frozen, pickled, smoked, and canned.

Much of the dried chile used in Texas cooking comes as a part of chili powder, a mixture of one or more types of chile with cumin and other spices. For the best and freshest chili powder, make your own from the recipe on page 135. If you're buying it packaged, look for blends with little or no salt and a full, slightly sweet taste. A prime powder should warm your tongue but not scorch it. Our recipes usually state a preference for the Gebhardt's brand, which is sold nationally, though a number of other Texas companies make fine products that have more limited distribution. Chili "seasonings" or "mixes" go a step further than powders, combining spices with onions, flour thickeners, and other ingredients.

Ground dried red chile, called for in many recipes, comes mostly from two similar chiles, the specially bred New Mexican pod, sometimes called a long red, and the more fruity and chocolate-like ancho. Usually a bit hotter than chili powder, and deeper red in color, the ground pods provide a rich, pure chile flavor. You can find them ready to use in packaged form, but when chile is the main flavor in a dish, you may want to grind your own dried whole pods rather than relying on a pre-ground product. Grinding your own takes only a few minutes and usually enhances the dish to some degree. Remove the stems and seeds from dried whole pods, toast the pods briefly in the oven at 300° F until they are lightly crisped, break them into several pieces, and then grind them in a blender. Two other less commonly used red chiles, mulatos and pasillas, offer similar amounts of heat and can be prepared in the same fashion.

A number of hotter chiles also come most commonly in a dried red form. The pea-sized chiltepins, which grow wild throughout southern Texas and other areas of the Southwest, and the closely related and equally diminutive pequíns both pack an amazing amount of firepower into a small shell. Two other cousins, chile de árbol and cayenne, add similar amounts of heat. Traditionally, chile de árbol is more common in dishes with Mexican roots and cayenne in those from Cajun country. At the mild end of the capsicum heat scale, paprika brings a sweet, earthy flavor to food rather than warmth, though some brands of the ground spice are virtually tasteless. Normally you find cayenne and paprika already powdered, and chiltepins, chiles pequíns, and chiles de árbols as dried pods that can be easily crushed with a mortar and pestle. With any of these or other dried chiles, look for a source that replenishes its supply frequently and buy just what you can use in a few months, keeping it in a cool, dry place.

Fresh chiles are typically used in their less mature green form, though one West Texas favorite, the güero or banana pepper, is used yellow-ripe. It's on the same heat level as the more familiar jalapeño, which is close to the center of the chile scale overall. Serranos are hotter than jalapeños, but can be used interchangeably in lesser amounts.

Definitely sharp but not incendiary, jalapeños became a popular accent flavor in Texas cooking several decades ago. They now appear in a variety of guises in addition to fresh. A number of companies pickle them in a liquid that makes a great marinade, and some outfits smoke them to make chipotles, which are sold dried or canned in a heady adobo sauce.

Fresh New Mexican green chiles, sometimes known as long greens or Anaheims, vary in heat, but all are milder than jalapeños and more robust and earthy in flavor. Along with poblanos, an acceptable substitute, they need to be roasted to remove the tough skin. Put the whole chiles in a single layer on a grill or on a cookie sheet beneath a broiler, and heat them until they are blistered and uniformly darkened. Transfer them to a sturdy plastic bag to steam, which loosens the skin and makes it easier to peel after the chiles are cool enough to handle. Remove the stems and seeds, and cut the pods into bite-size chunks. In many areas of the country, you can buy chopped frozen green chile without sacrificing too much of the fresh flavor, but avoid the bland canned variety unless nothing else is available.

In working with any chiles, but especially with the hotter varieties, wear rubber gloves if your skin irritates easily. Always refrain from touching your eyes, contact lenses, lips, or other sensitive body parts.

THE TRINITY GANG

Some Chinese chefs refer to a quartet of their favorite seasonings—garlic, ginger, green onion, and chile—as the Gang of Four. Texans have a Trinity Gang of their own—cumin, oregano, and garlic—that's a remarkably close cousin when you add chile to the trio, as you do in chili con carne and many other dishes.

Indigenous to the Southwest, cumin or *comino* (the Spanish name often used in Texas) comes in seed and powdered form. Serious Lone Star cooks buy the seeds, toast them in a heavy skillet for a couple of minutes, and crush them with a mortar and pestle or a spice mill, a process that most fully releases the earthy flavor.

The preferred oregano is the Mexican variety, which is more herbaceous in taste than the European alternative, an acceptable substitute. Most of our recipes containing garlic call for it fresh, except in dry mixes. Sometimes we suggest roasting the fresh garlic, to sweeten and mellow its taste. To do this, place individual cloves, with skins on, in a heavy skillet over low heat, and turn them until the skins darken on all sides and the cloves soften.

SASSY SAUCES

Texas cooks may use Louisiana-style hot pepper sauce even more than their neighbors on the other side of the Sabine. The king of the sauces, Tabasco, is so deeply entrenched in the state that the brand name appears frequently in Lone Star recipes. The McIlhenny Company makes this vintage liquid lightning by mashing Tabasco chiles with salt, aging the mixture in oak like a fine wine or whiskey, and combining it with vinegar before bottling. A number of competitors offer similar products based on other chiles, and most are adequate substitutes for Tabasco.

Texans also go for condiments that combine sweet and heat, incorporating them in everything from appetizers to meat marinades. Sugar and spice mix smartly in jalapeño jellies, horseradish-tinged Jezebel sauce, ketchup-with-a-kick chili sauce, and specialty items like D. L. Jardine's Texapeppa, a cousin of Jamaican Pickapeppa sauce. We give recipes for some of these and similar foods, and in "Mail-Order Sources" (pages 551–556) we list outlets for more.

Salsas are even bigger than other sauces in the state and more widely available in groceries and by mail. Much more than a dip, they flavor fried eggs, baked potatoes, our Pollo Kiev, and probably someone's yogurt. Our trio of recipes cover salsa basics, but in Texas experimentation is the essence of the dish and its uses.

Many Texas recipes gain pungency from mustard and horseradish, flavors popularized in the state by German and other central European settlers. A range of mustards are used. The purest taste comes from finely ground seeds in the form of powdered mustard, made usually with white or yellow seeds rather than the brown or black seeds found in Asian cooking. We have a preference for Colman's, in either the mild blend or the hotter "double superfine."

All-American yellow mustard, the hotdog condiment, appears in some dishes. A blend of the mildest seeds with turmeric for color, it provides a little mustard taste mixed with the tang of vinegar. A variation, jalapeño mustard, is becoming common in Texas recipes. It's available in many stores and by mail, but you can easily make your own by chopping a tablespoon (more or less, to taste) of pickled jalapeños and stirring them into a six-ounce jar of your favorite yellow mustard. Jalapeño mustard will keep indefinitely.

Zestier and deeper in flavor, prepared brown mustard is truer to central European roots. Creole mustard, developed by German Creoles in Louisiana, is the brown variety with horseradish and sometimes a touch of chile added. We especially like Zatarain's and McIlhenny's.

Native to central Europe, the horseradish root is more closely related to mustard than to horses or radishes. Most Texas recipes call for it prepared, which means grated and bottled with vinegar. Don't buy more than you plan to use in six months, because it can turn bitter. If you're fortunate enough to find the fresh root, it can be grated as needed and mixed with just enough white vinegar to bind it.

The Staff of Life

Few people today appreciate the tremendous importance of cornbread and biscuits on the American frontier. Without cornbread the state of Texas probably would have starved before it was born, and without biscuits the cowboy certainly would have had many more discouraging words about his home on the range.

Cornmeal and wheat flour, the basic ingredients of these pioneer staples, remain central components of Texas cooking. Get good and appropriate versions of each. Stone-ground cornmeal is preferable to steel-ground, the most common method of commercial processing. A medium-grind meal works best in cornbread, an extra-fine grind in spoonbread, and each makes an ideal coating for different fried dishes. We think the Adams Milling Company in Dothan, Alabama, produces some of the country's top cornmeal, though Arrowhead Mills of Hereford, Texas, comes very close and distributes more widely nationwide. Keep cornmeal in the freezer if you don't use it up quickly.

Grits and masa harina are also important ground-corn products. They come from dried hominy or pozole, made by treating corn with the mineral lime, or lye, which removes the hulls from the kernels and turns the kernels glutinous. In eastern Texas people grind the dried kernels coarsely into grits, and in the west they grind it more finely into masa harina, the basis of corn tortillas and tamales. With either, as with cornmeal, stone-ground varieties without preservatives are best. Again, keep them in the freezer or use them pronto.

Most Texas wheat is the hard red winter variety, which makes a superlative flour for yeast-bread baking, first popularized in the state by German and other central European settlers. The wheat's high gluten content helps form a strong but elastic dough. Arrowhead Mills makes an excellent minimally processed version of this flour distributed throughout the United States.

Biscuits and pie crusts require a low-gluten flour for tender, flaky results. Since biscuits were an import to Texas from Upper South settlers, it's not surprising that the finest flour for them still comes from Tennessee. White Lily Flour, available at grocery stores throughout the South and by mail, is ground from soft red winter wheat, which makes a less absorbent flour than hard varieties. It's so powder-like that it can be substituted for cake flour. While many people like the self-rising version of White Lily, with leavening and salt already added, we prefer the all-purpose alternative.

Standard all-purpose flours were developed to combine the best qualities of low-gluten soft wheat and high-gluten hard wheat, making a product suitable for a range of cooking needs. We prefer other flours for the specialized purposes mentioned above, but all-purpose flours work fine in most other situations.

Long Sweetin'

Americans used to distinguish between two types of sweetening, long and short. Today we rely heavily on the short style—such as sugar and honey—and tend to ignore the heavier flavoring potential of long sweeteners like molasses and cane syrup, both sugar-cane products.

Molasses is a brownish-black liquid produced by boiling the cane juice and extracting the sugar crystals. Successive boilings make light, dark, or blackstrap molasses. Choose dark, unsulphured varieties for a deep flavor in beans, marinades, gingerbread, and other baked goods. Blackstrap has become a fad in some circles, but we prefer leaving it to the cattle. Sorghum, another dark syrup, gets confused with molasses. Made from sorghum cane, a cereal grain, it's sweeter than molasses and something of an acquired taste.

Cane syrup comes from sugar cane ground to collect the juice, which is then cooked down until it's thick and golden brown. Harder to locate these days than molasses, cane syrup tastes milder and sweeter, though it's more full-bodied and less cloying than corn syrup, the usual modern substitute. McIlhenny cane syrup gets decent national distribution.

Cast in Iron

You can't cook chili in an aluminum pot or fried chicken in a stainless-steel skillet. It's technically possible, to be sure, but downright disrespectful of the food. Many traditional dishes simply taste best when cooked in cast iron, where they were usually born. If you didn't inherit a set of cast-iron pans, invest in at least one large all-purpose cast-iron skillet and set your mind on other pieces for the future, including a Dutch oven with a tight-fitting lid.

A cast-iron skillet allows you to fry anything short of a whale, but it can also do much more. Use it to toast spices like cumin seeds and to roast garlic cloves. For baking, cast-iron pans work better than others in developing crisp crusts on cornbread and caramelizing sugar on pineapple upside-down cakes.

If you're working with new cast iron, season it first. Rub the pan inside and out with lard, Crisco, or vegetable oil, and heat the pan in a 350° F oven for about an hour. Over the next few days, as time allows, repeat the process. After you start using a pan, clean it mainly with water and a sponge. Try to avoid using soap, which can undermine the effect of the seasoning. To guard against rust, always dry the pan with heat, either on the burner of the stove or in a warm oven.

Into the Frying Pan

Except for two vegetarians in Oregon, all the cooks in the country think they know how to fry food. The vast majority are wrong. Whether they are pan frying (with just enough fat to come up the sides of the food) or deep frying (where the food is completely submerged in oil), most Americans don't take full advantage of the taste and texture potentials in this method of cooking. When done right, frying is one of the most flavorful ways of preparing food, but all too often we settle for dishes that are greasy, soggy, or gummy instead of pert and crispy, for something that could have been baked to the same crunchiness, and for bites that collapse rather than burst beneath their crust.

In the recipes we give specific advice about frying various foods, but here we want to emphasize two important considerations for all fry cooking. First, never reduce the amount of oil called for in a recipe on the assumption you'll cut your intake of fat this way. Just the opposite would happen, because every dish requires a proper quantity of oil for the coating immediately to form a seal around the filling, trapping moisture inside the food and keeping grease outside, in the pan.

Second, make sure the oil is at the proper temperature when you start and throughout the frying. If the oil isn't hot enough, the food will absorb it, leaving a hard and greasy crust. If the oil is too hot, the coating will remain gummy inside and won't adhere well to the food. Don't overcrowd a frying pan, which would result in uneven cooking temperatures. It's better to cook in two or more batches rather than to rush to get everything done at once. In deep frying, and some other situations where the amount of oil is adequate, use a thermometer. Let the oil get ten degrees hotter than needed before adding the food, which will drop the oil temperature. Recheck the temperature if you cook successive batches of food.

The Oil Business

West Texas wildcatters aren't the only people whose fortunes rise and fall with oil. A home cook seeking real flavor and quality must know the basic properties of a wide range of oils and fats, even some currently in low esteem.

Most traditional recipes from the past used large amounts of saturated fat, well beyond what was useful for flavor. We have reduced the quantities significantly, and we have eliminated meat fat and hydrogenated oils entirely when they contribute little or nothing to the taste and texture of a dish. In many cases, however, saturated fat still works better in one way or another than monosaturated or polyunsaturated oils. Rather than dilute a dish, we leave it to you to moderate your intake of rich foods according to your needs. You can't do that, though, without understanding the options and their attributes.

GOING WHOLE HOG

"Hog's lard is the very oil that moves the machinery of life," according to Dr. John S. Wilson in *Godey's Lady's Book* in 1860. Few would maintain that view today, but we shouldn't completely dismiss lard, the rendered and clarified fat from pork. If you want the ultimate flakiness in biscuits, pie crusts, and pastries, you need the richness of lard, and its flavor adds considerably to some dishes like refried beans.

Most of the lard on the market now is processed to remove its naturally strong taste, leaving a mild nuttiness. Its consistency is similar to that of vegetable shortening. Although flavorful for frying, lard can't handle prolonged high temperatures or any reuse. Depending on the processing, it may be found in the supermarket at room temperature beside the vegetable shortening or in the refrigerated section near the butter. Keep it tightly wrapped in the refrigerator since it absorbs other flavors readily.

Salt pork and fatback provide a little lubrication to some traditional dishes and are, in small amounts, good for flavoring. Salt pork is cut from the sides or belly of the pig. It is salt-cured, like bacon, but not smoked. Fatback comes from the hog's backside and is not salted. Salt pork is usually simmered in water before use to eliminate some of its harsh salinity. Once that is done, it can be used interchangeably with fatback in most dishes. At the store look for either beside the bacon, or ask the butcher for a chunk. Fatback keeps about a week and salt pork two or three times longer. In Texas cooking, they commonly enhance greens, dried and fresh beans, and black-eyed peas.

Bacon drippings find broader application, flavoring a range of traditional dishes. Look for slab bacon that has been well smoked and is sliced thick. Texas slab bacon often comes with a black-pepper coating, a significant plus worth seeking out. Although your grandmother may have kept bacon drippings in a jar on the stove, it's better to keep any grease that you strain off meat in a closed jar in the refrigerator.

CATTLE CALL

The most flavorful beef fat is suet, a solid fat from the kidneys and loins. It was immensely popular in Texas cooking—particularly on the range—until recent decades, and it still has strong supporters in some parts of the state. We seldom use it, but if you want to give it a try, you can get it from your butcher. Suet keeps about a week.

Many nineteenth-century Texas visitors complained about the lack of butter in the state, despite the abundance of cattle, which were raised for beef instead of dairy products. Butter didn't catch on for cooking or anything else until it became widely available early in this century. If a recipe calls for any significant amount of butter, use the unsalted kind for a more delicate taste but be aware that it will spoil as quickly as a gallon of milk.

VEGETABLE SHORTENINGS AND OILS

Crisco brought out vegetable shortening about the same time that Texas stores started stocking much butter. Few places greeted the new product with such enthusiasm as the Lone Star State. A partially hydrogenated blend of vegetable oils, shortening turns semisolid at room temperature, making it a long-lasting, odorless alternative to lard. We think the original brand is still the best. A mixture of soybean and cottonseed oils, it stands up to prolonged cooking times and some careful reuse, and also fries some foods, like chicken, better than any other product.

Shortening also has beneficial properties in baking, though some people use it in too large a quantity, leaving a discernibly dull taste in baked goods. Avoid this by combining shortening with lard or butter.

Another hydrogenated vegetable oil product, margarine, has a dull flavor, too. We stick with butter or substitute a savory oil.

We recommend many oils in different recipes, some for their taste and others for their cooking properties. When you want a neutral oil, canola and corn are usually the top choices, though safflower and sunflower are also good options. All have high smokepoints, making them workhorses in frying. Peanut oil has a high smokepoint, too, and adds a hint of nuttiness to food as well. An oil of roasted peanuts, such as Loriva's, exudes intense aroma and flavor. When a dish calls for olive oil, it's often worth the expense of using the extra-virgin variety, normally heady in flavor.

The less refined an oil, the more it resembles the original food in character. Our recipes sometimes specify unrefined corn oil, which tastes of summer corn. Try Spectrum Naturals brand or Texas' Arrowhead Mills. Avoid using unrefined oil for tasks such as deep frying, because they have low smokepoints.

Specialty oils such as Texafrance's Roasted Garlic Essence can work wonders in salad dressings, marinades, and other preparations. A pioneer in the specialty oils field, Loriva has a full line of fascinating flavors. The growing availability of these and other oils may turn out to be as important to a new generation of home cooks as Crisco was to our grandparents.

Keep all oils in a cool, dark pantry, or refrigerate them if you don't think you'll finish them within a month or two.

Taking Stock

Frequently, stock is the most important difference between average and great home cooking. Until about fifty years ago, most Texans and other Americans used to keep a stockpot simmering almost constantly on the back of the stove. The liquid, which provides the essence of flavor in many traditional dishes, has no substitute. Store-bought cans and cubes of mystery substances are weak substitutes, usually long on salt, short on taste, and stiff on price.

Making your own stock is easy; it can be done in advance in large quantities; and, in this age of recycling, it's the perfect way to use your vegetable and meat trimmings as well as your pickle and peanut butter jars. Ideally, you should maintain a supply of beef, chicken, and seafood stocks, though chicken alone is a significant asset. Anyone who eats much game may want to keep game stock on hand, too. You don't need a precise recipe to make stocks, because depth of flavor doesn't depend on exact measurements. Start by saving your own ingredients and maybe begging scraps from your meatcutter. Keep trimmings and bones from raw or cooked poultry, beef, game, and seafood in separate plastic bags, and collect carrot peels, celery tops, and onion skins together to use in all of the stocks. Stash the ingredients in the freezer until you've got several pounds for a particular stock.

For real Texas taste, try to get some trimmings from smoked meats. If this isn't feasible, intensify the flavor by oven-roasting and browning the meat and vegetables for about 45 minutes at 375° F, or until they have turned into a deep brown mass (but avoid turning everything to charcoal). Seafood is the exception to the roasting rule, though smoked fish is still desirable for stock.

Toss the ingredients into a stockpot or large saucepan with a little garlic, a few peppercorns, and, if you have it, some parsley. Don't add salt; doing so could make it difficult to control the saltiness of dishes that use the stock. Cover the trimmings with double their volume in water, bring the pot to a boil, and then reduce the heat to low. Leave the pot uncovered, to evaporate the liquid and intensify the taste. Seafood stocks need only an hour or two to develop maximum flavor, but chicken and beef welcome a day (or two after-work evenings) of slow simmering. We usually cook the stock until about one-third of the original liquid remains, but you can reduce it further for greater richness and storage. When the stock is ready, strain it, and freeze it in small containers, for easy use later as needed.

REAL PIT-
SMOKED
BAR-B-Q

We arrived on the barbecue-grounds at about ten o'clock. More than two thousand people had already arrived, some from a distance of forty to fifty miles—old gray-bearded pioneers, with their wives, in ox-wagons; young men, profuse in the matter of yellow-topped boots and jingling spurs, on horseback; fair maidens in calico, curls, and pearl-powder, some on horseback, others in wagons and buggies. . . . A deep trench, three hundred feet long, had been dug. This trench was filled from end to end with glowing coals; and suspended over them on horizontal poles were the carcasses of forty animals — sheep, hogs, oxen, and deer—roasting over the slow fire. . . . It is claimed that this primitive method of preparation is the perfection of cookery, and that no meat tastes so sweet as that which is barbecued.

Alexander Sweet and John Knox,
On a Mexican Mustang through Texas

"*T*he perfection of cookery," Texans boasted to Alex Sweet and John Knox in 1880. Their descendants would say the same to visitors today. Barbecue has always been a matter of serious pride in Texas, as likely to stir passion as taxes or tight jeans.

We're talking real pit-smoked "Bar-B-Q," of course, not the suburban substitute scorched on a charcoal grill, the food equivalent of a walk on the wild side in Waxahachie. The genuine article cooks slowly at a low temperature from the heat and smoke of a wood fire. However cheap and tough the meat is before it goes in the pit, it comes out as succulent as a ripe peach and as tender as a grandmother's hug. Anyone who has tasted the result would dicker with the devil to get the secret of doing it at home.

We're going to save you and your soul from that fate. The secret's much simpler than we used to think, though you would never know that from reading cookbooks or food magazines. Until recently we believed the one and only way to get real barbecue today was to go to a real barbecue joint, a place such as Kreuz Market in Lockhart, Louie Mueller's in Taylor, or Angelo's in Fort Worth. We would drive hundreds of miles out of our way to get great "Q," convinced we could never match it in our backyard.

We tried everything at home except trapping a cow in the kitchen and burning the house. We made a barrel cooker out of a 55-gallon drum—the conventional approach—and we experimented with our Weber kettle grill for slow smoking—as a number of pretty cookbooks portray. Finally we even invested in a newfangled water smoker that looks like something dropped by a dinosaur on its way through the neighborhood. In most cases we got acceptable barbecue, sometimes even good, but not when we tackled brisket.

As Cactus Pryor once said, "It's common knowledge among the clergy that God invented beef briskets for Texans." The Almighty probably doesn't mind if we barbecue other things, but when a Texan has an Epiphany on the patio you can bet it's with brisket. If you can't count it among the meats you've mastered, you're stuck on the praying side of success.

The Secret of Real Backyard Bar-B-Q

We're almost ashamed about how simple the secret is—or we would be anyway if some other damned fool had just explained it before. All you have to do is buy or build a pit modeled on the ones used originally in the best of the old-fashioned barbecue joints. That's it. You cook brisket—and much more—as good as they do at Kreuz's, Louie Mueller's, Angelo's, or any of the other top dozen joints in Texas by using the same kind of pit and principles.

The first barbecue masters in human history—the ones who made supper the day fire was discovered—worked in open pits, much like the "trench" Alex Sweet and John Knox described. Early Texas settlers brought this method north from Mexico and west from Tennessee. The two traditions met in the central part of the state, where inventive German butchers took the idea and created modern Texas "Q" around the turn of the century.

These clever merchants perfected a type of closed pit, usually built of brick with a metal lid, that relied on smoke and heat from an external or offset wood fire. They came up with the contraption as a way to get rid of their worst cuts of meat, pieces they had to throw away before. Instead of accepting that loss, the butchers found they could dramatically enhance brisket and other poor fare through long, slow smoking. Closing the pit and putting the fire well away from the meat gave them better control of the cooking, and raising the pit above the ground cut down on the chiropractor bills.

What you need in your backyard is a small-scale version of that old German meat market pit. You don't want gas, electricity, charcoal, petroleum products, secret sauces, or any other recent refinements being pushed today at your local grilling emporium. To get real with barbecue you've got to return to the roots.

Prime Pits

Anyone with the time, the skills, and a lifetime address should consider building a brick pit. Those of us less fortunate may prefer to buy our way to glory, a time-honored prerogative in the Lone Star State.

An increasing number of companies, mostly in Texas, are manufacturing metal pits with fireboxes attached to the sides, as in the illustration. The design marks a major advance over 55-gallon drum cookers, giving you the same advantages as the real barbecue pros at a price comparable to that of a much more limited gas grill. You can burn wood logs, keep the flame away from the meat, maintain a constant low temperature for extended periods, and produce optimum amounts of smoke flavor. You regulate the heat with damper controls on the firebox and chimney.

We looked at all the brands we could find before settling on one for ourselves. The choice ultimately was the Pitt's and Spitt's pit that's pictured, a gem that cooks barbecue as good as we've ever had. With a variety of models starting at $595, the Houston company makes more expensive pits than some of its competitors, but the Pitt's and Spitt's pits are outstanding in looks, durability, and capability. Each pit features an offset firebox with quarter-inch plate walls, stainless-steel parts, an accurate thermometer, a water reservoir with a drain, and superior smoke drafting. Call 800-521-2947 for more information or stop by the Houston showroom.

A Pitt's and Spitt's pit is a capital investment to pass on to the kids, but you've got alternatives if the budget won't stretch that far into the future. Check at barbecue supply stores for similar smokers, or in national mail-order catalogs that sell outdoors gear. Just be sure you understand the trade-offs in price and quality, what you lose for what you save. If you restrict what you cook, you can also get along moderately well on your old Weber grill or barrel drum, as we'll discuss later in the chapter.

However you manage it, do some "Q." It could be the most fun you've ever had cooking, and the meals you make may get you elected to the Texas Hall of Fame.

The One-and-Only
Barbecued Brisket

*Despite being all the way up in Cambridge, Massachusetts, Chef Chris Schlesinger knows a bit about "Q." In **The Thrill of the Grill** he reckons "beef brisket just might be why the barbecue process was invented." This has the ring of truth, but the good chef goes astray when he claims that it's also the hardest of all meats to master. Anyone can do it to perfection in a brick or metal pit with an offset firebox.*

1 8- TO 12-POUND PACKER-TRIMMED BEEF
   BRISKET
2 CUPS LONE STAR DRY RUB (PAGE 27)
BOWL OF BEER MOP SAUCE FOR MEAT
   (PAGE 28)

Serves 20 to 25 people in Cambridge and a dozen in Houston

Be sure to get a packer-trimmed brisket, that is, one with a thick layer of fat on one side. On the day before the big event, pat the dry rub into every little pore on the brisket. Place the meat in a plastic trash bag and refrigerate it, preferably overnight.

Take the brisket out of the refrigerator first thing in the morning, to bring it closer to room temperature while you start your fire and warm your pit to about 210° F. After a couple of cups of coffee, when you and everything else are ready, put the brisket in the pit on the opposite side from the firebox. Be sure the untrimmed fat side is up, so the juices will help baste the meat.

Maintain a temperature between 180° F and 220° F until the brisket is well done, which takes 1 to 1¼ hours per pound. Every hour or so, when you feel an urge to look, dab the mop sauce on top of the blackening hunk. The mop isn't really necessary with brisket, because of the self-basting fat, but we believe in playing with your meat as much as your religion allows.

LEFTOVER BRISKET IS SUPER IN SANDWICHES. WARM THE MEAT, PULL IT INTO SMALL PIECES, AND PILE IT ONTO A HEATED FLOUR TORTILLA SPREAD GENEROUSLY WITH CREOLE OR YELLOW MUSTARD. WE TOP IT OFF WITH CHOPPED ONION, CHOPPED PICKLED VEGETABLES, CHOWCHOW, OR ALL THREE, WHICH WE LIKE BETTER WITH THE BRISKET THAN ANY BARBECUE SAUCE.

About the time the sun's setting, shut down the fire and remove the brisket. Let it sit 20 minutes, then cut the fatty top section away from the leaner bottom portion. An easily identifiable layer of fat will separate the two areas. Trim the excess fat from both pieces and slice them thin against the grain. If you wish, serve barbecue sauce on the side, but never risk insulting a connoisseur by slathering the stuff on the meat.

Variation: Smoke the fatty top section of the brisket for an additional 3 or 4 hours to make some great "burnt ends." The extra cooking makes this piece leaner and blacker, and tasty enough for a last meal. If you don't want to take the time for this on the same day, freeze the meat and put it back on the pit when you fire up again.

Lone Star Dry Rub

A dry rub is a mixture of spices that serves the same purpose as a marinade. It coats the surface of food, enhancing the flavor, and during the cooking process adds a crusty texture. This is an all-purpose rub, suitable on almost anything you barbecue. Add or subtract spices according to your tastes or to complement whatever you're smoking.

¾ CUP PAPRIKA
¼ CUP GROUND BLACK PEPPER
¼ CUP CHILI POWDER, PREFERABLY HOME-
    MADE (PAGE 135) OR GEBHARDT'S
¼ CUP SALT
¼ CUP SUGAR
2 TABLESPOONS GARLIC POWDER
2 TABLESPOONS ONION POWDER
1 TABLESPOON GROUND CAYENNE

Makes about 2 cups

Mix the spices thoroughly in a bowl.
    You can store leftover rub in a tightly sealed jar in the refrigerator, but it will lose potency over time.

The next time you're in Luling for the annual summer Watermelon Thump, have lunch downtown at the old City Market. The experts at the pit here fix such juicy brisket and links you might find yourself wanting to enter the watermelon seed-spitting contest. If you can reach 69 feet in the sport, you'll break the world record, currently held by a Luling pro.

Beer Mop Sauce

Some pitmasters would consider us slap-happy with our mop sauce because we use one with almost everything we barbecue. If you want to be frugal, lazy, or just technically correct, baste only food that will dry out in the cooking process. The mop adds moisture more than flavor, so it can contain anything wet, from water to wine. Always be sure to include plenty of oil when smoking anything that doesn't have a protective layer of fat, and never use ingredients that will burn (such as a ketchup-based barbecue sauce) before the last 30 to 45 minutes of cooking. These two versions of one basic recipe will mop up almost everything.

BEER MOP SAUCE FOR MEAT

12 OUNCES BEER
½ CUP VINEGAR, PREFERABLY CIDER OR WHITE
¼ CUP OIL, PREFERABLY CANOLA OR CORN
½ MEDIUM ONION, CHOPPED
2 GARLIC CLOVES, MINCED
2 TABLESPOONS LONE STAR DRY RUB
  (PAGE 27)
1 TABLESPOON WORCESTERSHIRE SAUCE

BEER MOP SAUCE FOR POULTRY AND FISH

12 OUNCES BEER
½ CUP FRESH LEMON JUICE
½ CUP OIL, PREFERABLY CANOLA OR CORN
½ MEDIUM ONION, CHOPPED
2 GARLIC CLOVES, MINCED
2 TABLESPOONS LONE STAR DRY RUB (PAGE 27)
1 TABLESPOON WHITE WINE WORCESTERSHIRE SAUCE OR 1½ TEASPOONS WORCESTERSHIRE SAUCE

Makes 2 to 3 cups

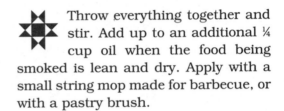 Throw everything together and stir. Add up to an additional ¼ cup oil when the food being smoked is lean and dry. Apply with a small string mop made for barbecue, or with a pastry brush.

Variations: Substitute stock for the beer, or inexpensive dry wine (red for the meat or white for the poultry or fish).

When he was elected Texas Governor in 1939 and 1941, "Pappy" O'Daniel invited everyone in the state to inaugural dinners in Austin. Some twenty thousand people showed up at the second shindig and consumed almost a pound of barbecue per person.

Ol' Red's Barbecue Sauce

*We're dedicating this recipe to our publisher because he's one of those unfortunate folks who grew up thinking barbecue was a charred chicken drowned in a "secret sauce" invented by Mr. Heinz. When we submitted a draft of this chapter without a barbecue sauce recipe, he thought we were smoking loco weed instead of brisket. We explained that real "Q" needs added flavor like Nolan Ryan needs a third arm, but he prevailed as usual with his business perspective, saying "look, errant authors, in the book trade purity went out with Cotton Mather." People talk like that in Boston. Anyway, we dug out one of our favorite Texas country cookbooks, Red Caldwell's **Pit, Pot and Skillet**, and borrowed this recipe. It's a terrific sauce, whether you use it on barbecue or something else, but be warned that it's hot. When our publisher tried it, friends had to dunk him in the Charles River to stop the howling. He never mentioned sauces again.*

2 TABLESPOONS OIL
4 CUPS CHOPPED ONIONS
¼ CUP MINCED FRESH JALAPEÑOS
¼ CUP MINCED FRESH SERRANOS (OR SUBSTITUTE ADDITIONAL JALAPEÑOS FOR A TOUCH LESS HEAT)
15 GARLIC CLOVES, MINCED
2 CUPS KETCHUP
1 CUP WORCESTERSHIRE SAUCE
1 CUP STRONG BLACK COFFEE
⅔ CUP DARK BROWN SUGAR
½ CUP CIDER VINEGAR
½ CUP LEMON JUICE
6 TABLESPOONS CHILI POWDER
3 TABLESPOONS PREPARED YELLOW MUSTARD
1 TABLESPOON SALT

Makes 8 cups

In a saucepan, heat the oil. Add the onions, jalapeños, serranos, and garlic, and cook them over low heat until soft. Add everything else, cover the pan, and simmer 40 minutes. Allow the mixture to cool to room temperature.

Strain out the remaining solids, liquify them in a food processor, and add them back to the strained liquid, stirring thoroughly. Set the sauce aside for several hours before serving to permit flavors to blend.

Refrigerate the sauce, covered, and use it as needed. It will keep for weeks.

Drunk and Dirty Tenderloin

From brisket in Texas to pork shoulder in North Carolina, traditional barbecue meats are tough, cheap cuts that need long, slow cooking before they're worth eating. The smoking process significantly enhances these meats, as it does many foods. We apply this principle here to the choicest cut of beef, the tenderloin. It's juicy and flavorful any way you cook it, but this smoked version is as luscious as any you'll find.

MARINADE

- 1 CUP SOY SAUCE
- ½ CUP BOURBON
- ¼ CUP WORCESTERSHIRE SAUCE
- 2 TABLESPOONS DARK BROWN SUGAR
- ½ TEASPOON POWDERED GINGER
- 4 GARLIC CLOVES, MINCED

- 2 POUNDS BEEF TENDERLOIN
- 2 TABLESPOONS COARSE-GROUND BLACK PEPPER
- 1 TEASPOON WHITE PEPPER
- ¼ CUP OIL, PREFERABLY CANOLA OR CORN

Serves 6

Combine the marinade ingredients. Place the whole tenderloin in a shallow dish and pour the mixture over the meat. Marinate the tenderloin for 4 to 8 hours in the refrigerator, turning occasionally, and a final hour at room temperature. Start a fire in the pit about the time you take the meat from the refrigerator, and get the temperature steady around 200° F.

Remove the tenderloin from the marinade and cover it thoroughly first with the black pepper, then the white pepper. In a skillet on the stove or on a hot outdoor grill, sear the meat several seconds on every side over high heat.

Split the marinade into two equal portions. Boil one half, add the oil, and use the mixture as a mop sauce, applying it to the meat every 15 to 20 minutes during the smoking process. Reserve the remaining marinade for a reduction sauce to serve with the tenderloin.

Place the meat in the pit and cook it at 180° F to 220° F until the internal temperature of the meat reaches 140° F, approximately 1½ to 2 hours. (Be careful not to overcook; tenderloin is always best rare to medium-rare. Use an instant-registering meat thermometer to check for doneness.) Remove the tenderloin from the pit and let it sit 15 minutes before slicing.

In the meantime, put the unused portion of marinade in a small, heavy saucepan, bring it to a boil, and reduce the heat to a simmer. Cook for 5 to 10 minutes until the marinade is reduced by one-fourth. Slice the tenderloin, and serve it with the sauce on the side.

Prime-Plus Short Ribs

When we see smoked prime rib on a restaurant menu, we always suspect the kitchen is more interested in its profit margin than its cooking. The best beef rib for slow smoking is the ugly, fatty short rib from the plate section, a cheap cut often made into stew meat.

5 TO 6 POUNDS BEEF SHORT RIBS
1 CUP LONE STAR DRY RUB (PAGE 27)
BOWL OF BEER MOP SAUCE FOR MEAT
   (PAGE 28)

GLAZE AND BARBECUE SAUCE

1½ CUPS KETCHUP
1 CUP BEER
¾ CUP CIDER VINEGAR
3 TABLESPOONS MINCED CILANTRO
3 TABLESPOONS DARK BROWN SUGAR
2 TABLESPOONS WORCESTERSHIRE SAUCE
2 GARLIC CLOVES, MINCED
2 TEASPOONS CUMIN SEEDS, TOASTED AND
   GROUND
1½ TEASPOONS ANISE SEEDS, TOASTED AND
   GROUND
1½ TEASPOONS SALT
1 TEASPOON TABASCO OR OTHER HOT PEPPER
   SAUCE

Serves 6

Massage each short rib with the dry rub. Place the ribs in a plastic trash bag, and put them in the refrigerator overnight.

The next day mix the mop sauce and prepare the pit for smoking. Place the ribs in the pit, fatty side up, and cook them between 200° F and 220° F for 5 hours. Until the last hour, baste with the mop sauce every 30 to 60 minutes.

While the ribs are smoking, prepare the glaze so it is ready to apply approximately 45 minutes before the meat is done. Mix the glaze ingredients in a saucepan, and bring them to a simmer, stirring frequently. Cook the mixture for 30 minutes.

Mop the glaze on the top and sides of the ribs twice during the last 30 to 60 minutes of cooking time. (Never apply glaze before the last hour or it will burn.) Return the remaining glaze to the stove, and simmer it until it's reduced by one-third, about 15 to 20 minutes.

After removing the ribs from the pit, allow them to sit 10 minutes, and then trim the fat. Serve them with the reduced glaze on the side.

PIT POINTER

We always barbecue more than we intend to eat that day. Most smoked food freezes well and can be reheated in a conventional oven without losing much of the original taste.

Texas Dry Ribs

In some parts of the country, particularly Memphis and Kansas City, pork spareribs are synonymous with barbecue. Texas barbecue joints tend to look at ribs differently, as something in a separate and lower culinary class from the main specialty. The sign out front might say something like "Wild Willie's BAR-B-Q and Ribs."

We smoke these spareribs Texas style, like brisket, and serve them in one of the popular Memphis manners, "dry," or without a glaze sauce. Make sure that you get thirteen-bone slabs of spareribs, instead of country or loin ribs, and that the chine bone is removed. The preferred size for barbecuing is "3 and down," meaning 3 pounds or smaller, a variable that depends on the weight of the pig when butchered. Don't fret if all you can find are larger slabs, but do smoke them a little longer, about 1 hour more for each extra pound.

⅓ CUP GROUND BLACK PEPPER

3 FULL SLABS PORK SPARERIBS, "ST. LOUIS CUT" (TRIMMED OF THE CHINE BONE AND BRISKET FLAP), PREFERABLY 3 POUNDS EACH OR LESS

⅔ CUP LONE STAR DRY RUB (PAGE 27)

BOWL OF BEER MOP SAUCE FOR MEAT (PAGE 28)

Serves 6

Apply the pepper evenly over the ribs, and then do the same with the dry rub. Place the slabs in a plastic trash bag, and put them in the refrigerator overnight.

The next day mix the mop sauce and prepare the pit for smoking. Cook the slabs between 200° F and 220° F until you can feel them crack a bit between the ribs when you bend the slabs with a gloved hand, approximately 3½ to 4 hours. Every 30 minutes baste both sides and turn them over. Allow the slabs to sit 10 minutes before slicing them into individual ribs.

> One of the few objections people raise to real barbecue is that it takes too long. Makes you wonder how those folks approach sex, baseball, and Larry McMurtry novels.

Bourbon-Glazed Ribs

This is our favorite "wet" spareribs recipe, finished at the end with a glaze that also serves as a barbecue sauce. Select spareribs using the same criteria described in the preceding recipe for Texas Dry Ribs.

⅓ CUP GROUND BLACK PEPPER

3 FULL SLABS PORK SPARERIBS, "ST. LOUIS CUT" (TRIMMED OF THE CHINE BONE AND BRISKET FLAP), PREFERABLY 3 POUNDS EACH OR LESS

⅔ CUP LONE STAR DRY RUB (PAGE 27)

BOWL OF BEER MOP SAUCE FOR MEAT (PAGE 28)

GLAZE AND BARBECUE SAUCE

¼ CUP UNSALTED BUTTER

¼ CUP OIL, PREFERABLY CANOLA OR CORN

2 MEDIUM ONIONS, MINCED

⅔ CUP BOURBON

⅔ CUP KETCHUP

½ CUP CIDER VINEGAR

½ CUP FRESH ORANGE JUICE

½ CUP MAPLE SYRUP

⅓ CUP UNSULPHURED DARK MOLASSES

2 TABLESPOONS WORCESTERSHIRE SAUCE

½ TEASPOON COARSE-GROUND BLACK PEPPER

½ TEASPOON SALT

Serves 6

✦ Apply the pepper evenly over the ribs, and then do the same with the dry rub. Place the slabs in a plastic trash bag, and put them in the refrigerator overnight.

The next day mix the mop sauce and prepare the pit for smoking. Cook the slabs at about 200° F to 220° F until you can feel them crack a bit between the ribs when you bend the slabs with a gloved hand, approximately 3½ to 4 hours. Until the last hour of cooking, baste both sides with the mop sauce and turn the ribs over every 30 minutes.

While the slabs are smoking, prepare the glaze so it is ready to apply approximately 45 minutes before the meat is done. Melt the butter in a large saucepan, add the oil, and cook 2 minutes over medium heat. Add the onions, and sauté for several minutes, until they begin to turn golden. Add the remaining glaze ingredients, and bring the mixture to a simmer, stirring frequently. Reduce the heat to low and cook until the mixture thickens, approximately 40 minutes.

During the last 30 to 60 minutes of smoking time, mop the glaze on the ribs twice. (Never apply it before the last hour or the glaze will burn.) Return the remaining glaze to the stove, and simmer it until reduced by one-third, about 15 to 20 minutes.

After removing the slabs from the pit, allow them to sit 10 minutes before slicing them into individual ribs. Serve them with the reduced glaze on the side.

Ranch-Style Fajitas

*Mexican ranchers and **vaqueros** in southwest Texas were some of the first pitmasters in the state. They learned early how to barbecue the least savory parts of the tough, stringy longhorns that once roamed freely in the region. Their major specialty in the past was a whole cow's head, often cooked overnight in an underground pit. That dish never caught on in Dallas, but another brush-country favorite has become the state-wide rage in recent decades. Fajita, or skirt steak, is the diaphragm muscle, once about as popular among suburbanites as a buzzard in the backyard. The term is frequently misused today to refer to almost any kind of grilled meat rolled in a flour tortilla, but the only true fajitas are made with beef skirt.*

MARINADE

12 OUNCES BEER

1 CUP OIL, PREFERABLY CANOLA OR CORN

½ MEDIUM ONION, SLICED

JUICE OF 2 LIMES

4 TO 5 GARLIC CLOVES, MINCED

1 BAY LEAF

2 TABLESPOONS WORCESTERSHIRE SAUCE

1 TABLESPOON CHILI POWDER, PREFERABLY
   HOMEMADE (PAGE 135) OR GEBHARDT'S

1 TEASPOON FRESH-GROUND BLACK PEPPER

1 TEASPOON CRUSHED CHILTEPINS OR CHILES
   PEQUÍNS

1 TEASPOON CUMIN SEEDS, TOASTED AND
   GROUND

2- TO 3-POUND WHOLE BEEF SKIRT, TRIMMED
   OF FAT AND MEMBRANE

WARM FLOUR TORTILLAS

PICO DE GALLO (PAGE 95) OR YOUR FAVORITE
   SALSA

Serves 6 to 8

Combine the marinade ingredients, and marinate the skirt in the mixture overnight in the refrigerator, turning it occasionally. Remove the meat from the refrigerator, and bring it to room temperature about the time you start a fire in the pit.

When the temperature reaches a steady level of 180° F to 220° F, place the skirt in the pit.

Boil the remaining marinade and baste the meat with it every 15 minutes. Smoke the skirt at 180° F to 220° F until it is almost done, approximately 1 hour.

If your pit has a grill area for cooking directly over the fire, move the meat there and sear it 1 to 2 minutes per side. This step, which can also be done on a charcoal grill, adds a pleasant crunchy texture, but isn't necessary for flavor. If you don't want to bother, smoke the meat a little longer until it is completely done.

Allow the skirt to sit for 10 minutes, and then slice it thin diagonally against the grain. Serve the meat on preheated flour tortillas with Pico de Gallo or another spicy sauce. If you want to be literal, this is a *taco de fajitas*, but most Texans know it simply by the name of the meat itself.

While Lyndon Johnson was president, another Texan, named Bobby Seale, was leading the Black Panther Party's opposition to the government. About the only thing the two men agreed on was barbecue. Years later, in 1988, Seale wrote a tribute to the "Q" he loved at his uncle's restaurant in Liberty, Texas, and showed how to duplicate it on a grill using marinades flavored with liquid smoke. Anyone determined to get barbecue taste off a covered grill should check out his book, *Barbeque'n with Bobby*.

PJ's Cheeky Chicken

We got this recipe from Wayne Whitworth, manufacturer of Pitt's and Spitt's pits, and named it for his delightful wife PJ. In barbecue cook-offs, she's been known to enter this standing-tall chicken with the wings raised to salute the judges. That probably doesn't hurt her chances, but she needs no trick to win. PJ's chicken makes all the rest taste like crowed-out roosters.

2 3- TO 4-POUND WHOLE CHICKENS
1 CUP OIL, PREFERABLY CANOLA OR CORN
1 CUP LONE STAR DRY RUB (PAGE 27)

INJECTION SAUCE
2 12-OUNCE CANS OR BOTTLES BEER
½ CUP OIL, PREFERABLY CANOLA OR CORN
½ CUP VINEGAR, PREFERABLY CIDER OR WHITE
2 TEASPOONS LONE STAR DRY RUB

MOP SAUCE
REMAINING INJECTION SAUCE
1 CUP UNSALTED CHICKEN STOCK
1 MEDIUM ONION, CHOPPED
1 TABLESPOON PREPARED JALAPEÑO OR
    YELLOW MUSTARD
1 TABLESPOON LONE STAR DRY RUB

2 12-OUNCE CANS BEER (BOTTLES WON'T DO
    THIS TIME)

Serves 4

Remove the organs from the cavity of the chickens. Massage the chickens thoroughly with oil, inside and out, and then cover them well with the dry rub. Work the oil and dry rub as far as possible under the skin without tearing it.

PJ and Wayne got married in style—real barbecue style. They were hitched between two pits at the barbecue cook-off at the Houston Livestock Show and Rodeo, and they celebrated the blessed event afterwards by serving "Q" to a thousand witnesses. The wedding cake was tiered layers of jalapeño cornbread topped with a Velveeta cheese frosting.

In a bowl, combine the ingredients for the injection sauce. With a kitchen syringe, inject the liquid deep into the breast and legs of each chicken in several spots; use ¼ to ½ cup in total. Add the mop sauce ingredients to the remaining liquid, and mix thoroughly.

Place the chickens in a plastic trash bag, and put them in the refrigerator to sit for at least 3 hours or overnight. Near the end of this time, stoke up the pit and bring the temperature to 220° F. While you wait, open the two beer cans and drink half—and only half—of each beer.

When you're ready to start smoking, remove the tops of the half-empty beer cans and fill them with some of the remaining injection and mop sauce. Take the chickens from the refrigerator, and insert the replenished beer cans into their cavities, balancing the birds so that they rest upright with their legs bent forward. The cans should sit flat on the pit grill, holding the chickens at attention while their insides are steaming and their outsides are smoking.

Cook the chickens for 3½ to 4 hours at 200° F to 220° F, mopping them with the remaining sauce every 20 minutes. When they are done their legs will move freely.

Variation: If you aren't willing to share your beer with the chickens, then stuff their cavity with quartered lemons and onions.

Smoking food in a pit requires more time than grilling it, but not as much close supervision. You have to be alert to flare-ups when grilling, and constantly mindful of not overcooking. With a pit you add wood every hour or so, check the temperature twice in the same period, and mop your vittles as needed. The separation of the meat and the flame prevents flare-ups, and the slow cooking keeps you from turning your dinner into coal.

Chicken's Little Livers

The livers that come in the cavity of a whole supermarket chicken can be smoked right along with the bird. When we have only a few, we nibble them as we cook, but sometimes we buy extras and serve them as appetizers.

MARINADE
¼ CUP FRUIT-FLAVORED VINEGAR

¼ CUP UNSALTED CHICKEN STOCK

¼ CUP OIL, PREFERABLY CANOLA OR CORN

⅓ MEDIUM ONION, CHOPPED

1 GARLIC CLOVE, MINCED

¼ TEASPOON POWDERED GINGER

¼ TEASPOON SALT

¼ TEASPOON FRESH-GROUND BLACK PEPPER

12 CHICKEN LIVERS, TRIMMED OF ANY
   MEMBRANE

4 SLICES SLAB BACON, SLICED IN THIRDS

Makes 1 dozen

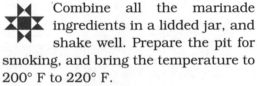 Combine all the marinade ingredients in a lidded jar, and shake well. Prepare the pit for smoking, and bring the temperature to 200° F to 220° F.

Place the chicken livers in a shallow nonreactive bowl. Pour enough marinade over the livers just to cover them. Marinate them at room temperature for 30 minutes, or in the refrigerator for 1½ to 2 hours. Reserve the remaining marinade.

Drain the livers. Wrap each liver with a piece of bacon, and secure the bacon with a toothpick. In a small saucepan, bring the reserved marinade to a boil, and remove it from the heat to use as a mop sauce.

Place the livers in the pit on a small grill rack, and smoke them at an average temperature of 200° F to 220° F for about 40 minutes, until the bacon is crisp. Apply the mop sauce several times during the cooking process.

> ### PIT POINTER
> If you're planning to cook bite-size tidbits or fish in your smoker or on the grill, it's worth investing in a portable grill rack with a small mesh and fireproof handles. You'll be able to lay out and remove all of your morsels in one quick step. Griffo Grill and Oscarware make models widely distributed in the United States.

Garlic-Spiced Turkey Breast

Smoking a full turkey makes for a very long day at the pit, but a breast can be cooked in less than half the time. The trick is keeping the bird juicy, which this method does.

INJECTION SAUCE
½ CUP GARLIC OIL
½ TEASPOON CAYENNE

15-POUND TURKEY BREAST

RUB
REMAINING INJECTION SAUCE
1 TABLESPOON FRESH-GROUND BLACK PEPPER
1 TEASPOON SALT

MOP SAUCE
3 CUPS UNSALTED TURKEY OR CHICKEN STOCK
⅓ CUP GARLIC OIL
1 TABLESPOON FRESH-GROUND BLACK PEPPER
½ TEASPOON CAYENNE

Serves 8

For the injection sauce, mix the garlic oil and cayenne in a small bowl. With a kitchen syringe, inject the mixture deep into the turkey breast in a half-dozen places, moving the needle around in each spot to shoot the liquid in several directions.

To make the rub, add the black pepper and salt to the remaining injection sauce, and mix thoroughly. Massage the turkey breast with the rub, working it as far as possible under the skin without tearing it. Place the turkey breast in a plastic trash bag, and put it in the refrigerator to sit overnight.

The next day prepare the pit and bring the temperature to about 200° F. Make the mop sauce: Combine the turkey or chicken stock, garlic oil, black pepper, and cayenne in a small bowl.

Place the turkey breast in the pit with the skin side up. Smoke it at about 200° F, applying the mop sauce to the breast every 20 minutes during the cooking process. The breast should be done in 5 to 6 hours, when the internal temperature reaches 180° F. Remove the meat from the pit, and allow it to sit for 15 minutes before carving.

Serve the sliced breast with the Chile Pecan Sauce for Turkey (page 211), if you like.

A BARREL OF FUN

*M*any people barbecue on barrel cookers converted from 55-gallon drums. These are better for grilling than for smoking, but they can manage either. Though they don't have an offset firebox like a proper pit, they can burn wood logs, their main advantage over a Weber kettle for smoking. Also, they have a bigger cooking area than other grills, allowing you to move the meat farther from the fire. The real attraction of the drums, however, is the homespun feel. They look like something Davy Crockett killed, and they let everyone know you're no drugstore dude.

A decent welder can build a barrel cooker from the illustration, but a few tips may help to get it right. Install a good thermometer in the lid, so you can check the temperature of the meat easily. Line the bottom of the barrel with sand and fire brick, which will keep logs from burning through and improve the cooker's heat retention. Most important, get solid, functional valves for the air vents on the chimney and the opposite side wall. Only by controlling the flow of air through the cooker can you regulate the heat. Remember to smoke slow and low, which will mean little or no flame from the wood fire.

Devilish Dove

Doves are small birds, but they're big-time game among Texas hunters. When sharp-eyed friends find their mark, this is how we cook the little critters as appetizers. If you find fresh yellow güero, or banana, chiles, substitute them for half the jalapeños for more color contrast.

2 DOZEN DOVES
2 TABLESPOONS OIL, PREFERABLY CANOLA OR
  CORN
½ CUP LONE STAR DRY RUB (PAGE 27)
24 LARGE FRESH JALAPEÑOS
1 MEDIUM ONION, CUT IN SLIVERS
12 SLICES SLAB BACON, SLICED IN HALF
  CROSS-WISE

Serves 6 to 8

Take the tiny breast from each dove, massage it with oil, and coat it with the dry rub. Save the rest of the bird for stock if desired. Cover and place in the refrigerator overnight.

As the pit is warming up to a cooking temperature of 200° F to 220° F, split the jalapeños along one side and seed them. Stuff a dove breast and a sliver or two of onion in each, wrap with a half piece of bacon, and secure the tidbit with a toothpick. Smoke about 30 to 40 minutes, until the bacon is crisp. These are fiery hot when served with the jalapeño still in place, so proceed cautiously. Tender-mouths may find the dove plenty picante eaten alone.

Variation: Substitute slices of chicken breast for the dove breast. Again, be wary about the jalapeño when serving.

Coke Stevenson, former governor of Texas, liked to brag about the size of watermelons on his cattle ranch. In an extra-hard winter, he claimed, the cowboys would hollow out one of the melons to shelter the herd.

Smoked Jalapeño Shrimp

Dean Fearing, Dallas chef, inspired this sizzling seafood dish. Like us, he advocates unrefined corn oil—a revelation to the tongue compared with the tasteless processed varieties.

MARINADE

⅓ CUP PICKLED JALAPEÑO SLICES

½ CUP JUICE FROM PICKLED JALAPEÑOS

JUICE OF 2 LIMES

4 TABLESPOONS CORN OIL, PREFERABLY UNREFINED

2 TABLESPOONS MINCED CILANTRO

4 GREEN ONIONS, SLICED

3 GARLIC CLOVES, MINCED

1 POUND LARGE SHRIMP (ABOUT 24 TO 30 SHRIMP)

½ CUP UNSALTED SEAFOOD STOCK OR WATER

Serves 4

In a food processor or blender, purée the marinade ingredients. Peel the shrimp, leaving the tails on. Clean and, if you like, devein them. Place the shrimp in a large nonreactive pan or bowl. One hour before you plan to begin smoking the shrimp, pour the marinade over them.

Remove the shrimp from the marinade, and, when the temperature is about 180° F to 200° F, place them in the pit on a small grill rack (as described on page 38). Add the stock or water to the remaining marinade, boil, and baste the shrimp at intervals of about 10 minutes. The shrimp should cook in about 30 minutes, but watch them carefully. They are ready when opaque, slightly firm, and light pink on the exterior. Serve them immediately, or wrap them in foil to keep them warm for up to 45 minutes.

Dean Fearing cooks at the Mansion on Turtle Creek, an uptown place by anyone's standards, but he and other Texas superchefs know how to get down. Fearing and Robert Del Grande, from Houston's Cafe Annie, formed a band called the Barbwires, and they and Stephan Pyles, of Dallas's Baby Routh, sometimes sneak away from their fancy tables to eat barbecue. One of their haunts is Clark's Outpost, a rustic restaurant in Tioga that serves some of the best calf fries in Texas in addition to terrific brisket and ribs.

Oh-My Oysters

This preparation works well with Gulf oysters and those from colder waters as well.

MARINADE
½ CUP BOTTLED CLAM JUICE
3 TABLESPOONS FRESH LEMON JUICE
3 TABLESPOONS EXTRA-VIRGIN OLIVE OIL
1 TABLESPOON COARSE-GROUND BLACK PEPPER
3 TO 4 GARLIC CLOVES, MINCED

12 OYSTERS, SHUCKED, BOTTOM SHELLS AND
   BRINE RESERVED
ABOUT 12 ICE CUBES
LIME WEDGES AND COARSE-GROUND BLACK
   PEPPER FOR GARNISH

Makes 1 dozen

In a lidded jar, combine the juices, oil, pepper, garlic, and any accumulated oyster brine. Cover the jar, and shake the marinade well.

Place the oysters in a small bowl. Pour the marinade over the oysters, and refrigerate them for 45 minutes to an hour.

Drain most of the marinade into a small pan. Place each oyster on a half-shell. Bring the marinade to a boil. Remove the pan from the heat, and set it aside.

Prepare your pit for barbecuing, bringing the temperature to 180° F to 200° F.

Put the ice cubes in an 8-by-8-inch or 9-by-12-inch baking pan, or in a deep pie pan. Place the oysters on a small grill rack (as described on page 38) and top the ice-filled baking pan with the grill rack.

Transfer the oysters to the pit, and smoke as far from the heat as possible. Check the oysters at 15- to 20-minute intervals, mopping them with a bit of marinade if they appear dry. Cook them about 45 minutes or until they become slightly firm but are still plump.

Serve the oysters warm, garnished with lime wedges and pepper.

PIT POINTER

As the recipes indicate, the ideal temperature for smoking most food is between 180° F and 220° F. All pits will fluctuate some, but when you're in that range you won't have a problem with much of anything except an impatient guest from north of the Red River. Don't worry if the temperature drifts up to 250° F or down to 160° F; just start making adjustments to get back to the right level.

PIT POINTERS

*F*or years scientists have warned backyard cooks about the danger of fat dripping on a hot fire, as often happens in the grilling process. The resulting smoke contains benzopyrene, a known carcinogen. You don't get that chemical reaction barbecuing in a pit with a water reservoir. The meat is never directly over the heat source and the fat falls harmlessly into water instead of on the hot metal below.

*W*e start our log fires using hickory chunks for kindling—or any other small pieces of hardwood on hand—and Weber Flamegos, white cubes made of natural, non-petroleum materials that ignite instantly and burn a good while. Stores with a decent selection of grilling supplies should carry both products. We would never use lighter fluid, which can bathe the food in petroleum fumes, or resinous kindling like fatwood, which supplies a bitter turpentine-like taste.

*O*ur Pitt's and Spitt's pit has a water reservoir directly below the cooking grill. We fill it with a garden hose before we begin smoking, up to a half-inch from the lip of the firebox opening. Fat drippings from the meat fall into the water, making the pit easy to clean through a side drain, and a little steam rises from the liquid to help keep the meat moist. It's a great idea. Look for such a system in any new pit you buy.

PIT POINTERS

*C*harcoal by itself does not produce smoke except when meat fat drips on it. That's why you barbecue with wood, preferably logs. You hear a lot of hype about the virtues of different types of wood, but the only thing that really matters is to burn hardwood, not a soft, resinous variety which would create an unpleasant bitter taste. With most food we notice little or no difference between smoking with oak, hickory, pecan, or fruit wood, the main options available to us. We usually avoid mesquite because it burns hot, the very reason it's great for grilling. If you have trouble finding an appropriate wood, check with local barbecue joints and other restaurants that offer smoked dishes to see where they get their supplies.

*B*arbecuing is a form of hot smoking, which is much different from the old preservation technique of cold smoking. Hot smoking cooks food, as does any other means of applying heat, and does little to keep it from spoiling. You must eat barbecue when it's done or refrigerate it. The cold smoking process relies on a combination of salt curing, temperatures below 100° F, and, in most cases, days of smoking to produce food that is dried more than cooked, and can be stored without refrigeration.

Peppered Catfish

You may never fry a catfish again after you try this.

6 8-OUNCE CATFISH FILLETS
½ CUP LONE STAR DRY RUB (PAGE 27)
⅓ CUP COARSE-GROUND BLACK PEPPER

MOP SAUCE
2 CUPS UNSALTED SEAFOOD OR CHICKEN STOCK
⅔ CUP OIL, PREFERABLY CANOLA OR CORN
JUICE OF 3 LIMES

Serves 6

Cover the catfish lightly and evenly with the dry rub. Place the fish in one or more plastic bags, and put the bags in the refrigerator for at least 3 hours or overnight.

Prepare the pit, bringing it to about 200° F. Remove the fish from the refrigerator, and gently pat the pepper into it.

In a bowl, mix the mop sauce ingredients. Place the fish on a small grill rack (as described on page 38), and place the grill rack in the pit. Smoke the fish at 180° F to 200° F until it is opaque and firm but flaky, approximately 1½ hours, dabbing the fish with the mop sauce every 15 minutes.

Serve the fish within a few minutes of removing it from the pit.

People in the Panhandle town of Dalhart know how to throw a really big barbecue. At the XIT Rodeo and Reunion each summer the organizers dig a huge trench, several hundred feet long, and fill it with more than a dozen cords of wood and over ten thousand pounds of beef. Using bulldozers and other heavy equipment, they cover the pit with sheet metal and dirt, and then dig it up again thirty hours later after the meat is smoked. The feed pays homage to cowboys who've worked the famed XIT Ranch, which once extended across three million acres in ten counties. The ranch was a Texas-size proposition from the beginning, when the state government traded the land to a Chicago construction company in exchange for building the largest capitol in the country in Austin.

Country Cabrito

Texans love to get your goat—and to cook it, too. Along with the West Indies and northern Mexico, the state is one of the goat-eating capitals of North America. The meat of choice is cabrito, milk-fed kid slaughtered between the spring and late summer at an age of 30 to 40 days and a weight of 10 to 15 pounds. (After goats start eating grass the flavor of the meat changes, and the bony critters get tougher, requiring more complex and spicy preparations.) Your meat market probably doesn't carry cabrito, but the butcher may be able to direct you to a source, particularly if you live in the Southwest.

1 10- TO 12-POUND CABRITO, QUARTERED

PASTE RUB
3 CUPS FRESH SAGE LEAVES
1 GARLIC HEAD, CLOVES SEPARATED AND PEELED
2 TEASPOONS SALT
2 CUPS OLIVE OIL (AN INEXPENSIVE KIND IS OK)

MOP SAUCE
2 CUPS UNSALTED CHICKEN OR BEEF STOCK, OR 2 CUPS BEER
1 CUP CIDER VINEGAR
1 CUP OLIVE OIL (AN INEXPENSIVE KIND IS OK)
¼ CUP CHOPPED FRESH SAGE
¼ CUP WORCESTERSHIRE SAUCE
4 TO 6 GARLIC CLOVES, MINCED

Of all the hundreds of cook-offs in Texas each year, our all-time favorite may be the World Championship Barbecue Goat Cook-Off in Brady, a Labor Day weekend party since 1974. While competitors from across the country barbecue for the judges, local pitmaster Gilbert Currie does the same for the public, smoking as many as 150 goats overnight for Saturday lunch.

Serves 6 to 8

Prepare the paste rub in a food processor: First process the sage, garlic, and salt until the sage and the garlic are chopped fine, and then add the olive oil in a slow stream, mixing thoroughly.

Rub the paste over the cabrito, covering the meat evenly. Place the cabrito in a plastic trash bag and refrigerate it overnight.

The next day prepare the pit for smoking, and mix the mop sauce ingredients in a bowl. Cook the cabrito between 200° F and 220° F about 1 hour per pound of weight for each quarter. Every 20 to 30 minutes, turn the meat and apply the mop sauce liberally. The skinny forequarters will be done earlier than the meaty hindquarters, which usually take 4 to 5 hours, depending on size. Don't skimp on the mop sauce; make up more if you need it.

When the meat is done, remove it from the pit, and allow it to sit 10 minutes before serving.

CONSUMPTION OF CABRITO IS ON THE RISE NATIONALLY, A BOON FOR TEXAS SINCE MUCH OF THE GOAT RAISED COMMERCIALLY COMES FROM THE STATE. IN TEXAS, THE POPULARITY OF GOAT MEAT GOES BACK TO THE EARLY YEARS, WHEN MANY RESIDENTS CONSIDERED IT A DELICACY COMPARABLE TO BEEF. EVEN *THE CATTLEMAN* IN 1950 PRAISED THE MEAT AND TALKED ABOUT HOW COMMON IT WAS IN RESTAURANTS ACROSS THE STATE——ROASTED, BARBECUED, IN POT PIES AND BURGERS, OR SERVED UP LIKE CORNED BEEF, WITH CABBAGE. LET'S HOPE THOSE DAYS ARE RETURNING.

The World's Greatest
Hamburger

This is how to cure a kid of McDonald's, shame an adult out of a Wendy's franchise, or even wean an Austinite from Dirty's Drive-in. Once you've eaten a slow-smoked burger none other will do.

2 POUNDS CHEAPEST GRADE GROUND BEEF
½ MEDIUM ONION, CHOPPED
**3 CHOPPED ROASTED GREEN CHILES, PREFER-
    ABLY NEW MEXICAN OR POBLANO, FRESH OR
    FROZEN**
½ CUP LONE STAR DRY RUB (PAGE 27)
**BOWL OF BEER MOP SAUCE FOR MEAT
    (PAGE 28)**

Serves 4

In a bowl, blend the ground beef, onion, and chiles with your hands. Form the mixture into four thick patties, and apply the dry rub thoroughly to all surfaces. Put the meat in the refrigerator for 1 to 2 hours to absorb the seasonings while you get the pit smoking and make the mop sauce.

Cook the patties about 1 hour at 180° F to 220° F, mopping every 15 minutes.

Try a bite of your hamburger before you reach for the mustard, mayonnaise, tomatoes, lettuce, or anything else. A couple of slices of sourdough bread makes a good bun, but other embellishments could distract from an experience that'll have you wrapping your bodily parts around the cook. The grease you're used to is on the bottom of the pit, displaced by a rich smoky flavor you never suspected from ground beef.

Ain't Momma's Meat Loaf

After you've had a smoked hamburger, you'll be looking for other things to do with ground beef in the pit. Try this next.

¼ CUP OL' RED'S BARBECUE SAUCE (PAGE 29) OR OTHER SPICY TOMATO-BASED BARBECUE SAUCE

BOWL OF BEER MOP SAUCE FOR MEAT (PAGE 28)

½ CUP MINCED ONION

½ GREEN OR RED BELL PEPPER, CHOPPED FINE

3 GARLIC CLOVES, MINCED

1 TABLESPOON OIL, PREFERABLY CANOLA OR CORN

1 TEASPOON FRESH-GROUND BLACK PEPPER

1 TEASPOON CAYENNE

1 TEASPOON SALT

½ TEASPOON CUMIN SEEDS, TOASTED AND GROUND

1¼ POUNDS GROUND BEEF

¾ POUND GROUND PORK

1½ CUPS DRY BREAD CRUMBS

3 TABLESPOONS SOUR CREAM

1½ TABLESPOONS WORCESTERSHIRE SAUCE

1 EGG

¼ CUP UNSALTED STOCK, PREFERABLY BEEF

Serves 6

Prepare the barbecue sauce, if necessary, and the mop sauce. Fire up the pit, and bring it to a temperature of 200° F to 220° F.

In a heavy skillet sauté the onion, bell pepper, and garlic in the oil until softened. Add the pepper, cayenne, salt, and cumin, and sauté an additional 2 to 3 minutes. Spoon the vegetable mixture into a large bowl.

Add the remaining ingredients, except the mop and barbecue sauces, and mix well with your hands. Mound the meat into a loaf pan.

Place the loaf pan in the pit. Maintain a temperature of 200° F to 220° F during the smoking process.

After 45 minutes, or when the meat has shrunk away from the sides of the pan, gently ease the meat loaf out of the pan and directly onto the surface of the pit's grill. Continue smoking the meat for an additional 1½ hours, dabbing it every 20 to 30 minutes with the mop sauce.

When 30 minutes of cooking time remain, apply the barbecue sauce to the top of the meat loaf. At the end of the cooking time, remove the meat loaf from the pit. Allow it to sit for 10 minutes.

Serve it warm, or refrigerate it to use later for sandwiches.

Lickety Links

The same German butchers who created modern Texas barbecue also made great link sausage, which they smoked with the brisket in the pit at the back of the meat market. Only the hardiest of home cooks today will want to grind and stuff their own sausage, but you can still get that old smoky flavor. If you use precooked links, get ones that were smoked originally because they won't be in your pit long enough to absorb much smoke there. We prefer to barbecue uncooked spicy sausage, but any kind will do. The biggest hits from our pit have been an uncooked, robust Italian sausage from San Francisco, and a Texas Hill Country deer sausage mixed with some pork and red and black pepper for seasoning.

12 6- TO 8-OUNCE LINKS OF ANY SAUSAGE

Serves 6

Warm the pit to 220° F, and put the sausage in it. Maintain a temperature of 220° F until the skin of the sausage looks ready to pop, which will take 30 minutes or more with precooked links and 2 hours plus with uncooked ones. In timing the latter, it's better to err on the side of caution. Cut one of the sausages open to check for doneness before eating any of them.

WE OFTEN SERVE SMOKED SAUSAGE WRAPPED IN A WARM FLOUR TORTILLA WITH JALAPEÑO MUSTARD AND SLICES OF ONION——A SANDWICH WE CALL A GERMAN BURRITO.

Founded in 1882, the Southside Market in Elgin is one of the oldest and best-known barbecue joints in Texas, famed for its "hot guts" sausage. It's not exactly an elegant establishment, even in the new roadside quarters, but its owner, Ernest Bracewell, Jr., made a nod to the niceties in 1983 by offering forks for the first time. He explained to a concerned reporter that the restaurant was getting too many people from the North who had never learned how to eat with their fingers.

No Baloney Bologna

The second most popular sausage in the United States, after frank-furters, bologna absorbs smoke flavor wonderfully.

1 2-POUND BOLOGNA SAUSAGE
½ CUP LONE STAR DRY RUB (PAGE 27)

Cover the bologna thoroughly with the dry rub. Place the meat in a plastic bag, and leave it in the refrigerator for 4 hours or overnight.

Smoke the bologna at 200° F to 220° F for 2 hours. Serve it sliced in sandwiches with chowchow, barbecue sauce, or mustard and onions.

Houston barbecue master Jim Goode based his sausage on an old family recipe developed by Czech settlers in Texas. He favors a coarse style, saying, "You should be able to still pick out chunks of meat. I don't like a sausage to look like a wienie."

If you enjoy wacky, outrageous people, or just want to learn more about "Q," attend a barbecue cook-off. Much more than a cooking contest, a good cook-off is a circus of characters and craziness. The biggest festival in Texas falls in February at the Houston Livestock Show and Rodeo, where you'll always find Pitt's and Spitt's pits featured. Competition warms up in late summer, when the heat seems to drive people amok at Taylor's International Barbecue Cook-off, Meridian's National Championship Barbecue Cookoff, and Nacogdoches' Do Dat Barbecue celebration. If none of these affairs fits your schedule, you can find hundreds of similar ones all across the state and the country, even as far from brisket land as Alaska and Wisconsin.

In *A Yankee in German America,* Vera Flach described life on a German hill country farm in the 1920s, when she moved to Texas from back East. Making sausage at home was one of the biggest cultural shocks. "Everywhere I looked there was meat. Mixed and reground, it was in dishpans, crocks, roasting pans—and sure, wash-tubs. . . . Lard, too, was everywhere—gallon ice cream cartons, two-pound coffee cans, big crocks, little crocks. . . . While the meat was being mixed, someone (good grief, not me!) was sent to the river with a washtub of entrails. There they were washed . . . and brought back to be sausage jackets." A half century after her first experience she said, "In all the years I have never eaten a bite of sausage after I saw it made." If you want to try making sausage yourself, consult the authoritative book by Bruce Aidells and Denis Kelly, *Hot Links and Country Flavors.*

Sweet Potatoes
with Honey-Mint Butter

We don't stoke up our pit just to smoke vegetables—or bologna for that matter—but once it's going we usually fill up the cooking space with an assortment of goodies, including sweet potatoes almost every time. They seem meant for smoking, whether you eat them plain or with something extra, as we do here.

4 SMALL SWEET POTATOES
OIL, PREFERABLY CANOLA OR CORN

HONEY-MINT BUTTER
4 TO 6 TABLESPOONS UNSALTED BUTTER
2 TEASPOONS HONEY
2 TEASPOONS CHOPPED FRESH MINT
SALT AND FRESH-GROUND BLACK PEPPER TO
  TASTE

MINT SPRIGS, OPTIONAL, FOR GARNISH

Serves 4

Bring the pit to a steady temperature between 180° F to 220° F. Prick the potatoes well in several spots, and rub a light film of vegetable oil over them. Place the potatoes in the pit, and cook them until they are soft, about 2 hours. The potatoes can sit for 15 minutes before serving, or up to an hour if you wrap them in foil.

While the potatoes cook, prepare the Honey-Mint Butter: Melt the butter and honey together in a small pan. Add the mint, and then the salt and pepper. Rewarm the butter, if necessary, just before eating.

To serve the sweet potatoes, slit open the top of each one and drizzle with the Honey-Mint Butter.

> MANY SWEET POTATO RECIPES COME OUT BETTER WITH PIT-COOKED SWEET POTATOES.

SMOKING ON A COVERED GRILL

*T*he drawing shows how to use a Weber kettle grill for slow smoking. The first step is to soak wood chips or chunks in water, the former for 30 minutes and the latter for 3 hours. We like a combination of both chips and chunks. Prepare some charcoal, and place a metal pan, half full of water, on the lower grill. The hot charcoal goes alongside, directly over one of the bottom vents. Put the wet wood on the coals, and set the food on the upper grill above the water pan and under the top vent of the closed lid. The only thing not visible in the illustration may be the most critical element, the ten-dollar grill thermometer next to the meat that lets you know when you're exceeding the low temperatures needed for real barbecue. You regulate the heat mainly with two key vents, the one on top and the vent below covered by the charcoal, opening them a notch to go up and closing them to head down. Leave the other bottom vents shut.

Smoking on a Weber grill takes practice and patience. We get the best results from items that occupy less than half the grill space and take under two hours to cook. The World's Greatest Hamburger (page 49) is a good starting point for a novice. With food that takes more than an hour to cook, be sure to replenish  the wood chips occasionally to keep the smoke coming. In some cases you'll also have to add more coals, preferably ones preheated in a charcoal chimney; they'll fit through the gap between the top grill handle and the kettle rim.

Smokin' Pepper Salad

We often fix this for lunch when we're barbecuing all day. It also makes a good side dish with smoked meats.

3 LARGE BELL PEPPERS, PREFERABLY 1 EACH
    OF RED, YELLOW, AND GREEN

1 SMALL ONION

1 FRESH NEW MEXICAN OR POBLANO GREEN
    CHILE

1 FRESH JALAPEÑO OR CHILE GÜERO (BANANA
    PEPPER) OR 1 TO 2 SERRANOS

3 LARGE GARLIC CLOVES

1 TABLESPOON CANOLA OR CORN OIL

1 TABLESPOON FLAVORED OIL, SUCH AS GARLIC
    OR ROASTED SAFFLOWER

1 TABLESPOON MINCED CILANTRO

¼ TO ½ TEASPOON CUMIN SEEDS, TOASTED AND
    GROUND

RED WINE VINEGAR TO TASTE

SALT TO TASTE

*Serves 2 as a main dish
or 4 as a side dish*

 Bring the pit to a steady cooking temperature between 180° F to 220° F.

Rub each of the bell peppers, the onion, the green chile, the jalapeño, and the garlic with enough canola or corn oil to coat their surfaces lightly. Arrange them on the pit's grill, and smoke them as far from the heat as possible until they are well-softened, about 30 minutes for the garlic and 75 minutes for everything else.

Put the bell peppers, green chile, and jalapeño in a plastic bag to steam. Remove the skins from the garlic and onion, chop them fine, and transfer them to a medium serving bowl. Remove the peppers from the bag, and pull the skin off each. Slice the bell peppers and green chiles into thin ribbons, and add them to the garlic and onion. Mince the jalapeño, and add about half of it to the bowl.

Stir in the flavored oil, the cilantro, the cumin, and a bit of vinegar and salt, and taste. Add more of the jalapeño or the other seasonings as you like.

Serve the salad warm or chilled.

PIT POINTER

Barbecue books are right when they tell you not to use a fork to move meat around, but they err in suggesting tongs as the best approach. You point a pair of those overgrown tweezers at a 10-pound brisket and the poor pincers are going to wilt in your hand. What you need are some nifty neoprene gloves, available at some barbecue supply stores (see "Mail-Order Sources"). They can handle anything and they clean quickly.

Cinnamon-Scented Squash

This is another option for lunch while you're tending the pit, or it can be refrigerated and reheated a day or two later for a side dish.

1 GOOD-SIZE ACORN SQUASH
1 TEASPOON OIL, PREFERABLY CANOLA OR
   CORN

CINNAMON BUTTER
4 TO 6 TABLESPOONS UNSALTED BUTTER
2 TEASPOONS DARK BROWN SUGAR
1 TEASPOON GROUND CANELA (MEXICAN CIN-
   NAMON) OR CINNAMON
½ TEASPOON GROUND DRIED RED CHILE,
   PREFERABLY NEW MEXICAN OR ANCHO

*Serves 2 as a main dish
or 4 as a side dish*

 Heat the pit for cooking, bringing it to a temperature of 180° F to 220° F.

Cut the squash in half, but don't remove the seeds (they will help keep it moist during the smoking). Rub the oil over the cut surfaces of the squash and on the outside. Place the squash halves, cut side down, on the pit's grill, and smoke them until they are tender, about 2 hours.

Prepare the Cinnamon Butter while the squash cooks: Melt the butter in a small pan or dish, and stir in the sugar, cinnamon, and chile. Keep the butter warm until needed.

When the squash is done, remove it from the pit. Scrape the seeds out of each squash half. If you are serving four, cut the halves into quarters. Spoon some of the Cinnamon Butter over each piece of squash.

PIT POINTER

You regulate temperature in the pit three ways. First in importance is the size and intensity of your fire. In an efficient, well-constructed pit you seldom need more than three logs burning at once, or more than a small flame going. The air-intake control is a close second in significance. You open it to increase the draft—which stirs the flame and raises the heat—or close it to dampen the blaze and reduce the temperature. The outtake adjustment on the smoke stack is most useful in reigning back a fire that's gotten too hot. Unless this happens, leave it fully open to keep the smoke circulating freely.

While-You-Wait Cheese

*This is the barbecue version of that wonderful Mexican dish **queso fundido** (baked cheese). When you're beginning to get hungry in the late afternoon and it's still hours before dinner, pop this in the pit.*

12-OUNCE PIECE MEDIUM CHEDDAR OR
  MONTEREY JACK CHEESE
1 TO 2 TEASPOONS CAJUN SEASONING OR LONE
  STAR DRY RUB (PAGE 27)
1 PICKLED OR FRESH JALAPEÑO, SLICED INTO
  THIN RINGS

*Serves 2 to 8, depending
on hunger levels*

 Bring the pit to a steady cooking temperature between 180° F to 220° F.

Place the cheese in a small baking dish. Sprinkle it with the seasoning and the jalapeño. Put the cheese in the smoker as far away from the heat as possible. Smoke the cheese until it is melted through, about 1½ hours. Avoid cooking it any longer, or it will become rubbery.

Serve the cheese immediately with warm flour tortillas, cut into quarters.

*W*ith the opening in 1887 of the first Tex-Mex restaurant, Marfa's Old Borunda Cafe, the culinary history of Texas emerged from the dark ages and entered the renaissance. . . . Along with chicken-fried steak and barbecue, Tex-Mex forms the Holy Trinity of our state's official cuisine. It is multileveled and richly dimensional, giving us taste, nutrition, history. . . . On the darker side it is responsible for unfortunate aberrations like Taco Bell and chili cookoff warfare.

Richard West, "Our Lady of the Taco," *Texas Monthly*

The sad truth is, outside Texas the fast-food franchisers have hijacked the proud Tex-Mex heritage and turned the food into big-bucks kiddie grub. Few folks in Oregon, Kansas, or New York ever ate at the Old Borunda, or any other authentic Tex-Mex restaurant, but almost everyone has had a plastic taco or two. Many have compared such a meal with one at a trendy nouvelle Southwestern–style restaurant—the kind now found all over the country—and concluded that Tex-Mex was riding the tailgate of regional cooking.

Not so. Tula Borunda Gutierrez would have shown them different a century ago in her Marfa cafe, and so could scads of cooks today in kitchens all over the state. When Tex-Mex is made right it's a bounty of flavors with the depth of bedrock. It may not be high on the scale of subtlety, but it'll have your taste buds dancing the fandango.

Chili Gravy and Yellow Cheese

The differences among Tex-Mex, Mexican, and other related styles of cooking are far from precise or definitive. They are in the kind of territory Texans love, where science yields to yarns. One night at San Antonio's Mi Tierra, when we might have been a bit downstream of the margarita flow, we had this vision about the birth of Tex-Mex cooking.

In the beginning God gave Texans the secret of chili gravy. No one in Mexico, New Mexico, California, or even the Garden of Eden knew about this sauce then, and they don't now. For eons Texans didn't do anything with the revelation except adapt it for bowls of red, a reasonable idea but hardly the whole enchilada. Finally the state's legendary lady hero, the Yellow Rose of Texas, shacked up with Santa Anna—only to help Sam Houston win Texas independence, of course. As part of the deal she got a few bites of El Presidente's Mexican combination plate. Ol' Yeller knew immediately the real purpose of chili gravy, and she passed along the discovery to friends such as Tula Borunda Gutierrez, Joe T. Garcia, and a Wisconsin farmer who dyed his cheese in her honor in thanks. Tex-Mex jumped to life when the chili gravy and the yellow cheese first seeped into a combo of enchiladas, tacos, tamales, rice, and beans.

They had all the basics in Mexico the whole time, but they used *queso blanco* (white cheese) and mild sauces without beef. You get a whole different perspective on the Battle of San Jacinto if you picture the Yellow Rose sitting around Santa Anna's tent wondering where the beef is. She knew where to find it, and so did other Texans, who ultimately began stuffing it up their tacos, enchiladas, and even tamales in place of Mexican pork, cheese, and chicken.

Meanwhile the independent-minded *paisanos* of New Mexico refused to be annexed or conquered by Texas. That left them without the beef too, though they compensated pretty well with a hardy sauce of pure chiles. The Spanish-speaking settlers of California went a different direction. Under the leadership of Friar Napa, they began developing contemporary Southwestern cuisine by grafting grapevines to corn stalks. In parts of Los Angeles today you still get a choice of red or white tortillas.

THE REAL-LIFE YELLOW ROSE OF TEXAS WAS EMILY MORGAN, A MULATTO SLAVE WHOM PRESIDENT SANTA ANNA OF MEXICO SEIZED AS SPOILS OF WAR WHILE HE WAS IN TEXAS IN 1836 TRYING TO SUPPRESS THE REBELLION AGAINST HIS RULE. LEGEND HAS IT THAT SANTA ANNA WAS SO SMITTEN WITH EMILY MORGAN'S EYES, WHICH SHONE LIKE DIAMONDS AND SPARKLED LIKE THE DEW, THAT HE PITCHED CAMP IN A VULNERABLE SPOT TO CHECK OUT THE REST OF HER ALLURES. SAM HOUSTON ATTACKED THAT AFTERNOON, WHEN SANTA ANNA WAS OCCUPIED IN HIS TENT, AND WON THE BATTLE OF SAN JACINTO AND TEXAS INDEPENDENCE. TEXANS LIKE TO BELIEVE THAT EMILY MORGAN SCHEMED HER SEDUCTION AS A PATRIOTIC PLOY AND THAT'S WHY SHE WAS "THE SWEETEST LITTLE ROSEBUD THAT TEXAS EVER KNEW."

El Huracán Chili Gravy

The variables in chili gravy are as infinite as the Odessa horizon. This version is heavy on the beef, uses scratch ingredients rather than a commercial chili powder, and is thickened by reduction and masa harina instead of wheat flour.

3 OUNCES DRIED RED CHILES (ABOUT 1
   DOZEN), PREFERABLY A COMBINATION OF
   ANCHO AND NEW MEXICAN (WE PREFER 8 OF
   THE FORMER AND 4 OF THE LATTER)
4 CUPS UNSALTED BEEF STOCK
1 POUND CHILI-GRIND GROUND BEEF
1 MEDIUM ONION, CHOPPED FINE
2 GARLIC CLOVES, MINCED
2 TABLESPOONS BACON DRIPPINGS, OPTIONAL
2 TEASPOONS CUMIN SEEDS, TOASTED AND
   GROUND
½ TEASPOON DRIED OREGANO, PREFERABLY
   MEXICAN
½ TEASPOON SALT
1 TABLESPOON MASA HARINA

Makes about 6 cups

 Preheat the oven to 300° F. Break the stems off the chile pods, and discard the seeds.

Place the pods in a single layer on a cookie sheet, and roast them in the oven at 300° F for about 5 minutes. Watch the pods closely, because they can scorch easily. Break each chile into several pieces.

In a blender, purée the pods with the stock. You will still be able to see tiny pieces of chile pulp, but they should be bound in a smooth, thick liquid. Set the purée aside.

In a medium saucepan or skillet, brown the meat with the onion and garlic. Drain the meat of excess fat. Add the bacon drippings, if you like, and return the pan to the heat. When the bacon drippings have melted, add the cumin, oregano, salt, and puréed chiles. Simmer the mixture for about 50 minutes, until the meat is tender and the liquid has thickened slightly. In a small bowl mix the masa harina with 2 table-

We named this chili gravy after Narciso Martínez, El Huracán del Valle (the Hurricane of the Valley). Martínez created *conjunto* music in the 1920s and thirties, blending the rhythms of the Mexican border with those he learned from the polkas and waltzes of Bohemian farmers in the Rio Grande Valley. The musical equivalent of Tex-Mex cooking, *conjunto* remains immensely popular in the southern part of the state and in migrant communities across the country.

spoons of the liquid, and stir the mixture back into the gravy. Simmer the gravy an additional 10 minutes.

Use the gravy with enchiladas, tamales, and other Tex-Mex dishes.

Variations: Some people prefer their chili gravy without the ground beef. Eliminate the meat, and sauté the onion and garlic in 4 tablespoons of lard or peanut oil, if you prefer. If you're eager to eat, you can speed up the preparation by starting with ½ cup chili powder (preferably either homemade, page 135, or Gebhardt's) instead of whole chile pods. In that case reduce the cumin and oregano by about half.

Beef Enchiladas

The idea of putting beef in enchiladas is sure and pure Texan. In all other forms of native Mexican and Southwestern cooking, cheese is the most common filling, followed in popularity by chicken. Even with meat inside the enchiladas, most Texans still top the dish with a beefy chili gravy, a combination as common in the state as tall hairdos at truck stops.

FILLING
1 POUND CHILI-GRIND LEAN GROUND BEEF
½ MEDIUM ONION, CHOPPED FINE
½ CUP UNSALTED BEEF STOCK
⅓ CUP CORN KERNELS, FRESH OR FROZEN
1 CHOPPED ROASTED GREEN CHILE, PREFERABLY POBLANO OR NEW MEXICAN, FRESH OR FROZEN
SALT TO TASTE

½ BATCH EL HURACÁN CHILI GRAVY (PAGE 63)
OIL, PREFERABLY CANOLA OR CORN, IF YOU ARE USING COMMERCIAL TORTILLAS
12 TO 16 CORN TORTILLAS
GRATED MILD CHEDDAR CHEESE, CHOPPED ONION, AND MINCED FRESH JALAPEÑO OR SERRANO, FOR GARNISH

Serves 4

In a medium skillet, fry the ground beef with the onions until the meat is gray. Pour off any excess fat. Add the stock, corn, green chile, and salt, and simmer, covered, for 10 minutes. The filling can be made a day ahead and reheated.

Preheat the oven to 350° F. Grease a medium baking dish. Warm the chili gravy, if it has been refrigerated.

If you use commercial tortillas, which are generally less fresh than homemade, they will need to be softened. Heat ½ to 1 inch of oil in a small skillet until the oil ripples. With tongs, dunk each tortilla in the oil just long enough for it to go limp, a matter of seconds. Don't let the tortilla turn crisp. Drain the tortillas lightly before proceeding. If you begin with fresh homemade tortillas, they will be soft enough to forgo the dip in oil.

With tongs, dip a tortilla in the gravy liquid to lightly coat it. Lay the tortilla on a plate, sprinkle 3 to 4 tablespoons of filling over it, and roll it up snugly. Transfer the enchilada to the baking dish. Repeat with the remaining tortillas and filling. Top the enchiladas with the remaining chili gravy, seeing that each enchilada is submerged in the sauce. Place the dish in the oven, and bake for 20 to 25 minutes, until the enchiladas are heated through and the sauce is bubbly. Remove the dish from the oven and sprinkle immediately with the cheese, onion, and jalapeño.

With a spatula, serve 3 to 4 enchiladas per person.

The Old Borunda Cafe remained in the same family until it closed in 1985. The last owner, Carolina Borunda Humphries, continued to do the cooking until illness forced her to shut the doors.

Variation: Enchilada plates can be prepared individually. Rather than use a baking dish, divide the rolled enchiladas among four plates, and spoon equal portions of the chili gravy over them. Bake 15 to 18 minutes.

Cheese Enchiladas

Texans used to fill cheese enchiladas with processed American cheese, popular because of its long shelf life and creamy consistency. At least one major chain of Tex-Mex restaurants still offers American cheese as an alternative, calling the variation "old-fashioned" cheese enchiladas. Real cheese is more common today.

FILLING

1½ POUNDS MILD CHEDDAR CHEESE, GRATED
½ MEDIUM ONION, CHOPPED FINE

1 BATCH EL HURACÁN CHILI GRAVY (PAGE 63)
OIL, PREFERABLY CANOLA OR CORN, IF YOU ARE USING COMMERCIAL TORTILLAS
12 TO 16 CORN TORTILLAS
GRATED MILD CHEDDAR CHEESE, CHOPPED ONION, AND MINCED FRESH JALAPEÑO OR SERRANO, FOR GARNISH

Serves 4

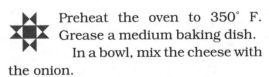 Preheat the oven to 350° F. Grease a medium baking dish.
In a bowl, mix the cheese with the onion.

Warm the chili gravy if it has been refrigerated.

If you use commercial tortillas, which may not be fresh, they will probably need to be softened. Heat ½ to 1 inch of oil in a small skillet until the oil ripples. With tongs, dunk each tortilla in the oil long enough for it to go limp, a matter of seconds. Don't let the tortilla turn crisp. Drain the tortillas lightly before proceeding. If you begin with fresh homemade tortillas, they will be soft enough to forgo the dip in oil.

With tongs, dip a tortilla in the gravy liquid to coat it lightly. Lay the tortilla on a plate, sprinkle about ¼ cup of filling over it, and roll it up snugly. Transfer the enchilada to the baking dish. Repeat with the remaining tortillas and filling. Top the enchiladas with the

---

The oldest Mexican restaurant chain in the country is El Fenix, started in Dallas by Mike Martínez in 1918. Originally from Mexico, Martínez learned to cook in the kitchen of the old Oriental (later Baker) Hotel, but was fired after his cooking became more popular than the chef's. When he opened the first El Fenix several months later, Martínez couldn't afford to hire help, so he pioneered the combination plate ordered by number as a way of keeping meal service simple.

remaining chili gravy, seeing that each enchilada is submerged in the sauce. Place the dish in the oven, and bake for 15 to 18 minutes, until the enchiladas are heated through and the sauce is bubbly.

Remove the dish from the oven, and sprinkle immediately with the cheese, onion, and jalapeño.

With a spatula, serve 3 to 4 enchiladas per person.

Hot Tamales

Tamales were the first Mexican dish to cross ethnic food lines in Texas and win broad acceptance. John C. Duval's experience may have been fairly typical among the Anglo pioneers. Around 1840 he and a traveling companion camped out near San Antonio. Their cook went to town to get corn and came back with rolls of husks he called "termarlers." The friend accused the cook of trying to feed them the roughage intended for the horses, but they later concluded the strange dish was excellent. Duval was so impressed he gave something of a recipe in his book **Early Times in Texas.**

FILLING

1½ POUNDS PORK LOIN

1 MEDIUM ONION, CHOPPED

1 BAY LEAF

2 CUPS WATER

2 TABLESPOONS OIL, PREFERABLY CANOLA OR CORN

2 GARLIC CLOVES, MINCED

1 TABLESPOON ALL-PURPOSE FLOUR

½ CUP CHILI POWDER, PREFERABLY HOMEMADE (PAGE 135) OR GEBHARDT'S

¾ TEASPOON SALT

¼ TEASPOON DRIED OREGANO, PREFERABLY MEXICAN

¼ TEASPOON CUMIN SEEDS, TOASTED AND GROUND, OPTIONAL

MASA

1 6-OUNCE PACKAGE DRIED CORN HUSKS

6 CUPS MASA HARINA

2 CUPS OIL, PREFERABLY CANOLA OR CORN

4½ CUPS WATER, OR MORE, AS NEEDED

1 TO 2 TABLESPOONS CHILI POWDER, PREFERABLY HOMEMADE (PAGE 135) OR GEBHARDT'S

2 TEASPOONS SALT

EL HURACÁN CHILI GRAVY (PAGE 63), GRATED MILD CHEDDAR CHEESE, AND MINCED ONION, FOR GARNISH

Makes 24 tamales of approximately 4 ounces each, about 8 to 12 main-dish servings

A day or two ahead, begin making the filling. Preheat the oven to 350° F.

Place the pork, onion, and bay leaf in a medium-size baking dish, and cover with the water. Bake for approximately 1½ hours, or until the meat is cooked through and pulls apart easily. Remove the pork from the broth. Set the meat aside to cool a few minutes, and refrigerate the broth. When the pork has cooled enough to handle, shred it fine, either with two forks or with the plastic dough blade in a Cuisinart or similar food processor. Refrigerate the broth, covered, overnight. The following day, strain the broth of fat solidified on its surface. If the broth doesn't measure 2 cups, add water to make 2 cups of liquid. Reserve the pork and the broth.

In a large, heavy skillet, warm the oil over medium heat, and add the garlic and pork. Sprinkle the flour over the mixture, and stir constantly for about a minute as the flour begins to brown. Add the chili powder, reserved broth, salt, oregano, and, if you like, cumin. Continue cooking over medium heat for about 30 minutes, or until the mixture has thickened and is almost dry. Watch carefully toward the end of the cooking time, stirring frequently to avoid burning. The filling will be meltingly tender. Reserve the mixture.

To prepare the corn husks, place them in a deep bowl or pan and cover them with hot water. Soak them 30 minutes, or until they are soft and pliable. Separate the husks, and rinse them under warm running water to remove any grit or brown silks. Soak the husks in more warm water until you are ready to use them.

To prepare the masa, the dough made from masa harina cornmeal, measure the masa harina into a large bowl. Add the oil, water, chili powder, and salt. Mix with a sturdy spoon, a powerful electric mixer, or your hands until smooth. When well-blended, the masa should have the consistency of a moist cookie dough.

To assemble the tamales, review the tips that follow this recipe. The amount of masa and filling used for each tamale should be approximately equal, but will vary depending on the size and shape of the tamale. To make 2 dozen 4-ounce tamales, use 2 tablespoons of masa and filling for each tamale.

Hold a corn husk flat on one hand.

Tamale vendors used to be common on the streets of Texas towns, selling homemade goods out of ten-gallon lard cans carried on the back or in a pushcart. The vendor cried out, "Hot tamales!" as he walked, stressing the last syllable compellingly. A nickel would buy a dozen during the Depression. Most of the customers were Anglos, because Mexican families could make their own more cheaply.

With a rubber spatula, spread a thin layer of masa across the husk and top with the filling. Roll the husk into the desired shape, using your imagination. Repeat the procedure until all the filling and masa are used.

Review the accompanying pointers on steaming the tamales. Cook the tamales over simmering water for 1 to 1¾ hours until the masa is firm and no longer sticks to the corn husk. Unwrap one tamale to check its consistency.

The tamales should be eaten warm. The corn husks are usually left on when the tamales are served unadorned, to be removed by each guest before eating. But when they're topped by chili gravy, as they often are, the husks are removed before the sauce is added. Sprinkle cheese and onion over the sauce before serving.

Variations: Tasty vegetarian tamales now abound, often stuffed with beans and cheese. We prefer a squash, corn, and cheese mixture. Instead of the meat filling, combine 1 cup roasted, chopped New Mexican green chile, 2 pounds grated zucchini, 2 cups corn kernels, 1

Most early tamale recipes called for meat from a pig's head, and in many areas of Texas that's still the pork used.

One Tex-Mex classic, cabrito or young goat, is regaining some of its old popularity in Texas. We like to barbecue cabrito, as described on page 47, but it's also good baked when you know what you're doing. Jorge and Ninfa Guerra perfected our favorite oven preparation at their colorful Austin restaurant, El Azteca. It's worth a special trip there to try it. Based partially on a secret old recipe from Jorge's uncle in Reynosa, the Guerra family's young goat is deep-fried at the end, giving it a wonderful contrast of textures.

tablespoon salt (or more, to taste), and 4 minced garlic cloves. Transfer the mixture to a colander, and let the accumulated liquid drain for at least 30 minutes. Stir in 2 cups grated mild cheddar cheese. Fill the masa as described above.

On the other end of the scale from this vegetarian option, some people insist that lard is better in the masa than oil, and some people prefer a beef filling made by draining the liquid from a favorite chili con carne.

TECHNIQUE TIPS

Tamales are a Texas Christmas treat, partially because their labor-intensive preparation is easier when enough people are around to make an assembly line. The work goes quickly with extra hands.

Clear off a table for your workspace, and line up the bowls of corn husks, dough, and filling. Have a towel and scissors handy, and a large plate or bowl for the wrapped tamales. If you are inexperienced, allow at least 2 hours for assembling the tamales. The assembly will go much faster with practice or additional help. Steaming requires another hour or more.

Tamales can be plump or thin and shaped as long cylinders or as rounded pouches. To assure that they cook fully, tamales should not be made any larger than described in the recipe, but they can be made smaller for appetizers.

Keep the dough loosely covered while you work. Spread it thin, on the smoother side of the corn husks, but not to the edges of the husks.

Top with filling spread more thickly through the dough's center, stopping short of the dough's edges. Roll the tamale, enclosing all the filling. Corn husks can be tied with strips of extra husk at both ends, or at the top of the pouch, or folded over at one end.

Depending on the size of the corn husks, you may have to overlap two husks to form one tamale. Spread the dough over the husks together, just as if they were one.

To cook the tamales, a large saucepan or small stockpot works best. Use a metal vegetable steamer or improvise with a baking rack or metal colander over about 2 inches of water. If you own a Chinese bamboo steamer, it will work, too. Place the tamales into the steamer, packing them loosely in opposite directions, or stand them on end. Allow enough space between them for the steam to rise effectively. Cover the pot, and cook over simmering water. You may need to use two steamers, or cook the tamales in two batches.

Toro Tacos

Many Tex-Mex tacos are made with ground beef. That's OK, especially when the meat is well seasoned, but chuck is much better. The preferred cut, if your butcher has it, is "eye of chuck," which contains a lot of beef flavor and shreds perfectly for tacos. The marinade adds real Tex-Mex punch.

1½ POUNDS EYE OF CHUCK

MARINADE

3 TABLESPOONS OIL, PREFERABLY CANOLA OR
    CORN
3 TABLESPOONS JALAPEÑO PICKLING LIQUID
1 TEASPOON CUMIN SEEDS, TOASTED AND
    GROUND
1 TEASPOON CHILI POWDER, PREFERABLY
    HOMEMADE (PAGE 135) OR GEBHARDT'S
2 GARLIC CLOVES, MINCED
1 CUP UNSALTED BEEF STOCK OR WATER
SALT TO TASTE
MINCED ONION AND FRESH OR PICKLED
    JALAPEÑO, OPTIONAL

18 TO 24 TACO SHELLS (PAGE 92)
YOUR FAVORITE SALSA (PAGES 95–97)
BITE-SIZE LETTUCE, CHOPPED TOMATOES, AND
    GRATED MILD CHEDDAR CHEESE OR CRUM-
    BLED ASADERO CHEESE (A TANGY MEXICAN
    CHEESE), FOR GARNISH

Serves 6

Prepare the filling: You can choose one of two methods for cooking the meat. Charcoal grilling is faster and more flavorful. Baking gives a slightly moister meat and may be easier some times of the year. Prepare the grill or preheat the oven to 350° F.

If you are grilling the meat, cut it into slices about ½ inch thick and place them in one layer in a shallow pan. If you plan to bake the meat, it's not necessary to slice it thinner than 1 inch.

In a small bowl, combine the oil, pickling liquid, cumin, chili powder, and garlic, and pour the marinade over the meat. Cover the meat, and refrigerate it at least 4 hours, or overnight, turning occasionally if the meat isn't thoroughly submerged in the marinade. Drain the meat, and bring it back to room temperature before proceeding. Save a tablespoon or two of the marinade if you plan to bake the meat.

If you are grilling the meat, place it over the coals when they are well covered with gray ash. Turn the meat once, and grill it until it is just cooked through, approximately 4 minutes per side.

To bake the meat, place it in a small baking dish with the stock or water and the reserved marinade. Cover the dish, and bake approximately 1¼ hours, or until the meat is cooked through and pulls apart easily.

Let the grilled or baked meat cool about 10 minutes, and then shred it. A food processor equipped with a plastic blade takes care of this step in quick measure. Salt the meat, and, if you like, add some onion, jalapeño, or both. Serve immediately, or refrigerate the filling for later reheating.

Serve the taco filling with the shells, salsa, and garnishes heaped on a platter or in separate bowls. Let everyone fill each of their taco shells with 2 or 3 tablespoons of filling, and top with the remaining ingredients.

Variations: For Texas soft tacos, wrap your fillings in warm flour tortillas rather than crispy corn shells. Since soft tacos are often made in the morning with leftovers from the previous night, we describe them in the chapter "Eye-Popping, Heart-Thumping Breakfasts" on page 426.

Carne Guisada

In the early years of statehood Tejanos made a stew similar to this except that carne *(meat) wasn't included in the name or very often in the pot either. Our version is based on the one served today at Guero's Taco Bar in Austin, a top-notch restaurant. Many guisadas cook on top of the stove, but the meat will be more tender if slow-baked. In either case, the stew should be thick, without much liquid. Guisada can be served by itself or as a filling in soft tacos.*

1¼ POUNDS BEEF TIPS CUT FROM A CHUCK ROAST, IN BITE-SIZE PIECES

2 TABLESPOONS ALL-PURPOSE FLOUR

1 TABLESPOON OIL, PREFERABLY CANOLA OR CORN

3 CELERY RIBS, CHOPPED

1 MEDIUM ONION, CHOPPED

1 TO 2 FRESH JALAPEÑOS, MINCED

1½ CUPS UNSALTED BEEF STOCK

1 TABLESPOON TOMATO PASTE

2 TEASPOONS CUMIN SEEDS, TOASTED AND GROUND

¼ TEASPOON CHILI POWDER, PREFERABLY HOMEMADE (PAGE 135) OR GEBHARDT'S

Serves 3 to 4 as a main dish, or 4 to 6 in tacos

Preheat the oven to 350° F.

Dust the meat cubes with the flour. Heat the oil over high heat in a skillet or Dutch oven. Brown the meat quickly. Add the remaining ingredients, and bring the mixture to a simmer on the stove. Cover the skillet, and place it in the oven. Bake about 2½ hours, until the meat falls apart at the touch. Serve warm.

Picadillo

The Tex-Mex equivalent of sloppy Joes, picadillo is heavy-duty comfort food. The ground meat can be beef, a combination of beef and pork, or sometimes venison. The savory mixture shows up in tacos and burritos, served on buns, or scooped atop tostada chips or Fritos.

1½ POUNDS LEAN GROUND BEEF
1 LARGE ONION, CHOPPED
2 GARLIC CLOVES, MINCED
1 14½-OUNCE CAN TOMATOES
2 MEDIUM BAKING POTATOES, CUT INTO BITE-SIZE CUBES
¼ CUP UNSALTED BEEF STOCK OR WATER
1 TEASPOON VINEGAR, PREFERABLY WHITE OR CIDER
1 CANNED CHIPOTLE CHILE WITH ½ TEASPOON ADOBO SAUCE
½ TEASPOON CUMIN SEEDS, TOASTED AND GROUND
½ TEASPOON SALT
½ BAY LEAF
1 TABLESPOON MINCED CILANTRO

Makes about 6 cups

In a skillet over medium heat, brown the ground beef with the onion and garlic. Pour off any accumulated grease. Add the remaining ingredients, except the cilantro. Simmer over medium-low heat for 20 to 25 minutes, stirring occasionally. Add a little water if the mixture appears dry. Serve the picadillo warm, sprinkled with the cilantro.

Variation: For Holiday Picadillo, add 1 chopped pear, ½ cup slivered almonds, ½ cup raisins, and ½ teaspoon ground canela (Mexican cinnamon) or cinnamon.

Gebhardt's Chili Powder is probably the oldest on the market and still the best in our book. German-born William Gebhardt, a New Braunfels resident, loved the famous fare of San Antonio's chili queens. In 1896 he figured out a formula for making their specialty from dried ingredients. He based the original chili powder on ground ancho chiles and a mix of spices such as cumin and garlic, still the core constituents today.

Ninfa's Fajitas

Ninfa Rodriguez Laurenzo opened a ten-table restaurant, Ninfa's, in Houston's eastside barrio in 1973. She cooked everything herself at first, modeling her dishes on ones her mother made years earlier in the Rio Grande Valley town of Harlingen. Over time Ninfa added new fare from Mexico, new restaurants, and new chefs, and within twenty years she was operating a dozen Ninfa's branches and a couple of dozen other eateries. One of the dishes she brought to Houston from the Valley, fajitas, swept the city and eventually the state. This is how Ninfa makes it.

2 SKIRT STEAKS, 1 TO 1¼ POUNDS EACH

MARINADE

1 LARGE ORANGE
2 LEMONS
¼ CUP PINEAPPLE JUICE
¼ CUP WHITE WINE
¼ CUP SOY SAUCE
¼ CUP WATER
3 DRIED CHILES DE ÁRBOL
1 TABLESPOON COARSE-GROUND BLACK PEPPER
1 GARLIC CLOVE, MINCED

16 TO 20 7-INCH FLOUR TORTILLAS, HEATED
NINFA'S MARINATED ONIONS (PAGE 88)
PICO DE GALLO (PAGE 95)
GUACAMOLE (PAGE 98)
TOMATO SLICES AND GREEN BELL PEPPER RINGS, OPTIONAL

Serves 8 generously

Trim the skirt steaks well of any membrane or fat. Place them in a shallow pan large enough to hold the meat in one layer.

For the marinade, grate 1 tablespoon of peel from the orange and 2 teaspoons peel from the lemons. Squeeze the orange to get approximately ¼ cup juice, and both lemons to get a similar amount of juice. Put the citrus zest and fresh-squeezed juices into a small bowl. Add the pineapple juice, wine, soy sauce, water, chiles, black pepper, and garlic, stirring to combine the ingredients. Pour the marinade over the skirt steaks. Let the

The oldest Tex-Mex cookbook we've found is *Gebhardt's Mexican Cookery for American Homes*, published by the San Antonio chili company in the 1930s. It wasn't until this period that enchiladas and tacos—or much else beyond chili and tamale variations—begin to appear in cookbooks.

meat marinate for at least 1 hour but not longer than 2 hours.

Prepare the grill, as Ninfa does, or preheat the broiler.

Drain the skirt steaks. Cook them about 3 inches above the coals or 4 inches below the broiler flame for about 5 to 6 minutes on each side, or until they are done to your taste. Remove the meat from the heat, and let it sit for 5 to 10 minutes. Slice the meat across the grain and diagonally into finger-length strips.

To assemble the fajitas, pile a platter

The biggest beef eaters in early Texas were the Mexican settlers in the southwestern part of the state. The Anglos who immigrated from the South favored pork until the second half of the nineteenth century, when they pushed farther west and learned both the cowboy trade and a love of beef from their Mexican neighbors.

high with the meat, and accompany the meat platter with the tortillas, onions, pico de gallo, guacamole, and, if you like, tomatoes and bell peppers. Let all assembled help themselves. For each serving, fill a flour tortilla with some of the meat and portions of the garnishes.

Variation: For pork tenderloin fajitas-style, pound 2 to 2½ pounds pork tenderloin to ½-inch thickness, removing any membrane. Marinate for 2 hours, and prepare as you would the skirt steaks.

In Mexican cooking, dishes such as tacos, tamales, and enchiladas are called *antojitos*. Literally "a little whim," the term can refer to appetizers at a meal or to typical native foods popular as street snacks. Traditional Mexicans seldom, if ever, eat the equivalent of a Tex-Mex combination plate, that is, a full dinner of *antojitos*. As Maria A. de Carbia said in the American edition of her Mexican cookbook (edited by Neiman Marcus chef Helen Corbitt), if you served a meal like that in her country the dessert of choice would be bicarbonate of soda.

Chicken a la Fajitas

Fajitas is the Spanish name for beef skirt, so a term like "chicken fajitas" doesn't make linguistic sense, however common it might be. The dish itself is definitely delicious, whatever you call it. This is Ninfa Laurenzo's recipe for chicken prepared fajitas-style, and it's a true match for her beef version.

2 TO 2¼ POUNDS BONELESS, SKINLESS
   CHICKEN BREASTS
3 TABLESPOONS WHITE WINE
6 TABLESPOONS UNSALTED BUTTER
1 TABLESPOON SOY SAUCE
2 GARLIC CLOVES, MINCED
1 TEASPOON FRESH-GROUND BLACK PEPPER
16 TO 20 7-INCH FLOUR TORTILLAS
NINFA'S MARINATED ONIONS (PAGE 88)
PICO DE GALLO (PAGE 95)
GUACAMOLE (PAGE 98)
TOMATO SLICES AND GREEN BELL PEPPER
   RINGS, OPTIONAL

Serves 8 generously

Prepare the grill, as Ninfa does, or preheat the broiler.

Pound the chicken breasts to ¾-inch thickness, and set them aside.

Heat a heavy skillet over high heat for 3 to 4 minutes. Pour the wine into the skillet, and boil it for 1 to 2 minutes to evaporate the alcohol. Reduce the heat to medium. Stir in the butter, soy sauce, garlic, and pepper, and cook until they are just combined, about 1 minute. Remove the skillet from the heat.

Dip the chicken breasts into the sauce, and turn them to coat them thoroughly.

Place the breasts 3 inches above the coals or 4 inches below the broiler flame. Grill or broil the chicken 3 to 5 minutes on each side, or until it is done to your taste. Remove the chicken from the heat, and let it sit for about 5 minutes. Slice the breasts into slim finger-length strips.

To assemble the fajitas, pile a platter high with the chicken strips, and accompany the platter with tortillas, onion, pico de gallo, guacamole, and if you like, the tomatoes and bell peppers. Let all assembled help themselves. For each serving, fill a tortilla with some of the chicken and portions of the garnishes.

In 1991 commercial Mexican salsa overtook ketchup as the top-selling condiment in the United States. This represented a major shift in American tastes. Before then ketchup had reigned supreme for over one hundred years.

Turkey Mole

The *Texas Almanac*—an indisputable source for hard-core trivia—says turkeys are among the state's oldest residents. They certainly were abundant in the early years of Anglo settlement, and became the wild game of choice for many hunters. This way of preparing the birds is relatively new in Texas, but ancient in Mexico, where **mole** is the queen of sauces.

SAUCE

12 OUNCES DRIED RED CHILE PODS, PREFERABLY A MIX OF ANCHOS, MULATOS, AND PASILLAS
6 TABLESPOONS SESAME SEEDS
4 TABLESPOONS PEANUT OIL
¾ CUP SLICED ALMONDS
6 GARLIC CLOVES, WITH SKINS ON
6 SMALL TOMATOES, PREFERABLY ROMAS OR ANOTHER ITALIAN PLUM VARIETY, WHOLE AND UNPEELED
2½ CUPS UNSALTED CHICKEN STOCK
JUICE OF 1 ORANGE
½ CUP RAISINS
½ CUP CHOPPED CILANTRO
1 MEDIUM ONION, CHOPPED
1 DAY-OLD CORN TORTILLA, TORN INTO QUARTERS
2 OUNCES UNSWEETENED CHOCOLATE
1½ OUNCES MEXICAN CHOCOLATE, PREFERABLY IBARRA (OR AN EQUAL AMOUNT OF BITTERSWEET CHOCOLATE WITH A PINCH OF CINNAMON)
1 CANNED CHIPOTLE CHILE, OPTIONAL
1 TEASPOON GROUND CANELA (MEXICAN CINNAMON) OR CINNAMON
1 TEASPOON ANISE SEEDS, TOASTED AND GROUND
½ TEASPOON FRESH-GROUND BLACK PEPPER
½ TEASPOON CUMIN SEEDS, TOASTED AND GROUND
½ TEASPOON SALT
⅛ TEASPOON GROUND CLOVES

HOT SLICED SMOKED TURKEY BREAST (PAGE 39) OR OTHER GOOD SMOKED OR ROASTED TURKEY
SPRIGS OF CILANTRO, OPTIONAL, FOR GARNISH
MINCED CILANTRO AND ONION, FOR GARNISH

Serves 10 to 12

Preheat the oven to 300° F. Break the stems off the chiles, and remove the seeds. Rinse the chiles, and transfer them to a baking sheet. Toast them for about 5 minutes, watching to make sure they don't burn. Turn off the oven. Transfer the chiles to a large saucepan, and cover them with water. Simmer over medium heat about 30 minutes, until the chiles are softened.

While the chiles simmer, prepare the seeds and nuts in a large, heavy skillet on top of the stove. First, toast the sesame seeds over medium heat. Watch them carefully. The seeds are done when fragrant, lightly browned, and popping merrily, a matter of several minutes. Don't let them burn. Spoon the seeds into a blender. Add 2 tablespoons of the oil to the warm skillet, and stir in the almonds. Sauté until the almonds are lightly colored and fragrant. Transfer them to the blender.

Wipe out the skillet with a paper towel, and increase the heat to medium-high. Scatter the garlic in the skillet, turning the cloves occasionally so that they soften and darken on all sides, a matter of a few minutes. Remove the garlic from the skillet, and set it aside. Add the tomatoes to the skillet, turning occasionally as they soften and darken. The skins will split a bit during the process. Remove the tomatoes, and set them aside until they are cool enough to handle.

Remove the skins from the garlic and tomatoes, stem the tomatoes, and add both to the blender.

Pour about 1½ cups of the stock into the blender. Purée the mixture for 2 to 3 minutes. The mixture will become smooth but a little grainy. Pour it into a large bowl.

The country's leading producer of commercial Mexican salsas is San Antonio's Pace Foods. David Pace developed the company's original product, Pace Picante Sauce, in 1947, and it's still made with the same recipe. One of the secrets is fresh jalapeños, used in amounts exceeding 25 million pounds a year.

TECHNIQUE TIPS

Mexicans make many different *moles*—complex, slightly sweet cooked sauces of varied chiles, chocolate, and ground seeds or nuts. This is a Texified version of a common Oaxacan *mole*. Though time-consuming to do, the roasting and toasting of the ingredients develops the multidimensional richness that marks a great *mole*. The sauce can be made a day ahead or frozen in batches.

For a fast and still tasty alternative, keep a jar or two of mole paste (a precooked blend of the key mole ingredients) on the pantry shelf. Heat it with a couple of teaspoons of peanut oil, a few squeezes of orange juice to taste, and enough chicken stock to make a sauce.

Drain most of the liquid from the chiles, reserving 1 cup of the liquid. Put the chiles and about ½ cup of the reserved liquid into the blender, and purée 1 to 2 minutes. Pour the chiles into the bowl of puréed tomatoes and almonds.

Add the remaining sauce ingredients to the blender, and purée for 2 to 3 minutes. This mixture, too, will become smooth but a little grainy. Pour it into the bowl, and stir the mixtures together.

Wipe out any tomato residue from the skillet, and add the remaining oil. Warm the oil over medium heat. Spoon in the *mole* sauce, and fry it for about 10 minutes, stirring up from the bottom constantly. The sauce should be thick but spoonable. Mix in a little of the reserved chile cooking liquid if it seems too thick. Cool and refrigerate the sauce for later reheating, or serve it immediately.

Arrange the turkey slices on a serving platter, and top generously with the *mole*. Surround the dish with sprigs of cilantro, if you like, and sprinkle with minced cilantro and onion.

Variations: For *mole* enchiladas, shred several cups of turkey or chicken and toss with a couple of tablespoons minced onion and cilantro. Assemble and cook as you do Beef Enchiladas (page 64), topped with *mole* sauce. Sprinkle with crumbled asadero or other fresh Mexican cheese, or with grated Monterey jack.

For a cocktail party, cube uncooked turkey or chicken, and marinate the cubes in orange juice with a little garlic and cilantro. Skewer the cubes, grill them, and serve them with the *mole* as a dipping sauce.

A common practical joke in the early years of Anglo settlement was to trick greenhorns into taking a mouthful of fiery chiles. Old-timers told newcomers the small red pods were sweet Texas strawberries.

Chipotle Chorizo

German settlers in Texas flavored their sausage with smoke. Mexican settlers used chile and other seasonings instead. You get the best of both worlds in this chorizo, made with smoky chipotle chile.

4 DRIED RED CHILES, PREFERABLY 2 ANCHO AND 2 NEW MEXICAN

1½ POUNDS GROUND PORK

½ CUP MINCED ONION

⅓ CUP CIDER VINEGAR

5 GARLIC CLOVES, MINCED

2 CANNED CHIPOTLE CHILES, MINCED

1 TO 2 TEASPOONS ADOBO SAUCE FROM CANNED CHIPOTLE CHILES

1 TEASPOON CUMIN SEEDS, TOASTED AND GROUND

1 TEASPOON SALT

½ TEASPOON CRUSHED CHILE PEQUÍN OR CAYENNE, OR MORE, TO TASTE

½ TEASPOON DRIED OREGANO, PREFERABLY MEXICAN

½ TEASPOON FRESH-GROUND BLACK PEPPER

¼ TEASPOON GROUND CANELA (MEXICAN CINNAMON) OR CINNAMON

¼ TEASPOON GROUND CORIANDER

Makes about 2 pounds

 Preheat the oven to 300° F. Break the stems off the chile pods, and discard most of the seeds.

Place the pods in a single layer on a cookie sheet, and roast them in the oven for about 5 minutes. Watch the pods closely, because they can scorch easily. Break each chile into several pieces. Transfer the chiles to a blender, and blend until they are evenly ground.

In a medium bowl, mix together the ground chile and all the other ingredients. Cover the bowl, and refrigerate it at least 8 hours and preferably 24. Use the chorizo as needed. Form it into patties, or fry it as is over medium heat until it is richly browned. It keeps, uncooked and refrigerated, at least a week.

As popular as jalapeños are in Texas cooking nowadays, they aren't a traditional Tex-Mex ingredient. Red chiles, such as the anchos used in chili powder, were the original favorites in the state. Jalapeños didn't catch on until recent decades. They reached craze status around 1976, when an Austinite set a world record by eating 108 in an hour. More recently, at the 1992 Jalapeño Festival in Laredo, Braulio Ramirez downed 141 of the fiery chiles in just 15 minutes.

Menudo

Menudo migrated to Texas from the Mexican state of Sonora, but the tripe stew may be more popular today on this side of the Rio Grande than anywhere across the border. The Texas claimant for the title "breakfast of champions," menudo is widely respected as a hangover cure.

1 CUP KOSHER SALT

1 CUP VINEGAR, PREFERABLY WHITE

2 POUNDS HONEYCOMB TRIPE

2 TABLESPOONS OIL, PREFERABLY CANOLA OR CORN

2 LARGE ONIONS, CHOPPED

4 TO 6 GARLIC CLOVES

2 TO 4 FRESH SERRANOS, MINCED, OR 1 TO 3 JALAPEÑOS, MINCED

6 CUPS UNSALTED CHICKEN STOCK

1 SMOKED HAM HOCK, PIG'S FOOT, PORK KNUCKLE, OR MEATY MARROWBONE, OR ¾ POUND OXTAILS (WE PREFER THE SMOKINESS OF THE HAM HOCK)

2 TABLESPOONS CHILI POWDER, PREFERABLY HOMEMADE (PAGE 135) OR GEBHARDT'S

1 TABLESPOON DRIED OREGANO, PREFERABLY MEXICAN

½ TEASPOON COARSE-GROUND BLACK PEPPER

SALT TO TASTE

1 14½- TO 16-OUNCE CAN HOMINY, DRAINED

½ CUP CHOPPED FRESH MINT, OPTIONAL

½ CUP CHOPPED CILANTRO, OPTIONAL

LIME WEDGES, FOR GARNISH

Serves 6 to 8

The day before you plan to serve it, clean the tripe. Mix together the salt and vinegar. Pour about ⅓ of the mixture into a large bowl, and add the tripe. Of numerous descriptions we've seen for cleaning tripe, Chris Schlesinger says it best in his *Thrill of the Grill*. Scrub the tripe "vigorously for 5 minutes, with a brush, as if the tripe were a dirty shirt collar." The kosher salt's rough texture acts as an abrasive. Rinse the tripe under cold running water, and repeat the process two more times. Transfer the tripe to a medium bowl, and cover it with cold water. Chill the tripe, covered, at least 8 hours; twice that long is fine. Change the water once about halfway through the chilling.

TECHNIQUE TIP

For menudo be sure to get honeycomb tripe, the most tender of the varieties. Tender is relative though, because all types start out tough and require long cooking. Tripe perishes quickly in its uncooked, uncleaned form, so start its preparation as early as possible. Look for tripe that is pale off-white at the market.

Remove the tripe from the refrigerator, and drain it. Slice the tripe into bite-size pieces, and place the pieces in a stockpot or large, heavy saucepan. Cover the tripe with cold water, and bring the water to a rapid boil over high heat. Boil the tripe 30 minutes. Drain the water from the tripe, discarding it, and reserve the tripe.

Rinse and dry the stockpot, and return it to the stove. Add the oil. Warm the oil over medium heat, and add the onions, garlic, and serranos. Sauté until they are soft, about 3 to 5 minutes. Add the stock and ham hock or other meat. Simmer the menudo over low heat 3 hours.

Remove the ham hock, discarding any bones or chunks of fat. Shred the meat, and reserve it. Add the chili powder, oregano, pepper, salt, and hominy.

Calvin Trillin, one of America's most passionate eaters, sniffs out good Mexican restaurants by looking for menudo on the menu. He's not interested in ordering the dish, but he knows that it's a sign of seriousness about the cooking.

Simmer another hour, or until the stew is cooked down and the tripe is tender. It will retain a little chewiness. Stir in the reserved ham hock or other meat, and, if you like, the mint and cilantro.

Serve the menudo steaming in large bowls with wedges of lime. Menudo will keep for several days.

Arroz Pilaf

The best Tex-Mex rice is a chili-scented pilaf, not the gloppy tomato "Spanish rice" concoction you find almost everywhere outside the state. This arroz is a perfect foil for enchiladas, beans, and other combo-plate fare.

2 TABLESPOONS PEANUT OIL OR LARD
2 GARLIC CLOVES, MINCED
1 MEDIUM ONION, CHOPPED FINE
1 CUP UNCOOKED RICE
2 SMALL TOMATOES, PREFERABLY ROMA OR
    ANOTHER ITALIAN PLUM VARIETY, CHOPPED
2 TEASPOONS CHILI POWDER, PREFERABLY
    HOMEMADE (PAGE 135) OR GEBHARDT'S
2 CUPS UNSALTED BEEF OR CHICKEN STOCK
¾ TEASPOON SALT

Serves 4 to 6

In a medium saucepan, heat the peanut oil or lard (we prefer to use peanut oil, but lard has its advocates). Sauté the garlic and onion over medium heat until softened. Add the rice, tomatoes, and chili powder, and sauté another couple of minutes, stirring to coat all the grains of rice with oil. Pour in the stock, sprinkle in the salt, and bring to a boil. Reduce the heat, cover the pan, and simmer the rice for 15 to 18 minutes, until all the liquid is absorbed.

Remove the pan from the heat, and let the rice steam, covered, for 5 to 10 minutes. Serve it immediately.

José Tafolla Garcia and his wife, Jesusita, both from the Mexican state of Michoacan, opened a four-table restaurant near the Fort Worth Stockyards on July 4, 1935. Originally they called it Joe's Barbecue and Mexican Dishes, and José's barbecue was the real specialty, with chili as a sideline. Over time an increasing number of customers made special requests for Jesusita's Mexican meals. After José's death, Jesusita wasn't able to manage both the barbecue and her own cooking, so she concentrated on the latter, and the renamed Joe T. Garcia's Mexican Dishes went on to become one of the top Tex-Mex restaurants in the state. The Garcias' daughter, Hope Garcia Lancarte, runs the operation today with the assistance of a dozen or two family members.

Sopa de Fideos

This "dry soup" often shows up in place of rice with home versions of Tex-Mex fare. Fideo, a type of vermicelli, is one of the Lone Star State's favorite pastas.

2 TABLESPOONS OIL, PREFERABLY CANOLA OR CORN
1 TABLESPOON BACON DRIPPINGS
5 OUNCES FIDEO OR VERMICELLI
1 MEDIUM TOMATO, CHOPPED
1 SMALL ONION, CHOPPED
½ GREEN BELL PEPPER, CHOPPED
2 GARLIC CLOVES, MINCED
1¼ CUPS UNSALTED CHICKEN OR BEEF STOCK
¾ TEASPOON SALT
¼ TEASPOON CUMIN SEEDS, TOASTED AND GROUND
DASH OF CAYENNE OR CRUSHED CHILE DE ÁRBOL, OR PINCH OF GROUND DRIED NEW MEXICAN OR ANCHO CHILE

Serves 4

Heat the oil and bacon drippings in a heavy skillet until medium-hot. Add to the oil the fideo or vermicelli, crumbled lightly from the "nests" in which it usually is sold. Sauté briefly, until the pasta is medium brown. Add the tomato, onion, bell pepper, and garlic, and continue heating for another couple of minutes, until the vegetables begin to soften. Pour in the stock, and sprinkle in the remaining seasonings. Cover the pan, reduce the heat to a low simmer, and cook until the liquid is absorbed and the pasta tender, about 20 minutes. Serve the sopa warm.

Texas cookbooks contained at least hints of Tex-Mex ideas from the beginning. In the earliest known cookbook, published in 1883, the Ladies Association of the First Presbyterian Church of Houston offered several versions of chili sauce in their "Sour Pickles" chapter. The Kute Kooking Klub of Honey Grove, Texas, put a similar recipe in its 1894 *K.K.K. Cook Book*. Two Austin ladies went further in 1891, when they included in their cookbook a whole chapter on "Mexican Receipts," featuring six dishes. Emma Davis and Anna Leigh, of Dallas, expanded on the options in 1909 in the "Chili and Tamales" category of their "400 recipes tested and proven to a point beyond failure."

Refried Beans

Refritos, or refried beans, are almost as central as tortillas to all Mexican and Tex-Mex cooking. The best versions are always made with lard or bacon drippings, but if you eat refritos with frequency, you may want to substitute peanut oil, which contributes a similar nutty richness to the adobe-colored purée.

¼ CUP LARD, BACON DRIPPINGS, OR PEANUT OIL
1 MEDIUM ONION, CHOPPED
2 GARLIC CLOVES, MINCED
3 CUPS FRIJOLES BORRACHOS (PAGE 86), OR
    OTHER WELL-SEASONED COOKED WHOLE
    PINTO BEANS, PLUS 1 CUP OF THE COOKING
    LIQUID
SALT TO TASTE
CREMA (PAGE 95) OR CRUMBLED ASADERO,
    MILD CHEDDAR, OR MONTEREY JACK CHEESE,
    FOR GARNISH
MINCED FRESH SERRANO OR JALAPEÑO, OP-
    TIONAL, FOR GARNISH

Serves 6

Warm the fat or oil in a heavy skillet over medium heat. Stir in the onions and garlic, and sauté until they are softened, about 3 minutes. Add the drained beans to the skillet, and mash them with a potato masher or Mexican-style bean masher, adding the liquid, a tablespoon at a time, until you reach a fairly smooth and moist consistency. Continue to cook, stirring up from the bottom with a spatula or large spoon, until the beans become a thick paste.

Serve the beans hot, topped with crema or cheese and, if you like, a sprinkling of serrano or jalapeño.

Variation: For a fat-free alternative to refritos, just mash well-seasoned beans with a few tablespoons of the cooking liquid instead of frying them. If other dishes on the plate are spicy, few people will notice the substitution.

TECHNIQUE TIP

When cooking dried beans, add salt toward the end of the cooking time, after the beans have softened well. If used earlier, the salt can hinder the softening process.

Frijoles Borrachos

These "drunken" beans make a great side or supper dish, and also work well for refritos. Plan on a total cooking time of about 2 to 2½ hours. The hardness of the water, the altitude, and the obstinacy of the particular beans can all affect the timing.

2 CUPS PINTO BEANS

6 CUPS WATER, OR MORE AS NEEDED

12 OUNCES BEER

2 TEASPOONS BACON DRIPPINGS OR PEANUT
   OIL

1 LARGE ONION, CHOPPED

2 GARLIC CLOVES, MINCED

2 FRESH JALAPEÑOS OR 1 TO 2 SERRANOS,
   CHOPPED

2 PICKLED JALAPEÑOS, CHOPPED

1 TEASPOON CHILI POWDER, PREFERABLY
   HOMEMADE (PAGE 135) OR GEBHARDT'S

1 TEASPOON SALT

Serves 6 to 8

 Pick through the beans and rinse them, watching for any gravel or grit. Soak the beans in water, enough to cover them by several inches, preferably overnight.

Drain the beans, and add them to a stockpot or a large, heavy saucepan. Cover them with the water and beer. Simmer the beans, uncovered, over low heat.

After 1 hour, stir the beans up from the bottom and check the liquid level. If there is not at least an inch more water than beans, add enough hot water to bring it to that level. Simmer the beans another 30 minutes, then check them again, adding water as needed.

When the beans are well softened, add the remaining ingredients, and continue simmering. Cook at least 15 more minutes, keeping the level of the water just above the beans. The beans are done when they are soft and creamy but not mushy, with each bean retain-

TECHNIQUE TIP

Soaking beans makes them cook faster, particularly at high altitudes, and, if you pour off the water before cooking, also eliminates some of the water-soluble flatulent substances. If you're in a rush, you can substitute a high-heat boiling for the lengthy soaking. Cover the beans with several inches of water, and bring them to a boil over high heat. Boil for 50 to 60 minutes, then drain off the water. Start the cooking with fresh water or stock.

ing its shape. There should be extra liquid at the completion of the cooking time, although the beans should not be soupy. If you want the liquid a little thicker, squash a few of the beans in the bottom of the pot with a potato or bean masher.

Serve the beans immediately, or cover them and keep them warm for as long as 1 hour. Or let them cool, and refrigerate or freeze them for later use.

> The huge El Chico chain started out modestly in the 1920s as Cuellar's Cafe in the small town of Kaufman. The business is still run by its founding family, as are many other old Tex-Mex restaurants in the state, however large or small.

Red-Hot Carrots

El Chico used to place a version of these carrots at each table with the condiments. We suspect the practice stopped because a friend of ours, Harriet Moyer, would go after every carrot in the restaurant when she came to dinner. She's now married to a doctor, which is probably a good thing for her stomach.

1 POUND CARROTS, SLICED INTO ROUNDS
1 TO 2 PICKLED JALAPEÑOS, CHOPPED
3 TABLESPOONS JALAPEÑO PICKLING LIQUID
2 TABLESPOONS OIL, PREFERABLY CANOLA OR CORN
2 TEASPOONS MINCED ONION
2 TEASPOONS CUMIN SEEDS, TOASTED AND GROUND
1 TEASPOON WHITE VINEGAR
1 GARLIC CLOVE, MINCED
PINCH OF SUGAR
SALT TO TASTE

Makes about 3 cups

Blanch the carrots in a saucepan of boiling water. Drain the carrots, rinse them in cold water, and drain them again. In a medium nonreactive bowl, mix together the remaining ingredients. Add the carrots to the marinade, and refrigerate them, covered, for at least 24 hours.

Taste the carrots, and adjust the seasoning if needed. The carrots will keep, refrigerated, for several days.

Ninfa's Marinated Onions

Ninfa Laurenzo serves these wonderful onions with fajitas, but we would eat them with anything from cake to cottage cheese.

2 CUPS UNSALTED BEEF STOCK
½ CUP SOY SAUCE
2 DRIED CHILES DE ÁRBOL, CRUSHED, OR 2
  FRESH JALAPEÑOS, CHOPPED
2 LARGE ONIONS, SLICED INTO THIN RINGS

 In a small saucepan, reduce the stock to 1 cup. Add the soy sauce and chiles, and stir.

Place the onions in a medium bowl, and pour the marinade over them. Cover the bowl, and refrigerate it for several hours or overnight.

Present the onions cold as a garnish, or heat them in the top of a double boiler and serve them warm. They will keep for at least 10 days.

The name Texas derives from the way the original Spanish colonists spelled an Indian word meaning ally or friend. A confederated group of Caddo tribes in the eastern part of the state called each other *tayshas*. The Spanish adopted the term and wrote it as *Tejas*, which became *Texas* over time.

Arnoldo De León's thorough study, *The Tejano Community, 1836-1900*, shows that the staples of the Mexican diet in nineteenth-century Texas were beans, corn tortillas, and chiles. On festive occasions the Tejanos fixed tamales, cabrito, and barbacoa (barbecue). Otherwise they ate much as their Anglo neighbors did, with an emphasis on simple preparations of eggs, game, domesticated stock, and home-grown produce. Some of the main dishes we associate with Tex-Mex cooking today—such as enchiladas and tacos—probably came up from Mexico later, though their essential ingredients were common in Texas from early on.

Ensalada de Nopales

Eating cactus sounds strange to some people, but the young, tender leaves of the prickly-pear cactus have been a delicacy in south Texas for two centuries. Usually roasted or grilled, the nopales have a mild vegetable crunch and tang that makes them a frequent addition to salads.

2 CUPS PREPARED NOPALES, SLICED IN THIN RIBBONS OR DICED

2 TO 3 TOMATOES, PREFERABLY ROMAS OR ANOTHER ITALIAN PLUM VARIETY, CHOPPED

¼ CUP SLICED GREEN ONIONS

2 GARLIC CLOVES, ROASTED (PAGE 9) AND MINCED

1 FRESH SERRANO OR JALAPEÑO, MINCED

JUICE OF ½ LIME

1 TO 2 TABLESPOONS EXTRA-VIRGIN OLIVE OIL

2 TABLESPOONS CRUMBLED OR GRATED MILD MEXICAN CHEESE, FRESCO OR ASADERO, OR MONTEREY JACK

1 TABLESPOON MINCED CILANTRO

Makes about 3 cups

Toss together the nopales, tomatoes, green onions, garlic, and chile with the lime juice in a medium bowl. Add just enough olive oil to bind the mixture together lightly. The salad can be served immediately or chilled several hours. Just before serving, mix in the cheese and cilantro, and spoon the mixture onto a serving plate.

Nopales are frequently called "tunas" in the Southwest, and some early Anglo settlers referred to them as "Texas figs."

TECHNIQUE TIP

In Texas and the Southwest, nopales (also called nopalitos) frequently can be bought fresh, especially at Hispanic and Latino markets. The spines have generally been removed. To prepare fresh nopales for salad, either grill the pads or boil them 30 minutes in lightly salted water. Change the water after the first 15 minutes of cooking. Outside the Southwest, look for canned nopales in Mexican food sections of supermarkets. Rinse the vinegary solution from the nopales before using them.

Albondiga Soup

Albondigas are Mexican meatballs. South of the border they are some-times made of seafood, but in Texas the most common core is beef or a com-bination of beef and pork. We use rice as the starch in the dish, though some people prefer finely minced corn tortillas, and we cut the usual greasiness by not cooking the albondigas completely in the soup.

SOUP

1 TABLESPOON PEANUT OIL
½ MEDIUM ONION, CHOPPED
3 GARLIC CLOVES, MINCED
½ TEASPOON CUMIN SEEDS, TOASTED AND
  GROUND
½ TEASPOON DRIED OREGANO, PREFERABLY
  MEXICAN
6 CUPS UNSALTED BEEF STOCK
2 CUPS CHOPPED SEEDED RED-RIPE TOMATOES
  OR CANNED CRUSHED TOMATOES
1 TO 2 CANNED CHIPOTLE CHILES
1 TO 2 TEASPOONS ADOBO SAUCE FROM
  CANNED CHIPOTLE CHILES
1 POTATO, PEELED AND CUBED
2 CARROTS, GRATED
1 TEASPOON SALT
½ CUP GRATED ZUCCHINI
¼ CUP UNCOOKED RICE

ALBONDIGAS

½ POUND GROUND BEEF
¼ POUND GROUND PORK
¼ CUP SHREDDED ZUCCHINI
1 EGG
1 GARLIC CLOVE, MINCED
3 TABLESPOONS UNCOOKED RICE
1 TABLESPOON MINCED CILANTRO
½ TEASPOON SALT
¼ TEASPOON CUMIN SEEDS, TOASTED AND
  GROUND

¼ TEASPOON DRIED OREGANO, PREFERABLY
  MEXICAN
CHOPPED CILANTRO AND MINT, OPTIONAL, FOR
  GARNISH

Serves 6

In a large, heavy saucepan or stockpot, heat the oil, and sauté the onion and garlic with the cumin and oregano until the vegetables are softened. Pour in the stock, and add the tomatoes, chipotle, potato, carrots, and salt. (The zucchini and rice will be added later.) Simmer the soup for 20 minutes while you form the albondigas.

In a bowl, combine all the meatball ingredients, and mix well. Form the mixture into small balls, about ¾- to 1-inch in diameter. In a large saucepan, bring to a boil enough water to cover the meatballs, and add them. Boil for 5 minutes to eliminate some of the grease. Drain the albondigas, discard-ing the cooking water. Add the albondi-gas, along with the reserved zucchini and rice, to the soup. Continue sim-mering the soup 30 minutes.

Serve the soup with generous sprin-klings of cilantro and mint, if you like.

Tortilla Soup

Tortilla soup originated in Mexico as a way to use old tortillas and left-over poultry, but it developed into one of the classics of the national cuisine. If you want the full flavor of the dish, don't skip the steps of roasting the garlic and broiling the onions. These actions add a smoky mellowness to the soup, which you can enhance even more by using smoked poultry.

8 CUPS UNSALTED CHICKEN STOCK
6 ROASTED GARLIC CLOVES, MINCED (PAGE 9)
½ CUP CHOPPED SEEDED RED-RIPE TOMATOES OR CANNED CRUSHED TOMATOES
1 MEDIUM ONION, HALF CHOPPED AND HALF SLICED INTO THIN RINGS
1 FRESH JALAPEÑO, SLICED INTO THIN RINGS
1 CHIPOTLE CHILE (WHOLE IF DRIED, OR MINCED IF CANNED)
1 TEASPOON DRIED OREGANO, PREFERABLY MEXICAN
2 CUPS SHREDDED COOKED CHICKEN OR TURKEY
JUICE OF 1 LIME
SALT TO TASTE
4 CORN TORTILLAS, SLICED INTO THIN STRIPS AND TOASTED OR BROILED UNTIL CRISP
CHOPPED CILANTRO, CUBED AVOCADO, AND CRUMBLED MEXICAN ASADERO CHEESE OR GRATED MONTEREY JACK CHEESE, FOR GARNISH

Serves 6

In a large, heavy saucepan, bring the stock to a boil. Reduce the heat, and simmer uncovered until the stock is reduced to approximately 6 cups.

Add the garlic, the tomatoes, the chopped half of the onion, the jalapeño, the chipotle, and the oregano to the stock. Continue to simmer, uncovered, over medium-low heat another 30 minutes. While the soup cooks, place the remaining onions (sliced) on a greased baking sheet, and broil them until they are softened and a little brown around the edges. Add the broiled onions, the chicken, and the lime juice to the soup, and continue simmering until the chicken is just heated through. If you have used a dried chipotle, remove the chile and either mince it and return it to the pan or discard it, depending on how spicy you want the meal.

To serve, place a small handful of tortilla strips in each bowl and pour the soup over. Pass the garnishes separately.

Corn Tortillas

Ready-made tortillas are now sold all across the country, from Tacoma to Tallahassee. Most taste like inner-tube patches, and most people don't know they shouldn't. Make your own to find out how flavorful fresh tortillas are. They aren't difficult as long as you use an inexpensive tortilla press, a wonderful gadget that substitutes for centuries of experience in patting out the masa by hand.

2 CUPS MASA HARINA
½ TEASPOON SALT
1¼ CUPS WARM WATER, OR MORE AS NEEDED

Makes 1 dozen 5- to 6-inch tortillas

Heat a dry griddle or heavy skillet over medium heat. In a large bowl, mix the ingredients with a sturdy spoon or your hands until the dough is smooth and forms a ball. A food processor can speed up this step. The dough should be quite moist, but hold its shape. Add a little more water or masa harina, if needed, to achieve the proper consistency.

Form the dough into twelve balls approximately 1½ inches in diameter. Cover the balls with plastic wrap to keep them from drying out. If any of the balls do dry out before cooking, knead more water into them. Unlike the dough for flour tortillas, this dough can be reworked.

Place one ball of dough between the two sheets of plastic sold with the tortilla press, or use two plastic sandwich bags. Press the ball in the tortilla press until it is flattened to the desired thickness, generally about ⅛ inch. Carefully pull the plastic from the round of dough, and lay the dough on the hot griddle or skillet. Cook the tortilla for 30 seconds. Flip it, and cook it for 1 minute on the other side. Then flip it back over to cook about 30 seconds longer on the first side. The tortilla will be speckled with brown flecks. Cover the cooked tortillas with foil to keep them warm while you shape and cook the remaining balls of dough.

Serve the tortillas warm in a napkin-lined basket with butter or salsa, or reserve them for another use. Tortillas taste best the day they are made.

Variation: To make taco shells, deep-fry corn tortillas in 350° F canola or corn oil. Use two forks to fold the tortilla in half quickly, and insert the tines of one fork in the fold so that the shell remains open about one-half inch. Fry just until crisp, usually less than a minute. Drain, and stuff with taco fillings.

Flour Tortillas

The very notion of flour tortillas would have bewildered Tejanos and Mexicans in the past. Corn and tortillas were so closely linked they seemed invented for each other, which is almost the case. The much newer flour version originated in the northern Mexican state of Sonora, and found greater acceptance across the border in the United States than in the southern part of Mexico. The same is true of dishes made with flour tortillas, such as burritos.

2 CUPS ALL-PURPOSE FLOUR
1 TEASPOON SALT
1½ TEASPOONS BAKING POWDER
1½ TEASPOONS OIL, PREFERABLY CANOLA OR CORN
¾ CUP LUKEWARM MILK OR WATER

Makes 6 to 8 tortillas, approximately 6 to 7 inches in diameter

Sift together the flour, salt, and baking powder into a large mixing bowl. Into the dry ingredients pour the oil, and mix with your fingertips to combine. Add the milk or water, working the liquid into the dough until a sticky ball forms.

Lightly dust a counter or pastry board with flour, and knead the dough vigorously for 1 minute. The mixture should be "earlobe-soft" and no longer sticky. Let the dough rest, covered with a damp cloth, for about 15 minutes. Divide the dough into 6 to 8 balls, cover them again with the damp cloth, and let them rest another 15 to 30 minutes (or refrigerate them up to 4 hours).

Lightly dust a counter or pastry board with flour, and roll out each ball of dough into a circle or oval approximately ¼ inch thick. A tortilla roller (much like a short section of broomstick) is easier to use than a conventional rolling pin. If you want nicely rounded tortillas, trim off any ragged edges and discard them. To avoid toughening the dough, roll it out only once.

Heat a dry griddle or heavy skillet over high heat for 5 minutes. Cook the tortillas 30 seconds on each side, or until the dough looks dry and slightly wrinkled, and a few brown spots form on both surfaces.

Serve the tortillas warm in a napkin-lined basket with butter or salsa, or reserve them for another use.

As recently as 1956 the head of instruction at Mexico City's Culinary Arts Institute, in a cookbook written for Americans, expressed distaste for flour tortillas. Josefina Velazquez de Leon said they were acceptable if you couldn't find masa harina for corn tortillas, but they wouldn't taste right.

Quintessential Quesadillas

An official of the Tortilla Industry Association, trying to boost sales, recently proposed broadening the appeal of quesadillas by calling them "cheese sandwiches." We figure this marketing whiz should take a Spanish course—as Jim Hightower once suggested to a political opponent—so he could become bi-ignorant.

8 FLOUR TORTILLAS

½ POUND MILD CHEDDAR CHEESE

2 TO 4 FRESH JALAPEÑOS, SLICED IN THIN RINGS

1 TO 2 TEASPOONS GROUND DRIED RED CHILE, PREFERABLY ANCHO OR NEW MEXICAN

FRIED CHIPOTLE CHORIZO (PAGE 80) OR BACON BITS, OPTIONAL

1 CUP SHREDDED RED CABBAGE, FOR GARNISH

1 CUP PICO DE GALLO (PAGE 95) OR OTHER SALSA

½ CUP CREMA (PAGE 95) OR SOUR CREAM

Serves 4

Preheat the oven to 350° F.

Arrange four of the tortillas on a baking sheet. Top with equal portions of the cheese. Scatter the jalapeño slices and a sprinkling of the ground dried red chile over each. Those who can't resist meat may want to add a bit of chorizo or bacon, but don't overdo it. The cheese should predominate. Top with the remaining tortillas.

Bake the quesadillas 12 to 15 minutes, or until the cheese melts and bubbles. Cut the double-decker tortillas into quarters. Transfer the wedges to a serving plate, and garnish with the cabbage, offering Pico de Gallo and Crema on the side.

What was the first full-fledged Tex-Mex restaurant in San Antonio? Most people assume it was the Original Mexican Restaurant on Losoya Street, which opened about 1900 and closed in the 1960s. That's probably wrong. A leading historian of the city, Charles Ramsdell, says that a Madame Garza ran an earlier establishment on the fringes of the red-light district as early as 1889. According to one patron it attracted both "the best people of the city" and a more colorful crowd from the local neighborhood.

Crema

This tangy thickened cream is the same as French crème fraîche and tops dishes from mole to quesadillas. It's even good on peach cobbler. While expensive in the stores, crema is easy and cheap to make at home.

1 CUP WHIPPING CREAM (PREFERABLY NOT ULTRA-PASTEURIZED)
2 TABLESPOONS BUTTERMILK

Makes about 1 cup

In a small glass or earthenware bowl, combine both ingredients. Cover the bowl loosely, and let it stand at room temperature for 8 to 24 hours, until the cream is thickened and tart. Stir it well, cover it tightly, and refrigerate it. Use it as needed. Crema keeps for up to 10 days.

Pico de Gallo

Literally translated as "beak of the rooster," pico de gallo is a superb salsa fresca, best when made with fresh fully-ripe tomatoes. It's associated with fajitas and a few other dishes, but it works well for many purposes.

3 SMALL RED-RIPE TOMATOES, DICED
½ BELL PEPPER, RED OR GREEN, CHOPPED
¼ CUP CHOPPED CILANTRO
⅓ CUP TOMATO JUICE
2 TABLESPOONS CHOPPED ONION
3 TO 4 FRESH JALAPEÑOS, MINCED
JUICE FROM ½ LIME
½ TEASPOON SALT, OR MORE, TO TASTE

Makes approximately 2 to 2 ½ cups

Combine all the ingredients in a medium bowl, and mix well. Refrigerate the salsa for at least 30 minutes for the flavors to develop. Serve it chilled, with fajitas, chips, or other dishes.

Year-Round Salsa

This is a good substitute for salsa fresca, handy in periods when fresh tomatoes and chiles aren't available. It's milder than Pico de Gallo, but if you wish you can make it more piquant with the addition of extra chile.

2 CUPS CANNED CRUSHED TOMATOES

2 FRESH OR PICKLED JALAPEÑOS, MINCED

1 TABLESPOON MINCED ONION

1 GARLIC CLOVE, MINCED

¼ TO ½ TEASPOON CAYENNE OR CRUSHED CHILE DE ÁRBOL

¼ TEASPOON SALT

GENEROUS PINCH OF CUMIN SEEDS, TOASTED AND GROUND

GENEROUS PINCH OF DRIED OREGANO, PREFERABLY MEXICAN

DASH OF WHITE VINEGAR, OPTIONAL

Makes about 2 ¼ cups

Stir all the ingredients together in a bowl, or, for a smooth sauce, purée them in the blender. Refrigerate the salsa for at least 30 minutes for the flavor to develop. Serve it with chips, warm tortillas, or other dishes.

If you want to get really down-home with Tex-Mex cooking, check out Lucy Garza's excellent *South Texas Mexican Cookbook*. Mrs. Garza tells how to prepare the dishes she was raised on in the Rio Grande Valley several decades ago. Among the favorites she describes are *chicharrones* (pork cracklings, a Christmas specialty), *cabeza en barbacoa* (barbecued beef head), and *tripas asadas* (grilled tripe). Other recipes range from a jalapeño bean dip to Mexican wedding cookies.

Salsa Verde Picante

This green salsa is sassy and sharp flavored, ideal when you want to warm up the crowd.

4 TO 5 SERRANOS

1 CUP CHOPPED FRESH TOMATILLOS, SKINNED AND BLANCHED, OR CANNED TOMATILLOS, DRAINED

1 CUP CHOPPED PREPARED NOPALES (SEE PAGE 89), FRESH OR CANNED, OR MORE TOMATILLOS

½ CUP MINCED CILANTRO

6 MEDIUM GREEN ONIONS, CHOPPED (GREEN AND WHITE PARTS)

2 GARLIC CLOVES, MINCED

1 TABLESPOON MINCED ONION

JUICE OF 1 LIME

½ TEASPOON SALT

Makes about 2 ½ cups

 Pierce each serrano with a fork, and hold it over the flame of a gas burner as if you are toasting a marshmallow. Or, if your stove is electric, pop the chiles under the broiler instead. When the skin is dark and blistered, place the chiles in a sandwich-size plastic bag to steam. As soon as the chiles are cool enough to handle, peel off the blistered skin. It's not necessary to remove all the skin—remnants will give a pleasant charred flavor to the salsa.

Combine all the ingredients in a medium bowl. Chill the salsa, covered, at least 30 minutes for the flavors to develop. Serve it with chips, warm tortillas, or other dishes. The salsa keeps, refrigerated, for 3 to 4 days.

Guacamole

Most versions of guacamole in this country are a travesty to this old and honored Mexican dish. It deserves to be done right. Use only Hass avocados, the dark bumpy-skinned variety, which are buttery-rich. If you can't find truly ripe tomatoes, leave them out.

2 LARGE RIPE HASS AVOCADOS
2 SMALL RED-RIPE TOMATOES, PREFERABLY
   ROMAS OR ANOTHER ITALIAN PLUM VARIETY,
   CHOPPED
⅓ CUP CHOPPED CILANTRO
2 TABLESPOONS CHOPPED ONION
JUICE OF 1 LEMON
1 JALAPEÑO, MINCED
1 GARLIC CLOVE, MINCED
½ TEASPOON SALT

Makes about 1½ cups

In a bowl, mash the avocado roughly, leaving a few toothsome chunks. Stir in the remaining ingredients. Serve within 30 minutes with chips, or as a garnish to other dishes.

TECHNIQUE TIP

Because guacamole darkens quickly, it is best made just before serving. The discoloration isn't harmful, but it's unappealing in appearance and flavor. Placing the avocado seed back in the mixture, as is often suggested, doesn't protect its emerald shade. If you have to hold the dip more than 30 minutes, place plastic wrap directly on its surface. The best way to cut down on last-minute preparations is to combine all the ingredients other than the avocados about an hour ahead of serving time. Just before eating, mash the avocados and fold in the remaining mixture.

Chile con Queso

This delightful dip and sauce has suffered the indignity of being homogenized into a glop that's poured on ballpark nachos. A real chile con queso, studded with tomato and green chile, bears little resemblance to the pretender.

1 TABLESPOON CORN OIL, PREFERABLY
   UNREFINED
⅓ MEDIUM ONION, CHOPPED
1 GARLIC CLOVE, MINCED
1 MEDIUM TOMATO, CHOPPED
⅓ CUP CHOPPED ROASTED GREEN CHILE,
   PREFERABLY NEW MEXICAN OR POBLANO,
   FRESH OR FROZEN
⅓ CUP UNSALTED CHICKEN STOCK
2 CUPS (8 OUNCES) GRATED MILD CHEDDAR
   CHEESE

Makes about 2 cups

Warm the oil in a small, heavy saucepan over medium heat. Sauté the onion and garlic until soft. Add the tomato, green chile, and stock, and bring the mixture to a simmer. Sprinkle in the cheese, and stir until it melts.

Serve the sauce immediately, or keep it warm in a water bath or chafing dish for up to an hour. Eat Chile con Queso with tostada chips or in other dishes such as Fried Cauliflower 'n' Queso (page 389) or Huevos con Queso (page 424).

Mystery Man Tostada Chips

An anonymous Mexican immigrant invented fried corn chips in San Antonio in the early decades of this century. He peddled them to restaurants around town and then in 1932 sold the business to Elmer Doolin for $100. The new owner named the chip a Frito, launching a company that became the giant Dallas-based Frito-Lay. In memory of the poor inventor, who returned to Mexico, make your own fresh chips, always better than any of the packaged brands.

12 5- TO 6-INCH CORN TORTILLAS
OIL, PREFERABLY CANOLA OR CORN, FOR DEEP FRYING
SALT OR GARLIC SALT TO TASTE

Makes 48 or 72 chips, depending on size, enough for 4 to 6 appetizer servings

Pour enough oil into a high-sided heavy skillet (a wok works too) to at least 2 inches in depth. Heat the oil to 375° F. If the oil smokes before reaching the proper temperature, it cannot be used for this recipe. Make sure you have fresh oil.

While the oil is warming, cut each tortilla into 4 or 6 wedges. Gently drop 6 to 8 wedges into the oil. When the chips are crisp and light golden, remove and drain them. Check the temperature again, and adjust the heat if necessary. Repeat the frying process with the remaining tortilla sections.

Salt the chips, if you like, and serve them warm. Tostada chips can be kept for up to 2 days in an airtight container. Rewarm the chips, uncovered, in a 250° F oven before serving.

Buñuelos

Puffy morsels related to Indian fry bread, New Mexican sopaipillas, and New Orleans beignets, buñuelos are especially popular at Christmas time. They are a bit of a bother for home cooks, but once you master them you won't regret the trouble. If you have access to fragrant Mexican cinnamon, called canela, use it for the topping, which is often sprinkled on dry for every-day purposes and cooked down as a syrup for special occasions. The canela has a warm mellow flavor that complements the buñuelos beautifully.

DRY TOPPING

¾ CUP SUGAR

2 TEASPOONS GROUND CANELA (MEXICAN CINNAMON) OR CINNAMON

SYRUP

1 CUP DARK BROWN SUGAR

1 TEASPOON GROUND CANELA (MEXICAN CINNAMON) OR CINNAMON

2 CUPS WATER

BREAD

4 CUPS ALL-PURPOSE FLOUR

1 TABLESPOON SUGAR

2 TEASPOONS SALT

2 TEASPOONS BAKING POWDER

¼ TEASPOON GROUND CANELA (MEXICAN CINNAMON) OR CINNAMON

1 TABLESPOON PLUS 1 TEASPOON OIL, PREFERABLY CANOLA OR CORN

1½ CUPS LUKEWARM MILK OR WATER

OIL, PREFERABLY CANOLA OR CORN, FOR DEEP FRYING

Makes 12 to 14 buñuelos, approximately 7 inches wide

 For the dry topping, mix the canela and sugar together in a small bowl or jar. Set the mixture aside.

If you prefer to make the syrup, combine the brown sugar and canela in a small, heavy saucepan. Add the water, and bring to a simmer. Let the mixture simmer until it thickens and forms a light syrup. Remove the pan from the heat, and set it aside. Rewarm the syrup, if necessary, before serving time.

For the bread, sift together the flour, sugar, salt, baking powder, and canela into a large mixing bowl. Pour the oil into the dry ingredients, and mix with your fingertips to combine. Add the water and milk, working the liquids into the dough until a sticky ball forms.

Lightly dust a counter or pastry board with flour, and knead the dough vigorously for 1 minute. The mixture should be "earlobe-soft" and no longer sticky. Let the dough rest, covered with a damp cloth, for 15 minutes. Divide the dough into 12 to 14 balls, about the size of golf balls. Cover the balls with the damp cloth, and let them rest for another 15 to 30 minutes (or refrigerate them for up to 4 hours).

Lightly dust a counter or pastry board with flour, and roll out each ball of dough into a circle about ¼ inch thick. It's OK if your buñuelos come out shaped like the state of Texas or even Illinois, but you can trim them into more circular shapes if you're a perfectionist. To avoid toughening the dough, you will want to roll it out only once, so discard any trimmings. Cover the buñuelos with the damp cloth. Don't stack the dough circles, because they are likely to stick together.

Pour enough oil into a high-sided, heavy skillet to measure at least 3 inches in depth. Heat the oil to 375° F. If the oil smokes before reaching the proper temperature, it cannot be used for this recipe. Make sure you have fresh oil.

Gently drop the first buñuelo into the hot oil. After sinking in the oil briefly, it should begin to puff and rise back to the surface. Don't spoon oil over the top of the frying bread as this would cause the bread to balloon up too much. When the buñuelo's top side has bubbled and risen more or less uniformly, turn it over with tongs. Cook the buñuelo until it is just light golden, remove it with tongs, and drain it on paper towels. Sprinkle the buñuelo with the dry cinnamon-sugar mixture, or drizzle syrup over it. Repeat the frying process for the remaining rounds of dough, adjusting the heat as necessary to keep the oil's temperature consistent. When all the buñuelos are ready, serve them immediately.

Variations: For anise-flavored buñuelos add 1 to 1½ teaspoons ground anise seeds to the dough.

Some folks make a fast-food version of buñuelos by frying flour tortillas until crispy and sprinkling them with the cinnamon-sugar topping.

Creamy Flan

This cream-cheese flan may surprise you with its unusual denseness and sinful richness. It bakes longer and at a lower temperature than most versions to achieve the proper texture.

CARAMEL
¼ CUP SUGAR

CUSTARD
1 14-OUNCE CAN SWEETENED CONDENSED MILK
14 OUNCES MILK (USE THE CONDENSED MILK
    CAN TO MEASURE)
3 OUNCES CREAM CHEESE, SOFTENED
4 EGGS
2 EGG YOLKS
1½ TEASPOONS VANILLA

Serves 8

Preheat the oven to 325° F.

For the caramel, set eight individual custard cups or an 8-cup soufflé dish within easy reach of the stove. Spoon the sugar into a heavy saucepan or skillet no larger than 1 quart. Cook over low heat, watching carefully as the sugar melts into a golden-brown caramel syrup. There is no need to stir unless the sugar is melting unevenly. When the syrup turns a rich medium-brown, remove the pan from the heat. Immediately pour about a teaspoon of caramel into the bottom of each custard cup, or pour all of it evenly in the soufflé dish. Tip the dish if needed to distribute the caramel. The hot syrup will harden almost immediately.

To make cleanup easier, place the pan in the sink and run water in it at once. Stay clear of the steam that will rise as the water hits the hot metal surface.

Put all the custard ingredients in a blender, and blend briefly until the mixture is smooth. Pour the mixture into the top pan of a double boiler. (If you don't have a blender, place the ingredients in the double boiler's top pan and beat with a whisk, or with a hand mixer at medium speed, for about 1 minute.) Heat the mixture over medium-low heat until it is warm throughout. Do not let the custard boil.

Pour the custard into the cups or dish, and place them in a baking pan large enough to accommodate all of the cups with a little room for air circulation. Add warm water to the pan, enough to cover the bottom third of the cups. Bake at 325° F 70 to 75 minutes for the small cups and 80 to 85 minutes for the larger dish, or until the custard is firm and light golden brown on top.

Remove the flan from the oven, and let it cool 15 to 20 minutes at room temperature. Cover the cups or dish, and refrigerate at least 4 hours or overnight.

Just before serving, take the cups from the refrigerator and uncover them. Unmold the flan by running a knife between the custard and the cup or dish. Cover each cup or the dish with a plate, and invert, giving the cup or dish a brief shake. The custard should drop to the plate. If not, try again. Serve the flan immediately. In the unlikely event you'll have leftovers, they can be kept for up to 2 days.

Pralines

Faintly perfumed with cinnamon, these creamy candies suffice as dessert after many a Tex-Mex meal.

1½ CUPS SUGAR
¾ CUP DARK BROWN SUGAR
½ CUP MILK
6 TABLESPOONS UNSALTED BUTTER
1½ CUPS PECANS, TOASTED AT 300° F FOR 5 TO 8 MINUTES
1 TO 2 STICKS GROUND CANELA (MEXICAN CINNAMON) OR CINNAMON
1½ TEASPOONS VANILLA

Makes a dozen large pralines

Grease a 2-foot-long sheet of waxed paper. Set it on several thicknesses of newspaper to avoid ending up with wax on your table or counter.

Combine all the ingredients in a heavy saucepan. Bring the mixture to a boil, and continue cooking over high heat, stirring constantly, until the mixture reaches the soft ball stage, 238° F to 240° F.

Remove the pan from the heat, and continue stirring as the candy cools. When the mixture becomes creamy and cloudy, and the pecans remain suspended while stirring, remove the canela. Quickly spoon the mixture onto the waxed paper, before the candy hardens in the pan. You can make pralines of any size, but most served in Texas are on the hefty side. For a dozen pralines, use about ⅓ cup of mixture for each. The pralines will set as they cool. Although best made the day they're served, the pralines can be kept, tightly covered, for several days.

CHAMPIONSHIP CHILI

*C*hili—real chili—chili Texas style, must have strength to chin itself, even with a big rock in the bottom of the pot. It will have the authority of a Marine buck sergeant.... It will make a poet sing of rhapsodious harmony in thunder, or inspire an umpire to toss coquettish kisses to the third-base wolves. It is an all-purpose invigorator, a reliable antibiotic for melancholy, and a prime mover when one's world seems to stand on dead center. It is a panacea to man in want or woe.

Joe E. Cooper, With or Without Beans; Being a compendium to perpetuate the internationally-famous Bowl of Chili (Texas Style) which occupies such an important place in modern civilization

$\mathcal{S}$ince Joe Cooper kicked off the chili cult in 1952, the friends of Texas red have spun an elaborate web of words about the ethereal essence of one of the simplest ideas in human history: flavoring meat with chiles and spices. A delightful if farcical clan, they expend paper and passion with the abandon of a French bureaucrat on points barely worth whittling with a butter knife. If it weren't so silly, it wouldn't be nearly so much fun.

The big question, discussed over and over, is who invented chili. The explanations range the globe and even beyond. One notion, reported at length by a prominent cookbook author, has a nun in seventeenth-century Spain learning the secret from American Indians during spiritual trances, when she would make incorporeal visits to the New World. A little closer to Earth, some speculate on a Mexican motherhood, a cowboy conception, and an accidental birth among Canary Islanders.

We suspect everyone is right, except perhaps the supporters of the flying nun theory. This may sound like a cop-out on our part, but it's actually closer to heresy. We reckon the culinary inspiration required for chili is so slight, there were probably thousands of different inventors at different times and places. All anyone needed for a patent was an appetite, a poor piece of meat, and an address in the vast region where chiles and other ingredients grow wild, an area encompassing much of the Southwest and Mexico. On many a day you had a choice of stewing up some kind of chili or waiting for the stagecoach to deliver a pizza.

The Savvy San Antonio Chili Queens

However simple in concept, chili can be a "bowl of blessedness," as Will Rogers called it, when the cook knows what to chunk in the pot and how to ladle it out. This is where the fabled chili queens of San Antonio enter the story. When they established their reign on the old Military Plaza around 1880, they turned a makeshift meal into an identifiable dish and served it with a flair that ensured instant popularity and lasting renown.

It must have been something like Mae West selling chicken tacos across the street from "the best little whorehouse in Texas." The chili queens hawked their goods from stands lining the plaza that was the nighttime hangout of every drifter, drinker, and rowdy in the wide-open San Antonio of the time. These were the customers, and the ladies competed for their favor by flirtation as well as fare. They might pin a rose over your heart, as one did to Stephen Crane, or hint at multiple ways to spice up your life. Whatever the means, the chili queens kept you coming back for more. By the turn of the century they had made chili a Texas institution.

High Noon at the Hoedown

From San Antonio, chili spread steadily around Texas and out to the farthermost corners of the country. It became a staple of the American Army diet well before World War I, and by the same time millions of housewives had learned to make it with commercial chili powder or at least serve it from a can.

Chili found its true home, however, in cheap, hole-in-the-wall cafes that offered only bowls of red and cups of coffee, available together for a nickel or dime. Especially after Prohibition and the start of the Depression, these greasy spoons became popular male hangouts, places where a fellow could toss his hat on the counter and enjoy a manly meal for very little. As the customers and the hard times disappeared during World War II, the chili joints closed. Most were only a memory by the early 1950s, when a couple of nostalgic Dallas newspapermen began sounding a loud alarm about the encroaching demise of their favorite food.

Joe Cooper's *With or Without Beans* and Frank X. Tolbert's later *A Bowl of Red* were calls to action quickly answered by a battalion of chiliheads. At first the recruits just met and exchanged recipes, but they soon discovered a way they could proselytize and play at the same time. They begat the chili cook-off, the ultimate missionary tool, when Tolbert stirred up a challenge in 1967 between Texas chili master Wick Fowler and Midwest humorist H. Allen Smith.

Smith had been brazen enough to write, for a national magazine, an article titled "Nobody Knows More About Chili than I Do," which debunked Texas red.

Tolbert tested the proffered recipe and declared it "a chili-flavored low-torque beef and vegetable soup." That led to the first World's Championship Chili Cookoff, in remote Terlingua, Texas, a high-noon event that ended in a draw but spawned a rollicking stream of successors.

At this point almost every town in Texas hosts a chili cook-off during the average year, and so do hundreds of other burgs across the country. Total

> Some people get riled up about the last letter in the spelling of *chili* or *chile*. Like most people today, we use an *i* when we're talking about Texas red and an *e* when we're referring to the fruit that provides much of the flavor in chili and other Southwestern dishes.

nationwide attendance approaches a million people. Three big annual events each claim to be *the* global championship, including two at the same time in tiny Terlingua, where the entire county population is under nine thousand in an area the size of Connecticut and Rhode Island combined. These days chili covers more ground than ever before, and still discharges a lot of hot air.

> O. Henry, who lived in Austin many years, loved to visit the chili queens. In one of his tales, "The Enchanted Kiss," a shy San Antonio drugstore clerk eats at one of the chili stands and hallucinates about being a Spanish conquistador who has survived hundreds of years by living on chili.

Your Own Chunk 'Em Chili

As the San Antonio chili queens taught the world, chili is more like a parade than a product, an expression of the cook's personality rather than codified chow. All the major recipes enjoy an element of eccentricity, and they often contradict each other with gleeful passion. Use the versions following as exemplars, not the final truth. Your ultimate goal as a chili cook is to create your own individual bowl of red. You can start by tinkering with a championship recipe or, like the chili queens, by chunking things in a pot and tasting the result until it's right for you. In either case the first step is to get a feel for the key ingredients. Beyond that, the only nuance is realizing that your best chili will always be the batch you're about to make.

MEAT
CHILE
IMAGINATION

Serves you and your friends

In your favorite pot, preferably cast iron, chunk in some combination of meat, chile, liquid, spices, and maybe more. Cook the mixture long and low. Taste it frequently during the last hour, adding any more of the basic ingredients that you think will improve the deep throaty flavor. Eat enough out of the pot to satisfy your immediate appetite, and age the rest in the refrigerator overnight before serving your friends.

Remember that chili is a meat dish, not a stew or soup, so you want plenty of meat relative to the other ingredients. The meat is usually beef, but you can find advocates for anything from venison to rattlesnake. Most chiliheads favor cheap cuts, which benefit the most from the slow cooking process. Cut the meat into small pieces, say ½-inch cubes, or buy it ground coarse in the style called "chili grind." Don't use hamburger, because it would turn to mush. In the past most cooks seared the meat in a lot of fat, leaving the chili swimming in grease, but the tendency today is to use a little vegetable oil or nothing at all.

The meat is the medium, but the chile is the message. You can use commercial chili powder, a mixture of chile and seasonings, but the pros generally start with dried chile pods, which they grind into powder after toasting the skins briefly in an oven or dry skillet and removing the stems and seeds. Anchos or New Mexican red chiles (or both) typically provide the basic flavor, and a smaller amount of cayenne, pequín, or another hot chile contributes some fire.

The meat and chile simmer in a liquid. Some folks make do with water, but others swear by beef stock, beer, or black coffee. The essential thing is to keep the amount moderate, so the chili isn't runny. If you need a thickener, even after long cooking, masa harina is the choice of most Texans. Some people use it just for the extra dimension of sweet corn taste.

The key spices are garlic, oregano, and cumin, each important to the full flavor of a traditional chili. Dedicated cooks usually seek out Mexican oregano, rather than European, and take the time to toast and grind their own cumin seeds.

The original chilis never contained tomatoes or onions, but they are common—and controversial—additions today. If you like onions, chop them small and add them early in the cooking process so they dissolve into the sauce. If you like tomatoes, some Texans will be sympathetic, but others will offer to buy you a bus ticket to Illinois.

Never, ever chunk in beans, at least in the Lone Star State. Serving them on the side is acceptable, even encouraged, but if you put them in the pot many chiliheads will be tempted to feature you as the exotic meat at their next cook-off.

A confident cook can make a good chili from these elementary guidelines. All the unknown inventors of chili, and all the champions who created the recipes below, started out in a similar chunk 'em fashion. That's the fascination of chili, and the challenge too.

Cincinnati is properly proud of its Three-, Four-, and Five-Way Chili, but Dallas's legendary Shanghai Jimmy was the king of options. At his hole-in-the-wall joint that was continually changing addresses, devoted customers ordered by the number, from one to eleven. The basic dish was chili and rice, a Number One. Jimmy added embellishments at each step up to his ultimate creation, a pint tub with rice, two scoops of chili, two kinds of cheese, chopped onions and celery, sweet pickle relish, oyster crackers, and, on the side for extra spice, a couple of salsas. Late in life Jimmy took up ice skating and relocated his business by a rink, calling the joint "Chili Rice on Ice is Nice."

Joe Cooper's Chili

*Joe Cooper's historic **With or Without Beans** wasn't a recipe book, but the original proselytizer did provide broad instructions for his own version of chili, reformulated here in faithful but contemporary terms. Cooper said his recipe, "like most all worth-while others, was conceived out of an uncertain past; born of a belief that no man can live long and prosper without good chili; reared in the confusion of trial and error; and now exists in maturity with the respect of neighbors and friends."*

¼ CUP OLIVE OIL

3 POUNDS LEAN BEEF, CHOPPED

1 QUART BEEF STOCK

2 BAY LEAVES, OPTIONAL

8 GROUND DRIED CHILE PODS, PREFERABLY
  ANCHO

3 TABLESPOONS PAPRIKA

10 GARLIC CLOVES, MINCED

1 TABLESPOON SUGAR

1 TABLESPOON SALT

1 TEASPOON GROUND CUMIN

1 TEASPOON DRIED OREGANO

1 TEASPOON CAYENNE, OR MORE, TO TASTE

½ TEASPOON BLACK PEPPER

6 TABLESPOONS CORNMEAL

3 TABLESPOONS ALL-PURPOSE FLOUR

Serves 4 to 6

In a large saucepan or Dutch oven, heat the olive oil over high heat. Add the meat and sear it. Stir constantly, cooking only until the meat is gray. Pour in the stock, and reduce the heat to a simmer. Add the bay leaves, and cover the pan. After about 20 minutes remove the bay leaves. Continue simmering the meat, stirring occasionally, for another 1½ hours.

Add the remaining ingredients except the cornmeal and flour. Simmer uncovered another 30 minutes, stirring fre-

The earliest Texas chili authority was E. DeGolyer, a Dallas oil millionaire and scholar. He concluded from his research that chili began as the "pemmican of the Southwest." In an adaptation of a Plains Indian food, frontiersmen pounded together dried beef, fat, chiles, and salt to make a nonperishable trail ration, a sort of chili brick. They boiled it in water for as tasty and nutritious a meal as you might find on the road in those days.

quently. Skim all accumulated fat from the chili.

In a small bowl, stir together the cornmeal and flour, and add enough water to make a thin paste. Mix the paste into the chili quickly, to avoid lumps, and cook 5 more minutes to eliminate the raw flour taste. Add a little extra stock or water if the chili seems stiff. Serve it hot.

Frank X. Tolbert's
Original Bowl of Red

*One pundit said that if chili were a religion, **A Bowl of Red** would be its Bible and Frank X. Tolbert its Moses. Courtesy of his family, this is the trailblazer's approach to making chili.*

12 DRIED ANCHO CHILES
3 POUNDS LEAN BEEF CHUCK, CUT IN THUMB-
  SIZE PIECES
2 OUNCES BEEF SUET
1 TABLESPOON GROUND CUMIN
1 TABLESPOON DRIED OREGANO
1 TABLESPOON CAYENNE
1 TABLESPOON TABASCO SAUCE
2 OR MORE GARLIC CLOVES, CHOPPED
1 TABLESPOON SALT
2 TABLESPOONS MASA HARINA, OPTIONAL

Serves 4 to 6

Break off the stems of the chiles, and remove the seeds. Place the chiles in a small saucepan, and cover them with water. Simmer the chiles for 30 minutes.

Purée the chiles in a blender with a bit of their cooking liquid to make a smooth, thin paste. Use as little liquid as possible, unless you want the chili to be soupy. Pour the chile purée into a Dutch oven or large, heavy saucepan.

In a heavy skillet, sear the meat in two batches with the beef suet until the meat is gray. Transfer each batch to the chile purée, then pour in enough of the chile cooking liquid to cover the meat by about 2 inches. Bring the chili to a boil, and then reduce the heat to a simmer. Cook the chili 30 minutes.

Remove the chili from the heat, and stir in the rest of the ingredients. Return the chili to the heat, and resume simmering for 45 minutes, keeping the lid on except to stir occasionally (too much stirring will tear up the meat). Add more chile cooking liquid only if you think the mixture will burn otherwise.

When 45 minutes are up, add the masa harina if you wish. Not only will it add a subtle, tamale-like taste to the chili, but it will thicken or "tighten" the chili. Cover the chili again, and simmer it for another 30 minutes, until the meat is done. During this last 30 minutes, do a lot of tasting to see if the seasoning suits you. Adjust the seasonings as you like, although you should go easy on the oregano to avoid ending up with a spaghetti sauce flavor. Take the chili off the heat, and refrigerate it overnight.

Skim as much fat as you wish from the chili before reheating it. Serve it hot.

Teddy Roosevelt's Rough Riders trained for the Spanish-American War in San Antonio during the heyday of the chili queens. When the civilian soldiers returned to their hometowns across the country, they brought back the memories and makings of an exotic, manly dish. The cult was a-borning.

Wick Fowler's Lazy-Way Chili

Frank X. Tolbert's favorite chili cook was the Austin newspaperman Wick Fowler, who defended the honor of Texas red against H. Allen Smith in the first Terlingua cook-off and won the 1970 event. The celebrity he gained through the brouhaha led him to create Wick Fowler's 2-Alarm Chili mix, a commercial facsimile of the seasonings he used in his scratch chili. The packaged product provides an easy, no-fuss way to make a solid chili, which can be tailored to your taste with the addition of some of the original scratch ingredients, such as Tabasco, chili powder, oregano, cumin, garlic, onions, cayenne, dried whole chiles, and chiles pequins. This rendition of Fowler's recipe comes from the International Chili Society.

2 POUNDS CHILI-GRIND GROUND BEEF
8 OUNCES TOMATO SAUCE
2 CUPS WATER
1 PACKAGE WICK FOWLER'S 2-ALARM CHILI
    SEASONING MIX
SALT TO TASTE

Serves 6

In a heavy saucepan or Dutch oven, sear the meat over high heat until it becomes gray. Add the tomato sauce and water, and all of the chili seasoning's ingredients except the masa harina. Cover the pan, and lower the heat to a simmer. Cook for about 75 minutes, stirring occasionally.

At the end of the 75 minutes, the meat should be quite tender. Skim off excess grease. Mix the masa harina with enough water to make a runny paste, and stir it into the chili quickly. Simmer the chili an additional 15 to 20 minutes, then add salt to taste.

Chill the chili overnight, if possible, and rewarm it before serving.

> The judge who voted first at the original World's Championship Chili Cookoff in 1967 cast a ballot for "Soupy" Smith, as she called him. A Lone Star Beer executive then opted for Fowler's entry. The last judge to taste was David Witts, a local land developer. He took a bite of Smith's chili, feigned convulsions, and fell to the floor. When he finally regained his voice, Witts declared that the Midwestern concoction had paralyzed his taste buds and left him unable to vote, forcing a draw.

H. Allen Smith's
Midwestern Chili

H. Allen Smith's chili recipe changed gradually over time, as most do. This is our composite of several versions he published in the 1960s and seventies, containing all his trademark ingredients. Accusing Texans of being gristle-lovers, Smith started his chili with tender, expensive cuts of meat. He also insisted on tomatoes and really tweaked Texans by throwing in bell peppers and beans.

2 TABLESPOONS OLIVE OIL
4 POUNDS CHILI-GRIND SIRLOIN OR TENDER-
   LOIN
1 QUART WATER
6 TO 12 OUNCES TOMATO PASTE
3 TO 4 MEDIUM ONIONS, CHOPPED
1 GREEN BELL PEPPER, CHOPPED
6 TO 8 GARLIC CLOVES, MINCED
3 TABLESPOONS OR MORE GROUND DRIED RED
   NEW MEXICAN CHILE FROM CHIMAYÓ
1 TABLESPOON GROUND CUMIN
1 TABLESPOON DRIED OREGANO
½ TEASPOON DRIED BASIL
SALT AND PEPPER TO TASTE
1 TO 2 16-OUNCE CANS PINTO OR PINK BEANS

Serves 6 to 8

In a Dutch oven or heavy saucepan, warm the olive oil over medium heat. Fry the meat in the oil until it is gray. Add the water and tomato paste, and stir to combine the mixture. Add the remaining ingredients, except the beans, and stir again. Reduce the heat to a simmer, cover, and cook for 2 to 3 hours, stirring occasionally.

Taste the chili, and correct the seasonings if needed. Add the beans, and cook the chili about 15 minutes more. Serve it hot.

Whatever you think of Smith's ingredients overall, you've got to appreciate his taste in chile pods. He was among the first writers to recognize and promote the virtues of red chiles from Chimayó, a small northern New Mexican village. The combination of weather and soil contribute to chiles with a perfect balance of sweetness and heat. In great demand these days, New Mexican pods from Chimayó will be proudly labeled as such and priced accordingly.

Smith was scheduled to battle Fowler a second time in Terlingua in 1968, but had to withdraw because of illness. His replacement was California champion Woody DeSilva, nicknamed "Wino" because of his propensity for champagne, which he applied liberally to himself and his chili during the contest. Once again the duel ended in a draw, this time because masked bandits stole the ballot box and threw it into an outhouse erected above a mine shaft.

C. V. Wood's
World's Championship Chili

Born in Texas and bred in Hollywood, C. V. Wood, Jr., helped design Disneyland and brought the London Bridge to the Arizona desert, but he was just as proud of winning two World's Championship Chili Cookoffs. His unorthodox recipe, provided courtesy of the International Chili Society, offended some purists but impressed the judges.

½ POUND BEEF SUET

1 TABLESPOON PLUS 2 TEASPOONS CHILI POWDER

1 TABLESPOON PLUS 1 TEASPOON SALT

1 TABLESPOON DRIED OREGANO

1 TABLESPOON GROUND CUMIN

1 TABLESPOON GROUND BLACK PEPPER

2 TEASPOONS SUGAR

1 TEASPOON MINCED CILANTRO

1 TEASPOON DRIED THYME

1 CUP BEER

1½ QUARTS CHICKEN STOCK

6 LONG GREEN CHILES, PREFERABLY NEW MEXICAN, ROASTED AND CHOPPED

4 15-OUNCE CANS WHOLE TOMATOES, PREFERABLY HUNT'S

¼ CUP MINCED CELERY

2 GARLIC CLOVES, MINCED

5 POUNDS CENTER-CUT PORK CHOPS, CUT INTO ⅜-INCH CUBES

4 POUNDS FLANK STEAK, CUT INTO ¼-INCH CUBES

3 MEDIUM ONIONS, CUT INTO ½-INCH PIECES

2 GREEN BELL PEPPERS, CUT INTO ⅜-INCH PIECES

1 POUND MONTEREY JACK CHEESE, GRATED

JUICE OF 1 LIME

Serves 12 to 16

In a skillet, render the suet over medium heat.

While the suet is melting, stir together the chili powder, salt, oreg-

"WOODY" WOOD WON THE THIRD TERLINGUA COOK-OFF IN 1969, BROUGHT A THRONE WITH HIM THE NEXT YEAR AND SAT OUT THE COMPETITION, TOOK THE TITLE AGAIN IN 1971, AND THEN ANNOUNCED HIS RETIREMENT AS THE "UNDEFEETED UNDENIA-BULL WORLD'S CHAMPION." SOME SOURPUSSES ATTRIBUTED HIS VICTORIES TO THE BEVY OF HOLLYWOOD STARLETS THAT HE BROUGHT ALONG AS CHEER-LEADERS.

ano, cumin, pepper, sugar, cilantro, and thyme in a bowl. Pour the beer over the spices, and mix until all lumps are dissolved. Pour the chicken stock into a Dutch oven or large, heavy saucepan, and spoon the beer mixture into it. Add the chiles, tomatoes, celery, and garlic to the stock.

After the suet is rendered, there should be 6 to 8 tablespoons of fat. Pour out about two-thirds of it, and reserve it. In two batches, brown the pork in the suet, adding more fat as needed. Spoon the pork into the stock mixture. Bring the mixture to a simmer, and simmer for 30 minutes.

Add more fat to the skillet, and brown the steak about a third at a time. Spoon the steak into the stock mixture, and simmer the mixture another hour.

Stir in the onion and bell pepper. Continue simmering for an additional 2 to 3 hours, stirring every 15 to 20 minutes, until the meat breaks down. Let the chili cool at room temperature for 1 hour. For optimum flavor, refrigerate it for about 24 hours.

Reheat the chili. About 5 minutes before serving, stir in the cheese and the lime juice.

Hot Pants Chili

Allegani Jani Schofield of Fredericksburg won the World's Championship Cookoff at Terlingua in 1974 with her famous Hot Pants recipe. The name came from the chili's effect on the eater as well as from Jani's attire, which an abashed Tolbert meekly described as "hot pants and sweater and nothing much else." One reporter said the combination of the cook and the chili set back planned parenthood by ten years. We're grateful to Jani for the latest version of the recipe, published originally in **Allegani Jani's Cookbook**.

2 TABLESPOONS OIL, PREFERABLY CANOLA OR
   CORN
4 POUNDS BEEF STEW MEAT, GROUND COARSE
   ONCE
2 MEDIUM ONIONS, CHOPPED FINE
GARLIC SALT AND LEMON PEPPER, TO TASTE
6 GARLIC CLOVES, CRUSHED
2 TEASPOONS CUMIN SEEDS
1 TABLESPOON WATER
1 POUND PEELED WHOLE TOMATOES WITH JUICE
¾ CUP BEER
4 OUNCES CHILI SEASONING
2 TABLESPOONS CHILI POWDER
1 TEASPOON SUGAR
1 TO 4 CHOPPED FRESH JALAPEÑOS, OPTIONAL
1 TABLESPOON *MOLE* PASTE
1 TEASPOON TABASCO SAUCE
1 TEASPOON SALT
1 QUART WATER
½ CUP MASA HARINA
GRATED CHEDDAR OR MONTEREY JACK CHEESE
   AND CHOPPED ONIONS, OPTIONAL, FOR
   GARNISH

Most early chili cook-offs barred women under ninety, a rule that reflected H. Allen Smith's contention that "no one should be permitted to cook chili while then and there being a female person." To combat the discrimination, Allegani Jani and friends organized the Hell Hath No Fury Chili Society and started the ladies-only Susan B. Anthony Memorial Cook-in in Luckenbach, which broke the official sex barrier. The chili chauvinists would have fared better against a north Texas twister.

Serves 5 to 6

In a large saucepan, warm the oil over medium heat. Add the meat and onions, season with the garlic salt and the lemon pepper, and fry the meat until it is well browned.

While the meat cooks, use a *molcajete* or mortar and pestle to make a paste from the garlic, cumin seeds, and 1 tablespoon water. Add the paste to the undrained meat.

In a blender, purée the tomatoes, beer, chili seasoning, chili powder, and sugar, and pour the mixture into the meat. Stir in as many jalapeños as

TECHNIQUE TIPS

Mole paste (a thick mixture of chiles, chocolate, and seeds) and a Mexican *molcajete* (the south-of-the-border version of a mortar and pestle) can be found in Mexican and Latino groceries.

The first women to cook at Terlingua showed up uninvited in 1970. One of the three party-crashers, Janice Constantine of Midland, arrived in a chauffeured Rolls Royce with a retinue of attendants who laid out an elaborate silver service with a candelabra. She cooked in a "mini-mini costume," as Tolbert called it, to the accompaniment of music provided by a tuxedoed violinist from the Midland-Odessa Symphony Orchestra.

your tongue can tolerate, the *mole* paste, the Tabasco, and the salt. Pour in the 1 quart water. Cover the chili, bring it to a simmer, and simmer it for 1 hour.

Uncover the pan, and cook the chili an additional 1½ hours, stirring occasionally.

Combine the masa harina with enough water to make a runny paste. Stir it into the chili quickly, to avoid lumps. Simmer the chili 30 minutes more to thicken it.

Serve the chili hot, passing the garnishes separately.

Hornadillo Chili

Not to be outdone by Allegani Jani Schofield and the other women competing in the ladies-only cook-off in his hometown, Luckenbach mayor Hondo Crouch developed his own chili recipe. A consummate prankster who called his village the "metropolis of mirth," Hondo liked his chili green instead of red, a reflection perhaps of the color he wanted to turn guests. In his own words, this is how Hondo described his "armadillo shell of bliss" to Allegani Jani.

1 MEDIUM ARMADILLO (SAVE THE SHELL)
OTHER STUFF

Dice the armadillo into chunks—do not grind. Next dye them pea green to produce the color for green chili. Use only "Ysleta Red" Chili Pods, grown only in Ysleta because the soil is peculiar. Grind 3 *comino* seeds vigorously. Add jigger of tequila, pinch of salt, slice of lime. (May be either taken internally or added to chili.) For chili thickening, put in a raw egg—two if they're cheap. And if you can borrow some, add olive oil. It's too expensive to buy. Add green onion tops and finely ground cedar bark. Sprinkle with green spinach or fresh watercress and serve on the half shell.

Will Rogers said he judged a town by the cafe chili it served. After trying hundreds of bowls across the Southwest, he awarded three stars to Coleman, Texas, whose local chili joint claimed to make its concoction from bull testicles.

THE FEDERAL GOVERNMENT ONCE INVITED HONDO TO REPRESENT TEXAS IN A CULTURAL EXCHANGE IN WASHINGTON, D.C. ALWAYS LOOKING FOR A LITTLE FUN, HE BOARDED THE PLANE WITH A PILLOWCASE TIED AT THE TOP WITH DECORATIVE RATTLESNAKE RATTLES. SOMEWHERE OVER TENNESSEE, HE GOT UP AND STARTED WANDERING THE AISLE, PEERING UNDER SEATS. FINALLY AN ELDERLY LADY GLANCED UP FROM HER KNITTING AND ASKED IF HE HAD LOST SOMETHING. HONDO REPLIED, "YES MA'AM, MY BABY RATTLERS GOT LOOSE OUT OF MY SACK."

PASSENGERS PANICKED, AND THE CAPTAIN RADIOED AHEAD TO DULLES AIRPORT TO ASK THE F.B.I. TO MEET THE FLIGHT AND CONFISCATE THE SNAKES. THE F.B.I. AGENTS GOT CONFUSED, THOUGH, AND GRABBED THE LADY'S KNITTING SACK, STOMPING IT FURIOUSLY WHILE HONDO SAUNTERED AWAY WITH THE PILLOWCASE TUCKED IN HIS BACK POCKET.

HONDO'S BUSINESS CARD READ:

HONDO CROUCH

IMAGINEER

AUTHORIZED DISTRIBUTOR

LUCKENBACH

Mind-Expanding Therapeutic Chili Verde

Not all green chilis are as strange as Hondo's. Even Tolbert acknowledged that many fine bowls of red were actually green, especially along the upper Rio Grande Valley near New Mexico. Houston chilihead Fred McMurray developed this recipe for St. Patrick's Day, and his friend Allegani Jani Schofield published it in her cookbook.

5 POUNDS TOP ROUND STEAK, TRIMMED AND CUBED

4 LARGE ONIONS, CHOPPED

2 CUPS NOPALES, CHOPPED (PAGE 89)

1 TABLESPOON SALT, OR MORE, TO TASTE

1 TABLESPOON PLUS 1 TEASPOON GROUND CUMIN

1 TABLESPOON DRIED OREGANO

7 FRESH JALAPEÑOS, CHOPPED

6 FRESH SERRANOS, CHOPPED

2 TO 3 GARLIC CLOVES, MINCED

7 CUPS WATER

12 GREEN CHILES, PREFERABLY NEW MEXICAN, ROASTED AND CHOPPED

12 PASILLA CHILES, ROASTED AND CHOPPED

5 LARGE TOMATOES, CHOPPED

12 OUNCES BEER

MASA HARINA, AS NEEDED

Serves 12

In a heavy saucepan over high heat, sear the meat, scraping it up from the bottom until it is evenly browned. Add half the onions and the nopales, salt, cumin, oregano, jalapeños, serranos, and garlic. Pour in 4 cups of the water, and stir well. Cover the pan, and bring the mixture to a simmer. Simmer for 2 hours.

Uncover the pan, and add the remaining water, the rest of the onions, the green chiles and pasilla chiles, the

A psychologist by training, Fred McMurray is one of the staunchest promoters of the therapeutic values of chili. His chilogical scientific tests have demonstrated conclusively that his chili is a biodegradable environmental enricher with tremendous aphrodisiac powers and the ability to heal preoperative lobotomy complications. It absolutely may or may not cure acute sobriety, frostbite, and grouchy dispositions.

tomatoes, and the beer, and simmer an additional hour, stirring occasionally.

If the chili seems thin, mix a few spoonfuls of masa harina together with enough water to make a runny paste, and stir it into the chili quickly, to avoid lumps. Cook the chili another 15 minutes.

Serve the chili hot. *Pozole* or pinto beans are good on the side.

Sam Pendergrast's Old-Time Texas Restaurant Chili

Abilene iconoclast Sam Pendergrast is fed up with the cook-off chilis of recent years. He says they suffer from CSWBG, the "Cubed Steak with Brown Gravy" syndrome, characterized by low-fat expensive meat cooked in a mild, lackluster sauce. Sam prefers the old cafe chilis of the 1940s, which he describes as "blood red, with an aroma of **cominos** *that could be whiffed at least a block away and precluded the necessity of outdoor advertising, hefty chunks of meat you could get your teeth into—along with authenticational bits of gristle—and a rich sauce featuring at least an eighth of an inch of grease." Sam's recipe—edited only slightly—and his chili observations come from his* **Zen Chili: The Real Terlingua and Other Boondoggles** *(third edition in progress).*

1 POUND FATTY BACON
2 POUNDS COARSE BEEF, EXTRA-LARGE CHILI GRIND
1 CUP CUMIN SEEDS
1 CUP GROUND DRIED RED CHILE, PREFERABLY NEW MEXICAN
¼ TEASPOON CAYENNE
CORNMEAL, OPTIONAL
SALT, PEPPER, AND GARLIC, TO TASTE
PAPRIKA, OPTIONAL

Serves 4

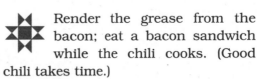 Render the grease from the bacon; eat a bacon sandwich while the chili cooks. (Good chili takes time.)

Sauté the beef in the bacon grease, over medium heat, for at least 10 minutes. Slowly add the cumin and red chile, a tablespoon or so of each at a time, until the mixture tastes and smells like chili. (This is the critical point: If you add all the spices at once, there is no leeway for personal tastes.) Let the mixture cook awhile between additions, and don't feel compelled to use all the spices.

Add water to avoid sticking or for soupier chili. SLOOOWLY add the cayenne, until smoke curls your eyelashes. Simmer the mixture at least 2 hours, until you can't resist ladling a bowlful for a sample. Skim the excess fat for dietetic chili, or mix the grease with a small amount of cornmeal and return it to the pot for thicker chili.

Finish with salt, pepper, and garlic to taste and, if you like, paprika to darken the chili. Continue simmering until served. Continue reheating until gone. (As with wine, time ennobles good chili.) The result should be a rich red, heavily cuminesque concoction with enough liquid to welcome crackers, some chewy chunks of meat thoroughly permeated by the distinctive spices, and an aroma calculated to lure strangers to the kitchen door.

The term *greasy spoon* was a literal signature for the old chili joints. They served big, thick bowls of red containing enough grease to lubricate a Model T. The original fat was beef suet, sometimes supplemented by pork fat, maybe bacon drippings or fatback.

Pedernales River Chili

Lyndon Johnson once loved the kind of greasy chili that Sam Pendergrast cooks. His doctor made him modify the recipe, though, when he suffered a heart attack during his tenure in the U.S. Senate. This became the new reduced-fat version, graciously provided by Mrs. Johnson.

4 POUNDS CHILI-GRIND BEEF CHUCK OR VENI-
   SON
1 LARGE ONION, CHOPPED
2 GARLIC CLOVES, MINCED
1 TEASPOON DRIED OREGANO, PREFERABLY
   MEXICAN
2 TABLESPOONS CHILI POWDER, OR MORE, TO
   TASTE
1 TEASPOON GROUND CUMIN
SALT TO TASTE
2 TO 6 DASHES TABASCO OR OTHER HOT PEP-
   PER SAUCE
2 CUPS HOT WATER
1½ CUPS CANNED WHOLE TOMATOES WITH
   JUICE

Serves 5 to 6

The Texas Legislature made chili the official state dish in 1977. Barbecue lovers said it was just another tasteless act from Austin, but supporters of chicken-fried steak claimed fraud, maintaining that L. T. Felty of Waxahachie bribed the politicians with his golden pots of chili.

You can follow the progression of chili across the country, and see it move from hot to mild, in the ingredients that were added over time. By 1920 many national cookbooks called for beans in chili. Two decades later, tomatoes became common.

Place the meat, onion, and garlic in a large, heavy frying pan or Dutch oven. Cook over medium heat until the meat is lightly browned.

Add the oregano, chili powder, cumin, salt, and hot pepper sauce. Pour in the water and tomatoes, and bring the chili to a boil. Reduce the heat to a simmer, and cook for 1 hour. Skim off any fat during the cooking.

Serve the chili hot.

Atascosa County Chili

Gloria Bledsoe Goodman gave us this recipe, which has been in her family for more than a century. It originated with Gloria's grandmother, Diega Faustina Ramon from San Luis Potosi, Mexico. Diega lived in Laredo after the death of her first husband until William Frazer Mather Ross drove his stagecoach into town, captured the young widow's heart, and moved her to a ranch in Atascosa County. The recipe hasn't changed since Diega's day except for the addition of tomato sauce, introduced by a cousin of Gloria's who sold the chili by the gallons to San Antonio society ladies.

2 WHITE ONIONS, CHOPPED FINE

2 GARLIC CLOVES, MINCED

1 TABLESPOON OIL OR BEEF SUET

2 POUNDS CHILI-GRIND BEEF

1 POUND CHILI-GRIND PORK (IF THE BUTCHER GRINDS THE PORK SPECIAL FROM A CUT WITH A BONE, TAKE THE BONE TOO.)

3 TABLESPOONS GEBHARDT'S CHILI POWDER

1 TABLESPOON CUMIN SEEDS

1 15-OUNCE CAN TOMATO SAUCE

1 TOMATO SAUCE CAN WATER

SALT TO TASTE

CAYENNE OR GROUND DRIED CHILE DE ÁRBOL TO TASTE

MASA HARINA, AS NEEDED

Serves 4 to 6

In a Dutch oven or heavy saucepan, fry the onions and garlic in the fat until they are limp. Add the beef and pork, and cook until the meat is just gray. Mix in the chili powder and cumin. Pour in the tomato sauce and water. If the butcher gave you some pork bones, toss them into the chili to add flavor (but remove them before serving).

Simmer the chili gently, adding salt to taste and cayenne or other chile at your peril. Cook at least 1 hour, preferably 2 hours or longer.

If the chili seems thin, stir a few spoonfuls of the masa harina together with enough water to make a runny paste, and stir the paste into the chili quickly, to avoid lumps.

Serve the chili hot. It is even better the following day. It makes a good sauce for Tex-Mex cheese enchiladas, too.

The official *Manual for Army Cooks*, published by the War Department in 1896, included one of the first written recipes for chili. It called for cooking pieces of round steak with rice, and making a separate sauce out of hand-squeezed chile pods softened in boiling water.

Old Buffalo Breath Chili

Our favorite treatise on chili, among the scores around, is John Thorne's **Just Another Bowl of Texas Red**, *a witty and wise pamphlet by the editor of the* **Simple Cooking** *newsletter. A former El Paso resident, Thorne urges readers not to fall into the recipe trap with chili—"the compelling logic of the dish is enough"—but he ultimately does give his own recipe, which we reproduce almost verbatim.*

5 POUNDS CHUCK ROAST, AT LEAST 3 INCHES
   THICK
10 TO 11 GARLIC CLOVES, CRUSHED
SALT TO TASTE
CHILI POWDER
¼ CUP OLIVE OIL
ABOUT 1 TO 2 CUPS BEEF BROTH
JUICE OF 1 LIME
2 TEASPOONS GROUND DRIED MILD RED CHILE,
   SUCH AS ANCHO OR NEW MEXICAN
2 TEASPOONS GROUND DRIED HOT RED CHILE,
   SUCH AS CAYENNE OR CHILE DE ÁRBOL
1 TABLESPOON CUMIN SEEDS, TOASTED AND
   GROUND
2 TEASPOONS DRIED OREGANO, PREFERABLY
   MEXICAN
CHILES PEQUÍNS TO TASTE
MASA HARINA, AS NEEDED

Serves 8

Two or three hours before you plan to begin making the chili, rub the chuck well with a mash made from two to three of the garlic cloves and salt. Sprinkle the meat with the chili powder to lightly coat it. Loosely cover it with plastic, and set it aside.

Fire up enough hardwood charcoal to sear the meat on an outdoor grill, preferably one with a cover. At the same time, soak a few handfuls of mesquite chips in water. When the coals are covered with gray ash, spread them out evenly, and scatter the damp mesquite chips on top. Then immediately set the meat over the smoke, about an inch from the coals. Cover the grill, and adjust the dampers to maintain a slow, steady heat. Let the meat sear for about 12 minutes (this process is meant to flavor, not cook, the meat), and turn it over to sear the other side for the same amount of time. Remove the meat from the heat, saving any juices on its surface, and transfer it to the refrigerator. Let it cool thoroughly, about 1 hour.

When the meat has cooled, trim away any surface fat or cartilage. With a sharp knife, cube the meat into the smallest pieces you have patience for, saving all the juices. Heat the olive oil in a large, heavy saucepan or Dutch oven over moderate heat. Mix in the remaining garlic, and sauté it until it turns translucent. Stir in the meat and all reserved meat juices, adding just enough beef broth to cover. Pour in the lime juice, and sprinkle in the rest of the seasonings, stirring and tasting as you do. Crumble in a few whole chiles pequins to bring the heat up to taste. (Don't try to adjust the seasoning perfectly though. It's easy to ruin a chili by correcting the flavors too soon—the long cooking will smooth and sweeten it.)

Turn the heat down as low as possible. Long cooking toughens, not tenderizes, if the chili is allowed to boil. Every half hour or so, stir the chili and taste for seasoning, adjusting as you wish. After the first hour, thicken

JOHN THORNE CALLS CHILI A "SAVORY CONCOCTION OF MEAT, GREASE, AND FIRE" AND WRITES THAT IT'S "THE NATURAL CHILD OF THE ARGUING STATE OF MIND. THERE'S NO RECIPE FOR IT, ONLY DISPUTATION, AND ALMOST ANYONE'S FIRST THOUGHT AFTER A TASTE OF SOMEBODY ELSE'S VERSION, NO MATTER HOW MUCH IT PLEASURES THE THROAT, IS THAT THEY COULD MAKE IT BETTER."

Will Rogers's favorite canned chili was Wolf Brand, which humbly originated in Corsicana, Texas, in 1921. The company's founder, Lyman T. Davis, did the canning in the back of his meat market at first. He named the product after his pet wolf, who was pictured on the label.

the chili as you like by adding the masa harina a teaspoon at a time. The chili should be ready to eat in 3 hours, although it will benefit from a night's aging in the refrigerator.

Serve the chili steaming hot in large, heavy bowls with an ample supply of soda crackers and a side of beans, but not much else except maybe hot black coffee or quart-size glasses of iced tea or a few frosty bottles of Lone Star beer. And after a good long while, we'll push things aside, lean back in our chairs, and start arguing.

Howling Coyote Chili

John Thorne's Old Buffalo Breath is our favorite traditional chili, but we're also partial to this unconventional version, our own chunk 'em creation. An all-pork chili, it's heavily influenced by the incendiary carne adovadas of New Mexico.

6 OUNCES (ABOUT 18) DRIED RED NEW MEXICAN CHILES, PREFERABLY FROM CHIMAYÓ

2 OUNCES (ABOUT 6) DRIED ANCHO CHILES

4 CUPS UNSALTED BEEF STOCK

½ MEDIUM ONION, CHOPPED

1 TEASPOON DRIED OREGANO, PREFERABLY MEXICAN

1 TEASPOON CUMIN SEEDS, TOASTED AND GROUND

1 TEASPOON WORCESTERSHIRE SAUCE

2 GARLIC CLOVES

½ TEASPOON SALT

3 POUNDS BONELESS PORK CHOPS, TRIMMED OF FAT AND CUT IN ½-INCH CUBES

Serves 6 to 8

Preheat the oven to 300° F.

Remove the stems and seeds from the chiles. Transfer them to a baking sheet. Toast them in the oven 8 to 10 minutes, watching carefully so as not to burn them. Remove them from the oven, and, when they are cool enough to handle, break each into two or three pieces.

In a blender, purée half the pods with 2 cups of the stock for about 1 minute. You should be able to see tiny pieces of chile pulp, but they should be bound in a smooth, thick liquid. Pour the liquid into a Dutch oven or large, heavy saucepan, preferably cast-iron. Repeat with the remaining pods and stock, adding the onion, oregano, cumin, Worcestershire, garlic, and salt to the batch as well. Pour this liquid into the pan, and stir.

Add the meat cubes, and bring the chili to a boil. Reduce the heat until the chili just barely simmers. Cover the chili and cook for 3 hours, stirring occasionally during the last 1½ hours.

Uncover the pan, and continue simmering for another 30 minutes, stirring frequently. The chili can be eaten immediately but is better if refrigerated overnight and reheated.

We serve it with icy Bohemia beer from Mexico and fresh flour tortillas.

A 1959 Mexican dictionary called chili con carne a "detestable food passing itself off as Mexican, sold in the U.S. from Texas to New York."

Fritos Pie

Because chili is best reheated rather than directly off the stove, it's great for leftovers. Texas cooks have developed many dishes just to use leftover chili. Daisy Dean Doolin created the best-known of these dishes in her San Antonio kitchen in 1932, making a savory pie out of her chili and the new corn chips that her son Elmer was selling. At the company Elmer founded, Dallas-based Frito-Lay, the dish later won official designation as "Fritos Corn Chips Chili Pie."

3 CUPS **FRITOS CORN CHIPS**
1 CUP CHOPPED ONION
1 CUP (4 OUNCES) GRATED MILD CHEDDAR
  CHEESE
2 ½ CUPS OF YOUR FAVORITE CHILI

Makes 4 to 6 servings

Preheat the oven to 350° F.

Spread 2 cups of the Fritos in a medium baking dish. Top the corn chips with half the onion and cheese. Pour the chili over the onion and cheese. Top with the remaining Fritos, onion, and cheese.

Immediately bake for 15 to 20 minutes, or until the pie is heated through and the cheese bubbles. Serve the pie hot.

Variation: We nostalgically prefer a pie served in individual-size Fritos bags, with a plastic spoon and a lot of paper napkins, which you eat standing up on a street corner downtown. Buy the snack-size packs of corn chips, slit open the side of each bag, and layer in hot chili with the onions and cheese.

Snackers around the world munch 16 million packages of Frito-Lay products daily. The company grinds up 600 million pounds of corn a year to satisfy our cravings for Fritos, Doritos, and similar morsels.

Chili Chile Skillet

This leftovers dish mixes ideas from three Texas favorites: chili, cornbread, and cobbler. You couldn't lose with it even if the cat fell in the skillet.

3 CUPS OF YOUR FAVORITE CHILI
¾ CUP CHOPPED ROASTED GREEN CHILES,
   PREFERABLY NEW MEXICAN OR POBLANO,
   FRESH OR FROZEN
½ CUP SOUR CREAM
1 RECIPE JUST GOOD PLAIN CORNBREAD BAT-
   TER (PAGE 317)

Serves 6 to 8

Preheat the oven to 400° F. Grease a 10-inch skillet, preferably cast-iron, and place it in the oven to heat while you prepare the other ingredients.

In a medium saucepan, heat together the chili, green chiles, and sour cream until the sour cream melts. Reserve the mixture.

Remove the skillet from the oven, and pour the cornbread batter into it. Top the cornbread batter with the chili mixture. Return the skillet to the oven, and bake about 30 minutes, until the cornbread has risen up through the chili and browned on top.

> Apart from tradition and Texas dogma, a practical reason to banish beans from chili is their tendency to spoil the leftovers. Beans don't keep well, and they turn mushy during reheating.

Chili Hominy Skillet

*This is another wonderful leftovers casserole, with the corn flavor in this case coming from nuggets of hominy or **pozole**.*

4 CUPS CANNED HOMINY OR COOKED *POZOLE*
4 CUPS OF YOUR FAVORITE CHILI
1 MEDIUM ONION, CHOPPED FINE
2 CUPS (8 OUNCES) GRATED MILD CHEDDAR
  CHEESE

Serves 6 to 8

Preheat the oven to 325° F. Grease a large, heavy skillet, preferably cast-iron. In it, layer half of the hominy or *pozole*, the chili, onion, and cheese. Repeat with the remaining ingredients. Bake for about 30 minutes, until the casserole is heated through and the cheese is bubbly.

Joe Cooper said, "The aroma of good chili should generate rapture akin to a lover's kiss." The statement became the motto of the Chili Appreciation Society International.

Personalized Chili Powder

If you want a scratch chili, but also like the convenience of a ready-made powder, package your own brand, avoiding commercial fillers like salt and unnecessary exotica like allspice. Adjust the seasonings to your taste. The recipe can easily be scaled up or down in size.

1½ OUNCES (ABOUT 6) DRIED RED CHILES OF MODERATE HEAT, PREFERABLY ANCHO AND NEW MEXICAN (WE MIX THEM 4 TO 2 RESPECTIVELY)

2 TO 5 (MORE OR LESS, TO TASTE) DRIED RED CHILES OF GREATER HEAT (WE CHOOSE EITHER CHILE DE ÁRBOL OR CAYENNE)

1½ TO 2 TABLESPOONS CUMIN SEEDS, TOASTED AND GROUND

1½ TO 2 TABLESPOONS GARLIC POWDER, PREFERABLY ONE THAT HASN'T SAT ON THE GROCER'S SHELF FOR 3 YEARS

1 TABLESPOON GROUND OREGANO, PREFERABLY MEXICAN

Makes about ¾ cup

Preheat the oven to 300° F.

Break the stems from all the chiles, and remove the seeds. Transfer the chiles to a baking sheet, and arrange them in a single layer. Place the pan in the oven. The chile de árbol or cayenne pods will be toasted first, so remove them after 4 or 5 minutes. Bake the larger pods an additional 4 or 5 minutes, until they are well dried.

When the chiles are cool enough to handle, break them into two or three pieces each and transfer them to a blender. Pulverize the pods briefly, until you have powder. Add the remaining ingredients, and blend just until they are combined.

Store the chili powder in a jar or other covered container for up to 3 months.

> The original chiles in Texas, the ones that grew wild in the state, were little round chiltepins, not the larger pods that became the preferred chili ingredient by the late nineteenth century.

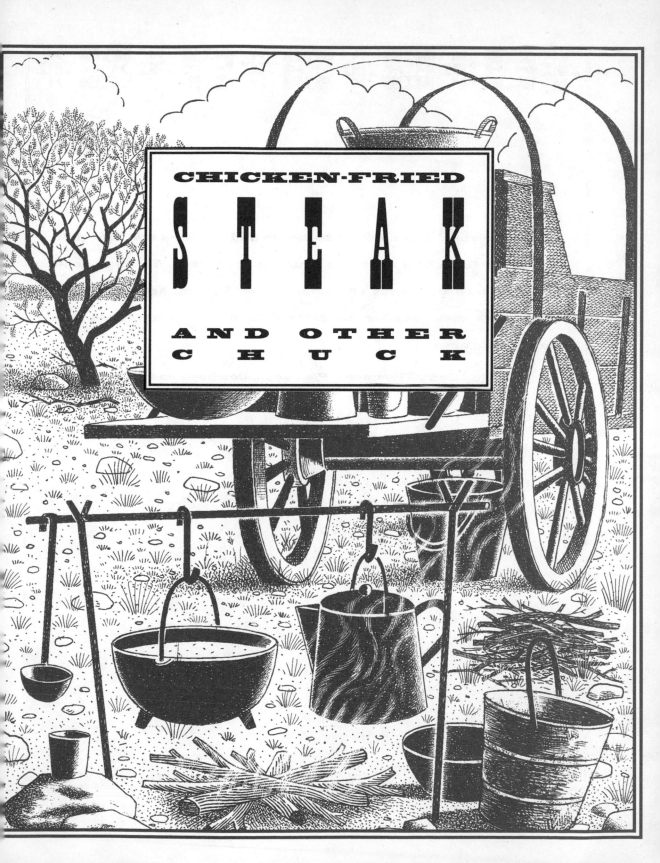

CHICKEN-FRIED STEAK AND OTHER CHUCK

As splendid and noble as barbecue and Tex-Mex are, both pale before the Great God Beef dish, chicken-fried steak. No single food better defines the Texas character; it has, in fact, become a kind of nutritive metaphor for the romanticized, prairie-hardened personality of Texas.

Jerry Flemmons, *Plowboys, Cowboys and Slanted Pigs*

If you ask a group of Texans to guess the most prominent feature of Heaven, at least half would say a steady diet of thick, juicy grilled steaks. That's just Heaven, though, and just talk. What they really like to eat here on this flawed Earth—what their base instincts crave more often than anything else—is a plate-size hunk of sorry beef pounded, battered, fried, and then drowned in a bucket of gooey gravy. Somehow, all that abuse heaped on a mean cut of meat produces Texas ambrosia, a golden slab of earthy perfection, the chicken-fried steak.

Not even football is more popular in the state, but Texans don't brag much about this humble dish. They'll get passionate over barbecue and Tex-Mex, and go loony with chili, while stuffing themselves into silence with chicken-fried steak. It's not embarrassment—an unknown emotion in Texas—but rather an assumption that CFSs are just something inherited, like being a good cusser. Texans come out of the womb knowing that they have a special relationship with chicken-fried steak, a divine dispensation granted no one else, and they keep quiet about it for the same reason that a pretty girl doesn't gloat to a plain one.

Home on the Range

That feeling, contrary to many in Texas, is buttressed by fact. Texans did inherit chicken-fried steaks, maybe not directly from God but at least from the next best source—the cowboy.

Texas was born rich in land and cattle, but neither were worth much at the time. Everywhere the first Anglo settlers ventured they found wild longhorns, descendants of cattle brought to the state by the original Spanish colonists. Some Texans, mainly of Mexican descent, rounded up the wild animals and pioneered ranching in the southwestern brush country, making money primarily from hides and tallow. These early ranchers and cowboys, *caballeros* and *vaqueros*, ate plenty of beef themselves, but they didn't have a profitable means of getting their cattle to distant meat markets.

The railroad became the way, when it reached Abilene, Kansas, in 1867. By then the five million cattle in Texas outnumbered people ten to one. Because of this supply and a growing demand for beef in thriving northern cities, the price per head was much higher in New York than in San Antonio. Anyone who could add, much less multiply, saw the potential, particularly since cattle reproduced each year. As one rancher remarked, the business was like running a house of prostitution—you could maintain your inventory no matter how much you sold.

The problem was getting the cattle to the railroad, and the solution to this was the cowboy. For a little over twenty years, up to 1890, the cowboy's life was devoted to driving vast herds north from Texas across open range, over legendary trails such as the Chisholm and the Goodnight-Loving. This was the job at its romantic peak, before it mutated into tending fences and attending rodeos. The cowboy's heroic period, which waned from natural causes, left an amazing legacy. The world had a new mythology, America had a mounted icon of individual freedom, Hollywood had hundreds of movies to make, and, best of all, Texas had the chicken-fried steak.

The Chuck and the Wagon

The open range the cowboys crossed on the great trail drives provided them with little sustenance. The cattle ate well on the grassy plains, but the men had to survive on beef and the meager rations they could pack for the long trek. They learned immediately to take along a resourceful cook to make their "chuck," as they called their food, and a chuck wagon to serve as a moving kitchen and cupboard.

The wagon was the cowboy's real home on the range, the place he went not only to eat, but to bed down, to talk, to treat cuts, to get some soap, to fetch a rope. When the outfit was plodding along the trail, making maybe ten miles a day, the wagon carried everyone's belongings, from bedrolls to horse hobbles. The back wall of the wagon folded down into a work table for the cook, exposing the chuck box, a warren of compartments containing all the provisions and utensils needed for months at a time.

Every few days the crew butchered one of their cattle, or preferably a stray, consuming the meat before it spoiled. On most days they ate beef for breakfast, dinner, and supper, always with coffee and sourdough biscuits. The cook usually cut the meat into thick slabs, dredged the steaks in flour, and fried them in suet or tallow. The diet might seem monotonous today, but the cowboys rarely tired of it.

When the trail days were done, and the cowboys settled back in Texas, they continued to yearn for those fried steaks. Before long every country cafe in Texas was happy to oblige, and every mamma was raising her kids on that same celestial chuck.

THE TEXAS RESTAURANT ASSOCIATION RECENTLY REPORTED THAT 90 PER-CENT OF ITS FOUR THOUSAND MEMBERS SERVE CHICKEN-FRIED STEAK. AN OFFICIAL CALCULATED THAT TEXANS ORDER EIGHT HUNDRED THOUSAND OF THE STEAKS A DAY, NOT COUNTING ANY THEY EAT AT HOME.

Original Chuck-Wagon
Fried Steak

This isn't the tastiest way to fry a steak, but you might find it fun. It's an authentic re-creation of what the cowboys ate on the open range, except that any steak you use will come out juicier and more tender than a cut of longhorn.

1 POUND CHEAP STEAK, CUT 1 INCH THICK
½ CUP BEEF SUET
SALT
¼ CUP ALL-PURPOSE FLOUR

Serves 1

Tenderize the steak by pounding it with a meat hammer or hacking it with a heavy knife. Melt the suet in a Dutch oven or thick cast-iron skillet until it is sizzling. Remove any cracklings.

Salt the steak, and dredge it thoroughly in flour. Cook it in the skillet, covered, approximately 5 minutes per side, or until it is well done. Serve it with Chuck-Wagon Sop.

THE DUTCH OVEN WAS THE CHUCK-WAGON COOK'S ALL-PURPOSE UTENSIL. A LARGE, DEEP, HEAVY IRON SKILLET WITH THREE LEGS AND A HEFTY LID, IT WAS USED BOTH FOR BAKING BISCUITS AND FRYING STEAKS.

Old cowboy saying: "Only a fool argues with a skunk, a mule, or the cook."

Chuck-Wagon Sop

Cowboys called their favorite steak gravy "sop." It wasn't a cream gravy in the early years, because there were no dairy products on the trail drives. This is the original version, as basic as it comes. Our Classic Cream Gravy, a more flavorful sop, follows.

½ CUP PAN DRIPPINGS
2 TABLESPOONS ALL-PURPOSE FLOUR
½ CUP WATER

Makes about 1 cup

When the Original Chuck-Wagon Fried Steak is cooked, pour off the top fat in the skillet, leaving about a half cup of suet, meat drippings, and excess cooked flour in the bottom of the pan. Place the skillet over medium heat. Stir in the new flour, mixing well and browning it lightly. Add the water, and simmer until the gravy is thick.

Serve the sop on the steak and some accompanying Sourdough Biscuits (page 157).

Variation: With a few adjustments, old-fashioned sop can still appeal to contemporary tenderfoot tastes. Reduce the amount of suet and drippings to ¼ cup, stir in a minced garlic clove, substitute beef stock for water, and add salt to taste and a liberal grind of black pepper.

The staples of the cowboy diet were beef, flour, coffee, beans, salt pork or bacon, syrup (usually molasses), and dried fruit. "Coosie" or "Cookie," as the cook was known, also carried salt, pepper, and baking soda, and, when feasible, sugar, spices, potatoes, and onions. In later years there was rice, and cans of corn and tomatoes, but these weren't always popular.

Classic Cream Gravy

Cream gravies took some time to catch on as the proper sop for fried steaks. Even after canned milk became available on the range, many cowboys scorned it as "canned cow." This is our version of a cream gravy for a modern chicken-fried steak, based on the old sop and some of that "canned cow."

¼ CUP PAN DRIPPINGS

3 TABLESPOONS ALL-PURPOSE FLOUR

2 CUPS EVAPORATED MILK

1 CUP UNSALTED BEEF STOCK

½ TEASPOON FRESH-GROUND BLACK PEPPER,
   PLUS MORE TO TASTE

SALT TO TASTE

Makes about 3 cups

After cooking a chicken-fried steak or similar dish, pour off the top fat through a strainer, leaving about ¼ cup of the pan drippings in the bottom of the skillet. Return any browned cracklings from the strainer to the skillet before starting on the gravy.

Place the skillet over medium heat. Sprinkle in the flour, stirring to avoid lumps. Add the evaporated milk and stock. Simmer until the liquid is thickened and the raw flour taste is gone, about 3 minutes. Stir the gravy up from the bottom frequently, scraping up any browned bits. Add the pepper and the salt to taste. The gravy should have a strong peppery flavor; add more pepper if it is needed.

Spoon the gravy over the steak and Prime-Time Mashed Potatoes (page 339), and serve immediately.

IN TEXAS DURING THE DEPRESSION, GRAVY BECAME A WAY OF STRETCHING A LITTLE MEAT TO FEED A FULL HOUSE-HOLD. RECALLING THOSE DAYS IN *MRS. BLACKWELL'S HEART OF TEXAS COOKBOOK: A TASTY MEMOIR OF THE DEPRESSION,* LOUISE B. DILLOW AND DEENIE B. CARVER SAY THE AMOUNT OF GRAVY WAS IN INVERSE PRO-PORTION TO THE AMOUNT OF MEAT, BUT THE GRAVY WAS ALWAYS FRESH. EVEN IN LEAN TIMES, STIFF LEFTOVER GRAVY WENT TO THE HOGS.

Braggin'-Rights Chicken-Fried Steak

In writing this chapter we tried every variation on chicken-fried steak that we could invent, coax from friends, or find in Texas cookbooks. We've included four other great recipes, but this was our personal favorite, the one we fine-tuned to become a family heirloom. Spicier and crunchier than most CFSs, it'll keep any cowboy or cowgirl from roaming the range.

1¾ TO 2 POUNDS ROUND STEAK, SLICED
  ½ INCH THICK AND TWICE-TENDERIZED BY
  THE BUTCHER
2 CUPS ALL-PURPOSE FLOUR
2 TEASPOONS BAKING POWDER
1 TEASPOON BAKING SODA
1 TEASPOON FRESH-GROUND BLACK PEPPER
¾ TEASPOON SALT
1½ CUPS BUTTERMILK
1 EGG
1 TABLESPOON TABASCO OR OTHER HOT PEP-
  PER SAUCE
2 GARLIC CLOVES, MINCED
VEGETABLE SHORTENING, PREFERABLY CRISCO,
  FOR DEEP FRYING

Serves 4

 Cut the steak into four equal portions. Pound the portions until each is about ¼ inch thick.

Place the flour in a shallow bowl. In a second dish, stir together the baking powder and soda, pepper, and salt, and mix in the buttermilk, egg, Tabasco, and garlic. The mixture will be thin. Dredge each steak first in flour and then in the batter. Dunk the steaks back into the flour and dredge them well, patting in the flour until the surface of the meat is dry.

Add enough shortening to a deep cast-iron skillet or Dutch oven to deep-fry the steaks in at least 4 inches of fat. Bring the temperature of the shortening to 325° F. Fry the steaks, pushing them down under the fat or turning them over as they bob to the surface, for 7 to 8 minutes, or until they are golden brown. Drain the steaks, and transfer them to a platter. Keep them warm while you prepare Classic Cream Gravy (page 144).

Place the steaks on separate plates, spoon Prime-Time Mashed Potatoes (page 339) next to them, and cover both generously with the gravy. Serve immediately.

Most cattlemen were of the sex suggested by the term, but a number of women breached the ranks from the beginning. Lizzie Johnson, who registered her brand in 1871 at the age of 29, even led a drive up the Chisholm Trail.

The Braggin'-Rights Chicken-Fried Steak and the other top versions that follow share several important characteristics.

The meat should be round steak, sliced no more than ½ inch thick. Some people chicken-fry more tender and expensive cuts, such as sirloin or even tenderloin, but the preparation does nothing for the meat. Other folks advocate veal, apparently unaware of the superiority of the similar German dish, wiener schnitzel. Venison is too lean for this cooking method.

You must pound the round steak as if you're training for a night of S&M. Let your butcher start the process by twice-tenderizing the meat at the store. When that's done, it should resemble a steak that wrestled with a waffle iron and lost. Then begin your own assault, pulverizing the meat with a mallet or other utensil until the sad-looking hunk has been reduced to about ¼ inch in thickness.

Fry the steak in a cast-iron skillet. If you don't have one, go out to eat.

Use only cream gravy on a CFS. The people who prefer brown gravy were born without the Texas chromosome.

The rest of the details are variables. People of decent moral sense and good taste genuinely differ on whether you soak the meat, dip it in batter or dredge it in flour, add much in the way of seasoning, use shortening or oil, and pan-fry or deep-fry.

Gary Cartwright's Chicken-Fried Steak

Gary Cartwright cooks chicken-fried steak almost as well as he writes. He favors marinating the meat in buttermilk for exactly 20 minutes—more makes it mushy—and double-dipping it in seasoned flour. We've used those tips in creating our version of his CFS.

1¾ TO 2 POUNDS ROUND STEAK, CUT ½ INCH THICK AND TENDERIZED BY THE BUTCHER
2 CUPS BUTTERMILK
2 CUPS ALL-PURPOSE FLOUR
½ TEASPOON SALT
½ TEASPOON FRESH-GROUND BLACK PEPPER
OIL, PREFERABLY CORN OR CANOLA, FOR FRYING

Serves 4

Cut the steak into four equal portions. Pound the portions, if needed, until each is about ⅛ to ¼ inch thick. Arrange the steaks in a shallow dish, and pour the buttermilk over them. Marinate the steaks in the buttermilk for 20 minutes, no longer.

Drain and blot the meat lightly to remove excess moisture from the surface. Reserve the buttermilk.

In a shallow dish, combine the flour with the salt and pepper. Dredge the steaks in the flour, dip them in the buttermilk, and dredge them again in the seasoned flour.

Pour enough oil into a cast-iron skillet so that the steaks will be half-immersed in it during the frying. Warm the oil over medium heat. Add

DON'T MESS WITH GARY CARTWRIGHT'S CHICKEN-FRIED STEAK: "PEOPLE WHO DIDN'T GROW UP IN TEXAS BELIEVE THAT CHICKEN-FRIED STEAK IS A PUT ON, LIKE THOSE JACKALOPE TROPHIES YOU SEE IN ROADSIDE SOUVENIR SHOPS. IT IS EVEN POSSIBLE, I SUPPOSE, FOR PEOPLE BORN AND REARED IN TEXAS TO BE SUSPICIOUS OF THIS ETHNIC CREATION—WITNESS THAT RENOWNED FOP, LARRY MCMURTRY, WHO ONCE WROTE THAT CHICKEN-FRIED STEAK LOOKS LIKE AN OLD PIECE OF WOOD WITH THE PAINT SANDED OFF. FOR ALL I KNOW, MCMURTRY HAS NEVER EATEN A REAL CFS; FOR ALL I KNOW, MCMURTRY WAS BORN IN NEW HAMPSHIRE, THE ILLEGITIMATE SON OF NOEL COWARD AND AIMEE SEMPLE MCPHERSON." —GARY CARTWRIGHT, "I AM THE GREATEST COOK IN THE WORLD," *TEXAS MONTHLY* (FEBRUARY, 1983)

the steaks and fry them, turning them carefully once, until the meat is fully cooked through and the coating is dark brown and crusty, about 8 minutes total. Drain the steaks, and transfer them to a platter. Keep them warm while you prepare a cream gravy from the drippings.

W. Park Kerr's
Chicken-Fried Steak

Park Kerr and his mother, Norma, are the talent behind El Paso Chile Company, a premier source for Texas salsas and condiments. The Kerrs make a superlative chicken-fried steak as well, using the tenets of the beaten-egg-and-cracker-crumb school of thought. They describe their recipe like this in their El Paso Chile Company's Texas Border Cookbook.

1¾ TO 2 POUNDS ROUND STEAK, CUT ½ INCH
    THICK AND TENDERIZED BY THE BUTCHER
SALT
FRESH-GROUND BLACK PEPPER
¾ CUP UNBLEACHED ALL-PURPOSE FLOUR
2 EGGS
1 TABLESPOON TABASCO OR OTHER HOT PEP-
    PER SAUCE
4 CUPS COARSELY CRUSHED SALTINE CRACKERS
    (ABOUT 1½ BAGS OF CRACKERS FROM A
    "FOUR-BAGGER" 1-POUND BOX)
¼ CUP CORN OIL
4 CUPS MILK

Serves 4

Cut the steak into four equal portions. Pound the portions, if needed, until each is about ¼ to ⅓ inch thick. Season each steak on both sides with a pinch of salt and one of

TECHNIQUE TIPS

Texas Highways once recommended a range of instruments for pounding a CFS, including the blunt end of a butcher knife, a hammer, a mallet, the butt end of a bottle, and the side of a saucer. The magazine quoted one restaurateur as saying to beat the meat into "the size of an L.P. record," which is about four times larger than a CD, in case you're too young to remember.

pepper, rubbing the salt and pepper into the meat.

Lightly beat the eggs with the hot pepper sauce. One at a time, dredge the steaks in the flour, then in the egg, then in the cracker crumbs. Reserve ¼ cup of the flour.

In a large cast-iron skillet over medium heat, warm the corn oil. Add the steaks, and cook them, turning them carefully once or twice, until the meat is fully cooked through and the crumb coating is brown and crisp, 8 to 10 minutes total. Drain the steaks. Transfer them to a platter, and keep them warm.

Pour all but 4 tablespoons of the fat from the skillet through a strainer, and discard it. Return any cracklings from the strainer to the skillet, and set the skillet over low heat. Whisk the reserved ¼ cup flour into the fat in the skillet, and cook over low heat, stirring and scraping, for 2 minutes. Gradually whisk in the milk. Raise the heat slightly, and bring the gravy to a simmer. Cook, stirring often and scraping the browned deposits from the bottom of the skillet, until the gravy has thickened, 5 to 6 minutes.

Taste the gravy, and adjust the seasoning.

Arrange the steaks on four plates. Spoon mashed potatoes next to the steaks, and top generously with the gravy. Serve immediately.

Cactus Pryor, an Austin radio personality, said he had a hand in "chicken-frying cosmopolitan Houston" in 1947. As the new program manager of an independent station competing against network giants, he proposed doing a "Houston Hoedown" during prime time. The owner objected at first, saying, "Man, we're uptown, have private clubs that serve mixed drinks and cafes that feature steaks that are not fried. This ain't no hick town." Pryor prevailed and so did the show, a big hit when radio was in its heyday.

Daddy-O's Hot-Times Chicken-Fried Steak

Bob "Daddy-O" Wade—the Texas artist who made the famous dancing frogs for the roof of Carl's Corner Truck Stop on Interstate 35—inspired this CFS marinated in jalapeño juice. Bob used to step lively around town until his wife Lisa tamed him and took him off to the mountains. These days Daddy-O's hankering for hot times is often satisfied by a chicken-fried steak.

1¾ TO 2 POUNDS ROUND STEAK, CUT ½ INCH THICK AND TWICE-TENDERIZED BY THE BUTCHER

1 CUP PLUS 2 TABLESPOONS PICKLING LIQUID FROM A JAR OF PICKLED JALAPEÑOS

2 EGGS

2 CUPS ALL-PURPOSE FLOUR

½ TEASPOON SALT

½ TEASPOON FRESH-GROUND BLACK PEPPER

VEGETABLE SHORTENING, PREFERABLY CRISCO, FOR FRYING

Serves 4

Cut the steak into four equal portions. Pound the portions, if needed, until each is about ⅛ to ¼ inch thick. Arrange the steaks in a shallow nonreactive dish, and pour 1 cup of the jalapeño liquid over them. Marinate the steaks in the jalapeño liquid for 2 hours. Most of the liquid will be absorbed into the steaks. Drain and blot lightly to remove excess moisture from the surface.

Mix the remaining jalapeño liquid with the egg in a shallow dish. Stir together the flour, salt, and pepper in another dish. Dredge the steak in the flour, then dip it in the egg, and back in the flour.

Put enough shortening into a cast-iron skillet so that the steaks will be half-immersed in it during the frying. Warm the fat over medium heat. Add the steaks and fry them, turning them carefully once, until the meat is fully cooked through and the crumb coating is brown and crisp, about 8 minutes total. Drain the steaks, and transfer them to a platter. Keep them warm while you prepare Classic Cream Gravy (page 144) from the drippings.

Place the steaks on separate plates, add Paris's Best French Fries (page 340), and cover both generously with the gravy. Serve immediately.

> The "Trucker Special" at Carl's Corner in Hillsboro is two chicken-fried steaks for only a dollar more than one.

Nuevo Laredo Chicken-Fried Steak

This nearly nouvelle CFS features a beer bath, border seasonings, and a crust made with masa harina, the specially-treated cornmeal used for tortillas and tamales.

1¾ TO 2 POUNDS ROUND STEAK, SLICED
   ½ INCH THICK AND TWICE-TENDERIZED BY
   THE BUTCHER
12 OUNCES BEER
2 GARLIC CLOVES, MINCED
1⅓ CUPS ALL-PURPOSE FLOUR
⅔ CUP MASA HARINA
2 TEASPOONS CUMIN SEEDS, TOASTED AND
   GROUND
1 TEASPOON GROUND DRIED RED CHILE,
   PREFERABLY NEW MEXICAN OR ANCHO
1 TEASPOON SALT
½ TEASPOON DRIED OREGANO, PREFERABLY
   MEXICAN
1 EGG
OIL, PREFERABLY CORN OR CANOLA, FOR DEEP
   FRYING

Serves 4

Cut the steak into four equal portions. Pound the portions, if needed, until each is about ⅛ to ¼ inch thick. Arrange the steaks in a shallow nonreactive dish, pour all but 2 tablespoons of the beer over them, and add the garlic. Marinate the steaks in the beer for at least 30 minutes and up to 2 hours.

While the steaks are soaking, combine the flour, masa harina, cumin, chile, salt, and oregano in a shallow dish. In another dish, mix the egg with the remaining 2 tablespoons of beer. Drain the steaks, and blot lightly with paper towels to remove excess moisture from the surface.

Dredge the steaks in the masa-flour mixture, then in the beer and egg. Dunk them back in the flour again, patting the flour in well to absorb moisture.

Add enough oil to a deep cast-iron skillet or Dutch oven to deep-fry the steaks. Bring the oil's temperature to 325° F, and deep-fry the steaks, pushing them down under the fat or turning them over as they bob to the surface, for 7 to 8 minutes, until they are medium brown. Drain the steaks, and transfer them to a platter. Keep them warm while you prepare Classic Cream Gravy (page 144) from the drippings.

Place the steaks on separate plates, spoon Prime-Time Mashed Potatoes with onion (page 339) next to them, and cover both generously with the gravy. Serve immediately.

Cowboy T-Bone

When contemporary cowboys aren't feasting on a CFS, they're likely to have a plain ol' thick and juicy T-bone, absolutely unadorned. They usually pan-fry it, or grill it over a hot mesquite fire, easily the best methods since broiling doesn't sear the surface properly.

4 1-POUND T-BONE STEAKS, 1½ INCHES THICK
SALT AND FRESH-GROUND BLACK PEPPER TO TASTE

Serves 4 cowboys

 Rub the steaks well with the salt and pepper, and allow them to come to room temperature.

To grill the steaks outdoors, fire up enough charcoal to form a single layer of coals beneath the meat. At the same time, put a few handfuls of mesquite chips in water to soak. When the coals are covered with gray ash, spread the mesquite chips on top. Place the steaks over the hot coals, and cover the grill, with the dampers open.

To pan-fry the steaks, warm a cast-iron skillet over high heat. Place the steaks in the skillet.

Cook the steaks to the desired doneness, about 6 to 8 minutes per side for medium rare. Some of the old cowboys preferred their meat just short of briquette stage, but that's a waste of a T-bone, a better cut of meat than the original cowhands had.

After removing the steaks from the heat, let them sit for about 5 minutes. Pour any accumulated pan juice over them, and serve them.

Houston's first restaurant with high culinary aspirations was Maxim's, opened in 1947. At the time it was the only place in the city that put sauce on food or served Belgian endive. While the menu was mainly haute cuisine, the most popular dish at business lunches was chicken-fried steak. When a French chef chided Camille Bermann, the owner of Maxim's, about offering such an unworthy entrée, Bermann flashed diamond-and-sapphire cuff links and proudly replied that he owed the gems to that lowly chuck.

Sonofabitch Stew

The sonofabitch was a special treat in cowboy country from the beginning, one of the few things the hands favored over a fried steak. They didn't get a sonofabitch often because it takes a day to cook and requires a calf's marrow gut, the connecting tube between the two stomachs of a cud-chewing animal. In a calf the marrow gut contains milk solids that give the stew its distinctive flavor. In case you can get this essential ingredient, we've given the recipe components in precise amounts. On the range, of course, cowboys simply killed a calf and used the quantities they found inside. They might have skipped some of the recommended steps, too, and perhaps added other ingredients like a skinned tongue or a "skunk egg" (onion).

1 POUND BEEF HEART, CUT IN SMALL PIECES

1 CUP BEEF SUET

1 WHOLE CALF MARROW GUT, CUT INTO SMALL RINGS

¼ POUND BEEF LIVER, CHOPPED

½ POUND BEEF KIDNEYS, CUBED

2 TABLESPOONS GROUND DRIED RED CHILE, PREFERABLY ANCHO OR NEW MEXICAN

SALT AND FRESH-GROUND BLACK PEPPER TO TASTE

1 POUND VEAL SWEETBREADS, MEMBRANES REMOVED, CUBED

1 POUND BEEF BRAINS

½ CUP ALL-PURPOSE FLOUR

Serves 6 to 8

 Place the heart in a small pan, cover it with water, and boil it for 30 minutes.

Melt ¾ cup of the suet over a low fire in a Dutch oven or a large cast-iron skillet. Brown the marrow gut and liver. Add the boiled heart, kidneys, chile, salt, and pepper, and cover the mixture with water. Bring to a boil, then reduce the heat to a simmer. Cook 6 to 7 hours, until the meat is tender and the liquid is creamy. Add the sweetbreads for the last 30 minutes of cooking.

Prepare the brains separately by removing the membranes, dredging the brains in flour, and cooking them in the remaining ¼ cup suet until they are beady in appearance. Add them to the stew just before serving.

Calf Fries

Once a year at the spring roundup, cowboys castrated and branded calves. They threw the freshly severed testicles into the branding-iron fire until the tough skin-like muscle on the outside split. When a cowboy got hungry, he peeled a testicle and ate it like a roasted chestnut. In polite company cowboys called the treat Rocky Mountain oysters, but it's better known today as "fries," in reference to the modern manner of preparation.

If you can get fresh testicles, they're as delicate as sweetbreads, and even the more common frozen ones are delicious after marinating in this way. Turkey testicles, though smaller, taste similar and can be substituted.

2 POUNDS CALF OR TURKEY TESTICLES, SKINNED

MARINADE

½ CUP DRY RED WINE

⅓ CUP OIL, PREFERABLY CANOLA OR CORN

⅓ CUP SOY SAUCE

½ MEDIUM ONION, CHOPPED

JUICE OF 1 LIME

1 TEASPOON CAYENNE

1 CUP ALL-PURPOSE FLOUR

¼ CUP MEDIUM-GRIND CORNMEAL, PREFERABLY STONE-GROUND

SALT AND FRESH-GROUND BLACK PEPPER TO TASTE

OIL, PREFERABLY PEANUT, FOR DEEP FRYING

Thaw the testicles, if necessary, and cut them into medallions. Put them in a bowl. Mix the marinade ingredients, pour the marinade over the testicles, and marinate the testicles for four hours in the refrigerator.

Mix the flour, cornmeal, salt, and pepper in a bowl. Roll each testicle in the mixture, dip it back in the marinade, and then roll it again in the flour.

Heat at least 3 inches of oil to 350° F. Place the testicles in the oil, using care not to splash yourself. Cook the testicles just until they are golden brown and tender. Don't overcook them, or they'll be tough. Serve the fries immediately. If you don't tell them, city guests will never guess what they're eating.

The first known Texas cookbook—published in 1883—doesn't include any batter-fried steaks. The closest recipe is one called "A Nice Way to Prepare Steak," which says to pound the meat well, fry it in a "very hot, dry" pan, and use the juice with butter, pepper, and salt to make a gravy that is poured over the steak.

Camp Potatoes

Chuck wagons didn't usually carry many potatoes because they would spoil. When possible, the cowboys set out with a small supply, and then consumed them early, often cooked in this way. Today, of course, potatoes are an essential part of a chicken-fry platter, as basic as cowhide to a football.

4 MEDIUM BAKING POTATOES, PEELED
6 SLICES SLAB BACON, DICED
1½ CUPS WARM WATER
SALT AND FRESH-GROUND BLACK PEPPER TO TASTE

Serves 4

Soak the potatoes in cold water for 30 minutes.

While the potatoes soak, fry the bacon in a large, heavy skillet or Dutch oven over medium heat until the bacon is browned and crisp. Remove it with a slotted spoon, drain it, and set it aside.

Drain the potatoes gently, and cut them into ¼-inch cubes. Add them to the bacon drippings, and pour the water over. Add the salt and pepper, and stir. Simmer the potatoes over low heat until the liquid is gone, about 30 minutes, stirring them up from the bottom frequently. The potatoes taste better if they are a little crusty, but don't let them stick or burn. If they get dry before becoming tender, add a little more water.

Stir in the reserved bacon, and serve the potatoes hot.

Cowboys wanted their steaks fried, big, and well done, which is what they got on the range. There are a lot of stories about ranch hands going into a city and getting steaks that were broiled, or small, or still pink inside. In one oft-told tale a cowboy sent back a steak to be cooked more, commenting, "I've seen cows git well that was hurt wors'n that."

Deceitful Beans

Easy to carry on trail drives, dried beans were popular with the cowboys, who called them such nicknames as "Mexican strawberries" and "whistle berries." The cook didn't have a wide range of ways to add flavor, but he managed well with what was available. We named this basic recipe in honor of the cowboy who labeled beans "deceitful"—" 'cause they talk behind your back." For a modern variation with less of the deceit, see Cowpoke Pintos (page 336).

2 CUPS BEANS, PREFERABLY PINTOS
¼ POUND SALT PORK, RINSED AND CUT IN
   1-INCH SQUARES ¼ INCH THICK
6 CUPS WATER, OR MORE, AS NEEDED
1 MEDIUM ONION, CHOPPED
2 TABLESPOONS UNSULPHURED DARK
   MOLASSES
½ TEASPOON DRY MUSTARD
½ TEASPOON FRESH-GROUND BLACK PEPPER
½ TEASPOON GROUND DRIED RED CHILE,
   PREFERABLY ANCHO OR NEW MEXICAN
1 TEASPOON SALT

Serves 6 to 8

Pick through the beans and rinse them, removing any gravel or grit. Soak the beans in water, enough to cover them by several inches, preferably overnight. (See page 86 for a quick-soak alternative.)

Place the salt pork in the bottom of a stockpot or a large, heavy saucepan. Drain the beans, add them to the pot, and cover them with 6 cups water. Add all the other ingredients except the salt, cover the pot, and bring the beans to a simmer. Simmer them over low heat for 1 hour.

Stir the beans up from the bottom, and check the liquid level. If there is not at least an inch more water than beans, add enough hot water to bring it to that level. Continue simmering the beans, checking every 30 minutes for the next two hours, and then every 15 minutes until they are finished, and adding water as needed to keep the level just above the beans. Add the salt near the end of the cooking time. The beans are done when they are soft and creamy but not mushy, with each bean retaining its shape. This should take a total cooking time of about 4 hours (the hardness of the water, the altitude, and the particular beans' obstinacy can all affect the timing). There should be extra liquid at the completion of the cooking, although the beans should not be soupy.

Cowboys always ate their beans with a spoon, and had sourdough biscuits and coffee on the side.

Sourdough Biscuits

A range cook's measure as a man was the quality of his sourdough biscuits. Many Texans still pride themselves on making these airy and slightly sour treats, though few follow the camp tradition of baking them over an open fire in a Dutch oven covered with glowing coals. If you don't already have sourdough starter, see the following recipe.

1 CUP SOFT-WHEAT FLOUR, PREFERABLY WHITE LILY

1½ TEASPOONS BAKING POWDER

1 TEASPOON SUGAR

SCANT ½ TEASPOON SALT

1 CUP SOURDOUGH STARTER

3 TABLESPOONS BACON DRIPPINGS OR BUTTER

Makes 1 dozen biscuits

Preheat the oven to 425° F.

Sift together the flour, baking powder, sugar, and salt into a medium bowl. Add the starter, and stir with a sturdy spoon until the flour is incorporated in the dough. It will remain sticky.

Flour a pastry board or your counter. Grease or flour your hands to make kneading the dough easier. Turn the dough out, and knead lightly a few times, just until it is smooth. The dough will remain soft. Pinch off pieces of dough about the size of eggs, or, for a more modern look, roll out the dough and cut it with a biscuit cutter.

Melt the bacon drippings (for real range flavor) or butter in a cast-iron skillet or Dutch oven. Dip one side of the biscuit in the fat, and then put it in the pan with its other side down. (Or melt the fat in a small dish, dip each biscuit in the fat, then place the biscuit on a baking sheet.) Arrange the biscuits so they just touch one another, which helps them rise.

Bake the biscuits 15 minutes. Serve them immediately.

COWBOYS LOVED THEIR SOURDOUGH BISCUITS SO MUCH THEY NICKNAMED THEM "DOUGH-GODS." WHEN THEY WANTED TO NETTLE THE COOK, A COMMON PASTIME, THEY MIGHT CALL HIS BISCUITS "SINKERS," "HOT ROCKS," OR "DOBIES," THE LATTER A REFERENCE TO THE DENSITY AND WEIGHT OF ADOBE BRICKS.

Sourdough Starter

Sourdough gets its start from the wild yeast in the air. Many contemporary recipes call for using packaged yeast, but the starter will develop a more interesting flavor without it. We like the approach of Jacqueline Higuera McMahan, a cookbook author who suggests using organic grapes. Their natural sugar helps feed the natural yeast to activate the starter. It takes 7 to 10 days to develop a good starter, but it can last you a lifetime.

1½ CUPS FLOUR (USE A SOFT-WHEAT FLOUR LIKE WHITE LILY IF THE PRIMARY USE OF YOUR FLOUR IS FOR BISCUITS; IF YOU VARY FREQUENTLY BETWEEN BISCUITS AND BREAD, USE ALL-PURPOSE FLOUR)

2 CUPS SPRING OR MINERAL WATER

1 BUNCH UNWASHED ORGANIC GRAPES, ON THE STEM

ADDITIONAL FLOUR AND WATER, AS REQUIRED

Stir the 1½ cups flour and 2 cups water together in a large plastic or earthenware bowl. Add the bunch of grapes, pushing it down into the gooey batter. Cover the bowl lightly, with cheesecloth or a dish-towel, so that the starter continues to get air. Leave the bowl in a warm place. Each day give the bowl another

Some lucky folks have sourdough starters that go back to the days of the Old West. The one we use may date to 1886, when Lafayette A. Brown supposedly carried it on a trail drive from Texas to Wyoming.

"Here then is the Holy Trinity of Texas. What the cod and fisherman and God meant to New England, the mustang, longhorn, and cowboy meant to Texas."—Joe Frantz, *Texas, a Bicentennial History*

tablespoon of flour and one of water, stirring to incorporate the additions. Within a couple of days the mixture should show signs of "starting," bubbling up a bit as yeasts feed on the starch and sugar. If this doesn't happen, throw the mixture out and begin again. Continue feeding the starter each day with the flour and water. If the mixture separates, stir it back together. After about 5 days, the starter will begin to smell sour. The smell won't be unpleasant, and won't overwhelm your kitchen. Let the starter ferment another few days, continuing to feed it. You'll end up with a mass that looks like a thick pancake batter. Remove the grapes with a slotted spoon, and discard them.

Cover the starter, and refrigerate it. Take the starter out of the refrigerator the evening before you plan to use it, or even a couple of days ahead for a more sour taste to the bread or biscuits. Every time you use the starter, replenish it. For each cup of starter you remove, add ½ cup flour and ½ cup water. Let it sit on the counter again for about a day before putting it back in the refrigerator. If you don't want to use the starter at least once every week or two, just feed it that often: Pour off about a half cup of starter, and add ¼ cup flour and ¼ cup water.

Properly tended, the starter can last for years, developing more complexity over time. It can be used for sourdough pancakes, breads, and other dishes in addition to biscuits.

Richard Bolt, a veteran chuck-wagon cook, said that one of his most important jobs was keeping the sourdough starter in good condition. On cold nights he wrapped his earthenware crock of starter in a blanket and slept with it. Bolt's rule was that it's "as temperamental as a woman so treat it like your wife."

Dried and Fried Fruit Pies

The most common dessert on the range was dried fruit, usually peaches, apples, or apricots, often stewed up with plenty of sugar. "Cookie" might also add sugar to biscuit dough and fry it, as a rudimentary but tolerable doughnut. Enterprising cooks, who were paid more than even the top riders and cowhands, created fried fruit pies as a combination of the two desserts. This recipe takes a few liberties with the original dish, adding jam for extra fruit taste and sweetness, and lightening up the lard pastry.

FILLING

1½ CUPS DRIED APRICOTS
1½ CUPS WATER
½ CUP APRICOT JAM OR PRESERVES
¼ CUP FINELY MINCED PECANS OR DRY BREAD
  CRUMBS

1 RECIPE FLAKY PIE CRUST (PAGE 513)
VEGETABLE SHORTENING, PREFERABLY CRISCO,
  FOR DEEP FRYING
SUGAR

Makes 8 pies

In a small, heavy saucepan, combine the apricots with the water. Simmer over low heat until the fruit is plump and soft and most of the water has been absorbed, about 25 minutes. Add more water if needed.

Drain the apricots and chop them. Mix the apricots in a small bowl with the jam or preserves, and the nuts or bread crumbs. Refrigerate the filling, if you wish, for as long as 24 hours.

Roll the pie dough out ⅛ to ¼ inch thick. Cut it into rounds with the top of a coffee can or with a large round biscuit or cookie cutter. Spread equal portions of filling on each round, moisten the dough edges lightly, and fold the rounds over into half-moon shapes. Crimp the edges with a fork.

One cowboy commented that a chuck-wagon cook "is a sort of human that was kicked in the head by a brindle cow or a cross-grained mule when very young. . . . They're temperamental as wimmin too; an' like the bosses, don't need no sleep neither." —Quoted in Ramon Adams, *Come and Get It*

In a heavy saucepan or Dutch oven, heat at least 4 inches of shortening to 350° F. Fry the pies in batches, turning them over midway through the cooking, after they rise to the surface. Remove them when they are golden brown and crispy, about 3 minutes. Drain them, and sprinkle them with sugar. Let them cool for at least 5 minutes before eating.

Variations: The pies can be baked rather than fried. Place them on a greased baking sheet, brush them with a little beaten egg (1 egg is enough for this batch of pies), sprinkle them with sugar, and bake them at 375° F for about 20 minutes, or until they are lightly browned.

Experiment with other dried fruit or jam fillings. Try dried peaches simmered in peach nectar with a touch of jalapeño jam, or dried apples with cider, a splash of applejack, and cinnamon.

The early cowboys loved their longhorn steaks, but not everyone thought highly of the animals or their meat. Two journalists, Alex Sweet and John Knox, said the Texas longhorn is "principally composed of lean rib roasts and soup bones attached to a wide-spreading pair of horns. Her time is mostly taken up in eating grass and in trying to lose herself."

Vinegar Pie

Don't skip over this one too fast. Vinegar pie is much better than it sounds. When chuck-wagon cooks had no dried fruit, they learned to substitute vinegar fermented from apple cider. Some of the resulting pies, when made without much spice, taste similar to lemon pies. Our version adds a generous amount of spice, making it more like a pumpkin pie.

UNBAKED SINGLE FLAKY PIE CRUST (PAGE 513)

FILLING
¼ CUP UNSALTED BUTTER
1 CUP SUGAR
5 TABLESPOONS ALL-PURPOSE FLOUR

1 TABLESPOON GROUND CINNAMON
1 TEASPOON GROUND ALLSPICE
½ TEASPOON GROUND CLOVES
2 ½ CUPS WATER
4 EGGS
6 TABLESPOONS CIDER VINEGAR, PREFERABLY UNREFINED

Makes 1 pie

Preheat the oven to 400° F. Bake the pie crust for 10 minutes. Remove the crust, and reduce the heat to 350° F.

Make the pie filling: In the top pan of a double boiler, beat the butter and sugar together with a hand mixer. Add in the flour and spices, and beat well. Beat in the water, eggs, and vinegar.

Place the pan over its water bath, and cook over medium-low heat until the filling is thick, stirring frequently. Pour the filling into the partially baked crust. Bake for 30 minutes, until the filling is the consistency of jellied cranberry sauce.

Serve the pie hot or at room temperature.

Boiling is one of the worst ways to fix coffee, but it was the only method the cowboys knew. Using a pound or more of coffee per gallon of water, they ground the beans, boiled the water, added the coffee, cooked it on a hot fire until it was plenty strong, and sprinkled in cold water to settle the grounds. To make your own campfire coffee, use a heaping tablespoon of ground coffee per cup of water, and boil them together for 10 minutes, or until the brew suits your taste, if it ever does. Sprinkle in some cold water, and serve.

THE MAIN COURSE

*T*he Texas Longhorn made more history than any other breed of cattle the civilized world has known. . . . In picturesqueness and romantic realism his name is destined for remembrance as long as the memory of man travels back to those pristine times when waters ran clear, when free grass waved a carpet over the face of the earth, and America's Man on Horseback—not a helmeted soldier, but a booted cowboy—rode over the rim with all the abandon, energy, insolence, pride, carelessness and confidence epitomizing the booming West.

J. Frank Dobie, *The Longhorns*

*T*he ultimate Texan in many ways, "Pancho" Dobie loved his cattle. He made the Longhorn—capitalized, you note—into the bovine equivalent of the Alamo, a mythic symbol of freedom and frontier fortitude. With Dobie's help the scraggly animal left a more lasting brand on Texas than it ever received on its own hide.

The longhorn is long gone, except at a few ranches and on a university pasture in the center of Austin, but Texans still treat cattle with the devotion most Americans reserve for movie stars and pet dogs. The benefit of this beatification, in the state and out, is the beef we get, not just the tastier meat Texans produce today but the multitude of imaginative ways they cook it. The truth is, Dobie aside, most Texans prefer their cattle on the platter rather than the hoof, and they have perfected a range of beef preparations, from "The Texas Classics" covered earlier to these distinctive dishes.

Bourbon-Molasses Marinated Tenderloin

After drinking this bourbon and molasses cocktail, tenderloin takes on a sweet smokiness, like a bar full of honky-tonk angels.

MARINADE

1 MEDIUM ONION, CHOPPED FINE
½ CUP BOURBON
¼ CUP UNSULPHURED DARK MOLASSES
2 TABLESPOONS WORCESTERSHIRE SAUCE
1 TEASPOON SWEET MUSTARD
¼ TEASPOON POWDERED GINGER
PINCH OF CRUSHED CHILE DE ÁRBOL OR
   CAYENNE

1 TO 1½ POUNDS BEEF TENDERLOIN, CUT INTO
   8 MEDALLIONS
SALT AND FRESH-GROUND BLACK PEPPER TO
   TASTE
2 SLICES SLAB BACON, CHOPPED
1 TABLESPOON OIL, PREFERABLY CANOLA OR
   CORN

Serves 4

In a small bowl, combine the marinade ingredients. Place the tenderloin medallions in a shallow nonreactive dish, and pour the marinade over the meat. Cover the meat, and refrigerate it for 2 to 4 hours, turning it once. Remove it from the refrigerator 20 to 30 minutes before cooking.

Drain the medallions, and salt and pepper them. Reserve ½ cup of the marinade.

In a large cast-iron skillet, fry the bacon over medium heat until it is browned and crispy. Remove it with a slotted spoon, and drain it. Set aside the bacon, and reserve the drippings.

Stir the oil into the drippings, raise the heat to medium-high, and add the medallions. Cook them rare, about 3 minutes, turning once. Remove the steaks, pour the reserved marinade

TECHNIQUE TIP

It's hard to go wrong with tenderloin. The aptly named cut comes from the middle of an animal's back, an area that stays lusciously tender because it does little work.

Pan frying is a better method of preparing a steak at home than broiling because you can sear the surface of the meat at a much hotter temperature in a skillet than under the broiler of a typical home oven.

into the skillet, and raise the heat to high. Scrape up any browned bits from the bottom, and stir the marinade as it thickens into a glaze, which requires about 1 to 2 minutes. Working quickly, return the steaks to the skillet briefly to coat them with the glaze on both sides. Transfer the medallions to a decorative platter, sprinkle the bacon over, and serve immediately.

Steak Dunigan

When Texans visit Santa Fe, New Mexico, their favorite quick getaway, they flock to the Pink Adobe Restaurant for this superlative steak. Restaurateur Rosalea Murphy named it after Pat Dunigan from Abilene, who always asked for green chile on his steak.

1 TO 2 TABLESPOONS CHAR CRUST (SEE "TECHNIQUE TIP," PAGE 170) OR UP TO 1 TABLESPOON HICKORY SALT (ROSALEA RECOMMENDS SPICE ISLANDS OR SCHILLING)
2 14- TO 15-OUNCE NEW YORK SIRLOIN STRIP STEAKS

SAUCE
2 TABLESPOONS OLIVE OIL
1 MEDIUM ONION, CHOPPED FINE
1 CUP CHOPPED ROASTED GREEN CHILE, PREFERABLY NEW MEXICAN, FRESH OR FROZEN
¼ TEASPOON DRIED OREGANO
¼ TEASPOON MINCED CILANTRO
¼ TEASPOON SALT
1 TEASPOON MINCED JALAPEÑO, OPTIONAL
4 TABLESPOONS UNSALTED BUTTER
4 LARGE MUSHROOMS, SLICED THIN

*Serves 2 at the Pink Adobe
or 4 of average appetite*

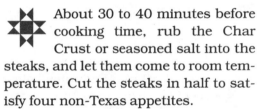 About 30 to 40 minutes before cooking time, rub the Char Crust or seasoned salt into the steaks, and let them come to room temperature. Cut the steaks in half to satisfy four non-Texas appetites.

Prepare the sauce: Heat the oil in a small saucepan, and add the onion. Sauté it briefly, until it is soft. Add the remaining ingredients, including the jalapeño if you want the extra heat, and cook for 5 minutes. Keep the sauce warm.

Heat the butter in a small skillet, and add the mushrooms. Sauté them until they are soft, about 5 minutes. Keep them warm, too.

Grill or pan-fry the steaks to the desired doneness, turning them once. Transfer the steaks to a platter. Spread the mushrooms over the tops of the steaks. Cover each steak equally with the green chile sauce. Serve the steak immediately.

Steak Peggy Sue

French chefs had a good idea with Steak Diane, but this variation is more true to a Texan's heart.

1 POUND BEEF TENDERLOIN, CUT INTO 8
    MEDALLIONS
2 TO 3 TEASPOONS CHAR CRUST OR SALT AND
    COARSE-GROUND BLACK PEPPER TO TASTE
4 TABLESPOONS UNSALTED BUTTER
2 TABLESPOONS MINCED ONION
2 TABLESPOONS BRANDY
1 TABLESPOON WORCESTERSHIRE SAUCE
1 TEASPOON BROWN MUSTARD
1 TEASPOON FRESH LEMON JUICE
2 TABLESPOONS MINCED PARSLEY

Serves 4

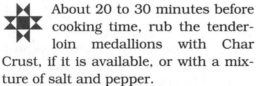 About 20 to 30 minutes before cooking time, rub the tenderloin medallions with Char Crust, if it is available, or with a mixture of salt and pepper.

Warm 1 to 2 tablespoons of the butter over medium-high heat. Pan-fry the medallions to the desired doneness, turning once. This takes only a few minutes.

Remove the medallions from the pan, and arrange them on a serving platter. Keep them warm while you make the sauce.

Add the remaining butter to the pan drippings, and reduce the heat to medium. Stir in the onion, and cook it until it is well softened. Pour the brandy into the pan, and ignite it. After the flame has died, add the Worcestershire, mustard, and lemon juice, and heat them through. Sprinkle in the parsley, and stir.

Spoon the sauce over the steaks, put on a Buddy Holly record, and serve immediately.

TECHNIQUE TIP

Anyone who grills or pan-fries steaks should check out Char Crust, a savory dry rub from Chicago. Bernard Silver's family developed the rub when they owned a popular steakhouse. They sell it primarily to restaurants, but individuals can order by mail. Contact the company at 3015 North Lincoln Avenue, Chicago, Illinois 60657, 312-528-0600.

Beef 'n' Brew Stew

Back in the 1930s some cattlemen sponsored a contest among cowboys for their favorite stew recipes. The winning entry was called "Stew without Them Goddamn Carrots." This is a different stew recipe, our personal favorite. With apologies to that cowboy, it does contain those contrary carrots.

4 SLICES SLAB BACON, CHOPPED

2 TABLESPOONS ALL-PURPOSE FLOUR

2 TEASPOONS GROUND DRIED RED CHILE, PREFERABLY NEW MEXICAN

1½ TEASPOONS SALT, OR MORE, TO TASTE

1 TEASPOON DRY MUSTARD

¾ TEASPOON CUMIN SEEDS, TOASTED AND GROUND

½ TEASPOON CAYENNE

½ TEASPOON FRESH-GROUND BLACK PEPPER

2 ½ POUNDS SIRLOIN, CUT IN ½- TO ¾-INCH CUBES

2 CUPS CHOPPED ONIONS

3 CUPS BEER

2 CUPS UNSALTED BEEF STOCK

2 TABLESPOONS TOMATO PASTE

1 TABLESPOON PLUS 1 TEASPOON UNSULPHURED DARK MOLASSES

1½ CUPS PEARL ONIONS, PEELED

6 CARROTS, CUT INTO THICK CHUNKS

2 MEDIUM BAKING POTATOES, CUT INTO CHUNKS, PLACED IN WATER TO PREVENT DISCOLORATION

Serves 8 hearty eaters

Preheat the oven to 325° F.

Fry the bacon in a large, heavy skillet over medium heat until the bacon is crisp. Remove it with a slotted spoon, drain it, and set it aside. Keep the bacon drippings warm in the skillet.

While the bacon is cooking, combine the flour, chile, salt, mustard, cumin, cayenne, and black pepper in a medium plastic or paper bag. In batches, add the sirloin to the seasoned flour mixture, and shake to coat each cube.

Turn the heat under the skillet to medium-high. In batches, add the sirloin cubes and brown them. Don't overcrowd the meat, or it won't brown properly.

With the slotted spoon, transfer the sirloin to a small stockpot, Dutch oven, or four-quart oven-proof pan. Add the chopped onions to the skillet, and sauté them in the remaining bacon grease until they are soft. If the mixture is dry, add a couple of tablespoons of water, being sure to scrape up all the browned bits remaining in the skillet. Transfer the onions to the stockpot or pan. Pour the beer and stock over the meat, add the tomato paste and molasses, and stir well.

Place the stew in the oven, and bake it for about 1½ hours. Add the remaining onions, the carrots, and the potatoes. Bake the stew 1½ hours longer (another 15 minutes won't hurt it if you're busy). At the end of the baking time the liquid should have reduced to a light sauce. If it remains thinner than you prefer, heat the pan or dish on the stove over medium-high heat to thicken it. Add the reserved bacon, and more salt if needed.

You can eat the stew immediately, but it will develop more flavor if you chill it overnight. Reheat it before serving.

Variation: If you are firing up your barbecue pit on the same day that you make this stew, you can add an earthy flavor to the stew by placing it in the smoker for an hour.

Cattle industry sales were rolling along strong in the 1970s, but then "the wheels fell off the wagon," as G. C. Smith from Texas A&M puts it. Consumers, concerned about saturated fat and cholesterol, pushed the industry into breeding slimmer cattle and trimming meat more closely. In case it's lean meat you're looking for, these cuts of beef are the lowest in fat: top round, top loin, round tip, eye of round, sirloin, and tenderloin.

TECHNIQUE TIP

The most important tip we can give you about beef, or any meat, for that matter, is to find a reputable butcher or meatcutter with high standards. Look for a market that cuts and grinds to order, perhaps does some aging, and has people who take an interest in you and what you're cooking. Good butchers can tell you the best cut they have for what you plan to do, and you should always take their advice over any cookbook's. Be willing to pay for top-quality meat and advice.

Picante Pot Roast

This luscious dish works best with chuck, preferably the boneless shoulder cut. When cooked long and slow, chuck shreds as easily as cotton and absorbs these lively seasonings as smartly as a biscuit takes gravy.

1 3-POUND BONELESS SHOULDER CHUCK ROAST
3 TO 4 GARLIC CLOVES, SLIVERED
1 TO 2 PICKLED JALAPEÑOS, SLIVERED
LONE STAR DRY RUB (PAGE 27) OR A SIMILAR
    BLEND OF DRY SOUTHWESTERN SEASONINGS
2 TABLESPOONS BACON DRIPPINGS OR OIL,
    PREFERABLY CANOLA OR CORN
¼ CUP ALL-PURPOSE FLOUR
2 10-OUNCE CANS RO-TEL TOMATOES AND
    GREEN CHILES, OR AN EQUAL QUANTITY OF
    PEELED WHOLE TOMATOES PLUS 1 TO 2
    CHOPPED ROASTED GREEN CHILES, PREFER-
    ABLY NEW MEXICAN
½ TO 1 CUP UNSALTED BEEF STOCK
6 SMALL CARROTS, CUT IN HALVES
1½ MEDIUM ONIONS, SLICED IN RINGS

Serves 6 to 8

Insert the garlic and jalapeño slivers into openings in the meat's surface. Rub the meat well with the dry rub or other seasoning blend, and let it sit about 30 minutes to come close to room temperature.

Preheat the oven to 300° F.

Heat the bacon drippings (for more flavor) or oil in a heavy lidded skillet or Dutch oven. Dredge the meat in the flour, and brown it in the drippings or oil. Turn off the heat. Pour in the tomatoes and ½ cup of stock, and add the carrots and onions to the pan. Cover the pan tightly, and bake the roast for 4 hours.

Check the meat after 3 hours, and add more stock if it is getting dry. If it seems a little soupy, uncover it for the last 30 minutes of baking. The meat should be falling-apart tender when done. Serve the meat and vegetables hot.

TECHNIQUE TIP

To zip up anything requiring canned tomatoes, try Ro-Tel Tomatoes and Green Chiles. Carl Roettele figured that Texas and the rest of the country were ready for a little verve in the often bland world of canned tomatoes, so he created the product to "jump-start your heart." See "Mail-Order Sources" (page 555) if you can't find the tomatoes in your supermarket.

Garlic-Stuffed Sirloin

The garlic in this dish mellows during the two stages of its cooking and adds richness to the top sirloin, a leaner and more tender cut than the bottom sirloin. We prefer the meat grilled over charcoal and mesquite, but you can also bake it.

FILLING

1 MEDIUM GARLIC HEAD, BAKED FOR ABOUT AN
   HOUR AT 350° F
1 TABLESPOON PLUS 1 TEASPOON OLIVE OIL
½ CUP SLICED GREEN ONIONS

1 3-POUND BONELESS TOP SIRLOIN STEAK,
   ABOUT 2 INCHES THICK
SALT AND FRESH-GROUND BLACK PEPPER TO
   TASTE

Serves 6 to 8

On an outdoor grill, fire up enough charcoal to form a single layer of coals beneath the meat. At the same time, put a few handfuls of mesquite chips in water to soak.

Make the filling: Break the garlic head apart, and squeeze each soft clove from its skin. In a small skillet, heat 1 tablespoon of the oil. Add the garlic, mashing it in the oil with a fork to form a rough purée. Stir in the green onions, and cook a minute or two, until the onions are limp. Remove the pan from the heat, and let the filling cool while you ready the meat.

Trim any fat from the sirloin, and cut a horizontal slit through it to form a pocket the length of the steak (don't cut the meat through to the other side).

Spread the remaining teaspoon of olive oil in a thin film over the sirloin.

Salt and pepper the meat inside and out.

Spoon the filling into the pocket of the sirloin. Use toothpicks as needed to secure the stuffing.

Allow the charcoal to gray, spread the mesquite chips on top of the coals, and lay the steak on the grill. Cover the meat with the grill lid or a foil tent. Grill the sirloin on one side for 15 minutes, and turn it. Cook it another 10 to 15 minutes, to the desired doneness, and serve immediately.

Before refrigeration, beef preservation techniques did little to attract people to the meat. Drying maintained the flavor well but made beef hard to chew. The U.S. Army relied on salted beef, but the soldiers scorned it as "salt horse." Canning caught on in the early decades of this century, but it worked better for fruits and vegetables than for meats.

Marinated Flank Steak

Flank is the good-news, bad-news cut of beef. It can be as tough as John Wayne's boots, but if you know how to tame it, the meat has great flavor. We give you a choice of two marinades here, and then use a combination of quick cooking and thin slicing against the grain to make this steak purr. We recommend charcoal-grilling, but the steak can also be broiled.

2 FLANK STEAKS TOTALING ABOUT 2 ½ POUNDS

PEPPA MARINADE
½ CUP SOY SAUCE
⅓ CUP PICKAPEPPA OR TEXAPEPPA SAUCE
¼ CUP WORCESTERSHIRE SAUCE
3 TABLESPOONS DRY RED WINE
3 TABLESPOONS RED WINE VINEGAR
2 TABLESPOONS DARK BROWN SUGAR
2 GARLIC CLOVES, MINCED

RED-EYE MARINADE
1 CUP STRONG BLACK COFFEE
½ CUP TOMATO SAUCE
¼ CUP UNSALTED BUTTER
¼ CUP WORCESTERSHIRE SAUCE
1 TABLESPOON DARK BROWN SUGAR
1 TABLESPOON COARSE-GROUND BLACK PEPPER

Serves 6 to 8

Place the steaks in one layer in a shallow nonreactive pan. Combine the ingredients for one of the two marinades, and pour the marinade over the steaks. Cover the pan, and refrigerate it at least 12 hours, preferably twice that long. Turn the meat occasionally during the marinating.

Fire up enough charcoal to form a single layer of coals beneath the meat, if you are grilling outdoors, or heat the broiler.

Remove the steaks from the marinade, reserving the liquid if you used the Peppa version. Discard the red-eye marinade, which would become bitter if reheated.

Grill the meat uncovered over hot, ashen-gray coals for 4 to 5 minutes per side, or until the steaks are done to your taste. Broiling should take about the same amount of time. Let the meat rest 5 to 10 minutes before slicing it thin, across the grain.

If you used the Peppa marinade, bring the liquid to a boil in a small saucepan, allowing it to reduce by about a third, a matter of just a few minutes. Spoon some of it over the sliced meat.

Serve the meat immediately.

> The first known Texas cookbook, published in 1883, says "all fresh meat" should be boiled first—20 minutes per pound—so that "the outer part contracts and the internal juices are preserved."

West Texas Ja-lop-eno Steak

This is another version of marinated flank steak, concocted and named by Mike Shannon, a political consultant, when he was living in the Midland-Odessa area. Spicy hot and full of tang, it begs to be charcoal-grilled.

1½ POUNDS FLANK STEAK, SLICED THIN ACROSS THE GRAIN
JUICE FROM 1 14-OUNCE JAR OF PICKLED JALAPEÑOS

Serves 4 to 6

Roll the steak strips into coils, and secure the coils with toothpicks. Place them in a single layer in a shallow nonreactive pan. Pour the pickling liquid over the meat. Cover the pan, and refrigerate it at least 12 hours, preferably twice as long.

On an outdoor grill, fire up enough charcoal to form a single layer of coals beneath the meat. When the coals are ashen gray, spread them evenly.

Remove the meat from the marinade, and cook it on the uncovered grill over the hot coals for 2 to 3 minutes per side, or until the meat has reached the desired degree of doneness. Take out the toothpicks, and serve the steak immediately.

Madisonville's Sidewalk Cattlemen's Association Celebration, held each June, had its origins in jest. In 1941 Henry B. Fox, publisher of the *Madisonville Meteor*, wrote a humorous column about people who wore cowboy boots but didn't own cattle, and then announced the formation of the Sidewalk Cattlemen's Association to regulate such behavior in Madison County. Some boor at the Associated Press took Fox seriously, and sent out a national wire story on the new group. A little girl in Boston named Audrey Mangan, who wanted some cowboy boots, wrote the Association for its OK. When the post office forwarded the letter to the *Meteor*, Fox decided to fly Audrey down for a barbecue and a pair of boots, inaugurating the annual Celebration.

Fajitas Borrachas

*The darling of the beef business these days, fajitas aren't above getting drunk (**borrachas**) on tequila, a sure way to soften up any tough critter.*

2 SKIRT STEAKS, 1 TO 1¼ POUND EACH,
  TRIMMED OF MEMBRANE AND FAT

MARINADE

1 CUP RED WINE VINEGAR
½ CUP TEQUILA
¼ CUP OIL, PREFERABLY CANOLA OR CORN
JUICE OF 3 LIMES
4 GARLIC CLOVES, MINCED
3 TABLESPOONS DARK BROWN SUGAR
3 FRESH JALAPEÑOS, MINCED
1 TABLESPOON WORCESTERSHIRE SAUCE
2 TEASPOONS FRESH-GROUND BLACK PEPPER
1 TEASPOON DRIED OREGANO, PREFERABLY
  MEXICAN
1 TEASPOON CUMIN SEEDS, TOASTED AND
  GROUND
SALT TO TASTE

16 TO 20 7-INCH FLOUR TORTILLAS, HEATED
NINFA'S MARINATED ONIONS (PAGE 88)
PICO DE GALLO (PAGE 95)
GUACAMOLE (PAGE 98)

Serves 8 generously

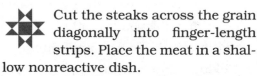 Cut the steaks across the grain diagonally into finger-length strips. Place the meat in a shallow nonreactive dish.

Combine all the marinade ingredients in a bowl, mix them well, and pour them over the meat. Refrigerate the meat, covered, between 8 and 24 hours.

Place a cast-iron or other heavy skillet on the stove over high heat. Drain the meat strips, and fry them, in batches if necessary, for 1 to 2 minutes.

To serve, pile a platter high with the meat, and accompany the meat platter with the tortillas, onions, Pico de Gallo, and Guacamole. Let all assembled help themselves by filling flour tortillas with some of the meat and portions of the garnishes.

TECHNIQUE TIP

Texans marinate fajitas (skirt steaks) in almost anything, including Italian salad dressing, pineapple juice, pickled jalapeño juice, soy sauce, beer, and Coke.

South Texas Sweetbreads

Some people today recoil at the thought of eating thymus glands, or sweetbreads, but the meat was extremely popular in Texas around the turn of the century. When prepared properly, sweetbreads are a wonderful delicacy, much milder than most organ meats and creamy in texture. This recipe is involved but not difficult, and the tasks can be spread over a couple of days.

2 POUNDS VEAL SWEETBREADS

4 TABLESPOONS OIL, PREFERABLY CANOLA OR CORN

1 TO 1½ TABLESPOONS FRESH LIME JUICE

SALT TO TASTE

⅓ CUP PEPITAS (SHELLED RAW PUMPKIN SEEDS)

1 CUP STOCK, PREFERABLY VEAL OR CHICKEN

2 SLICES SLAB BACON, CHOPPED

½ SMALL ONION, CHOPPED FINE

½ SMALL RED BELL PEPPER, CHOPPED FINE

1 FRESH SERRANO, MINCED

PINCH OF DARK BROWN SUGAR, OPTIONAL

Serves 4 to 6

Soak the sweetbreads in very cold water for at least 4 hours, or overnight, changing the water several times in the first hour. Drain the sweetbreads, and transfer them to a saucepan. Add enough water to cover them, and bring the water to a boil. Reduce the heat, and simmer for about 8 minutes (don't overcook the sweetbreads, or they will become tough). Drain the sweetbreads, and plunge them into ice water.

When they are cool, peel off as much of the outer membrane as possible, taking care to keep the sweetbreads intact. Transfer them to a shallow nonreactive dish. Mix together 3 tablespoons of the oil and 1 tablespoon of the lime juice, and pour the mixture over the sweetbreads. Place a plate on top of the sweetbreads to weight them down. Refrigerate the sweetbreads 2 to 8 hours.

Drain the sweetbreads, and cut them into medallions. Salt them lightly, and set them aside.

Warm a heavy skillet over high heat. Add the pepitas, and toast them briefly until they are fragrant and popped. Transfer them to a blender. Pour in the stock, and purée the mixture. Reserve it.

TECHNIQUE TIP

Veal sweetbreads are the most delicate. Select meat that is white, signifying its youth, rather than red. It should be firm and plump-looking. Unprepared sweetbreads perish easily, so plan to begin their preparation the day you buy them.

Warm the same skillet over medium heat, and fry the bacon until it is browned and crisp. Remove it with a slotted spoon, and drain it. Reserve the bacon and drippings.

Stir the remaining tablespoon of oil into the bacon drippings, and warm the fat over medium heat. Add the sweetbreads, and sauté them until they are lightly crisped and colored. Remove them to a serving plate with a slotted spoon, make a foil tent over the plate, and keep the plate warm.

Add the onion, bell pepper, and serrano to the drippings, and sauté them 3 to 4 minutes. Pour in the pepita and stock mixture, and heat it through. Taste the sauce, and adjust the seasoning, adding a little more lime juice and a pinch of brown sugar, if you like. Spoon the sauce over the sweetbreads, scatter the bacon over the sauce, and serve immediately.

Wiener Schnitzel

German immigrants to towns such as Fredericksburg and New Braunfels brought this traditional version of veal cutlet from the mother country. Simple, straightforward, and sensational, schnitzel is a natural for Texas because it's a bit like a chicken-fried steak with a younger piece of meat.

4 VEAL CUTLETS, ABOUT 4 TO 6 OUNCES EACH
½ CUP ALL-PURPOSE FLOUR
SALT AND FRESH-GROUND BLACK PEPPER TO TASTE
2 EGGS, BEATEN LIGHTLY WITH 1 TABLESPOON WATER
1¼ CUPS FINE-TEXTURED DRY BREAD CRUMBS
¾ CUP UNSALTED BUTTER
1 LEMON, CUT IN HALF

Serves 4

 Pound the veal very thin, to about ⅛ to ¼ inch in thickness.

In a shallow bowl, combine the flour with a bit of salt and pepper, but don't overdo the seasoning. Wiener schnitzel shouldn't be as assertively spiced as some chicken-fried steaks.

Place the eggs in a second shallow dish, and the bread crumbs in a third.

Melt the butter in a heavy skillet over medium heat. Dip each schnitzel

One nineteenth-century visitor to New Braunfels said he heard so much German spoken that "I got a sore throat listening to it."

in the flour, egg, and bread crumbs. Immediately sauté the schnitzels, turning them once, until they are golden brown, about 10 minutes. Transfer the schnitzels to a serving platter, and squeeze the juice from one lemon half over them. Garnish with lemon wedges cut from the other lemon half, and serve immediately.

Beef Rouladen

More old Texas cookbooks include rouladen than any other German-inspired beef dish, including sauerbraten. We found as many as five different versions per book.

1 TO 1¼ POUNDS TOP ROUND STEAK, TRIMMED OF FAT AND CUT INTO 4 EQUAL PIECES
2 TABLESPOONS BROWN OR GERMAN MUSTARD
2 SLICES SLAB BACON, CUT IN HALF CROSSWISE
2 SMALL TOMATOES, PREFERABLY ROMAS OR ANOTHER ITALIAN PLUM VARIETY, CHOPPED
½ TO 1 LARGE DILL PICKLE, CHOPPED
1 MEDIUM ONION, MINCED
SALT AND FRESH-GROUND BLACK PEPPER TO TASTE
1 TABLESPOON UNSALTED BUTTER
1 TABLESPOON OIL, PREFERABLY CANOLA OR CORN
1 CUP UNSALTED BEEF STOCK
½ CUP DRY RED WINE
1 GARLIC CLOVE, MINCED

Serves 4

Preheat the oven to 325° F.
Pound each piece of steak into an approximate rectangle about ¼ inch thick. Spread about 1 teaspoon mustard on each steak. Lay a piece of bacon over the mustard. Sprinkle about 1 tablespoon tomato, 1½ tablespoons dill pickle, 2 teaspoons onion, and salt and pepper over each steak. Reserve the remaining quantities of all toppings. Roll up each steak snugly, and secure the rolls with toothpicks.

TECHNIQUE TIP

Round steaks, which come from a section of the hind leg, usually benefit from moist-heat cooking because of their toughness. Top round, which we use for the rouladen, is the best cut, and the only one worthy of a dry cooking method such as grilling.

In a cast-iron skillet, Dutch oven, or heat-proof baking dish, warm the butter and oil together over medium-high heat, and brown the beef rolls quickly. Pour the stock and wine over the rouladen, and scatter the garlic and all remaining toppings over them. Cover the pan, place it in the oven, and bake 1½ hours, until the meat is very tender. Transfer the meat to a serving platter, and spoon some of the sauce over each roll. Serve the rouladen hot.

Texas has more bovine residents than any other state, over 13 million head at last count, not much shy of the total human population. Almost half of the agricultural income in the state comes from beef cattle, and nearly all of the 254 counties produce more revenue from cattle than any other farm or ranch commodity.

Dutch Brisket

Most recipes for cooking brisket indoors produce pale imitations of pit-smoked brisket. This recipe, however, comes from someone who has never tasted barbecued brisket, the mother of a recent Dutch immigrant, Peter Noom. It's a dish to die for—literally, perhaps, because of its richness, unless you save it for special occasions. Use margarine rather than butter because butter can't stand up to the long cooking time required.

1 SMALL FULLY-TRIMMED BRISKET, ABOUT 3½ TO 4 POUNDS, SLICED INTO STRIPS ½ TO ¾ INCH THICK
SALT AND CAYENNE
3 TO 4 STICKS MARGARINE
4 CUPS UNSALTED BEEF STOCK

Serves 10 to 12

 Rub the brisket strips with a moderate amount of salt and all the cayenne you can handle.

Let them sit from 30 minutes to several hours.

In a large, heavy skillet, melt a stick of margarine. Fry a quarter to a third of the brisket strips in the margarine over medium-high heat, turning them frequently, until they are dark brown and a little crispy, about 15 to 20 minutes. Transfer the brisket, with the margarine it was cooked in, to a stockpot or large, heavy saucepan. Add a little stock to the skillet to loosen any browned cracklings, and add them to the stockpot. Repeat this process, two or three times, with the remaining margarine and brisket.

When all the brisket has been fried, pour the remaining stock over it, submerging as much of the meat as possible in the liquid. Cover the stockpot, and simmer over low heat on the stove for 4 hours, or until the strips are meltingly tender.

You can eat the brisket immediately, but it gains flavor in the refrigerator for a day or two. Reheat it in the pot, and drain the slices before serving.

Fort Worth got its "Cowtown" nickname from its busy Stockyards, one of the biggest cattle auction grounds in the country from the turn of the century through the 1940s. The last of the major yards left in 1971, and the area is now a national historic district, with museums, shops, restaurants, and, not to be missed, Billy Bob's Texas, "the world's largest honky tonk."

Milagro Meat Loaf

Almost any kitchen crime can be called a meat loaf, but our version is so good one legislator threatened it with a sin tax. We named it after the **milagros**, *or miracle charms, sold outside major churches in Mexico, because the recipe transforms a mundane dish into a family heirloom.*

1 TABLESPOON UNSALTED BUTTER
½ CUP MINCED ONION
½ GREEN OR RED BELL PEPPER, CHOPPED FINE
2 GARLIC CLOVES, MINCED
1 TEASPOON FRESH-GROUND BLACK PEPPER
1 TEASPOON CAYENNE
1 TEASPOON SALT
½ TEASPOON CUMIN SEEDS, TOASTED AND GROUND
1¼ POUNDS LEAN GROUND BEEF
¾ POUND GROUND PORK
1½ CUPS DRY BREAD CRUMBS
¼ CUP TOMATO-BASED BARBECUE SAUCE

3 TABLESPOONS SOUR CREAM
1 TABLESPOON WORCESTERSHIRE SAUCE
1 EGG
MILK, AS NEEDED
ADDITIONAL BARBECUE SAUCE, OPTIONAL

Preheat the oven to 350° F.
Melt the butter in a heavy skillet. Add the onion, bell pepper, and garlic, and sauté until they are softened. Stir in the black pepper, cayenne, salt, and cumin, and sauté an additional 2 or 3 minutes.

Spoon the vegetable mixture into a large bowl.

Add to the bowl the remaining ingredients, except the milk, and mix well with your hands. The meat should feel quite moist but not soupy. If it is too dry, add milk a tablespoon or two at a time until the consistency is right.

Mound the meat into a 9-by-5-inch loaf pan. Bake the meat, uncovered, for 40 minutes. Raise the oven temperature to 400° F, and continue baking another 20 to 30 minutes. If you wish, brush with an additional tablespoon or two of barbecue sauce in the last 10 minutes.

Serve the meat hot or cold. The meat loaf makes great leftovers and sandwiches.

Variation: Milagro Meat Loaf makes a great filling for stuffed peppers. Cut the tops off red or green bell peppers, and remove the seeds. Spoon the uncooked meat loaf mixture loosely into the peppers. Place the peppers in a baking dish with a few tablespoons of stock or water. Bake 40 minutes at 350° F, and about 10 minutes more at 400° F. Baste with barbecue sauce in the last few minutes, or top with a sprinkling of grated cheddar cheese.

Old Dave's Original Burger

Frank X. Tolbert, the famous chili promoter, made a strong case for Athens, Texas, as the home of the hamburger. According to Tolbert's research, a lunch counter owner named Fletcher Davis, better known as "Old Dave," invented the hamburger in the late 1880s as his menu specialty. His version was a greasy piece of ground beef placed between slices of hot home-baked bread, and served with a mixture of mustard and mayonnaise, a big slice of Bermuda onion, and pickles. Davis took the concoction to the St. Louis World's Fair in 1904, where he sold it on the midway out of "Old Dave's Hamburger Stand," directly across from an Indian show featuring Geronimo. McDonald's Restaurants' "Hamburger University" agrees that the sandwich first appeared at the fair, but attributes the invention to an unknown vendor.

**6 TO 8 OUNCES GROUND CHUCK, IN A PATTY
½ INCH THICK
2 THICK SLICES HOME-STYLE SOURDOUGH
BREAD
PREPARED MUSTARD AND MAYONNAISE, MIXED
IN EQUAL PORTIONS
ONION AND DILL PICKLE SLICES, FOR GARNISH**

Makes 1 burger

In a cast-iron or other heavy skillet, sear the meat on both sides over high heat. Reduce the heat to medium-low, and cook the meat until it is done to your taste.

While the meat cooks, warm the bread in the oven on low heat, making sure the bread doesn't toast. Remove it from the oven, and spread one piece with dollops of mustard and mayonnaise, a thick slice of onion, and a few pickles. Place the patty, undrained, on the other piece of bread, allowing the bread to absorb the grease before you form the sandwich.

Take a bite, savor, and sing the praises of Old Dave.

TECHNIQUE TIP

For the best ground beef, ask your butcher to twice grind a piece of chuck, top or bottom round, or rump, with enough fat to make up about 20 percent of the whole.

O.T. Special Burger

Martin's Kum-Bak in Austin, an old-fashioned drive-in restaurant better known as Dirty's, is one of America's great hamburger joints, a place where the owners could make a good living just selling sniffs of the grill. This is our version of one of Dirty's specialties, named after the Old Timer who flips the meat behind the short-order counter, which is definitely the best place to sit.

10 TO 12 OUNCES GROUND CHUCK, IN **2** EQUAL-SIZE, ½-INCH-THICK PATTIES
2 SLICES AMERICAN CHEESE
1 OR **2** SLICES COOKED BACON, CUT IN HALF CROSSWISE
1 HAMBURGER BUN
MAYONNAISE
2 ICEBERG LETTUCE LEAVES
2 TOMATO SLICES

Makes 1 double burger

SOME PEOPLE DON'T SEEM TO UNDERSTAND WHAT BURGERS ARE ALL ABOUT. AT THE "21" CLUB, NEW YORKERS PAY $24 FOR A BURGER THAT DOESN'T HAVE ENOUGH GREASE TO OIL A PAPER AIRPLANE.

In a cast-iron or other heavy skillet, fry the patties over medium-high heat. About two minutes before they are cooked to your preference, top each patty with a slice of cheese and one or two bacon pieces.

While the meat cooks, warm the bun in an oven on low heat. Remove the bun, and smear both sides with mayonnaise. Add the lettuce and tomato to the bottom half, then top with both burgers, undrained, and perch the top half of the bun over the whole elaborate concoction. Eat immediately.

Old Texas lore claims children shouldn't eat mustard, because it would make their feet stink.

Texas Grilled Cheese

This burger is based on Dirty's other big seller, the D. H. Special, even sexier than the novelist with the same initials.

6 OUNCES GROUND CHUCK, IN A PATTY LESS
   THAN ½ INCH THICK
2 THIN SLICES ONION, PULLED APART INTO
   INDIVIDUAL RINGS
2 SLICES INEXPENSIVE WHITE BREAD
DILL PICKLE SLICES
2 SLICES AMERICAN CHEESE
2 TOMATO SLICES

Makes 1 burger

 With your fingers or a spatula, press half the onion rings into each side of the meat.

In a cast-iron or other heavy skillet, fry the patty over medium-high heat to the desired doneness. While the meat cooks, toast the bread lightly, and top each hot slice with a sprinkling of pickles and a piece of cheese. Pop the burger and onions between the two slices. Lay the sandwich in the hot skillet or on a hot grill, and cook it, turning once, until the cheese melts into the meat. Serve the burger hot.

The Texas A&M student body devours over 130 tons of hamburger annually.

Tamale Pie

Tamale pie, a superb casserole, can be made with pork, but in Texas the meat is usually beef. The dish offers a lot of hearty tamale flavor without all the work of the dish that inspired it.

FILLING

1 POUND LEAN GROUND BEEF

1 MEDIUM ONION, CHOPPED

1 GREEN BELL PEPPER, CHOPPED

2 GARLIC CLOVES, MINCED

1 CUP CORN KERNELS, FRESH OR FROZEN

1 CUP CHOPPED FRESH TOMATOES OR 1 CUP CANNED CRUSHED TOMATOES

½ CUP UNSALTED BEEF STOCK

¼ CUP RAISINS, OPTIONAL

¼ CUP SLICED PIMIENTO-STUFFED GREEN OLIVES

1 TABLESPOON CHILI POWDER, PREFERABLY HOMEMADE (PAGE 135) OR GEBHARDT'S

2 TEASPOONS CUMIN SEEDS, TOASTED AND GROUND

½ TEASPOON SALT, PLUS MORE TO TASTE

½ TEASPOON DRIED OREGANO, PREFERABLY MEXICAN

TOPPING

2 CUPS UNSALTED BEEF STOCK

1 CUP MASA HARINA

½ TEASPOON CHILI POWDER, PREFERABLY HOMEMADE (PAGE 135) OR GEBHARDT'S

½ TEASPOON SALT

1 EGG, SEPARATED

½ CUP (2 OUNCES) GRATED MILD OR MEDIUM CHEDDAR CHEESE

CREMA, OPTIONAL (PAGE 95)

Serves 6

 Preheat the oven to 350° F. Grease a medium baking dish.

Make the filling: In a large skillet, sauté the ground beef, onion, bell pepper, and garlic until the meat is lightly browned. Pour off any accumulated fat. Mix in the corn, tomatoes, stock, raisins, and olives. Stir in the chili powder, the cumin, ½ teaspoon salt, and the oregano. Cook, uncovered, over medium-low heat for 20 minutes. At the end of the cooking, the mixture should no longer be soupy. Taste, and add more salt if you like. If it seems too moist, raise the heat and cook another minute or two.

While the filling cooks, prepare the dough topping: In a heavy saucepan, bring the stock to a boil, and gradually add in the masa harina, stirring

Each June, Goliad, Texas, runs a hundred longhorn steers through its main streets for the "fastest parade in history." The Stampede started with the 1976 Bicentennial, and was so much fun the town made it an annual event.

constantly. Sprinkle in the chili powder and salt. Reduce the heat, and continue stirring until the masa is good and stiff, 8 to 10 minutes. Remove the pan from the heat. In a small bowl, beat the egg yolk, and stir it into the masa. In another small bowl, beat the egg white until stiff, and fold it into the masa.

Spoon the filling into the baking dish. Spread the batter over it. Top with the grated cheese. Bake the pie for 30 minutes, or until it is slightly puffed and lightly browned.

If you like, spoon a tablespoon or two of crema over each serving. The crema will melt into delicious rivulets around the hot pie. Cut the pie, and place slices on individual plates.

CHICKEN, PORK AND OTHER BARNYARD FARE

*T*he meal was spread on a plain pine table without cover. We did not at first know that it was a pine table, owing to the fact that it did not seem to have been washed since the Texas revolution. Supper consisted of coffee without milk, flies without butter, corn-bread, and "fry." "Fry" means rancid bacon charred by the action of fire.

Alexander Sweet and John Knox,
On a Mexican Mustang through Texas

*M*ost Texas visitors in the nineteenth century praised the German and Mexican food they encountered but constantly complained about the frontier fare of Southern settlers. Mostly from Tennessee and nearby areas, these Anglo pioneers lived contentedly on a subsistence level, getting by much of the time on the cornbread and fried pork they served Alex Sweet and John Knox. By and large, they agreed with the journalists' host, who told the travelers that this food was more "wholesome and better fur the stomach, than the high-toned slops you git in the cities."

Whatever the merits of their cooking, the early Southerners did raise their own staples, and over time they established a farming tradition that still thrives in many rural areas of the state. They grew corn from the beginning and kept semidomesticated hogs and a few chickens. Unlike the people who continued to push west into cattle country, their meat of choice remained pork throughout the nineteenth century and then became chicken for the first half of the twentieth century. Farmers could raise these animals in the barnyard, unlike beef cattle, and could even butcher them at home and preserve the pork. Beef may hold sway today—largely because of the spread of electrical refrigeration and freezing after World War II—but Texas has a long legacy of lighter and leaner farm-raised fare.

Hopkins County Chicken Stew

This stew has been a tradition in Hopkins County longer than anyone can recollect. The annual World Champion Hopkins County Stew Contest goes back thirty years, and the dish itself may date to the earliest decades of Anglo settlement in east Texas. Bill Elliot of the Sulphur Springs Chamber of Commerce speculates that the stew developed as a way of celebrating the end of the school year. Each student brought something for the school's kitchen pot, a huge iron kettle hung over an open wood fire. Although chicken is the meat of choice these days, Bill figures that squirrel and venison went into the pot originally, because folks at the time would have been reluctant to eat their egg-laying chickens. Hopkins County schools still serve the stew, now several times a month, and the cafeteria recipe even won the Stew Contest one year. That version inspired this one.

2 POUNDS CHICKEN PARTS, PREFERABLY BREASTS OR THIGHS

4 CUPS UNSALTED CHICKEN STOCK

2 ½ TEASPOONS SALT

4 MEDIUM BAKING POTATOES, DICED

1 LARGE ONION, DICED

2 CUPS CANNED CRUSHED TOMATOES

1 15-OUNCE CAN TOMATO SAUCE

2 TEASPOONS CHILI POWDER, PREFERABLY HOMEMADE (PAGE 135) OR GEBHARDT'S

2 TEASPOONS PAPRIKA

1 TEASPOON COARSE-GROUND BLACK PEPPER

2 CUPS CORN KERNELS, FRESH OR FROZEN

1 16-OUNCE CAN CREAM-STYLE CORN

2 TABLESPOONS UNSALTED BUTTER

Serves 6 to 8

Assuming you don't have a huge iron pot, use a Dutch oven or heavy stockpot for cooking the stew. Place the chicken in the pot with the stock and salt. Over medium heat, simmer the chicken until it is tender and cooked through, about 15 to 20 minutes. With a slotted spoon, remove the chicken, and set it aside until it is cool enough to handle.

TECHNIQUE TIP

Some people insist the stew should cook a long time, as much as seven hours. We haven't found the extra cooking time worth the effort, but if you want to try it, be sure to stir the stew often.

Bring the stock back to a simmer, and add the potatoes and onion. Simmer until the potatoes are cooked through, about 15 minutes. In the meantime, skin, bone, and shred or dice the chicken. Return it to the pot, along with the tomatoes, tomato sauce, chili powder, paprika, and pepper. Bring the mixture to a simmer again. Add both types of corn and the butter. Cover the pot, and continue simmering the stew for at least 30 minutes, until it is quite thick. Stir the stew up from the bottom frequently to prevent scorching, and add a little water if it starts to get dry. Don't let it boil—that would toughen the chicken.

The stew is tasty with cornbread. In Hopkins County, though, it's usually served with fistfuls of crackers, slices of cheese, and plenty of pickles.

AS WITH CHILI, EVERYONE HAS A THEORY ON WHAT SHOULD AND SHOULDN'T GO INTO HOPKINS COUNTY CHICKEN STEW. A SUGGESTION THAT TOMATO PASTE BE SUBSTITUTED FOR WHOLE TOMATOES OR SAUCE ONCE INCITED A LIVELY TWO-WEEK DEBATE IN THE *DALLAS MORNING NEWS*. DISCUSSIONS OF FRESH VERSUS CANNED CORN CAN GET EVEN MORE CONTENTIOUS.

The World Champion Hopkins County Stew Contest, held each September in Sulphur Springs, is great fun. Inexpensive tickets allow you to wander around the city park sampling the seventy or eighty entries, most being cooked by contestants in period dress stirring iron cauldrons. Young women might want to enter the Cover Girl Contest, where dimples and curls count less than the ability to drive a tractor, milk a cow, and pluck a chicken.

Old Texas lore claimed that eating chicken gizzards gave girls large breasts. Try them in the Classic Cream Gravy—the gizzards, that is.

East Texas Fried Chicken

*In our travels through Texas, we've found fried chicken seasoned with oranges, jalapeños, garlic, mustard, cayenne, and cumin. We've found it batter-dipped and cornmeal-coated, pan-fried and deep-fried, and cooked in lard, bacon drippings, shortening, and a multitude of oils, mainly corn, canola, safflower, and sesame. Forget the gimmicks. Nothing tops this recipe. We owe the secrets to a couple of serious pros, Lula Mae Austin, a Dallas cook, and the author James Villas, who devotes an entire chapter to frying chicken in his wonderful **American Taste**.*

3 TO 4 CUPS BUTTERMILK

2 TEASPOONS TABASCO OR OTHER HOT PEPPER SAUCE

2 TO 3 TEASPOONS SALT

1 TEASPOON FRESH-GROUND BLACK PEPPER

3½ TO 4 POUNDS CHICKEN PARTS

1½ CUPS ALL-PURPOSE FLOUR

1½ POUNDS (3 CUPS) SHORTENING, PREFERABLY CRISCO

3 TABLESPOONS BACON DRIPPINGS

Serves 6

At least 2½ hours (and up to 12 hours) before you plan to eat, mix the buttermilk, Tabasco or other sauce, ½ teaspoon of the salt, and ¼ teaspoon of the pepper in a shallow dish. Add the chicken parts, turning to coat them well with the mixture. Cover the dish, and refrigerate it.

About 20 minutes before you plan to fry the chicken, bring it to room temperature. Sprinkle the remaining salt and pepper into a medium-size paper bag, and add the flour. Set the bag aside.

In a 10- to 12-inch cast-iron skillet, melt the shortening over high heat. Add the bacon drippings to the skillet. When small bubbles form on the surface, reduce the heat slightly. Place a large brown paper sack near the stove for draining the chicken.

Starting with the dark pieces, take a piece of chicken out of the marinade, shake off the excess liquid, and drop it into the bag of seasoned flour. Shake the bag well so that the piece is coated thoroughly. Remove it from the bag, and lower it gently into the skillet, skin-side down. Repeat until all the chicken is in the skillet, arranging it so that all the pieces cook evenly. The pieces should fit snugly together, although they shouldn't stick to each other. Reduce the heat to medium, and cover the skillet. Fry the chicken exactly 17 minutes.

Lower the heat slightly, take off the cover, and use tongs to turn over the chicken gently. Fry it uncovered for another 17 minutes.

Remove the chicken with the

tongs—it will be a deep, rich brown—and lay it on the paper sack to drain.

Serve the chicken hot with Prime-Time Mashed Potatoes (page 339) and Classic Cream Gravy (page 144) made with the pan drippings.

Variation: Among all the possible variations on fried chicken, we're partial to the jalapeño-garlic version we enjoyed a few years ago at the Kerrville Folk Festival. Just add to the buttermilk a couple of minced pickled jalapeños with 1 or 2 tablespoons of their pickling liquid and a half-dozen garlic cloves. Serve the chicken with pickled jalapeño slices.

Pilgrim's Pride grew from a feed-store in Pittsburg, Texas, to one of the nation's largest chicken producers. Owner "Bo" Pilgrim still lives close to the headquarters in a multimillion-dollar mansion locals call "Cluckingham Palace."

TECHNIQUE TIPS

Fried chicken deserves perfection. These half-dozen hints help you get there.

• Avoid supermarket-style mass-produced poultry parts. Find yourself a good meat market that takes pride in its chickens, and have it cut up a whole chicken for you. Or do it yourself.

• Always use a well-seasoned cast-iron skillet at least 10 inches in diameter. Never substitute anything with an electric cord or a decorator color.

• Soaking the chicken adds moisture to the meat. Don't skimp on the soaking time.

• Yes, you have to use Crisco and bacon drippings. They make a big difference in taste and texture. If you follow our instructions carefully, though, the chicken will absorb little of the fat it's fried in.

• Never cook the chicken in more than ½ inch of oil or you will deep-fry it, even if you're using a skillet. Deep-fried chicken does not have the proper balance of crispy exterior and juicy interior.

• Do not reheat fried chicken. Any leftovers are better cold.

Chicken and Dumplings

When Huey P. Long, the Louisiana politico, promised Depression-era voters a chicken in every pot, people on both sides of the Sabine River drooled over the idea of chicken and dumplings. This was Sunday Dinner Number 2 then, a close second to fried chicken, and even preferable if you had an old bird—like any of Huey's—that was too tough for the skillet.

CHICKEN

1 STEWING CHICKEN, ABOUT 5 POUNDS, CUT UP
ABOUT 8 CUPS UNSALTED CHICKEN STOCK
3 CELERY RIBS, CHOPPED
3 CARROTS, SLICED
1 MEDIUM ONION, CHOPPED
2 TEASPOONS SALT
2 GARLIC CLOVES, MINCED
1 BAY LEAF
½ TEASPOON COARSE-GROUND BLACK PEPPER
½ TEASPOON MACE OR A PINCH OF NUTMEG

DUMPLINGS

2 CUPS SIFTED ALL-PURPOSE FLOUR
1 TABLESPOON BAKING POWDER
1 TEASPOON SALT
2 EGGS, LIGHTLY BEATEN
⅔ CUP MILK
2 TABLESPOONS CHOPPED PARSLEY
½ TEASPOON COARSE-GROUND BLACK PEPPER

CHOPPED PARSLEY, FOR GARNISH

Serves 6 to 8

ALLEN'S FAMILY-STYLE MEALS IN SWEETWATER SERVES THE BEST SIX-DOLLAR MEAL IN TEXAS AND MAYBE THE WORLD. THE ALLENS HAVE BEEN FRYING CHICKEN FOR THE PUBLIC SINCE THE 1940S, AND TODAY THEY BRING IT TO THEIR COMMUNAL TABLES WITH BRIMMING BOWLS OF SERVE-YOURSELF VEGETABLES, BREADS, AND DESSERTS. ON OUR LAST VISIT, THERE WERE A DOZEN DOWN-HOME VEGETABLES TO SAMPLE, BUT THE FRIED CHICKEN WAS STILL THE STAR. IN *ROAD-FOOD*, ROVING WRITERS JANE AND MICHAEL STERN DESCRIBE IT AS "SHEATHED IN A LOVELY, CRACKLING-CRISP CRUST, JUICY AND LOADED WITH FLAVOR INSIDE, A PERFECT BLEND OF SPICE, CRUNCH, JUICE, AND BALMY BIRD SAVOR." THAT'S THE IDEA, SURE ENOUGH.

Place the chicken in a stockpot, and pour in enough stock just to cover it. Add the rest of the chicken ingredients, and bring the mixture to a boil. Reduce the heat to a simmer, cover, and cook about 1 hour.

With a slotted spoon, remove the breasts to a plate, and continue simmering for another 30 minutes. Remove the remaining chicken, setting it aside with the breasts, and reserve the broth.

When the chicken is cool enough to handle, shred the meat, and discard the skin and bones. Transfer the chicken to a large serving dish, and keep it warm.

While the chicken is cooking, mix up the dumpling batter. Some Texas recipes make noodle-style dumplings in strips, but we prefer the fluffy biscuit-like option. Sift the flour together with the baking powder and salt into a medium bowl. Add the remaining ingredients, and combine lightly. Don't overmix. For lighter dumplings, let the batter sit at least 10 minutes, and up to an hour, before using it.

About twenty minutes before you plan to eat, bring the broth to a boil.

Drop the batter into the broth by tablespoons. Reduce the heat to a simmer, cover the pot, and cook the dumplings 15 minutes.

Spoon the dumplings and the thickened mixture of broth and vegetables over the chicken, top with parsley, and serve immediately.

Variation: Maybe only in Texas would a cook think of this. For fast dumplings, cut flour tortillas into small wedges, and cook them in the broth for several minutes until they are soft. Few friends will guess what you've done—unless, of course, they do it, too.

THE DAUGHTERS OF THE REPUBLIC OF TEXAS, WHO OPERATE THE ALAMO, SUPPLIED THIS BIT OF TURN-OF-THE-CENTURY ADVICE ON TENDERIZING CHICKEN: "IN COOKING TOUGH FOWL OR MEAT, ONE TABLESPOON OF VINEGAR IN THE WATER WILL SAVE NEARLY TWO HOURS OF BOILING."

King Ranch Chicken Casserole

The origin of this dish and its connection to the King Ranch are mysteries, but it is the Lone Star of casseroles, well known and loved all over the state.

SAUCE

2 TABLESPOONS UNSALTED BUTTER
2 GARLIC CLOVES, MINCED
¼ TEASPOON GROUND DRIED RED CHILE,
  PREFERABLY ANCHO OR NEW MEXICAN
PINCH OF GROUND CUMIN
2 TABLESPOONS ALL-PURPOSE FLOUR
¾ CUP UNSALTED CHICKEN STOCK
½ CUP MILK
2 TABLESPOONS SOUR CREAM
SALT AND FRESH-GROUND BLACK PEPPER TO
  TASTE

FILLING

1 TABLESPOON UNSALTED BUTTER
½ MEDIUM ONION, CHOPPED
½ MEDIUM GREEN BELL PEPPER, CHOPPED
¼ CUP CHOPPED ROASTED GREEN CHILE,
  PREFERABLY NEW MEXICAN OR POBLANO,
  FRESH OR FROZEN
6 OUNCES MUSHROOMS, CHOPPED FINE
½ CUP DICED TOMATOES, FRESH OR CANNED
2 TABLESPOONS PIMIENTOS
OIL FOR FRYING, PREFERABLY CANOLA OR CORN
8 CORN TORTILLAS
2 TO 3 CUPS DICED OR SHREDDED COOKED
  CHICKEN (SMOKED CHICKEN IS ESPECIALLY
  FLAVORFUL)
1½ CUPS GRATED MILD CHEDDAR CHEESE
¼ CUP SLICED PIMIENTO-STUFFED GREEN
  OLIVES
¼ CUP SLICED GREEN ONIONS

Serves 6

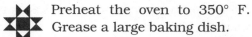 Preheat the oven to 350° F. Grease a large baking dish.

In a medium skillet, melt the butter. Add the garlic, chile, and cumin, and sauté 1 to 2 minutes. Sprinkle in the flour, and stir. Pour the chicken stock and milk into the skillet slowly, stirring continuously to avoid lumps. Simmer the sauce about 3 minutes, or until it has thickened.

The King Ranch is known for almost everything except chicken. It's the largest spread in Texas today—though less than a third the size of the XIT at its peak—and runs some sixty thousand head of cattle, mostly Santa Gertrudis, a beefy breed the ranch developed to replace stringy longhorns. You would think the land and cattle would produce ample income, but the owners were deep in debt until they discovered oil in the 1940s. Now thousands of oil and gas wells keep them comfortable down on the ranch.

Stir in the sour cream, salt, and pepper. Reserve the sauce. (It can be made ahead and refrigerated.)

Prepare the filling: Melt the butter in a skillet. Add all the filling ingredients, and sauté until they are softened and well combined. Reserve the filling.

Heat about ½ inch of the oil in a small skillet. With a pair of tongs, dunk the tortillas, a couple at a time, in the oil for a few seconds, just long enough to soften them. If you have made your own fresh tortillas (page 92), this step can be eliminated.

In the baking dish, layer half of the tortillas and the chicken, a third of the sauce, and one-half each of the filling, cheese, green olives, and green onions. Spoon on another third of the sauce, and then repeat the layering with the remaining ingredients, ending with the rest of the sauce. Bake the casserole 30 minutes, until it is heated through and bubbly.

Both-Ways Chicken Gumbo

Gumbo sailed down the Gulf from New Orleans to Galveston and Houston on the earliest ships that plied those waters. Most recipes call for either okra or filé powder to aid in thickening, but this version benefits from the flavors of both.

1 2½- TO 3-POUND CHICKEN, OR 2½ TO 3
    POUNDS CHICKEN PARTS
4 CUPS UNSALTED CHICKEN STOCK
½ POUND ANDOUILLE OR OTHER HOT, SMOKY
    SAUSAGE
ABOUT 3 TABLESPOONS OIL, PREFERABLY
    CANOLA OR CORN
¼ CUP ALL-PURPOSE FLOUR OR PREBROWNED
    FLOUR (SEE TECHNIQUE TIP)
1 CUP SLICED OKRA, FRESH OR FROZEN
1 MEDIUM ONION, CHOPPED
3 CELERY RIBS, CHOPPED
1 MEDIUM GREEN BELL PEPPER, CHOPPED
2 GARLIC CLOVES, MINCED
1 14½-OUNCE CAN WHOLE TOMATOES,
    UNDRAINED

1 CUP V-8 JUICE
½ CUP SLICED GREEN ONIONS
2 BAY LEAVES
2 TEASPOONS WORCESTERSHIRE SAUCE
¾ TEASPOON DRIED THYME
¾ TEASPOON SALT
¼ TEASPOON FRESH-GROUND BLACK PEPPER
¼ TEASPOON WHITE PEPPER
¼ TEASPOON CAYENNE
1 TEASPOON FILÉ POWDER
SEVERAL SPLASHES TABASCO OR OTHER HOT
    PEPPER SAUCE

Serves 6 to 8

Place the chicken in a large saucepan with the stock. Bring the stock to a boil, reduce the heat, and simmer until the chicken is very tender, about 45 to 60 minutes. Remove the chicken from the stock, and reserve both.

When the chicken has cooled enough to handle, shred it, and transfer it to a plate or bowl.

Brown the sausage in a Dutch oven or stockpot over medium-low heat. With a slotted spoon, remove it from the pot, leaving the rendered fat, and add the sausage to the reserved chicken. Refrigerate the chicken and sausage.

Eyeball the amount of fat remaining in the skillet, and add enough oil to bring it up to about ¼ cup. Warm the oil and meat drippings over medium-high heat. Add the flour, and stir constantly until a medium-brown roux forms. The time will depend on whether you use uncooked or browned flour.

When the roux has reached the right shade, turn off the heat. Quickly stir in the okra, onion, celery, bell pepper, and garlic. When the sizzling stops, slowly pour in the reserved chicken stock, stirring to combine. Add the tomatoes, V-8 juice, green onions, bay leaves, Worcestershire sauce, thyme, salt, peppers, and cayenne, and bring the mixture to a boil over high heat. Reduce the heat, and simmer the gumbo about 45 minutes. Stir in the chicken, sausage, and filé powder. Heat through, and taste, adjusting the seasoning or adding a bit of Tabasco for a little more kick. Serve the gumbo hot over rice, in bowls.

TECHNIQUE TIP

Many Cajun and Creole dishes require a roux, a flour-and-fat base. Joe Cahn, the indomitable founder of the New Orleans School of Cooking, teaches a little trick to speed up the process of making a roux. Spoon some all-purpose flour into a baking pan, place it in a moderate oven (about 350° F), and bake it for a couple of hours, stirring it once or twice as it cooks. The flour will turn a deep golden brown. It will keep indefinitely if it is stored in a tightly covered jar. Substitute it for uncooked flour when you start a roux.

Chicken Spaghetti

During the Depression, meat was hard to afford, and during World War II, it was seldom available, even in Texas. Most of the substitute dishes disappeared when the hard times did, but this combination of chicken and spaghetti remained popular in the state. It made Texas cookbooks by 1949 and has continued to get good press ever since.

12 OUNCES COOKED SPAGHETTI, STILL WARM

1 TABLESPOON UNSALTED BUTTER

2 TABLESPOONS BACON DRIPPINGS

1 LARGE ONION, CHOPPED

3 CELERY RIBS, CHOPPED

1 GREEN BELL PEPPER, CHOPPED

1 CUP MINCED MUSHROOMS (ABOUT 10 TO 12 MEDIUM)

3 GARLIC CLOVES, MINCED

1 TEASPOON WORCESTERSHIRE SAUCE

2 TEASPOONS CHILI POWDER, PREFERABLY HOMEMADE (PAGE 135) OR GEBHARDT'S

1 TABLESPOON ALL-PURPOSE FLOUR

1½ CUPS BEER OR UNSALTED CHICKEN STOCK

3 RIPE TOMATOES, PREFERABLY ROMA OR ANOTHER ITALIAN PLUM VARIETY

¼ CUP CHILI SAUCE, PREFERABLY HOMEMADE (PAGE 406)

¾ CUP HALF-AND-HALF

2 TABLESPOONS MINCED PARSLEY

2 CUPS DICED OR SHREDDED COOKED CHICKEN

½ CUP SLICED PIMIENTO-STUFFED GREEN OLIVES

2 CUPS GRATED MEDIUM CHEDDAR CHEESE (8 OUNCES)

Serves 6

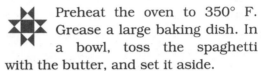 Preheat the oven to 350° F. Grease a large baking dish. In a bowl, toss the spaghetti with the butter, and set it aside.

Warm the bacon drippings in a skillet over medium heat. Cook the onion, celery, bell pepper, mushrooms, garlic, Worcestershire sauce, and chili powder together until the vegetables are well softened, about 15 minutes; cover the skillet if the mixture appears to be getting dry. Sprinkle in the flour, stirring to incorporate it, and add the beer or stock, the tomatoes, and the chili sauce. Bring the mixture to a boil, reduce the heat to a simmer, and cook the sauce for 30 minutes, until it has thickened slightly and reduced a bit. Remove the pan from the heat, and stir in the half-and-half and parsley. Pour the sauce over the spaghetti, and toss well.

West Texas bumper sticker: "Support Beef. Run Over A Chicken."

Layer half the spaghetti-and-sauce mixture in the baking dish. Top with half each of the chicken, olives, and cheese. Add the other half of the spaghetti, and top with the remaining chicken, olives, and cheese. (The casserole can be assembled ahead to this point, covered, and refrigerated overnight. Remove it from the refrigerator 30 minutes before baking it.)

Bake the casserole 25 minutes, or until the cheese melts and the sauce bubbles heartily around the edges. Serve the casserole hot.

The demand for pesticide- and drug-free products led A. M. "Buddy" Lindeman and his son David to start raising Buddy's Natural Chickens. In south central Texas, near Gonzales, the Lindemans nourish their healthy chicks to maturity in airy houses with space to roam, without using growth stimulants or antibiotics. While some companies take pride in their high-tech processing plants, the Lindemans are equally enthusiastic about their unautomated facility, which assures greater quality control and minimizes the chance of salmonella contamination. Call 210-379-8782 for information on stores that stock the chickens.

Traditionally, in much of Texas, the only meals as big as Thanksgiving and Christmas dinners were on days the preacher came to call. Everyone washed up well and put on their Sunday best. Mom brought out a scrubbed and ironed white tablecloth and real glasses to replace the usual jelly jars. You chased down a couple of chickens, wrung their necks, and fried them fresh, to serve with plenty of potatoes, cream gravy, hot biscuits, and probably a gooey cobbler. Since the preacher ate like this regularly, dad always left the table wondering how he had missed his true vocation.

Peanut-Roasted Chicken

This idea goes back to Virginia, where many future Texas families set-tled first, and features one of the Lone Star State's favorite legumes. Taking the trouble to rotate and baste the bird rewards you with juicy meat and a crispy skin.

1 3- TO 3½-POUND CHICKEN
1 TABLESPOON ROASTED PEANUT OIL
½ TABLESPOON UNSALTED BUTTER
SALT AND FRESH-GROUND BLACK PEPPER TO
   TASTE
½ MEDIUM ONION, SLICED
½ CUP RAW PEANUTS
1 CUP UNSALTED CHICKEN STOCK
20 GARLIC CLOVES, UNPEELED
½ CUP WHITE WINE OR ADDITIONAL UNSALTED
   CHICKEN STOCK

Serves 3

 Preheat the oven to 400° F. Grease the rack of a small roasting pan.

Slip your fingers under the chicken's skin, and loosen it, being careful not to tear it. Massage the oil into the flesh and inside the cavity. Rub the butter over the chicken's skin. Salt and pepper the chicken generously in-side and out. Fill the cavity with the onion and ¼ cup of the peanuts.

Place the chicken on the rack in the roasting pan, breast up, and roast it for 15 minutes. Turn the chicken on one side, add the garlic cloves to the pan, and baste the chicken with a lit-tle stock. Reduce the heat to 350° F and cook the bird 15 minutes more. Turn the chicken on its other side, add the remaining ¼ cup of peanuts to the pan, and baste again. Cook 15 minutes longer, and turn the bird back-side up. Pour the wine or addi-tional stock over it, and roast it for another 15 minutes. Turn the chicken breast up again, and baste it with the pan juices and a little more stock. After 15 more minutes, the chicken should be golden brown with a crispy skin. The total cooking time is 1¼ hours.

Remove the chicken from the oven. Spoon out the onion and peanuts from its cavity, and add them to the roasting pan. Transfer the chicken to a serving platter, cover it with a foil tent, and let it sit for 10 to 15 minutes before carving it.

Pour the contents of the roasting pan and the wine or remaining stock into a blender or food processor, and purée. Strain the sauce, reheat it if needed, and serve it in a gravy boat along with the roast chicken.

Chicken Pot Pie

British colonists brought steak-and-kidney pies with them across the Atlantic, but little except the crust survived the climb over the Appalachian Mountains. We think Texans probably knew by instinct that chicken would be much better than kidneys inside the dough. Some versions have just a single top crust, but wrapping the filling with two flaky crusts doubles the pleasure.

FLAKY PIE CRUST* (SEE PAGE 513)

FILLING

½ CUP HALF-AND-HALF

2 GARLIC CLOVES, CHOPPED

1 FRESH JALAPEÑO, CHOPPED

4 WHOLE CLOVES

3 TABLESPOONS UNSALTED BUTTER

½ MEDIUM ONION, CHOPPED FINE

2 CELERY RIBS, CHOPPED

⅓ MEDIUM RED BELL PEPPER, CHOPPED FINE

3 CUPS UNSALTED CHICKEN STOCK

1½ CUPS DICED CARROTS

1 CUP PEARL ONIONS, PEELED

1 SMALL RED POTATO, DICED

½ CUP CORN KERNELS, FRESH OR FROZEN

½ CUP PEAS, FRESH OR FROZEN

1½ POUNDS BONELESS CHICKEN BREAST OR
    THIGH MEAT, OR A COMBINATION, CUT IN
    BITE-SIZE CHUNKS

2 TABLESPOONS ALL-PURPOSE FLOUR

1 TEASPOON SALT

½ TEASPOON FRESH-GROUND BLACK PEPPER

½ TEASPOON DRY MUSTARD

3 TABLESPOONS MINCED PARSLEY

Serves 6

* If you like, replace the water in the pie crust recipe with cold chicken stock thinned to the consistency of water.

Preheat the oven to 400° F.

In a small pan over low heat, warm the half-and-half with the garlic, jalapeño, and cloves until tiny bubbles just surface around the edges. Remove the pan from the heat, set it aside, and let the spices steep.

Melt the butter in a large saucepan over medium heat. Add the onions, celery, and bell pepper, and sauté them until they are soft, 2 to 3 minutes. If the mixture seems dry, cover it for a minute or two while it cooks.

Pour the chicken stock into the saucepan, and bring it to a simmer. Stir in the carrots, pearl onions, and potato, and cook until the vegetables are just tender, about 10 minutes. Add the corn, and continue cooking for another 3 minutes, until the corn has just cooked through. Stir in the peas, and immediately take the pan from the heat. With a slotted spoon, remove the vegetables from the broth, and place them in a medium bowl.

Return the pan with the broth to the stovetop. Add the chicken to the broth, and poach it over low heat about 3 to 4 minutes, or until it is cooked through. With a slotted spoon, remove the chicken, and add it to the bowl of vegetables. Measure the remaining stock. Return it to the saucepan, and reduce it to 1½ cups.

In a small bowl, stir together the flour, salt, pepper, and dry mustard. Spoon in a few tablespoons of the hot stock, and mix well. Stir the flour mixture back into the stock in the saucepan, and bring the stock to a boil. Reduce the heat, and simmer the mixture for two to three minutes, until it is well thickened. Strain the spices from the reserved half-and-half, and discard them. Add the half-and-half to the sauce, and heat it through.

Mix the sauce with the vegetables and chicken. Sprinkle in the parsley, and stir well. Taste the filling, and adjust the seasonings as desired.

Place the bottom crust into a 9-inch pie pan, pour in the filling, and top it with the second crust. Prick a few steam vents in the top crust. Bake the pie at 400° F for 20 minutes. Reduce the oven temperature to 350° F, and bake for an additional 30 minutes. Check the pie about halfway through the cooking time, and cover the edges with foil if they appear to be browning too quickly. The crust should be lightly browned when the pie is done. Serve the pie hot.

The now-huge East Texas broiler chicken industry developed right after World War II, filling the gap caused by the decline of cotton cultivation. The East Texas Poultry Festival in early October celebrates the broilers with a competition and auction that annually raises over thirty thousand dollars for charity.

Fiesta Chicken Casserole

Many casseroles are bland combinations of prefab canned and processed foods—pretend dishes for people who want to fool themselves into thinking that they are cooking. We love the blend of flavors in a good casserole, though, and we sort through the schlock in search of them. This recipe is a definite winner, thanks to the creative labors of Cicily Cross of Tenaha, who made the original version the 1986 cook-off winner at the East Texas Poultry Festival in Center.

CASSEROLE

1 RECIPE NOT-CREAM-OF-MUSHROOM SOUP
(PAGE 363)
10 OUNCES FRESH SPINACH
1 CUP SOUR CREAM
½ CUP CHOPPED ROASTED GREEN CHILES,
PREFERABLY NEW MEXICAN OR POBLANO,
FRESH OR FROZEN
¼ CUP CHOPPED ONION
2 TABLESPOONS CHOPPED PIMIENTO
1 GARLIC CLOVE, MINCED
½ TEASPOON SALT
¼ TEASPOON CUMIN SEEDS, TOASTED AND
GROUND
DASH OF TABASCO OR OTHER HOT PEPPER
SAUCE
2 TO 3 CUPS DICED OR SHREDDED COOKED
CHICKEN
1 CUP (4 OUNCES) GRATED MONTEREY OR
JALAPEÑO JACK CHEESE
½ CUP (2 OUNCES) GRATED SHARP CHEDDAR
CHEESE

TOPPING

2 EGGS, SEPARATED
1 CUP ALL-PURPOSE FLOUR
¾ CUP MILK

¼ CUP UNSALTED BUTTER, SOFTENED
PAPRIKA

Serves 6

Heat the oven to 375° F. Grease a deep baking dish.

In a medium bowl, combine the soup, spinach, sour cream, chiles, onion, pimiento, garlic, salt, cumin, and Tabasco or other hot sauce. In another bowl, combine the chicken with the cheeses.

Spoon half of the spinach mixture into the prepared dish. Top it with half of the chicken mixture. Repeat with the remaining spinach and chicken.

In a medium bowl, beat the egg whites until stiff peaks form. Spoon the whites into a small bowl, using the original bowl to beat together the egg yolks, flour, milk, and butter. (It's not necessary to wash the whisk or beaters in between.) Beat the batter for 2 minutes, and then fold in the egg whites gently. Spoon the batter over the casserole, and sprinkle the top liberally with paprika. Bake for 40 to 45 minutes, or until the topping is a deep golden brown and a toothpick inserted into it comes out clean. Remove the casserole from the oven, and let it sit for 10 to 15 minutes before serving.

Pollo Kiev

Back when we were less concerned about the amount of butter we consumed, Chicken Kiev was one of our favorite dishes. This is our new version, with salsa in place of the saturated fat.

¾ CUP PICO DE GALLO (PAGE 95) OR OTHER
  CHUNKY FRESH SALSA
4 BONELESS AND SKINLESS CHICKEN BREAST
  HALVES
SALT AND FRESH-GROUND BLACK PEPPER TO
  TASTE
1 CUP SALTINE CRACKER CRUMBS
1½ TEASPOONS CUMIN SEEDS, TOASTED AND
  GROUND
1 EGG
1 TABLESPOON OIL, PREFERABLY CANOLA OR
  PEANUT
OIL FOR DEEP FRYING, PREFERABLY CANOLA OR
  PEANUT OR A COMBINATION OF BOTH

Serves 4

On a piece of waxed paper laid over a plate, spoon out the salsa into four portions, and shape the portions into rectangular mounds. Place the plate in the freezer until the salsa mounds are solid, a minimum of at least 1 hour. (You can do this step a day ahead if you like.)

Pound the chicken breasts to about a ¼-inch thickness. Lightly salt and pepper both sides of the chicken.

Remove the salsa mounds from the freezer, and place one in the center of each chicken breast. Working quickly, carefully roll the chicken up around the salsa, tucking the ends in well and completely enclosing the salsa. Place the rolled chicken breasts, seam side up, on a plate, cover them, and transfer them to the freezer for about 1 hour.

Combine the cracker crumbs with the cumin. Shortly before cooking, lightly beat the egg with the tablespoon of oil. Roll the chicken in the cracker crumbs, then in the egg, and then again in the cracker crumbs.

In a heavy saucepan, heat to 325° F enough oil to cover the chicken by at least 1 inch. Fry the chicken rolls for 7 to 8 minutes, until they are a deep golden brown. Serve them immediately.

Margarita Chicken Breasts

Margarita flavors spice up these chicken breasts and may enliven you, too. This is a great dish for grilling outside on a summer evening, but it can be baked as well.

4 BONELESS, SKINLESS CHICKEN BREASTS

MARINADE

¼ CUP TEQUILA
2 TABLESPOONS FRESH LIME JUICE
1 TEASPOON LIME ZEST
1 TABLESPOON HONEY
1 TABLESPOON MINCED CILANTRO
1 TABLESPOON CORN OIL, PREFERABLY
  UNREFINED
1 SMALL FRESH JALAPEÑO, MINCED
½ TEASPOON DRIED TARRAGON
½ TEASPOON SALT
FRESH-GROUND BLACK PEPPER TO TASTE

Serves 4

Arrange the chicken in a single layer in a nonreactive dish. Mix the marinade ingredients together, and pour the mixture over the chicken. Cover the chicken, and refrigerate it 8 hours or overnight. Turn it at least once.

If you want to grill the chicken, fire up enough charcoal to form a single layer of coals beneath the breasts, and heat the coals until they are covered with gray ash. If you want to bake the chicken, preheat the oven to 450° F.

Drain the chicken, reserving the marinade in a small saucepan. If you are grilling the chicken, cook it, uncovered, over medium-hot coals until it is cooked through, basting it with some of the marinade. If you are baking, place the breasts in a small oven-proof dish, and cover it tightly. Bake the chicken 15 to 18 minutes, until it is cooked through, uncovering it for the last two to three minutes.

With either cooking method, let the chicken sit for 5 to 10 minutes after it cooks. In the meantime, bring the reserved marinade to a boil, and boil it for at least 4 minutes, reducing the liquid slightly. Taste it, and adjust the seasoning. Cut each chicken breast into thin slices, arrange them on a platter or individual plates, and top them with the sauce made from the marinade. Serve the breasts hot.

> DON'T CONFUSE FRIED TURKEY WITH TURKEY FRIES. BOTH ARE COOKED IN HOT OIL, BUT ONE'S A BIRD AND THE OTHER IS ITS BALLS. THE TESTICLES ARE COOKED LIKE CALF FRIES (PAGE 154).

Chile Pecan Fried Turkey

Over the past couple of decades, a passion for fried turkey swept out of Cajun Louisiana into southeastern Texas. We picked up the idea from some Houston friends. Fried turkey requires a heavy-duty outdoor gas cooker capable of putting out 35,000 BTUs of heat. Read the instructions carefully before jumping into this one.

½ CUP LONE STAR DRY RUB (PAGE 27)
½ CUP UNSALTED CHICKEN OR TURKEY STOCK
2 TABLESPOONS GARLIC-FLAVORED OIL
2 TABLESPOONS MELTED UNSALTED BUTTER
1 TEASPOON WHITE VINEGAR
1 12-POUND TURKEY
PEANUT OIL FOR DEEP FRYING, ABOUT 5 GALLONS
CHILE PECAN SAUCE FOR TURKEY (PAGE 211)

Serves 8 to 10

The night before you plan to fry the turkey, place 2 tablespoons of the dry rub in a small bowl, and mix it with the stock, oil, butter, and vinegar. If your bird has one of those little pop-up attachments that tells you when the turkey is done, remove it to avoid melting it or otherwise making it go haywire. Inject the liquid into the bird at 2-inch intervals, making several injections going in different directions at each hole. Go deep into the meat with the needle. Inject the breast most fully. Rub a little of the mixture over and under the skin, too. Massage the remaining dry rub into the turkey's cavity and under the skin. Transfer the bird to a plastic trash bag, and refrigerate it overnight.

Take the turkey out of the refrigerator 1 hour before you plan to begin frying it. Remove it from the bag, and let it air-dry. While the turkey recovers from its chill, assemble everything needed for frying.

Position a heavy-duty butane burner on a sturdy surface that won't be hurt by any drips of oil. Set a heavy stockpot capable of holding at least 8 to 10 gallons on the burner. Have on hand a metal basket large enough for the bird to rest in, a deep-fry thermometer, a kebob skewer, pot holders, something to wipe up any grease spills, and a couple of sturdy long-handled utensils, either forks or spoons. On a baking sheet, arrange at least three thicknesses of brown paper bags for draining the turkey after it's cooked. Think through the process of how you're going to get the bird into and out of the hot oil. If possible, have a second person available to assist with those tasks.

Transfer the turkey to the frying basket. Pour the oil into the stockpot. The oil absolutely must be fresh. Use enough to submerge the bird by at least 6 inches, remembering that it will displace some of the oil, and avoiding overfilling the pot. Heat the oil to 325° F.

Lower the turkey into the oil. The oil temperature will drop a good bit. Adjust the heat as needed to maintain an oil temperature of 275° F to 280° F.

Keep an eye on the turkey throughout the cooking time, 6 to 7 minutes per pound. Wipe up any grease splatters as they occur. If a portion of the turkey isn't staying submerged, use your long-handled spoons or forks to readjust its position or push it back under the oil's surface.

When the turkey is ready, it will have turned a deep, dark brown. Stick a skewer into the breast to check its doneness. The juices should run clear.

Carefully remove the basket with the turkey from the oil. Dislodge the bird from the basket, and drain it on the paper bags, placing it breast down for about 5 minutes and then turning it over to drain and rest another 15 minutes.

Transfer the bird to a platter, carve it, and serve it with the Chile Pecan Sauce.

THE KIND OF OUTDOOR GAS COOKER USED FOR FRIED TURKEY IS ALSO GREAT FOR FISH AND SEAFOOD FRIES, CRAWFISH BOILS, AND BLACKENING FOOD IN THE STYLE OF PAUL PRUDHOMME. LOOK FOR THE COOKERS AT STORES THAT HANDLE GRILLS, SMOKERS, AND OTHER OUTDOOR EQUIPMENT, OR CALL MAIL-ORDER SUPPLIERS SUCH AS PITT'S AND SPITT'S (SEE "MAIL-ORDER SOURCES," PAGE 552).

Chile Pecan Sauce for Turkey

This sauce was inspired by a more complex one that Dean Fearing developed for the Mansion on Turtle Creek in Dallas. We use it on fried, baked, and smoked turkeys.

1 TABLESPOON OIL, PREFERABLY CANOLA OR
   CORN
2 TABLESPOONS MINCED ONION
2 FRESH JALAPEÑOS, MINCED
2 GARLIC CLOVES, MINCED
1 TABLESPOON CHILI POWDER, PREFERABLY
   HOMEMADE (PAGE 135) OR GEBHARDT'S
1 TEASPOON CUMIN SEEDS, TOASTED AND
   GROUND
2 CUPS UNSALTED STOCK, PREFERABLY TURKEY
   OR CHICKEN
1 TEASPOON WORCESTERSHIRE SAUCE
½ CUP CHOPPED PECANS, TOASTED
1 TABLESPOON UNSALTED BUTTER
SALT TO TASTE

Makes about 2 cups

Warm the oil in a saucepan over medium heat. Add the onion, jalapeños, and garlic, and sauté them until they are softened. Stir in the chili powder and cumin, and cook 2 more minutes, until the spices are fragrant. Pour in the stock and the Worcestershire sauce, and simmer the mixture until it has reduced by one-third, about 30 minutes. (The sauce can be made ahead to this point early in the day. Reheat it before proceeding.) Stir in the pecans and the butter and salt to taste. Serve the sauce warm.

The late Bob Wills, "the King of Western Swing," came from Turkey, Texas. The town honors its favorite son each April on Bob Wills Day, which features lots of music and a barbecue lunch at the Bob Wills Center. If that's not enough for you, visit the Bob Wills Monument, the Bob Wills Museum, or the Bob Wills Cafeteria.

Baker Hotel Turkey and Rarebit Sandwich

Yet another glass tower replaced the Baker Hotel in downtown Dallas many years ago, but we still treasure a version of the lunchroom's most popular sandwich.

RAREBIT SAUCE

¾ CUP HALF-AND-HALF OR BEER

1 TABLESPOON UNSALTED BUTTER

1 EGG YOLK, LIGHTLY BEATEN

1½ CUPS (6 OUNCES) GRATED SHARP CHEDDAR CHEESE

1 TEASPOON WORCESTERSHIRE SAUCE

½ TEASPOON DRY MUSTARD

½ TEASPOON PAPRIKA

½ TEASPOON SALT

4 SLICES SOURDOUGH WHITE BREAD

4 SLICES TOMATO

10 TO 12 OUNCES SLICED SMOKED TURKEY BREAST

4 SLICES SLAB BACON, COOKED CRISP

Makes 2 sandwiches

In the top of a double boiler, warm the half-and-half or beer with the butter. Add a tablespoon of the hot liquid to the egg yolk in a small bowl, and mix. Stir the egg into the liquid. Add the cheese, stirring until it has melted evenly. Mix in the Worcestershire sauce, mustard, paprika, and salt. When the sauce is hot through and bubbly, remove it from the heat.

Heat the broiler.

Toast the bread or, if you prefer, leave it soft. Lay two slices on each of two heatproof plates. Arrange half of the tomato, turkey, and bacon over the bread on each plate. Spoon half of the rarebit sauce over each sandwich.

Pop the open-face sandwiches under the broiler momentarily, until the sauce is bubbly.

Serve the sandwiches piping hot. You will want to eat them with knives and forks.

A BRITISH DISH, RAREBIT HAS BEEN POPULAR IN TEXAS SINCE THE TURN OF THE CENTURY AT LEAST. THERE ARE LONE STAR RECIPES IN OUR *HOME COOK BOOK*, PUBLISHED IN AUSTIN IN 1891, AND IN THE 1909 DALLAS OPUS, *THE TEXAS "FOUR HUNDRED" COOKBOOK; 400 RECIPES TESTED AND PROVEN TO A POINT BEYOND FAILURE.*

Monday Night Ham Loaf

Try this traditional loaf if you have leftovers from a Sunday ham, and consider making the dish even if it requires a special trip to the store. Like meat loaf, this pork cousin makes great sandwiches, hot or cold.

1 POUND SMOKED HAM, SUCH AS HORMEL
  CURE 81
1 TABLESPOON OIL, PREFERABLY CANOLA OR
  CORN
1 ONION, CHOPPED
¾ POUND GROUND PORK
1 CUP SALTINE CRACKER CRUMBS
2 EGGS
1 CUP MILK
1 TABLESPOON PREPARED YELLOW MUSTARD
1 TABLESPOON WORCESTERSHIRE SAUCE
1 TABLESPOON VINEGAR, PREFERABLY CIDER
¼ TEASPOON GROUND CLOVES
SALT TO TASTE

GLAZE
2 TABLESPOONS APPLE CIDER
2 TABLESPOONS DARK BROWN SUGAR
2 TEASPOONS PREPARED YELLOW MUSTARD

Serves 6 to 8

If you are buying ham especially for the dish, ask the butcher to grind it for you. Or run it through a meat grinder or mince it fine in a food processor.

Preheat the oven to 350° F.

Warm the oil in a small skillet over medium heat. Add the chopped onion, and sauté it briefly until it is softened. Combine the onion with all the other ingredients in a medium bowl, mixing well. The mixture will be quite moist but shouldn't be soupy. Place the meat in a loaf pan, and smooth its surface. Bake the ham loaf about 1 hour.

While the loaf bakes, combine the glaze ingredients in a bowl. After the ham loaf has baked 45 to 50 minutes, brush it with the glaze, and continue baking for another 10 to 15 minutes.

Remove the pan from the oven, and let it sit for at least 10 minutes before cutting the loaf. Serve the ham loaf hot, at room temperature, or cold.

DALLASITES USED TO GO DOWN-TOWN TO CELEBRATE SPECIAL EVENTS, OFTEN AT THE BAKER HOTEL OR JUST ACROSS THE STREET AT THE STILL-STANDING ADOLPHUS. IN THE BAKER'S PEACOCK TERRACE, PATRONS STRUTTED ACCOUTREMENTS WORTHY OF THE NAMESAKE BIRD. THE ADOLPHUS, NOT TO BE OUT-DONE, SPORTED THE CENTURY ROOM, WITH AN ICE-SKATING RINK IN ITS CENTER AND CABARET PERFORMANCES.

Grilled Pork Tenderloin with Peach Sauce

This is a superb way to prepare tenderloin, which is as lean as chicken, but try it only at the height of the peach season. The peaches have to be at their peak of flavor to match the lusciousness of the tenderloin, the prime cut of pork. The timing makes this a wonderful dish to grill outdoors over mesquite.

3 PORK TENDERLOINS, ABOUT 10 TO 12
  OUNCES EACH

MARINADE

½ CUP OIL, PREFERABLY CANOLA OR CORN
JUICE OF 2 LIMES
2 TEASPOONS GROUND DRIED RED CHILE,
  PREFERABLY ANCHO OR NEW MEXICAN
1 GARLIC CLOVE, MINCED
¼ TEASPOON CINNAMON
SALT AND PEPPER TO TASTE

SAUCE

½ POUND (ABOUT 2 MEDIUM) RIPE JUICY
  PEACHES, SKINNED AND PITTED
3 TABLESPOONS UNSALTED BUTTER
1 GARLIC CLOVE, MINCED
JUICE OF 1 LIME
1 TEASPOON WORCESTERSHIRE SAUCE
1 TEASPOON GROUND DRIED RED CHILE,
  PREFERABLY ANCHO OR NEW MEXICAN
¼ TEASPOON CINNAMON
SALT TO TASTE
PINCH OF DARK BROWN SUGAR, OPTIONAL

MINCED CILANTRO, FOR GARNISH

Serves 6

At least 4 hours before cooking and preferably the night before, place the pork in a nonreactive dish. Mix the marinade ingredients together, and pour the marinade over the pork. Cover the dish, and place it in the refrigerator, turning the meat occasionally.

Take the meat from the refrigerator 30 to 45 minutes before you plan to cook it. At about the same time, put

Southern settlers in Texas came to the state with a love of ham, but they didn't bring the elaborate curing and smoking techniques found in places like Smithfield, Virginia. The process of making true country hams—which are very rare today—requires a full year and a settled situation, uncommon luxuries on the frontier.

a few handfuls of mesquite chips in water to soak, and fire up enough charcoal to form a single layer of coals beneath the meat.

To make the sauce, purée the peaches in a food processor or blender. Warm the butter in a skillet over medium heat, add the garlic, and sauté it a minute or two. Stir in the peaches and the remaining ingredients, except for the sugar. Continue cooking the sauce for 15 minutes. Taste it, and adjust the seasoning, adding the brown sugar if it is needed to heighten the fruitiness. Keep the sauce warm while you grill the pork.

When the charcoal is covered with gray ash, spread the mesquite chips on top. Drain the pork, discarding the marinade, place the meat over the coals, and cover the grill, with the dampers about halfway open. Grill the tenderloins, turning them several times to assure even cooking, until their internal temperature taken on an instant-read thermometer measures 155° F to 160° F, about 12 minutes. Don't overcook them. Baste the pork with a few tablespoons of the sauce during its last few minutes on the grill.

Let the meat stand for about 5 minutes before carving it into medallions. Spoon some of the sauce over the medallions, and sprinkle them with cilantro. Serve the meat with the rest of the sauce on the side.

Hog killings were important annual events in many areas of Texas well into the twentieth century. Timing was critical. You needed a sustained period of cold weather to ensure the meat didn't spoil, so you waited until early winter, perhaps until Thanksgiving or Christmas. Some meat was salted away, some ground into sausage, some pickled. Almost everything became food, including the intestines (chitlings), skin (cracklings), and head (headcheese).

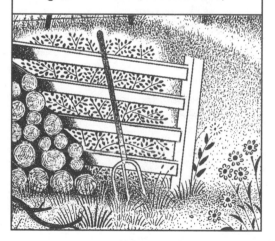

Pork Loin Texa-cruz

Peaches aren't the only fruit that pairs well with pork. In this tender, long-cooked loin, tropical fruits combine with chile for a south-of-the-border tang reminiscent of Veracruz.

3½- TO 4-POUND BONELESS CENTER-CUT PORK
    LOIN
1 TABLESPOON GROUND DRIED RED CHILE,
    PREFERABLY ANCHO OR NEW MEXICAN
SALT AND FRESH-GROUND BLACK PEPPER TO
    TASTE

FILLING
¾ CUP CHIPOTLE CHORIZO (PAGE 80) OR GOOD
    STORE-BOUGHT CHORIZO
1 EGG
½ MEDIUM ONION, MINCED
TOPS OF 2 TO 3 GREEN ONIONS, SLICED,
    OPTIONAL

SALSA
1 CUP FRESH ORANGE JUICE
2 SMALL RIPE TOMATOES, PREFERABLY ROMA
    OR ANOTHER ITALIAN PLUM VARIETY
1 SMALL RIPE BANANA, CHOPPED
½ MEDIUM ONION, MINCED
1 FRESH JALAPEÑO, MINCED
1 TEASPOON GROUND DRIED RED CHILE,
    PREFERABLY ANCHO OR NEW MEXICAN
2 GARLIC CLOVES, MINCED
DASH OF CIDER VINEGAR, OPTIONAL

1 TABLESPOON OIL, PREFERABLY CANOLA OR
    CORN

Serves 8

Preheat the oven to 350° F. Grease a baking dish.

Slice a pocket lengthwise through the center of the pork loin. Rub the loin inside and out with the chile, salt, and pepper. Set it aside.

In a small bowl, mix together the chorizo with the egg and the onion. Stuff the loin with the chorizo mixture, and tie it closed with string.

In another bowl, combine the salsa ingredients, except for the vinegar. If the mixture seems too sweet, add a bit of vinegar to correct the balance. Spoon about half of the salsa in the baking dish.

Warm the oil in a heavy skillet over medium-high heat. Add the loin, and brown it quickly on all sides. Transfer the meat to the baking dish, and pour the remaining salsa over it. Cover the dish, and bake the meat for about 1½ hours, basting it frequently, until the internal temperature taken on an instant-read thermometer measures 155° F to 160° F.

Remove the pork from the oven, and allow it to rest 10 to 15 minutes before carving it. Pour off any accumulated fat from the salsa. Ladle some of the salsa over the slices, and pass the rest separately.

Stuffed Pork Chops

These succulent chops are stuffed with a moist cornbread dressing. Ask your butcher to cut a pocket to the bone in each chop—or do it yourself (it's not difficult with a thin, sharp knife).

STUFFING

4 TABLESPOONS UNSALTED BUTTER

½ MEDIUM GREEN BELL PEPPER, CHOPPED FINE

⅓ MEDIUM ONION, CHOPPED FINE

1 CELERY RIB, CHOPPED FINE

1 CUP CORNBREAD CRUMBS

1 DOZEN PITTED PRUNES, CHOPPED

2 TABLESPOONS CHOPPED PARSLEY

1½ TEASPOONS MINCED FRESH SAGE

¼ TEASPOON DRY MUSTARD

SALT TO TASTE

½ TO 1 CUP UNSALTED STOCK, PREFERABLY CHICKEN OR VEAL

4 DOUBLE-THICK CENTER-CUT PORK CHOPS

Serves 4

Preheat the oven to 350° F.

Melt 3 tablespoons of the butter in a small skillet. Add the bell pepper, onion, and celery, and sauté them until they are soft. Spoon the vegetables into a bowl, and stir in the bread crumbs, about two-thirds of the chopped prunes, the parsley, 1 teaspoon of the sage, the dry mustard, and salt. Mix well. Stuff about one-quarter of the mixture into the pocket of each pork chop.

Melt the remaining butter in a skillet large enough to hold the four chops. Brown the chops lightly on both sides. Pour ½ cup of the stock over the chops. Scatter the remaining prunes and sage in the skillet, cover it, and bake the chops for 1½ to 1¾ hours, until they are very tender. Check about halfway through the baking time, and add more stock if it appears to be cooking away.

Let the chops sit for about 10 minutes after removing them from the oven. Then spoon the pan sauce over the chops and serve them.

Pandering politicians dip into the "pork barrel" today to "bring home the bacon" to their constituents. The imagery is apt. The real pork barrels of the past were heavy wood casks filled with a thick brine solution that preserved side slabs of meat. You dug out a piece of salty, fatty pork and fried it for the main part of a meal, or perhaps stuck it in a simmering pot to flavor greens or a soup.

Yam and Pork Chop Skillet

The natural sweetness of yams or other sweet potatoes complements pork, which is why they often appear together on Southern tables. This is a typically Texan skillet supper. Shoulder chops start out a little tougher and fattier than their center-cut cousins, but they are cheaper, richer in flavor, and quite tender when cooked this way.

2 SLICES SLAB BACON, CHOPPED

4 PORK CHOPS CUT FROM THE SHOULDER, OR AS NEAR THE SHOULDER AS YOUR BUTCHER CAN PROVIDE

2 CELERY RIBS, CHOPPED

2 MEDIUM SWEET POTATOES, SLICED

1 LARGE ONION, SLICED AND SEPARATED INTO RINGS

1 GREEN BELL PEPPER, SLICED IN RINGS

½ TEASPOON DRIED THYME

½ TEASPOON DRIED MARJORAM

1 14½-OUNCE CAN WHOLE TOMATOES, UNDRAINED

1 TABLESPOON WORCESTERSHIRE SAUCE

SEVERAL DASHES OF TABASCO OR OTHER HOT PEPPER SAUCE

SALT AND FRESH-GROUND BLACK PEPPER TO TASTE

¼ CUP UNSALTED CHICKEN STOCK

Serves 4

✴ Fry the bacon over medium heat in a cast-iron or other heavy skillet large enough to accommodate all four chops. Remove it with a slotted spoon when it is brown and crisp, and set it aside.

Brown the chops in the bacon drippings. Reduce the heat to low, leaving the chops in the skillet. Scatter the celery around the chops, and then top them with layers of sweet potato, onion, and bell pepper. Sprinkle the thyme and marjoram over the vegetables, and pour the tomatoes and their juice over all. Top with the Worcestershire sauce, Tabasco, and salt and pepper.

Cover the skillet, and cook the chops over medium-low heat about 1 hour, until they are cooked through and tender. Check the dish a couple of times during the cooking, adding a little of the stock if the mixture appears to be getting dry.

Remove the skillet from the heat, and let it sit, covered, for 10 to 20 minutes before serving the chops.

Before refrigeration, salt curing was the foremost means of preserving both pork and beef. Treated this way, pork is the tastier of the two meats, which was one of the principal reasons for its popularity even in cow country.

Crown Pork Roast
with Sauerkraut
and Potato Dumplings

From the 1850s to the 1920s, a stream of Czech emigrants left Bohemia and Moldavia for the United States, and many settled in the area bounded by Houston, San Antonio, and Dallas. These families were serious about meat and potatoes, and the meat was always pork, as in this elegant crown roast. Call your butcher ahead for the roast, formed by tying the rib section of the loin into a circle.

½ MEDIUM ONION, GRATED

2 TEASPOONS PAPRIKA

SALT AND FRESH-GROUND BLACK PEPPER TO TASTE

5-POUND CROWN PORK ROAST (10 TO 12 CHOPS)

TEX-CZECH SAUERKRAUT (PAGE 387)

1 CUP UNSALTED STOCK, PREFERABLY CHICKEN OR BEEF

POTATO DUMPLINGS

3 MEDIUM BAKING POTATOES

2 TEASPOONS SALT

2 TABLESPOONS DRY BREAD CRUMBS

1 EGG

2 TABLESPOONS GRATED ONION

½ TEASPOON PAPRIKA

¼ TO ½ CUP ALL-PURPOSE FLOUR

2 CUPS STOCK, PREFERABLY CHICKEN OR BEEF, SALTED TO TASTE

2 TO 4 TABLESPOONS UNSALTED BUTTER, MELTED

Serves 6 to 8

Preheat the oven to 350° F.

In a small bowl, mix the onion with the paprika, salt, and pepper into a thick paste. Rub the paste all over the roast, and transfer the roast to a roasting pan. Fill the roast's center with the sauerkraut.

Bake the roast for 1½ hours, basting frequently with the stock and accumulated pan juices, until the internal temperature taken on an instant-read thermometer measures 155° F to 160° F. Drizzle stock over the sauerkraut, too, but if it appears to be getting too dry, cover it with a small piece of foil.

While the pork is roasting, prepare the dumplings: Boil the potatoes in a

> Texas has the largest rural Czech population in the United States.

saucepan with enough generously salted water to cover them. When the potatoes are done, remove them with a slotted spoon, reserving their water. When they are cool enough to handle, grate or rice the potatoes into a medium bowl. Add the salt, bread crumbs, egg, onion, ¼ teaspoon of the paprika, and ¼ cup of flour. Blend the mixture with a fork until it is well combined and a bit lightened. Add more flour if it is needed for the dough to hold together. Flour your hands lightly, and roll the dough into golf-ball-size dumplings. Transfer the dumplings to a plate, cover them lightly, and set them aside until the pork is done.

Remove the pork from the oven, cover it loosely with foil, and let it rest for 15 to 20 minutes. Meanwhile, finish the dumplings: Add the stock to the reserved potato water, and bring the liquid to a boil. With a slotted spoon, gently lower the dumplings into the liquid. Reduce the heat, and simmer the dumplings 8 to 10 minutes, or until they are lightly firm. Drain the dumplings well, and discard the liquid.

Using a sturdy spatula, transfer the roast to a platter. Arrange some of the dumplings on and in the sauerkraut.

Transfer the remaining dumplings to a serving bowl, drizzle them with the melted butter, and sprinkle them with the remaining paprika.

At the table, serve the sauerkraut and dumplings inside the roast first, and then carve the roast by slicing between the bones to separate the individual chops.

Descendants of pigs brought by the Spanish, wild hogs ranged freely around Texas during the frontier period and provided some of the pork that pioneers ate. Alex Sweet and John Knox said the hams were juicier than "a hind leg of an iron fire dog, but not quite so fat as a pine knot." These skeptics claimed that the meat couldn't be enhanced by breeding with better stock: "The only way to improve him is to cross him with a railroad train."

Pork and Apple Stew

Supported by the Dallas County Heritage Society, the now-closed Brent Place restaurant in Dallas's Old City Park used to serve a savory pork pie, one of the menu's many traditional Texas dishes. That pie, studded with apples and vegetables, spurred us to concoct a stew with similar flavors.

6 SLICES SLAB BACON, CHOPPED

2 MEDIUM ONIONS, CHOPPED

4 CARROTS, SLICED

1 GREEN OR RED BELL PEPPER, CHOPPED INTO BITE-SIZE CHUNKS

2 GARLIC CLOVES, MINCED

2 ½ POUNDS BONED PORK LOIN END, CUT INTO BITE-SIZE CUBES

2 TABLESPOONS ALL-PURPOSE FLOUR

2 TEASPOONS SALT

½ TEASPOON FRESH-GROUND BLACK PEPPER

1 TABLESPOON OIL, PREFERABLY CANOLA OR CORN, OPTIONAL

3 CUPS STOCK, PREFERABLY CHICKEN OR VEAL

2 CUPS APPLE CIDER

½ CUP BOURBON

1 TABLESPOON TOMATO PASTE

1 TABLESPOON CREOLE MUSTARD

2 TEASPOONS DRIED THYME

2 TABLESPOONS UNSALTED BUTTER

1 TART APPLE, SUCH AS GRANNY SMITH OR JONATHAN, PARED AND SLICED INTO BITE-SIZE PIECES

18 PEARL ONIONS, PEELED

½ POUND MUSHROOMS, SLICED (WILD VARIETIES ARE ESPECIALLY GOOD)

2 TABLESPOONS MINCED PARSLEY

JUICE OF ½ LEMON

Serves 6 to 8

Preheat the oven to 325° F.

Fry the bacon in a large skillet over medium heat until it is brown and crisp. Remove the bacon with a slotted spoon, and reserve it. Add the onions, carrots, bell pepper, and garlic, and cook them in the remaining bacon drippings until the onion has softened, 3 to 5 minutes. With a slotted spoon, remove the vegetables, and spoon them into a large baking dish or Dutch oven.

Mix the flour, salt, and pepper, and dust the pork lightly with the mixture. Brown the pork in the bacon drippings, in batches if necessary, adding the oil if the skillet gets too dry. Spoon the pork cubes into the baking dish.

Pour the stock, cider, and bourbon over the meat and vegetables. Add the tomato paste, mustard, and thyme, stirring well. Bring the stew to a boil on top of the stove, and then place it in the oven and bake it for 2 hours.

Melt the butter in a medium skillet. Add the apple, pearl onions, and mushrooms, and toss them to coat them with the butter. Sauté them until the apple begins to soften and the mushrooms go limp. After the stew has baked for 2 hours, stir this mixture into it, and cook it for another

45 minutes to 1 hour, until the meat, vegetables, and fruit become very tender and the liquid is nicely thickened. The stew can be made ahead to this point (it actually tastes better if it is served the day after it is made).

Just before serving, add the parsley, a good squeeze of lemon, and the reserved bacon to the stew. Serve the stew hot, over lightly buttered noodles, if you like.

Chorizo-Rice Casserole

This sausage casserole is something of a cross between a Tex-Mex picadillo and a Cajun jambalaya.

½ POUND CHIPOTLE CHORIZO (PAGE 80) OR
    GOOD STORE-BOUGHT CHORIZO
1 MEDIUM ONION, CHOPPED
2 GARLIC CLOVES, MINCED
2 SMALL TOMATOES, PREFERABLY ROMA OR
    ANOTHER ITALIAN PLUM VARIETY, CHOPPED
2 CELERY RIBS, CHOPPED
1 MEDIUM RED-SKINNED POTATO, DICED
½ MEDIUM GREEN BELL PEPPER, CHOPPED
¾ CUP UNCOOKED RICE
½ CUP CURRANTS OR RAISINS
1 TABLESPOON CHILI POWDER, PREFERABLY
    HOMEMADE (PAGE 135) OR GEBHARDT'S
½ TEASPOON CUMIN SEEDS, TOASTED AND
    GROUND
1¾ CUPS UNSALTED BEEF OR CHICKEN STOCK
½ CUP CHOPPED ROASTED, SALTED PEANUTS
2 TABLESPOONS CHOPPED CILANTRO

Makes 4 to 6 servings

Preheat the oven to 350° F.

In a large oven-proof skillet, preferably cast-iron, brown the chorizo over medium heat, breaking it into small pieces. Pour off the accumulated fat as necessary to leave no more than about 1 tablespoon. Add the onion, garlic, tomatoes, celery, potato, and bell pepper to the chorizo, and continue cooking, stirring occasionally, until the vegetables are limp and somewhat tender. Add the rice, currants or raisins, chili powder, and cumin, and cook another 5 minutes, stirring frequently. Pour in the stock, cover the dish, and bake the casserole for 45 to 50 minutes, or until the liquid is absorbed and the rice is tender.

Remove the casserole from the oven, and stir in the peanuts and cilantro. Serve the casserole immediately.

*W*ild turkeys, ducks, geese, haunches of venison were displayed beside roast beef, pork, red-fish, Irish and sweet potatoes, pumpkin and apple pie, and an abundant supply of whiskey, brandy, and Hollands, without which a fête in Texas is nothing thought of.

Anonymous report on a Galveston wedding feast in the 1840s, quoted in John Q. Anderson, *Tales of Frontier Texas*

When Pecos Bill was a baby, his father fed him jerked game, whiskey, and onions for breakfast one morning. Bill's mother weaned him immediately after that, according to the story, and by the time Pecos Bill was three, he had killed his first panther and eaten a piece of the flank raw.

Like the state's mythical hero, Texas grew up on game. Even most of the cattle and hogs ran wild until the middle of the nineteenth century, and deer, bear, and turkeys were far more common than people. Settlers relied on their rifles for meat of all kinds, and anyone who couldn't hunt couldn't count on making it through the winter.

Most of the game tasted a little like Pecos Bill's raw panther—tough and pungent. When the pioneers had their druthers, they'd usually choose a flour biscuit instead. After domesticated animals became as abundant as game and Texans grew accustomed to the milder taste, they began looking for ways to temper wild flavors. Hunters learned the importance of proper field dressing when their quarry was intended for the table, and more recently farmers and ranchers have started raising and harvesting game in ways that ensure its appeal to today's palate.

Because of such improvements, game is enjoying a surge in popularity across the country. Texas cooks, with their generations of experience, are helping to lead the way. Their modern preparations of game balance a hint of the old wildness with a new fullness of flavor, transforming an ancient necessity into a tamed and tasty modern meal.

Peppered Venison Steaks

This venison preparation, like our others, was developed for store-bought meat, farmed or harvested for peak flavor. All the recipes work fine with hunted game, but the tenderness and taste will depend on a variety of factors, including the age of the animal, its food supply, and the way it was handled in the field. These superb steaks can be grilled or pan-fried.

4 VENISON BACKSTRAP (LOIN) STEAKS, 4 TO 6
    OUNCES EACH, CUT 1 INCH THICK

MARINADE

1 CUP DRY RED WINE
1 CUP OIL, PREFERABLY ROASTED SAFFLOWER
    OR CANOLA
1 MEDIUM ONION, CHOPPED
3 TABLESPOONS CREOLE MUSTARD
1 TEASPOON DRIED OREGANO, PREFERABLY
    MEXICAN
2 GARLIC CLOVES, MINCED

4 TABLESPOONS COARSE-GROUND BLACK
    PEPPER
1½ TEASPOONS SALT
1 TABLESPOON OIL, PREFERABLY ROASTED SAF-
    FLOWER OR CANOLA, IF FRYING

Serves 4

If the venison is frozen, thaw it in red wine to keep the meat moist. Reserve the wine to use as a part of the marinade.

Purée the marinade ingredients together in a blender or food processor. Arrange the venison steaks in a shal-low nonreactive dish, and pour the marinade over them. Refrigerate them at least 4 hours and preferably over-night.

Drain the steaks, reserving the marinade in a small saucepan. Com-bine the pepper with the salt. Rub each steak with equal portions of the pepper-salt mixture, and let the steaks sit, tightly covered, at room temperature for 30 to 45 minutes.

If you will be grilling outside, fire up enough charcoal to form a single layer of coals beneath the meat.

Meanwhile, bring the marinade to a boil. Then reduce the heat, and sim-mer the marinade until it is reduced by half. Taste, and adjust the season-ing. You can add another splash of wine to the marinade at this point to heighten its flavor. Keep the sauce warm while you prepare the steaks.

For grilling, place the steaks over hot coals that are covered with gray ash. For pan frying, place the tablespoon of oil in a heavy skillet, bring the heat to medium-high, and add the venison. Cook the steaks until they are rare or medium rare, about 2 minutes per side. If the steaks were pan-fried, deglaze the pan by adding the sauce to it and scraping up any browned bits.

Serve the steaks immediately with a bowl of the sauce on the side. Buttered noodles are a good accompaniment for soaking up the sauce.

Venison Medallions
with Roasted Sweet Onion Jam

Texas restaurant chefs such as Stephan Pyles, Dean Fearing, and Robert Del Grande have played a major role in reviving interest in game and in inspiring new styles of preparation. This recipe grew out of a venison loin dish that Pyles used to serve at his now-closed Routh Street Cafe in Dallas.

8½-INCH-THICK VENISON BACKSTRAP OR LOIN MEDALLIONS, ABOUT 3 OUNCES EACH

JAM

1 LARGE SWEET ONION, SKIN ON

½ GARLIC HEAD, SKINS ON

1 MEDIUM CARROT

1 TEASPOON OIL, PREFERABLY CANOLA OR CORN

½ CUP UNSALTED GAME OR BEEF STOCK

1 TABLESPOON UNSALTED BUTTER

1 CHIPOTLE CHILE, CANNED IN ADOBO SAUCE

1 TEASPOON UNSULPHURED DARK MOLASSES

1 TEASPOON RED WINE VINEGAR

SALT TO TASTE

DRY RUB FOR GAME (PAGE 229) OR CHAR-CRUST RUB (PAGE 170)

1 TABLESPOON OIL, PREFERABLY CANOLA, IF YOU ARE FRYING

Serves 4

 If the venison is frozen, thaw it in red wine to keep the meat moist.

Preheat the oven to 350° F.

Coat the onion, garlic, and carrot with the oil, and place them in a baking dish. Bake the vegetables until they are lightly browned and well softened. The garlic and carrot can be removed from the oven with tongs after about 45 to 50 minutes. The onion will require about 90 minutes baking time. Remove the outer skin from the onion and garlic. Cut the onion in quarters and the carrot in thirds. Process the three vegetables in a food processor or blender with the stock, butter, and chipotle until they reach a chunky, jamlike consistency. Add one-half each of the molasses and vinegar, then taste, adding the rest of either as needed, depending on the vegetables' natural sweetness. Salt the jam to taste, and reserve it.

Coat each of the medallions in dry rub, and let them sit, tightly covered, at room temperature for 20 to 30 minutes.

If you will be grilling outdoors, fire up enough charcoal to form a single layer of coals beneath the meat.

Close to serving time, warm the onion jam. For grilling, place the steaks over hot coals that are covered with gray ash. For pan frying, place the tablespoon of oil in a heavy skillet, bring the heat to high, and add the venison. Cook the medallions until they are rare or medium rare, about 1 to 1½ minutes per side.

Serve two medallions per person with a large dollop of the onion jam.

TECHNIQUE TIPS

The lack of fat in venison requires some adjustments in the way you normally cook meat.

When you grill, broil, or sauté a choice cut of tender venison, cook the meat rapidly for less time than you allow beef. You want to sear the outside while leaving the inside rare or medium rare. Baste the surface during the cooking, and slice the cooked meat across the grain.

Less tender cuts of venison should be cooked in moisture, as by stewing or braising. Allow more time than you would for other kinds of meat.

When venison comes frozen, thaw it in red wine or buttermilk, depending on which best complements the rest of the preparation.

Hunters usually grind all venison except the backstrap into sausage (mixed with about 25 percent pork), chili meat, or hamburger. To cook a ground venison patty, brown it quickly over high heat, reduce the heat to low, add a little red wine or meat stock to the pan, and cook, covered, until the meat is rare to medium.

Don't expose cooked venison to the air for long. If you cannot serve it immediately, wrap it in foil to prevent it from drying out. Slice it just before serving.

Dry Rub for Game

Dry rubs work as well with game as they do with barbecue, enhancing flavor and adding a light crust to the finished dish. This all-purpose rub for deer, antelope, and other game meats can be modified easily to your taste by adding or subtracting ingredients.

¾ CUP PAPRIKA
¼ CUP GROUND BLACK PEPPER
¼ CUP SALT
¼ CUP DARK BROWN SUGAR
2 TABLESPOONS GARLIC POWDER
2 TABLESPOONS ONION POWDER
1 TABLESPOON CAYENNE
1 TABLESPOON MINCED DRIED ORANGE ZEST
10 TO 12 JUNIPER BERRIES, CRUSHED IN A
   MORTAR AND PESTLE OR SPICE MILL
½ TEASPOON GROUND CLOVES

Makes about 2 cups

Mix the spices thoroughly in a bowl.

Store the rub in a tightly sealed jar in the refrigerator. It keeps indefinitely but loses potency over time.

VENISON IS MEAT FROM DEER, OF COURSE, BUT ALSO FROM ANTELOPE, ELK, CARIBOU, MOOSE, AND REINDEER. WHAT YOU FIND MOST OFTEN IN LONE STAR STORES IS SOUTH TEXAS ANTELOPE, A NATIVE OF THE HIMALAYAN FOOTHILLS THAT WAS BROUGHT TO THE STATE DECADES AGO AND NOW LIVES IN THE WILD ON THE RANGELAND OF THE KING RANCH. THE LARGE HERDS ARE HARVESTED REGULARLY AND PRODUCE LEAN MEAT THAT TASTES SOMETHING LIKE VEAL.

Mustard-Coated Venison Loin

The mustard coating in this dish helps keep the loin moist and adds a felicitous flavor as well.

1 BONELESS LOIN OF VENISON (ABOUT 3 POUNDS)
MARINADE FOR PEPPERED VENISON STEAKS (PAGE 226), *WITHOUT* THE MUSTARD
DRY RUB FOR GAME (PAGE 229), OR SALT AND PEPPER TO TASTE

PASTE

6 GREEN ONIONS, CUT INTO 1-INCH LENGTHS
3 TABLESPOONS CHOPPED PECANS
3 GARLIC CLOVES
2 FRESH SAGE LEAVES OR ¼ TEASPOON DRIED SAGE
¼ CUP PLUS 2 TABLESPOONS PREPARED HONEY MUSTARD

1 TABLESPOON OIL, PREFERABLY CANOLA OR CORN, FOR FRYING

Serves 6 to 8

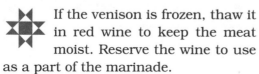 If the venison is frozen, thaw it in red wine to keep the meat moist. Reserve the wine to use as a part of the marinade.

Place the venison in a nonreactive dish, and pour the marinade over it. Refrigerate it at least 4 hours, preferably overnight. Remove the venison from the marinade, and blot it dry. Reserve 3 tablespoons of the marinade. Rub the meat with the dry rub or a mixture of salt and pepper, and let it sit at room temperature, covered tightly, for 30 to 45 minutes.

Preheat the oven to 375° F.

In a food processor, mince together the onions, pecans, garlic, and sage. Spoon in the mustard, and process until the mixture is a thick paste.

Add the oil to a skillet, and heat it almost to smoking. Add the venison, and sear it on all sides. Transfer the loin to a small roasting pan.

Pour the reserved marinade around the venison. Spread the meat with a thick coating of the mustard paste. Bake the venison until an instant-read thermometer inserted into it registers 125° F, about 20 minutes. Don't overcook the venison, or it will toughen. Let the meat rest, covered, for 5 minutes.

Slice the meat across the grain, and serve it.

> I've encountered one person in my lifetime who did not have a special recipe for removing the wild taste from venison. He was a vegetarian from Tibet who did not know what meat was."
> —Cactus Pryor, *Inside Texas*

Glazed Saddle of Venison

A whole saddle of venison is the animal's back from just behind the shoulders to just in front of the hind legs. This dish calls for the entire saddle (approximately 12 to 15 pounds) of an axis deer, or a similar-size quarter saddle of an antelope, a much larger animal. The saddle makes a magnificent party presentation.

1 12- TO 15-POUND VENISON SADDLE
DRY RUB FOR GAME (PAGE 229)
2 CUPS UNSALTED GAME OR BEEF STOCK
¼ CUP OIL, PREFERABLY CANOLA OR CORN
¼ CUP BRANDY
JUICE OF 1 ORANGE
1 CUP GINGER PRESERVES
1 CUP JALAPEÑO JELLY OR JAM, PREFERABLY
　HOMEMADE (PAGE 395)

Serves 18 to 20

The night before you plan to serve the venison, massage it well with the dry rub. Save a tablespoon or two of the rub for "mopping" (basting) the meat the next day. Transfer the meat to a plastic garbage bag, and refrigerate it.

Take the venison from the refrigerator about 1 hour before you plan to begin cooking it. Preheat the oven to 450° F. Combine the stock, oil, brandy, and reserved dry rub in a small bowl. This mixture is for mopping the meat. In another bowl, mix the orange juice, preserves, and jelly for the glaze.

Transfer the venison to a large roasting pan. Bake 20 minutes, mopping once. Reduce the oven temperature to 350° F, and continue baking, mopping frequently, until an instant-read thermometer measures about 125° F (plan on a total baking time of 15 to 17 minutes per pound). The meat should be rare to medium rare; it's critical to avoid overcooking such a prime piece of venison. Brush on the glaze twice during the last 10 minutes of cooking.

Remove the roasting pan from the oven, and transfer the venison to a platter. Tent the saddle with foil, and let the meat sit for 15 minutes before carving it. Spoon some of the pan drippings over the meat before serving.

Mark Kristen's Red Deer Farm in Bellville, Texas, raises majestic red deer, bred in England for centuries and extensively farmed in New Zealand. Kristen markets venison and also trains others in the business, which is likely to boom in the years ahead.

Venison Scaloppine with Blackberry Sage Sauce

A Dean Fearing dish from Dallas's Mansion on Turtle Creek inspired this recipe, which pairs plump blackberries and thin scallops from the naturally tender upper hind leg.

SAUCE

1 POUND BLACKBERRIES, FRESH OR FROZEN
1½ CUPS FRUITY RED WINE
1½ CUPS UNSALTED GAME OR BEEF STOCK
2 MEDIUM ONIONS, CHOPPED
10 TO 12 FRESH SAGE LEAVES OR 1 TEASPOON
  DRIED SAGE
1 TEASPOON SALT
1 TABLESPOON DARK BROWN SUGAR
1 TABLESPOON UNSALTED BUTTER

1½ POUNDS VENISON SCALOPPINE, CUT
  AGAINST THE GRAIN IN SLICES ⅓ INCH THICK
SALT AND FRESH-GROUND BLACK PEPPER TO
  TASTE
1 TABLESPOON OIL, PREFERABLY CANOLA OR
  CORN
FRESH SAGE SPRIGS, OPTIONAL, FOR GARNISH

Serves 4

 If the venison is frozen, thaw it in red wine to keep the meat moist.

In a heavy saucepan, combine the blackberries, wine, stock, onion, sage, and salt. Simmer the mixture over low heat for 30 minutes, until the blackberries have disintegrated and the sauce has reduced somewhat. Strain the sauce, extracting as much liquid as possible from the solids, and return it to the saucepan. Taste it, and add as much of the sugar as necessary to offset the tartness of the berries without masking their pleasant tang. Continue cooking the sauce until it has reduced to about 1½ cups. Whisk the butter into the sauce. Refrigerate the sauce, covered, or keep it warm while preparing the venison.

Sprinkle the venison lightly with salt and pepper. Heat the oil in a heavy skillet until it is almost smoking. Add the venison, and stir-fry it for a minute or two, searing the meat on all sides.

Ladle the sauce over the meat, and add sage leaves, if you like, for garnish. Serve the scaloppine immediately.

> HUNTERS LOOKING TO IMPROVE THE TASTE OF THEIR GAME CAN FIND GOOD FIELD TIPS IN JUDITH AND RICHARD MOREHEAD'S *THE NEW TEXAS WILD GAME COOKBOOK* AND IN MIKE HUGHES'S *THE BROKEN ARROW RANCH COOKBOOK*.

Broken Arrow Ranch Venison Pot Roast

Mike Hughes's Broken Arrow Ranch has stimulated much of the current interest in wild game in Texas and across the country. Mike's knowledgeable assistant, Kathy Reeves, gave us this recipe, which works especially well with South Texas antelope. We prefer the meat cooked in a Crockpot, but you can use the oven, too.

1 3-POUND VENISON CHUCK ROAST
SALT AND FRESH-GROUND BLACK PEPPER TO
   TASTE
2 TABLESPOONS ALL-PURPOSE FLOUR
1 TABLESPOON OIL, PREFERABLY CORN OR
   CANOLA
1 LARGE ONION, SLICED
¼ CUP CIDER VINEGAR, PREFERABLY UNRE-
   FINED
2 TABLESPOONS DARK BROWN SUGAR
1 TABLESPOON WORCESTERSHIRE SAUCE
2 TEASPOONS PREPARED YELLOW MUSTARD
2 GARLIC CLOVES, MINCED
1 14 ½-OUNCE CAN WHOLE TOMATOES WITH
   JUICE

Serves 6

 Preheat the oven to 300° F, unless you're using a Crock-pot.
   Rub the roast with a generous coating of salt and pepper, and dredge it in the flour. Warm the oil over medium-high heat, and brown the roast quickly.
   Place the venison in a Dutch oven

A scuba diver, civil engineer, and founder of the world's largest underwater salvage and service company, Mike Hughes bought the six-thousand-acre Broken Arrow Ranch in the Texas Hill Country in 1982 to pursue a plan for the harvesting and marketing of nonnative wild game. Through the Texas Wild Game Cooperative, he now oversees the professional hunting and field dressing of exotic animals on over one hundred and fifty Texas ranches. The Broken Arrow Ranch sells much of the meat to fine restaurants but also offers it to individuals in some retail stores and by mail order. See "Mail-Order Sources" (page 555) for additional information.

or heavy baking dish, or in the Crockpot. Add all the other ingredients, pouring the tomatoes in last.

Bake the meat 4 to 5 hours in the oven, or 12 to 13 hours in the Crockpot. The pot roast will be "falling apart" tender if it has cooked long enough.

Variation: To turn the pot roast into a one-dish meal, add big chunks of carrots and potatoes about two-thirds of the way through the cooking time.

Back in the 1930s, World War I flying ace Eddie Rickenbacker was one of the first people to release exotic game animals on Texas ranches for hunting purposes.

IN THE UNITED STATES, NATIVE WILD GAME SPECIES SUCH AS WHITETAIL DEER ARE PUBLIC PROPERTY AND CANNOT BE HUNTED OR RAISED FOR PROFIT. THE VENISON SOLD IN STORES COMES PACKAGED FROM FOREIGN COUNTRIES, PARTICULARLY NEW ZEALAND, OR FROM AMERICAN RANCHES WHERE NONNATIVE ANIMALS ARE FARM-RAISED OR HUNTED IN THE WILD. A 1985 SURVEY IDENTIFIED OVER ONE HUNDRED TWENTY THOUSAND EXOTIC GAME ANIMALS ON THE LOOSE IN TEXAS, RANGING FROM AXIS DEER TO SOUTH TEXAS ANTELOPE.

South Texas Venison Stew

This flavorful stew makes a value-minded meal out of venison, which can be expensive meat. It's another good dish for a Crockpot.

1 POUND VENISON STEW MEAT, CUT IN ½-INCH CHUNKS

1 TEASPOON SALT

1 TEASPOON COARSE-GROUND BLACK PEPPER

1 TEASPOON CUMIN SEEDS, TOASTED AND GROUND

½ TEASPOON OREGANO, PREFERABLY MEXICAN

2 TABLESPOONS OIL, PREFERABLY CANOLA OR CORN

1 MEDIUM ONION, DICED

1 MEDIUM RED BELL PEPPER, DICED

2 GARLIC CLOVES, MINCED

1½ CUPS UNSALTED GAME, BEEF, OR CHICKEN STOCK

½ CUP DRIED APRICOTS, DICED

⅓ CUP CHILI SAUCE, PREFERABLY HOMEMADE (PAGE 406)

1 14½-OUNCE CAN HOMINY OR 2 CUPS COOKED *POZOLE*

2 CUPS COOKED BLACK BEANS (CANNED BEANS ARE ACCEPTABLE IF THEY ARE RINSED BEFORE USING)

JUICE OF 1 LIME

1 TABLESPOON MINCED CILANTRO PLUS MORE, OPTIONAL, FOR GARNISH

Serves 4

Preheat the oven to 325° F, unless you're using a Crockpot. Toss the venison cubes lightly with a mixture of the salt, pepper, cumin, and oregano. Warm the oil over medium-high heat, and brown the meat quickly. With a slotted spoon, remove the venison from the oil, and place it in a Crockpot, Dutch oven, or other heavy pot. Sauté the onion, bell pepper, and garlic in the oil remaining in the pan until they have softened. Spoon the vegetables into the pot with the venison. Add the stock, apricots, and chili sauce, stir to combine, and cover the pot. Cook the stew in the Crockpot 10 to 12 hours or bake it 3 to 4 hours in the oven, until the venison is very tender.

During the last half-hour of cooking, mix the *pozole* and beans into the stew. Take the stew off the heat, and stir in the lime juice and the tablespoon of cilantro.

Serve the stew hot, with more cilantro, if you like.

Health considerations are one reason behind the increasing popularity of game. Venison contains about one-third the calories of beef and one-eighth the fat. Because of the low fat content, it freezes well, which is fortunate since you usually find it frozen at a meat market.

Llano Smothered Doves

Doves are seldom available commercially—unlike the other game we cover—but they are the favorite fall game bird of most Texas hunters. Their popularity has spawned hundreds of family recipes, some routine and some exceptional. This imaginative variation on typical smothered-dove dishes comes originally from the Ratliss family in Llano.

12 WHOLE DOVES, DRESSED
SALT AND FRESH-GROUND BLACK PEPPER TO
   TASTE
¼ CUP OLIVE OIL
1 MEDIUM ONION, CHOPPED
1 GARLIC CLOVE, MINCED
½ TEASPOON DRIED ROSEMARY
1 CUP UNSALTED CHICKEN STOCK
½ CUP SHERRY
½ CUP WHIPPING CREAM
DASH OF BITTERS
1 TABLESPOON ALL-PURPOSE FLOUR

Serves 4

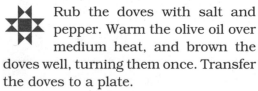 Rub the doves with salt and pepper. Warm the olive oil over medium heat, and brown the doves well, turning them once. Transfer the doves to a plate.

To the hot oil, add the onion, garlic, and rosemary, and sauté until the onion has softened. Return the doves to the skillet, and add the stock and sherry. Bring the liquid to a simmer, adjust the heat, and cover the skillet. Simmer the doves for 30 minutes.

Transfer the doves to a serving platter, and keep them warm. Pour the cream and bitters into the pan juices. Put the flour into a small bowl. Spoon a few tablespoons of the warm liquid into the flour, and then stir the flour mixture into the contents of the skillet. Bring the sauce to a boil, and cook it until it has slightly thickened, about 3 minutes. Taste, and adjust the seasoning.

Pour the gravy over the doves, and serve them. White rice is a good accompaniment.

TECHNIQUE TIP

Livers from small birds such as dove and quail make good additions to stocks, soups, and stews.

Chiltepin Doves

A pea-sized, orange-red chile with a sharp, searing heat, chiltepins grow wild in the dove country of south Texas. If you can't find them, substitute half the number of dried chiles pequins, a close relative.

12 WHOLE DOVES, DRESSED
14 WHOLE CHILTEPINS
SALT AND FRESH-GROUND BLACK PEPPER
12 SLICES SLAB BACON
1 CUP CHICKEN STOCK

Serves 4

Preheat the oven to 350° F.

Place one chiltepin—a little goes a long way—in the cavity of each dove. Reserve the two remaining chiles. Rub salt and pepper into the skins of the birds. Wrap each dove with a strip of bacon, making sure that the breast is covered especially well. Secure the bacon with toothpicks.

Transfer the doves to a baking dish that will hold them snugly in a single layer. Pour the stock over the doves, and add the two remaining chiltepins to the dish. Cover the dish, and bake the birds for 1½ hours. Remove the lid, and continue baking 20 to 30 minutes, until the liquid has reduced a bit and the bacon has browned.

Transfer the doves to a platter, discarding the greasy cooking liquid. Let the doves sit for 5 to 10 minutes, and serve them. The chiltepins will have perfumed the doves from both inside and out. Caution diners who are not certified "pepper bellies" against eating the chile pods.

Texas children have made chiltepins an instrument of torturous amusement for generations, sneaking them into the candy of other kids, for example. Sometimes their mothers get even by washing out foul mouths with the tiny chiles, which are far more effective than soap at emblazoning a lesson.

Grilled Stuffed Doves

The grapes in this outdoor-grilled dish help keep the doves moist and add a surprise taste.

12 WHOLE DOVES, DRESSED
DRY RUB FOR GAME BIRDS (PAGE 239), OR
   SALT AND PEPPER TO TASTE
24 SEEDLESS GRAPES, HALVED
6 SLICES SLAB BACON, HALVED
¼ CUP UNSALTED BUTTER
1 GARLIC CLOVE, MINCED
JUICE OF 2 LEMONS
1 TEASPOON WHITE WINE WORCESTERSHIRE
   SAUCE

Serves 4

Massage the dry rub or a mixture of salt and pepper into the skins of the birds. Place the doves in one or more large plastic bags, and allow them to sit in the refrigerator for at least 1 hour, or until the grill is ready.

Fire up enough charcoal to form a single layer beneath the doves. When the coals are covered in gray ash, spread them in the grill, and allow them to cool to a moderate heat.

Remove the doves from the refrigerator, and place four grape halves in the cavity of each bird. Place a half slice of bacon across the breast of each dove, securing the bacon with a toothpick.

Melt the butter in a small saucepan set on the grill. Add the garlic, and heat it through. Stir in the lemon juice and Worcestershire sauce, and keep the mixture warm.

Baste the doves frequently with the butter mixture while grilling them. Turning them occasionally, cook them until the bacon is browned and lightly crisped, approximately 10 minutes. Serve the birds warm.

If you've had your fill of chili and barbecue cook-offs, you might want to try the Championship Dove Cook-Off in Coleman, Texas, in the heart of hunting country. Held during the fall season, it's open to anyone who brings three or more of their own doves to cook.

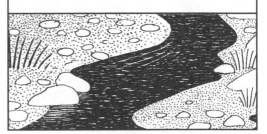

Dry Rub for Game Birds

This all-purpose blend of dry seasonings imparts extra flavor to dove, quail, pheasant, wild turkey, and other fowl in a variety of dishes. Adjust the ingredients to your own taste or to complement what you're cooking.

2 TABLESPOONS PICKLING SPICE, CRUSHED IN A
    MORTAR AND PESTLE OR SPICE MILL
1 TABLESPOON COARSE-GROUND BLACK
    PEPPER
1 TABLESPOON SALT
1 TABLESPOON DARK BROWN SUGAR
2 TEASPOONS WHITE PEPPER
2 TEASPOONS DRY MUSTARD
2 TEASPOONS POWDERED GINGER
1 TEASPOON CAYENNE
1 TEASPOON GROUND NUTMEG
6 TO **8** JUNIPER BERRIES, CRUSHED IN A MOR-
    TAR AND PESTLE OR SPICE MILL

Makes about ½ cup

Stir all the ingredients together in a small bowl.

Store the rub in a tightly closed jar. It keeps indefinitely but loses its potency over time.

Dallas bon vivant Diana Clark once shocked her Stanford University friends by cutting class to go duck hunting with her father. One incredulous professor thought her story was a Texas tall tale until she presented him with a plucked and dressed mallard drake packed in ice.

Pan-Fried Quail Picante

If you've eaten quail, it was probably fried, the most popular preparation of the bird in Texas, the rest of the country, and in northern Mexico as well. These are done border-style, with a spicy brown gravy.

8 QUAIL, WHOLE OR SPLIT, ABOUT 6 TO 7
   OUNCES EACH

3 CUPS MILK

2 GARLIC CLOVES, MINCED

1 CUP ALL-PURPOSE FLOUR

1 TABLESPOON GROUND DRIED RED CHILE,
   PREFERABLY NEW MEXICAN OR ANCHO

½ TEASPOON CUMIN SEEDS, TOASTED AND
   GROUND

½ TEASPOON SALT

¼ TEASPOON FRESH-GROUND BLACK PEPPER

PINCH OF CINNAMON

OIL, PREFERABLY CORN OR CANOLA, FOR
   FRYING

3 CUPS UNSALTED CHICKEN STOCK

Serves 4

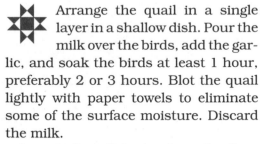 Arrange the quail in a single layer in a shallow dish. Pour the milk over the birds, add the garlic, and soak the birds at least 1 hour, preferably 2 or 3 hours. Blot the quail lightly with paper towels to eliminate some of the surface moisture. Discard the milk.

In a shallow dish, combine the flour with the chile, cumin, salt, pepper, and cinnamon. Dredge the quail in the seasoned flour. Reserve ¼ cup of the flour mixture.

Add enough oil to a cast-iron skillet to measure 1 inch in depth, and heat the oil to 350° F. Fry the quail for 3 to 4 minutes on each side, until they are golden and crispy outside and juicy when you crack open the crust. Transfer the quail to a serving platter, and keep them warm.

Pour off all but ¼ cup of the oil through a strainer, and discard it. Return any cracklings from the strainer to the skillet. Warm the drippings over medium heat, and add the reserved seasoned flour, stirring well to avoid lumps. Pour in the stock, and simmer, stirring often, until the liquid has thickened into a rich brown gravy, about 3 minutes. Taste, and adjust the seasoning. Pour the gravy into a gravy boat.

Serve the quail immediately, and pass the gravy separately.

Farm-raised quail are becoming more common in American stores. Nancy Dierker's Southwest Texas Quail Farm, near Uvalde, one of the first operations of its kind in the state, raises a type of coturnix quail that is juicier than the native bobwhites. See "Mail-Order Sources" (page 554) for more information.

Fig-Filled Grilled Quail

Say this one three times fast.

8 WHOLE QUAIL, ABOUT 6 TO 7 OUNCES EACH
1½ TO 2 CUPS MOLASSES-BACON VINAIGRETTE
   (PAGE 297)
4 FRESH FIGS (OR DRIED FIGS SIMMERED IN
   WATER UNTIL SOFT), HALVED

Serves 4

Combine the quail with the vinaigrette in a nonreactive dish. Cover the dish, and refrigerate it. Marinate the quail at least 4 hours, and up to 12, turning them occasionally.

About 30 minutes before cooking, take the quail from the refrigerator, and drain the birds gently. Save about ½ cup of the marinade. Stuff each quail with a fig half.

Fire up enough charcoal to form a single layer beneath the quail. When the coals are covered with gray ash, spread them in the grill, and allow them to cool for several minutes to medium-hot.

John Nance Garner, the former vice president, helped Harry Truman carry Texas in the 1948 presidential election by hosting a well-publicized quail breakfast for the candidate in Garner's hometown of Uvalde.

Grill the quail about 12 to 14 minutes total, turning them frequently and basting them with the reserved vinaigrette. Expect the cooked quail to be a little pinker than chicken. Avoid overcooking them.

Remove the figs, and transfer the quail and figs to a platter. Serve them hot. Encourage diners to use their fingers when eating the tiny birds.

TECHNIQUE TIP

Quail is often cooked whole because deboning the tiny birds is a time-consuming nuisance. Commercially marketed quail may be partially deboned or even cut into drumsticks and boneless breasts, but that won't affect the preparation method.

Honey-Roast Quail
with Cornbread Dressing

Big-Foot Wallace said that Indians could tell when and where white pioneers were approaching because bees would position their hives fifty miles in front of any encroaching settlement.

8 QUAIL, ABOUT 6 TO 7 OUNCES EACH

MARINADE
½ CUP OIL, PREFERABLY CANOLA OR CORN
¼ CUP HONEY
JUICE OF 2 LIMES
2 GARLIC CLOVES, MINCED
1 TO 2 FRESH SERRANOS OR 1 JALAPEÑO, MINCED
½ TEASPOON DRIED THYME

DRESSING
1 RECIPE DAY-OLD JUST GOOD PLAIN CORNBREAD (PAGE 317) OR OTHER DRY CORNBREAD SUFFICIENT TO YIELD 4 CUPS OF CRUMBS
6 TABLESPOONS UNSALTED BUTTER
1 MEDIUM ONION, CHOPPED
2 CELERY RIBS, CHOPPED
2 TO 3 FRESH SERRANOS OR 1 TO 2 JALAPEÑOS, MINCED
2 GARLIC CLOVES, MINCED
⅓ CUP CHOPPED PECANS, OPTIONAL
1 TEASPOON DRIED THYME
½ TEASPOON SALT, OR MORE, TO TASTE
1 EGG, LIGHTLY BEATEN
1 TO 1½ CUPS UNSALTED CHICKEN STOCK

Serves 4

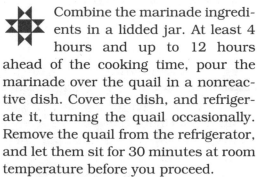 Combine the marinade ingredients in a lidded jar. At least 4 hours and up to 12 hours ahead of the cooking time, pour the marinade over the quail in a nonreactive dish. Cover the dish, and refrigerate it, turning the quail occasionally. Remove the quail from the refrigerator, and let them sit for 30 minutes at room temperature before you proceed.

Preheat the oven to 450° F. Grease the rack of a roasting pan and a large baking dish.

Crumble the cornbread into a medium bowl. Warm the butter in a heavy skillet over medium heat. Add the onion, celery, serranos or jalapeños, and garlic, and sauté them briefly until they are softened. Mix in the pecans, if you like, and the thyme and salt, and heat the mixture another minute or two. Spoon the vegetable mixture over the bread, add the egg, and mix lightly. Stir in ⅓ cup of the stock.

Measure out 1½ cups of dressing to stuff the birds, and reserve it. Add more stock to the remaining dressing, until it is very moist but short of soupy. Spoon it into the baking dish.

The dressing needs to bake 25 minutes. We suggest putting it, covered, in the oven 15 to 18 minutes ahead of the quail, and then uncovering it when adding the quail, so that both can be removed at the same time.

Fill the cavity of each quail loosely with a few tablespoons of the reserved dressing. Some folks like to truss their quail, but this isn't necessary. Transfer the quail to the rack of the roasting pan. Roast the quail 8 to 10 minutes, until they are well browned.

Remove the dressing from each bird's cavity, and serve each diner two quail, accompanied with the dressings that were cooked inside and outside the birds.

Duck farming in the United States goes back to 1873, when a clipper ship brought three dozen Pekin ducks from China, where the breed had been raised for centuries. This breed is still the most common in the country and is widely available in stores.

Roast Pheasant
with Jambalaya Dressing

Once plentiful in America, including on the high plains of Texas, wild pheasants are too gamy in taste for most people today. We prefer the more delicate farm-raised birds, which are similar to free-range chickens in flavor. An assertively flavored rice dressing makes a great accompaniment.

2 PHEASANTS, ABOUT 2½ TO 3 POUNDS EACH

6 TABLESPOONS UNSALTED BUTTER, SOFTENED

2 GARLIC CLOVES, MINCED

½ TEASPOON TABASCO OR OTHER HOT PEPPER SAUCE

½ TEASPOON WORCESTERSHIRE SAUCE

½ TEASPOON SALT

½ TEASPOON FRESH-GROUND BLACK PEPPER

JAMBALAYA DRESSING

1 TABLESPOON OLIVE OIL

½ POUND ANDOUILLE OR OTHER SPICY SMOKED SAUSAGE

1 MEDIUM ONION, CHOPPED

1 RED BELL PEPPER, CHOPPED

2 CELERY RIBS, CHOPPED

2 GARLIC CLOVES, MINCED

1 TEASPOON DRIED THYME

1 BAY LEAF

1 TEASPOON SALT

½ TEASPOON DRY MUSTARD

½ TEASPOON FILÉ POWDER

½ TEASPOON FRESH-GROUND BLACK PEPPER

½ TEASPOON WHITE PEPPER

¼ TEASPOON CAYENNE

2½ CUPS CHICKEN STOCK

2 CUPS CANNED CRUSHED TOMATOES

1¼ CUPS UNCOOKED RICE

6 GREEN ONIONS, SLICED

½ CUP UNSALTED CHICKEN STOCK

Serves 6

Start preparing the pheasants the night before you plan to roast them. In a food processor or with a mixer, combine the butter with the garlic and other seasonings until you have a smooth mixture. Loosen the pheasants' skin with your fingers, being careful not to tear it. Rub the pheasants inside and out with the seasoned butter, especially under the breast skin. Place the birds in a plastic garbage bag, and refrigerate them overnight.

Remove the pheasants from the refrigerator about 1 hour before you plan to begin cooking. Preheat the oven to 375° F. Grease a large baking dish and the rack of a roasting pan.

While the pheasants are coming to room temperature, prepare the dressing: Warm the oil in a large, heavy skillet over medium heat. Add the sausage, and fry it until it is well browned, about 10 minutes. Transfer the sausage to the baking dish. Reduce the heat to medium-low, and add the onion, bell pepper, celery, garlic, thyme, bay leaf, salt, mustard, filé, black pepper, white pepper, and cayenne. Cover the skillet, and cook until the vegetables are softened, about 10 to 12 minutes, stirring occasionally. Pour in the stock and the tomatoes, and bring the mixture to a boil. Add the rice, cover, and simmer about 20 minutes, until the liquid is absorbed. Stir in the green onions. Spoon the rice into the baking dish, mixing it with the sausage.

Transfer the pheasants breast-side down to the roasting pan. Cover the jambalaya, and place it and the pheasants in the oven. After 15 minutes, turn the pheasants breast-side up with the help of sturdy long-handled spoons. Again, try to avoid tearing the skin. Baste the birds with some of the stock and accumulated pan juices, and continue basting frequently during the remaining baking time. Cover the breasts with foil toward the end of the cooking time if they appear to be browning too quickly, but keep basting. Allow a total baking time of about 40 to 45 minutes, until the juices run pink when the birds are pierced with a skewer and the dressing is heated through.

Take the pheasants from the oven when they are done, tent them with foil, and let them sit for 10 to 15 minutes before carving them. Accompany them with the hot Jambalaya Dressing.

Pheasant never achieved the same status in the United States that it once enjoyed in Europe, where it was prized as a banquet bird because of its plumage and the wild, gamy taste, usually intensified by hanging the dead pheasant by the neck until it began to decompose.

Braised Pheasant
with Sauerkraut

Central European cooking traditions in Texas inspire this richly flavored dish. Braising keeps the pheasant moist.

1 3- TO 3½-POUND PHEASANT
SALT AND FRESH-GROUND BLACK PEPPER TO
    TASTE
1 SMALL ONION, STUDDED WITH 4 WHOLE
    CLOVES
3 SLICES SLAB BACON, CHOPPED
½ POUND UNCOOKED SMOKY SAUSAGE, SLICED
2 TABLESPOONS OIL, PREFERABLY CANOLA OR
    CORN
¼ CUP CHOPPED ONION
2 GARLIC CLOVES, MINCED
2 POUNDS SAUERKRAUT, PREFERABLY NOT A
    CANNED VARIETY
1 CUP UNSALTED CHICKEN STOCK
6 TO 8 JUNIPER BERRIES, BRUISED
1 TEASPOON COARSE-GROUND BLACK PEPPER

Serves 4 to 6

Preheat the oven to 350° F.

Rub the pheasant lightly with salt and pepper inside and out. Stuff the pheasant with the clove-studded onion. Truss the bird.

In a heavy skillet or Dutch oven, fry the bacon until it is browned and crisp. With a slotted spoon, remove the bacon, and reserve it. Add the sausage slices to the warm drippings, and brown them. Remove them with a slotted spoon, and set them aside.

Pour the oil into the meat drippings, and warm it over medium heat. Lightly brown the pheasant, and remove it from the drippings. Spoon in the onion and garlic, and cook until the onion has softened. Add the sauerkraut, and stir to coat it with the drippings.

Make a nest for the pheasant in the middle of the kraut. Set the pheasant in its nest, and pour the chicken stock over it. Scatter the juniper berries and pepper in the dish, and bring the stock to a boil.

Cover the dish, and place it in the oven. Bake the pheasant 1½ hours. After about 1 hour, scatter the reserved sausage over the pheasant.

When the pheasant is done, remove the dish from the oven, transfer the kraut and sausage to a platter, and sprinkle the bacon over the kraut. Place the pheasant on top, and serve.

Quack in a Sack

When Camille Bermann opened Maxim's in Houston in 1948, he found patrons had a fascination with his fish *en papillote*. Before long, he decided that they were just intrigued to see something cooked in a paper sack. Maybe so, but Texas home cooks have been using the same technique for decades with this duck dish. The recipe is good with both wild and domestic fowl.

1 MEDIUM-SIZE HEAVY BROWN PAPER SACK
OIL TO COAT THE SACK
1 4 ½- TO 5-POUND DUCK
SALT AND FRESH-GROUND BLACK PEPPER TO
   TASTE
½ TEASPOON POWDERED GINGER
1 APPLE, QUARTERED AND CORED
1 ONION, QUARTERED

Serves 2 to 3

 Preheat the oven to 400° F. Grease the rack of a roasting pan. Coat the paper sack thickly with oil.

If the duck is a fattier domestic species, prick its skin all over with a fork, being careful not to pierce the flesh. Rub the bird inside and out with salt, pepper, and ginger. Insert the apple and onion into the cavity.

Transfer the duck to the roasting pan, breast-side up. Roast the bird 30 minutes. Remove the pan from the oven, and pour off the accumulated fat. Pick up the duck by inserting a sturdy spoon into its cavity, and transfer the bird, breast-side up, to the oiled bag. Tie the sack tightly closed with kitchen twine.

Return the "quack" in its sack to the roasting pan. Return the pan to the oven. Reduce the oven temperature to 350° F, and roast the duck an additional 45 minutes. Remove the pan from the oven, open the sack, and insert an instant-read thermometer in the duck. If the internal temperature is not 155° F to 160° F, continue cooking the duck in the bag until the temperature reaches 155° F. Remove the duck from the oven, and let it sit in the sack for 5 to 10 minutes before carving it.

Serve the duck with the apple and onion chunks, if you wish.

> WILD DUCKS ARE LEANER THAN THEIR DOMESTIC COUSINS AND MORE ASSERTIVE IN TASTE, WITH DARK, RICH MEAT. COOKS OFTEN REDUCE THE FAT OF FARM-RAISED DUCKS BY PRICKING THE SKIN AND STEAMING THEM FOR ABOUT 30 MINUTES, AND THEY MAY LARD AND BASTE WILD ONES TO KEEP THEM FROM DRYING OUT. THE PAPER-SACK TREATMENT ELIMINATES SOME OF THE FUSS IN BOTH CASES.

Sage-Grilled Duck Breasts

Flocks of wild ducks fly south each year from Canada to help harvest the rice crop in Texas and Arkansas. Hunting is highly regulated today, but some marksmen and -women still bag their limit of tasty mallard drakes, pintail drakes, and teal.

If you start with prime young duck breasts, from either wild or domestic birds, this recipe makes a delectable dish.

4 DUCK BREAST HALVES, ABOUT 4 TO 5 OUNCES
    EACH
SALT AND FRESH-GROUND BLACK PEPPER TO
    TASTE
¼ CUP UNSALTED BUTTER, SOFTENED
1 TABLESPOON FRESH SAGE LEAVES
1 GARLIC CLOVE, CHOPPED
ADDITIONAL FRESH SAGE LEAVES, FOR GARNISH

Serves 4

 Fire up enough charcoal to form a single layer beneath the duck breasts.

Rub the duck breasts with salt and pepper under and over their skin.

In a food processor, combine the butter, sage, and garlic, processing until the mixture is smooth. Rub equal portions of the seasoned butter under and over the skin.

When the charcoal is covered with gray ash, place the breasts skin-side down over the hot coals. Cook 4 to 5 minutes, until the skin is well browned and crispy. Turn the breasts over, and move them a few inches from the hottest part of the fire, cooking another 2 to 4 minutes for medium rare meat. The butter dripping on the coals may cause some flare-ups, so watch the grill carefully and douse any conflagrations.

Let the breasts sit at room temperature for 5 minutes, and then slice each on the diagonal, serving some of the crispy skin with each breast. Transfer the slices to a platter or individual plates, and serve.

TECHNIQUE TIP

Don't bother with wild ducks that feed on fish. There are ways to alleviate the fishy taste, but the results aren't worth the trouble.

Hasenpfeffer

German hasenpfeffer, a classic in Texas as well as the mother country, is a superb way to cook either wild or domestic rabbit.

MARINADE

¾ CUP RED WINE VINEGAR

½ CUP DRY RED WINE

¾ CUP UNSALTED STOCK, PREFERABLY CHICKEN

1 MEDIUM ONION, CHOPPED

2 CELERY RIBS, CHOPPED

2 TABLESPOONS PICKLING SPICE

1 BAY LEAF

½ TEASPOON SALT

1 TEASPOON FRESH-GROUND BLACK PEPPER

6 JUNIPER BERRIES, BRUISED

1 RABBIT, CUT IN 8 SERVING PIECES

1½ CUPS ALL-PURPOSE FLOUR

½ TEASPOON SALT

½ TEASPOON FRESH-GROUND BLACK PEPPER

2 TABLESPOONS UNSALTED BUTTER

¼ CUP BRANDY

1 TABLESPOON PLUS 1 TEASPOON CURRANT JAM OR JELLY

½ CUP SOUR CREAM

Serves 3 to 4

Combine the marinade ingredients, and pour the marinade over the rabbit pieces in a non-reactive bowl. Cover the bowl, and refrigerate the rabbit pieces for 24 hours.

Remove the rabbit pieces from the marinade, and lightly pat them dry with paper towels. Reserve the marinade. Combine the flour, salt, and pepper in a paper bag. Put the rabbit pieces in the bag, and dredge them in the seasoned flour.

Heat the butter in a skillet, and brown the rabbit pieces. Pour the marinade over them, and simmer over medium-low heat for about 1 hour, or until the meat is tender and cooked through. With tongs or a slotted spoon, remove the rabbit pieces from the pan, and place them on a serving platter. Keep the meat warm while finishing the sauce.

Pour the pan drippings through a sieve, pressing on the solids to release as much flavor as possible. Discard the solids. Reheat the drippings, reducing them over high heat, if necessary, to make about 1 cup of sauce. Add the brandy and jam to the sauce, stirring until the jam is melted. Remove the sauce from the heat, and stir in the sour cream.

Taste, add more salt and pepper if you like, and pour the sauce over the rabbit pieces. Serve the rabbit immediately.

> Similar in taste to chicken, rabbit has virtually no fat and fewer calories per pound than almost any other meat.

Robust Rabbit Loins

Save this simple preparation for tender loins from farm-raised rabbits. A homemade chili sauce, such as our Rojo, is a lusty complement to the luscious meat.

8 RABBIT LOINS, ABOUT 2 TO 3 OUNCES EACH

SALT AND FRESH-GROUND BLACK PEPPER TO TASTE

¼ TEASPOON CAYENNE

2 TABLESPOONS UNSALTED BUTTER

2 TABLESPOONS OIL, PREFERABLY PEANUT

2 SMALL TART APPLES, SUCH AS GRANNY SMITHS, CHOPPED

2 TABLESPOONS CHOPPED ROASTED SALTED PEANUTS

½ CUP CHILI SAUCE, PREFERABLY ROJO (PAGE 406) OR ANOTHER HOMEMADE VARIETY

DASH OF CIDER VINEGAR, OPTIONAL

Serves 4

 Rub the rabbit loins with salt and pepper, and sprinkle the cayenne over them lightly.

In a heavy skillet, warm the butter and oil together over medium-high heat. Sauté the loins until they are lightly browned and just cooked through, two minutes or less per side, depending on their size. With tongs, remove the rabbit loins to a platter, and keep them warm while preparing the sauce.

Reduce the heat to medium, and add the apple to the drippings, sautéing it briefly until the fruit is softened but still a little crunchy. Stir in the peanuts and the chili sauce, and heat the mixture through. Taste, and adjust the seasoning, adding a dash of vinegar to balance the sweetness if it is needed. The sauce should be thick and chunky.

Arrange two tenderloins each, sliced if you like, on four individual plates, and top each loin with a few spoonfuls of the sauce.

In *The New Texas Wild Game Cookbook*, Judith and Richard Morehead estimate that two million Texas hunters spend some $600 million a year on licenses, guns, transportation, clothing, camping equipment, ammunition, and other expenses of their sport.

Roast Wild Turkey

The common holiday turkey, bred for white meat, is very different from the wild variety, which is now being farm-raised in various areas of the country. The wild ones have a dark, dense flesh, with a rich, almost smoky flavor, reminiscent of duck.

6 TABLESPOONS UNSALTED BUTTER, SOFTENED
2 GARLIC CLOVES, MINCED
1 CANNED CHIPOTLE CHILE, MINCED
½ TEASPOON SALT
½ TEASPOON FRESH-GROUND BLACK PEPPER
1 8- TO 10-POUND WILD TURKEY, FRESH OR
   FROZEN
1½ CUPS UNSALTED TURKEY OR CHICKEN STOCK
SALT AND FRESH-GROUND BLACK PEPPER TO
   TASTE

Serves 6 to 8

Start preparing the turkey the night before you plan to cook the bird. In a food processor or mixer, combine the butter with the garlic and other seasonings until the mixture is smooth. Loosen the turkey's skin with your fingers, being careful not to tear it. Rub the turkey inside and out with the butter, especially under the breast skin. Place the bird in a plastic garbage bag, and refrigerate it overnight.

Remove the turkey from the refrigerator about 1 hour before you plan to begin cooking it. Preheat the oven to 450° F. Grease the rack of a roasting pan.

Transfer the turkey breast-side down to the roasting pan. Roast it in this position for 1 hour, reducing the oven temperature to 325° F after the first 20 minutes. Turn the turkey breast-side

TECHNIQUE TIP

Game shot in the wild reacts with an adrenaline surge that tightens the muscles. On all except the most tender cuts of store-bought venison, use a soak to loosen muscle fibers and draw out some bodily fluids. Buttermilk is the best soak for most purchased meat, but for older, gamier animals you need a vinegar-water soak mixed in the proportion of a gallon of water to 1 tablespoon of salt and ¼ cup of vinegar. Place the venison in the liquid in a plastic bag, and put it in the refrigerator overnight.

up, using sturdy long-handled spoons. Again try to avoid tearing the skin or piercing the flesh. Baste the bird with some of the stock and accumulated pan juices. Allow a total roasting time of about 13 to 15 minutes per pound, until the internal temperature reaches 155° to 160° F. Continue basting every 20 to 30 minutes during the remaining roasting time. The breast can be covered with foil toward the end if it appears to be browning too quickly, but keep basting.

Take the turkey from the oven when it is done, tent it with foil, and let it sit for about 20 minutes before carving it. Add any remaining stock to the drippings, scrape up any browned bits from the bottom of the roasting pan, and pour the liquid into a small saucepan. Degrease the liquid. Bring it to a boil, and reduce it as needed to make a thin sauce that can be spooned over the bird like gravy. Add salt and pepper to taste.

NATIVE TO THE AMERICAS, TURKEYS USED TO ROAM FREELY IN MUCH OF TEXAS AND THE UNITED STATES. EVEN AFTER BEING EXTENSIVELY HUNTED, THEY REMAINED MORE COMMON THAN CHICKENS IN SOME AREAS EVEN IN THE EARLY NINETEENTH CENTURY, AND THEY OFTEN COST LESS TO BUY. BEN FRANKLIN, ALWAYS THE SAGE, WANTED THEM NAMED THE NATIONAL BIRD.

Slice the turkey thin, and serve it on a platter with the sauce. If you like, accompany the turkey with the dressing used in the recipe for Honey-Roast Quail with Cornbread Dressing (page 242).

Other wild game varieties eaten in Texas include rattlesnake, armadillo, squirrel, opossum, and javelina. For many years, the San Antonio Reptile Gardens at the Witte Museum served free fried rattlesnake every Sunday afternoon.

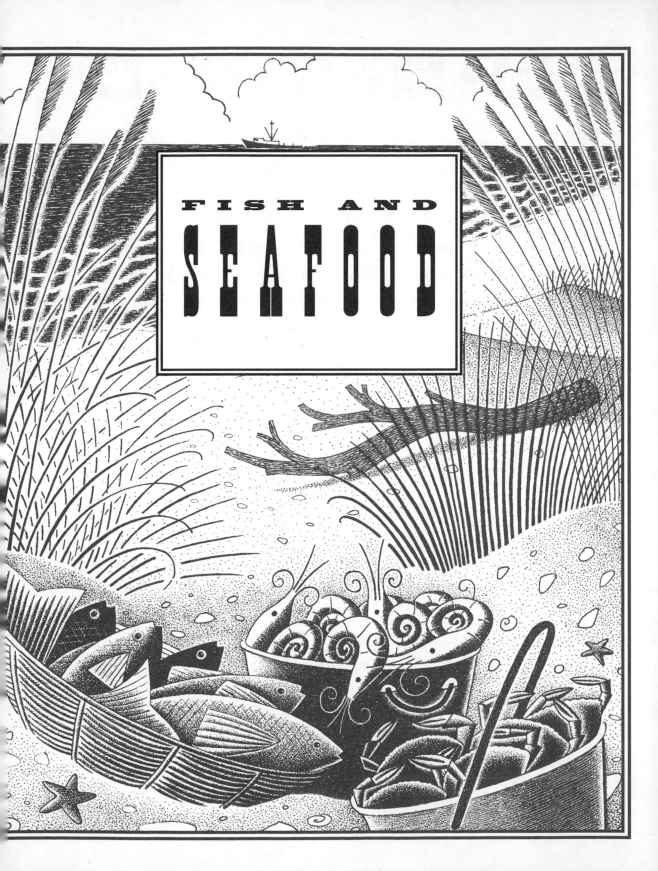

FISH AND SEAFOOD

*H*ere a while back there's a fellow telling another fellow 'bout how he caught a fish weighed 500 pounds. This other fellow told him, says, "Well, I caught one that had swallowed a coal oil lantern that was still burning." This fellow that had caught the big fish says, "I don't believe that." Second fellow says, "Well, you cut off part of your fish and I'll blow that lantern out."

Told by George Tull in *The Loblolly Book II*

*S*omehow it never mattered whether you liked fish. It didn't even matter if you actually caught one. The important thing was going to the river and bragging about your time there.

When it came to cooking and eating fish and seafood, many Texans turned up their noses, partially because until recent decades much of the available supply smelled. Galveston, Houston, and other settlements along the Gulf were the only places where you could count on freshness and variety, as well as any amount of ice, which had to be brought in by boat in the early years. Farther inland, Texans ate a little freshwater fish, but it wasn't a major part of their diet as long as cooking oils were limited to meat fats.

Despite the limitations, cooks along the coast gradually developed a strong seafood tradition, influenced by New Orleans and by the Texas propensity for frying anything that moves. With improvements in refrigeration, food processing, and vegetable oils, the Gulf style flourished and spread slowly around the state. Today, when a Texan talks big about fish, it's more likely to concern the one on the plate than the one that got away.

Bona Fide Fried Shrimp

Most of the fried shrimp in the United States looks and tastes like it was wiped off the bottom of a boot. Sometimes we think only Texans treat the dish seriously, particularly people like the Gaido brothers in Galveston, who have volunteered the frying tips below. This is a double-dip version, using both cornmeal and flour for a wonderful, crunchy coating.

2 POUNDS MEDIUM OR LARGE SHRIMP,
    PEELED, WITH TAILS
1½ CUPS MEDIUM-GRIND CORNMEAL, PREFER-
    ABLY STONE-GROUND
1½ CUPS ALL-PURPOSE FLOUR
1 TABLESPOON PAPRIKA
1 TABLESPOON FRESH-GROUND BLACK PEPPER
1½ TEASPOONS WHITE PEPPER
1½ CUPS BUTTERMILK
2 TO 3 GARLIC CLOVES, MINCED
SEVERAL SPLASHES OF TABASCO OR OTHER
    HOT PEPPER SAUCE OR PICKLED JALAPEÑO
    BRINE
OIL FOR DEEP FRYING, PREFERABLY CANOLA OR
    PEANUT
SASSY SEAFOOD COCKTAIL SAUCE (PAGE 258)

Serves 4 to 6

Devein the shrimp if you wish. Definitely butterfly them, slicing down the curved lower side and pressing the shrimp open.

In one small paper sack, place the cornmeal; in another, the flour, paprika, and black and white pepper, shaking to combine everything. Mea-sure the buttermilk into a small bowl, and add the garlic and Tabasco or other sauce to it.

Paul and Mike Gaido's father opened the family's famous Galveston restaurant in 1911. Even in its early decades, Gaido's was the master fry house of the Texas Gulf, everyone's favorite stop for perfectly cooked fresh fish and seafood.

Pour the oil into a heavy saucepan, filling the pan to a level of at least 4 inches, but no more than half full (to avoid the possibility of overflows during cooking). Heat the oil to 350° F. If the oil smokes before reaching the correct temperature, it cannot be used for deep frying. Use only fresh oil.

Plan to cook the shrimp in batches, coating only as many as will go into the pan at a time. Drop the shrimp in the bag of seasoned flour, shaking well to coat them thoroughly. Then remove the shrimp, shaking off any excess flour, dip them in the buttermilk, and shake them in the bag of cornmeal. Remove the shrimp, shaking off the excess cornmeal, and fry them 2 minutes, until they are golden brown. Drain them. Repeat with the remaining shrimp.

Serve the shrimp immediately with the seafood cocktail sauce.

Aransas Pass, Texas, calls itself the "Shrimp Capital of the World" and celebrates the title each September at its Shrimporee. We've always yearned to be a double winner at the event, taking both the shrimp-eating contest and the outhouse race.

TECHNIQUE TIPS

Paul and Mike Gaido provide this advice about frying seafood and fish:

Batter-coat fish and seafood to seal in moisture. If you fry correctly, very little of the oil seeps into the food.

Don't use the same breading or coating indiscriminately for different fish and seafood. The idea is to match flavors and textures, which vary among the critters you're cooking.

Use a fresh vegetable oil for deep frying. At Gaido's Restaurant, the kitchen works with soybean oil, but any oil with a high smoking point, such as canola or peanut, is a good option.

Deep-fry fish and seafood at 350° F.

Never overcrowd the pan, or the temperature will drop substantially and you'll end up boiling your batter-coated fish instead of frying it. Always check the oil temperature before beginning a new batch.

Sassy Seafood Cocktail Sauce

This sauce is great for fried shrimp, boiled shrimp, or almost anything that once lived in the Gulf of Mexico. Use the suggested proportions as a guide, mixing, squeezing, and splashing in the ingredients until the flavor is right for you. If you want the sauce sassy, though, don't skimp on the horseradish and lime.

1½ CUPS KETCHUP
⅓ CUP PREPARED HORSERADISH
JUICE OF 1 LEMON
JUICE OF 1 LIME
½ TEASPOON WORCESTERSHIRE SAUCE
SPLASH OR TWO OF TABASCO OR OTHER HOT
   PEPPER SAUCE

Makes about 2 cups

Mix all the ingredients together in a small bowl, and then refrigerate the sauce at least 30 minutes. The sauce keeps for several days.

The best commercial seafood sauce we've found is New Canaan Farms' Jalapeño Shrimp Sauce. The owner, Tim Tingle, and his son created the original version when they were eating at a Gulf seafood house that featured a mammoth salad bar, from which they took their improbable but inspired mix of ingredients. See "Mail-Order Sources" (page 554) for additional information.

Shrimp Rémoulade

Gennie's Bishop Grill in Dallas proudly displays a sign that says the kitchen cooks for "Texans, not Frenchmen." Even Gennie probably likes rémoulade, though, despite its Gallic origins. It became a Texas favorite after the good neighbors in Louisiana transformed it into a premier Gulf shrimp sauce.

4 CUPS WATER

2 TABLESPOONS SHRIMP- AND CRAB-BOIL SEASONING, SUCH AS ZATARAIN'S

1½ POUNDS MEDIUM SHRIMP, UNPEELED, WITH TAILS

SAUCE

½ CUP MAYONNAISE

2 CELERY RIBS, CHOPPED

5 TO 6 GREEN ONIONS, CHOPPED

¼ CUP MINCED PARSLEY

2 TABLESPOONS PREPARED CREOLE MUSTARD

1 TABLESPOON KETCHUP

1 TABLESPOON LEMON JUICE

2 TEASPOONS PREPARED HORSERADISH

2 TEASPOONS WHITE WINE WORCESTERSHIRE SAUCE OR 1 TEASPOON REGULAR WORCESTERSHIRE SAUCE

1 TEASPOON PAPRIKA

1 GARLIC CLOVE, MINCED

½ TEASPOON TABASCO OR OTHER HOT PEPPER SAUCE

½ TEASPOON SALT

LETTUCE LEAVES

LEMON WEDGES, OPTIONAL, FOR GARNISH

*Serves 4 as a main dish
or 6 as an appetizer*

A couple of hours before you plan to eat, prepare the shrimp: Put the water and the boil seasoning in a saucepan. Bring the water to a boil, reduce the heat, and simmer 5 or 10 minutes. Add the shrimp, and simmer them until they are just cooked through and pink, a matter of only a couple of minutes. Drain the shrimp, discarding the cooking liquid, and refrigerate them until they are cold. Peel the shrimp, leaving their tails on, and, if you wish, devein them.

Place all of the sauce ingredients in a blender or food processor, and purée them until they are smooth. Refrigerate the sauce until you are ready to use it. It can be made a day ahead. Before serving, taste the sauce, and adjust the seasonings. It should have a tangy assertiveness and a touch of heat that builds pleasantly in your mouth after a few bites.

When you are ready to serve the shrimp, arrange the lettuce leaves on plates, top them with the shrimp, and drizzle each plate with a few tablespoons of the sauce. Garnish with lemon wedges, if you like.

• The Gulf provides superlative fish and seafood, but pollution has contaminated the supply in some areas. Use a little caution.

• Find a reputable source, such as a market that specializes in seafood. Good suppliers should be able to tell you where the fish is from, how long it has been out of the water (not just when they got it), how it was transported, and how it has been stored.

• Observe the fish. It should look fresh and smell briny but not fishy. The skin and eyes should glisten on a whole fish, and fillets and seafood should look moist and firm.

• Talk to your supplier about what you plan to do with a particular fish. Many fishes are reasonably interchangeable in recipes, and a good dealer can suggest substitutes that may be a day fresher or several dollars per pound cheaper.

• Look for fresh seafood, but remember that some high-quality products are shipped frozen. This is often true with shrimp. The frozen shrimp may be better than the "fresh" down the block, if the latter has been out of the water two weeks.

• Be willing to pay for your supplier's expertise and high-quality ingredients. You'll find an ample reward at the table.

Texiana Shrimp and Rice

This Texas variation on a Cajun jambalaya blends Louisiana and Southwestern flavors.

1½ POUNDS LARGE SHRIMP

3 TABLESPOONS OIL, PREFERABLY CANOLA OR CORN

2 MEDIUM ONIONS, CHOPPED

2 GARLIC CLOVES, MINCED

1 LARGE GREEN BELL PEPPER, CHOPPED

¼ CUP CHOPPED ROASTED GREEN CHILE, PREFERABLY POBLANO OR NEW MEXICAN, FRESH OR FROZEN

1 TEASPOON CUMIN SEEDS, TOASTED AND GROUND

1 TEASPOON DRIED OREGANO, PREFERABLY MEXICAN

1 TEASPOON WHITE PEPPER

1 TEASPOON SALT

1 BAY LEAF

1½ CUPS UNCOOKED RICE

3 CUPS SHRIMP OR SEAFOOD STOCK

2 TABLESPOONS FRESH LEMON JUICE

6 GREEN ONIONS, SLICED

⅓ CUP CHOPPED CILANTRO

Serves 6

Peel, and, if you wish, devein the shrimp. Save the shells for stock. Refrigerate the shrimp until you are ready to use them.

Warm the oil in a heavy skillet or Dutch oven over medium heat. Add the onions, garlic, green pepper, and green chile, and sauté them, stirring occa-sionally, until the onions have soft-ened, about 5 minutes. Add the dried seasonings and the rice, stirring to coat all the grains, and cook another couple of minutes. Add the stock and the lemon juice, and bring the liquid to a boil. Cover the skillet, reduce the heat to medium-low, and simmer 18 minutes. Check the mixture toward the end of the cooking time, and stir if the rice appears to be sticking. Add the shrimp and the sliced green onions, stirring to incorporate them. Cook 2 to 3 minutes more.

Remove the skillet from the heat, and let the shrimp and rice sit, cov-ered, for 10 minutes. Then sprinkle the cilantro over the dish, and serve it immediately. Eat any leftovers the next day.

Texas has its own Cajun popula-tion, concentrated in the south-eastern part of the state. Some Cajuns crossed the Sabine River into Texas from Louisiana during the first years of the Republic, and more came early in this cen-tury with the oil boom.

Grilled Pickled Shrimp

We like to grill these pickled shrimp, but you don't have to take that last step. They're also tasty cold, just out of the marinade, and many Texans eat them that way.

1 TO 1½ POUNDS MEDIUM SHRIMP

MARINADE

⅔ CUP UNSALTED SHRIMP OR FISH STOCK OR WATER

1 MEDIUM ONION, CHOPPED IN BITE-SIZE SQUARES

2 TEASPOONS SHRIMP- AND CRAB-BOIL SEASONING, SUCH AS ZATARAIN'S

⅔ CUP OIL, PREFERABLY MILD-FLAVORED OLIVE OR ROASTED SAFFLOWER

⅔ CUP WHITE WINE VINEGAR

¼ CUP LEMON JUICE

2 TABLESPOONS CAPERS

1 TEASPOON SUGAR

½ TEASPOON SALT

¼ TEASPOON TABASCO OR OTHER HOT PEPPER SAUCE

PIMIENTO-STUFFED GREEN OLIVES, APPROXIMATELY 1 CUP

*Serves 4 as a main course
or 6 to 8 as an appetizer*

 Peel the shrimp, and, if you wish, devein them. Place them in a shallow nonreactive pan or bowl.

Combine the stock or water, the onion, and the boil seasoning in a small saucepan. Bring the liquid to a boil, reduce the heat, and simmer about 5 minutes. Remove the pan from the heat, and add all the remaining ingredients except the green olives. Pour the warm marinade over the shrimp, mix well, and marinate, refrigerated, at least 8 hours and preferably 24.

If you will be grilling the shrimp, fire up enough charcoal to form a single layer beneath the shrimp.

Drain the shrimp and the onions, and alternate them on skewers with the green olives. The presentation looks especially nice if you skewer one end of a shrimp, slide on an olive, and skewer the shrimp's other end, with

---

Henry Ford invented charcoal briquets for home use. His original cars had a lot of wood parts, which left his plants drowning in odd, discarded bits of wood. Ford turned the pieces into charcoal and sold them through his auto dealers for use in wood stoves. The briquets didn't catch on until the 1950s, however, when backyard grilling became popular.

onion sections between the shrimp. The skewers can be readied in advance and then returned to the marinade until just before cooking.

For grilling, cook the shrimp over medium-hot ashen-gray coals for a minute or two on each side, until the shrimp are just firm. Avoid overcooking them, or they will toughen. You can also broil the shrimp indoors, for the same amount of time. Serve the shrimp hot.

Cornmeal-Crusted Fried Oysters

In most places, oyster connoisseurs eat the little bivalves raw. Contrary to a point of honor, Texans usually fry them.

1 PINT SHUCKED OYSTERS WITH THEIR LIQUOR
1 EGG
2 CUPS MEDIUM-GRIND CORNMEAL, PREFERABLY STONE-GROUND
½ TEASPOON SALT
CAYENNE TO TASTE
OIL FOR DEEP FRYING, PREFERABLY CANOLA OR PEANUT
SASSY SEAFOOD COCKTAIL SAUCE (PAGE 258) OR YOUR FAVORITE SALSA, OPTIONAL
LIME OR LEMON WEDGES, OPTIONAL, FOR GARNISH

Serves 4

Remove the oysters from their liquor, and drain them. Measure 2 tablespoons of the briny juice into a shallow dish, add the egg, and beat well. In a small paper sack, combine the cornmeal, salt, and cayenne.

Drop the oysters into the sack, a few at a time, and shake the sack to coat them with the cornmeal. Dip each oyster in the egg mixture, and then coat the oysters again in cornmeal.

Pour the oil into a heavy pan to a depth of at least 4 inches. Heat the oil to 350° F. Deep-fry the oysters, in batches, for 2½ to 3 minutes, depending on their size. The cornmeal coating should be medium-golden and crispy.

Eat the oysters unadorned, or serve them with cocktail sauce or salsa and plenty of lemon or lime wedges.

> As Jonathan Swift noted verily, "He was a bold man that first ate an oyster."

Pepper-Poached Oysters

The peppery seasoning in this dish heightens the lively, briny taste of a good oyster. Mark Miller, Southwest chef, introduced us to the combination of flavors, having discovered it himself in Mexico's Yucatan. The idea originated with Gulf oysters, but any large, plump variety works well. If you have the oysters shucked at the store, be sure your seafood merchant saves the bottom shells and the liquor for you.

24 LARGE OYSTERS WITH LIQUOR (SHELLS
  RESERVED)
1 8-OUNCE BOTTLE CLAM JUICE
1½ TABLESPOONS BLACK PEPPERCORNS
2 GARLIC CLOVES, ROASTED (PAGE 9)
½ TEASPOON SALT
SCANT ¼ TEASPOON GROUND ALLSPICE
1 BAY LEAF
3 TABLESPOONS EXTRA-VIRGIN OLIVE OIL
JUICE OF 1 MEDIUM LIME
LIME WEDGES, FOR GARNISH

Makes 24 oysters on the half shell

Drain the oysters, and pour their liquor into a small saucepan. The amount will vary depending on the particular batch of oysters and the skill of the shucker. Add enough of the clam juice to the liquor just to cover the oysters. Bring the liquid to a boil, add the oysters, and reduce the heat to a simmer. Poach the oysters about 3 to 4 minutes, or until their edges curl and they begin to plump. With a slotted spoon, remove the oysters immediately, and set them aside. Reserve the poaching liquid.

With a mortar and pestle or a mini–food processor, combine the peppercorns, garlic, salt, and allspice until they form a paste. Add two tablespoons

TECHNIQUE TIPS

Whether you are frying oysters, cooking them another way, or popping them raw, keep these pointers in mind in the market:

• For the most tender oysters, choose those small for their species.

• Oysters are highly perishable and should be shucked as close to serving time as is practical.

• Shucked oysters should be plump and smell briny but not unpleasant.

• If your oysters come packaged in their liquor, it should be clear, not cloudy.

of the oyster poaching liquid to the paste, and blend the paste.

Drop the bay leaf into the poaching liquid, and return it to a boil. Reduce the liquid to about ½ cup. Stir in the spice paste, and then add the oysters. Remove the saucepan from the heat, and stir in the olive oil and lime juice.

Refrigerate the oysters in the poaching liquid, covered, for at least 30 minutes and up to 1 hour.

Place the oysters on the half shells with about a teaspoon of the liquid for each. Garnish the oysters with lime wedges, and serve them.

Texas Blue Crab Cakes

Blue crabs get their name from the color of their shells and claws. They can be expensive, particularly away from the Gulf, but this recipe stretches a little of the succulent meat a long way.

1 EGG, LIGHTLY BEATEN

2 TABLESPOONS MAYONNAISE

2 TEASPOONS PREPARED CREOLE MUSTARD

2 TEASPOONS PREPARED HORSERADISH

2 TEASPOONS WORCESTERSHIRE SAUCE

1½ TEASPOONS CRAB-BOIL SEASONING, SUCH AS ZATARAIN'S

1 TEASPOON COARSE-GROUND BLACK PEPPER

¼ TEASPOON SALT

SEVERAL DASHES OF TABASCO OR OTHER HOT PEPPER SAUCE

1 POUND CRABMEAT, PICKED OVER TO REMOVE ANY SHELLS

¾ CUP SALTINE CRACKER CRUMBS (ABOUT 1½ OUNCES)

½ CUP MINCED RED BELL PEPPER

3 TABLESPOONS OLIVE OIL

1 TABLESPOON UNSALTED BUTTER

LEMON WEDGES, FOR GARNISH

Makes 8 crab cakes

In a large bowl, stir together the egg, mayonnaise, mustard, horseradish, Worcestershire sauce, Old Bay seasoning, pepper, salt, and Tabasco. Gently mix in the crabmeat, cracker crumbs, and bell pepper. For the ideal combination of crisp exterior and creamy interior, form eight patties ¾ inch thick.

Warm the oil and butter together over medium-high heat. Fry the crab cakes 5 to 7 minutes on each side, or until they are golden. Drain them.

Serve the cakes immediately. They are so flavorful that they require little more than a squeeze of lemon juice for accompaniment.

Pan-Fried Soft-Shell Crabs

At a stage in the blue crab's development, it sheds its shell to grow a new, bigger one. At this point, it's a soft-shell crab, edible in its delectable entirety. Mike and Paul Gaido's perfect preparation of soft-shells inspired this recipe.

½ CUP ALL-PURPOSE FLOUR

1 TEASPOON DRIED OREGANO

SALT AND FRESH-GROUND BLACK PEPPER TO TASTE

½ CUP MILK

2 EGGS

6 GARLIC CLOVES

3 CUPS SALTINE CRACKER CRUMBS (ABOUT 6 OUNCES)

3 TABLESPOONS UNSALTED BUTTER

3 TABLESPOONS OLIVE OIL

8 SOFT-SHELL CRABS

Serves 4

In a shallow dish, stir the flour together with the oregano, salt, and pepper. In a second dish, mix together the milk and eggs. In a food processor, mince the garlic. Add the cracker crumbs to the garlic, and process until the crumbs are ground fine. Transfer the crumbs to another dish.

In a large, heavy skillet, warm the butter and oil together over medium-high heat. Dip each crab lightly first in the flour, next in the egg mixture, and then in the cracker crumbs. Add the crabs to the skillet, in two batches if necessary, and pan-fry them 6 to 8 minutes, turning them once.

Drain the crabs, and serve them immediately.

In their delightful book *Eats: A Folk History of Texas Food*, Ernestine Sewell Linck and Joyce Gibson Roach offer a trove of Lone Star lore related to cooking and eating. The old-timers, according to their research, said you should go fishing when the bluebonnets are in bloom, the cows are grazing, and the west wind is blowing.

ABC Sandwich

A sandwich good enough for a dinner entrée, the ABC was a specialty at the now-defunct Pittman House Restaurant in Dallas. Maybe the initials should be reversed, since the avocado and bacon play supporting roles for C, the crab star.

1 CUP MAYONNAISE
½ CUP MINCED GREEN ONIONS
2 TABLESPOONS BRANDY
¼ TEASPOON COARSE-GROUND BLACK PEPPER
18 SLICES TOASTED WHOLE-WHEAT BREAD
LEAF LETTUCE
12 OUNCES CRABMEAT, PICKED OVER WELL TO
    REMOVE ANY SHELLS
TOMATO SLICES
12 SLICES SLAB BACON, CUT IN HALF, COOKED
    CRISP, AND DRAINED
2 AVOCADOS, SLICED

Makes 6 sandwiches

 In a small bowl, combine the mayonnaise, green onion, and brandy, mixing well.

For each sandwich, spread three pieces of bread with a portion of the mayonnaise mixture. Cover the first slice of bread with lettuce leaves, 2 ounces of crabmeat, and one or two tomato slices. Add the second slice of bread, and top it with four half-slices of bacon, a layer of avocado slices, another tomato slice or two, and more lettuce. Cover with the third slice of bread, secure the sandwich with toothpicks, if you like, and slice it in half.

Serve the sandwiches immediately. Try them with a side of Rangerette Sweet Potato Chips (page 457).

"He can catch more fish in a given time than any . . . ordinary liar I have met. The gigantic bass, the enormous trout, the tremendous catfish, that he has hooked, and that eventually got away [would] fill six refrigerator cars, besides all the men, women, and children in Southwestern Texas."—Alex Sweet and John Knox, describing a typical fisherman, in *On a Mexican Mustang Through Texas*

Boiled Crawfish

Kids all over Texas used to fish for "crawdads" with a piece of string and a small hunk of fat, sometimes cooking the tails on tin-can lids over a fire down by the creek. These days, the feasters are more likely to be adults, perhaps at a crawfish boil, a common food event in the southeastern part of the state.

10 POUNDS LIVE CRAWFISH

2 ORANGES, CUT INTO THICK ROUNDS

2 LEMONS, CUT INTO THICK ROUNDS

1 GARLIC HEAD, CLOVES SEPARATED AND PEELED

¼ CUP SALT

2 TABLESPOONS GROUND BLACK PEPPER

1 TABLESPOON CHILI POWDER, PREFERABLY HOMEMADE (PAGE 135) OR GEBHARDT'S

2 TEASPOONS CAYENNE

2 BAY LEAVES

8 TO 12 SMALL NEW POTATOES

4 EARS CORN, CUT IN HALF

1 POUND SMALL BOILING ONIONS

SALT, FRESH-GROUND BLACK PEPPER, AND CAYENNE TO SPRINKLE OVER THE CRAWFISH AND VEGETABLES

Serves 4

Rinse the crawfish well. To make sure you remove all the mud or debris, put them into a large pot or bucket of water, and let them sit for about 30 minutes. (You can skip this soaking process if your crawfish are farm-raised and "purged" of mud.)

While the crawfish bathe, pour 4 to 5 gallons of water into a large stockpot. Add to it the oranges, lemons, garlic, salt, black pepper, chili powder, cayenne, and bay leaves. Bring the water to a boil, and cook the spices 10 to 15 minutes. Add the potatoes, corn, and onions. After the liquid returns to a boil, cook the vegetables for 5 minutes.

Drain the crawfish from their soaking bath, and add them to the stockpot. After the liquid again returns to a boil, cook the crawfish for 10 to 12 minutes.

Remove the pot from the heat, cover it, and let the crawfish and vegetables steep in the liquid for 10 minutes. Drain the liquid from the pot.

> THE FAT IN THE HEADS OF CRAWFISH IS SO RICH AND DELICIOUS THAT IT CAN BE SUBSTITUTED FOR AN EQUAL AMOUNT OF BUTTER IN MOST CRAWFISH DISHES. IN TEXAS AND LOUISIANA, SUCKING THE HEADS FOR THE JUICE IS A RISQUÉ RITUAL, NOT TO BE MISSED.

Freshwater crustaceans related to lobsters, crawfish have a texture similar to shrimp, which can be substituted for them in our recipes. The flavor of crawfish is distinctive, however, so they are worth seeking out. From November through early summer, try to find them live, although whole blanched crawfish also work well. If a recipe calls for crawfish tails and you want to start from whole crustaceans, buy about five to six pounds for every pound of tails required. The shells are tougher than a shrimp's, but soft enough for most people to crack and peel with their hands. Save the shells for stock.

Buying crawfish tails, already blanched and peeled, takes care of much of the work, but you lose the head fat. Avoid blanched tails that are un-curled, an indication that the crawfish were already dead when cooked. Frozen crawfish can be good, but sometimes taste a little rancid.

Serve everything heaped on big platters, with plenty of newspapers on the side to soak up drippings from the ritual of peeling and eating, all done with the fingers. Sprinkle salt, pepper, and cayenne over the crawfish and vegetables as you eat, and, after you break off the tails, be sure to suck the fat from the crawfish heads. It's a gloriously messy feast.

Texas towns like to crow about their catches. At least three Gulf coast burgs host annual festivals honoring crawfish; Fulton stages the Oysterfest; Crystal Beach salutes crabs; and Orange sponsors the International Gumbo Cook-off.

Gaido's Deviled Crawfish Balls

The Gaido brothers offer a bounty of crawfish preparations at their landmark Galveston restaurant. This is a home-style version of one of their best.

1 STICK UNSALTED BUTTER
½ CUP CHOPPED ONION
½ CUP CHOPPED CELERY
1 GARLIC CLOVE, MINCED
2 TEASPOONS CAJUN CHEF HOT SAUCE (SEE BELOW) OR 1 TO 2 TEASPOONS OTHER HOT PEPPER SAUCE
2 TEASPOONS WORCESTERSHIRE SAUCE
1 TEASPOON CAYENNE
3 CUPS COARSE-GROUND WHITE BREAD CRUMBS
1 POUND BLANCHED CRAWFISH TAILS, CHOPPED
SALT AND FRESH-GROUND BLACK PEPPER TO TASTE
¼ CUP ALL-PURPOSE FLOUR
OIL, PREFERABLY CANOLA, FOR DEEP FRYING

Makes about 2 ½ dozen balls, enough for 5 to 6 appetizer servings

Melt the butter in a skillet. Add the onion, celery, and garlic, and sauté them until they are soft. Stir in the hot pepper sauce, Worcestershire sauce, and cayenne, and then the bread crumbs and crawfish tails. Taste the mixture, and add salt and pepper as desired. Remove the pan from the heat. Form the mixture into 1-inch balls, and roll them in the flour to coat them lightly.

Heat the oil to 350° F in a heavy high-sided saucepan. If the oil smokes before reaching the correct temperature, it cannot be used for deep frying. Use only fresh oil. Fry the balls in batches to avoid overcrowding them.

Cook the balls until they are golden brown, drain them, and serve them immediately.

No matter how many dictionaries you're toting with you, don't call a crawfish a "crayfish" along the Gulf coast. If you do, you'll probably have to suck a few heads in public to prove you're OK.

TECHNIQUE TIP

Cajun Chef is the brand of hot pepper sauce the Gaidos prefer. Although similar to Tabasco, it's slightly milder and less acidic. Both sauces are distributed nationally, but Cajun Chef isn't as common. If you substitute Tabasco, start with about half the recommended amount.

Crawfish Étouffée

Étouffée means "smothered," a preparation that Cajuns perfected.

¼ CUP OIL, PREFERABLY CANOLA OR CORN
¼ CUP UNSALTED BUTTER
½ CUP ALL-PURPOSE FLOUR OR PREBROWNED
  FLOUR (PAGE 200)
2 CUPS CHOPPED ONIONS
1 CUP CHOPPED CELERY
1 GREEN BELL PEPPER, CHOPPED
2 GARLIC CLOVES, MINCED
1 BAY LEAF
¾ TEASPOON SALT
¼ TEASPOON DRIED THYME
¼ TEASPOON FRESH-GROUND BLACK PEPPER
¼ TEASPOON WHITE PEPPER
¼ TEASPOON CAYENNE
3 CUPS UNSALTED CRAWFISH OR OTHER
  SEAFOOD STOCK
1 POUND BLANCHED CRAWFISH TAILS
½ CUP SLICED GREEN ONIONS
1 TABLESPOON MINCED PARSLEY
COOKED RICE

Serves 4

In a cast-iron skillet, warm the oil and butter together over medium-high heat. Sprinkle in the flour, and stir constantly until the roux turns a deep chocolate-brown. (If you are using prebrowned flour, this process will take only about 3 minutes, saving you 30 to 35 minutes.) Add the onion, celery, bell pepper, garlic, bay leaf, salt, thyme, peppers, and cayenne, and remove the pan from the heat. Continue stirring until the sizzling stops.

Heat the stock in a large, heavy saucepan. Add spoonfuls of the roux-and-vegetable mixture to the stock, continuing to stir after each addition. When all the roux has been combined fully, reduce the heat to a simmer, and cook for 20 minutes. The étouffée can be made ahead to this point and refrigerated, but rewarm it before continuing.

Add the crawfish tails, and simmer another 5 to 7 minutes, until the tails are cooked through.

Stir in the green onions and parsley, and remove the étouffée from the heat. Serve it immediately, over rice.

SOME ONE HUNDRED AND FIFTY TEXAS CRAWFISH FARMS HARVEST ABOUT TWO MILLION POUNDS OF CRUSTACEANS A YEAR. THE FARMERS "PURGE" THEIR CRAWFISH OF IMPURITIES BEFORE SHIPPING THEM, BY HOLDING THEM IN TANKS OF CLEAN WATER FOR ONE TO TWO DAYS. PURGED CRAWFISH KEEP LONGER, TASTE BETTER, AND KEEP YOUR KITCHEN A LOT CLEANER THAN THEIR MUDDY WILD COUSINS. SEE "MAIL-ORDER SOURCES" (PAGE 553) FOR HOME-DELIVERY INFORMATION.

Gulf Gumbo

Gumbos go back a long way in Texas. The first known cookbook published in the state, a Houston collaboration, contained a half-dozen different recipes—one more than the number of lemon pies—plus instructions for making filé powder, a common gumbo ingredient.

½ POUND ANDOUILLE OR OTHER HOT SMOKY
   SAUSAGE
3 TO 4 TABLESPOONS OIL, PREFERABLY CANOLA
   OR CORN
¼ CUP ALL-PURPOSE FLOUR OR PREBROWNED
   FLOUR (SEE PAGE 200)
2 MEDIUM ONIONS, CHOPPED
2 MEDIUM BELL PEPPERS, PREFERABLY
   1 GREEN AND 1 RED, CHOPPED
3 CELERY RIBS, CHOPPED
3 GARLIC CLOVES, MINCED
6 CUPS UNSALTED SEAFOOD STOCK
1 TABLESPOON FILÉ POWDER
1 BAY LEAF
½ TEASPOON FRESH-GROUND BLACK PEPPER
½ TEASPOON CAYENNE
½ TEASPOON DRIED THYME
¼ TEASPOON WHITE PEPPER
¾ POUND PEELED MEDIUM SHRIMP
½ TO ¾ POUND CRABMEAT, PICKED OVER TO
   REMOVE ANY BITS OF SHELL
10 TO 12 SHUCKED OYSTERS, IN THEIR LIQUOR
1 DOZEN GREEN ONIONS, SLICED
COOKED RICE

Serves 6 to 8

In a Dutch oven or heavy stockpot, brown the sausage over medium-low heat. With a slotted spoon, remove the sausage from the rendered fat, and reserve it. Eyeball the amount of fat remaining in the skillet, and add enough oil so that it measures about ¼ cup. Warm the oil and meat drippings over medium-high heat. Sprinkle in the flour, and, stirring constantly, cook it over high heat until a medium-brown roux forms. (If you are using prebrowned flour, this process will take 2 to 3 minutes, saving you 25 to 30 minutes.)

When the roux reaches the right shade, reduce the heat to medium, and add the onions, bell peppers, celery, and garlic. Continue cooking and stirring for about 3 minutes. Slowly pour in the seafood stock, stirring to incorporate it. Add the filé, bay leaf, black pepper, cayenne, thyme, and white pepper, and simmer the mixture about 45 minutes. Stir in the reserved sausage, shrimp, crab, oysters, and green onions, and heat them through.

Serve the gumbo hot over rice in bowls.

THE CHOCTAW INDIANS DISCOVERED THE FLAVORING AND THICKENING PROPERTIES OF GROUND SASSAFRAS LEAVES, WHICH WE KNOW AS FILÉ.

Variation: To make gumbo-stuffed peppers, mix rice with the gumbo. Bake seeded, cored bell peppers at 350° F for 25 minutes in a dish with a bit of seafood stock. Spoon the gumbo into the peppers, and bake them another 25 minutes.

Rice-Stuffed Redfish

We prefer to cook this elegant Gulf dish on a charcoal grill, but it's just as good from the oven.

2 TABLESPOONS UNSALTED BUTTER
½ CUP CHOPPED PECANS
1 CELERY RIB, MINCED
6 GREEN ONIONS, SLICED
1 CUP BROWN RICE, PREFERABLY TEXMATI
2 ¼ CUPS UNSALTED SEAFOOD OR CHICKEN STOCK
1 TEASPOON WORCESTERSHIRE SAUCE
1 3-POUND WHOLE REDFISH OR RED SNAPPER, COMPLETELY BONED
1 TABLESPOON OIL, PREFERABLY CANOLA OR CORN
SALT AND FRESH-GROUND BLACK PEPPER TO TASTE
1 TEASPOON LEMON ZEST, CHOPPED FINE
¼ CUP CHOPPED PARSLEY
LEMON SLICES AND ADDITIONAL SLICED GREEN ONIONS, FOR GARNISH

Serves 4

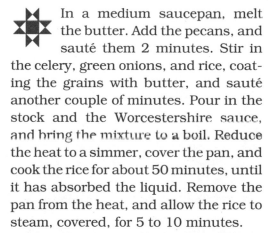

In a medium saucepan, melt the butter. Add the pecans, and sauté them 2 minutes. Stir in the celery, green onions, and rice, coating the grains with butter, and sauté another couple of minutes. Pour in the stock and the Worcestershire sauce, and bring the mixture to a boil. Reduce the heat to a simmer, cover the pan, and cook the rice for about 50 minutes, until it has absorbed the liquid. Remove the pan from the heat, and allow the rice to steam, covered, for 5 to 10 minutes.

While the rice stuffing cooks, fire up enough charcoal to form a single layer under the fish, or preheat the oven to 350° F. Lay the fish on a cookie sheet or other work surface. Rub it inside and out with the oil, and then massage in a sprinkling of salt and pepper.

When the rice is ready, mix the lemon zest and parsley into it. Fill the fish's cavity with as much of the rice mixture as will fit easily. Press lightly to flatten the fish a bit.

To grill the fish: When the charcoal is covered with gray ash, transfer the fish to a greased grill basket, grill rack (see page 38), or large piece of heavy-weight foil, and place it over the coals. Cover the grill with its lid or foil. To bake the fish: Transfer the fish to a shallow baking dish. In either case, spoon the remaining rice into a small baking dish, cover it, and heat it alongside the fish.

Grill or bake about 8 to 10 minutes per inch of fish. Turn the fish once carefully. A long, sturdy spatula helps the process.

When the fish is cooked, transfer it to a serving platter, surround it with the rice baked separately, and top it with the lemon slices and green onions. Cut the fish crosswise to serve, scooping up some of the rice filling with each portion of fish.

Orange-Marinated Gulf Fish

For this charcoal-grilled preparation, use firm fish fillets from snapper, redfish, or grouper, which hold up better than fragile fish such as flounder.

MARINADE

JUICE OF 2 ORANGES, APPROXIMATELY
⅔ CUP
ZEST OF 1 ORANGE, MINCED
6 TABLESPOONS SHERRY
6 TABLESPOONS OIL, PREFERABLY PEANUT
2 GARLIC CLOVES, MINCED
1 TEASPOON PREPARED CREOLE MUSTARD
¼ TEASPOON SALT
¼ TEASPOON FRESH-GROUND BLACK PEPPER

4 6-OUNCE FIRM WHITE FISH FILLETS
ORANGE WEDGES AND ADDITIONAL ORANGE
ZEST, FOR GARNISH

Serves 4

 Fire up enough charcoal to form a single layer beneath the fish.

Combine all the marinade ingredients in a lidded jar, and shake the jar well.

Lay the fillets in a single layer in a nonreactive pan. Pour the marinade over the fish, and let the fish sit at room temperature for 30 minutes.

Drain the fillets, reserving the marinade. Bring the marinade to a boil, and then simmer it for several minutes.

When the charcoal is covered with gray ash, place the fillets on the grill. Cook the fish until it is opaque and flaky, about 4 to 5 minutes per half-inch of thickness. Turn over the fish halfway through the cooking time, basting with the marinade then and shortly before the fish is done.

Serve the fish garnished with orange wedges and a sprinkling of orange zest.

Athens, Texas, announced plans in 1992 to build the Freshwater Fishing Hall of Fame. You can bet the trophies will be tastier than any in Cooperstown.

Snapper Vera-Texana

Snapper Veracruzana, probably the most popular fish dish in Mexico, is too often drowned in a pasty tomato sauce, even south of the border. If that's the only way you've had the dish, prepare yourself for a revelation, particularly if you use fresh tomatoes picked at their peak season.

4 6-OUNCE RED SNAPPER FILLETS OR OTHER
   FIRM-FLESHED WHITE FISH FILLETS
JUICE OF 3 LIMES
SALT AND FRESH-GROUND BLACK PEPPER

SAUCE

2 TABLESPOONS EXTRA-VIRGIN OLIVE OIL
1 MEDIUM ONION, CHOPPED
2 GARLIC CLOVES, MINCED
1 POUND VERY RIPE FRESH TOMATOES, CHOPPED,
   OR 2 CUPS CANNED CRUSHED TOMATOES
¼ CUP SEAFOOD STOCK OR BOTTLED CLAM JUICE
¼ CUP CHOPPED PARSLEY
⅓ CUP SLICED PIMIENTO-STUFFED GREEN OLIVES
1 TO 2 PICKLED JALAPEÑOS, CHOPPED
1 TEASPOON JALAPEÑO PICKLING LIQUID
1 TABLESPOON CAPERS
1 BAY LEAF
2 TEASPOONS WHITE WINE WORCESTERSHIRE
   SAUCE
1 TEASPOON DRIED OREGANO, PREFERABLY
   MEXICAN
½ TEASPOON COARSE-GROUND BLACK PEPPER
¼ TEASPOON GROUND CINNAMON

LIME WEDGES, OPTIONAL, FOR GARNISH

Serves 4

 At least 30 minutes and up to 1¼ hours before you plan to serve the dish, place the fish fillets in a single layer in a shallow non-reactive dish. Pour half the lime juice over the fish, and sprinkle each fillet with salt and pepper. Refrigerate the fish if you plan to marinate it longer than 30 minutes.

In a skillet or other heavy, shallow pan, heat the olive oil until it is fragrant. Add the onions, and cook them over medium heat for about 10 minutes, or until they are very soft and just beginning to brown. Stir them occasionally. Add the garlic, and sauté another minute or two. Mix in the tomatoes (and any juice they have given off) and the remaining sauce ingredients. Cook the sauce over medium heat for 10 to 15 minutes, and then stir in the remaining lime juice. The sauce can be made a couple of hours ahead. Warm it before proceeding.

Drain the fish fillets, and arrange them on top of the sauce in the skillet, pushing each into the sauce just a bit. Immediately before serving them, poach the fillets, covered, until they are just cooked through and flaky, about 5 to 7 minutes. Don't overcook the fish.

Serve the fish immediately, giving each guest a fillet surrounded by a small sea of the sauce. Garnish the fish with lime wedges, if you like.

Ceviche

The lime juice in ceviche chemically "cooks" the seafood, magically changing its character in a matter of minutes. In this version, the scallops provide a nice contrast in texture and flavor to the Gulf fish. Truly fresh seafood is critical to the right taste.

¾ POUND RED SNAPPER, GROUPER, OR OTHER FIRM-FLESHED WHITE FISH, SLICED IN BITE-SIZE PIECES

¼ POUND SCALLOPS (SMALL BAY SCALLOPS CAN BE USED AS IS; LARGER SEA SCALLOPS SHOULD BE HALVED)

⅓ CUP FRESH LIME JUICE

2 TABLESPOONS FRESH ORANGE JUICE

1 AVOCADO, PEELED, SEEDED, AND CUBED

1 TOMATO, PREFERABLY ROMA OR ANOTHER ITALIAN PLUM VARIETY, CHOPPED

¼ CUP FINELY DICED RED BELL PEPPER

3 TABLESPOONS FINELY DICED ONION

1 PICKLED JALAPEÑO, MINCED

1 TABLESPOON JALAPEÑO PICKLING LIQUID

1 FRESH SERRANO OR ½ FRESH JALAPEÑO, SLICED IN VERY THIN RINGS, OPTIONAL

1 TO 2 TABLESPOONS EXTRA-VIRGIN OLIVE OIL

1 TABLESPOON CHOPPED CILANTRO

¼ TEASPOON SALT

DICED YELLOW TOMATO OR YELLOW BELL PEPPER, OPTIONAL, FOR MORE COLOR

LIME WEDGES, FOR GARNISH

Makes 4 appetizer portions

 In a nonreactive bowl, marinate the fish and scallops in the lime and orange juices for 30 to 45 minutes. Drain the liquid from the bowl, and gently mix in all the remaining ingredients except the lime wedges. Refrigerate the ceviche 30 to 45 minutes.

Spoon the ceviche into parfait glasses, margarita glasses, or glass bowls to show off its colors. Garnish with the lime wedges, and serve.

"I DISCOVERED CEVICHE ONE BLISTERING HOT DAY WHILE DRINKING BEER UNDER A *PALAPA* NEAR ZIHUATANEJO'S GRUBBY DOWNTOWN BEACH. AFTER EVERY FOURTH OR FIFTH CARTA BLANCA I DRANK, THE OLD LADY WHO RAN THE PLACE SERVED A BOWL OF CHOPPED FISH, ONIONS, AND PEPPERS. I'M NOT WILD ABOUT FISH, BUT THIS DIDN'T TASTE FISHY. IT TASTED REFRESHING AND MADE ME BELIEVE I WAS ON THE ROAD TO LONG LIFE AND PROSPERITY. I'D EATEN SEVERAL BOWLS BEFORE I REALIZED THE FISH WAS RAW."—GARY CARTWRIGHT, "I AM THE GREATEST COOK IN THE WORLD," *TEXAS MONTHLY*, FEBRUARY 1983

Flounder Fillets with Smoked Catfish Stuffing

One early Texas cookbook called for stuffing fish with Irish potatoes. You'll like this approach much better.

1¾ TO 2 POUNDS FLOUNDER OR SOLE FILLETS

STUFFING
6 TO 8 OUNCES SMOKED CATFISH
½ CUP DRY BREAD CRUMBS
¼ CUP CHOPPED CELERY
¼ CUP CHOPPED ONION
1 EGG WHITE, LIGHTLY BEATEN
¼ TEASPOON PAPRIKA
1 TO 2 TABLESPOONS MILK

2 TABLESPOONS UNSALTED BUTTER
JUICE OF ½ LEMON
PAPRIKA AND FRESH-GROUND BLACK PEPPER
  TO TASTE
LEMON WEDGES, OPTIONAL, FOR GARNISH

Serves 4

Preheat the oven to 350° F. Butter a medium baking dish. Cut the flounder into eight pieces of equal size, about 3 to 4 ounces each, and set it aside.

Remove the catfish from the bones (easily accomplished), if necessary, and place the fish sections in the bowl of a food processor. Add the rest of the stuffing ingredients except the milk, and process them together briefly. The stuffing should be thoroughly blended together but not puréed to oblivion. Add as much of the milk as is needed to moisten the mixture without making it soupy.

Spoon equal portions of the stuffing onto half of the fillets. Top each "stuffed" fillet with one of the remaining fillets. Place the fish in the baking dish, dot it with the butter, and sprinkle it with the lemon juice, paprika, and pepper. Bake for 20 minutes, until the flounder is opaque and flaky.

Serve the stuffed fillets with lemon wedges, if you like.

> YOU CAN FIND SMOKED CATFISH IN MANY SUPERMARKETS, BUT OFTEN YOU CAN GET A BETTER VERSION BY MAIL (SEE "MAIL-ORDER SOURCES," PAGE 556).

Fried Catfish

This is the classic style of preparation, spiced up a bit, for Texas's favorite freshwater fish. We use peanut oil for the frying, after years of experimenting with other options.

In Texas, catfish almost always appears whole or in fillets averaging about ½ pound each. Cut your fillets into smaller pieces if you prefer.

2 POUNDS CATFISH FILLETS

2 CUPS BUTTERMILK

2 TO 3 TEASPOONS TABASCO OR OTHER HOT
   PEPPER SAUCE

1 GARLIC CLOVE, MINCED

1½ CUPS MEDIUM-GRIND CORNMEAL, PREFER-
   ABLY STONE-GROUND

½ CUP EXTRA-FINE-GRIND CORNMEAL,
   PREFERABLY STONE-GROUND, OR
   ALL-PURPOSE FLOUR

2 TEASPOONS PAPRIKA

2 TEASPOONS SALT

1 TEASPOON FRESH-GROUND BLACK PEPPER

CAYENNE TO TASTE

PEANUT OIL FOR PAN FRYING

LEMON WEDGES, PINK TARTAR SAUCE (PAGE
   281), OR TABASCO OR OTHER HOT PEPPER
   SAUCE, FOR GARNISH

Serves 4 to 6

✦ In a shallow nonreactive dish, soak the catfish fillets in the buttermilk, Tabasco, and garlic. Refrigerate the fillets for at least 1 hour and up to several hours.

Combine the cornmeals, paprika, salt, pepper, and cayenne, and spread the mixture on a plate or in a shallow bowl.

Pour enough oil into a cast-iron skillet to reach halfway up your fillets. Heat the oil to 350° F. If the oil begins to smoke before reaching the proper temperature, it should not be

In Uncertain, Texas, the residents pride themselves on having a lot of uncertainties, but not when it comes to their catfish. Home to some of the best catfish in the state, the small town on Caddo Lake got its name because boats have to make their way through a maze of cypress trees in the water to find the landing.

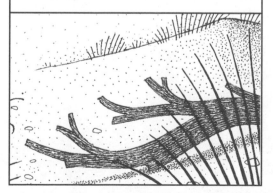

used for this recipe. Always start with fresh oil.

While the oil is heating, drain the fillets, and lay them in the cornmeal mixture one at a time, coating both sides well. Gently place a few pieces of fish in the skillet, frying them in batches if necessary. Fry the fillets a total of about 5 minutes per half-inch of thickness, turning them once. Adjust the heat as necessary to get a deep golden brown crust and a flaky interior.

Drain the fillets. Transfer the fish to a warm platter. (Don't put them in the oven.) Serve the fish immediately, with the lemon wedges, Pink Tartar Sauce, or Tabasco. Pepper 'Puppies (page 284) add another level of crunch to the plate.

Variation: For catfish nuggets with Creole mustard sauce, cut the fillets into 1-inch nuggets, and prepare and fry them as above, reducing the cooking time accordingly. Serve with Rémoulade Sauce (page 259).

Texans tend to think of jalapeños as a Lone Star treasure, but they came originally from Jalapa (or Xalapa), the capital of the Mexican state of Veracruz. Cooks in that area used jalapeños in traditional dishes long before Texans did.

Pink Tartar Sauce

The traditional accompaniment to all fried fish, tartar sauce benefits from a touch of tomato.

¾ CUP MAYONNAISE

3 TABLESPOONS SWEET PICKLE RELISH
(HELLISH SWEET RELISH, PAGE 409, GIVES
IT A GOOD KICK)

1 TABLESPOON PLUS 1 TEASPOON CAPERS

1 TABLESPOON PREPARED CREOLE MUSTARD

1 TABLESPOON KETCHUP

JUICE OF ½ LEMON

SALT AND CAYENNE TO TASTE

Makes about 1¼ cups

In a small bowl, combine the mayonnaise, relish, capers, mustard, ketchup, and half the lemon juice. Taste the mixture, and add a little more lemon juice, if needed, and salt and cayenne. Refrigerate the sauce at least 30 minutes. It keeps for several days.

FRIED CATFISH AND PINK TARTAR SAUCE MAKE A SUPER SANDWICH. BEFORE FRYING THE FISH, FRY TWO SLICES OF BACON FOR EACH DINER, AND PREPARE THE TARTAR SAUCE. HAVE SOME GOOD SOFT ROLLS, TOMATO SLICES, AND LETTUCE ON HAND. CUT THE CATFISH FILLETS INTO SECTIONS OF ABOUT 4 OUNCES EACH, AND PREPARE AND FRY THEM AS USUAL. COMBINE THE FRIED FISH ON THE ROLLS WITH THE BACON, TOMATO, LETTUCE, AND A GENEROUS DOLLOP OF THE TARTAR SAUCE.

Catfish Fillets
with Pecan-Butter Sauce

Frying is such a common way to fix catfish, a Texan could grow up thinking the fish are born with a cornmeal crust. This is a fast and flavorful alternative preparation, best with the thinnest fillets you can find.

1½ POUNDS CATFISH FILLETS, CUT INTO FOUR
    PIECES ABOUT 6 OUNCES EACH
CAJUN OR CREOLE SEASONING
1 TABLESPOON PLUS 1 TEASPOON ALL-PURPOSE
    FLOUR
1 TABLESPOON OIL, PREFERABLY CANOLA OR
    CORN
1 TABLESPOON UNSALTED BUTTER
½ CUP SEAFOOD STOCK OR BOTTLED CLAM
    JUICE
JUICE OF 1 LEMON
2 TEASPOONS WORCESTERSHIRE SAUCE
SALT TO TASTE, OPTIONAL
¼ CUP CHOPPED PECANS, TOASTED
2 TABLESPOONS MINCED PARSLEY

Serves 4

Rub the catfish fillet pieces with as much Cajun or Creole seasoning as you wish. Lightly dust each piece of fish with the flour.

Warm the oil and butter together over medium-low heat. Add the fish pieces, and cook them 3 minutes on each side. Thin fillets (about ⅛ inch) will cook completely in 6 minutes and begin to flake; fat fish will be a little underdone. Both states are acceptable at this stage. Pour in the stock, lemon juice, and Worcestershire sauce.

Remove the fillets that are cooked through as soon as they are coated with the sauce. Fillets that require longer cooking can simmer in the sauce another minute or two.

Transfer the fillets to individual plates or a platter. Stir the salt (if needed), pecans, and parsley into the sauce, and spoon equal portions over each piece of fish. Serve the fish immediately.

Batter-Dipped Fried Fish

Along with barbecues and crawfish boils, fish fries are a popular way to raise money in Texas for churches, schools, and volunteer fire departments. These two batters are perfect for these occasions or for your own smaller parties. The first makes a light crunchy coating, rather like tempura. The second is thicker and flakier. Both work well with any white fish.

LIGHT BATTER

1 CUP ALL-PURPOSE FLOUR
3 TABLESPOONS PAPRIKA
2 TEASPOONS SALT
12 OUNCES BEER
2 TEASPOONS PREPARED YELLOW MUSTARD

FLAKY BATTER

1 CUP ALL-PURPOSE FLOUR
1 TEASPOON BAKING POWDER
1 TEASPOON SALT
½ TEASPOON SUGAR
⅛ TEASPOON NUTMEG
8 OUNCES BEER
1 EGG, LIGHTLY BEATEN

2 POUNDS MILD-FLAVORED FISH FILLETS, CUT
   IN EQUAL PIECES OF SEVERAL OUNCES EACH
PEANUT OIL FOR DEEP FRYING
PINK TARTAR SAUCE (PAGE 281)
PEPPER 'PUPPIES (PAGE 284)
TABASCO OR OTHER HOT PEPPER SAUCE
LEMON WEDGES

Serves 4 to 6

 For either batter, stir together the dry ingredients, and then mix in the liquid ingredients. Have the fish ready to dip into the batter before you heat the oil.

Fill a large, heavy pan with at least 4 inches of oil. Don't fill the pan more than half full. Heat the oil to 350° F. If the oil begins to smoke before reaching the proper temperature, it cannot be used for this recipe. Always start with fresh oil.

Dip the fish in the batter a few pieces at a time, taking care to avoid overcrowding the pieces. Fry the fish until it is golden brown, 3 to 4 minutes, and drain it. Repeat the process until all the fish is fried.

Serve the fish with the Pink Tartar Sauce, Pepper 'Puppies, Tabasco, and plenty of lemon wedges. The fish is good English-style, too, with malt vinegar.

> Catfish raised or sold commercially usually average 1 to 3 pounds—puny, by some standards. In 1965, Mrs. Joe Cockrell of Austin reeled a 36.5-pound channel cat out of the Pedernales River, setting the state record.

Pepper 'Puppies

These slightly spicy hushpuppies can be fried right along with the batter-dipped fish in the preceding recipe, and they'll go equally well with any other fried fish.

¾ CUP MEDIUM-GRIND CORNMEAL, PREFERABLY
  STONE-GROUND
⅓ CUP FLOUR, PREFERABLY A SOFT-WHEAT
  FLOUR LIKE WHITE LILY
½ TEASPOON BAKING POWDER
¼ TEASPOON BAKING SODA
¼ TEASPOON SALT
½ CUP BUTTERMILK
1 EGG, LIGHTLY BEATEN
3 TABLESPOONS MINCED ONION
1 TEASPOON COARSE-GROUND BLACK PEPPER
1 GARLIC CLOVE, MINCED
PEANUT OIL FOR DEEP FRYING

Serves 4 to 6

In a medium bowl, stir together the cornmeal, flour, baking powder, baking soda, and salt. Mix in the buttermilk, egg, onion, black pepper, and garlic, combining the ingredients thoroughly.

Pour enough oil into a skillet or other pan to measure at least 1½ inches in depth. Heat the oil to 350° F. Gently spoon in the hushpuppy batter a tablespoonful at a time. Try a test 'puppy first. It should quickly puff up and, when done, be deep golden brown on the outside. Cut into it to make sure it is cooked throughout. Adjust the heat if necessary. Then fry the rest of the 'puppies.

Drain the hushpuppies, and serve them hot with fried fish.

Salmon Patties

Away from the Gulf, the most common fish in Texas until recent decades was salmon—canned salmon. All the early cookbooks contain recipes for it, particularly patties or croquettes, which continue to be popular. We start these from fresh salmon, adding another dimension to the dish.

2 EGG WHITES, LIGHTLY BEATEN

2 TABLESPOONS MINCED PARSLEY

2 TABLESPOONS MINCED ONION

1 TABLESPOON PREPARED CREOLE MUSTARD

1 TABLESPOON WHITE WINE WORCESTER-
   SHIRE SAUCE OR 1½ TEASPOONS REGULAR
   WORCESTERSHIRE SAUCE

1 TABLESPOON MAYONNAISE

¼ TEASPOON SALT

SCANT ¼ TEASPOON WHITE PEPPER

2 CUPS COOKED, FLAKED SALMON

½ CUP SALTINE CRACKER CRUMBS

¼ CUP MINCED RED OR GREEN BELL PEPPER,
   OR A MIXTURE OF BOTH

ADDITIONAL SALTINE CRACKER CRUMBS,
   OPTIONAL

3 TABLESPOONS OIL, PREFERABLY CANOLA OR
   CORN

1 TABLESPOON UNSALTED BUTTER

Serves 4

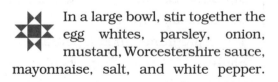 In a large bowl, stir together the egg whites, parsley, onion, mustard, Worcestershire sauce, mayonnaise, salt, and white pepper.

Gently mix in the salmon, cracker crumbs, and bell pepper. Form the mixture into individual patties. This amount makes about twelve 2-inch patties. If you like a crunchy exterior, coat the patties in additional cracker crumbs.

Heat the oil and butter together in a skillet, and fry the patties in batches until they are golden brown on both sides. Drain the patties, and serve them immediately.

Baked Bass
with Spicy Citrus Sauce

This recipe works equally well with black bass fresh from the lake and store-bought striped or white bass. A version in Nick Bennack's **Tastes of Deep South Texas** *provided our initial inspiration.*

MARINADE

¼ CUP CORN OIL, PREFERABLY UNREFINED
2 TABLESPOONS FRESH LIME JUICE
2 GARLIC CLOVES, MINCED
¼ TEASPOON SALT
¼ TEASPOON FRESH-GROUND BLACK PEPPER

4 6-OUNCE BASS FILLETS

SAUCE

4 TABLESPOONS CORN OIL, PREFERABLY
  UNREFINED
4 GREEN ONIONS, SLICED
2 GARLIC CLOVES, MINCED
2 FRESH JALAPEÑOS, MINCED
½ MEDIUM BELL PEPPER, PREFERABLY RED, DICED
½ CUP FRESH ORANGE JUICE
1 TABLESPOON ORANGE ZEST, MINCED
2 TABLESPOONS SLICED PIMIENTO-STUFFED
  GREEN OLIVES

Serves 4

Preheat the oven to 400° F.

Combine the marinade ingredients. About 30 minutes before you intend to bake the fish, pour the marinade over the bass fillets in a shallow nonreactive dish.

While the fish marinates, make the sauce: Heat the corn oil in a medium skillet, and add the green onions, garlic, jalapeños, and bell pepper. Sauté the vegetables a few minutes until they have softened, and add the orange juice and zest. Simmer the sauce over medium heat until the orange juice reduces to a syrupy consistency. Add the olives, and heat through. Reserve the sauce, keeping it warm while you prepare the fish.

Grease a shallow baking dish. Drain the fish gently, and transfer it to the baking dish. Bake it until it is cooked through, about 4 to 5 minutes per ½-inch of thickness. Watch it carefully to avoid overcooking it.

Transfer the fish to a serving plate, and top the fillets with the sauce. Serve the fish hot.

Big bass, known in fishing lingo as "lunkers," are the stars of a Texas program called Operation Share A Lone Star Lunker. Hoping to breed larger fish, the state Parks and Wildlife staff encourages fishermen to free bass over 13 pounds.

SUPPER
AND SIDE DISHES

HEARTY
SALADS
AND BREADS

*I*f the good Lord wanted man to eat grass, He'd a made him into a cow.

Anonymous cowboy (quoted by Ramon Adams in *Come an' Get It*)

$\mathcal{T}$exans have always loved their "doughgods," or biscuits, and other kinds of bread, but green salads have had more trouble getting respect than a cowboy in a bowler hat. As recently as 1949 Arthur and Bobbie Coleman, in their excellent *The Texas Cookbook*, called their salad chapter "Petticoat Doings."

Tastes have changed a good deal since then, but even folks reluctant about lettuce will enjoy many of these dishes. They are robust in a Texas style and as versatile as a campaigning politician. Served individually, many make fine starters or accompaniments at main meals. Served together in a combination of a salad and bread, they make a hearty supper. Either way they'll earn your esteem.

In the same year the Colemans published *The Texas Cookbook*, Jane Trahey brought out *A Taste of Texas* on behalf of Neiman Marcus. Contrary to the Colemans, she claimed Texans loved salads. What Trahey meant, it turns out from her recipes, were dishes like applesauce, or avocado filled with cranberry sherbet.

Creamy Peanut Coleslaw

Slaw has always been the most popular type of green salad in Texas. In the past, local cookbooks sometimes treated it separately from other salads, devoting whole chapters just to slaws.

1 CUP MAYONNAISE
¼ CUP PLUS 2 TABLESPOONS CIDER VINEGAR
¼ CUP PLUS 2 TABLESPOONS SUGAR
2 TABLESPOONS MILK
1 GARLIC CLOVE, MINCED
½ TEASPOON BEAU MONDE SEASONING (FROM
    SPICE ISLANDS) OR CELERY SALT
1 MEDIUM CABBAGE HEAD, SHREDDED
2 TO 3 CARROTS, SHREDDED
2 TABLESPOONS MINCED ONION
¾ CUP CHOPPED ROASTED SALTED PEANUTS
SALT TO TASTE

Serves 6

In a lidded jar, shake together the mayonnaise, vinegar, sugar, milk, garlic, and Beau Monde or celery salt until they are well blended.

Place the cabbage, carrots, and onion in a large bowl. Pour the dressing over the vegetables and toss them together.

Chill the coleslaw at least 1 hour. Just before serving, stir the peanuts into the slaw. Taste, and add salt as desired. The slaw keeps well for several days.

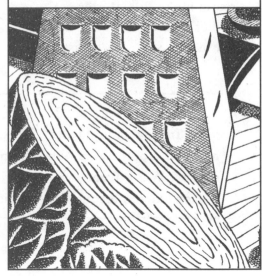

Until recent decades green was the last color you would find in any Texas salad except slaw. Potatoes were the most common ingredient, followed by chicken, eggs, seafood, fruit, and gelatin.

Sweet-Sour Kraut Salad

This tangy German dish is served in central Texas almost as frequently as coleslaw.

1 POUND SAUERKRAUT, PREFERABLY NOT A
  CANNED VARIETY
⅔ CUP SUGAR
⅓ CUP CIDER VINEGAR
⅓ CUP MINCED SWEET ONION (SUCH AS TEXAS
  1015, VIDALIA, OR WALLA WALLA) OR ¼ CUP
  REGULAR ONION
2 CARROTS, SHREDDED FINE
2 CELERY RIBS, CHOPPED
½ SMALL GREEN BELL PEPPER, CHOPPED
2 TABLESPOONS CHOPPED PIMIENTO
2 TABLESPOONS OIL, PREFERABLY CANOLA OR
  CORN
1 TABLESPOON MUSTARD SEEDS
DASH OF GROUND CLOVES

Serves 4 to 6

 Drain, rinse, and drain again the sauerkraut. Place it in a large bowl.

Heat the sugar and vinegar together until the sugar has dissolved. Pour it over the kraut.

Add the remaining ingredients and toss well. Refrigerate the salad, covered, at least 1 hour. The salad keeps well for several days and can be made ahead easily.

The source of so many things cantankerous, Austin was probably the place where green salads first took root in Texas. In the decade after World War II a couple of young, adventuresome chefs began putting salads on the tables of two of the capital's top restaurants. Mary Faulk Koock provided the inspiration at Green Pastures, and Helen Corbitt led the way at the Driskill Hotel.

Not-Quite-Granny's
Wilted Lettuce

When lettuce first appeared on Texas farm tables, it was usually in a "wilted" form. Early recipes called for a heap of hot bacon grease, but you can get plenty of that flavor with a lot less saturated fat.

10 TO 12 CUPS TORN LEAF LETTUCE

4 TO 6 RADISHES, SLICED THIN

2 TABLESPOONS EXTRA-VIRGIN OLIVE OIL

1 TABLESPOON BACON DRIPPINGS

¼ TO ½ CUP CHOPPED SWEET ONION (TEXAS 1015, VIDALIA, WALLA WALLA, OR MAUI) OR GREEN ONIONS

1 GARLIC CLOVE, MINCED

1 TEASPOON SUGAR

¼ TEASPOON SALT

1 TABLESPOON CIDER VINEGAR, PREFERABLY UNREFINED

Serves 4 to 6

Place the lettuce in a large bowl. Add the radishes.

In a skillet, warm the olive oil and bacon drippings together over medium heat. Stir in the onion and garlic, and cook them until they are limp. Sprinkle in the sugar and salt, and stir until they are dissolved. Remove the skillet from the heat and add the vinegar.

Pour the warm dressing over the greens and mix well, until the lettuce is well wilted. Like cooked spinach, it will reduce substantially in volume.

Serve the salad warm or at room temperature.

> EAST TEXAS PIONEERS PICKED AND ATE WILD GREENS, PARTICULARLY POKE, BUT THEY DIDN'T MUNCH THEM RAW. INSTEAD THEY BOILED THE GREENS WITH SALT PORK, BOTH TO TENDERIZE THEM AND TO ADD FLAVOR. WILTED SALADS WERE A NATURAL EVOLUTION, PROBABLY DONE FIRST WITH POKE, A TASTY, LEAFY WEED WITH POISONOUS BERRIES AND ROOTS.

Special Dressings for Green Salads

Though wilted lettuce salads are still popular in the state, most Texans today favor crisp, cool greens with assertive dressings. Any of the following trio of toppings adds Lone Star flavor to crunchy lettuces such as romaine and iceberg, and both vinaigrettes also pair well with the more tender leaf lettuces.

Ranch Dressing

Ranch dressings now are ubiquitous on grocery-store shelves because the original homemade version was so good. It still is, and it doesn't take long to make. In Texas it's served on everything from lettuce to baked potatoes.

¾ CUP MAYONNAISE
½ CUP BUTTERMILK
1 TABLESPOON MINCED PARSLEY
2 TEASPOONS MINCED ONION
1 TO 2 GARLIC CLOVES, MINCED
½ TEASPOON COARSE-GROUND BLACK PEPPER
¼ TEASPOON SALT
SPLASH OF WHITE VINEGAR, OPTIONAL

Makes approximately 1½ cups

Combine all the ingredients in a large lidded jar and shake them well. Chill at least 30 minutes. The dressing keeps, refrigerated, at least 5 days.

Variation: For jalapeño ranch dressing, add one or two minced fresh or pickled pods.

Mint Vinaigrette

Vinaigrettes are recent arrivals in Texas, but this one thrives on mint, an old Lone Star favorite.

6 TABLESPOONS EXTRA-VIRGIN OLIVE OIL
3 TABLESPOONS MINCED FRESH MINT
2 TABLESPOONS CIDER VINEGAR, PREFERABLY
   UNREFINED
1 GARLIC CLOVE, MINCED
½ TEASPOON SALT

Makes approximately ⅔ cup

Combine all the ingredients in a lidded jar and shake them well. For the best flavor, refrigerate the dressing at least 30 minutes. The dressing keeps well for several days.

Variation: To make cilantro vinaigrette, replace the mint with cilantro. It's especially good over avocados or paired with Southwestern spices.

Salads seem today like a natural way to control weight, but people had other ideas in the past. In the 1920s Ida Chitwood, a Texas food chemist and cookbook author, advocated an elaborate diet fortified with laxatives to reduce your stomach to "little boy size," so you would eat less in the future. She also recommended exercise, because it brought body oils to the surface, where they could be washed off, as a way of shedding pounds.

Molasses and Bacon Vinaigrette

This robust vinaigrette mimics the smoky sweetness of wilted lettuce salads.

4 OUNCES SLAB BACON, CHOPPED

1 GARLIC CLOVE, MINCED

¼ CUP EXTRA-VIRGIN OLIVE OIL

1 TABLESPOON PLUS 2 TEASPOONS UNSUL-
PHURED DARK MOLASSES

1 GREEN ONION, SLICED

DASH OF TABASCO OR OTHER HOT PEPPER
SAUCE

SALT AND FRESH-GROUND BLACK PEPPER TO
TASTE

2 TO 4 TABLESPOONS RED WINE VINEGAR

Makes approximately ⅔ cup

In a small skillet, fry the bacon over medium heat until it is browned and crisp. With a slotted spoon, remove the bacon, drain it, and reserve it. Stir in the garlic and sauté it for a quick minute.

Reduce the heat to low and mix in the oil, molasses, green onion, Tabasco, salt, pepper, and 2 tablespoons of the vinegar. Taste, and add more vinegar if you prefer.

Serve the dressing warm. (It can be refrigerated and reheated.) Sprinkle the reserved bacon over the salad, if you like.

WHEN TEXANS FINALLY BEGAN CONSUMING GREEN SALADS IN QUANTITY, INVARIABLY THE MAIN INGREDIENT WAS ICEBERG LETTUCE, ABOUT THE ONLY VARIETY SOLD IN GROCERY STORES UNTIL RECENTLY. IT LACKED THE EARTHY FLAVOR OF MOST GREENS, BUT IT PROVIDED THE PERFECT CRISP PLATFORM FOR THE STOUT DRESSINGS TEXANS CAME TO LOVE.

Crunchy Carrot-Raisin Salad

This salad is a lively twist on the usual creamy combinations of carrots and raisins.

4 CARROTS, SLICED INTO THIN ROUNDS
¾ CUP RAISINS
½ MEDIUM GREEN BELL PEPPER, DICED FINE
2 TABLESPOONS MINCED ONION
6 TABLESPOONS PEANUT OIL
2 TO 3 TABLESPOONS CIDER VINEGAR
2 TEASPOONS SUGAR
½ TEASPOON SALT PLUS MORE TO TASTE

Serves 4 to 6

 In a medium bowl, combine the carrots, raisins, bell pepper, and onion.

In a lidded jar, mix together the oil, vinegar, sugar, and ½ teaspoon salt. Pour the dressing over the carrot mixture and toss well to coat. Refrigerate the salad at least 2 hours, preferably overnight.

Taste the salad, and add salt if you like. The salad keeps well for several days.

Helen Corbitt was such an influence on Texas cooks a few decades ago that she once created a run on sour cream in Houston. Demand for the product skyrocketed overnight after Corbitt taught a cooking class that featured a horseradish–sour cream dressing.

Hill Country Broccoli Salad

We got the idea for this dish—a kind of broccoli slaw—from Mike Hughes's Broken Arrow Ranch Cookbook.

3 CUPS (ABOUT 1½ POUNDS) CHOPPED FRESH BROCCOLI
⅓ TO ½ CUP SLICED PIMIENTO-STUFFED GREEN OLIVES
⅓ CUP SLICED GREEN ONIONS
¼ CUP MAYONNAISE
1 TEASPOON FRESH LEMON JUICE
SALT AND FRESH-GROUND BLACK PEPPER TO TASTE

Serves 4

In a large bowl, toss together all the ingredients, including a generous grind of black pepper. Refrigerate the salad, covered, for a couple of hours. Serve the salad chilled. The salad keeps for 2 days.

Gail Borden, Jr., the nineteenth-century Texan who created the process for condensing milk, also invented the dehydrated beef biscuit. Meant to be portable chow for armies, it was a powder made from beef extract and flour. You added water, heated the mixture, and had a hefty meal. From all reports Borden should have stuck with milk.

Roasted Corn Salad

Much of the flavor in this salad comes from roasting the corn on a charcoal grill, a step definitely worth the extra effort. Remove the silks, but not the husks, from the ears of corn and soak the ears in water for a few minutes before grilling. Lay the ears over medium-hot coals and a few presoaked mesquite chips, and cook them, covered, for about 30 minutes, turning them occasionally.

5 EARS CORN ON THE COB, ROASTED
1 TO 2 SMALL TOMATOES, CHOPPED
1 CELERY RIB, DICED FINE
2 TABLESPOONS MINCED CILANTRO
2 TABLESPOONS MINCED SWEET ONION (SUCH
   AS TEXAS 1015, VIDALIA, OR WALLA WALLA)
   OR SLICED GREEN ONIONS
3 TABLESPOONS EXTRA-VIRGIN OLIVE OIL
1 TABLESPOON CIDER VINEGAR
1 CANNED CHIPOTLE CHILE, MINCED
1 TO 2 TEASPOONS ADOBO SAUCE FROM
   CANNED CHIPOTLE CHILES
2 TEASPOONS FRESH LIME JUICE
¼ TEASPOON SALT
LETTUCE LEAVES, FOR GARNISH

Serves 6

Remove the kernels from the ears of corn, slicing deeply enough to cut through the milky bottom portion of the kernels, but avoiding the cob.

Place the corn in a medium bowl, and mix in the tomatoes, celery, cilantro, and onion. In a small lidded jar, shake together the remaining ingredients, and pour them over the corn. Serve the salad at room temperature or chilled, on the lettuce leaves.

Corn was the first major crop cultivated in Texas and the most important staple during the pioneer period. Spanish and Mexican settlers made it into tortillas and Anglos made it into cornbread, the staff of life in both cases. In a good year, some said, a farmer could grow corn so tall and thick, it took two experienced woodcutters a full day to chop down one stalk. The only other way to harvest it, they claimed, was to shoot the ears off the stalks with a hunting rifle.

Texas Three-Bean Salad

This variation on a common dish takes advantage of a German-style sweet-sour dressing that is similar to some dressings used in potato salads. When you're in a hurry, substitute canned kidney and garbanzo beans, but stick with fresh green beans.

2 CUPS COOKED KIDNEY BEANS

2 CUPS COOKED GARBANZO BEANS

2 CUPS COOKED GREEN BEANS OR YELLOW WAX BEANS, OR A COMBINATION OF THE TWO

2 TABLESPOONS OIL, PREFERABLY CANOLA OR CORN

2 SLICES SLAB BACON, CHOPPED

1 MEDIUM ONION, CHOPPED

2 GARLIC CLOVES, MINCED

1 TABLESPOON ALL-PURPOSE FLOUR

¾ CUP PLUS 1 TABLESPOON CIDER VINEGAR

¾ CUP UNSALTED CHICKEN STOCK

¼ CUP SUGAR

2 TEASPOONS PREPARED YELLOW MUSTARD

1 TEASPOON PAPRIKA

2 CELERY RIBS, CHOPPED

½ MEDIUM GREEN BELL PEPPER, CHOPPED

¼ CUP MINCED PARSLEY

SALT AND FRESH-GROUND BLACK PEPPER TO TASTE

Serves 6 to 8

Combine the beans in a large bowl.

Warm the oil in a saucepan over medium heat. Add the bacon and fry it until it is brown and crisp. With a slotted spoon, remove the bacon from the pan, drain it, and reserve it. To the bacon drippings and oil, add the onion and garlic, and cook them over medium heat until they are softened. Mix in the flour. Pour in the vinegar and stock, stirring, and add the sugar, mustard, and paprika. Simmer the dressing for about 10 minutes total, adding the celery and bell pepper in the last couple of minutes. They should be softened slightly, but retain some crunch. Remove the saucepan from the heat, and stir in the parsley. Taste, and add salt and pepper as you wish. Stir the dressing into the beans.

Chill the salad, covered, for at least 2 hours. Stir in the reserved bacon before serving. The salad keeps for several days.

Calico Black Runner Bean Salad

This one's dedicated to Bill's mom, Lois Gilder, who lives in Dallas. A few years ago she discovered how much she likes fresh vegetable combinations with vinaigrette dressings.

1 POUND DRIED BLACK RUNNER BEANS,
   SCARLET RUNNER BEANS, OR LIMA BEANS
1 TEASPOON SALT
1 BAY LEAF
KERNELS CUT FROM 1 EAR OF ROASTED OR
   BOILED CORN
1 MEDIUM TOMATO, CHOPPED
1 SMALL ONION, DICED
1 MEDIUM BELL PEPPER (RED, GREEN, OR
   YELLOW, OR A MIX OF COLORS), DICED
2 TABLESPOONS CHOPPED CILANTRO
1 TEASPOON PAPRIKA
MINT VINAIGRETTE (PAGE 296)

Serves 6

Presoak the beans: In a large saucepan, cover the beans with several inches of water. Bring the pot of beans to a boil, and reduce the heat to a simmer. Add the salt and bay leaf to the beans after the beans have begun to soften. Plan on a total cooking time of at least 2 hours. Add more hot water to the beans as needed. Stir gently to avoid gouging the sleek black exteriors of the beans. When the beans are soft but have not yet begun to break down, drain and rinse them.

Place the beans in a large bowl, add the remaining ingredients, and toss lightly. Refrigerate the salad for at least 1 hour, preferably several hours.

Dora's Macaroni Salad

Macaroni salads with cheese and peas are popular all over Texas, from the Gulf waters to Sweetwater. This version came to us via Dorothy Hicks, whose stepmother Dora Thompson lived much of her life in Amarillo. Like all good natural cooks, Dora would toss in approximate amounts of ingredients until the salad tasted "right"—a little sweet, a little savory, and bound by just enough mayonnaise to make it moist. Today Dorothy uses a smaller amount of cheese and substitutes nonfat yogurt for at least half of the mayo. The salad still tastes great.

1 POUND MACARONI, PREFERABLY SMALL
   ELBOWS OR SHELLS, COOKED AND DRAINED
6 TO 8 OUNCES MILD OR MEDIUM CHEDDAR
   CHEESE, CUT IN SMALL CUBES
1½ CUPS BABY PEAS, FRESH OR FROZEN
1 MEDIUM GREEN BELL PEPPER, CHOPPED
1 MEDIUM ONION, CHOPPED
¾ CUP SWEET PICKLE RELISH
½ CUP MAYONNAISE
¼ CUP PIMIENTOS, CHOPPED
WHITE PEPPER TO TASTE

Serves 6 to 8 generously

In a large bowl, mix together all the ingredients. Refrigerate the salad, covered, for at least 1 hour to develop the flavors. The salad keeps well for several days.

Variation: For additional flavor in this salad, add a clove or two of garlic, or some chopped green olives.

Jalapeño Rice Salad

*A winning recipe from the Laredo Jalapeño Festival inspired this salad.
It combines several Texas favorites—jalapeños, pimientos (alone and in
green olives), and marinated artichoke hearts.*

2 CUPS COOKED RICE
1 6-OUNCE JAR MARINATED ARTICHOKE
   HEARTS, SLICED THIN, WITH MARINADE
⅓ CUP MAYONNAISE
2 CELERY RIBS, CHOPPED FINE
3 TABLESPOONS SLICED PIMIENTO-STUFFED
   GREEN OLIVES
2 TO 3 TABLESPOONS MINCED PICKLED
   JALAPEÑOS
2 TABLESPOONS CHOPPED PIMIENTOS
2 TABLESPOONS MINCED PARSLEY
3 GREEN ONIONS, SLICED
PINCH OF SUGAR
LETTUCE LEAVES, OPTIONAL, FOR GARNISH

Serves 6

In a medium bowl, mix the rice with the other ingredients, except the lettuce. Cover the salad and chill it for at least 30 minutes. Serve the salad cold, on top of the lettuce leaves if you like.

The Jalapeño Festival is part of Laredo's ten-day celebration of George Washington's birthday, the largest event in the nation in honor of the first president. First celebrated in 1898, the fiesta also includes a Mexican-style rodeo and a waiters' race, in which competitors must carry a tray with a glass of champagne and an open bottle. It's all great fun, but ol' George may have had different ideas about his legacy.

Grapefruit-Avocado Salad with Poppyseed Dressing

Jeremiah Tower, San Francisco superchef, once mused ruefully that his epitaph will likely read, "He invented black bean cake." Texas trailblazer Helen Corbitt is equally identified with this salad, a delightful combination of flavors.

3 GRAPEFRUIT, PREFERABLY A TEXAS RUBY-
   RED VARIETY, PEELED AND SECTIONED
3 RIPE HASS AVOCADOS, SLICED
LETTUCE LEAVES OR SHREDDED RED CABBAGE,
   FOR GARNISH
POPPYSEED DRESSING (PAGE 306)

Serves 6

Just before mealtime, arrange the grapefruit sections and avocado slices decoratively on the lettuce. Drizzle some poppyseed dressing over the salad and serve more on the side.

TECHNIQUE TIP

For the most attractive presentation of the grapefruit, start with whole fruits. Peel each, removing the bitter white pith. Working with a sharp, flexible knife, slice into each fruit along both sides of its membranes, cutting to the core. The sections will release. A little practice makes the process easy.

NO TEXAS CHEF HAS EVER INFLU-ENCED HOME COOKING IN THE STATE AS MUCH AS HELEN CORBITT DID A GENERATION AGO. A DEMURE NEW YORKER, SHE MOVED TO AUSTIN, WORKED AS AN INSTRUCTOR AT THE UNIVERSITY OF TEXAS, AND THEN MOVED ON TO THE DRISKILL HOTEL AND A HOUSTON COUNTRY CLUB BEFORE SET-TLING IN DALLAS AT THE NEIMAN MARCUS ZODIAC ROOM. CORBITT INTRODUCED THE STATE TO FRESH HERBS, FISH THAT WASN'T DEEP-FRIED, PEP-PER MILLS, AND OLIVE OIL, AMONG MANY FOOD BLESSINGS.

Poppyseed Dressing

This dressing, an integral part of Helen Corbitt's grapefruit and avocado creation, today appears in many other Texas fruit-flavored salads.

¼ CUP SUGAR

¼ CUP HONEY

¼ CUP WHITE VINEGAR

2 TABLESPOONS FRESH LEMON JUICE

1 TEASPOON DRY MUSTARD

1 TEASPOON GRATED ONION

½ TEASPOON SALT

1 TEASPOON PAPRIKA, OPTIONAL

1 CUP OIL, PREFERABLY CANOLA OR CORN

1 TABLESPOON POPPYSEEDS

Makes about 2 cups

In a food processor or with a mixer, combine all the ingredients except the oil and the poppyseeds. Pour in the oil and continue mixing until the dressing is thick. Blend in the poppyseeds. Drizzle the dressing over Grapefruit-Avocado Salad or another fruit salad. Refrigerated, the dressing keeps for a couple of weeks. If it separates, process or mix it again before using.

TECHNIQUE TIP

If you don't want to make your own poppyseed dressing, there's a good commercial version based on the recipe Helen Corbitt made legendary. La Martinique still mixes the dressing by hand. If you would like it shipped to your door, see "Mail-Order Sources" (page 555) for additional information.

Betty's Ambrosia Salad with Lemon Dressing

A heavenly concoction of fresh citrus and tropical fruits, ambrosia shows up in some of the earliest Lone Star cookbooks and still graces many Texas tables at Thanksgiving and Christmas. Cheryl's mother, Betty, perfected our family preparation, a little different from most. Many supermarkets now offer fresh pineapple already cut into rounds or bite-size chunks, but in a pinch the canned variety will do.

1 POUND FRESH PINEAPPLE SLICES OR CHUNKS
  IN JUICE
½ CUP SUGAR
2 TEASPOONS CORNSTARCH
2 TABLESPOONS FRESH LEMON JUICE
1 TABLESPOON FRESH ORANGE JUICE
1 EGG, LIGHTLY BEATEN
3 TO 5 BANANAS
¼ TO ½ CUP (1 TO 2 OUNCES) GRATED MILD
  CHEDDAR CHEESE
½ CUP SHREDDED COCONUT

Serves 4 to 6

With a strainer, drain the pineapple. Measure 1 cup of juice, and set it aside. Cut the pineapple into very small chunks or tidbits, and reserve them.

Make the dressing: In a heavy saucepan over medium heat, stir the sugar and cornstarch together. Pour in the pineapple juice slowly, stirring to eliminate any lumps. Add the lemon and orange juices and the egg, simmering until thickened, about 8 to 10 minutes. Stir frequently. Cool the dressing.

Slice the bananas into thin rounds and arrange half of them in a serving bowl. Top them with half of the pineapple chunks and half of the dressing. Repeat the layers, and sprinkle on the cheese and coconut. Refrigerate the salad, covered, for at least 1 hour before serving. The salad is best the day it's made.

Fig and Cantaloupe Salad

This is a tasty, if unusual, blend of two of the state's foremost fruits.

8 FRESH FIGS, SLICED INTO SIXTHS
2 CUPS CANTALOUPE CHUNKS (FROM ABOUT ½
   MEDIUM CANTALOUPE)
¼ CUP CHOPPED FRESH MINT
¼ CUP PECAN PIECES, TOASTED

DRESSING

½ CUP SOUR CREAM OR YOGURT
1 TABLESPOON PLUS 1 TEASPOON HONEY
1 TABLESPOON PLUS 1 TEASPOON FRESH LIME
   JUICE

4 THIN CANTALOUPE WEDGES
FRESH MINT LEAVES, FOR GARNISH

Serves 4

 In a medium bowl, combine the figs, cantaloupe, mint, and pecans.

Make the dressing: In a small bowl, stir together the sour cream or yogurt, honey, and lime juice. Pour the dressing over the fruit and toss them together lightly. The salad can be refrigerated until it is ready to serve, but it is best eaten within a few hours of preparation.

To serve, place a cantaloupe wedge on each person's plate. Spoon the salad in the hollow of each wedge. Garnish each serving with mint leaves.

> The most arid corner of Texas produces the juiciest cantaloupes. The well-irrigated alkaline soil of Pecos, along with its western sunlight and its half-mile-high altitude, yields succulent fruit.

TECHNIQUE TIP

There are a couple of ways to tell a good cantaloupe from an inferior one. First, check the stem. It should be completely gone, leaving only a smooth, shallow basin known as a "full slip." You also should be able to smell a full-bodied fruity aroma.

Smoked Turkey and
Cantaloupe Salad

This salad gets some of its flavor from curry powder. The East Indian blend of spices has appeared in Texas cookbooks for over a century, but Helen Corbitt popularized its contemporary use in the state.

2 CUPS SHREDDED OR CUBED SMOKED TURKEY
½ MEDIUM CANTALOUPE, DICED
¾ CUP PECAN PIECES, TOASTED
2 CELERY RIBS, CHOPPED
2 GREEN ONIONS, SLICED
1 TEASPOON CURRY POWDER
PINCH OF SALT
⅓ CUP MAYONNAISE
⅓ CUP SOUR CREAM OR YOGURT
LETTUCE LEAVES AND THIN CANTALOUPE
    WEDGES, FOR GARNISH

Serves 4 to 6

In a medium bowl, combine the turkey, cantaloupe, pecans, celery, onions, curry powder, and salt. Mix in the mayonnaise and sour cream or yogurt, and toss the ingredients together. Refrigerate the salad, covered, for about an hour.

Arrange the lettuce leaves and cantaloupe wedges on each plate, and top them with mounds of the salad.

Pecos, Texas, residents celebrate their favorite crop at the Cantaloupe Festival in August, when they carve melons in the shape of their own faces and compete in a look-alike contest. The next day the festival goes aloft as airplane pilots try to bomb targets with cantaloupes.

Triple-A Chicken Salad

This combination of apricots, apples, and almonds is a triple play in any league. It's based on a recipe from the Dallas Junior League's best-selling South of the Fork *cookbook.*

1 TO 1½ CUPS POPPYSEED DRESSING (PAGE
   306)
½ CUP DRIED APRICOTS, CUT IN HALVES OR
   QUARTERS
1½ POUNDS SHREDDED COOKED CHICKEN,
   CHILLED
½ CUP SLICED GREEN ONIONS
½ TEASPOON MINCED LEMON ZEST
½ CUP SLICED ALMONDS, TOASTED
1 TART APPLE, SUCH AS GRANNY SMITH, SLICED
   THIN
LETTUCE LEAVES, FOR GARNISH

Serves 4 to 6

In a medium bowl, combine the poppyseed dressing with the apricots. Let the bowl sit for 30 minutes to 1 hour. Mix in the chicken, green onions, and lemon zest.

Refrigerate the salad, covered, if you wish. Shortly before serving, stir the almonds and apple into the salad. Mound the salad on lettuce leaves.

The Junior League of Dallas has been publishing cookbooks since the Great Depression. The first one, called simply *Cook Book,* came out in 1935.

Shelby County Egg Salad

Egg salads have been a winner on Texas tables for well over a century. This version, created by Jason Griffin of Center, won a cook-off at the 1986 East Texas Poultry Festival.

6 HARD-BOILED EGGS, GRATED FINE OR SIEVED
¼ CUP PLUS 2 TABLESPOONS MINCED
    PIMIENTO-STUFFED OLIVES
¼ CUP PLUS 1 TABLESPOON MAYONNAISE
2 TABLESPOONS MINCED GREEN ONIONS
2 TABLESPOONS MINCED PARSLEY
1 TABLESPOON PREPARED DIJON MUSTARD
SALT AND FRESH-GROUND BLACK PEPPER TO
    TASTE
LETTUCE LEAVES, OPTIONAL, FOR GARNISH

Makes about 2 cups

Combine all the ingredients together in a medium bowl, and mix thoroughly. Refrigerate the salad, covered, at least 30 minutes. Serve the salad atop lettuce leaves or spread it in a sandwich. Leftovers can be kept a couple of days.

You can win with more than egg salads at the East Texas Poultry Festival, held in Center in early October. We particularly enjoy the Flying Chicken Contest, where athletic birds fly as far as they can from a roost on a 12-foot-high mailbox.

Miss Sterett's Shrimp Salad

This is an updated version of a pioneering dish Willie Mae Sterett served in the 1950s at the S&S Tea Room, then the leading spot for ladies' luncheons in Dallas.

SHRIMP

4 CUPS UNSALTED SEAFOOD STOCK
1 MEDIUM ONION, CHOPPED
TOPS OF 3 TO 4 CELERY RIBS
2 TABLESPOONS SALT
2 BAY LEAVES
½ TEASPOON DRIED THYME
1½ POUNDS MEDIUM SHRIMP, UNSHELLED

SALAD

½ CUP MAYONNAISE
3 TABLESPOONS MINCED PARSLEY
1 TABLESPOON EXTRA-VIRGIN OLIVE OIL
1 TABLESPOON FRESH LEMON JUICE
3 TO 4 CELERY RIBS, CHOPPED FINE
½ TEASPOON PREPARED DIJON MUSTARD
¼ TEASPOON DRIED THYME

LETTUCE LEAVES, FOR GARNISH

Serves 4

In a large saucepan, combine the stock with the onion, celery, and seasonings. Bring the liquid to a boil, and boil for 10 to 15 minutes, reducing the liquid slightly. Add the shrimp, immediately reduce the heat to a simmer, and cook the shrimp 2 to 4 minutes, until the shells have turned pink and the shrimp are firm. Don't overcook the shrimp. Drain the liquid from the shrimp, and put them in the freezer for about 10 minutes, until they are cool.

When the shrimp are cool, peel and devein them, and slice each in half lengthwise. Place the shrimp in a bowl and gently mix in the remaining ingredients. Chill the salad, covered, for 30 minutes or longer before serving. Mound the salad on the lettuce leaves.

TECHNIQUE TIP

The shrimp salad is deceptively simple. For best results, get top-quality shrimp and cook them only briefly but with a lot of seasoning. The shrimp soak up just enough of the flavor to enhance their natural briny sweetness. Don't be alarmed by the amount of salt in the cooking liquid; the shrimp absorb little of it.

Catfish Salad

Even Willie Mae Sterett wouldn't have dared serve this dish. In her prime, catfish was relegated to the plates of poor folks. It's gained in stature only recently, partially through the support of authorities such as Craig Claiborne, who calls it "one of the prized fishes of American waters."

¾ CUP CHOPPED CELERY

½ CUP CHOPPED DILL PICKLE PLUS 1 TABLE-
SPOON PICKLING LIQUID

½ CUP SLICED PIMIENTO-STUFFED GREEN
OLIVES

2 HARD-BOILED EGGS, CHOPPED

3 TABLESPOONS MAYONNAISE

3 TABLESPOONS YOGURT OR ADDITIONAL
MAYONNAISE

2 TABLESPOONS PREPARED HORSERADISH

2 TABLESPOONS CAPERS

3 GARLIC CLOVES, MINCED

JUICE OF 1 LEMON

1 TEASPOON SALT

1½ POUNDS CATFISH FILLETS, SMOKED,
BROILED, OR GRILLED, AND FLAKED

1 OR 2 DASHES OF TABASCO OR OTHER HOT
PEPPER SAUCE, OPTIONAL

LETTUCE LEAVES, FOR GARNISH

Serves 4 to 6

In a medium bowl, mix together the celery, pickle, olives, eggs, mayonnaise, yogurt, horseradish, capers, garlic, lemon, and salt, and toss together well. Add the catfish to the other ingredients, mixing gently. Taste, and adjust the seasoning, adding Tabasco if you like. Chill the salad for at least 1 hour for the flavors to mingle together. Serve the salad atop the lettuce leaves.

Miss Sterett occasionally got peeved at the tastes of her wealthy clients. She once complained, "Here we are, overnight from the Gulf, and they have no interest in seafood. It's just pure damned ignorance.... If these women would try to be a little cosmopolitan, you wouldn't have to practically break their arms to get them to take something they haven't been eating since they were kids."

Shivering Elizabeth Salad

We once tried to improve this traditional dish with fresh fruit, but the result wasn't half as good as Mary Jane Mallard's version in **A Texas Hill Country Cookbook,** *the state's best collection of congealed, or gelatin-based, salads. We went back to a recipe very close to Mrs. Mallard's.*

2 11-OUNCE CANS MANDARIN ORANGES
2 TABLESPOONS FRESH LEMON JUICE
1 3-OUNCE PACKAGE ORANGE GELATIN
1 PINT ORANGE SHERBET, SOFTENED
2 TABLESPOONS SOUR CREAM

DRESSING

½ CUP SOUR CREAM
½ CUP YOGURT
½ CUP MANGO OR PEACH CHUTNEY, PURÉED
2 TABLESPOONS FRESH LEMON JUICE
ZEST OF 1 LEMON, OPTIONAL

Serves 6 to 8

Oil a 6- to 8-cup decorative mold.

With a strainer, drain the oranges, reserving them and their syrup. Pour the lemon juice into a measuring cup. Add enough orange syrup to make ¾ cup of liquid. Heat the liquid in a medium saucepan, and stir in the gelatin until it is dissolved. Add the sherbet and sour cream to the warm gelatin and stir until they are well combined. Transfer the pan to the refrigerator and chill 30 to 40 minutes, or until the gelatin turns syrupy.

Stir in the drained oranges and pour the gelatin into the prepared mold.

Chill it until it sets, 1 to 2 hours.

Make the salad dressing while the gelatin sets: Combine all the ingredients, except for 1 tablespoon of the lemon juice, in a small bowl and stir them well. Add the additional lemon juice, if needed, for tartness. The dressing may be made a day ahead, if it is covered and refrigerated.

Unmold the salad shortly before serving time. Serve it topped with the dressing.

THE MAKERS OF JELL-O DESERVE CREDIT FOR PROMOTING SALADS IN TEXAS AND OTHER PARTS OF THE COUNTRY DECADES AGO. THEY MARKETED THEIR SWEETENED GELATIN AS AN APPETIZING WAY TO EAT FRUITS AND VEGETABLES, AND THE IDEA CAUGHT ON LIKE BEER AT A BARBECUE. SOME PEOPLE TODAY TAKE AN UPPITY VIEW ABOUT CONGEALED SALADS, BUT THEY ARE STILL THE MOST POPULAR POTLUCK DISHES IN TEXAS.

Dr Pepper Cherry Salad

Texans will mix almost anything with gelatin. We even found, in an old San Angelo cookbook, a congealed salad with peanut butter. Dr Pepper may sound odd, too, but this is a combination that works.

1 17-OUNCE CAN SWEET BLACK CHERRIES
1 8-OUNCE CAN CRUSHED PINEAPPLE IN ITS
　OWN JUICE
1 TABLESPOON FRESH LEMON JUICE
2 3-OUNCE PACKAGES CHERRY GELATIN
12-OUNCE CAN OR BOTTLE DR PEPPER
1 CUP CHOPPED PECANS, TOASTED

Serves 6

Oil a 6-cup decorative mold. With a strainer, drain the liquid from the cherries and the pineapple, and reserve the liquid. Slice the cherries in half, and reserve them along with the pineapple. Add the lemon juice to the liquid from the canned fruit. Measure the liquid and add enough water to make 2 cups. Bring the liquid to a boil.

Place the gelatin in a medium bowl.

Pour the boiling liquid over it and stir until the gelatin is dissolved. Mix in the Dr Pepper. Refrigerate until the gelatin turns syrupy, about 45 minutes to 1 hour.

Fold the fruit and pecans into the gelatin. Pour the gelatin into the mold, and chill it again until the mixture sets firmly, another hour or two. Unmold the salad, and serve it.

A SIMILAR CONGEALED SALAD, POPULAR THROUGHOUT THE SOUTH, IS MADE WITH COKE, RC COLA, OR EVEN 7 UP. WE THINK THE TEXAS SOFT DRINK GIVES THIS ONE THE EDGE.

In *The Texas Cookbook*, Arthur and Bobbie Coleman offered an ingenious explanation for the state's fascination with congealed salads. They reckoned that gelatin is "particularly appropriate to Texas, coming as it does from cows."

Seafoam Salad

A 1927 Texas cookbook suggested dressing up pears for a salad by dye-ing one half of each pear green and the other half pink, and then sticking cloves in each to represent stems. The approach in this salad is just as color-ful and tastes better.

2 16-OUNCE CANS PEARS (IN LIGHT SYRUP OR
  THEIR OWN JUICE)
1 3-OUNCE PACKAGE LIME GELATIN
1 CUP COTTAGE CHEESE
½ CUP MAYONNAISE
JUICE FROM 1 LIME
1 TEASPOON PREPARED HORSERADISH

Serves 6

Oil a 6-cup decorative mold.
Drain the pears and chop them fine. Reserve the fruit, and measure 1 cup of the pear liquid, discarding the rest or saving it for another use. In a small pan, bring the pear liquid to a boil. Sprinkle in the gelatin and stir it until it dissolves.

In a medium bowl, combine the cottage cheese, mayonnaise, lime juice, and horseradish. With a mixer, beat the ingredients well. Pour in the gelatin mixture and beat just to combine.

Refrigerate the mixture until it is thickened, 30 to 45 minutes. Fold in the pears. Pour the gelatin into the mold. Chill the salad, until the gelatin sets firmly, at least 1 hour. Unmold the salad shortly before serv-ing it.

When wheat was available in early Texas it was used for bis-cuits, a special treat at the time. John Duval recalled how he cele-brated the republic's indepen-dence from Mexico with a big meal of biscuits—"none of your little flimsy affairs, such as are usually seen on fashionable tables, but good solid fat fellows, each as big as a saucer."

Just Good Plain Cornbread

We dedicate this recipe to Governor Ann Richards, famed for cajoling legislators late at night at the Mansion with a silver tongue and a plate of golden cornbread.

1 TABLESPOON OIL, PREFERABLY CORN OR CANOLA

1½ CUPS MEDIUM-GRIND CORNMEAL, PREFERABLY STONE-GROUND

½ CUP ALL-PURPOSE FLOUR

3 TABLESPOONS SUGAR

1 TABLESPOON BAKING POWDER

1 TEASPOON SALT

1 TEASPOON BAKING SODA

1½ CUPS BUTTERMILK

3 EGGS, LIGHTLY BEATEN

3 TABLESPOONS UNSALTED BUTTER, MELTED

Serves 6 to 8

 Grease a 10-inch cast-iron skillet with the oil. Place the empty skillet in a cool oven, and set the oven at 400° F.

In a medium bowl, stir together the cornmeal, flour, sugar, baking powder, salt, and baking soda. Pour in the buttermilk and eggs, and gently mix by hand until the mixture is thoroughly blended. Stir in the melted butter.

Remove the skillet from the oven, pour the batter into the skillet (the batter will sizzle), and return it to the oven. Bake the bread for 18 to 20 minutes, or until it begins to brown on top and a toothpick inserted in the center comes out clean. Serve the cornbread warm.

"Crumblin'" is a time-honored way of drinking your cornbread. Take a big glass—the kind you'd use for iced tea—and crumble in enough cornbread to fill it about three-fourths full. Add enough buttermilk to top off the glass, and spoon down the mushy mixture as you would a thick malt.

Jalapeño Cornbread

Jalapeño cornbread is so popular in Texas that many people assume, as Frank X. Tolbert once claimed, that it's an "old border recipe." In truth the dish is probably younger than rock and roll, but it's still a sure-fire approach to a classic concept, usually spicier, heavier, and moister than regular cornbread.

4 TABLESPOONS OIL, PREFERABLY CANOLA OR CORN
1 CUP MEDIUM-GRIND CORNMEAL, PREFERABLY STONE-GROUND
1 CUP ALL-PURPOSE FLOUR
2 TABLESPOONS SUGAR
1 TABLESPOON BAKING POWDER
1 TEASPOON SALT
1 CUP BUTTERMILK
1 CUP CORN KERNELS, FRESH OR FROZEN
1 CUP (4 OUNCES) GRATED SHARP CHEDDAR CHEESE
3 EGGS, LIGHTLY BEATEN
3 TO 4 FRESH OR PICKLED JALAPEÑOS, MINCED
2 TABLESPOONS MINCED ONION
2 TABLESPOONS SOUR CREAM
¼ CUP UNSALTED BUTTER, MELTED

Serves 6 to 8

Grease a 10-inch cast-iron skillet with 1 tablespoon of the oil. Place the empty skillet in a cool oven, and set the oven to 400° F.

In a medium bowl, stir together the cornmeal, flour, sugar, baking powder, and salt. Pour in the buttermilk,

In one form or another—and the variations were many—cornbread was a mainstay of the Texas diet in the pioneer period. Not everyone loved it, though. An English visitor complained that the staple was "a modification of sawdust," and another traveler railed against having to stay in "the usual cornbread-and-coffee sort of hotel."

TECHNIQUE TIPS

These tips apply to any cornbread recipe:

• For the best results, use a stone-ground cornmeal like Arrowhead Mills or Adams. (If you can't find stone-ground cornmeal locally, see "Mail-Order Sources," page 553, for information.)

• Keep the cornmeal in the freezer for freshness.

• Make the cornbread in a heavy skillet, preferably cast-iron, to get the crispest crusts; baking pans make poor substitutes.

and add the corn, cheese, eggs, jalapeños, onion, and sour cream. Gently mix by hand until the mixture is thoroughly blended. Stir in the melted butter and the remaining oil.

Remove the skillet from the oven, pour the batter into the skillet (the batter will sizzle), and return it to the oven. Bake the cornbread for 30 minutes, or until it begins to brown on top. Serve the cornbread warm.

Spoonbread

The most elegant preparation of cornmeal in Southern cooking, spoonbread migrated to Texas before the Civil War. As the name implies, it was originally made as a bread, but more recently it's also served as a soufflé-like side dish, suitable for any meal of the day.

1 CUP WATER

1 CUP BUTTERMILK

½ CUP MILK

½ CUP CORN KERNELS, FRESH OR FROZEN

2 TABLESPOONS CORN OIL, PREFERABLY UNREFINED

2 TABLESPOONS CHOPPED RED BELL PEPPER

1 TEASPOON SALT

¼ TEASPOON WHITE PEPPER

¾ CUP FINE-GRIND CORNMEAL, PREFERABLY STONE-GROUND

3 EGGS, SEPARATED

Serves 4 to 6

 Preheat the oven to 425° F. Grease a 10-inch cast-iron skillet or a shallow 9-by-12-inch baking dish.

Over medium heat, combine all the ingredients except the cornmeal and eggs in a large, heavy saucepan, and bring the liquid to a simmer. Sprinkle the cornmeal over the hot liquid and

SPANISH AND MEXICAN SETTLERS IN TEXAS USUALLY GROUND CORN IN A *METATE,* A STONE TOOL DESIGNED SPECIFICALLY FOR THE PURPOSE. THE EARLY ANGLOS HAD TO IMPROVISE. FREQUENTLY THEY USED A HOLLOWED-OUT TREE STUMP, CUT TO A CONVENIENT HEIGHT FOR THE WOMAN OF THE HOUSE SO SHE COULD POUND THE CORN INTO MEAL WITH A LARGE WOODEN PESTLE.

stir it in well. After incorporating all of the cornmeal and eliminating any lumps, remove the pan from the heat. Set the mixture aside to cool slightly.

Beat the egg yolks together until they are light yellow and frothy. Stir the yolks into the cornmeal. Beat two of the egg whites (saving the third for another use) until soft peaks form. Fold the whites into the cornmeal, and combine lightly. Pour the mixture into the prepared skillet or dish. Bake the bread for about 30 minutes, or until it is set and just a bit browned. Serve it immediately.

Buttermilk Biscuits

Before the invention of baking powder, cooks always used buttermilk in biscuits to make them rise. This still works today, but the distinctive flavor is the only real reason you should need to prefer buttermilk to regular milk.

2½ CUPS SOFT-WHEAT FLOUR, PREFERABLY
   WHITE LILY
1½ TABLESPOONS SUGAR
2 TEASPOONS BAKING POWDER
½ TEASPOON BAKING SODA
½ TEASPOON SALT
3 TABLESPOONS LARD, WELL CHILLED
2 TABLESPOONS VEGETABLE SHORTENING,
   PREFERABLY CRISCO, WELL CHILLED
1 CUP BUTTERMILK, WELL CHILLED

*Makes about 8 to 10 3-inch
or 12 to 14 2-inch biscuits*

 Position the rack in the middle of the oven, and preheat the oven to 450° F. Grease a baking sheet.

Sift together the dry ingredients into a large bowl. Repeat the sifting three times. With a pastry blender or large fork, blend in the lard and shortening until a coarse meal forms. Pour in the buttermilk, and stir together the wet and dry ingredients just until a sticky dough forms.

Flour your hands and a pastry

> Baking powder wasn't available in Texas until the 1890s, and it didn't catch on fully at first. Some men suspected it made life too easy for women and might be poisonous.

You won't go wrong with any biscuit recipe if you follow these hints:

• Use a low-gluten soft-wheat flour like White Lily. If you can't find it locally, see "Mail-Order Sources" (page 553).

• Sift the flour before measuring it, and then sift it together with the other dry ingredients several times for lightness.

• Lard produces the flakiest, best-textured biscuits. You can substitute shortening for some of the lard and still get a fine result, but this is not the place to use vegetable oils.

• Chill the fat and the bowl, and work quickly to keep the fat from melting. All the grains of flour need to be surrounded with fat so that water will not activate the flour's gluten. If that happens, you'll get a hard, heavy biscuit.

• Invest in a good biscuit cutter with sharp edges that cut clean and an open top that allows air to escape, so that the dough rises properly.

• Pat the dough out only once. Rerolled biscuit dough takes on weight like a sumo wrestler. This doesn't apply to the recipe for Masa Biscuits, which can have the dough rerolled once because there's less gluten to toughen the mixture.

• For even cooking, turn the baking sheet around in the oven halfway through cooking, and, if you bake more than a single sheet, reverse the positions of the sheets in the oven.

board or counter. Turn the dough out and knead it gently, only four to six times. Pat the dough until it is about ½ inch thick. Cut it with a 2- or 3-inch-round biscuit cutter or a round cookie cutter.

Transfer the biscuits to the baking sheet, arranging them so that they just touch each other. Bake the biscuits about 10 minutes, or until they are raised and golden brown. (At the halfway point, turn the baking sheet from front to back.)

Serve the biscuits hot with butter or topped with cream gravy.

Kerr Family Masa Biscuits

The delicate corn flavor in these biscuits comes from masa harina, a treated cornmeal. The absence of gluten in the masa makes the biscuits especially tender. We include them courtesy of Norma and Park Kerr, who feature them in their El Paso Chile Company's Texas Border Cookbook. Like the Kerrs, we eat them split, buttered, and slathered with jalapeño jelly.

3¾ CUPS UNBLEACHED ALL-PURPOSE FLOUR

1½ CUPS MASA HARINA

2 TABLESPOONS PLUS 1 TEASPOON BAKING POWDER

1 TEASPOON SALT

1 STICK UNSALTED BUTTER, WELL CHILLED AND CUT INTO SMALL PIECES

½ CUP VEGETABLE SHORTENING, WELL CHILLED AND CUT INTO SMALL PIECES

2 CUPS BUTTERMILK, CHILLED

Makes 12

 Position racks in the upper and middle thirds of the oven, and preheat the oven to 450° F.

In a large bowl, stir together 3½ cups of the flour and the masa, baking powder, and salt. With a pastry blender or large fork, blend in the butter and shortening until the mixture resembles a coarse and slightly lumpy meal. Stir in the buttermilk until a soft, crumbly dough is formed.

Sprinkle the work surface with half the remaining flour. Turn the dough out, gather it into a ball, and briefly knead it, just until it holds together. Flatten the dough, sprinkle it with the rest of the flour, and roll it out until it is about 1 inch thick. Form the biscuits with a 3-inch-round cutter, and transfer them to two ungreased baking sheets, spacing the biscuits about 2 inches apart. Gather the scraps into a ball, roll it out to a 1-inch thickness, and cut out the remaining biscuits.

Set the baking sheets on the racks, and bake the biscuits about 15 minutes, or until they are golden and crisp. At the halfway point, exchange the position of the sheets on the racks from top to bottom and from front to back. Serve the biscuits hot or warm.

IN TEXAS AND MANY AREAS OF THE SOUTH, CAUTIOUS COOKS USE YEAST IN THEIR BISCUITS ALONG WITH BAKING POWDER AND SODA, GIVING THEM TRIPLE LEAVENING POWER. KNOWN AS ANGEL OR BRIDE'S BISCUITS, THEY'RE MORE LIKELY TO RISE TO THE HEAVENS THAN A DALLAS DO-GOODER.

Sweet Potato Biscuits

Another tasty variation on buttermilk biscuits, these feature sweet pota-toes, a staple in Texas since pioneer days.

8 OUNCES COOKED SWEET POTATO, WELL CHILLED

⅓ CUP BUTTERMILK, WELL CHILLED

1 CUP SOFT-WHEAT FLOUR, PREFERABLY WHITE LILY

1½ TEASPOONS BAKING POWDER

1 TEASPOON SUGAR

½ TEASPOON SALT

¼ TEASPOON BAKING SODA

3 TABLESPOONS LARD OR VEGETABLE SHORT-ENING, PREFERABLY CRISCO, WELL CHILLED

Makes about 12 to 14 2-inch biscuits

Preheat the oven to 450° F. Grease a baking sheet.

Purée the sweet potato and buttermilk together in a food proces-sor or blender.

Sift the dry ingredients together into a bowl. With a pastry blender or large fork, cut in the lard or shortening, until the mixture resembles coarse meal. With a spoon or spatula, fold in the sweet potato mixture. Blend it to-gether well with the dry ingredients, but don't overmix.

On a floured board or counter, knead the dough gently, for about six turns. Pat it out, and cut it with a bis-cuit cutter or round cookie cutter dipped in flour.

Transfer the biscuits to the baking sheet, and bake them 12 to 14 min-utes, until they are raised and lightly browned on the top edges. At the halfway point, exchange the position of the sheets on the racks from top to bottom and from front to back. Serve the biscuits immediately.

Variation: A little chile can enhance sweet potato biscuits. Add 2 teaspoons ground dried red chile, preferably New Mexican, to the dry ingredients when sifting.

Flour figured prominently in the development of country-and-Western music in Texas. The great Bob Wills, inventor of Western swing, won his initial fame on a Fort Worth live-radio show sponsored by Light Crust flour. When he fell out with the crusty president of the company, "Pappy" O'Daniel, he changed the name of his band from the Light Crust Doughboys to the Texas Playboys and ultimately went into a partnership with General Mills to market Play Boy flour.

Edna's Sunday Rolls

Throughout much of this century in Texas, biscuits were the everyday bread in most homes, and yeast rolls were the Sunday dinner treat. This recipe comes from Dallas cook Edna McGlothen, who made these light, soft rolls every week for many years for the big family meal.

2 PACKAGES YEAST
¼ CUP WARM WATER
1 CUP MILK
¾ CUP SUGAR
½ CUP UNSALTED BUTTER
2 TABLESPOONS VEGETABLE SHORTENING,
   PREFERABLY CRISCO
1 TEASPOON SALT
2 EGGS
1 CUP MASHED POTATOES
4½ TO 5 CUPS FLOUR, PREFERABLY A HARD
   WINTER-WHEAT FLOUR FOR BREAD BAKING
MELTED BUTTER

Makes about 2 to 2½ dozen rolls

In a large bowl, dissolve the yeast in the water.

Warm the milk, sugar, ½ cup butter, shortening, and salt together in a small, heavy pan over low heat, just until the butter and shortening melt. Set the pan aside to cool to lukewarm. Add the liquid to the yeast, and let the mixture sit for 5 minutes. Mix in the eggs and potatoes. Stir in as much of the flour as is needed to form a soft dough. Cover the bowl with a towel, and let the dough rise until it has nearly doubled in size, about 1½ to 2 hours.

Sprinkle a counter with some of the remaining flour, and knead the dough for a couple of minutes to make it smooth and elastic. Add in a little flour, if needed, to make the dough more workable. Roll the dough out to a ¼- to ½-inch thickness. Cut it into rounds with a 3-inch biscuit cutter. Brush half of each roll's top with melted butter and fold the unbuttered half over it, so that the upper half extends about ½ inch beyond the lower half. Arrange the rolls on a greased baking sheet with the rounded side of each roll just touching the flat side of the roll next to it. Allow the rolls to sit, covered, for 1 hour or until they are doubled in size.

Preheat the oven to 400° F. Bake the rolls for 10 minutes. Reduce the temperature to 350° F, and bake the rolls an additional 10 to 12 minutes, or until they are nicely browned. Serve the rolls hot.

In her 1981 book *The Only Texas Cookbook*, Linda West Eckhardt aptly describes the desirable thickness of biscuit dough by saying it should be as plump as the pad of a prickly-pear cactus.

Poppyseed Cheese Bread

When poppyseeds aren't populating Texas salad dressings, they're popping up in breads.

¾ CUP UNSALTED BUTTER

⅓ CUP SUGAR

5 EGGS

½ CUP MILK

2 FRESH JALAPEÑOS, MINCED

2 TABLESPOONS POPPYSEEDS

1 CUP (4 OUNCES) GRATED MILD CHEDDAR
   CHEESE

3 OUNCES CREAM CHEESE

1 CUP ALL-PURPOSE FLOUR

1 CUP MEDIUM-GRIND CORNMEAL, PREFERABLY
   STONE-GROUND

2 ½ TEASPOONS BAKING POWDER

1 TEASPOON SALT

Makes 1 9-by-5-inch loaf

Preheat the oven to 375° F. Grease a 9-by-5-inch loaf pan.
Cream together the butter and sugar with an electric mixer or food processor. Add the eggs, and blend them in. Add the milk, jalapeños, poppyseeds, and cheeses, mixing well after each addition. Sift together the remaining ingredients, and add the dry mixture to the batter, about one-third at a time, mixing well after each addition.

Spoon the batter into the pan. Bake the bread about 40 minutes, or until a toothpick inserted in the center comes out clean. Serve the bread warm or at room temperature.

Restaurants abuse the term *Texas toast,* using it to signify any oversized piece of white bread toasted in any old way. Originally, the name referred to how the bread was cooked, which was closer to frying than toasting. The cook slathered the bread with butter and warmed it on the grill beside the steaks and burgers, where it absorbed some of the meat drippings. It's still a tasty way to eat white bread.

Corn and Jalapeño Jam Muffins

Hot and sweet go together in Texas—and these muffins—like moonshine and moonlight.

1¼ CUPS ALL-PURPOSE FLOUR
¾ CUP MEDIUM-GRIND CORNMEAL, PREFERABLY STONE-GROUND
1 TABLESPOON BAKING POWDER
½ TEASPOON SALT
¼ TEASPOON CAYENNE
¾ CUP BUTTERMILK
¼ CUP UNSALTED BUTTER, MELTED
3 TABLESPOONS SUGAR
2 EGGS
1½ CUPS CORN KERNELS, FRESH OR FROZEN
¾ CUP JALAPEÑO JELLY OR JAM, PREFERABLY HOMEMADE (PAGE 395)

Makes 12 muffins

Preheat the oven to 375° F. Grease the muffin tins.

Sift together the flour, cornmeal, baking powder, salt, and cayenne in a bowl, and set it aside. In another, larger bowl, beat together the buttermilk, butter, and sugar. Mix in the eggs, followed by the corn, blending well after each addition. Add the flour mixture, and stir to combine lightly.

Spoon about half of the batter—it will be a bit stiff—into the muffin tins, filling each cup just one-third full. Drop a dollop of jelly, about 1 teaspoon, on top of the batter in each cup. Top with the remaining batter, covering the jelly completely for each muffin.

Bake the muffins 22 to 24 minutes, until they are deep golden. Serve them warm.

TECHNIQUE TIP

Jalapeño and other chile jellies lately seem to have passed oil wells in profitability, judging by the relative abundance of each. If you can find them, try the brands from the Travis County Farmers' Market and El Paso Chile Company, two of the best. The Stonewall Chili Pepper Company makes excellent hotter versions with serranos, chiles pequíns, and cayennes. All three brands can be delivered to your door; see "Mail-Order Sources" (pages 551–556).

Gillespie County Peach Muffins

Richard West once said in **Texas Monthly** *that you shouldn't worry if you were never promised a rose garden—a peach from Gillespie County would substitute nicely.*

2 CUPS ALL-PURPOSE FLOUR

2 TEASPOONS GROUND CINNAMON

1 TEASPOON POWDERED GINGER

¾ TEASPOON SALT

¾ TEASPOON BAKING SODA

¼ TEASPOON BAKING POWDER

2 EGGS

¾ CUP DARK BROWN SUGAR

¾ CUP OIL, PREFERABLY HALF WALNUT AND
    HALF CANOLA

1 TEASPOON VANILLA

1¾ CUPS (ABOUT 2 LARGE) CHOPPED PEACHES

⅔ CUP CHOPPED PECANS, TOASTED

¼ CUP POPPYSEEDS

Makes 12 muffins

Preheat the oven to 400° F. Grease the muffin tins.

Sift together the flour, cinnamon, ginger, salt, baking soda, and baking powder into a bowl, and set it aside. In another, larger bowl, beat together the eggs with the brown sugar, oil, and vanilla. Fold in the peaches, pecans, and poppyseeds. Add the flour mixture, and lightly stir to combine.

Spoon the batter into the prepared muffin tins. Bake the muffins 22 to 25 minutes, or until they are browned and a toothpick inserted in the center of a muffin comes out clean. Serve the muffins warm or at room temperature.

Farmers first grew wheat commercially in Texas near Sherman in the 1830s. The acreage expanded greatly by the 1850s because of rapid settlement in the state and the introduction of a Mediterranean wheat that adapted well to the climate in north Texas. This made flour affordable for the first time, and biscuits soon took the place of cornbread in the state's diet.

Greer Garson's Garlic Muffins

While Dallas's Greer Garson is best known for her movies, she also deserves recognition as a muffin maker. This is a variation on one of her favorite recipes.

1 TABLESPOON UNSALTED BUTTER

4 GARLIC CLOVES, MINCED

2 CUPS ALL-PURPOSE FLOUR

1 TABLESPOON BAKING POWDER

1 TABLESPOON SUGAR

¾ TEASPOON SALT

¾ CUP MILK

½ CUP OIL, PREFERABLY CANOLA OR CORN (OR
    SUBSTITUTE 1 TO 2 TABLESPOONS OF GARLIC
    OIL FOR AN EQUAL AMOUNT OF REGULAR OIL)

3 OUNCES CREAM CHEESE, SOFTENED

2 EGGS, LIGHTLY BEATEN

2 TABLESPOONS MINCED CHIVES

2 TABLESPOONS SESAME SEEDS, TOASTED

Makes 12 muffins

Preheat the oven to 400° F. Grease the muffin tins.

In a small skillet, warm the butter over medium heat. Sauté the garlic in the butter until it is tender, and reserve it.

Sift together the flour, baking powder, sugar, and salt into a bowl, and set it aside. In another bowl, beat together the milk, oil, cream cheese, and eggs. Stir in the chives and the reserved garlic. Add the flour mixture, and gently stir to combine.

Spoon the batter into the prepared muffin tins, and sprinkle with sesame seeds. Bake the muffins 20 minutes, or until they are lightly browned and a toothpick inserted in the center of a muffin comes out clean. Serve the muffins warm or at room temperature.

> Even after his split with Bob Wills, "Pappy" O'Daniel continued to sell his Light Crust flour on country-music radio. His shows became popular entertainment during the Depression and eventually propelled him into the governor's office. He went from there to the U.S. Senate, defeating Lyndon Johnson for the seat in 1941, but he was never as preeminent in politics as he was in pitching flour.

BEANS, 'TATERS AND OTHER KEEPERS

I can't remember when this love affair began. Perhaps it was the first time I looked into Hedy Lamarr's eyes. I was sitting in the front row of the theater, and she was on the silver screen.... The next time I looked into those eyes they were swimming in their natural juices and cozying up to hunks of backstrap. And even today, all these years later, I think of Hedy Lamarr every time I eat black-eyed peas.

Cactus Pryor, *Inside Texas*

*T*raditional Texas side dishes rely heavily on *keepers*—vegetables, legumes, and grains that don't require canning or refrigeration for a long shelf life. In addition to their staying power, these staples usually grow well in the state without a lot of fuss, and they make stalwart accompaniments to meaty main dishes. Black-eyed peas, pinto beans, white potatoes, sweet potatoes, onions, noodles, and rice were practical foods for pioneer folk, and over the generations they became Lone Star comfort foods, often eaten today alone or with a salad as a more-than-sufficient supper. These dishes are Texas love bites, the way to a mate's heart or just some good-time self-gratification.

Texas Caviar

Along with the pinto bean, the black-eyed pea is Texas's most-loved legume. Helen Corbitt, the mother of modern Texas cooking, prepared them like this. Her famous recipe didn't call for bell pepper, but green pepper and jalapeño are common additions today.

1 POUND DRIED OR FROZEN BLACK-EYED PEAS

6 CUPS UNSALTED CHICKEN STOCK

¾ CUP CORN OIL, PREFERABLY UNREFINED

¼ CUP CIDER VINEGAR, PREFERABLY UNRE-
FINED

1 SMALL GREEN BELL PEPPER, CHOPPED

½ CUP CHOPPED SWEET ONION (SUCH AS
TEXAS 1015, VIDALIA, OR WALLA WALLA) OR
¼ CUP REGULAR ONION

2 ROASTED GARLIC CLOVES (PAGE 9)

1 TEASPOON COARSE-GROUND BLACK PEPPER

½ TEASPOON SALT, OR MORE, TO TASTE

Serves 4 to 6

In a large saucepan, cover the peas by at least 1 inch with stock. Bring the liquid to a boil over high heat. Reduce the heat to a simmer, and cook the peas until they are tender, anywhere from 45 minutes to 1½ hours depending on your peas. (Frozen peas generally cook faster.) Stir occasionally, and add more stock or water if the peas begin to seem dry before they are done.

Drain the peas. In a large bowl, toss them together with the remaining in-gredients. Refrigerate the peas, covered, at least 2 hours, preferably overnight. The peas get tastier over several days. Serve the peas chilled.

Some fancy-food eaters think of black-eyed peas as Southern backwoods fare. In truth they are a global delicacy, first cultivated in Asia eons ago. African slaves brought seeds to the New World in 1674 and the little pearls spread in a snap throughout the South.

Black-Eyed Peas
with Ham Hocks

This is an assertively seasoned version of the oldest, most popular way to cook black-eyed peas, a method imported to Texas from the Deep South.

2 POUNDS DRIED OR FROZEN BLACK-EYED PEAS
10 TO 12 CUPS WATER
1 POUND SMOKED HAM HOCKS (1 OR 2 HOCKS)
1½ MEDIUM ONIONS, CHOPPED
1 LARGE GREEN BELL PEPPER, CHOPPED
¼ CUP CIDER OR WHITE VINEGAR
2 TABLESPOONS PURE LIQUID HICKORY SMOKE, OPTIONAL
1 TEASPOON FRESH-GROUND BLACK PEPPER
½ TEASPOON CELERY SEEDS
3 GARLIC CLOVES, MINCED
2 BAY LEAVES
1 TEASPOON SALT, OR MORE, TO TASTE

Serves 8 to 10

Put all the ingredients, except the salt, into a good-size stockpot, and bring them to a boil. Reduce the heat to a simmer, and cook until the peas are very tender, but not mushy, about 45 minutes to 1½ hours. (Frozen peas generally cook faster.) Stir occasionally, adding more water if necessary. Add the salt toward the end of the cooking time, after the other flavors have mingled together. The peas should have some extra liquid when cooked, but they should not be soupy. Serve the peas warm. They keep for 5 to 7 days in the refrigerator, and they freeze well.

A traditional way of eating these black-eyed peas is to scoop them on top of cornbread and add a sprinkling of chopped onions. Serve Tabasco or another hot pepper sauce on the side.

Hoppin' John

Another Southern classic, Hoppin' John vaulted westward across the Sabine River all the way from the Carolinas. Everywhere the dish contains black-eyed peas and rice, but other seasonings vary with the locale and the cook. Most Texans make it a bit spicy, some adding dried chile and calling it "Hoppin' Juan." We like it that way, but we prefer the vinegar tang of Tabasco with the peas and rice.

1 POUND DRIED OR FROZEN BLACK-EYED PEAS

6 CUPS UNSALTED CHICKEN STOCK

1½ MEDIUM ONIONS, CHOPPED

1 MEDIUM GREEN OR RED BELL PEPPER,
   CHOPPED

¼ POUND SALT PORK, RINSED AND DICED

2 TEASPOONS CIDER VINEGAR

2 GARLIC CLOVES, MINCED

2 BAY LEAVES

1½ TEASPOONS FRESH-GROUND BLACK PEPPER

1 TEASPOON TABASCO OR OTHER HOT PEPPER
   SAUCE

1 TEASPOON DRIED THYME

1 TEASPOON SALT, OR MORE, TO TASTE

ADDITIONAL STOCK, AS NEEDED

1 CUP UNCOOKED RICE

*Serves 6 as a side dish
or 4 as a main course*

In a large saucepan, combine the black-eyed peas with the stock. Add the onions, bell pepper, salt pork, vinegar, garlic, bay leaves, pepper, Tabasco, thyme, and salt, and simmer until the peas are cooked through and soft. Don't let them get mushy. Expect the cooking time to be at least 45 minutes and up to 1½ hours. Frozen peas generally cook faster.

Drain the cooking liquid from the peas into a large measuring cup. You will need 2½ cups of liquid to cook the rice. Discard any extra liquid, or add stock to equal the 2½ cups. Pour the liquid back into the peas, add the rice to the pot, and simmer over medium heat 20 minutes or until the rice is cooked through. Remove the pan from the heat, and let the rice and peas steam with the lid on for 5 to 10 minutes. Serve the dish hot with more Tabasco or a pepper vinegar.

Marinated Rice, Black-Eyed Pea, and Corn Salad

In this salad, a trio of Texas favorites do-si-do smartly with a South-western dressing.

2 CUPS COOKED RICE

2 CUPS COOKED BLACK-EYED PEAS (SEE TEXAS CAVIAR, PAGE 332, FOR COOKING INSTRUCTIONS)

2 CUPS COOKED CORN KERNELS (ROASTED CORN IS ESPECIALLY GOOD; SEE PAGE 300)

6 GREEN ONIONS, SLICED THIN

2 TO 3 PICKLED JALAPEÑOS, MINCED

¼ CUP PLUS 2 TABLESPOONS OIL, PREFERABLY CANOLA OR CORN

2 TABLESPOONS CIDER VINEGAR

1 TABLESPOON FRESH LIME JUICE

1 TEASPOON UNSULPHURED DARK MOLASSES

1 TEASPOON CHILI POWDER, PREFERABLY HOMEMADE (PAGE 135) OR GEBHARDT'S

½ TO 1 TEASPOON CUMIN SEEDS, TOASTED AND GROUND

¼ TEASPOON SALT, OR MORE, TO TASTE

Serves 6 to 8

In a large bowl, combine the rice, black-eyed peas, corn, onions, and jalapeños. In a lidded jar, mix together the remaining ingredients. Pour them over the rice mixture. Refrigerate the salad, covered, at least 2 hours, preferably twice that long. The salad keeps well for several days.

In his famous *A Bowl of Red*, Frank X. Tolbert tells about a friend's amazing diet, which included some days with only black-eyed peas. He drank black-eyed-pea pot likker for breakfast, with pepper sauce, and at noon he might have a pea cocktail and a sandwich spread with butter, onions, and cold peas. For dinner the friend pulled out all the stops, downing more pot likker and consuming a big bowl of peas with cornbread, butter, and buttermilk.

Cowpoke Pintos

Pinto beans have always been as popular in the western and southern parts of Texas as black-eyed peas were in the eastern and northern sections. Cowboys in particular thrived on chuck-wagon pintos. This zestier version adds some newer ingredients.

1 POUND DRIED PINTO BEANS, SOAKED
   OVERNIGHT
8 CUPS WATER
12 OUNCES COCA-COLA
1 14½-OUNCE CAN WHOLE TOMATOES,
   UNDRAINED
1½ MEDIUM ONIONS, CHOPPED
¼ TO ½ CUP TOMATO-BASED BARBECUE SAUCE
2 TO 3 SLICES SLAB BACON, CHOPPED
3 TABLESPOONS CHILI POWDER, PREFERABLY
   HOMEMADE (PAGE 135) OR GEBHARDT'S
2 TABLESPOONS WORCESTERSHIRE SAUCE
4 GARLIC CLOVES, MINCED
3 TO 4 FRESH SERRANOS OR 2 TO 3
   JALAPEÑOS, MINCED
2 TEASPOONS CUMIN SEEDS, TOASTED AND
   GROUND
1 TEASPOON SALT, OR MORE, TO TASTE

Serves 4 to 6

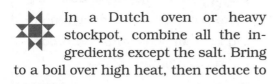 In a Dutch oven or heavy stockpot, combine all the ingredients except the salt. Bring to a boil over high heat, then reduce to a simmer. Cook slowly, stirring up from the bottom occasionally, for at least 2 hours, adding more water if the beans begin to seem dry. Stir in the salt in the last few minutes of cooking. The beans should hold their shape but be soft and just a little soupy. Serve them in bowls with a bit of the cooking liquid.

THE COCA-COLA IN THE RECIPE ADDS FLAVOR, BUT IT ALSO PURPORTEDLY HELPS TO REDUCE THE GASEOUS EFFECT OF BEANS. OTHER INGREDIENTS YOU CAN USE WHEN SERVING BEANS TO COMPANY INCLUDE CARROTS AND EPAZOTE, AN HERB THAT'S ALSO CALLED MEXICAN TEA. NOTHING MUCH WORKS IF YOU GO DANCING AFTERWARD.

Wayne's Wonderful $50 Beans

This is the ultimate way to cook pinto beans, definitely extravagant and definitely worth it. We got the idea from Houston barbecue wizard Wayne Whitworth, president of Pitt's and Spitt's. His company's address is in "Mail-Order Sources" (page 552), in case you're compelled to send a thank-you card—which is likely, after you taste these jewels.

1 SMOKED BONE-IN HAM, ABOUT 10 POUNDS

⅓ CUP COARSE-GROUND BLACK PEPPER

3 POUNDS PINTO BEANS, SOAKED OVERNIGHT

2 ONIONS, CHOPPED

12 GARLIC CLOVES, MINCED

1 TABLESPOON TABASCO OR OTHER HOT PEPPER SAUCE

1 TABLESPOON DRIED EPAZOTE ("MEXICAN TEA")

SALT TO TASTE

Serves 12

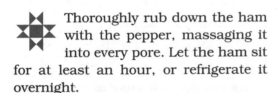 Thoroughly rub down the ham with the pepper, massaging it into every pore. Let the ham sit for at least an hour, or refrigerate it overnight.

Place the ham in a large stockpot. Fill the pot with water to cover the ham by several inches. Let the pot simmer over low heat about half a day, covered, until the meat literally falls apart.

Remove the ham and bone, and reserve the meat for another use. Add the pintos and the rest of the ingredients, except the salt, to the broth.

Barely simmer the beans for 3 to 4 hours, stirring them occasionally, until they are quite soft but still hold their shape. Add a little more water if the beans begin to look dry. Stir in the salt in the last few minutes of the cooking time. The pintos can be kept warm for another hour, covered, over very low heat. Serve the beans hot.

TECHNIQUE TIP

When cooking beans, stir them up from the bottom frequently for the creamiest results. Never stir up any beans, however, that are stuck to the bottom of the pan. Forget about those beans, and salvage the rest by pouring them into another pot. Begin cooking again with a little more water.

Hart Stilwell's Baked Beans

This recipe goes back originally to Hart Stilwell, the frontier novelist, who made a rough version of these beans over campfires on hunting and fishing trips. Marie Riha, who lived in Alamo, Texas, refined the dish for household use and passed it along to her daughter, Frances Poteet. The beans are sweetly delicious. If you don't have a Texan's sweet tooth, reduce the amount of brown sugar a bit.

2 POUNDS COOKED NAVY BEANS OR OTHER
   WHITE BEANS
1½ CUPS TOMATO JUICE
1 CUP CHOPPED PECANS, TOASTED
¾ CUP DARK BROWN SUGAR
¾ CUP STRONG BLACK COFFEE
½ MEDIUM RED ONION, CHOPPED
½ CUP KETCHUP
½ CUP BOURBON
4 SLICES SLAB BACON, CHOPPED
1 CARROT, GRATED FINE
2 TABLESPOONS UNSULPHURED DARK
   MOLASSES
2 TABLESPOONS DRY MUSTARD

Serves 8 to 10

Preheat the oven to 350° F.

Mix all the ingredients together in a large bowl. Pour the ingredients into a baking dish. Bake the beans, uncovered, about 1½ hours, or until they have thickened and cooked down, with a "skin" just beginning to form on the top of the beans. The beans reheat well and keep for several days.

Many people know they should eat black-eyed peas on New Year's Day for good luck during the year, but no one seems to know who made this fortunate discovery. Some writers credit farmers in Athens, Texas, the "Black-Eyed Pea Capital of the World" and home of the annual Black-Eyed Pea Jamboree. The idea may be older than Athens, however; one pea popper says it's an ancient custom in Egypt and India.

Prime-Time Mashed Potatoes

These are our special-occasion mashed potatoes, wonderfully fluffy but very rich. For everyday eating, we substitute more milk for the half-and-half and cut down the butter by several tablespoons.

2 POUNDS BAKING POTATOES, SCRUBBED, HALF OF THEM PEELED
1 TABLESPOON SALT
6 TO 8 TABLESPOONS UNSALTED BUTTER
1 CUP WHOLE MILK
½ CUP HALF-AND-HALF
SALT AND FRESH-GROUND BLACK PEPPER TO TASTE

Serves 6 to 8

Place the potatoes in a large, heavy pan, and cover them with water by at least 1 inch. Add the salt. Cook the potatoes over moderate heat until they are tender, about 25 to 35 minutes, depending upon their size. Drain the potatoes.

While the potatoes cool slightly, pour the milk and half-and-half into a medium pan, and scald them. Watch that the mixture doesn't foam over as it heats. Reserve the mixture, and keep it warm.

When the potatoes are cool enough to handle, rice or mash all but one of the potatoes back into their original pan. Cut the 1 reserved potato into chunks, and add it to the pan for a little lumpiness. Put the pan over low heat, and stir the potatoes continuously for 2 or 3 minutes to dry them out thoroughly.

Add 6 tablespoons of the butter, a tablespoon or two at a time, stirring

TECHNIQUE TIPS

These hints apply to any mashed potato recipe:

• Although waxy red potatoes have their advocates, mealy baking potatoes such as russets absorb liquid better.

• To flavor the potatoes fully, use the amount of salt listed in the recipe.

• Don't cool potatoes in their cooking water, or they'll taste watery.

• Don't skip the drying stage. It will help the potatoes later absorb the milk and butter.

• Recipes that give absolute amounts of milk and butter aren't realistic. Many factors, including the time of harvest, affect how much the potatoes will absorb well.

well after each addition. Pour in about 1 cup of the warm milk mixture, about ¼ cup at a time, while continuing to stir. Add more if the potatoes can absorb it without becoming soupy. Stir in all or part of the remaining butter too, if the potatoes can absorb the additional fat. Taste the potatoes for seasoning, and add salt, if needed, and pepper.

Although they are best served right away, you can keep the potatoes up to 1 hour in the top of a double boiler. Serve them unadorned or topped with Classic Cream Gravy (page 144).

Variations: You can add 8 to 12 garlic cloves, or even more if you're a big fan of garlic, to the potatoes as they cook. Mash the cloves along with the potatoes when both are soft. Instead, or additionally, you can mix in a chopped, sautéed onion after you add the butter.

Paris's Best French Fries

Anyone can fry potatoes, but few people know how to make memorable French fries. This is the way the best cooks in Paris, Texas, do it. The difference is some extra steps, all worth the time for superb taste and texture.

4 TO 6 MEDIUM BAKING POTATOES, PEELED OR UNPEELED
ICE CUBES
PEANUT OIL OR LARD FOR DEEP FRYING (SEE TECHNIQUE TIP)
SALT, CAJUN SEASONING, OR BOTH

Serves 4

We prefer the peels on, and, besides, leaving them on means less work. Slice the potatoes into fat matchsticks, about ⅜ inch in diameter, and put them into a bowl of cold water. Place the bowl in the refrigerator. Soak the potatoes in the water for at least 1 hour, preferably 2 hours, to eliminate much of the starch.

Pour off the water, add more cold water to cover, and toss in a half-dozen ice cubes. Place the bowl in the refrigerator. Soak the potatoes in the ice water about 30 minutes, to firm them up again. Drain them well on a dish towel or paper towels, drying off each matchstick. Then roll up the potatoes in another dry towel. You want no remaining moisture.

In a large, heavy saucepan, heat 3 to 4 inches of oil to 340° F. Add the potatoes in batches, and partially fry them about 4 minutes. They should just begin to color. Drain the potatoes. This step can be done 30 to 40 minutes before eating.

Just before serving, reheat the oil to

360° F, and fry the potatoes again for 3 to 4 minutes, or until they are golden brown. Drain the potatoes again. We favor shaking them in a brown-paper sack into which we have sprinkled the salt or Cajun seasoning. Serve the fries hot.

Variation: For "wet" Rio Grande–style French fries, ladle warm Chile con Queso (page 99) over the potatoes before serving them. If you want extra spice, top everything with jalapeño slices.

T E C H N I Q U E   T I P

Although lard breaks down at sustained high temperatures, it works well for the short cooking time of French fries and yields the crispiest results. Lard also adds a distinctive taste, which some folks like but doesn't seem to us to enhance the potatoes. Peanut oil, which is more healthful, produces a crisp fry too, and we think its flavor is a better complement for the potatoes.

Your grandmother probably didn't make French fries. They are largely a legacy of 1950s drive-in restaurants and their successors, the fast-food chains of today.

Presidential Stuffed Potatoes

Stuffed or twice-baked potatoes rank just behind mashed and fried spuds as Texas favorites. Frequently they are flavored with sour cream, cheddar cheese, and maybe bacon or green onion. Henry Haller, who was the chef at the White House during the Lyndon Johnson administration, created a more imaginative version for the president and his family. Although the dish is not for dieters, this version is lighter than the original recipe.

6 SMALL OR 3 LARGE BAKING POTATOES
OIL, PREFERABLY CORN OR CANOLA
3 TABLESPOONS UNSALTED BUTTER
2 SLICES SLAB BACON, CHOPPED
½ CUP SLICED GREEN ONIONS
⅓ TO ½ CUP MILK
½ CUP SOUR CREAM
2 EGG YOLKS
1 TABLESPOON MINCED CHIVES
¾ TO 1 TEASPOON SALT
¼ TEASPOON WHITE PEPPER
GENEROUS PINCH OF NUTMEG
2 TABLESPOONS GRATED PARMESAN CHEESE
PAPRIKA

Serves 6

Preheat the oven to 375° F.
Rub the potatoes well with the oil, and prick them with a fork so steam can escape. Bake the potatoes for 1 hour, or until they are soft when pierced through. Remove the potatoes, but leave the oven on.

In a small skillet, melt the butter over medium heat. Add the bacon, and fry it until it is browned and crisp. Remove the bacon with a slotted spoon, drain it, and set it aside. Add the green onions to the butter, and sauté them over low heat until they are softened.

Cut the warm potatoes in half lengthwise. Scoop out the insides, and reserve the potato "shells." Rice the potatoes or beat them in a medium bowl until they are fluffy, adding ⅓ cup of the milk and mixing well. Stir in the sour cream, egg yolks, chives, salt, pepper, and nutmeg. Add the remaining milk if the mixture seems dry.

Spoon the potato mixture back into the shells, mounding it attractively. The potatoes can be made ahead to this point, if they are covered and refrigerated, but plan to allow a few extra minutes of baking to compensate for the cold stuffing. Sprinkle the cheese evenly over the potatoes, and add a healthy dash of paprika on top.

Transfer the potatoes to a baking dish, and bake them for 20 minutes, until they are heated through and lightly browned.

Jalapeño Potatoes

Inspired by a recipe in the 1968 Houston Junior League Cookbook, this is what we cook when we have an urge for scalloped potatoes. The original was one of the earliest jalapeño recipes published for polite company.

3 POUNDS BAKING POTATOES, PEELED OR UNPEELED

1½ TABLESPOONS SALT

4 TABLESPOONS UNSALTED BUTTER

4 TABLESPOONS UNREFINED CORN OIL OR ADDITIONAL UNSALTED BUTTER

1 MEDIUM GREEN BELL PEPPER, CHOPPED

8 TO 10 GREEN ONIONS, SLICED

3 GARLIC CLOVES, MINCED

4 OUNCES PIMIENTOS, DICED

⅓ CUP PICKLED JALAPEÑOS, SLICED, PLUS 1 TABLESPOON JALAPEÑO PICKLING LIQUID

2 TABLESPOONS ALL-PURPOSE FLOUR

2 CUPS EVAPORATED MILK

2 CUPS (8 OUNCES) GRATED MILD OR MEDIUM CHEDDAR CHEESE

Serves 6 to 8

Place the potatoes in a large, heavy pan, and cover them with water by at least 1 inch. Add the salt. Cook the potatoes over moderate heat until they are tender, about 25 to 35 minutes depending upon the size of the potatoes. Drain the potatoes, and, when they are cool enough to handle, slice them very thin.

Preheat the oven to 350° F. Grease a large baking dish.

Warm the butter and oil in a saucepan over medium heat. When the butter has melted, add the bell pepper, onions, and garlic, and sauté them until they are softened. Stir in the pimientos, the jalapeños, and the jalapeño liquid. Sprinkle the flour over the vegetables, and mix it in. Pour the milk in gradually, stirring to avoid lumps. Simmer briefly until the mixture is thickened. Remove the pan from the heat, add the grated cheese, and mix well.

Alternate layers of potatoes and sauce in the baking dish, ending with some of the sauce. Cover the dish tightly, and bake for 50 minutes to 1 hour, until the potatoes are very soft and much of the sauce has been absorbed. Serve the potatoes hot.

The potatoes can be assembled a day ahead and refrigerated. Bring the dish back to room temperature before baking.

When Mary Faulk Koock opened her celebrated Green Pastures restaurant in Austin after World War II, she fed her children the same fine fare that the patrons got. After a couple of weeks of filet mignon the kids revolted, wailing that they wanted to go back to *real* food—pinto beans.

Sweet and Savory Potato Salad

The Texas Constitution—or some serious authority at least—prohibits picnics without potato salad. This one will get you named in an amendment. It's made with mealy baking potatoes (such as russets), instead of the sturdier red tubers, so that some of the potato chunks will disintegrate.

6 MEDIUM BAKING POTATOES, PEELED

1½ CUPS MAYONNAISE

3 TO 4 TABLESPOONS SWEET PICKLE RELISH,
  PLUS 1 TO 2 TABLESPOONS JUICE

1 TABLESPOON PLUS 1 TEASPOON PREPARED
  YELLOW MUSTARD

1 TABLESPOON CIDER OR WHITE VINEGAR

½ TEASPOON WORCESTERSHIRE SAUCE

½ TEASPOON SALT

¼ TO ½ TEASPOON FRESH-GROUND BLACK
  PEPPER

¼ TO ½ TEASPOON TABASCO OR OTHER HOT
  PEPPER SAUCE

6 GREEN ONIONS, SLICED

4 HARD-BOILED EGGS, CHOPPED

3 CELERY RIBS, CHOPPED

1 TO 2 TABLESPOONS MILK, OR MORE, FOR
  THINNING

Serves 6 to 8

In a large pan of boiling salted water, cook the potatoes over high heat until they are tender, about 15 to 20 minutes. Drain the potatoes, rinse them in cold water, and drain them again. Set them aside to cool.

Combine the mayonnaise, pickle relish and juice, mustard, vinegar, Worcestershire, salt, pepper, and Tabasco in a small bowl. Set the bowl aside.

Place the green onions, eggs, and celery in a large bowl. Chop the cooled potatoes into bite-size chunks. Add the chunks to the bowl, mixing them gently with the other ingredients. Pour the mayonnaise mixture into the bowl, and stir until the ingredients are well blended. Taste your creation, adding a little more sweet pickle relish, mustard, vinegar, or salt to adjust it to your crowd. If the salad seems a little dry, add the milk, a tablespoon at a time. It should look moist but not soupy. Cover the salad, and chill it for at least 2 hours, preferably overnight. Serve the salad cold. It will keep well for several days.

Variation: You can substitute leftover mashed potatoes for the potato chunks. If you do, start with a couple of tablespoons less mayonnaise, adding more if you think it's needed. Leave out the milk completely.

A Dilly of a Potato Salad

This is a different style of potato salad from the sweet and savory version, but we like it just as well. We got the approach from Bobby Seale's **Barbeque'n with Bobby**, *in which he attributes his inspiration to family traditions in East Texas.*

4 MEDIUM BAKING POTATOES, PEELED
¾ CUP MAYONNAISE
½ MEDIUM ONION, CHOPPED
**⅓ CUP CHOPPED DILL PICKLE, PLUS 1 TABLE-
    SPOON DILL-PICKLE BRINE**
2 HARD-BOILED EGGS, CHOPPED
1 CELERY RIB, CHOPPED
½ GREEN BELL PEPPER, CHOPPED
½ RED BELL PEPPER, CHOPPED
2 TABLESPOONS MINCED PARSLEY
½ TEASPOON PAPRIKA
½ TEASPOON SALT
DRIED OR FRESH DILL, OPTIONAL
PAPRIKA, FOR GARNISH

Serves 6 to 8

In a large pan of boiling salted water, cook the potatoes over high heat until they are tender, about 15 to 20 minutes. Drain the potatoes, rinse them in cold water, and drain them again. Set them aside to cool.

Combine the mayonnaise, onion, dill pickle and brine, eggs, celery, green and red bell peppers, parsley, paprika, and salt in a large bowl. Cut the potatoes into bite-size chunks and stir them into the mixture. Taste the salad, adjusting the seasoning as you prefer. Add a little dill if you like an herby tang.

Refrigerate the salad for at least 2 hours, or overnight. Sprinkle paprika generously over the salad shortly before serving it. Serve the salad cold. It keeps well for several days.

> Potato salads have been around Texas almost as long as oil. We haven't found a single nineteenth- or early twentieth-century Texas cookbook that doesn't contain at least one recipe, and most have several.

German Hot Potato Salad

Red waxy potatoes, which hold their shape when cooked, are best for this warm salad. They're tossed with a heated, tangy-sweet dressing, which is fortified with a Bavarian beer, if you like.

8 MEDIUM RED POTATOES, PEELED OR
   UNPEELED
1½ CELERY RIBS, CHOPPED FINE
½ GREEN BELL PEPPER, CHOPPED FINE
2 HARD-BOILED EGGS, GRATED
¼ CUP SLICED GREEN ONIONS, TOPS ONLY
4 SLICES SLAB BACON, CHOPPED
½ MEDIUM ONION, CHOPPED
1 GARLIC CLOVE, MINCED
2 TEASPOONS ALL-PURPOSE FLOUR
½ TEASPOON DRY MUSTARD
¼ TEASPOON SALT
¼ TEASPOON FRESH-GROUND BLACK PEPPER
¾ CUP BEER OR UNSALTED CHICKEN STOCK
6 TABLESPOONS CIDER VINEGAR, PREFERABLY
   UNREFINED
1 TABLESPOON PLUS 1 TEASPOON SUGAR

Serves 6 to 8

In a large pan of boiling salted water, cook the potatoes over high heat until they are tender, about 15 to 20 minutes. Drain the potatoes, rinse them in cold water, and drain them again. Set them aside to cool.

Place the celery, bell pepper, eggs, and green onions in a large bowl. Slice the potatoes thick, and add them to the bowl.

In a skillet over medium heat, fry the bacon until it is browned and crisp. With a slotted spoon, remove the bacon. Drain it, and set it aside. Add the onion and garlic to the warm bacon drippings, and cook them briefly, until they are softened. Sprinkle in the flour, mustard, salt, and pepper, and stir to combine. Pour in ½ cup of the beer or stock, the vinegar, and the sugar, and bring the sauce to a boil. Reduce the heat, and simmer for 2 to 3 minutes.

Pour the sauce over the potato mixture, and toss to combine. The result should be moist but not runny. If the salad seems dry, add some or all of the remaining beer or chicken stock. Taste, and adjust the seasoning. The salad should have plenty of pizzazz from the vinegar but should not be overly tart. Add the bacon shortly before serving.

Although most frequently served hot, the salad is good chilled as well.

Potato-Barley Soup

This hearty soup is based on a recipe in the Dallas Czech Club's book, Generation to Generation: Czech Foods, Customs, and Traditions, Texas-Style.

3 MEDIUM BAKING POTATOES, PEELED OR UN-
   PEELED, CHOPPED IN BITE-SIZE CHUNKS
½ CUP PEARL BARLEY
1 ONION, CHOPPED
2 TABLESPOONS FRESH OR 1 TABLESPOON
   DRIED DILL
1½ TEASPOONS SALT, OR MORE, TO TASTE
6 CUPS UNSALTED CHICKEN STOCK
2 HARD-BOILED EGGS, SIEVED OR GRATED
¾ CUP SOUR CREAM

Serves 6

Unlike this Tex-Czech specialty, many soups are too thin for Lone Star tastes. Arthur and Bobbie Coleman, in one of the best Texas cookbooks of recent decades, called their soup chapter "Crybaby Feed."

In a stockpot, combine the potatoes, barley, onion, dill, salt, and chicken stock, and bring to a boil over medium-high heat. Reduce the heat, and simmer, covered, 50 minutes to 1 hour, until the potatoes and barley are both very tender. Pour in a little water if the mixture begins to dry out. It should be thick but still soupy. Remove the pot from the heat, and stir in the eggs and sour cream. Serve the soup hot.

Candied Yams

A longtime star on Texas holiday tables, candied yams are often sugary enough to serve as a dessert. This version is sweet, but it is better balanced than some, leaving room for the potato to shine.

2 TO 2 ½ POUNDS (ABOUT 3 MEDIUM) SWEET
   POTATOES, PEELED AND SLICED ¼ TO ⅓ INCH
   THICK
½ CUP FRESH ORANGE JUICE
⅓ CUP DARK BROWN SUGAR
¼ CUP UNSALTED BUTTER
2 TO 3 TABLESPOONS SHERRY
1 TABLESPOON LIGHT CORN SYRUP
½ TEASPOON SALT
½ CUP CHOPPED PECANS, TOASTED
MARSHMALLOWS (WE PREFER THE MINIATURE
   KIND)

Serves 6

Preheat the oven to 350° F. Grease a medium baking dish.

Place the sweet potato slices in a medium saucepan, and cover them with water. Bring the water to a boil, and cook the potatoes until they are just tender, about 15 minutes.

While the potatoes cook, combine the orange juice, brown sugar, butter, sherry, corn syrup, and salt in a small saucepan, and warm them over medium-low heat.

When the potatoes are tender, drain them. Layer half of them in the baking dish. Scatter about half the pecans over the potatoes, and, if you're inclined, toss in a few marshmallows, too. Pour half of the sauce over the potatoes. Top with the remaining potatoes and pecans. Scatter as many marshmallows as your sweet tooth allows, and drizzle with the remaining sauce.

Bake the yams, uncovered, 35 to 45 minutes, or until much of the sauce is absorbed and the potatoes and marshmallows have melded together in a white-capped sea of orange. Serve the yams warm.

Tequila-Tipsy Yams

We need a dose of candied yams occasionally, but these days we usually prefer this recipe, or the one that follows this one, as a holiday substitute.

4 TABLESPOONS UNSALTED BUTTER
1¼ POUNDS SWEET POTATOES, PEELED AND
  GRATED
1½ TABLESPOONS SUGAR
1½ TABLESPOONS TEQUILA
JUICE OF ½ MEDIUM LIME
SALT AND FRESH-GROUND BLACK PEPPER TO
  TASTE
LIME WEDGES, FOR GARNISH

Serves 4

Melt the butter in a 9- to 10-inch skillet or saucepan. Add the grated potatoes, patting them down with a spatula into a solid layer. Sprinkle the sugar over the potatoes, and cook, uncovered, for about 15 minutes over medium heat. Every few minutes, scrape the potatoes up from the bottom and then pat them back down firmly. The potatoes are ready when they are soft and a little translucent, though still holding their shredded shape, and the sugar has begun to caramelize.

Before removing the pan from the heat, pour in the tequila and lime juice, and sprinkle the potatoes with salt and pepper. Toss the ingredients one more time with the spatula, and turn the potatoes into a bowl. Serve the potatoes hot, with lime wedges.

George Washington Carver improved and popularized sweet potatoes in the early twentieth century. Before then, most Americans regarded them as second-rate fare. One Texas settler left the state in 1845, telling neighbors that "dry beef, black coffee, sweet potatoes, and other hard features of your country would ruin me." The best an 1891 Austin cookbook could offer on the spud was a recipe called "A Good Receipt for Poor Sweet Potatoes."

Sweet Potato, Pecan, and Bacon Compote

This recipe was inspired by a dish Dean Fearing developed at the Mansion on Turtle Creek as an accompaniment to molasses-marinated beef tenderloin. Our simpler compote doesn't require any sous-chefs and is equally good with a holiday ham or turkey.

4 SLICES SLAB BACON, CHOPPED

2 TABLESPOONS UNSALTED BUTTER

½ MEDIUM ONION, CHOPPED FINE

½ POUND MUSHROOMS, PREFERABLY WILD, SLICED THIN

¼ CUP UNSALTED CHICKEN STOCK

1 TABLESPOON CIDER VINEGAR

1 TABLESPOON DARK BROWN SUGAR

2 TEASPOONS UNSULPHURED DARK MOLASSES

½ TEASPOON WORCESTERSHIRE SAUCE

½ TEASPOON FRESH-GROUND BLACK PEPPER

¼ TEASPOON DRIED THYME

¼ TEASPOON CHILE CARIBE OR OTHER CRUSHED MEDIUM-HOT RED CHILE

PINCH OF POWDERED GINGER

SALT TO TASTE

¾ POUND (ABOUT 1 MEDIUM) SWEET POTATO, PEELED AND DICED IN BITE-SIZE PIECES

1 DOZEN PEARL ONIONS, BLANCHED AND PEELED

½ CUP CANDIED PECANS (PAGE 479)

Serves 4 to 6

 In a large skillet, fry the bacon over medium heat until it is browned and crisp. With a slotted spoon, remove the bacon from the rendered drippings, drain it, and reserve it. Melt the butter in the drippings. Add the onion and the mushrooms, and sauté them over medium heat until they are softened, 2 or 3 minutes.

Add to the skillet the stock, vinegar, brown sugar, molasses, Worcestershire sauce, pepper, thyme, chile, ginger, and a touch of salt, and mix well. Stir in the sweet potatoes, and simmer over medium heat 2 or 3 minutes. Add the pearl onions, cover the pan, and continue to cook another 7 to 10 minutes, until both the potatoes and onions are tender. The dish can be made ahead to this point 1 hour in advance of your meal; if you do make it ahead, cover the pan at this point.

Uncover the pan, and cook another couple of minutes, stirring continually, until the sauce reduces to a glaze. Sprinkle in the pecans and the reserved bacon, and stir to mix them in. Taste, add a little more salt if you like, and serve.

Sweet Potato Hash Browns

These hash browns go as well with pork or venison as French fries do with a hamburger.

1 LARGE SWEET POTATO (ABOUT 1 POUND), PEELED AND GRATED
⅓ MEDIUM ONION, GRATED OR MINCED
1 EGG
¼ CUP ALL-PURPOSE FLOUR
2 TEASPOONS DARK BROWN SUGAR
SALT AND FRESH-GROUND BLACK PEPPER TO TASTE
OIL FOR FRYING, PREFERABLY CANOLA OR CORN

Serves 4

In a medium bowl, mix together all the ingredients except the oil. Form the mixture into eight small patties. (This step can be done 1 hour or so ahead. Refrigerate the patties until you are ready to use them.)

Warm ⅛ inch of oil in a heavy skillet over medium-high heat. Place the patties in the skillet, frying in two batches if necessary. Fry the patties for 3 to 4 minutes or until they are browned and crispy. Drain the patties, and serve them hot.

In some parts of the country farmers used to grow black-eyed peas to feed cattle, calling the beans cowpeas. When Union troops in the Civil War burned Southern crops, according to some stories, they passed over pea fields because they couldn't imagine anyone eating the animal fodder. Makes you wonder how they won, with smarts like that.

Ham-Stuffed Yams

If you like bacon in a baked potato, you'll love ham in a yam.

2 MEDIUM SWEET POTATOES

OIL, PREFERABLY CANOLA OR CORN

1 TABLESPOON UNSALTED BUTTER

2 TABLESPOONS SOUR CREAM

1 TABLESPOON PLUS 2 TEASPOONS PREPARED
  BROWN MUSTARD

1 TABLESPOON PLUS 1 TEASPOON DARK BROWN
  SUGAR

1 TEASPOON PAPRIKA, PLUS MORE FOR
  GARNISH

½ TEASPOON DRIED THYME

½ TEASPOON SALT

½ TO ¾ CUP WARM MILK

¾ CUP MINCED HAM, PREFERABLY WELL
  SMOKED, SUCH AS HORMEL CURE 81

Serves 4

Preheat the oven to 375° F.

Scrub the potatoes well, prick them in several spots, and coat them with a light film of oil. Place them on a baking sheet, and bake them until they are very soft, 1¼ hours or more, depending on the size of the potatoes. Reduce the heat to 350° F.

Remove the potatoes from the oven, and let them cool a few minutes. Slice each one in half horizontally. Scoop out the potato from each skin, being careful not to scrape through the skin. Reserve the potato shells.

Mash the potatoes well with a potato masher or a ricer. Put the mashed potatoes in a medium bowl, and vigorously mix in the butter and sour cream. Add the mustard, brown sugar, paprika, thyme, and salt. Mix in the milk, about ¼ cup at a time, adding as much as the potatoes can absorb to become light but not soupy. Fold in the minced ham.

Spoon the potato filling back into the shells, mounding it up in the center. (The potatoes can be prepared to this point a few hours ahead and refrigerated.)

Transfer the potatoes to a small baking dish. Sprinkle each potato liberally with paprika. Bake the potatoes 15 minutes, or until they are heated through. (Allow an extra 5 to 10 minutes if your potatoes were refrigerated.) Serve the potatoes hot.

Chili Onion Rings

These are best with sweet onions such as Noondays or Texas 1015s, a variety named for its October planting date, but they work well with nippier onions, too.

3 LARGE ONIONS, PREFERABLY SWEET (SUCH AS TEXAS 1015, VIDALIA, OR WALLA WALLA)

3 TO 4 CUPS BUTTERMILK

2 CUPS ALL-PURPOSE FLOUR

2 TEASPOONS SALT

2 TEASPOONS CHILI POWDER, PREFERABLY HOMEMADE (PAGE 135) OR GEBHARDT'S

1 TEASPOON GROUND DRIED RED CHILE, PREFERABLY NEW MEXICAN

1 TEASPOON SUGAR, IF YOU ARE NOT USING SWEET ONIONS

PEANUT OIL, FOR DEEP FRYING

Serves 4

Cut the onions into ¼-inch slices. In a nonreactive dish, soak the onions in the buttermilk for 30 to 60 minutes. In a brown-paper sack, combine the flour, salt, chili powder, chile, and, if it is needed, sugar. Drain the onions, and dredge them in the seasoned flour.

Pour at least 4 inches of oil into a heavy saucepan at least twice that deep. Heat the oil to 375° F. If the oil smokes before reaching the correct temperature, it cannot be used for deep frying. Use only fresh, unused oil.

Fry the onions, in batches, about 2 to 3 minutes, or until they are golden. For the crispiest results, drain the onions on paper towels and spread them on a serving platter. Don't pile them into a basket, where they are likely to get soggy. Serve the onions immediately.

TEXAS 1015S ARE THE STATE'S BEST-KNOWN SWEET ONIONS. SOME OF THE YELLOW BEAUTIES GROW AS LARGE AS GRAPEFRUIT AND ARE MILD ENOUGH TO MUNCH LIKE APPLES. LIKE OTHER SWEET ONIONS, 1015S MATURE DURING THE WINTER MONTHS, WHEN SHORTER DAYS INHIBIT THE DEVELOPMENT OF THE ACID THAT MAKES ONIONS PUNGENT. MOST SWEET ONIONS ARE AVAILABLE ONLY FROM APRIL THROUGH JUNE.

Onion Bread Pudding

A savory twist on a popular dessert, this bread pudding is particularly good with sweet onions.

1 TABLESPOON OIL, PREFERABLY CORN OR
   CANOLA
1 TABLESPOON UNSALTED BUTTER
½ MEDIUM ONION, PREFERABLY SWEET (SUCH
   AS TEXAS 1015, VIDALIA, OR WALLA WALLA),
   CHOPPED FINE
1 GARLIC CLOVE, MINCED
4 CUPS OF BITE-SIZE PIECES WHITE OR WHOLE-
   WHEAT BREAD, LIGHTLY TOASTED
½ CUP (2 OUNCES) GRATED SHARP CHEDDAR
   CHEESE
½ CUP MILK
¼ CUP HALF-AND-HALF
2 EGGS
1 TABLESPOON MINCED PARSLEY
PINCH OF CAYENNE
SALT TO TASTE

Serves 4 to 6

Preheat the oven to 350° F. Grease a baking dish.

Warm the oil and butter together in a small skillet over medium heat. Add the onion and garlic, and cook them a couple of minutes, until they are softened. Spoon the onion and garlic into a bowl, and add the re-maining ingredients, mixing well. The mixture should be very moist but not soupy. Pour it into the prepared dish. Bake the pudding 30 minutes, or until it is lightly browned and crusted on top. Serve it hot.

THE EAST TEXAS TOWN OF NOONDAY PRIDES ITSELF ON SWEET ONIONS THAT ARE AS GOOD AS TEXAS 1015S, VIDALIAS, MAUIS, AND WALLA WALLAS. THE RESIDENTS CELEBRATE THE CROP EACH JUNE IN A FESTIVAL THAT FEATURES AN "ONIONHEAD" CONTEST FOR BABIES AND BALD MEN AND A TEAR-JERKER STORYTELLING COMPETITION, IN WHICH CONTESTANTS TRY TO MAKE THE JUDGES CRY BY PEELING AN ONION AND TELLING A SAD TALE.

Popeye Noodles

German and Czech settlers, not Italians, introduced pasta in Texas. They began making Old World noodles as soon as flour became widely available in the state, in the mid-nineteenth century. The idea caught on quickly with the general population. In this dish noodles are paired with fresh spinach.

2 CUPS WHOLE MILK

2 CUPS EGG NOODLES

¼ TEASPOON SALT, OR MORE, TO TASTE

1 TABLESPOON UNSALTED BUTTER

2 TABLESPOONS CHOPPED ONION

10 TO 12 OUNCES FRESH SPINACH, CHOPPED

GENEROUS GRIND OF BLACK PEPPER

PINCH OF NUTMEG

1 HARD-BOILED EGG, GRATED OR SLICED,
   OPTIONAL

Serves 4

 Place the milk, noodles, salt, and butter in a large, heavy saucepan. Over low heat, cook the noodles in the milk, stirring occasionally, until they are softened and the milk has been almost completely absorbed. The noodles should be very soft and creamy in texture.

In a skillet, melt the butter over medium heat. Add the onion, and cook it briefly until it is softened. Stir in the spinach, and cook it until all the leaves are wilted.

Mix the spinach into the noodles and heat through, sprinkling in the pepper and nutmeg at the end. The egg can be added at the table, but we think the dish is rich enough, and plenty tasty, without it.

Garlic-Cheese Grits

Coarse-ground dried hominy cooked up as a stiff porridge, grits can be bland by themselves. Texans usually liven up the dish, often in this way.

1 CUP GRITS (SEE TECHNIQUE TIP)
1 TEASPOON SALT
2 TABLESPOONS UNSALTED BUTTER
½ MEDIUM ONION, MINCED
4 GARLIC CLOVES, MINCED
2 CUPS (8 OUNCES) GRATED SHARP CHEDDAR
  CHEESE
2 EGGS, LIGHTLY BEATEN
1 TEASPOON PAPRIKA
¼ TO ½ TEASPOON TABASCO OR OTHER HOT
  PEPPER SAUCE

Serves 4 to 6

 Preheat the oven to 300°F. Grease a 9-by-11-inch baking pan.

In a large saucepan (grits will expand in volume during the cooking), bring 6 cups of water to a boil. Sprinkle in the salt and grits, a handful at a time, stirring constantly. Reduce the heat to a simmer, and cook the grits about 25 minutes, until they are thickened and soft in texture. Stir the grits occasionally as they cook.

While the grits are cooking, melt the butter over medium heat in a small skillet. Add the onion and garlic, and cook them until they are well softened. Remove the skillet from the heat, and set it aside.

Take the grits off the heat. Stir in the onion-garlic mixture and the cheese, eggs, paprika, and Tabasco. Pour the grits into the prepared pan. Bake for 1 hour, or until the grits are lightly firm and slightly browned.

Let the grits sit at room temperature for at least 5 to 10 minutes before serving. Serve them warm or at room temperature, cut into squares or wedges.

Variation: For spicier grits, use jalapeño jack cheese instead of sharp cheddar, or combine them half and half.

TECHNIQUE TIP

Avoid "instant" grits, which are as phony as instant mashed potatoes. The 5-minute version called "quick" is acceptable (for this recipe, reduce the cooking time accordingly), but you get maximum flavor with the 30-minute variety.

Sour Cream-Chile Rice

In this robust rice dish, soothing sour cream offsets the heat of green chiles.

3 CUPS COOKED RICE
¾ CUP SOUR CREAM
½ CUP CHOPPED ROASTED GREEN CHILE, PREFERABLY NEW MEXICAN OR POBLANO, FRESH OR FROZEN
½ TEASPOON GROUND CORIANDER
SALT TO TASTE
1 CUP (4 OUNCES) GRATED MONTEREY JACK CHEESE
PAPRIKA

Serves 6

Preheat the oven to 350° F. Grease a baking dish.

In a bowl, stir together the rice, sour cream, chile, coriander, and salt. Spoon half the mixture into the baking dish and top with half the cheese. Spoon the remaining rice over the cheese and bake the rice, covered, 20 minutes. Uncover the rice, and top it with the remaining cheese and a liberal dusting of paprika. Continue baking for 5 more minutes, until the cheese melts. Serve the rice hot.

In recent decades two national groups competed for the honor of promoting black-eyed peas. Elmore Torn of Taylor, Texas, father of the actor Rip Torn, founded and led the National Black-Eyed Pea Association. James J. Kilpatrick, the syndicated Washington columnist, headed the Black-Eyed Pea Society of America.

Texas Pilaf

A new strain developed for its rich aroma and flavor, long-grain Texmati rice grows in southeast Texas. It's the first choice for this pilaf, in which pecans heighten the rice's natural nuttiness.

2 TABLESPOONS UNSALTED BUTTER
½ CUP CHOPPED PECANS
1 CUP BROWN RICE, PREFERABLY TEXMATI
2¼ CUPS UNSALTED STOCK (CHOOSE THE STOCK
   TO MATCH WHATEVER YOU'RE PAIRING THE
   DISH WITH)
1 TEASPOON WORCESTERSHIRE SAUCE
SALT TO TASTE
6 GREEN ONIONS, SLICED THIN

Serves 4

Melt the butter in a heavy saucepan over medium heat. Add the pecans, and sauté them 2 minutes. Stir in the rice, coating the grains with butter, and sauté another minute or two. Pour in the stock, Worcestershire sauce, and salt, and bring the rice to a boil. Reduce the heat to a simmer, cover the rice, and cook it 45 to 50 minutes, until the liquid is absorbed. Open the pan just long enough to sprinkle in the onions. Allow the rice to steam, covered, for a few more minutes. Serve the rice hot.

Japanese immigrants at the turn of the last century helped make rice a major Texas crop. They moved to the state at the urging of the Houston Chamber of Commerce, which was eager to boost the local economy. With their first harvest in 1904, Kiyoaki Saibara and other Japanese farmers nearly doubled previous rice yields.

American Indians taught Virginia colonists how to make hominy out of the native corn, using ashes and water to remove the skin of dried kernels. Right away the British newcomers began grinding the hominy into grits, which they carried with them as far as Texas in the next stages of western migration.

FARM·FRESH VEGETABLES

*N*othing but a damn vegetarian.

Sam Houston, dismissing a political rival

$\mathcal{S}$am Houston meant his comment as a curse, but you could interpret it as a compliment. Being a vegetarian in early Texas would have required more courage and resourcefulness than winning any battle Houston ever fought. Few people grew any vegetables other than corn and sweet potatoes, and some settlers held green vegetables in such disdain that they swore you risked your life by eating two in the same meal.

A little of the old attitude lingers in the state, but it's a lot easier to be a vegetable lover today. Texas farmers grow an abundance of fresh produce, and many are now selling it direct to consumers at an increasing number of farmers' markets. Just as important, over the years Texas cooks have developed, adapted, or adopted a variety of hearty garden dishes that appeal to meat-eaters and vegetarians alike. Houston would still feel at home in his old republic, but he would have to update his rhetoric.

Jalapeño Spinach Casserole

When vegetables finally took root in Texas, casserole dishes led the way to acceptance and success. Still a sure-fire winner on a Texas table, they often contain processed cheese and canned soup, which we replace with lighter and tastier ingredients that are almost as simple. This is a personal favorite, first discovered in the 1976 Dallas Junior League Cookbook but with fresher ingredients this time around.

3 TABLESPOONS UNSALTED BUTTER

4 OUNCES MUSHROOMS, SLICED

3 CELERY RIBS, CHOPPED

½ MEDIUM ONION, CHOPPED

2 TABLESPOONS MINCED PICKLED JALAPEÑO, PLUS JALAPEÑO PICKLING LIQUID TO TASTE

1 POUND FRESH SPINACH, CHOPPED

1 RECIPE NOT-CREAM-OF-MUSHROOM SOUP (PAGE 363)

1 CUP (4 OUNCES) GRATED MILD CHEDDAR CHEESE

SALT TO TASTE

⅓ CUP SALTINE CRACKER CRUMBS

Serves 4 to 6

Preheat the oven to 350° F. Butter a medium baking dish.

Melt the butter in a heavy saucepan over medium heat. Add the mushrooms, celery, onion, and jalapeño, and sauté the vegetables briefly, until they are softened. Top the sautéed vegetables with the spinach. Cover the pan, and continue cooking for several more minutes to wilt the spinach.

Stir the soup substitute into the spinach, add the cheese, and stir well. Taste, and add salt or a little jalapeño pickling liquid to give the spinach more tang.

Spoon the spinach mixture into the baking dish, and top it with the cracker crumbs. Bake the casserole 25 minutes, or until it is heated through and bubbly. Serve the casserole warm.

If you're driving around Texas, you won't find more local flavor than at a farmers' market. The Texas Department of Agriculture publishes a list of places and times, available free by calling 512-463-7593 in Austin.

Not-Cream-of-Mushroom Soup

Many vegetable casseroles call for canned cream of mushroom soup. We've come up with a more flavorful substitute that takes less than ten minutes to prepare. You can even make soup out of it, by adding stock or milk to thin the blend.

2 TABLESPOONS UNSALTED BUTTER
¾ CUP MINCED MUSHROOMS
¼ CUP MINCED ONION
2 TABLESPOONS ALL-PURPOSE FLOUR
6 OUNCES EVAPORATED MILK (SKIMMED
  EVAPORATED MILK WORKS FINE), OR
  1 5-OUNCE CAN OF EVAPORATED MILK
  PLUS 2 TABLESPOONS MILK
⅛ TEASPOON WHITE PEPPER
SALT TO TASTE, OPTIONAL

Makes about 1⅓ cups, enough to replace 1 can of cream of mushroom soup in other recipes

Melt the butter in a medium skillet. Add the mushrooms and onion, and cook them over moderate heat until they are soft, about 5 minutes. Sprinkle the flour over the mushroom mixture, and cook for another minute or two, stirring continuously. Mix in the milk and white pepper, and remove the skillet from the heat. We don't normally add salt here, preferring to add it instead to the finished dish, but it can be sprinkled in now if you wish.

Use this preparation as a substitute for canned cream of mushroom soup concentrate. Refrigerate it, covered, until it is needed. It keeps 3 to 4 days in the refrigerator, and it can be frozen.

The Campbell Soup folks estimate that 80 percent of the cream of mushroom soup they sell goes into other dishes.

Broccoli Rice Casserole

Despite his much-publicized aversion to broccoli, even George Bush would probably like this casserole, a perennial potluck dish in the ex-president's adopted state.

2 CUPS COOKED RICE
1 TABLESPOON UNSALTED BUTTER
1¼ POUNDS FRESH BROCCOLI, CHOPPED
½ CUP CHOPPED ONION
¾ CUP (3 OUNCES) GRATED MILD CHEDDAR
   CHEESE
1 RECIPE NOT-CREAM-OF-MUSHROOM SOUP
   (PAGE 363)
¼ TEASPOON OR MORE SALT

Serves 4 to 6

Preheat the oven to 350° F. Grease a medium baking dish. Place the cooked rice in a medium bowl.

Boil or steam the broccoli and onion until both are tender. Drain them, and add them to the rice. Mix in the cheese and soup substitute, and add salt to taste. The mixture should be moist but not drippy. Spoon it into the baking dish. Cover the casserole, and bake it 25 to 30 minutes, until it is heated through and slightly bubbly. Serve the casserole hot.

George Bush's presidential library is housed at Texas A&M, the university that helps keep the state second only to California in broccoli production.

Eggplant Casserole

The sage in this casserole complements the eggplant delightfully. If you're a fan of the herb, use the larger amount recommended.

1 MEDIUM EGGPLANT, PEELED AND CUBED

1 SMALL ONION, CHOPPED

¾ CUP PLUS 2 TABLESPOONS DRY BREAD
   CRUMBS, PREFERABLY CORNBREAD

1 CUP (4 OUNCES) GRATED MILD CHEDDAR
   CHEESE

2 TABLESPOONS MILK

1 TABLESPOON UNSALTED BUTTER

1 TO 2 TEASPOONS MINCED FRESH SAGE, OR ¼
   TO ½ TEASPOON DRIED

¼ TEASPOON OR MORE SALT

FRESH-GROUND BLACK PEPPER TO TASTE

1 EGG, LIGHTLY BEATEN

Serves 6

Preheat the oven to 350° F. Grease a medium baking dish.

    Place the eggplant and onion in a medium saucepan, and add salted water to cover. Bring the vegetables to a boil, reduce the heat to a simmer, and cook 20 to 25 minutes, until the vegetables are very soft. Drain the liquid from the eggplant and onion, and purée them together in a food processor or blender, or mash them until they are smooth with a fork or potato masher. Mix in ¾ cup of the bread crumbs and ¾ cup of the cheese, reserving the rest of both. Add the milk, butter, sage, salt, and pepper. When the seasonings are adjusted to your taste, mix in the egg.

    Spoon the mixture into the baking dish. Top it with the reserved bread crumbs and cheese. Bake the casserole, uncovered, 25 to 30 minutes. Serve it immediately.

Yellow Squash and Hominy Casserole

The original El Paso recipe for this casserole had the vegetables drowning in a sea of butter, cheese, and sour cream. We like it much better when you can taste the squash and hominy, which go well together.

2 TABLESPOONS CORN OIL, PREFERABLY
 UNREFINED
½ MEDIUM ONION
1 POUND YELLOW SQUASH, CHOPPED IN
 BITE-SIZE CUBES
2 TABLESPOONS DICED RED BELL PEPPER OR
 PIMIENTO
1 PICKLED JALAPEÑO, MINCED, PLUS 1
 TEASPOON PICKLING LIQUID
¼ TEASPOON DRIED OREGANO, PREFERABLY
 MEXICAN
2 TABLESPOONS MILK
1¾ CUPS (1 CAN) HOMINY
3 TABLESPOONS SOUR CREAM
½ CUP (2 OUNCES) GRATED SHARP CHEDDAR
 OR JALAPEÑO JACK CHEESE
3 TO 4 TABLESPOONS CRUSHED TOSTADAS OR
 OTHER CORN CHIPS

Serves 4

Preheat the oven to 325° F. Grease a baking dish.

In a skillet, warm the oil over medium heat. Add the onion, and cook it until it is well softened, but not browned, about 5 minutes. Mix in the squash, bell pepper or pimiento, jalapeño and pickling liquid, and oregano, and continue cooking until the vegetables are limp. Add the milk, reduce the heat slightly, and cover the pan. Simmer the mixture 15 to 20 minutes, or until the squash is very soft. Remove the pan from the heat, and stir in the hominy and sour cream.

Layer half the vegetable mixture into the prepared baking dish, and sprinkle it with half the cheese. Top with the remaining mixture and cheese. Sprinkle the crushed tostadas over the top. Bake the casserole 30 to 35 minutes, and serve it immediately.

A New World vegetable, squash was one of the staples of the American Indian diet, along with corn and beans. It remains popular in Texas, especially the yellow crookneck variety. Urban cafeterias, from Lubbock's Furr's chain to Dallas's upscale Highland Park Cafeteria, count baked squash casseroles among their best-loved dishes.

Calabacitas

A common preparation of summer squash in West Texas, calabacitas came originally from New Mexico.

2 TABLESPOONS CORN OIL, PREFERABLY
   UNREFINED
3 MEDIUM ZUCCHINI OR YELLOW SQUASH (OR A
   COMBINATION OF THE TWO), HALVED
   LENGTHWISE AND SLICED
1 MEDIUM ONION, CHOPPED
2 CUPS CORN KERNELS, PREFERABLY FRESH
½ CUP CHOPPED ROASTED GREEN CHILE,
   PREFERABLY NEW MEXICAN OR POBLANO,
   FRESH OR FROZEN
¼ CUP MILK
1 TEASPOON DRIED OREGANO, PREFERABLY
   MEXICAN
½ TEASPOON SALT
1 TABLESPOON MINCED FRESH MINT, OPTIONAL
CRUMBLED MILD FRESH GOAT CHEESE OR
   GRATED CHEDDAR CHEESE, OPTIONAL

Serves 6

In a large skillet, heat the oil. Add the squash and onion, and sauté the vegetables over medium heat until they begin to wilt. Add the corn, green chile, milk, oregano, and salt. Cook, covered, over low heat until the vegetables are tender, about 15 to 20 minutes. Remove the skillet from the heat. If you like, mix in the mint and cheese, and serve immediately.

> Much of Texas's fresh produce comes from the Lower Rio Grande Valley, one of the most productive corners of the United States. Commercial cultivation began as soon as the railroad reached the area, in 1904, and accelerated after 1914, when growers developed grapefruit and orange trees especially adapted to the local soil and climate.

Grilled Squashalitos

These baby squash are a succulent summer accompaniment to other grilled dishes.

12 TO 16 WHOLE BABY SQUASH, PREFERABLY A COMBINATION OF ROUND OR OVAL GREEN AND YELLOW VARIETIES
GARLIC OIL OR OTHER FLAVORED OIL

Serves 4

 Fire up enough charcoal to form a single layer of coals beneath the squash.

Rub each squash generously with oil. Skewer the squash.

When the charcoals are covered with gray ash, place the skewers over the coals. Cook the squash 10 to 15 minutes, basting occasionally with oil, until they are tender. Serve the squash hot.

Fresh produce was often rare and expensive in Texas in the early years. In 1838 one devoted Galveston husband sold a town lot to buy his wife several boxes of fresh cherries.

The Travis County Farmers' Market in Austin is one of the state's liveliest. Market Master Hill Rylander promotes Texas as the "Capsicum Capital of the World," and has erected a monument on the grounds to reinforce the claim. The vendors sell plenty of hot peppers, but just about everything else as well.

Baked Acorn Squash

This is a variation on the cinnamon-scented squash served at Gennie's Bishop Grill in the Oak Cliff neighborhood of Dallas.

1 ACORN SQUASH
4 TABLESPOONS UNSALTED BUTTER
1 TABLESPOON DARK BROWN SUGAR
1 TEASPOON GROUND CANELA (MEXICAN CINNAMON) OR CINNAMON
1 TEASPOON VANILLA
PINCH OF GROUND CLOVES
PINCH OF SALT

Serves 4

 Preheat the oven to 350° F. Grease a baking sheet and a baking dish.

Halve the squash lengthwise. Transfer the squash, cut side down, to the baking sheet, and bake the squash until it is tender, about 45 minutes. Don't turn off the oven.

While the squash cooks, melt the butter in a small pan, and stir in the remaining ingredients. Keep the mixture warm until it is needed.

Cut each squash section in half. Arrange the squash, cut sides up, in the baking dish. Spoon the butter and seasonings equally over the sections. Bake the squash another 15 minutes, until it is very soft. Serve the squash hot.

> MAYBE IT'S $15 INSTEAD OF 15 MINUTES: THE SIGN IN GENNIE'S BISHOP GRILL ONE-UPS ANDY WARHOL—"IF OUR PRICES WERE HIGHER, WE'D BE FAMOUS."

East Texas
Honeyed Collard Greens

A touch of sweetening is common in Texas and Southern vegetable dishes. Collard greens pair nicely with honey, as Bobby Seale showed us in his Barbeque'n with Bobby.

3 TO 3½ POUNDS COLLARD GREENS OR KALE, TOUGH STEMS REMOVED, COARSELY CHOPPED

1 SMOKED HAM HOCK (ABOUT 1 POUND)

4 MEDIUM ONIONS, CHOPPED

2 GREEN OR RED BELL PEPPERS, CHOPPED

¾ CUP CIDER VINEGAR, PREFERABLY UNREFINED

¼ CUP PURE LIQUID HICKORY SMOKE

4 FRESH JALAPEÑOS, MINCED

2 TABLESPOONS HONEY

3 GARLIC CLOVES, MINCED

2½ TEASPOONS COARSE-GROUND BLACK PEPPER

2 TEASPOONS CELERY SEEDS

8 CUPS WATER

Serves 8

Combine all the ingredients in a large pot, and bring them to a boil. Simmer the pot, covered, about 2 hours. Remove the ham hock; when it is cool enough to handle, remove the meat from it in small chunks or shreds, and return the meat to the pot. Reheat the greens briefly, if necessary. The greens can be kept over very low heat another hour. Serve them warm with some of the liquid, the pot likker. Leftovers keep for several days.

Lula Mae Austin, who grew up in Clarksville, near Paris, in East Texas, helped us shape this book by sharing with us her fond reminiscences about a lifetime of cooking and eating. Her family added sugar rather than honey to greens, and often did the same with their other garden vegetables.

Spinach Tejano

Spanish settlers brought spinach from their native country to the New World. This dish salutes that legacy with Tex-Mex seasoning.

1½ TABLESPOONS BACON DRIPPINGS OR OLIVE
    OIL
3 TABLESPOONS MINCED ONION
1 TEASPOON CHILI POWDER, PREFERABLY
    HOMEMADE (PAGE 135) OR GEBHARDT'S
1½ POUNDS FRESH SPINACH, CHOPPED
SALT TO TASTE

Serves 4

Warm the bacon drippings or oil in a skillet over medium heat. Add the onion, and sauté it briefly over medium heat, until it is softened. Mix in the chili powder, and cook until it is fragrant. Stir in the spinach, and heat until it is wilted and warmed through. Add salt to taste, and serve the dish warm.

Variation: For a complementary flavor, add a handful of yellow or red cherry tomatoes, and warm them through with the spinach.

The Texas spinach industry dates back to the first decade of the twentieth century, when M. H. Crockett of Manor defied the agricultural experts and became one of the largest growers in the country. The state now leads all others in spinach cultivation, raising 40 percent of the nation's production.

Creamed Spinach

This is a hearty Tex-Czech specialty.

2 POUNDS FRESH SPINACH
3 SLICES SLAB BACON, CHOPPED
2 TABLESPOONS UNSALTED BUTTER
2 GARLIC CLOVES, MINCED
1 MEDIUM ONION, CHOPPED
2 TABLESPOONS ALL-PURPOSE FLOUR
1½ CUPS HALF-AND-HALF
½ TEASPOON SALT
¼ TEASPOON NUTMEG
¼ TEASPOON FRESH-GROUND BLACK PEPPER
1 OR 2 DASHES OF TABASCO OR OTHER HOT
  PEPPER SAUCE

Serves 4 to 6

Cook the spinach in a small amount of boiling salted water until it is wilted. Drain the spinach, rinse it in cold water, and drain it again, squeezing out the excess moisture. Chop the spinach and reserve it.

In a medium skillet, fry the bacon until it is browned and crisp. Remove the bacon with a slotted spoon, drain it, and reserve it. Add the butter to the warm bacon drippings. Add the garlic and onion, and sauté them until they are soft. Stir in the flour, and cook the mixture for a couple of minutes, stirring constantly. Add the half-and-half a few tablespoons at a time, stirring to avoid lumps. Add the seasonings and the reserved spinach and bacon. Serve the dish warm.

In the heart of Texas's Winter Garden region, Zavala County calls itself the "Spinach Capital of the World." The most prominent feature of Crystal City, the county seat, is a statue of Popeye, erected decades ago during the Depression.

Greens Soup
with Cornbread Dumplings

Try this tasty way to clear out the refrigerator. One version we like uses chard, mustard greens, carrot tops, and beet greens. If the greens have tender stems, you can include these as well as the tops, but chop the stems into small pieces.

1 RECIPE JUST GOOD PLAIN CORNBREAD
   BATTER (PAGE 317)
2 POUNDS MIXED GREENS (MUSTARD, TURNIP,
   COLLARD, DANDELION, AND BEET GREENS,
   SPINACH, LAMB'S QUARTERS, CHARD, KALE,
   AND CARROT TOPS ALL CAN BE USED),
   TOUGH STEMS REMOVED, COARSELY
   CHOPPED
1 ONION, CHOPPED
2 OR 3 CELERY RIBS, CHOPPED
½ TO 1 GREEN BELL PEPPER, CHOPPED
2 GARLIC CLOVES, MINCED
6 CUPS UNSALTED CHICKEN STOCK
1 TABLESPOON PAPRIKA
2 TEASPOONS CIDER VINEGAR, PREFERABLY
   UNREFINED
2 TEASPOONS CREOLE OR CAJUN SEASONING
½ TEASPOON FRESH-GROUND BLACK PEPPER
½ TEASPOON DRIED THYME
1 MEDIUM BAKING POTATO, PEELED OR
   UNPEELED, DICED
1 CUP CORN KERNELS, FRESH OR FROZEN

Serves 4 to 6

Measure out ½ cup of the cornbread batter, and reserve it.

For cornbread to serve on the side, bake the rest of the batter according to the recipe, but reduce the baking time by about 3 minutes.

Into a stockpot or large saucepan, toss the mixed greens, onion, celery, bell pepper, garlic, chicken stock, paprika, vinegar, Creole seasoning, pepper, and thyme. Bring the mixture to a boil, reduce the heat to a simmer, and cook for 1 hour, stirring occasionally.

Knox County, the "Vegetable Capital of North Texas," celebrates its crops in the Vegetable Festival each summer. In some events, contestants make human faces and other sculptured forms out of their favorite vegetables.

Add the potato to the soup. Simmer the soup an additional 20 minutes, until the greens and potato are tender.

Spoon out about half the soup, and purée it in a food processor or blender. Return the purée to the pan, add the corn, and bring the soup back to a simmer. Add the reserved cornbread batter by teaspoons to the simmering soup. Cover the soup, and cook it 15 minutes more, or until the dumplings are tender.

Ladle the soup into bowls, and serve it immediately with warm cornbread on the side.

TECHNIQUE TIP

Like unrefined oils, unrefined vinegars offer more of the character of their source. Unrefined cider vinegar smells distinctly of the fall's apple harvest.

Minted Beets

Minus a half-cup of butter, this recipe comes from a 1950 cookbook, **Favorite Dallas County Recipes**, *compiled by the Dallas County Home Demonstration Clubs.*

6 TO 7 MEDIUM BEETS (TO YIELD ABOUT 3 CUPS WHEN COOKED AND SLICED), TRIMMED
1 TABLESPOON UNSALTED BUTTER
¼ TEASPOON GROUND CLOVES
2 TABLESPOONS PEACH, APRICOT, OR JALAPEÑO JELLY
1 TABLESPOON FRESH LEMON JUICE
2 TO 2½ TABLESPOONS MINCED FRESH MINT

Serves 4 to 6

Preheat the oven to 350° F. Place the beets in a covered dish, and bake them approximately 1 hour. The beets are done when they can be pierced easily with a knife or skewer.

Allow the beets to cool until they can be easily handled. Peel the beets, and slice them.

Melt the butter in a medium saucepan, and add the beets and cloves. Over medium heat, warm the beets, stirring occasionally. After a couple of minutes, add the jelly and lemon juice, stirring to combine. Remove the pan from the heat, and stir in the mint. Serve the beets hot or at room temperature.

The Home Demonstration Clubs that developed this recipe were part of Texas A&M's Extension Service. The service provided home-economics guidance to the state's rural areas, which in 1950 included most of Dallas County.

Shiner's Soused Carrots

A success with any beer, this recipe comes from the Spoetzl Brewery in the tiny town of Shiner, Texas. The beer adds complexity to the glaze.

8 MEDIUM CARROTS, SLICED INTO THIN
   ROUNDS OR MATCHSTICKS
1 CUP BEER
1 TABLESPOON UNSALTED BUTTER
1 TO 2 TEASPOONS SUGAR
PINCH OF GROUND NUTMEG
SALT AND COARSE-GROUND BLACK PEPPER TO
   TASTE

Serves 4

In a saucepan, cover the carrots with the beer. Simmer the carrots over medium-low heat for 15 minutes, or until they are almost tender. Drain the carrots, reserving them and ¼ cup of the cooking liquid.

Melt the butter in a skillet over medium heat, and add the carrots. Sauté the carrots for 1 minute. Add the reserved cooking liquid, sugar, nutmeg, salt, and pepper. Cook the carrots 4 to 5 minutes more, stirring frequently, until the sauce reduces to a glaze. Serve the carrots hot.

Creole Green Beans
and Potatoes

Some early Texas cookbooks paid scant attention to vegetables because the writers assumed everyone knew how to boil them into submission. Occasionally the lengthy cooking works, as in this recipe, even though the time here is less than half of what you find in old recipes.

2 TABLESPOONS OIL, PREFERABLY CANOLA OR
   CORN
1 LARGE ONION, CHOPPED
1 BELL PEPPER, PREFERABLY RED, CHOPPED
2 CELERY RIBS, CHOPPED
½ CUP CHOPPED PARSLEY
2 GARLIC CLOVES, MINCED
2 BAY LEAVES
4 CUPS UNSALTED CHICKEN STOCK
2 POUNDS FRESH GREEN BEANS, SLICED IN
   2-INCH LENGTHS
2 TABLESPOONS CIDER VINEGAR
1 TEASPOON FRESH-GROUND BLACK PEPPER
¾ TEASPOON SALT, OR MORE, TO TASTE
1 TO 2 TABLESPOONS PURE LIQUID HICKORY
   SMOKE, OPTIONAL
3 MEDIUM BAKING POTATOES, CUT IN BITE-SIZE
   CHUNKS
¾ TEASPOON FILÉ POWDER

Serves 6 to 8

In a large, heavy pot, warm the oil over medium heat. Add the onion, bell pepper, celery, parsley, garlic, and bay leaves, and sauté until the vegetables soften.

Pour in the chicken stock, and add the green beans, vinegar, pepper, salt, and, if you like, the liquid smoke. Bring the mixture to a boil. Reduce the heat, and simmer 30 minutes. Add the potatoes, and cook another 20 to 25 minutes, until the potatoes are tender. Stir in the filé powder, and remove the pot from the heat. Serve the dish warm.

Once the filé powder has been added, the vegetables can be reheated, but they should not be boiled. The dish keeps for several days.

TEXANS OFTEN LIKE SMOKE FLAVOR IN VEGETABLE DISHES; THEY GET IT BY ADDING PIECES OF SMOKED MEAT OR LIQUID SMOKE. STONEWALL JACKSON SEEMS TO HAVE INVENTED LIQUID SMOKE DURING A BARBECUE, BY DISSOLVING TAR (FROM BURNED WOOD) IN WATER. IN THE "PURE" COMMERCIAL PRODUCT TODAY, TARS AND RESINS ARE REMOVED, MAKING IT A "NATURAL FOOD" IN U.S. DEPARTMENT OF AGRICULTURE CLASSIFICATIONS.

Granny's Green Beans

*Actually these beans are better than Granny's, because they aren't cooked quite as long. Nobody would consider them **al dente**, but they still have some life left and, sure enough, the flavor of Grandma's.*

1½ POUNDS FRESH GREEN BEANS, CUT INTO
   1- TO 2-INCH LENGTHS
3 CUPS UNSALTED CHICKEN STOCK
¼ POUND CHUNK FATBACK OR BACON
½ MEDIUM ONION, CHOPPED FINE
1 TABLESPOON COARSE-GROUND BLACK
   PEPPER
SALT TO TASTE

Serves 4 to 6

Place all the ingredients in a large saucepan. Cover the saucepan, and simmer over medium heat for 35 to 45 minutes, until the beans are very tender but not mushy. Discard the fatback or bacon.

Serve the beans warm. They reheat easily.

> A TEXAS COOKBOOK FROM THE 1880S SAYS GREEN BEANS SHOULD BE BOILED WITH BACON FOR THREE TO FOUR HOURS, "UNTIL QUITE TENDER."

Stuffed Bell Peppers

Vegetable- and rice-stuffed peppers gained popularity during World War II. One of our old recipes describes them as "easy on points," the rationing system in place at the time. This version adds more vegetables than most cooks used fifty years ago.

6 MEDIUM BELL PEPPERS, RED, GREEN, OR A
   COMBINATION OF THE TWO
1 12-OUNCE CAN V-8 JUICE, REGULAR OR SPICY
1 TABLESPOON UNSALTED BUTTER OR UNRE-
   FINED CORN OIL
2 GARLIC CLOVES, MINCED
1 TEASPOON GROUND CUMIN
1 CUP CORN KERNELS, FRESH OR FROZEN
2 SMALL TOMATOES, PREFERABLY ROMA OR
   ANOTHER ITALIAN PLUM VARIETY, CHOPPED
1 SMALL YELLOW SQUASH OR ZUCCHINI,
   CHOPPED FINE OR GRATED
1 TO 2 FRESH JALAPEÑOS, MINCED
4 GREEN ONIONS, SLICED
2 CUPS COOKED RICE
1 EGG, BEATEN
1 TABLESPOON MINCED CILANTRO
1 CUP (4 OUNCES) GRATED MONTEREY JACK
   CHEESE
SALT AND FRESH-GROUND BLACK PEPPER TO
   TASTE

Serves 6

 Preheat the oven to 350° F. Grease a baking dish that can hold the peppers snugly upright.

Slice off the tops of the peppers, and remove the seeds and cores. If any of your peppers won't stand upright, slice a little off the bottom, being careful not to cut into the pepper's cavity. Chop the pepper trimmings, and reserve them.

Pour about one-third of the V-8 juice into the baking dish. Place all the peppers in the dish, and bake them, empty, about 20 minutes.

While the peppers bake, prepare the filling: Melt the butter in a medium skillet. Sauté the garlic with the cumin over medium heat for 1 minute. Add the corn, tomatoes, squash, jalapeños, and reserved pepper trimmings. Cook the vegetables until they are softened, sprinkling in the green onion shortly before removing the skillet from the heat. Mix in the rice, egg, cilantro, and ¾ cup of the cheese. Add salt and pepper to taste, keeping in mind that the V-8 juice will contribute flavor.

Remove the peppers from the oven, and stuff each with a portion of the rice-and-vegetable mixture. Top with the remaining ¼ cup of cheese. Pour the rest of the V-8 juice on and around the peppers. Bake the stuffed peppers for 30 minutes longer.

Serve the peppers warm, spooning some of the sauce over each one.

Green Chile Corn with Cream Cheese

The Hicks family of Amarillo introduced us to this dish. The Dallas actress Morgan Fairchild also claims it as a favorite in a Texas celebrity cookbook. This version is a little spicier than either of theirs.

2 TABLESPOONS UNSALTED BUTTER
1 GARLIC CLOVE, MINCED
6 OUNCES CREAM CHEESE, CUT IN SEVERAL
    CHUNKS
¼ CUP MILK
4 CUPS CORN KERNELS, FRESH OR FROZEN
½ CUP CHOPPED ROASTED GREEN CHILE,
    PREFERABLY NEW MEXICAN OR POBLANO,
    FRESH OR FROZEN
½ TEASPOON SALT, OR MORE, TO TASTE
¼ TEASPOON FRESH-GROUND BLACK PEPPER
¼ CUP DRY BREAD CRUMBS
PAPRIKA

Serves 6

Preheat the oven to 350° F. Grease a medium baking dish.

In a saucepan, melt the butter over medium heat. Sauté the garlic in the butter until it is soft. Add the cheese and milk, and reduce the heat to low. Cook, stirring occasionally, until the cheese melts. Remove the saucepan from the heat. Mix in the corn and green chile, and add salt and pepper to taste. Pour the mixture into the baking dish. Top with the bread crumbs, and sprinkle paprika over the top. Bake 25 minutes, or until the casserole is bubbly. Serve it immediately.

Texas Veggie Trio

Potatoes, onions, and corn on the cob, simmered together with a lot of seasonings, make a great accompaniment for smoked or grilled meat and seafood.

2 QUARTS SALTED WATER
1 TABLESPOON CHILI POWDER
3 CORN EARS, HALVED
6 SMALL NEW POTATOES
6 TO 12 BOILING ONIONS
BUTTER, SALT, AND ADDITIONAL CHILI POWDER

Serves 6

In a large saucepan or small stockpot, bring the water and 1 tablespoon chili powder to a boil. Add the vegetables, and reduce the heat to a simmer. Cook the vegetables until they are tender, about 15 minutes. Serve them hot with butter and sprinklings of salt and chili powder.

TECHNIQUE TIP

If you're trying to cut saturated fat, don't substitute margarine for the butter here. Instead, try unrefined corn oil, which has a buttery corn taste all its own.

Flash-Fried Okra

A U.S. Department of Agriculture survey named okra, eggplant, and turnips as the three vegetables people like the least. Some people must not know how to cook them. No one who has tasted fried okra is going to vote against it.

1 TO 1¼ POUNDS OKRA PODS, PREFERABLY
   UNDER 2½ INCHES EACH
ICE WATER
2 TEASPOONS SALT
2 CUPS MEDIUM-GRIND CORNMEAL, PREFER-
   ABLY STONE-GROUND
OIL, PREFERABLY PEANUT, FOR DEEP FRYING

Serves 4

Place the okra in a bowl, and cover it with ice water. Add the salt, and refrigerate the okra for 30 minutes to plump it up.

Spoon the cornmeal into a medium-size brown-paper bag. Drain the okra, and cut it into thin rounds.

Pour the oil into a heavy saucepan, to a depth of at least 3 inches. Heat the oil to 360° F.

Dredge the okra in the cornmeal. Fry the okra until the cornmeal deepens slightly in color, a matter of seconds. Drain the okra, and serve it immediately.

> Some Texans will fry almost anything, including dill pickles, Camembert cheese, hog brains, turkey testicles, and avocados.

Okra, Tomato, and Corn Skillet

This medley of garden treats sings of summer days.

1 TABLESPOON UNSALTED BUTTER
1 TABLESPOON UNREFINED CORN OIL OR
   ADDITIONAL UNSALTED BUTTER
4 OUNCES OKRA PODS, SLICED IN THIN
   ROUNDS
¼ CUP (ABOUT 4) SLICED GREEN ONIONS
½ MEDIUM GREEN BELL PEPPER, CHOPPED
1 GARLIC CLOVE, MINCED
2 MEDIUM TOMATOES, PEELED AND CHOPPED
½ CUP CORN KERNELS, FRESH OR FROZEN
2 TABLESPOONS CHOPPED PARSLEY
SCANT ½ TEASPOON SALT
¼ TEASPOON CELERY SEEDS
¼ TEASPOON FRESH-GROUND BLACK
   PEPPER
¼ TEASPOON FILÉ POWDER

Serves 4

Warm the butter and oil in a saucepan over medium heat. Sauté the okra, green onions, bell pepper, and garlic until they are just softened, about 3 to 4 minutes. Add the remaining ingredients, except the filé powder, and cover the saucepan. Simmer 5 to 7 minutes, until the okra and corn are tender. Stir in the filé powder in the last minute of the cooking time. Serve the dish warm.

African slaves brought okra to the New World from their native continent and made it a mainstay in the Southern diet.

Stewed Tomatoes

Your experiences in the school cafeteria may have given you an aversion to stewed tomatoes. This recipe will bring them back into your favor.

2 SLICES SLAB BACON, CHOPPED

1 SLICE BREAD, CUBED IN BITE-SIZE PIECES
   AND TOASTED

1 CELERY RIB, CHOPPED FINE

2 TABLESPOONS MINCED ONION

1½ POUNDS VERY RIPE TOMATOES, CUT INTO
   WEDGES

1 TO 2 TEASPOONS DARK BROWN SUGAR

1 TEASPOON PAPRIKA

¾ TEASPOON SALT

½ TEASPOON FRESH-GROUND BLACK PEPPER

Serves 4

In a skillet over medium heat, fry the bacon until it is browned and crisp. With a slotted spoon, remove the bacon from the rendered drippings. Drain it, and reserve it. Add the bread cubes to the hot drippings, and toss them lightly. Remove them with a slotted spoon, and reserve them.

Stir the celery and onion into the remaining drippings, and sauté them for about 1 minute. Add the tomatoes and the additional seasonings, and cook for about 15 minutes, until the tomatoes are juicy and tender. Just before serving, mix in the reserved bread cubes and bacon. Serve the tomatoes hot.

EUROPEAN EXPLORERS FOUND TOMATOES GROWING WILD IN SOUTH AMERICA AND TOOK THEM BACK HOME——AS AN ORNAMENTAL PLANT RATHER THAN A FOOD. FOR CENTURIES MOST PEOPLE CONSIDERED THEM POISONOUS, EVEN THOUGH A FEW FRENCH AUTHORITIES INSISTED THEY WERE "LOVE APPLES." THOMAS JEFFERSON GREW TOMATOES AS EARLY AS 1781, BUT THE VAST MAJORITY OF AMERICANS SHUNNED THEM UNTIL THE EARLY TWENTIETH CENTURY.

Fried Green Tomatoes

Just before fall's first freeze, every tomato plant in the world seems to burst forth with fruit that doesn't stand a chance of getting ripe and juicy. Frying saves the hard green "love apples," and, when you add another reputed aphrodisiac, cumin, you're really ready for winter.

4 MEDIUM GREEN TOMATOES
½ CUP FLOUR
1 TEASPOON SALT
½ TEASPOON CUMIN SEEDS, TOASTED AND GROUND
¼ TEASPOON FRESH-GROUND BLACK PEPPER
2 PINCHES OF SUGAR
1 EGG
1 TABLESPOON MILK
½ CUP MEDIUM-GRIND CORNMEAL, PREFERABLY STONE-GROUND
CANOLA OIL OR VEGETABLE SHORTENING, PREFERABLY CRISCO, FOR PAN FRYING

Serves 4

Slice the tomatoes ¼ inch thick. In a small bowl, combine the flour with the salt, cumin, pepper, and sugar. In another small bowl, beat the egg with the milk. Place the cornmeal in a third small bowl.

Dredge each tomato slice in the seasoned flour, then dip it briefly in the milk mixture. Finally, dip it in the cornmeal.

In a large, heavy skillet, heat a thick film of oil or shortening. Add the tomatoes, and fry them over medium heat, turning them once. Cook the tomatoes 2 to 3 minutes per side, until they are golden brown and crispy. Serve them hot.

You may not think of cumin as a dessert flavoring, but in past centuries—as late as the nineteenth—cooks added it to cakes to stimulate a little passion in the diners.

Rot Kohl

As one historian remarked, German immigrants came to Texas with tenacity, thrift, and vinegar. This cabbage dish draws on all three.

2 TABLESPOONS BACON DRIPPINGS

1 MEDIUM ONION, CHOPPED

1 SMALL CABBAGE HEAD, SHREDDED (ABOUT 4 CUPS)

2 APPLES, GRATED

¼ CUP CIDER VINEGAR, PREFERABLY UNREFINED

¼ CUP WATER

3 TABLESPOONS DARK BROWN SUGAR

1 TEASPOON SALT

¼ TEASPOON GROUND CLOVES

COARSE-GROUND BLACK PEPPER TO TASTE

Serves 4 to 6

Warm the bacon drippings in a saucepan over medium heat. Add the onion, and sauté it briefly until it is limp. Stir in the remaining ingredients, and reduce the heat to a simmer. Cover the saucepan, and cook 20 minutes, until the cabbage is tender.

While Rot Kohl generally is served hot, leftovers are tasty right out of the refrigerator.

German and Czech settlers loved cabbage, an Old World vegetable, but other Texans were suspicious. Some claimed that it would make your skin scaly and thick.

Tex-Czech Sauerkraut

The first Czech immigrants made their sauerkraut from scratch, but you can do an authentic-tasting version much more quickly today.

1 POUND SAUERKRAUT, PREFERABLY NOT
  CANNED
1½ CUPS UNSALTED STOCK, PREFERABLY BEEF
  OR CHICKEN
1 MEDIUM BAKING POTATO, PEELED AND
  GRATED
3 TABLESPOONS CHOPPED ONION
1 TEASPOON CARAWAY SEEDS
GENEROUS GRIND OF BLACK PEPPER
1 TABLESPOON ALL-PURPOSE FLOUR

Serves 4 to 6

Drain the sauerkraut, rinse it, and drain it again. Place it in a saucepan with all the ingredients except the flour. Simmer the kraut over medium heat for about 20 minutes. With a slotted spoon, remove the kraut to a serving platter.

Add a couple of spoonfuls of the cooking broth to the flour. Stir them together, and add the flour to the pan. Cook just a few minutes, until the broth thickens and the raw flour taste disappears. Pour the sauce over the kraut, and serve. The dish usually accompanies roast pork or *klobase*, a stalwart Czech sausage.

Variation: Some cooks add a tablespoon of brown sugar or some bacon to their kraut.

As master of ceremonies for Lyndon Johnson's first presidential barbecue dinner, Cactus Pryor shared his sympathy with Ludwig Erhard, the West German chancellor, about the difficulty of barbecuing sauerkraut.

Stewed Cabbage

This idea comes from Threadgill's in Austin, a great home-cooking restaurant that makes stewed cabbage you can eat all day.

2 SLICES SLAB BACON, CHOPPED
½ MEDIUM ONION, CHOPPED
1 GARLIC CLOVE, MINCED
1 MEDIUM CABBAGE HEAD, SLICED
1½ CUPS CANNED CRUSHED TOMATOES
1 CUP UNSALTED CHICKEN STOCK
1 TABLESPOON TOMATO PASTE
½ TO 1 TEASPOON SUGAR
¼ TEASPOON FRESH-GROUND BLACK PEPPER
SEVERAL DASHES OF TABASCO OR OTHER HOT
    PEPPER SAUCE
SALT TO TASTE

Serves 4 to 6

In a skillet or large saucepan, cook the bacon until it is browned and crisp. With a slotted spoon, remove the bacon from the rendered drippings. Drain it, and reserve it. Add the onion and garlic to the drippings, and sauté them until they are softened. Add the cabbage and all the other ingredients except the Tabasco and salt. Stir well, cover the pan, and simmer for about 20 minutes. The cabbage should be soft and tender, but not cooked to oblivion, in a moderately thick sauce. If it seems a little thin, raise the heat and cook an additional couple of minutes, uncovered. Add Tabasco and salt to taste.

Serve the cabbage immediately. Refrigerated, the cabbage keeps a couple of days.

> The spot that's now Threadgill's restaurant was originally Kenneth Threadgill's gas station and country-music hangout, where Janis Joplin got her start.

Fried Cauliflower 'n' Queso

"Cauliflower is nothing but cabbage with a college education," Mark Twain claimed. *If so, this dish has a Ph.D. in Texas taste.*

1 LARGE CAULIFLOWER
2 CUPS ALL-PURPOSE FLOUR
1½ CUPS BUTTERMILK
1 EGG
2 TEASPOONS BAKING POWDER
1 TEASPOON BAKING SODA
1 TEASPOON TABASCO OR OTHER HOT PEPPER
  SAUCE
1 GARLIC CLOVE, MINCED
¾ TEASPOON SALT
1 RECIPE CHILE CON QUESO (PAGE 99)

Serves 6

Break the cauliflower into flowerettes, and transfer them to a large saucepan. Cover the cauliflower with salted water, and bring it to a boil. Cook until the cauliflower is tender but not mushy. Drain the cauliflower and reserve it.

Place the flour in a shallow bowl. In a second dish, stir together the baking powder and soda, pepper, and salt, and mix in the milk, egg, Tabasco, and garlic. The mixture will be thin. Dredge each flowerette first in the flour and then in the batter. Dunk the flowerettes back into the flour.

Add enough oil to a heavy, deep skillet or stockpot to deep-fry the flowerettes in at least 4 inches of oil. Heat the oil to 350° F. Fry the cauliflower in batches for 3 to 4 minutes, until it is golden brown. Drain the cauliflower, top it with Chile con Queso, and serve it hot.

Specialty vegetables have become a big business in Texas. Lone Star farmers now raise taro, bok choy, daikon, ginger, celeriac, Jerusalem artichokes, and more. Part of the demand has been fueled by an influx of Asian immigrants in recent decades.

COUNTRY CANNING

I love long life better than figs.

Charmian, in William Shakespeare's *Antony and Cleopatra*

*T*hat's fair, Ol' Bard, but what about fig preserves? The real question for some of us isn't about long life, or even whether to be or not to be, but whether we would want to bother perpetuating the species if we couldn't have our fig preserves.

As soon as Americans began preserving food through canning, in the mid-nineteenth century, Texans began turning the new necessity into a passionate pleasure. Not satisfied with simply laying away the bounty of summer and fall for the lean months after, Lone Star cooks developed an amazing array of treats, from chili sauces to chowchows, pepper mangoes to pickled peaches.

The canning craft declined a couple of generations ago, but it's being revived by a combination of forces, including renewed interest in specialty products, diet considerations, and the ease of working with food processors. Savvy Texans today, like their grandmothers, can put together a relish tray that glistens like the dew and tempts like a forbidden fantasy.

Life-Enriching Fig Preserves

When Bill was a kid, one of the most compelling reasons to visit Grandmother in Buda, Texas, was her fig preserves, a chunky, syrupy concoction that magically transformed white bread into manna. She picked the figs each fall off the two trees in the backyard and then cooked and canned them much as we do today.

3 POUNDS FRESH FIGS, STEMMED AND HALVED
   (ABOUT 8 TO 9 CUPS)
4 CUPS SUGAR
1 CUP WATER
1 TEASPOON POWDERED GINGER
1 TABLESPOON FRESH LEMON JUICE
1 THIN SLICE OF LEMON FOR EACH JAR

Makes 6 to 7 half-pints

 Prepare the canning jars according to the manufacturer's directions.

Combine the figs, sugar, water, and ginger in a heavy pot, and bring the mixture to a boil over high heat. Boil for 10 minutes, skimming off any foam that rises to the surface. Reduce the heat to a simmer, and cook 45 to 50 minutes, stirring up from the bottom frequently toward the end to avoid scorching. The mixture should be reduced to a thick purée. Remove the pan from the heat, and stir in the lemon juice.

With clean hands, place a lemon slice in each jar, standing it upright against the side. Pack the preserves around it, leaving ¼ inch of headspace. Process the jars in a water bath according to the manufacturer's directions, usually 10 minutes.

> FIGS ARE AN ANCIENT DELIGHT, TREASURED FOR SUCCULENCE IN ASSYRIA AND BABYLON FIVE THOUSAND YEARS AGO. CLEOPATRA NIBBLED THEM, AS DID HER ATTENDANT CHARMIAN, AND ANTONY'S FELLOW ROMANS FORCE-FED THEM TO GEESE TO HELP CREATE THE ORIGINAL FOIE GRAS.

Calico Jalapeño Jam

Jalapeño jellies and jams of various types probably outnumber blue-bonnets in Texas. This is a chunky, thick, and colorful version. Like other preparations, it enhances a variety of Lone Star dishes and makes a wonderful snack on top of cream cheese and crackers.

2 CUPS CHOPPED GREEN, RED, AND YELLOW BELL PEPPERS (ABOUT 3 SMALL TO MEDIUM PEPPERS)

⅓ CUP CHOPPED FRESH JALAPEÑOS (ABOUT 4 TO 6 JALAPEÑOS), GREEN OR RED

5½ CUPS SUGAR

1½ CUPS CIDER VINEGAR, PREFERABLY UNREFINED

1 CUP LIGHT BROWN SUGAR

2 TABLESPOONS FRESH LIME JUICE

2 3-OUNCE PACKAGES LIQUID PECTIN, SUCH AS CERTO

Makes about 7 half-pints

 Prepare the canning jars according to the manufacturer's directions.

Combine all the ingredients except the pectin in a large saucepan or stockpot. Bring the mixture to a boil over high heat, and boil vigorously for 1 minute. Immediately stir in the pectin. Bring the mixture back to a rolling boil, and boil for 1 minute more.

Spoon the jam into the prepared jars, leaving ¼ inch of headspace. Process in a water bath according to the manufacturer's directions, generally 10 minutes.

The jam may take several hours to set.

A growing number of small Texas companies make fine specialty jams, jellies, and preserves. One of the best firms is Fischer and Wieser, also known as Das Peach Haus, in Fredericksburg. Mark Fischer and Case Wieser produce over fifty different fruit condiments, including spicy Jalapeach Preserves and luscious Old-Fashioned Peach Preserves. See "Mail-Order Sources" (page 554) for ordering information.

Apple-Tequila Jelly

Tequila is a distinctive yet subtle addition to this jelly, which is lower in sugar than most. Your family and friends will have a hard time guessing what gives the apples such an intriguing taste.

4 CUPS APPLE CIDER (WITH NO SUGAR ADDED)
6 TABLESPOONS TEQUILA
3 CUPS SUGAR
2½ TABLESPOONS SURE-JELL LIGHT PECTIN
½ TEASPOON UNSALTED BUTTER

Makes about 7 half-pints

 Prepare the canning jars according to the manufacturer's directions.

Pour the cider and tequila into a large, heavy saucepan. Place 2 tablespoons of the sugar in a small bowl, and stir in the Sure-Jell Light, mixing well. Add the Sure-Jell Light mixture and the butter to the cider.

Bring the liquid to a full rolling boil over high heat, stirring constantly. Quickly stir in the remaining sugar, and bring the mixture back to a full rolling boil again, continuing to stir. Boil 1 minute. Remove the pan from the heat. Skim off any foam, although the addition of the butter should prevent much from forming.

Fill the reserved jars to within ⅛ inch of their tops. Process them in a water bath according to the manufacturer's directions, generally 10 minutes.

The jelly may take several hours to set.

Many cultures have ascribed erotic qualities to apples. In ancient Greece, if a boy tossed an apple to a girl, it was a proposal; a catch was an acceptance. The Athenian sage Solon, fearing overindulgence of some kind, forbade bridal couples from eating more than one apple between them on their wedding nights.

Texas Port Jelly

Wine jelly may sound like a trendy new idea, but the first known Texas cookbook, published in 1883, carried a recipe. This jelly is made with a full-bodied port, such as the ones from the Messina Hof Winery in Bryan, Texas. It goes great with game.

2 CUPS GOOD-QUALITY PORT
3 CUPS SUGAR
1 TABLESPOON LEMON JUICE
2 CINNAMON STICKS, BROKEN IN HALF
1 3-OUNCE PACKAGE LIQUID PECTIN, SUCH AS
  CERTO

Makes about 4 half-pints

 Prepare the canning jars according to the manufacturer's directions.

Combine the port, sugar, lemon juice, and cinnamon sticks in a heavy saucepan, and bring the mixture to a boil over high heat. Stir to help dissolve the sugar. Boil vigorously for 2 minutes, remove the pan from the heat, and immediately add the pectin.

Most Texas wineries now market jellies made from their grapes. We particularly like Messina Hof's Jalapeño Blush Jelly.

Spoon the jelly into the prepared jars, leaving ¼ inch of headspace. Place a piece of cinnamon stick in each jar. Process the jars in a water bath according to the manufacturer's directions, generally 10 minutes.

TECHNIQUE TIP

Jellies gel because of pectin, which is found in fruit. Commercial pectin, usually distilled from apples or citrus, comes powdered and in liquid gel-packs. Both kinds work well when combined with sugar and acid, but they shouldn't be substituted for each other. Low methoxyl pectins such as Sure-Jell Light are chemically treated to gel with substantially less sugar than regular powdered pectins. They are a little trickier to use but worth the trouble when you want a lower level of sweetness.

If this small batch of jelly is to be used soon, the processing can be skipped, but keep the jelly refrigerated.

Variation: Fortified wines like port make some of the best jellies, but any wine you like to drink can be used. Just substitute your favorite vintage, and eliminate the cinnamon sticks.

TECHNIQUE TIP

For a full discussion of canning, check out Jeanne Lesem's *Preserving Today*, a revised and expanded version of her 1975 *Pleasures of Preserving and Pickling*. Another helpful resource is the Ball Corporation's *Blue Book*, available from the canning products giant based in Muncie, Indiana. The book is updated every few years for the latest on techniques, recipes, and safety considerations.

Jim Hightower, former commissioner of the Texas Department of Agriculture, started the Taste of Texas program in 1983. Condiments and other foods that carry the Taste of Texas logo are made by Texas companies using Texas food products. The businesses range from familiar corporations like Wolf Brand Chili in Richardson to small-scale entrepreneurs like Z's and Key's Bees, honey producers in Point.

Bonham Pear Butter

You don't have to use good eating pears, such as Bartletts and Boscs, for this recipe. Texans make this butter as a tasty way to enjoy coarser pears, like Kieffers, which are more common in the state.

**4 POUNDS PEARS, PREFERABLY KIEFFERS,
   PEELED, CORED, AND CHOPPED**
2 CUPS SUGAR
1 CUP FRESH ORANGE JUICE
¼ CUP PEAR BRANDY
1 TO 2 TABLESPOONS FRESH LEMON JUICE

Makes about 5 half-pints

 Prepare the canning jars according to the manufacturer's directions.

Combine the pears, sugar, orange juice, brandy, and 1 tablespoon of the lemon juice in a heavy saucepan. Bring the mixture to a boil over high heat. Reduce the heat to a simmer, and cook slowly until the pears are very tender, about 30 to 35 minutes.

Spoon the mixture into a food processor or blender, and purée it, in batches if necessary, until it is smooth. Return the mixture to the heat, and simmer over low heat, stirring frequently, until it is very thick, another 25 to 30 minutes. Taste, and add the remaining lemon juice, if you like.

Spoon the mixture into the prepared jars, leaving ¼ inch of headspace. Process according to the manufacturer's directions, usually 10 minutes.

Anyone who thinks canning is a lost craft hasn't been to the State Fair of Texas lately. If you can't make it in person, check out the winning entries in the annual cookbooks, published by Elizabeth Peabody, the fair's Creative Arts head, since the 1970s. The Texas Sesquicentennial collection, from 1986, is particularly good.

Persimmon Chutney

Chutneys combine fruit with vinegar, sweetening, spices, and sometimes hot chiles. Peaches are the most common fruit used in Texas, but persimmons work well, too. Try this as an accompaniment to grilled or roasted meats or as an appetizer with crackers and cream cheese or mild goat cheese. If you plan to use the chutney within a few weeks, it doesn't have to be canned, though you should still start with sterilized jars and store it in the refrigerator.

2 POUNDS RIPE PERSIMMONS
1 CUP CHOPPED ONIONS
½ CUP WHITE VINEGAR
¼ CUP WATER
¼ CUP RAISINS
¼ CUP DARK BROWN SUGAR
1 TABLESPOON UNSULPHURED DARK MOLASSES
1 TABLESPOON MUSTARD SEEDS
½ TEASPOON POWDERED GINGER
½ TEASPOON WHITE PEPPER

Makes 4 to 5 half-pints

 Prepare half-pint canning jars according to the manufacturer's directions.

Split the skins of the persimmons, and spoon out the soft flesh. Combine the fruit and other ingredients in a heavy saucepan. Simmer the mixture over low heat for 40 to 45 minutes, stirring occasionally, until it is very thick. Add a little more water if the mixture starts to be sticky.

Spoon the chutney into the prepared jars, and screw on the lids. Refrigerate the jars, or process them in a water bath for 10 minutes. If you are processing, leave about ¼ inch headspace.

The chutney is best if it is allowed to gain flavor for a couple of days.

Texans started growing persimmons, a late fall fruit, in 1894, importing the trees from China and Japan.

> **TECHNIQUE TIP**
>
> Supermarket persimmons are often unripened, giving their taste an unpleasant blast of tannin. Allow the bright orange fruit to sit a few days at room temperature. The flavor should hint of apricots, but the texture should be juicier and more voluptuous.

Drunken Cranberry Sauce

This fruit sauce isn't actually canned, because it keeps at least two weeks in the refrigerator, longer than it will last at Thanksgiving or Christmas.

1 12-OUNCE BAG CRANBERRIES
1 TO 1¼ CUPS SUGAR
¼ TEASPOON GROUND CINNAMON
DASH OF NUTMEG
¼ CUP BOURBON

Makes about 2 cups

Preheat the oven to 350° F.
Combine the cranberries, sugar, cinnamon, and nutmeg in an 8-inch square pan, and cover the pan with aluminum foil. Bake 50 minutes to 1 hour, until the cranberries have softened and become juicy. Uncover the pan, and immediately stir in the bourbon. The alcohol will evaporate, leaving just the liquor's warm, smoky essence. Refrigerate the sauce, covered, until ready to serve.

Texans made their first jellies and jams out of wild berries and fruits. Mustang grapes, *agaritas* (a type of currant), and apple-like mayhaws were particularly popular for canning. Some of these and other heirloom ingredients are making a comeback in commercial products. For a true taste of the past, check with the companies listed in "Mail-Order Sources" (pages 553–554).

Watermelon Pickles

Hard to find at the local grocery, these morsels will make you a believer if you try them just once. Just save the rind from the next watermelon you eat, and take a little time over the following three days to complete a series of simple steps.

FIRST-DAY INGREDIENTS

RIND OF ONE LARGE WATERMELON, ABOUT 16
    CUPS CUBED
¾ CUP PICKLING SALT
1 GALLON WATER

SECOND-DAY INGREDIENTS

8 CUPS SUGAR
4 CUPS WHITE VINEGAR
2 LEMONS, SLICED THIN
1 TABLESPOON WHOLE CLOVES
1 TABLESPOON WHOLE ALLSPICE
4 CINNAMON STICKS, BROKEN IN HALF
¼ TEASPOON MUSTARD SEEDS

Makes about 8 pints

The first day. This is the toughest part of the process. Cut the watermelon rind into manageable chunks. Scrape all the remaining red meat from the inside of the rind. Then pare off the hard green outer skin with a small knife. It's not difficult, but it takes a while. Cube the rind into bite-size pieces.

In a large bowl, dissolve the salt in the water. Transfer the rind cubes to the salted water, and weight the rind pieces down with a plate to keep them submerged. Find an out-of-the-way corner of your kitchen for the bowl, and soak the cubes about 24 hours.

The second day. Combine all the second day's ingredients in a large saucepan. Bring them to a boil, and simmer the syrup for about 5 minutes.

While the syrup simmers, drain the cubes, rinse them, and drain them again. Rinse the bowl the cubes were soaking in, and return them to it. Pour the hot syrup over the cubes, place the bowl back in its original resting place, cover it lightly, and let it sit another 24 hours, more or less.

The third day. Sterilize pint canning jars according to the manufacturer's directions.

Pour the cubes and syrup into a

WATERMELONS REQUIRE HOT WEATHER TO REACH A PEAK OF FLAVOR, BUT AFTER HARVESTING THEY KEEP BEST IN A DARK, COOL PLACE. UNTIL THE DAYS OF MODERN REFRIGERATORS, PEOPLE OFTEN STORED THEM UNDER THEIR BEDS.

large pan, and bring the mixture to a boil. With a slotted spoon, pack the cubes lightly into the prepared jars, dividing the lemon slices equally among the jars. Pour the syrup over the cubes, adding equal amounts to each jar and filling to within ½ inch of the top. Process the jars in a water bath for 10 minutes.

Allow the pickles to sit for at least one week before you indulge.

Gingered Cantaloupe Pickles

As rare as watermelon pickles on supermarket shelves, these cantaloupe cousins have an assertive gingery sweetness and tang. They're made from the meat of the melon rather than the rind, and they work best with one of the underripe specimens found so often in chain groceries.

½ CUP PICKLING LIME
2 QUARTS WATER
2 SMALL CANTALOUPES, ABOUT 3½ POUNDS TOTAL
5 CUPS SUGAR
2½ CUPS VINEGAR, PREFERABLY DISTILLED WHITE
⅓ CUP MINCED CRYSTALLIZED GINGER

Makes 7 to 8 half-pints

 The first day. Dissolve the pickling lime in the water, following the directions on the package.

Cut the cantaloupe meat from the rind, and slice it into bite-size chunks of similar size and shape. Add the cantaloupe to the lime solution, and let it stand about 4 hours at room temperature.

Drain the cantaloupe, rinse it, and drain it again. Return the fruit to the bowl, cover it with more water, and let it stand at room temperature for about 2 hours.

Drain the cantaloupe once more. Return the fruit to the bowl, and add the rest of the ingredients. Stir well to dissolve all of the sugar. Weight the fruit with a plate, and let it sit overnight.

The second day. Transfer the cantaloupe and liquid to a large saucepan. Bring the mixture to a boil quickly. Boil vigorously for about 1¼ hours, until the liquid has reduced to a thick syrup.

While the cantaloupe cooks, sterilize half-pint canning jars according to the manufacturer's directions.

With a slotted spoon, divide the fruit chunks evenly among the jars, filling them to within ½ inch of their tops.

Pour the syrup evenly over the cantaloupe. Process the jars in a water bath for 10 minutes.

Let the pickles sit at least a week to develop their flavor.

Hill Country Pickled Peaches

One of many Texas canned peach preparations, this pickled version uses firm-textured peaches. You can complete the recipe in one day if you start early, or you can spread the steps over two days.

8 POUNDS PEELED WHOLE PEACHES, SMALL TO
   MEDIUM IN SIZE, RIPE YET STILL FIRM
6 CUPS SUGAR
4 CUPS VINEGAR
2 CUPS WATER
4 CINNAMON STICKS
1½ TABLESPOONS WHOLE CLOVES
2 TEASPOONS POWDERED GINGER
½ TEASPOON WHITE PEPPER

Makes 4 quarts

Combine all the ingredients in a heavy saucepan. Bring the mixture to a rolling boil over high heat. Boil until the peaches can be pierced easily with a fork, a matter of minutes; do not allow them to soften. Remove the pan from the heat, and let the peaches sit in the syrup at room temperature for at least 8 hours or overnight.

Prepare quart canning jars according to the manufacturer's directions.

Return the pan to the stove, and bring the mixture back to a boil. Spoon the peaches into the jars, wedging them in, and divide the syrup and spices equally among the jars. Leave about ½ inch of headspace in each jar. Process the jars for 20 minutes.

For the best taste, store the peaches for at least 2 weeks before serving them.

IN OLD TEXAS COOKBOOKS, PICKLING PREPARATIONS WERE AMONG THE MOST ELABORATE. ONE RECIPE FOR PICKLED PEACHES CALLED FOR SLICING THE FRUIT IN HALF, FILLING THE CENTERS WITH A CHUTNEY-STYLE MIXTURE OF MORE PEACHES, MUSTARD, GINGER, AND OTHER INGREDIENTS, AND THEN SEWING THE HALVES BACK TOGETHER BEFORE PICKLING.

Molasses Mustard

When frontier children complained about their food, a common parental rebuff was, "Help yourself to the mustard." This pungent one would have been a treat, particularly with grilled or smoked meat. Even without canning, it lasts as long as a Houston summer.

½ CUP DRY MUSTARD
4 TABLESPOONS BEER
2 TABLESPOONS UNSULPHURED DARK
   MOLASSES
2 TABLESPOONS CIDER VINEGAR
¼ TEASPOON GROUND CINNAMON
¼ TEASPOON GROUND ALLSPICE
¼ TEASPOON FRESH-GROUND BLACK PEPPER
⅛ TEASPOON GROUND CLOVES

Makes about 1 cup

Place all the ingredients in a small bowl, mix them together well, cover, and refrigerate. Let the mustard mellow at least 24 hours. It keeps indefinitely.

The original pickle potentate, H. J. Heinz, installed the first electric sign in New York City. It was a 40-foot-long pickle that used twelve hundred bulbs during an era when few homes had even one.

Chili Sauce Rojo

Not to be confused with sauces of red chiles, common around El Paso, a chili sauce is a ketchup with character. The short season for fresh red chiles coincides with the height of tomato season, allowing you to can a blazing crimson ketchup. A classic chili sauce by Helen Witty inspired our Rojo.

14 CUPS (ABOUT 7 POUNDS) SKINNED AND COARSELY CHOPPED TOMATOES, PREFERABLY ROMA OR ANOTHER ITALIAN PLUM VARIETY

3 CUPS (ABOUT 6 MEDIUM) MINCED RED BELL PEPPERS

3 CUPS (ABOUT 3 LARGE) MINCED ONIONS

1 CUP (ABOUT 4 MEDIUM) MINCED FRESH LARGE RED CHILES, PREFERABLY NEW MEXICAN, OR ¾ CUP (ABOUT 8 MEDIUM) MINCED RED JALAPEÑOS

1 CUP (2 TO 3 RIBS) MINCED CELERY

3 GARLIC CLOVES, MINCED

3 CUPS CIDER VINEGAR

1 CUP DARK BROWN SUGAR

½ CUP LIGHT CORN SYRUP

¼ CUP PICKLING SALT

1 TABLESPOON MUSTARD SEEDS

2 TEASPOONS GROUND CINNAMON

1½ TEASPOONS GROUND CLOVES

TABASCO OR OTHER HOT PEPPER SAUCE, OPTIONAL

Makes about 7 pints

Place all the ingredients, except the Tabasco, in a stockpot. Bring the mixture to a boil, reduce the heat, and simmer for about 2½ hours, stirring occasionally. The mixture is ready when it has cooked down to a thick sauce. Stir it more fre-quently toward the end of the cooking time to prevent it from sticking. The seasoning can be adjusted near the end, with a few splashes of Tabasco added if the heat level is not sufficient. We sometimes add another tablespoon or so of brown sugar.

Sterilize pint canning jars and lids according to the manufacturer's directions.

When the sauce is ready, pour it into the jars, filling them to about ¼ inch from their tops. Process the jars in a water bath for 15 to 20 minutes.

For peak flavor, allow the sauce to sit at least 1 week before using it.

TECHNIQUE TIP

Tomatoes intended for fresh eating make a fine chili sauce, too, but they have to be treated a little differently because of their higher water content. Cut the tomatoes into wedges, and squeeze out most of the liquid and seeds before chopping. The cooking time will be closer to 3 hours.

Hot Cha Chowchow

Texas chowchows usually pack more pepper punch then their counter-parts elsewhere, and this one is certainly no exception.

2 POUNDS (4 TO 5 MEDIUM) GREEN TOMATOES
1½ POUNDS (ABOUT 1 HEAD) WHITE CABBAGE
1 POUND ONIONS, PREFERABLY SWEET
2 LARGE BELL PEPPERS, PREFERABLY 1 RED AND 1 GREEN
6 TO 8 FRESH JALAPEÑOS
3 TABLESPOONS PICKLING SALT
2½ CUPS CIDER VINEGAR
1½ CUPS SUGAR
2 TABLESPOONS PICKLING SPICE
1 TABLESPOON CELERY SEEDS
1 TABLESPOON MUSTARD SEEDS
2 TEASPOONS POWDERED GINGER

Makes about 5 pints

Chop all the vegetables in batches in a food processor. Chowchow is usually chopped fine, but stop short of puréeing it. You want some fresh vegetable texture to remain.

Place all the vegetables in a large bowl, and sprinkle them with the salt. Let the vegetables sit for at least 2 hours and up to 4 hours, stirring them occasionally. They will release a good bit of liquid while they rest.

Prepare pint canning jars according to the manufacturer's directions.

Bring the vinegar, sugar, and spices to a boil in a large pan or stockpot. Reduce the heat, and simmer 10 minutes. Drain the vegetables—don't rinse them—add them to the pan, and continue simmering for another 10 minutes. Bring the mixture to a rolling boil, and boil for 2 to 3 minutes.

Spoon the chowchow into the prepared jars, leaving at least ½ inch headspace, and process them for 10 minutes.

Let the chowchow sit a week to develop its flavor.

Chowchows often sport an abundance of ingredients. Other items found frequently in Texas chowchows include cauliflower, cinnamon, allspice, and turmeric.

Caddo Lake Relish

A good use for end-of-the-season green tomatoes, this zingy relish is a less complex variation on chowchow. In Caddo Lake fishing camps, the cooks usually serve it with fresh-caught fried fish and hushpuppies.

5 POUNDS (10 TO 12 MEDIUM) GREEN
  TOMATOES
1 POUND ONIONS
1 CUP CHOPPED FRESH JALAPEÑOS
2 CUPS CIDER VINEGAR, PREFERABLY
  UNREFINED
1½ CUPS SUGAR
¼ CUP PICKLING SALT

Makes about 6 pints

 Prepare pint canning jars according to the manufacturer's directions.

Coarsely chop the tomatoes, onions, and jalapeños in batches in a food processor, and reserve them. Combine the vinegar, sugar, and salt in a stockpot, and bring to a boil over high heat. Add the vegetables and boil the mixture vigorously for 2 to 3 minutes.

Spoon the relish into the prepared jars, leaving ½ inch of headspace. Process the jars in a water bath for 10 minutes.

To this day, the *Ball Blue Book*, the original bible of preserving, contains charts that tell a family of any size precisely how many jars of canned goods it will need to make it through the winter.

Hellish Sweet Relish

This pickle relish adds more zest to food than any store-bought variety.

2½ POUNDS CUCUMBERS, PREFERABLY SMALL
 PICKLING CUKES, CHOPPED FINE
1 POUND (ABOUT 3 MEDIUM) BELL PEPPERS,
 PREFERABLY RED AND YELLOW, CHOPPED
 FINE
3 FRESH GREEN CHILES, PREFERABLY NEW
 MEXICAN OR POBLANO, CHOPPED FINE
2 LARGE ONIONS, CHOPPED FINE
2 TABLESPOONS PICKLING SALT
3 CUPS CIDER VINEGAR
1¼ CUPS SUGAR
1½ TABLESPOONS PICKLING SPICE
2 CINNAMON STICKS
1 TEASPOON TURMERIC
1 TEASPOON MUSTARD SEEDS
½ TEASPOON GROUND NUTMEG

Makes 6 to 7 pints

Combine the cucumbers, bell peppers, chiles, and onions in a large bowl, and mix in the salt, which will release liquid from the vegetables. Weight the vegetables with a plate to keep them submerged. Set them aside for at least 12 hours and up to 24.

Drain and rinse the vegetables, and drain them again. Transfer the mixture to a stockpot or large saucepan. Add the remaining ingredients, and bring the mixture to a simmer over medium-low heat. Cook the mixture about 1 hour, stirring occasionally, until it is well thickened.

Prepare the canning jars according to the manufacturer's instructions.

When the relish is cooked, remove the cinnamon sticks, and spoon the rest into the prepared jars, leaving ¼ inch of headspace. Process the jars in a water bath according to the manufacturer's directions, usually 10 minutes.

Let the relish sit at least a week to develop its flavor.

A few early Texas condiments you may not find at Safeway today: Green Tomato Soy, Plum Pickles, Peach Chips, Cucumber Ketchup, Pickled Raisins, and Onion Jelly.

Slang Jang

This chunky uncooked relish—practically the Southern equivalent of salsa—doesn't need canning, making it a fast and fresh alternative to our others.

1 LARGE, VERY RIPE TOMATO, CHOPPED
2 CELERY RIBS, CHOPPED
1 MEDIUM GREEN BELL PEPPER, CHOPPED
1 MEDIUM ONION, CHOPPED
¾ CUP VINEGAR, PREFERABLY WHITE
¼ CUP WATER
¼ TO ½ TEASPOON SALT
¼ TEASPOON SUGAR
1 WHOLE DRIED CAYENNE OR CHILE DE ÁRBOL, CRUMBLED

Makes about 3 cups

In a bowl, combine all the ingredients, and mix them well. Try a spoonful, and adjust the salt, sugar, and cayenne to your taste.

Refrigerate the relish at least 30 minutes to develop the flavor. Slang Jang keeps about a week.

During his many years as a congressman from central Texas, Jake Pickle collected a pantry's worth of pickles in all forms. His name inspired such political slogans as "Our Pickle is a peach," "Pickle is a dilly," "We relish Pickle for Congress," and "We don't wanna beet Pickle."

Okra Pickles

These are some of the most popular pickles in Texas, threatening to supplant fried okra as the preparation of choice for the vegetable.

2 POUNDS SMALL WHOLE OKRA

3 CUPS VINEGAR, PREFERABLY CIDER

1 CUP WATER

2 TABLESPOONS PICKLING SALT

2 TEASPOONS TABASCO OR OTHER HOT PEPPER SAUCE

2 TEASPOONS WHITE WINE WORCESTERSHIRE SAUCE

FOR EACH JAR

1 TO 2 SMALL WHOLE DRIED CHILES, PREFERABLY PEQUÍN, DE ÁRBOL, OR CAYENNE

1 GARLIC CLOVE

1 FRESH DILL "HEAD" WITH SEEDS

¼ TEASPOON MUSTARD SEEDS

Makes approximately 4 pints

 In a large bowl, soak the okra in cold water for about 1 hour to plump it.

While the okra soaks, sterilize the canning jars according to the manufacturer's directions.

Shortly before the okra finishes its bath, combine the vinegar, water, salt, Tabasco, and Worcestershire sauce in a medium saucepan, and bring the mixture to a boil. Simmer the pickling liquid while you prepare the okra and spices in their jars.

With clean hands, snugly pile the okra vertically into the sterilized jars, leaving about ½ inch of space at the top of each jar. Add the chiles, garlic, dill, and mustard seeds to each jar.

Ladle the hot pickling liquid over the okra in each jar, covering the okra but leaving about ½ inch of head-space. Process the jars in a water bath according to the manufacturer's directions, generally 10 minutes.

Let the pickles sit for at least a week before serving them.

TALK O' TEXAS PRODUCES SUPERB PICKLED OKRA, AVAILABLE WIDELY IN SUPERMARKETS IN THE SOUTH AND SOUTHWEST.

Pickled Jalapeños

This Texas classic is one of the quickest and easiest pickles to make at home.

3 CUPS CIDER VINEGAR

2 TABLESPOONS HONEY

2 TABLESPOONS OLIVE OIL

2 TABLESPOONS PICKLING SPICE

2 TEASPOONS SALT

2 POUNDS FRESH JALAPEÑOS, WHOLE OR
    SLICED INTO ROUNDS

4 GARLIC CLOVES

12 BLACK PEPPERCORNS

Makes 4 pints

 Prepare the canning jars according to the manufacturer's directions.

In a nonreactive saucepan, combine the vinegar, honey, oil, pickling spice, and salt, and bring the mixture to a boil over high heat. Reduce the heat to very low, and simmer the mixture while you pack the jars.

Arrange equal quantities of the jalapeños, garlic, and peppercorns in each jar. Pour the hot liquid over the peppers, leaving ½ inch of headspace. Process the jars in a water bath according to the manufacturer's directions, generally 10 minutes.

Store the pickled peppers for at least a week before eating them.

D. L. Jardine's in Austin makes great pickled jalapeños, distributed under the trademark Texas Popcorn. More stores are stocking sweet pickled jalapeño slices, too, such as Jardine's Texas Hot Wheels and the Hot and Sweet Jalapeños from Tastes of the Southwest. See "Mail-Order Sources" (page 551).

Garlic Dill Pickles

These dills may make your day over and over, all winter long. Try them with any kind of sandwich or by themselves as a low-calorie snack.

4 POUNDS 3- TO 4-INCH PICKLING CUCUMBERS
2 CUPS WATER
2 CUPS VINEGAR, PREFERABLY DISTILLED
    WHITE
⅓ CUP SUGAR
¼ CUP PICKLING SALT
2 TABLESPOONS PICKLING SPICE

FOR EACH JAR
1 FRESH DILL "HEAD" WITH SEEDS
1 BAY LEAF
2 TO 3 GARLIC CLOVES
1 SMALL DRIED HOT CHILE SUCH AS A PEQUÍN,
    CAYENNE, OR DE ÁRBOL
½ TEASPOON MUSTARD SEEDS

Makes about 7 pints

 Prepare pint canning jars according to the manufacturer's directions.

Slice the cucumbers into quarters lengthwise.

Combine the water, vinegar, sugar, and salt together in a large pan. Many cookbooks say to tie the pickling spice in a piece of cheesecloth or to put it in a large teaball before adding it to the pickling liquid. We like the look of the spice in the jars, though, so we toss it into the pot along with the other ingredients. Bring the liquid to a boil, reduce the heat, and simmer it for 15 minutes.

With clean hands, pack the cucumber spears snugly in the prepared jars. Add the dill, bay leaf, garlic, chile, and mustard seeds to each jar. Pour the hot liquid over the cucumbers, leaving ½ inch of headspace. Process the jars in a water bath for 10 minutes.

For best flavor, let the pickles sit for at least a week before serving them.

Crispy Picante Sweet Pickles

The mineral lime helps keep these hot and sweet cucumber slices crisp. The process of making them takes several days but isn't complicated.

FIRST-DAY INGREDIENTS
4 POUNDS 3- TO 4-INCH PICKLING CUCUMBERS
1 CUP PICKLING LIME
4 QUARTS WATER

SECOND-DAY INGREDIENTS
7½ CUPS CIDER VINEGAR
4½ CUPS SUGAR
2 TEASPOONS PICKLING SPICE
1½ TEASPOONS PICKLING SALT
¾ TEASPOON WHOLE CLOVES
¾ TEASPOON CELERY SEEDS
8 CHILES PEQUÍNS

Makes 7 to 8 pints

The first day. Slice the cucumbers into thin rings. In a large nonreactive bowl, dissolve the pickling lime in the water according to the manufacturer's directions, and add the cucumber slices. Let them stand about 24 hours.

The second day. Drain the cucumbers, rinse them, and drain them again. Rinse out the bowl, and return the cucumbers to it. Cover the cukes with cool water, and let them stand another 2 to 3 hours.

While the cucumbers sit, make the syrup: In a medium saucepan, combine the second day's ingredients, and bring them to a boil over high heat. Reduce the heat to a simmer,

stirring the mixture as needed to dissolve the sugar. Remove the pan from the heat.

Drain the cucumbers again well, and return them to the bowl. Pour the syrup over the cucumbers, cover them loosely, and let them sit at least 12 hours and up to 24.

The third day. Prepare pint canning jars according to the manufacturer's directions.

Transfer the pickles and syrup to a stockpot. Bring them to a boil over high heat, and boil vigorously for 30 minutes, until the cucumbers appear translucent.

Spoon the pickles and equal amounts of syrup into the jars, leaving ½ inch of headspace. Make sure each jar gets a chile. Process the jars in a water bath for 10 minutes.

For peak flavor, store the pickles for at least 1 week before eating them.

John Landis Mason's design and patent of a glass jar with a screwtop lid revolutionized the process of airtight sealing in the mid-nineteenth century, and made Mason's name synonymous with canning jars.

Five-Day Cinnamon Cukes

Pickles made with red-hot candies may sound goofy, but they taste delightful and provide a touch of Christmas color.

FIRST-DAY INGREDIENTS

16 LARGE UNWAXED CUCUMBERS
1 CUP PICKLING LIME
4 QUARTS WATER

SECOND-DAY INGREDIENTS

½ CUP VINEGAR
½ OUNCE RED FOOD COLORING
2 QUARTS PLUS **2** CUPS WATER
5 CUPS SUGAR
2 CUPS WHITE VINEGAR
¾ CUP RED-HOT CINNAMON CANDIES
8 CINNAMON STICKS

Makes about 8 pints

The first day. Peel the cucumbers and slice them lengthwise. Scoop out the seeds with a spoon or melon baller. Slice the cucumbers thin.

In a large nonreactive bowl, dissolve the pickling lime in the 4 quarts water according to the manufacturer's directions, and add the cucumbers. Let the cucumbers stand about 24 hours.

The second day. Drain the cucumbers, rinse them, and drain them again. Rinse out the bowl, and return the cucumbers to it. Cover the cukes with cool water, and let them stand another 2 to 3 hours.

While the cucumbers sit, combine the vinegar, food coloring, and the 2 quarts water in a medium saucepan. Bring the mixture to a boil over high heat. Add the cucumbers, reduce the heat, and simmer 2 hours. Drain the cucumbers again well, and return them to the bowl.

Combine the 2 cups water and the remaining ingredients in a pan, and bring them to a boil. Pour the syrup over the cucumbers, cover them loosely, and let them sit at room temperature about 24 hours.

The third day. Drain the syrup off into a saucepan, and bring it to a boil. Pour it back over the cucumbers, and cover them again.

The fourth day. Repeat the previous day's process.

The fifth day. You're almost there. Prepare pint canning jars according to the manufacturer's directions.

Transfer the cucumbers and the syrup to a saucepan, and bring them to a boil. Spoon the pickles into the jars, dividing the syrup equally and making sure each jar gets a cinnamon stick. Leave ½ inch of headspace. Process the jars in a water bath for 10 minutes.

The pickles taste best if allowed to sit for at least 1 week before eating them.

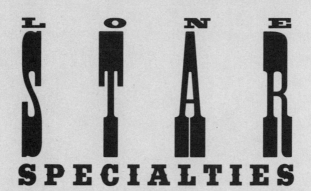

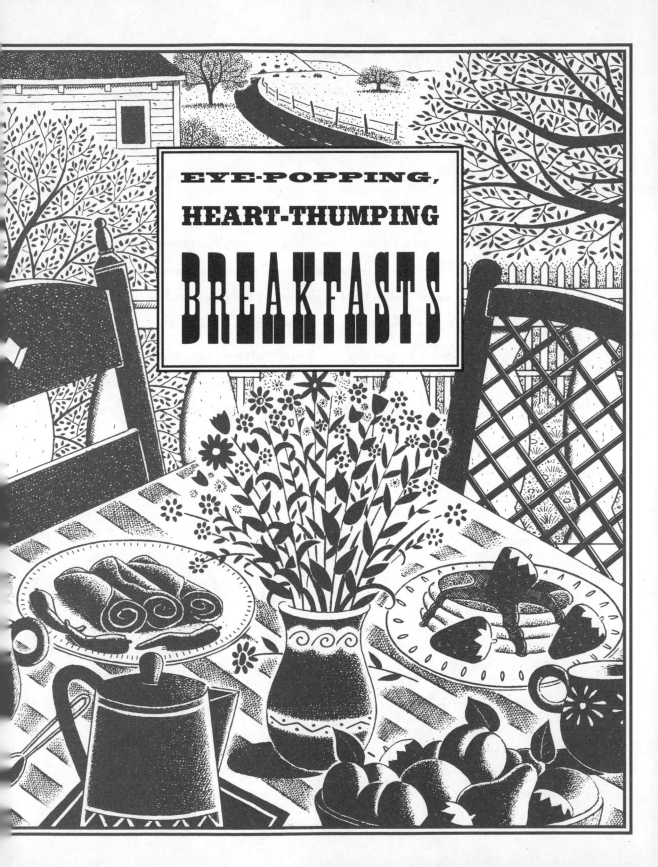

EYE-POPPING,
HEART-THUMPING
BREAKFASTS

I might have known that everything French had frog in it in some shape or other.... I made out a tolerable breakfast on other things, but would have been much better satisfied if I could have had four or five pounds of roasted buffalo-meat and a "marrow gut."

Texas pioneer Big-Foot Wallace, when he was served
fried frog legs for breakfast in New Orleans, quoted in
John C. Duval's *The Adventures of Big-Foot Wallace*

*T*exans have always been inclined to start the day in a big and snappy way. They treat breakfast like an uprising rather than an arising, a bellow instead of a yawn. It's no time for the subtle or dainty, for flaky croissants or fancy eggs. It's a time instead for robust flavor, for some sugar and spice, for locomotion. Breakfast in Texas stirs your juices.

Migas

A Tex-Mex masterpiece, migas takes its name from the Spanish word for "crumbs," a reference to the tortilla chips mixed in with the scrambled eggs. This recipe is easily doubled or tripled.

4 EGGS

1 TABLESPOON WATER

1 TABLESPOON SALSA, HOMEMADE (PAGE 96) OR STORE-BOUGHT

1 TABLESPOON BACON DRIPPINGS

¼ CUP CHOPPED GREEN BELL PEPPER

¼ CUP CHOPPED ONION

12 TO 16 TOSTADA CHIPS, BROKEN INTO BITE-SIZE PIECES

½ CUP (2 OUNCES) GRATED SHARP CHEDDAR CHEESE OR MONTEREY JACK

2 TEASPOONS MINCED CILANTRO, OPTIONAL, FOR GARNISH

Serves 2

 In a small bowl, beat the eggs lightly with the water and the salsa. Set the bowl aside.

In a heavy skillet, warm the bacon drippings over medium heat. Add the bell pepper and onion, sautéing them until they are limp. Pour in the eggs and stir them up from the bottom of the skillet as they cook. About a minute before the eggs are done, add the chips, stirring them in well. Remove the eggs from the heat, and stir in the cheese, reserving a little to scatter over the top. Sprinkle the cilantro over the eggs, too, if you like.

Serve the migas immediately with warm flour tortillas and more salsa or picante sauce.

Variation: You can substitute fresh corn tortillas for the tostada chips. Cut the tortillas into thin strips, and sauté them in the bacon drippings along with the bell pepper and onion. They will become a little chewy and crispy.

TECHNIQUE TIP

Eggbeaters or similar egg substitutes work well in migas, as they do in all our recipes that require beaten eggs. We've kept the amount of cheese moderate, here and elsewhere, but you can reduce saturated fat further by cutting the quantity or replacing a portion of it with low-fat cheese. You can also use vegetable oil in place of the bacon drippings.

Huevos Rancheros

Texas versions of this popular Mexican breakfast dish are often spicier than those you find elsewhere, including south of the border. These El Paso huevos rancheros get their punch from a combination of jalapeños and New Mexico green chiles.

RANCHERO SAUCE

1 TABLESPOON OIL, PREFERABLY CANOLA OR CORN

1 MEDIUM ONION, CHOPPED

2 GARLIC CLOVES, MINCED

1 MEDIUM GREEN BELL PEPPER, CHOPPED

½ CUP CHOPPED ROASTED GREEN CHILES, PREFERABLY NEW MEXICAN, FRESH OR FROZEN

1 TO 2 FRESH JALAPEÑOS, MINCED

4 TO 6 SMALL RIPE TOMATOES, PREFERABLY ROMA OR ANOTHER ITALIAN PLUM VARIETY, CHOPPED

1 TABLESPOON WHITE VINEGAR

2 TEASPOONS SUGAR

1 TEASPOON CUMIN SEEDS, TOASTED AND GROUND

½ TEASPOON SALT, OR MORE, TO TASTE

⅓ CUP CHOPPED CILANTRO

1 TABLESPOON FRESH LIME JUICE

OIL FOR PAN FRYING, PREFERABLY CANOLA OR CORN

8 CORN TORTILLAS

8 EGGS

½ CUP (2 OUNCES) GRATED MONTEREY JACK OR MILD CHEDDAR CHEESE

CREMA (PAGE 95) OR SOUR CREAM, CILANTRO SPRIGS, AND AVOCADO SLICES, OPTIONAL, FOR GARNISH

Serves 4

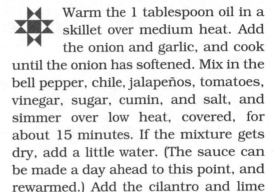 Warm the 1 tablespoon oil in a skillet over medium heat. Add the onion and garlic, and cook until the onion has softened. Mix in the bell pepper, chile, jalapeños, tomatoes, vinegar, sugar, cumin, and salt, and simmer over low heat, covered, for about 15 minutes. If the mixture gets dry, add a little water. (The sauce can be made a day ahead to this point, and rewarmed.) Add the cilantro and lime juice during the last minute or two of cooking.

Just before serving time, get out four plates.

Heat about ½ inch oil in a skillet. Dip the tortillas into the oil, one or two at a time, and cook them for a few seconds until they are soft and pliable. Drain the tortillas on paper towels. Arrange two tortillas overlapping on each plate.

Pour most of the oil from the skillet into a small bowl, leaving only enough to coat the skillet's surface generously.

Place the skillet back on the stove, and heat the oil over low heat. Fry the eggs in batches. Add a little of the reserved oil when the pan becomes dry. Top each tortilla with a fried egg. Alternatively, the eggs can be poached in the simmering sauce.

Sprinkle a couple of tablespoons of the cheese over each serving of eggs, and top with equal portions of the sauce. Serve the eggs immediately with crema or sour cream, cilantro, and avocado on the side, if you like. Huevos rancheros are almost always accompanied by refried beans (page 85).

Variation: Start the sauce by frying ¾ pounds of Chipotle Chorizo (page 80) or a good store-bought variety. Omit the oil in the sauce, using the chorizo's rendered drippings instead. Complete the dish according to the recipe.

Huevos con Queso

Whoever Benedict of egg fame was, he or she wasn't from the Lone Star State. Texans would never choose a wimpy hollandaise topping for eggs when they could have a hard-hitting chile-cheese sauce.

UNSALTED BUTTER

8 THIN SLICES CANADIAN BACON

8 EGGS

4 MEXICAN BOLILLOS (SMALL YEAST ROLLS AVAILABLE AT MEXICAN BAKERIES OR SOME LATINO OR HISPANIC MARKETS) OR ENGLISH MUFFINS

1 TO 1½ CUPS WARM CHILE CON QUESO (PAGE 99)

CHOPPED TOMATO AND SLICED GREEN ONION TOPS, OPTIONAL, FOR GARNISH

Serves 4

Warm enough butter in a skillet to form a thin film when melted. Fry the bacon until it is lightly crisped, and drain it. The eggs can be fried in the meat drippings and butter or poached.

Split and toast the bread, and butter the halves. Transfer two halves to each person's plate. Place a bacon slice on each piece of bread, and top with the eggs and equal portions of Chile con Queso. Serve the dish hot, garnished with the tomato and onion, if you wish.

CANADIAN BACON DOESN'T HAVE MUCH TO DO WITH CANADA OR BACON. IT'S ACTUALLY SMOKED EYE OF PORK LOIN, AND SOME OF THE BEST IS MADE IN TEXAS. TRY THE VERSION FROM RANCH HOUSE MESQUITE-SMOKED MEATS IN THE HILL COUNTRY BURG OF MENARD. SEE "MAIL-ORDER SOURCES" (PAGE 556) FOR ORDERING INFORMATION.

Nest Eggs

Jayne Bridges of Center, Texas, developed this dish, which won her a prize at the 1986 East Texas Poultry Festival.

6 SHREDDED WHEAT CEREAL BISCUITS, CRUSHED

3 TABLESPOONS UNSALTED BUTTER, MELTED

1 CUP (4 OUNCES) GRATED MILD CHEDDAR CHEESE

6 EGGS

6 TABLESPOONS MILK

SALT, FRESH-GROUND BLACK PEPPER, AND PAPRIKA TO TASTE

Serves 6

Preheat the oven to 350° F. Grease six custard cups.

In a small bowl, toss the cereal and butter until they are well combined. Set aside 3 tablespoons of the cereal, and divide the rest evenly among the custard cups. Press the mixture evenly against the bottoms and sides of the cups. Divide one-half of the cheese equally among the custard cups, and break an egg into each cup. Spoon 1 tablespoon of milk over each egg, and sprinkle it with salt and pepper. Cover with the remaining cheese, and spread about ½ tablespoon of the reserved cereal around the edge of each cup. Sprinkle the top of each cup with paprika.

Place the custard cups on a baking sheet. Bake for 15 to 20 minutes, or until the eggs are firm. Serve the eggs hot.

THE 1924 *PRESBYTERIAN PHILATHEA COOKBOOK* FROM GONZALES, TEXAS, IS FULL OF RECIPES USING SHELLS OR NESTS OF SHREDDED WHEAT CEREAL FOR EVERYTHING FROM STRAWBERRIES TO OYSTERS. IT'S ALSO THE EARLIEST TEXAS COOKBOOK WE'VE FOUND THAT LISTS EACH RECIPE'S INGREDIENTS SEPARATELY FROM THE COOKING INSTRUCTIONS, A BIG IMPROVEMENT IN READABILITY.

George Lang, the food guru, once said that "a well-developed breakfast fantasy can be more interesting than many people's sexual fantasies." His own scenario involved a date with Sophia Loren, some chamber music, and Peter Ustinov serving warm brioche while commenting on the news of the day.

Breakfast Tacos

Simple in concept and execution, however tasty, a breakfast taco is a flour tortilla folded or wrapped around anything on the stove. Some of the best fillings are leftovers from the night before, particularly Carne Guisada (page 72), Refried Beans (page 85), and Picadillo (page 73). Other good options include scrambled eggs, fried potatoes, chorizo (page 80), and German sausage. For a bountiful buffet, offer several of the fillings and at least one salsa.

6 CUPS ASSORTED FILLINGS (THOSE MEN-
   TIONED ABOVE OR OTHERS), WARMED
1 DOZEN 6-INCH FLOUR TORTILLAS, WARMED
1 CUP (4 OUNCES) GRATED MILD CHEDDAR
   CHEESE
1 CUP (4 OUNCES) GRATED PEPPER JACK OR
   MONTEREY JACK CHEESE
ONE OR MORE SALSAS (PAGES 95–97)
MELTED BUTTER
CHOPPED CILANTRO, OPTIONAL

Serves 4

Preheat the broiler. Grease a baking sheet.

Set out all the fillings, the tortillas, cheeses, and salsa in bowls or baskets. Top the tortillas with spoonfuls of filling, and fold them in half. Brush the tacos lightly with butter, and transfer them to the baking sheet. Pop them under the broiler for a couple of minutes, until they are slightly crisp on top.

Serve the tacos immediately with cheese and salsa, plus cilantro, if you like.

"Gradually I'm learning to like, respect, and even trust those who don't share my taste for good Bourbon, thick mutton chops, and genuine country ham, but never, repeat never, could I develop a really meaningful rapport with anyone who doesn't appreciate a wholesome and relaxing breakfast—and I mean the type of breakfast all Americans used to enjoy and not this silly thing called brunch."—James Villas, *American Taste*

High Plains Hash

This is a sure-fire way to get someone's attention in the morning, particularly if you use smoked meat and two jalapeños.

2 TABLESPOONS OIL, PREFERABLY CORN OR
  CANOLA
1 TABLESPOON UNSALTED BUTTER
2½ CUPS DICED PEELED OR UNPEELED
  POTATOES
1½ CUPS DICED ONION
1 CUP DICED RED BELL PEPPER
1 TO 2 FRESH JALAPEÑOS, MINCED
4 CUPS SHREDDED BARBECUED BRISKET OR
  ROAST BEEF
¾ CUP UNSALTED BEEF STOCK
1 TABLESPOON PREPARED YELLOW MUSTARD
1 TABLESPOON KETCHUP
1 TEASPOON COARSE-GROUND BLACK PEPPER
SALT TO TASTE

Serves 4

Warm the oil and butter together in a heavy skillet over medium heat. Add the potatoes, onion, bell pepper, and jalapeño, and sauté for 10 minutes. Mix in the remaining ingredients. Simmer, covered, for 10 minutes, stirring the mixture up from the bottom once after 6 or 7 minutes and patting it back down. Uncover the skillet, and continue cooking another minute or two until the liquid is absorbed and the mixture just begins to get crusty on the bottom. Serve the hash hot.

The inventor of Post Toasties and other cereals, C. W. Post moved to Texas at the turn of the century to create a model city. Still called Post today, the original community experimented with health care, strange crops, and the use of dynamite for rain-making.

Sausage and Apple Strata

Sometimes called overnight casseroles in Texas, stratas make breakfast a breeze because you do most of the preparation the evening before.

1 POUND UNCOOKED SMOKY SAUSAGE, CRUM-
   BLED OR SLICED THIN
2 TART APPLES, CHOPPED
5 EGGS
1½ CUPS MILK
1½ TEASPOONS DRY MUSTARD
½ TEASPOON SALT
¼ TEASPOON FRESH-GROUND BLACK PEPPER
1 SMALL LOAF GOOD-QUALITY WHITE BREAD
1 TABLESPOON CHOPPED FRESH SAGE OR 1½
   TEASPOONS DRIED
1 CUP (4 OUNCES) GRATED MONTEREY JACK
   CHEESE
1 CUP (4 OUNCES) GRATED SMOKED CHEDDAR
   OR MEDIUM CHEDDAR CHEESE

Serves 6

Grease a 9- to 10-inch baking dish.

In a skillet, fry the sausage. Add the apple, and sauté over low heat until the apple is soft.

Whisk the eggs in a medium bowl. Add the milk, dry mustard, salt, and pepper, and mix well. Cut the bread into ½-inch slices. Dip the bread into the milk and egg mixture, and wedge a single layer of the bread into the bottom of the prepared dish. Top it with half of the sausage and apple, the sage, and the cheeses. Pour half of the milk-egg mixture over the assembled ingredients. Repeat the layering with the remaining ingredients, concluding with the milk and eggs. Cover the strata, and refrigerate it overnight.

Remove the strata from the refrigerator about 30 minutes before you want to bake it. Preheat the oven to 350° F.

Bake the strata 50 to 55 minutes, or until it is puffed, golden, and set in the center. Serve it immediately.

Other chapters cover some multipurpose dishes often served at breakfast, including Menudo (page 81) and Biscuits (pages 157 and 320–323) with Classic Cream Gravy (page 144).

Broccoli-Cheese Strata

An easy overnight casserole like the previous recipe, this one is healthful enough for a vegetarian and hearty enough for a halfback.

3 CUPS CHOPPED BROCCOLI
1 TABLESPOON OLIVE OIL
½ MEDIUM RED BELL PEPPER OR 2 OUNCES PIMIENTOS
½ MEDIUM ONION, CHOPPED
1 GARLIC CLOVE, MINCED
1 CUP BUTTERMILK
4 EGGS, LIGHTLY BEATEN
½ TEASPOON SALT
½ TEASPOON FRESH-GROUND BLACK PEPPER
1 SMALL LOAF GOOD-QUALITY WHITE BREAD
1½ CUPS COTTAGE CHEESE
1½ CUPS (6 OUNCES) GRATED SHARP CHEDDAR CHEESE

Serves 6

 Blanch the broccoli in a pot of boiling salted water. Drain it, rinse it in cold water, and drain it again. Set it aside.

Warm the oil in a skillet over medium heat. Add the bell pepper or pimientos, onion, and garlic, and cook until the vegetables are softened. Remove the pan from the heat, and stir in the buttermilk, eggs, salt, and pepper.

Grease a casserole dish approximately 10 to 12 inches in diameter. Cut the bread into ½-inch slices. Dip the bread in the buttermilk mixture, and wedge a single layer of the bread into the bottom of the prepared dish.

Top with half the broccoli, cottage cheese, and cheddar cheese. Pour half the remaining buttermilk-egg mixture over the assembled ingredients. Repeat the layering with the remaining ingredients, concluding with the last of the buttermilk and eggs. Cover the strata, and refrigerate it overnight.

Remove the strata from the refrigerator about 30 minutes before you want to bake it. Preheat the oven to 350° F.

Bake the strata 50 to 55 minutes, or until it is puffed, golden, and lightly set in the center. Serve the strata immediately.

The strata doesn't reheat well, so if you don't think the whole recipe will be eaten, make it in two dishes, cooking the second batch the following day.

> In Mrs. Beeton's nineteenth-century *Book of Household Management*, the original Heloise said, "The moral and physical welfare of mankind depends largely on its breakfasts."

Sausage Upside-Down Cornbread

Like a strata, this is a complete one-dish meal. The recipe comes from East Texas. We substitute chorizo for the original German sausage.

1 POUND BULK CHORIZO (CHIPOTLE CHORIZO, PAGE 80, OR STORE-BOUGHT)
1 MEDIUM ONION, CHOPPED
1 MEDIUM GREEN BELL PEPPER, CHOPPED
1 CUP (4 OUNCES) GRATED MILD OR MEDIUM CHEDDAR CHEESE
1 RECIPE JUST GOOD PLAIN CORNBREAD BATTER (PAGE 317)

Serves 6

Preheat the oven to 400° F.

In a cast-iron skillet, fry the chorizo with the onion and bell pepper over medium heat until the chorizo is cooked through and the vegetables are very soft. Pour off and discard any fat from the skillet.

Arrange the sausage in a layer in the skillet, and sprinkle the cheese over it. Spoon the cornbread batter over the cheese. Bake about 20 minutes, or until the cornbread is lightly browned.

Remove the skillet from the oven, and let the dish stand for 5 minutes. Run a knife around the edge of the cornbread. Invert the skillet onto a plate. Serve the cornbread immediately.

During the years of the Texas Republic, Pamela Mann served big breakfasts in Houston at her Mansion House Hotel. Not puny herself, she took pride in her ability to evict rowdies and vagabonds single-handed. In 1839, a jury convicted Mann of forgery and sentenced her to death, but President Mirabeau B. Lamar pardoned her.

Chilaquiles Casserole

*In Mexico, **chilaquiles** means, colloquially, "broken-up old sombreros." The resemblance is strictly visual.*

TOMATILLO SAUCE

SALSA VERDE PICANTE, WITH ALL TOMATILLOS
(PAGE 97)
½ CUP CREAM
½ CUP UNSALTED CHICKEN STOCK
SALT AND FRESH-GROUND BLACK PEPPER TO
TASTE

CASSEROLE

OIL FOR FRYING, PREFERABLY CORN OR CANOLA
1 DOZEN STALE CORN TORTILLAS (THICKER
TORTILLAS ARE BEST—USE A COUPLE OF
EXTRA TORTILLAS IF YOURS ARE ON THE SLIM
SIDE)
1¼ CUPS CUBED COOKED CHICKEN
½ MEDIUM ONION, SLICED IN THIN RINGS
2 CUPS CRUMBLED OR GRATED CHEESE,
PREFERABLY QUESO BLANCO, ASADERO, OR
MONTEREY JACK
CREMA (PAGE 95) OR SOUR CREAM, THINNED
SLIGHTLY WITH MILK, FOR GARNISH

Serves 4 to 6

Mix together the salsa, cream, and chicken broth in a saucepan over medium-high heat. Bring the sauce to a boil, then reduce the heat, and simmer the sauce 10 minutes, until it has reduced slightly (there should be about 2½ cups). Add salt and pepper to taste, and set the sauce aside.

Preheat the oven to 350° F. Grease a shallow baking dish. Cut the tortillas into sixths.

Heat about ½ inch of oil in a skillet over medium heat. Add some of the tortilla wedges, frying them briefly until they are golden and chewy, but not as crisp as tostada chips. Drain the wedges on paper towels. Repeat until all the wedges are fried.

Dip the wedges in the tomatillo sauce, and lay them all in the bottom of the baking dish. Sprinkle the chicken, onion, and cheese over the tortilla wedges. Top the dish with the remaining tomatillo sauce. Then bake the casserole for 20 to 25 minutes, until it is bubbly. Serve the casserole hot with the crema or sour cream on the side or drizzled over the top.

To simplify the last-minute tasks, the tomatillo sauce can be made and the tortilla wedges fried the night before. Don't assemble the casserole, though, until shortly before baking, or the tortillas will get too soggy.

Old Texas lore says it's good luck to dream of eggs—unless they are broken, which is a sure sign of misfortune.

Jalapeño Pie

Called a pie because it's served in slices, this Texas treat is actually a casserole of jalapeños, cheese, and eggs, supported here by a cornmeal crust that's a Paul Prudhomme innovation. Like most versions of the dish, this is for folks who like some real sparks to get themselves ignited in the morning.

¼ CUP PLUS 2 TABLESPOONS MEDIUM-GRIND CORNMEAL, PREFERABLY STONE-GROUND

½ TEASPOON SUGAR

½ TEASPOON BAKING POWDER

1 CUP BUTTERMILK

½ CUP MILK

2 TABLESPOONS UNSALTED BUTTER

1 GARLIC CLOVE, MINCED

1½ CUPS CHOPPED ONIONS

6 TO 7 FRESH JALAPEÑOS, SLICED IN VERY THIN RINGS

1 TEASPOON GROUND DRIED RED CHILE, PREFERABLY NEW MEXICAN OR ANCHO

1¼ TEASPOONS CUMIN SEEDS, TOASTED AND GROUND

1 TEASPOON FRESH-GROUND BLACK PEPPER

½ TEASPOON SALT, OR MORE, TO TASTE

2 TABLESPOONS OIL, PREFERABLY CANOLA OR CORN

8 EGGS

2 CUPS (8 OUNCES) GRATED SHARP CHEDDAR CHEESE

Serves 6 to 8

Preheat the oven to 350° F.

Toast the cornmeal in a heavy 12-inch skillet, preferably cast-iron, until it is fragrant and just beginning to brown. The cornmeal turns quickly from lightly brown to burnt, so keep an eye on it. Stir in the sugar and the baking powder. Pour the cornmeal mixture into a medium bowl, add the buttermilk and milk to it, and stir everything together well. Set the bowl aside.

Wipe the skillet free of any clinging cornmeal, and then melt the butter in it over medium heat. Add the garlic and onion, and cook them until the onion has softened. Add the jalapeños, red chile, cumin, black pepper, and salt, and cook for 5 minutes more. Spoon the mixture into a small bowl, and reserve it.

Wipe out the skillet again, and add the oil, heating it until it is quite hot but not smoking.

Spoon the cornmeal batter into the skillet. It will pop and sizzle. Remove the skillet from the heat immediately. The batter will partially cook as it cools. After 2 minutes, top it with the jalapeño mixture, spread evenly. In a medium bowl, whisk the eggs together until they are foamy, and pour them over the jalapeño mixture. Top the eggs with the cheese.

Bake the pie for 30 minutes, or until it is lightly puffed and golden. Allow it to cool 10 to 15 minutes. Then slice it in wedges, and serve it. Leftovers can be reheated.

Potato Pancakes
with Nutmeg Applesauce

Originally from Germany, potato pancakes are still a favorite in Fredericksburg and other German towns, and nowadays pop up all around Texas.

APPLESAUCE

2 CUPS APPLESAUCE
½ TEASPOON GROUND NUTMEG

PANCAKES

2 CUPS FINELY GRATED UNCOOKED BAKING POTATOES
2 EGGS
3 TABLESPOONS MINCED ONION
2 TABLESPOONS ALL-PURPOSE FLOUR
1 TABLESPOON THIN-SLICED GREEN ONION TOPS
SCANT 1 TEASPOON SALT
½ TEASPOON COARSE-GROUND BLACK PEPPER
⅛ TEASPOON GROUND NUTMEG
OIL FOR PAN FRYING, PREFERABLY CANOLA OR CORN
1 TO 2 TEASPOONS BACON DRIPPINGS, OPTIONAL

Serves 4

 Combine the nutmeg with the applesauce, and reserve it. It can be refrigerated or served warm.

Arrange the potatoes on a dish towel, and roll up the towel jelly roll–style. Wring it, squeezing as much moisture as possible from the potatoes.

Place the potatoes in a medium bowl, and add the eggs, onion, flour, green onions, salt, pepper, and nutmeg. Stir well.

Heat a skillet over medium-high heat, and add about ¼ inch of oil. (For extra flavor, you can add a teaspoon of bacon drippings.) Spoon the batter into the hot pan, making cakes about 3 inches wide. Cook the pancakes until they are a deep golden brown on both sides, about 4 to 5 minutes total. Repeat as necessary until all the batter is used (you should get about eight pancakes). Add more oil or bacon drippings if they are needed.

Serve the pancakes immediately with the applesauce on the side.

Given the popularity of potatoes in German cooking today, it's ironic that Prussians refused to eat spuds until around 1720, when King William I threatened to cut off their noses as an alternative.

Cornmeal and Rice Pancakes

These griddle cakes from southeast Texas are supremely versatile. Serve them either sweet, with syrup and butter, or savory, with salsa and chunks of avocado.

½ CUP EXTRA-FINE-GRIND CORNMEAL, PREFER-
ABLY STONE-GROUND
½ CUP ALL-PURPOSE FLOUR
¾ TEASPOON SALT
½ TEASPOON BAKING SODA
1 TEASPOON SUGAR (INCREASE TO 1 TABLE-
SPOON IF YOU INTEND TO SERVE THE PAN-
CAKES SWEET)
1½ CUPS COOKED WHITE RICE
2 CUPS BUTTERMILK
2 EGGS, SEPARATED
2 TABLESPOONS UNSALTED BUTTER, MELTED
OIL, PREFERABLY CANOLA OR CORN, FOR PAN
FRYING

Serves 4

 Into a medium bowl, sift together the cornmeal, flour, salt,
baking soda, and sugar.

In a separate bowl, mix together the rice, buttermilk, egg yolks, and butter. Stir the mixture into the dry ingredients. Combine only lightly, leaving a few lumps.

Beat the egg whites until they form soft peaks. Fold the egg whites into the batter.

Smear a griddle or skillet with a film of oil, and heat it until a few drops of water sprinkled onto it sizzle and dance. Spoon the batter onto the grid-dle in individual portions about 4 inches in diameter. Flip the pancakes when air bubbles form on their surfaces. When browned lightly on both sides, the pancakes are done. You should be able to make twelve to sixteen 4-inch pancakes. Serve them immediately.

Variation: Brown rice is a good substitute for white rice in the savory version of the pancakes.

Many old cookbooks specified the quantities of yeast needed in recipes by price. In early Texas tomes, the typical amount was five cents' worth.

Peanut Butter French Toast with Jalapeño Jelly Syrup

Kids of all ages love this one.

JALAPEÑO JELLY SYRUP

4 TABLESPOONS UNSALTED BUTTER

2 CUPS PLUS **1** TABLESPOON JALAPEÑO JELLY OR JAM, PREFERABLY HOMEMADE (PAGE 395)

¾ CUP CORN SYRUP

¾ CUP CREAMY PEANUT BUTTER

1 TABLESPOON HONEY

12 SLICES WHITE BREAD

4 EGGS

½ CUP MILK

BUTTER OR OIL, PREFERABLY CANOLA OR CORN, FOR PAN FRYING

Serves 4

Melt the butter in a small saucepan over low heat. Add the 2 cups jelly and corn syrup, and stir to combine. Set the syrup aside, keeping it warm.

In a small bowl, combine the peanut butter with the honey and 1 tablespoon jelly. Spread equal portions of the mixture on half of the bread slices. Top each slice with another slice of bread. Cut the sandwiches in half on the diagonal.

Whisk together the eggs and milk. Dip the sandwich halves into the mixture, soaking both sides well.

Heat a griddle or heavy skillet. Add a small amount of butter or oil, and fry the sandwich halves, in batches, until they are golden brown.

Serve each guest three sandwich halves, and pass the warm jalapeño jelly syrup separately.

> A DOCTOR DEVELOPED PEANUT BUTTER AS A HEALTH FOOD FOR THE ELDERLY AND PROMOTED IT NATIONALLY AT THE 1904 ST. LOUIS WORLD'S FAIR, THE SAME EXPOSITION THAT INTRODUCED THE HAMBURGER.

> When desperate, nineteenth-century Texans sometimes made "coffee" out of dried and roasted mesquite beans, the pod-packed seeds of the scraggly tree.

Tortilla French Toast

*We adapted this savory twist on French toast from a recipe in an El Paso Junior League cookbook, **Seasoned with Sun**.*

2 EGGS
½ TEASPOON SALT
¼ CUP MILK
8 FLOUR TORTILLAS (THE THICKER THE BETTER)
2 TABLESPOONS UNSALTED BUTTER
2 TABLESPOONS OIL, PREFERABLY CANOLA OR CORN
SALSA, DICED AVOCADO, AND GRATED CHEDDAR CHEESE, FOR GARNISH

Serves 4

 Preheat the oven to 300° F. Place four plates in the oven to warm.

Combine the eggs, salt, and milk in a shallow dish. Add the tortillas one or two at a time, and soak them as you would French toast, turning once to coat them evenly.

Heat about ½ tablespoon each of the butter and oil in a heavy skillet. Fry the tortillas one at a time, cooking until they are browned lightly on each side and adding more butter and oil as needed. Place a pair of tortillas on each of the plates, arranging the tortillas side by side but overlapping a bit. Don't cover them.

Top the tortillas with salsa, some chunks of avocado, and a generous sprinkling of cheese. Serve the French toast immediately.

In his overblown book on Texas, *The Super-Americans*, English writer John Bainbridge said, "Good public eating is harder to find than oil." He claimed that outside the cities, he found himself "at the mercy of cooks and countermen who, to judge by the food they serve, are barely able to conceal their homicidal instincts." He obviously never ate breakfast in a Texas country cafe.

"Morning food is the only really good food that you can eat in your pajamas."—Margaret S. Fox and John Bear, *Morning Food*

San Saba Pecan Waffles
with Cajeta Sauce

German settlers popularized waffles in Texas, but this version owes its sparkle to a Mexican caramel sauce, cajeta, made with goat's milk. We named them for San Saba County, where we like to get the pecans that provide their substance.

CAJETA

1 QUART GOAT'S MILK
1 CUP SUGAR
1 TABLESPOON CORN SYRUP
¼ TEASPOON BAKING SODA

WAFFLES

1 CUP PECANS, TOASTED
1 CUP ALL-PURPOSE FLOUR
¾ CUP MEDIUM-GRIND CORNMEAL, PREFERABLY
  STONE-GROUND
2 TABLESPOONS SUGAR
2 TEASPOONS BAKING POWDER
½ TEASPOON SALT
3 EGGS, SEPARATED
1½ CUPS MILK
6 TABLESPOONS UNSALTED BUTTER, MELTED

ADDITIONAL BUTTER

Serves 4

Make the cajeta: In a large, heavy saucepan, combine the milk, sugar, and corn syrup, and cook over medium heat. When the mixture comes to a boil, add the baking soda, which will cause the milk to bubble merrily. Return the pan to the stove, and lower the heat so that the milk simmers steadily. Cook the milk 40 to 45 minutes, stirring occasionally at the beginning and frequently toward the end. The milk will thicken and turn golden brown. It should be the consistency of a spoonable syrup.

Cajeta can be used immediately or stored in the refrigerator, covered, to be used as needed. When rewarming it, add a little water or milk if the caramel seems too thick.

Make the waffles: Preheat a waffle iron according to the manufacturer's directions.

TECHNIQUE TIP

A little tangier than cow's milk, goat's milk is generally stocked by health food stores and is showing up in many supermarkets. Some stores stock only an evaporated canned version, a reasonable substitute. Use 2 cups of the evaporated version, adding 2 additional cups of water or regular milk.

Place ¾ cup of the pecans in a food processor, and chop them very fine. Add the flour and cornmeal, and process until the mixture reaches the consistency of meal. Add the sugar, baking powder, and salt, and process until the ingredients are blended. Transfer the mixture to a large bowl.

In another bowl, whisk the egg yolks together with the milk and butter. Stir the liquid mixture into the dry, just until they are combined.

Beat the egg whites in another bowl until stiff peaks form. Fold the whites gently into the batter.

Cook the waffles in the iron according to the manufacturer's directions.

Serve the waffles hot, accompanied by butter, the rest of the pecans, and warm cajeta.

CAJETA TAKES AN HOUR OR SO TO MAKE AND THEN KEEPS INDEFINITELY, BUT YOU CAN FIND JARS OF IT IN MEXICAN MARKETS WHEN YOU WANT AN EVEN QUICKER RESULT. CAJETA IS ALSO GOOD ON ICE CREAM AND ANGEL FOOD OR POUND CAKE, AND WITH MANGOES, PEACHES, OR SAUTÉED BANANAS.

BRING YOUR NUTCRACKER TO SAN SABA IN THE FALL FOR THE ANNUAL PECAN FESTIVAL AND VENISON CHILI COOK-OFF. THE NUMBER OF PECAN VARIETIES WILL ASTOUND YOU.

Caramel Pecan Sticky Rolls

Ruth Bauer, a New England artist and a displaced Texan, makes these superb cinnamon rolls for her annual Christmas brunch, using a largess of Lone Star pecans shipped by her uncle.

ROLLS

1 PACKAGE YEAST
¼ CUP WARM WATER
½ CUP MILK
½ CUP UNSALTED BUTTER
⅓ CUP SUGAR
½ TEASPOON SALT
½ TEASPOON VANILLA
2 EGGS
2¼ TO 2½ CUPS ALL-PURPOSE FLOUR
1 TABLESPOON GROUND CINNAMON
½ CUP DARK BROWN SUGAR

TOPPING

I CUP DARK BROWN SUGAR
½ CUP PECAN PIECES, TOASTED
¼ CUP UNSALTED BUTTER, CUT IN SEVERAL
   PIECES
6 TABLESPOONS CORN SYRUP

Makes about 1 dozen rolls

 Sprinkle the yeast over the warm water in a small bowl, and let it dissolve.

Heat the milk and ¼ cup of the butter together in a small saucepan until the butter is melted. Pour the milk and butter into a large mixing bowl, and stir in the sugar, salt, and vanilla. Let the mixture cool to lukewarm, and add the yeast. Beat in the eggs. Gradually mix in the flour, adding only as much as is needed to make a smooth dough. Turn the dough out onto a floured surface, and knead until it is satiny. Rinse and dry the bowl, and coat it lightly with oil. Place the dough back in the bowl, and turn it over so that it is covered with a film of oil. Cover the bowl with a towel, and set the bowl aside in a warm place until the dough rises to double its original size, about 1½ hours.

While the dough is rising, butter a 9-by-12-inch baking pan. Prepare the topping: Scatter the brown sugar, pecans, and butter bits in the dish, and drizzle with the corn syrup. Place the pan in the oven, and set the oven to 350° F. Heat the pan for a few minutes, until the butter has melted and the syrup is runny. Remove the pan from the oven, but leave the oven on. Stir the mixture if it has melted unevenly. Set the pan aside.

Knead the dough lightly, and roll it out into a rectangle about 10 inches by 12 inches. Melt the final ¼ cup of butter, and spread it on the dough. Sprinkle with the cinnamon and brown sugar.

Roll up the dough carefully from one of the rectangle's longer sides. Cut the roll into slices about 1 inch thick. Arrange the slices over the topping in the baking pan. Cover the pan loosely, and let the dough rise until it is doubled in size again.

Bake the rolls 30 minutes or until they are golden brown. Run a knife around the inside edge of the pan and invert the rolls onto a plate or tray.

Serve the rolls immediately, or let them cool and reheat them, covered, the following morning.

> **WAVERLEY ROOT, THE FOOD HISTORIAN, SPECULATED THAT PECANS DEVELOPED ORIGINALLY IN TEXAS AND SPREAD FROM THERE TO OTHER AREAS OF THE UNITED STATES, WHICH HAS A VIRTUAL WORLDWIDE MONOPOLY ON THE NUT EVEN TODAY.**

Gingered Banana Bread

Tropical fruits arrived early in Texas because the state's ports were closer to many of the growing areas than were other shipping points in the United States. This combination of bananas and ginger preserves makes an especially moist bread.

1¾ CUPS ALL-PURPOSE FLOUR
2½ TEASPOONS BAKING POWDER
½ TEASPOON SALT
½ CUP SUGAR
⅓ CUP UNSALTED BUTTER, AT ROOM TEMPERATURE
2 EGGS
1½ CUPS MASHED RIPE BANANAS
⅓ CUP GINGER PRESERVES
¼ CUP SOUR CREAM
¾ TEASPOON LEMON ZEST
¾ CUP CHOPPED PECANS, TOASTED, OPTIONAL

Makes 1 loaf

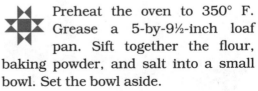 Preheat the oven to 350° F. Grease a 5-by-9½-inch loaf pan. Sift together the flour, baking powder, and salt into a small bowl. Set the bowl aside.

With a mixer, cream the sugar and butter together until the mixture is light and fluffy. Add the eggs, one at a time, beating well after each addition. Beat in the bananas, preserves, sour cream, lemon zest, and, if you wish, pecans. Spoon in the flour about a third at a time, mixing until the batter is well combined.

Pour the batter into the prepared pan, and bake 60 to 65 minutes, or until a toothpick inserted in the center comes out clean.

Serve the bread warm. Folks with a sweet tooth will like to spread more ginger preserves on each slice.

Rice Fritters

Early Texas cookbooks often featured fritters, but this variation is a more recent dish from the southeastern part of the state. It is perhaps influenced by calas, a better-known deep-fried rice pastry from New Orleans. We prefer these fritters with Texmati or another variety of naturally nutty basmati rice.

2 CUPS COOKED RICE
2 EGGS, LIGHTLY BEATEN
¼ CUP SUGAR
¼ CUP ALL-PURPOSE FLOUR
2½ TEASPOONS BAKING POWDER
½ TEASPOON LEMON OR ORANGE ZEST
¼ TEASPOON VANILLA
¼ TEASPOON GROUND CANELA (MEXICAN CINNAMON) OR CINNAMON
OIL FOR DEEP FRYING, PREFERABLY CANOLA OR CORN
POWDERED SUGAR, OPTIONAL, FOR GARNISH

Serves 4

 Combine all the ingredients except the oil and the powdered sugar in a medium bowl.

Heat at least 4 inches of oil to 375° F in a heavy saucepan. If the oil smokes before reaching the correct temperature, it cannot be used for deep frying. Use only fresh, unused oil.

Drop the batter by heaping tablespoons into the oil. As the fritters rise to the surface, turn them in the oil so they cook evenly. Fry until the fritters are puffed and golden, 4 to 5 minutes. Remove them from the oil with a slotted spoon, fishing out any renegade pieces of fritter and rice. Drain.

Serve the fritters immediately, with powdered sugar if you like.

Canary Island Doughnuts

This San Antonio specialty is called a doughnut, but it's closer to an empanada. The anise flavor in our recipe comes from seeds of the spice and from Pernod, a widely available liqueur.

FILLING

1 POUND (ABOUT 1 LARGE) BOILED OR BAKED
   SWEET POTATO, MASHED
1½ CUPS CHOPPED TOASTED ALMONDS
¾ CUP SUGAR
¼ CUP MILK
2 TABLESPOONS PERNOD
1 TEASPOON ANISE SEEDS, TOASTED AND
   GROUND
1 TEASPOON LEMON ZEST
PINCH OF CINNAMON

PASTRY

8 CUPS ALL-PURPOSE FLOUR
1 CUP SUGAR
1 TABLESPOON BAKING POWDER
1 TEASPOON SALT
1 TEASPOON LEMON ZEST
¾ CUP VEGETABLE SHORTENING, PREFERABLY
   CRISCO, CHILLED
¼ CUP UNSALTED BUTTER, CHILLED
ICE WATER

CANOLA OIL OR VEGETABLE SHORTENING,
   PREFERABLY CRISCO, FOR DEEP FRYING
POWDERED SUGAR

Makes 2 dozen "doughnuts"

 In a medium bowl, combine all the filling ingredients. Refrigerate at least 1 hour, or overnight.

Sift together the flour, sugar, baking powder, and salt into a large bowl. Sprinkle in the lemon zest. Cut in the shortening and butter with a pastry blender or fork. Add ice water a tablespoon at a time, adding only the minimum needed to barely hold the dough together. Wrap the dough in plastic, and refrigerate it for at least 1 hour, or overnight.

Roll the dough out ¼ inch thick on a floured pastry board or counter. With a biscuit cutter, cut out 4-inch rounds. Top each round with about 2 tablespoons of filling. Fold the round in half, pinch the edges to seal them, and crimp them with a fork.

Add the oil or shortening to a heavy saucepan to a depth of at least 4 inches, and heat to 350° F. If the oil smokes before reaching the correct temperature, it cannot be used for deep frying. Use only fresh, unused oil.

Fry the doughnuts until they are lightly browned, about 2 to 3 minutes. Drain them, and sprinkle them with powdered sugar. Serve them immediately.

> In 1731, King Philip V of Spain sent a group of Canary Islanders to help settle and build San Antonio. Some people claim these pioneers invented chili, and it's certain they gave us these doughnuts.

Creamy Peach, Prune, or Poppyseed Kolaches

Airy breads with sweet or savory fillings, kolaches are the Czechs' best-known contribution to Texas cooking. We show how to make them with three different fillings.

2 PACKAGES DRY YEAST
½ CUP LUKEWARM WATER
¼ CUP UNSALTED BUTTER, SOFTENED
¼ CUP VEGETABLE SHORTENING, PREFERABLY CRISCO
¼ CUP PLUS 1 OR 2 TABLESPOONS SUGAR
2 EGG YOLKS
⅔ CUP MILK
1 TEASPOON SALT
4 CUPS ALL-PURPOSE FLOUR
MELTED BUTTER, FOR TOPPING

1 RECIPE CREAMY PEACH, PRUNE, OR POPPYSEED FILLING (SEE BELOW)

Makes 3 dozen kolaches

 In a small bowl, combine the yeast with the lukewarm water. Set the bowl aside.

In a large bowl, cream together the butter, shortening, and ¼ cup sugar until the mixture is light and fluffy. Mix in the egg yolks, milk, and salt, combining well. Stir in the dissolved yeast and the flour, and mix until the ingredients are thoroughly blended into a soft dough. Cover the dough with a towel, and set the dough aside to rise to about double in size, approximately 1 to 1½ hours.

While the dough rises, choose and prepare one of the three fillings. The recipes for the fillings follow these instructions.

Grease a baking sheet. Pinch off pieces of dough about one-and-a-half times the size of a golf ball, flatten the balls slightly, and transfer them to the baking sheet. Place the balls at least 1 inch apart, and brush them liberally with the melted butter. Set them aside to double in size again, about 45 minutes to 1 hour.

With your thumb, gently indent the top of the dough. Make the holes especially deep if you plan to use

the poppyseed or creamy peach filling. Spoon in a couple of teaspoons of filling, and, with the poppyseed or creamy peach versions, coax the dough over the filling. Let the kolaches rest again for 15 to 20 minutes.

Preheat the oven to 425° F.

Bake the kolaches for 10 to 12 minutes, until they are golden brown.

Remove the pan from the oven, immediately brush the kolaches with more butter, and sprinkle them with the remaining sugar. Transfer them to a rack, and let them cool.

The kolaches should be tender, somewhat like a light buttery Danish. They're best eaten the day they're made.

CREAMY PEACH FILLING

2 CUPS SMALL-CURD COTTAGE CHEESE, DRAINED IN A SIEVE OR CHEESECLOTH FOR 30 TO 45 MINUTES
½ CUP PEACH BUTTER
1 EGG
1 TABLESPOON SUGAR
1 TABLESPOON UNSALTED BUTTER, MELTED
½ TEASPOON NUTMEG

To make the creamy peach filling, squeeze any accumulated liquid from the cheese. Mix the cheese with the remaining ingredients in a bowl.

PRUNE FILLING

1 POUND DRIED PRUNES
1 TEASPOON VANILLA
1 CUP SUGAR
1 TEASPOON FRESH LEMON JUICE
1 TEASPOON LEMON ZEST

To make the prune filling, put the prunes into a saucepan, and cover them with water. Add the vanilla, and simmer until the prunes have softened, about 15 minutes. Drain and pit the prunes, and chop them in a food processor with the sugar, lemon juice, and lemon zest. Or chop the prunes by hand, and then add the sugar, lemon juice, and lemon zest.

POPPYSEED FILLING

¾ CUP SUGAR
2 TEASPOONS CORNSTARCH
1½ CUPS POPPYSEEDS
¾ CUP WHOLE MILK
¾ TEASPOON ALMOND EXTRACT

 To make the poppyseed filling, stir together the sugar and cornstarch in a small bowl. Set the bowl aside.

Grind the poppyseeds in a blender with about half the milk. Place the poppyseed mixture and the remaining milk in a large, heavy saucepan, and bring the mixture to a boil over medium-high heat. Reduce the heat to a simmer, and stir in the reserved sugar-and-cornstarch mixture and the almond extract. Simmer, stirring often, until very thick—a matter of a few minutes.

> Commenting on Texas tall tales, Artemus Ward once said, "The trouble with Texans is that they know so many things which ain't so."

TECHNIQUE TIPS

Some kolache recipes call for "proofing" the yeast in milk, but the fat in milk can actually hinder the yeast's development. It's best to "proof" the yeast in water first and then to add milk later for tenderness.

You can make kolaches with sausage or almost any type of cooked fruit filling. Don't use jelly, though, because it's too runny. The fruit needs to be cooked to fruit-butter consistency.

Make the center depressions carefully so the bread doesn't go flat.

Enclose cheese-based fillings, like the creamy peach, and poppyseed fillings totally with dough. Stiffer fillings like prune can peer out the top.

Don't skimp on the amount of butter brushed on the dough.

When Bum Phillips, the former Houston Oilers coach, judged a kolache competition once, he was so impressed with the sausage-stuffed entry that he offered to trade two draft choices for an extra pastry to go.

Many Texas towns stage Czech heritage celebrations. Two of the best occasions to get your fill of kolaches, sausage, strudel, and dancing are the West Fest on Labor Day weekend in West and, in the spring, the National Polka Festival in Ennis, which features four halls of rousing polka bands.

The term *Texan*, worn so proudly in the state today, used to be controversial. Early residents referred to themselves as "Texians," and many of them didn't cotton to a change. An editorial in the *Texas Monument* in 1851 called *Texan* a "wretched barbarism." When someone uses the word, the editor wrote, "we involuntarily look to see if he has the lock-jaw, or if he has ice in his mouth."

Mazarine Coffee Cake

Early German settlers in Texas commonly ate three regular meals plus two minimeals. The midmorning snack, called a second breakfast, usually featured coffee cake washed down with coffee or milk. There are many local versions, but we like the almond and raspberry flavors in this one.

CAKE

1⅓ CUPS ALL-PURPOSE FLOUR

1½ TEASPOONS BAKING POWDER

¼ TEASPOON SALT

½ CUP UNSALTED BUTTER, SOFTENED

⅓ CUP SUGAR

1 EGG

2 TABLESPOONS SOUR CREAM

¼ CUP RASPBERRY JAM

FILLING

½ CUP UNSALTED BUTTER, AT ROOM TEMPERA-
TURE

⅓ CUP SUGAR

1 CUP ALMONDS, TOASTED AND GROUND

1 TEASPOON ALMOND EXTRACT

2 EGGS

TOPPING

¼ CUP RASPBERRY JAM

¼ CUP POWDERED SUGAR MIXED WITH 2 TEA-
SPOONS LEMON JUICE, OPTIONAL

Makes an 8- or 9-inch coffee cake

 Preheat the oven to 350° F. Grease an 8- or 9-inch round or square baking dish.

Sift together the flour, baking powder, and salt into a small bowl. Set the bowl aside.

With a mixer, cream together the butter and sugar in a large bowl until the mixture is light and fluffy. Add in the egg, sour cream, and jam, beating well. Mix in the dry ingredients, about a third at a time, until they are well combined. Spoon the mixture into the prepared pan, pressing it along the sides as well as the bottom.

Using the same bowl and beaters (it isn't necessary to wash them first), prepare the filling: Cream the butter and sugar together, and then add the almonds, almond extract, and eggs, mixing until the ingredients are well combined. Pour the filling over the cake batter.

Bake the cake for 40 minutes, remove it from the oven, and spoon dollops of raspberry jam over it. Return the cake to the oven for 5 to 10 minutes, until the filling is set and the cake is golden brown. Remove the pan from the oven.

If you like, top the cake with the powdered sugar–lemon juice mixture. Slice the cake, and serve it warm.

FOOTBALL FOOD

*I*f he was married to Racquel Welch, he'd expect her to cook.

Dallas Cowboys' quarterback Don Meredith,

on the perfectionism of his coach, Tom Landry

(quoted by Wallace O. Chariton in *This Dog'll Hunt*)

*A*t the very least, Don, Racquel ought to be able to throw together some munchies for a Monday night football game. These snacks are simple enough on the whole, and they will satisfy someone as demanding as Landry and even someone with as many moves as Meredith. They are versatile tidbits adaptable for anything from TV treats to party fare. In a land where hors d'oeuvres could get confused with horse burrs, they make a good substitute for a predinner course, and enough of them can cover for a full meal on Super Bowl Sunday.

Even Helen Corbitt, the mother of cultured cooking in Texas, wouldn't call her first courses "hors d'oeuvres." The famed Neiman Marcus chef referred to such goodies as "finger food," perhaps a better way of saying "football food" if you're catering to the ladies' luncheon crowd.

Higginbotham Cheese Wafers

Cheese wafers, also called cheese straws, pop up as a snack in Texas as often as you used to see Bob Lilly in the other team's backfield. Our recipe is a variation on one found in two delightful cookbooks, **This Little Higgy Went to Market** *and* **This Little Higgy Stayed Home**, *collections of family recipes published by Dallas's Higginbotham family and distributed as gifts to lucky friends.*

2 CUPS (8 OUNCES) GRATED SHARP CHEDDAR
   CHEESE
1 CUP UNSALTED BUTTER, SOFTENED
1 TABLESPOON GRATED ONION
2½ CUPS ALL-PURPOSE FLOUR
1 TEASPOON SALT
½ TEASPOON COARSE-GROUND BLACK PEPPER
½ TEASPOON CAYENNE

Makes 9 to 10 dozen wafers

In a food processor, combine the cheese, butter, and onion. Stir the dry ingredients together in a small bowl, and add them by batches to the cheese mixture. Process thoroughly.

Remove the dough from the processor, and shape it into several rolls of manageable lengths. The Higginbothams make their rolls about the diameter of a quarter; we roll ours closer to a fifty-cent piece (if you can remember what one of those looks like). Wrap each roll tightly in plastic wrap, and refrigerate the rolls for at least 1 hour before slicing them into rounds ¼ inch thick. You can keep the dough in the refrigerator for a week or in the freezer for several months, slicing off the quantity desired.

Preheat the oven to 425° F. Place the wafers ½ inch apart on an ungreased baking sheet. Bake for 3 to 5 minutes, or until the edges of the wafers are lightly colored.

Serve the wafers warm or at room temperature. They keep for a week if they are tightly covered.

Variation: For some extra crunch, and another flavor, add ½ to 1 cup of minced pecans to the dough.

Big-Foot Wallace had his own version of athletic padding. J. Frank Dobie tells how the frontiersman, surrounded by Indians, protected himself by stuffing his clothes with hard-shelled hickory nuts. The attackers fired a volley of arrows at Big-Foot and then fled in terror when the arrows just bounced off.

"Deaf" Smith Jalapeños

These unlikely jalapeños, stuffed with peanut butter, are always a popular snack in Texas, but don't serve them to any inexperienced chile eaters.

1 DOZEN MEDIUM TO LARGE PICKLED JALAPEÑOS
APPROXIMATELY ¾ CUP PEANUT BUTTER

Makes 2 dozen stuffed chiles

Slice the jalapeños in half lengthwise. Spoon peanut butter into each half, mounding it generously. The jalapeños can be served immediately or refrigerated, covered, for several hours. Remove them from the refrigerator 30 minutes before serving.

Variation: Cream cheese also works well as a filling; so does a combination of cream cheese and peanut butter.

ONE OF THE BEST COMMERCIAL PEANUT BUTTERS WAS NAMED AFTER ERASTUS "DEAF" SMITH, A HERO OF THE TEXAS REVOLUTION. SMITH SPIED FOR THE INSURGENTS, HELPING HOUSTON DEFEAT SANTA ANNA. HIS NAME SEEMS TO CARRY PARTICULAR CACHET IN THE FOOD WORLD; IT ALSO DESIGNATES A STONE-GROUND FLOUR.

In Texas, football themes can inspire whole cookbooks. In 1981, the Ex-Students' Association of the University of Texas came out with *Cook 'em Horns*. Not to be outdone, Texas A&M a few years later published its own collection of recipes, called *Aggies, Moms, and Apple Pie*.

Armadillo Eggs

Well, not really, but you can probably fool your aunt from Duluth.

2 CUPS LARGE, UNPITTED GREEN OR BLACK
    OLIVES, DRAINED
½ CUP OLIVE BRINE
½ CUP EXTRA-VIRGIN OLIVE OIL
½ CUP BEER
¼ CUP WHITE VINEGAR
2 GARLIC CLOVES, MINCED
2 CAYENNES OR CHILES DE ÁRBOL
1 BAY LEAF
¾ TEASPOON CHILI POWDER, PREFERABLY
    HOMEMADE (PAGE 135) OR GEBHARDT'S
½ TEASPOON CUMIN SEEDS, TOASTED AND
    GROUND

Makes 2 cups marinated olives.

Place the olives in a bowl. Shake the remaining ingredients together in a lidded jar, and pour the marinade over the olives. Let the mixture marinate for at least 2 days (longer, if you can), stirring occasionally. Unlike most gridiron stars, the olives get better with age.

The Aggies had a big hand in introducing "fine dining" in Texas. For a half century, from 1878 to 1928, Bernard Sbissa ran the central A&M kitchen with New Orleans finesse. He loved to prepare elaborate banquets for the students on special occasions. At one dinner, Sbissa's appetizers included green sea turtle Mikado, oyster cocktails, and broiled rockfish maître, and the entrées ranged from fresh lobster Newburg to imported smoked tongue.

Jícama Texicana

From Mexico originally but now easy to find in the States, jícama is a root vegetable that tastes something like a cross between a water chestnut, an apple, and a turnip. In the market, a near-sighted quarterback could mistake a large whole jícama for a football. A little chili powder and lime is all the seasoning it needs.

1 JÍCAMA, ABOUT 1 POUND
JUICE AND ZEST OF 1 LIME
CHILI POWDER, PREFERABLY HOMEMADE
   (PAGE 135) OR GEBHARDT'S, TO TASTE
SALT TO TASTE

Makes 1 pound of "matchsticks"

Peel the jícama, and slice it into fat matchsticks. Transfer it to a bowl, cover it with water, and refrigerate it for 30 minutes. Drain it.

Arrange the jícama on a platter, and sprinkle it with the lime juice and zest, the chili powder, and, if you wish, some salt. If you like, serve the jícama with additional chili powder on the side.

Maverick Ham Rolls

Variations on these ham rolls have been the most fashionable party snack in San Antonio for over one hundred years, since they were first introduced by Albert and Jane Maury Maverick. A San Antonio native, Albert met Jane in her home state at the University of Virginia. The recipe had been in Jane's family for many years, and the couple brought it with them to Texas on their honeymoon trip in 1877.

12 BOLILLOS (MEXICAN ROLLS) OR OTHER
   SMALL, STURDY YEAST ROLLS
1 POUND SMOKED HAM, CHOPPED OR SLICED
¼ CUP CHOPPED DILL PICKLE
2 TO 4 TABLESPOONS DILL PICKLE BRINE
¼ CUP CHOPPED CELERY
2 TABLESPOONS CHOPPED ONION
2 TABLESPOONS PREPARED YELLOW MUSTARD
6 TABLESPOONS UNSALTED BUTTER, MELTED

Makes 2 dozen rolls

Preheat the oven to 350° F.

Slice the bolillos in half lengthwise, and carefully hollow out the centers. Set aside the bread "shells," and toast the centers briefly until lightly browned.

Place the toasted centers in a food processor, and process until crumbs form. Add the ham, the pickle, 2 tablespoons of the pickle brine, the celery, the onion, and the mustard. Process until the mixture forms a rough spread, but stop short of puréeing it. Taste, and add as much of the remaining pickle juice as you like. Set the mixture aside.

Brush the bolillo "shells" with about ⅔ of the butter. Fill them with the ham mixture, and transfer them to a baking sheet. Brush the tops with the remaining butter. Bake the rolls for 15 minutes, or until the bread is lightly browned and the rolls are heated through.

Serve the rolls hot.

The Mavericks are one of the most illustrious families of Texas. The founder of the clan, Samuel Augustus Maverick, signed the Texas Declaration of Independence and also gave us the term "maverick" to signify unbranded cattle, which he owned, and independent-minded people, which his family bred. A century later, Maury Maverick, serving as mayor of San Antonio, inspired the city to start development of its now-famous Riverwalk.

Rangerette Sweet Potato Chips

You don't have to fix your own chips for the dips that follow, but these homemade chips will kick off the show as well as their namesake, the Kilgore Rangerettes, do.

3 MEDIUM (ABOUT 2 TO 2¼ POUNDS) SWEET POTATOES
ICE CUBES
PEANUT OIL, FOR DEEP FRYING
SALT
CHILI POWDER, PREFERABLY HOMEMADE (PAGE 135) OR GEBHARDT'S, OR CAJUN OR CREOLE SEASONING

Serves 4 to 6

Wash the sweet potatoes, and, if you wish, peel them. (We prefer the peels on, and besides, leaving them on is less work.) Slice the sweet potatoes to chip thinness with a food processor or, more laboriously, by hand.

Toss the chips into a bowl of cold water, and soak them for 30 minutes to eliminate some of the starch.

Pour off the water, add more cold water to cover, and toss in a half-dozen ice cubes. Refrigerate the chips to firm them, about 30 minutes. Drain them well on a dish towel, drying off each chip. Then roll up the chips in another dry towel—you want no remaining moisture.

Heat at least 3 inches of oil to 375° F in a large, heavy saucepan. If the oil smokes before reaching the correct temperature, it cannot be used for deep frying. Use only fresh, unused oil. Add the potatoes in batches, and fry them just a minute or two, until they are slightly colored and crisp. Drain them.

Sprinkle the chips with salt and chili powder or Cajun or Creole seasoning, and serve them warm.

Variation: Regular potato chips can be made from scratch by the same method. If you want corn chips instead, see page 100 for a homemade version.

> The high-kicking Kilgore Rangerettes were the original football drill team, the inspiration for a Texas tradition. Gussie Nell Davis created the concept in 1940, envisioning a wholesome chorus line of cowgirls to entertain at football games. From the beginning, the Rangerettes had to be able to kick their boots above their stylish Stetsons on the field, while keeping their knees together at all other times.

Double-Whammy
Green Chile Dip

The double whammy in this dip, as punchy as an Earl Campbell run, comes from the combination of fresh and dried green chile. The smoky dried variety packs intense flavor, though it's not always easy to find. If you can't locate it, substitute another ½ cup of fresh green chile. In this case you'll have a single-whammy dip, but it'll still be as snappy as a Bum Phillips quip.

1 OUNCE DRIED NEW MEXICAN GREEN CHILE
8 OUNCES SOUR CREAM
1 TABLESPOON CHOPPED ROASTED GREEN
    CHILE, PREFERABLY NEW MEXICAN OR
    POBLANO, FRESH OR FROZEN
2 GARLIC CLOVES, ROASTED (PAGE 9) AND
    MINCED
½ TEASPOON MINCED ONION

Makes 1¼ to 1½ cups dip

Place the dried green chile in a blender or spice mill, and grind briefly until the chile is powdered. In a small bowl, combine the powdered chile with the sour cream. Mix in the remaining ingredients. Refrigerate the dip for at least 1 hour to develop its flavors. It keeps well for 3 or 4 days.

Serve this dip with Rangerette Sweet Potato Chips (page 457), Mystery Man Tostada Chips (page 100), or store-bought chips.

Potato chips owe their origin to a chef's frustration with railroad magnate Cornelius Vanderbilt. Dining at the Moon Lake resort in Saratoga, New York, in 1853, Vanderbilt sent back his fried potatoes twice, claiming they were too thick. To spite him, the chef prepared a new dish of potatoes sliced paper-thin, fried, and salted, knowing Vanderbilt would have a dickens of a time eating them with a fork. To everyone's surprise, he loved them, and the Saratoga Crunch Chip was born.

Babe's Dip

This cilantro-jalapeño dip, as potent as the preceding one, we named for Mildred "Babe" Didrikson Zaharias, probably the greatest athlete Texas ever produced. Babe never let the fans down, and neither will this recipe.

2 CUPS SOUR CREAM
½ CUP MINCED CILANTRO
2 TO 3 PICKLED JALAPEÑOS, MINCED
3 GARLIC CLOVES, ROASTED (PAGE 9) AND MINCED
2 TEASPOONS GRATED ONION
¼ TEASPOON SALT, OR MORE, TO TASTE

Makes about 2½ cups dip

Mix all the ingredients together in a medium bowl. Cover the bowl, and chill the dip at least 1 hour. The dip keeps for several days but loses a little of its cilantro flair. It's good with either potato or corn chips.

A Port Arthur native, Babe Zaharias set two world records and won three medals in the 1932 Olympics before turning pro as a golfer. A member of the LPGA Hall of Fame, she once won an incredible seventeen consecutive golf tournaments.

TECHNIQUE TIP

Lighten up your dips with one of several tricks: Instead of regular sour cream, use a light version, or substitute low-fat yogurt for half the sour cream. Most people don't notice much difference in taste in a dip between normal mayonnaise, high in fat, and the slimmer alternatives. The same goes for Neufchâtel cheese, sometimes marketed as "light cream cheese," in place of regular cream cheese.

Ninfa's Green Sauce

If the couch potatoes in your crowd like guacamole, they'll leap goal-posts to get to this spicy avocado dip. Ninfa Laurenzo created it as a signature dish for her Houston chain of Ninfa's restaurants.

4 FRESH OR CANNED TOMATILLOS (ABOUT 6 TO 8 OUNCES), DRAINED (IF CANNED) AND CHOPPED

3 MEDIUM GREEN TOMATOES, CHOPPED

3 GARLIC CLOVES, MINCED

1 TO 2 FRESH JALAPEÑOS, CHOPPED

3 MEDIUM HASS AVOCADOS, HALVED, SEEDED, AND PEELED

1½ CUPS SOUR CREAM

1 TABLESPOON MINCED CILANTRO

¼ TEASPOON SALT, OR MORE, TO TASTE

Makes about 4 cups dip

> **TECHNIQUE TIP**
>
> If you can't find tomatillos, you can omit them. Ninfa suggests adding a squeeze or two of lemon juice to replace their tang.

In a medium saucepan, simmer the tomatillos and tomatoes with the garlic and jalapeños for 15 minutes, or until their liquid has evaporated.

While the tomatillo mixture simmers, place the avocados in a blender. Spoon the thickened tomatillo mixture into the blender. Add the sour cream, cilantro, and salt, and blend for up to 5 minutes to create a smooth purée. Taste, and add more salt if needed.

Serve the sauce immediately with tostada chips, or refrigerate it for later use. Ninfa's makes this sauce fresh every day, but we've kept it overnight, and it has remained tasty and hasn't turned gray the way guacamole does.

> In 1990 the *Houston Chronicle* selected Ninfa's Green Sauce as one of the 1980s' best developments in the city.

Prairie Fire Dip

This is one of Helen Corbitt's most famous dishes. The use of jalapeños, uncommon at the time, made the dip seem as hot as a prairie fire, hence the name. Chili is a more recent addition to the conflagration and can be omitted if you prefer to stay truer to the classic form.

2 TABLESPOONS UNSALTED BUTTER

2 TABLESPOONS OIL, PREFERABLY CANOLA OR CORN

⅓ MEDIUM ONION, CHOPPED FINE

1 GARLIC CLOVE, MINCED

2 CUPS COOKED PINTO BEANS, WITH ¼ CUP COOKING LIQUID RESERVED

1¾ CUPS GRATED MONTEREY JACK OR MILD CHEDDAR CHEESE

2 PICKLED JALAPEÑOS, CHOPPED FINE

2 TO 3 TEASPOONS JALAPEÑO PICKLING LIQUID

1 CUP CHILI CON CARNE, OPTIONAL

¼ CUP SLICED GREEN OLIVES, OPTIONAL

Makes 3½ to 4 cups dip with chili and 2½ to 3 cups without

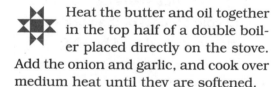 Heat the butter and oil together in the top half of a double boiler placed directly on the stove. Add the onion and garlic, and cook over medium heat until they are softened.

Fill the bottom half of the double boiler with water, and insert the top half onto the bottom. Spoon 1½ cups of the beans into the pan, and mash them with a potato masher or bean masher (used for refried beans). Alternatively, put the beans through a ricer or sieve before adding them to the pan. Don't purée the beans in a food processor or blender, which would make them pasty.

When the beans are well mashed, add the remaining ½ cup of beans, 1½ cups of the cheese, the jalapeños and their liquid, and the chili if you are including it. Heat everything together, stirring frequently, until the cheese is melted, adding bean liquid as needed if the dip seems dry.

Pour the hot dip into a chafing dish or heatproof bowl on a warming tray. Sprinkle with the remaining cheese and, if you like, the olives. Serve Prairie Fire hot with chips or crackers.

Variation: Some people omit chili and use a mild fresh goat cheese in place of all or part of the Monterey jack or cheddar.

Why hasn't some Texas high school named its football team the Prairie Fires? In pioneer days, a prairie fire was as menacing a prospect as a Comanche raid, and even today the name might conjure more dread than actual monikers such as Ricebirds, Ducks, and Purple Rock Crushers.

Layered Bean Dip

All bean dips owe a debt to Helen Corbitt's Prairie Fire, but some today have gotten more complex and flavorful than the model. We like this one, based on a dip served at Guero's Taco Bar in Austin. If you're in a hurry, you can even make a decent version with canned beans.

1½ CUPS REFRIED BEANS (PAGE 85)
1 CUP PICADILLO (PAGE 73), OPTIONAL
½ CUP SOUR CREAM
1 CUP GUACAMOLE (PAGE 98)
1 CUP PICO DE GALLO (PAGE 95)
½ CUP GRATED MILD CHEDDAR CHEESE
PICKLED JALAPEÑO SLICES, OPTIONAL

Makes about 5 cups

Heat the Refried Beans and, if you like, the Picadillo in separate saucepans until they are bubbly. Spoon the beans into the bottom of a medium serving dish, and top them with the Picadillo. Layer each of the other ingredients in the order listed.

Serve this dip warm with tostada chips.

PICADILLO, GUACAMOLE, AND PICO DE GALLO ALL MAKE GOOD DIPS BY THEMSELVES. SEE TEX-MEX TREASURES (PAGES 59–104) FOR RECIPES.

Dallas's Fair Park is home to two venerable institutions, the Cotton Bowl and the "corny dog." A vendor at the state fair invented the batter-dipped-hot-dog-on-a-stick years ago, and it's still sold at most of the park's 175 restaurants and food booths.

Quick Chowchow Dip

You can make this one faster than Roger Staubach could release a pass.

½ CUP HOT CHA CHOWCHOW (PAGE 407) OR
   YOUR FAVORITE COMMERCIAL VARIETY
½ CUP PREPARED BROWN MUSTARD

Makes 1 cup dip

 In a small bowl, mix together the chowchow and the mustard.

Serve the dip with crackers, with sausage slices, or in ham sandwiches.

Texas League Crawfish Dip

Football is such a mania in Texas, you might not know that baseball was the state's first professional team sport and a source of considerable pride in the past. We named this dip not for the tepid Texas League of today but for its mighty predecessor of the early twentieth century, when the stars included Tris Speaker, Rogers Hornsby, Dizzy Dean, Carl Hubbell, and Hank Greenberg. Those fellows could cook crawdad tails with anyone.

½ CUP SOUR CREAM
3 OUNCES CREAM CHEESE, SOFTENED
2 TEASPOONS WORCESTERSHIRE SAUCE
3 TABLESPOONS CHOPPED TOMATO
3 TABLESPOONS CHOPPED CELERY
3 TABLESPOONS MINCED ONION
2 GARLIC CLOVES, ROASTED (PAGE 9) AND
   MINCED
½ TEASPOON FRESH-GROUND BLACK PEPPER
¼ TEASPOON SALT
⅛ TEASPOON CAYENNE
½ POUND COOKED CRAWFISH TAILS, CHOPPED

Makes about 2½ cups dip

 Mix all the ingredients except the crawfish in a medium bowl until they are well combined. Fold in the crawfish. Cover the bowl, and chill the dip at least 1 hour.

Serve this dip with crackers or small slices of bread, or scoop it up with celery sticks.

George Bush Dunk

If you think George Bush was full of bunk about broccoli, dunk it to him in this savory sausage-and-broccoli blend.

½ POUND SPICY BULK BREAKFAST SAUSAGE
¾ POUND FRESH BROCCOLI, CHOPPED
2 TABLESPOONS UNSALTED BUTTER
1½ TABLESPOONS FLOUR
1 CUP MILK
SALT TO TASTE

Makes about 3 cups dunk

Brown the sausage in a skillet over medium heat. Drain off any accumulated fat, and transfer the sausage to a dish. Set the dish aside.

Steam the broccoli in a saucepan until it is tender but not mushy. Rinse it under cold water, so that it keeps its bright color, drain it, and set it aside with the sausage.

In the skillet used for the sausage, melt the butter over low heat. Sprinkle in the flour, and cook 2 to 3 minutes, stirring continuously. Pour in the milk slowly, stirring to keep the sauce smooth.

Add the sausage and broccoli, and heat through. Taste, and add as much salt as you like. Thin the mixture with a little milk if it seems overly stiff.

Serve the dunk in a chafing dish or heatproof bowl on a warming tray. It's best with those Texas chips, Fritos, in the size made for dipping.

Tris Speaker (lifetime batting average of .344) and Rogers Hornsby (the highest average in National League history—.358) not only starred in the Texas League but also came from the state. Other native baseball greats include Ernie Banks, Frank Robinson, and Nolan Ryan.

Bush's favorite game, golf, has always been big in Texas. In addition to the incomparable Babe Zaharias, pro stars from the state include four other LPGA Hall of Famers, Ben Hogan, and Lee Trevino.

Tequila-Almond Dunk for Fruit

This is the most healthful tequila cocktail you'll find at a Texas party, particularly if you substitute yogurt for half of the sour cream.

2 CUPS SOUR CREAM
¼ CUP GROUND TOASTED ALMONDS
3 TABLESPOONS TEQUILA, PREFERABLY GOLD
1 TABLESPOON PLUS **1** TEASPOON DARK BROWN
    SUGAR, OR MORE, TO TASTE
1 TABLESPOON FRESH ORANGE JUICE
1 TABLESPOON MINCED ORANGE ZEST
1 TEASPOON FRESH LIME JUICE
1 TEASPOON MINCED LIME ZEST

Makes about 2½ cups dunk

 Mix all the ingredients together in a medium bowl. Cover the mixture and chill it, preferably overnight.

Serve the dunk with fruit such as seedless grapes and pear slices (dipped in lemon juice) during football season, and strawberries, pitted cherries, or chunked melon, piled high, for a cooling summer treat. The dunk can also be thinned with milk and served as a dressing over fruit.

If you're cooking for dieting players or cheerleaders, check out *Mrs. Ida Chitwood's Choice Recipes, Food Charts and Reducing Methods,* published in Fort Worth in 1927. Mrs. Chitwood says the first step in losing weight is to shrink the stomach by eating nothing for nine days except either three grapefruit or four half-pint glasses of buttermilk daily. You can continue eating grapefruit afterward, but not buttermilk because it becomes fattening, she says, when consumed with solid food.

Spicy Apple Dip

Apple and spice go nice with both fruit and chips.

1¼ CUPS RANCH DRESSING, HOMEMADE (PAGE 295) OR STORE-BOUGHT
1 GRANNY SMITH OR OTHER TART APPLE, CHOPPED FINE
1 TO 2 TEASPOONS FRESH LEMON JUICE
1 TEASPOON PREPARED HORSERADISH
½ TEASPOON GROUND CINNAMON
¼ TEASPOON GROUND NUTMEG
¼ TEASPOON GROUND MACE

Makes approximately 2 cups dip

Mix all the ingredients together in a medium bowl. Cover the dip, and chill it at least 1 hour. Serve this dip with Rangerette Sweet Potato Chips (page 457), wheat crackers, or apple and pear slices dipped in diluted lemon juice.

Beer Cheese

The Spoetzl Brewery in Shiner, Texas, came up with this long-lasting, make-ahead spread. Pack it, if you like, in several small containers so that you can pull out a fresh one when unexpected guests arrive.

1 POUND SHARP CHEDDAR CHEESE, GRATED
½ CUP BEER
1 TABLESPOON WORCESTERSHIRE SAUCE
2 TEASPOONS MINCED ONION
2 GARLIC CLOVES, MINCED
½ TEASPOON DRY MUSTARD
¼ TEASPOON TABASCO OR OTHER HOT PEPPER SAUCE

Makes about 2½ cups spread

Mix all the ingredients together in a food processor or mixer. Pack the cheese into crocks or a bowl, and cover tightly.

The cheese is best after at least a day's mellowing, and it keeps for a couple of weeks. Serve it with crackers or bread.

Wonder what they would have called their high school teams in these old, defunct Texas towns: Cream, Pancake, Bacon, Onion, Okra, and Bean Creek?

Pimiento Cheese

As popular in Texas as peanut butter, pimiento cheese is best, we think, when it's not as sweet as the commercial versions. If your childhood memories insist on extra sugar, add another spoonful of pickle relish.

1 POUND MEDIUM CHEDDAR CHEESE
½ CUP MAYONNAISE
4 OUNCES (ABOUT ¼ CUP) PIMIENTOS WITH JUICE
2 TABLESPOONS SWEET PICKLE RELISH
2 TEASPOONS MINCED ONION

Makes about 3 cups spread

In a food processor, grate the cheese. Add the rest of the ingredients, and process until the mixture becomes a smooth purée. Pack the mixture in a bowl, and refrigerate the bowl, covered, for at least 30 minutes.

Pimiento cheese keeps up to 5 days. Serve it with crackers or the favorite white bread from your childhood.

Variation: For a spicy pimiento cheese, use our Hellish Sweet Relish (page 409) in place of the regular sweet relish, or add 1 tablespoon, more or less, of minced pickled jalapeños to the cheese mixture before processing it.

TECHNIQUE TIPS

Tailgate parties in a stadium parking lot are as treasured a tradition in Texas as football itself. Most of the morsels in this chapter are ideal for the occasion, but keep a few general strategies in mind:

• Take foods that are not only easily transported but also easy to eat. Limit silverware to one fork per person.

• Wrap hot foods in layers of foil surrounded by newspaper.

• The best desserts are sheet cakes in covered pans, cookies, and brownies.

• Pack some wet cloth wipes for hands and plastic trash bags to simplify the cleanup.

Jezebel Sauce
and Cream Cheese

You can fix this treat faster than Coach Darrell Royal snapped up three hundred-pound recruits for the University of Texas. Some versions of this sauce—sometimes referred to as Jeff Davis sauce—are more potent than this one, but you can increase the firepower easily by adding an extra tablespoon of horseradish.

SAUCE

1 CUP ORANGE MARMALADE OR PEACH OR
    APRICOT PRESERVES, OR A COMBINATION
⅔ CUP APPLE JELLY
5 TABLESPOONS CREOLE MUSTARD OR PRE-
    PARED BROWN MUSTARD
¼ CUP PREPARED HORSERADISH
1 TEASPOON COARSE-GROUND BLACK PEPPER

1 POUND CREAM CHEESE

Makes about 2 cups sauce

Combine all the sauce ingredients in a small bowl, and mix well. Refrigerate for a day or two for the best flavor, although the sauce is tasty from the start. It keeps indefinitely.

Serve the sauce over the cream cheese. We use about a cup with 8 ounces of cheese. Accompany with crackers.

Jezebel sauce enhances smoked meats, too. We especially like mini-sandwiches of turkey or ham with sharp cheddar on split biscuits topped with a dollop of the sauce.

TECHNIQUE TIP

If you don't want to make your own Jezebel Sauce, Tastes of the Southwest in Tyler and New Canaan Farms in Dripping Springs make excellent commercial versions. Both are listed in "Mail-Order Sources" (page 551).

See "Country Canning" (pages 391–415) for more ideas on pickles, relishes, and other condiments to complement your munchies.

Smoked Catfish Spread

You can find the smoked catfish needed for this spread in many super-markets, but in most cases you can get better versions by mail (see "Mail-Order Sources," page 556).

8 OUNCES SMOKED CATFISH FILLET, BROKEN INTO SMALL PIECES
4 OUNCES CREAM CHEESE
2 TABLESPOONS UNSALTED BUTTER
1 TO 1½ TABLESPOONS MILK
2 TEASPOONS MINCED ONION
1½ TEASPOONS BRANDY
1 TEASPOON FRESH LEMON JUICE
¼ TEASPOON TABASCO OR OTHER HOT PEPPER SAUCE
SALT AND FRESH-GROUND BLACK PEPPER TO TASTE

Makes approximately 2 cups spread

Place all the ingredients in the bowl of a food processor or mixer, and mix well. Pack the mixture into a small serving bowl, and refrigerate the mixture, covered, at least 30 minutes and as long as 48 hours.

Serve the spread with crackers or bread.

At Texas Christian University, they call their team mascot the horned frog, but everyone else in the state knows the little critter as a horny toad. Actually a lizard, the animal has been around Texas for eons and once was as popular a curiosity as the armadillo is today.

Devilish Eggs

Deviled eggs are as popular in Texas as a Cowboys cheerleader who's buying a round at a honky tonk.

12 HARD-BOILED EGGS, SHELLED
2 TABLESPOONS HELLISH SWEET RELISH
(PAGE 409) OR COMMERCIAL SWEET
PICKLE RELISH MIXED WITH MINCED
PICKLED JALAPEÑO TO TASTE
2 TABLESPOONS PREPARED YELLOW MUSTARD
2 TABLESPOONS MINCED PARSLEY
1 TABLESPOON MINCED ONION
1 TABLESPOON MINCED CELERY
½ TEASPOON PAPRIKA, PLUS MORE FOR
GARNISH
¼ CUP MAYONNAISE
¼ CUP SOUR CREAM OR ADDITIONAL
MAYONNAISE
¼ TO ½ TEASPOON SALT, TO TASTE
ADDITIONAL PARSLEY, OPTIONAL, FOR GARNISH

Halve the eggs lengthwise. Remove the yolks, and place them in a bowl. Using a fork or your fingers, crumble the yolks. Add the relish, mustard, parsley, onion, celery, and paprika, mixing lightly. Stir in the mayonnaise and sour cream, a few tablespoons at a time, checking the consistency before committing yourself to the full amount of either. Taste the yolk mixture, and add salt and more of anything you especially like.

Spoon, or pipe with a pastry tube, the yolk mixture into the egg whites. Sprinkle the eggs generously with more paprika. Place them on a serving tray with egg-shaped indentations, or on a regular plate with a bed of parsley to keep the eggs from sliding around. Refrigerate the eggs, covered, until just before serving time.

DEVILED EGGS HAVE BEEN A TEXAS FAVORITE FOR MANY YEARS. THE HOUSTON PRESBYTERIAN LADIES, WHO AUTHORED THE FIRST KNOWN TEXAS COOKBOOK BACK IN 1883, INCLUDED THREE DIFFERENT RECIPES FOR WHAT THEY CALLED "STUFFED" EGGS.

Bacon-Wrapped Watermelon Pickles

These are as simple as they are scrumptious.

SLICES OF SLAB BACON, CUT INTO THIRDS

WATERMELON PICKLES, HOMEMADE (PAGE 402) OR STORE-BOUGHT

Preheat the oven to 400° F.

Wrap a slice of watermelon pickle in a piece of bacon and secure the bacon with a toothpick. Repeat with as many pickles and bacon slices as you like. Bake 13 to 15 minutes, until the bacon is brown and crisp. Drain, and serve.

Pete Gent, the author of *North Dallas Forty* and a former Dallas Cowboy, once told a rookie skimming the team play book, "Don't bother reading it, kid; everybody gets killed at the end."

Venison Meatballs

Who wants to eat Swedish meatballs during a game when you can have some real game?

SAUCE

1 1-POUND CAN CRANBERRY SAUCE

½ CUP CHILI SAUCE, PREFERABLY HOMEMADE
(PAGE 406)

⅓ CUP ORANGE JUICE

2 TABLESPOONS CIDER VINEGAR

2 TABLESPOONS DRIED CRANBERRIES,
OPTIONAL

1 TABLESPOON PICKAPEPPA OR JARDINE'S
TEXAPEPPA SAUCE (SEE "MAIL-ORDER
SOURCES," PAGE 551)

½ TEASPOON POWDERED GINGER

MEATBALLS

1½ POUNDS GROUND VENISON

½ POUND GROUND PORK

¾ CUP DRY BREAD CRUMBS

½ CUP SLICED GREEN ONION

¼ CUP MINCED PARSLEY

3 TABLESPOONS PICKAPEPPA OR JARDINE'S
TEXAPEPPA SAUCE

2 TABLESPOONS FRESH ORANGE JUICE

2 GARLIC CLOVES, MINCED

1 EGG

½ TEASPOON POWDERED GINGER

OIL, PREFERABLY PEANUT, FOR FRYING

Makes about 3 dozen meatballs

 Combine all the sauce ingredients in a heavy saucepan, and simmer over low heat 30 minutes. Add water if the sauce becomes overly thick. Keep the sauce warm.

Place all the meatball ingredients in a bowl, and mix well. You can use a spoon, but we prefer to do this with our hands. Form the mixture into balls about 1 inch in diameter.

Pour a thick film of oil into a heavy skillet, and warm the oil over medium heat. Fry the meatballs until they are lightly browned, in batches to avoid overcrowding. Since venison can dry out quickly, you may want to fry a test meatball to make sure your timing is correct.

Combine the meatballs and any pan drippings with the warm sauce.

Serve the meatballs hot, with toothpicks.

Wing Dings

The citizens of Buffalo should be begging for chicken wings as saucy and sassy as these.

SAUCE

1 CUP BEER
¼ CUP UNSULPHURED DARK MOLASSES
¼ CUP CREAMY PEANUT BUTTER
¼ CUP WORCESTERSHIRE SAUCE
1½ TABLESPOONS CHILI POWDER, PREFERABLY
   HOMEMADE (PAGE 135) OR GEBHARDT'S
JUICE OF 1 MEDIUM LIME
½ TEASPOON DRY MUSTARD
¼ TEASPOON ANISE SEEDS, TOASTED AND
   GROUND
¼ TEASPOON SALT

1½ DOZEN CHICKEN WINGS

Makes 3 dozen pieces

 Preheat the oven to 350° F. Grease a large baking pan or dish.

Combine the sauce ingredients in a large, heavy pan. Simmer them over medium heat 15 to 20 minutes, until they have reduced to a thick sauce.

While the sauce simmers, prepare the chicken wings. With a cleaver or butcher knife, remove the wing tips. Then cut each wing in half at the joint.

Add the wings to the sauce, and stir to coat them. Ladle the wings and the sauce into the baking dish. Bake for 25 minutes, then stir the wings in the sauce. Turn the heat up to 425° F, and bake an additional 10 minutes, or until the sauce glazes the wings.

Serve the wings hot.

University of Texas students sing "The Eyes of Texas" at football games as though it's a hymn, but actually the song originated as a prank. An early president of the university liked to admonish students to remember always that "the eyes of Texas are upon you." In 1903, as part of a minstrel show, an undergraduate mocked the phrase by setting it to the tune of "I've Been Working on the Railroad."

Savory Swirls

Tasty and filling, this is a good snack when you've got a lot of line-backers to feed.

¾ POUND CHORIZO OR OTHER BULK SAUSAGE

1 TEASPOON CHILI POWDER, PREFERABLY
   HOMEMADE (PAGE 135) OR GEBHARDT'S,
   OPTIONAL

SALT TO TASTE

1 RECIPE BUTTERMILK BISCUIT DOUGH
   (PAGE 320)

2 CUPS (8 OUNCES) GRATED MILD CHEDDAR
   CHEESE

¾ CUP CHOPPED ROASTED GREEN CHILE,
   PREFERABLY NEW MEXICAN OR POBLANO,
   FRESH OR FROZEN

Makes 2 dozen rolls

Position the rack in the middle of the oven, and preheat the oven to 425° F. Grease a baking sheet.

In a skillet, fry the sausage over medium heat until it is browned. Pour off and discard any accumulated fat. Stir in the chili powder, if you like, and salt, and cook another minute or two. Set the sausage aside to cool.

On a floured board or counter, roll the biscuit dough out into a rectangle ¼ inch thick. Top it evenly with the sausage. Sprinkle the cheese and green chile over the meat.

Starting from one of the long sides of the rectangle, roll up the dough jelly roll–style. Make the roll snug but not overly tight—the dough needs a little room to expand during baking. Put the roll in the freezer for 10 minutes. Remove it, and slice it into ½-inch pinwheels. Transfer the pinwheels to the baking sheet.

Place the baking sheet in the oven. After about 5 minutes, turn the baking sheet from front to back. Bake for about 10 minutes total, until the swirls are raised and golden. Serve them hot.

Artichoke Nibbles

This is hardly the most sophisticated way to eat artichokes, but these nibbles have been a long-term winner in Texas kitchens. They are both easy to make and tasty.

2 6-OUNCE JARS MARINATED ARTICHOKE HEARTS

1 SMALL ONION, CHOPPED FINE

2 GARLIC CLOVES, MINCED

4 EGGS

¼ CUP DRY BREAD CRUMBS

¼ TEASPOON DRIED OREGANO

¼ TEASPOON FRESH-GROUND BLACK PEPPER

¼ TEASPOON TABASCO OR OTHER HOT PEPPER SAUCE

2 CUPS (8 OUNCES) SHREDDED SHARP CHEDDAR CHEESE

2 TABLESPOONS CHOPPED PARSLEY

Makes about 32 bite-size squares

Preheat the oven to 325° F. Grease an 8-inch-square pan.

Drain the marinade from one of the jars of artichoke hearts into a small skillet. Heat the marinade, and add the onion and garlic. Cook until the vegetables are soft, stirring occasionally.

Drain the second jar of artichoke hearts, saving the marinade for another purpose, if you wish. Chop all the artichoke hearts, and place them in a medium bowl. Add the eggs, bread crumbs, oregano, pepper, Tabasco, and the marinade mixture. Stir in the cheese and the parsley. Spoon the mixture into the baking pan. Bake for 30 minutes, or until the mixture is set.

Let the mixture cool for 15 or 20 minutes before cutting it into bite-size squares. Serve the squares warm or chilled.

The Cowboys' "Too Tall" Jones may have had a few inches on Texas pioneer Sarah Borginnis, but not much else. When she served as a cook for U.S. troops during the Mexican War, the soldiers nicknamed her "Great Western" for being the tallest, toughest fighter in camp.

Deep-Fried Grits
with Jezebel Sauce

This is a great way to use leftover grits, but it's also worth making up special. The frying creates a crunchy exterior, though the inside remains creamy, and the Jezebel sauce adds zing.

1 RECIPE GARLIC-CHEESE GRITS (PAGE 356), CHILLED AT LEAST 2 HOURS AND UP TO 2 DAYS

OIL, PREFERABLY CANOLA, FOR DEEP FRYING

JEZEBEL SAUCE, PREFERABLY HOMEMADE (PAGE 468)

Makes about 4 to 5 dozen squares

Cut the grits into bite-size tidbits about 1½ inches square. Transfer the squares to several thicknesses of paper toweling to absorb any surface moisture.

Pour enough oil into a heavy saucepan to measure at least 3 inches in depth. Heat the oil to 350° F. If the oil smokes before reaching the correct temperature, it cannot be used for deep frying. Use only fresh oil.

Fry the squares in batches for about 1 minute, until they crisp up and brown slightly. Drain them.

Serve the squares hot with Jezebel Sauce on the side.

Texas Trash

El Paso Chile Company has now trademarked the name "Texas Trash"—and has kindly allowed us to use it—but this Lone Star take on Chex cereal party mixes goes back further than the firm.

6 CUPS MIXED CHEX CEREALS
2 CUPS PRETZEL STICKS
2 CUPS FRITOS CORN CHIPS
2 CUPS PECAN HALVES
½ CUP OLIVE OIL
4 GARLIC CLOVES, HALVED
2½ TABLESPOONS WORCESTERSHIRE SAUCE
2 TEASPOONS CAJUN OR CREOLE SEASONING
1 TEASPOON GROUND DRIED RED CHILE,
   PREFERABLY NEW MEXICAN OR ANCHO
1 TEASPOON TABASCO OR OTHER HOT PEPPER
   SAUCE

Makes 12 cups party mix

Preheat the oven to 250° F.

In a large bowl, stir together the cereal, pretzels, Fritos, and pecans. In a small skillet, warm the oil over medium heat, and add the garlic. Cook the garlic until it is well softened, remove it with a slotted spoon, and discard it. Stir the remaining seasonings into the skillet, and then pour the seasoned oil over the cereal mixture. Stir well to coat the mixture evenly.

Transfer the mixture to a large baking pan (we use our turkey roaster), and bake it for 1 hour, stirring every 15 minutes.

Spoon the Trash onto brown-paper bags to cool.

Eat the Trash while it is still a bit warm, or serve it at room temperature by the generous bowlful. Texas Trash can be kept, tightly covered, for up to 3 days, but it's best served the day you make it.

Variation: To make your own distinctive Trash, add Corn Nuts, Chee-tos, Cheerios, Goldfish cheese crackers, or anything crunchy that sounds good to you. If you don't want to do any of the work, call El Paso Chile Company (see "Mail-Order Sources," page 551) to get a batch of their superb version delivered to your door.

Little Devils

These chile peanuts are as naturally matched with beer as Baylor University is with Waco.

2 TABLESPOONS PEANUT OIL, PREFERABLY
   ROASTED
2 GARLIC CLOVES, MINCED
3 TEASPOONS CHILI POWDER, PREFERABLY
   HOMEMADE (PAGE 135) OR GEBHARDT'S
2 TO 3 TEASPOONS GROUND DRIED RED CHILE,
   PREFERABLY NEW MEXICAN OR ANCHO
1 TEASPOON SALT, OR MORE, TO TASTE
1 POUND (ABOUT 3 CUPS) RAW PEANUTS

Makes 3 cups spiced peanuts

Preheat the oven to 350° F.

In a heavy skillet, warm the oil over low heat. Add the garlic, and sauté it briefly until it is softened. Stir in the chili powder, chile, and salt, and mix well. Sprinkle in the peanuts, and stir to coat them.

Transfer the peanuts to a baking sheet. Bake them 10 minutes, or until they are lightly browned. Transfer them to absorbent paper. Let them cool before serving.

Stored in a closed jar, the peanuts will keep several weeks.

Candied Pecans

Keeping a full bowl of these around will make you a two-touchdown favorite with the fans.

1 CUP WATER
½ CUP SUGAR
½ CUP UNSULPHURED DARK MOLASSES
2 TEASPOONS GROUND DRIED RED CHILE,
    PREFERABLY NEW MEXICAN OR ANCHO
½ TEASPOON SALT
2 CUPS PECAN HALVES

Makes about 2½ cups candied pecans

 Preheat the oven to 250° F. Grease a 9-by-12-inch baking dish.

In a heavy saucepan, bring all the ingredients except the pecans to a boil over high heat. Add the pecans, stir well, and reduce the heat to a simmer. Cook the pecans for 10 to 12 minutes, stirring occasionally, until the syrup has been well reduced.

With a slotted spoon, transfer the pecans to the baking dish. Bake the nuts for about 1¼ hours, stirring them about halfway through the cooking time. When ready, the pecans will be dark brown and crunchy. Stir them a few more times, and transfer them to waxed paper to cool.

Tightly covered, the pecans will keep at least a week.

*R*ight there in the saintly town of Dallas, the Vatican City, as you might call it, of the Baptist church, the cow-made millionaires pay an exorbitant price for, and get drunk on, a grade of rot-gut at which the aforementioned goatherders of Sierra County, New Mexico, would turn up their noses in disgust. In fact, and I state this on the very highest authority, the drinking industry of the State of Texas, under its present Baptist management, has now sunk to such a low level that many men who were once known to hundreds of bartenders as qualified judges of good whiskey are today known to as many bootleggers as inveterate guzzlers of chock beer.

Owen P. White, an El Paso writer, during Prohibition

*N*othing has ever aroused passion in Texas like booze. For a hundred years, from the 1870s to the 1970s, the prohibition issue dominated politics, sermons, and social mores. The epic struggle, a battle for the soul of Texas, pitted a hard-drinking, hell-raising frontier tradition against the sober and self-righteous values of the strongest church in the state. Everyone chose sides, and the sinners relished their deviltry as much as the saints savored their virtue. Over the years, the conflict produced more bravado, pious posturing, humor, and foolishness than all the sessions of the state legislature combined.

The winner was iced tea. It was the only drink everyone loved, something the most dedicated tipplers and teetotalers could swig together, the sure way not to offend anyone at the table. A couple of Waco soft drinks, Dr Pepper and Big Red, won a following, too, and eventually beer and wine rose up the social ranks into a different and more acceptable class than demon rum. In the meantime, hard spirits just got hardier, and their fans developed a number of cocktails featuring high-octane local flavors.

The result today is a wide range of Texas beverages to mix and match for different occasions. You aren't likely to be attacked anymore for what you do or don't serve, but there's no reason to take chances. Just in case, it's worth knowing about Texas convictions and conventions.

> IN THEIR 1891 COOKBOOK, *OUR HOME COOK BOOK*, MRS. PAUL THORNTON AND MRS. I. V. DAVIS OF AUSTIN WROTE, "ICED TEA IS A NECESSARY BEVERAGE IN SOUTHERN SUMMERS." THE POPULAR DRINK ORIGINATED IN THE NINETEENTH CENTURY AS A WARM WEATHER ALTERNATIVE TO COFFEE, THE FAVORITE BREW OF THAT PERIOD, BUT THESE DAYS TEXANS DRINK ICED TEA YEAR-ROUND, WITHOUT REGARD TO THE TEMPERATURE.

BEVERAGES TO BOAST ABOUT

Traditional Texas Tea

In truth, there are two traditional iced teas in Texas, as different to their partisans as bourbon and milk. The only variation between them—sugar—may seem to outsiders like a matter of personal preference, but in Texas the choice approaches a statement on moral character. The sweetening set usually adds sugar—a lot of it—before serving the tea, leaving you little option about how you want it, and the nonsweeteners will avert their eyes if you reach for sugar, as though you might pick your nose next.

6 TEASPOONS LOOSE BLACK TEA OR 6 TEA BAGS
1 QUART COLD WATER
ICE
SUGAR, OPTIONAL
LEMON WEDGE, FOR GARNISH

Serves 1 Texan

Place the loose tea or tea bags in a large teapot.

Pour the water into a tea kettle or saucepan (always use fresh cold water for best results). Bring the water to a vigorous boil, and, at once, pour it over the tea. Don't allow the water to boil more than a minute or two, or the tea could become clouded by mineral deposits in the water. Top the teapot with the lid, and allow the tea to steep about 5 minutes. The tea should get good and dark since it will be diluted by the ice. Discard the tea bags, or, if you are working with loose tea, plan to strain it through a small strainer before serving.

Let the tea stand at room temperature until it is needed. When you pour it, use a good number of ice cubes, but don't overdo it the way fast-food franchises always seem to do. Serve the tea in a barrel-size plastic glass or 1-quart Mason jar for an authentic touch. Add sugar, if you like, and a hefty wedge of lemon. Always offer refills. Iced tea tastes best the day it's made.

Variation: On hot summer days, make "sun tea" outside. Put the tea and cold water in a jar, and set it out to soak up some rays. You'll have tea in a couple of hours, but give it twice that long for full flavor.

> Hot tea has always been rare in Texas, except for a variety made from sassafras root. Sassafras tea was a traditional beverage in East Texas, used in the spring to "thin the blood," and it's still as good a way to fight a cold as any we know.

Minted Iced Tea

*Morton Gill Clark had to revise the first draft of his 1970 cookbook, **The Wide, Wide, World of Texas Cooking**, to add an iced tea recipe. He got so many complaints from Texas reviewers about the absence of the beloved drink that he made it the lead-off recipe in the book. Clark suggested serving a mint syrup on the side for a sweetener, similar to what we do here.*

MINT SYRUP

1 CUP SUGAR
1 CUP WATER
½ CUP MINT LEAVES

TRADITIONAL TEXAS TEA (PAGE 484)
FRESH MINT SPRIGS, FOR GARNISH

Serves 1 Texan

Boil the syrup ingredients together in a small pan until the sugar dissolves and the liquid is clear. Set it aside; it will steep as it cools. When it has cooled to room temperature, strain the syrup into a creamer or other small pitcher.

Offer a gargantuan glass of Traditional Texas Tea over ice, accompanied by the mint syrup. Garnish with the mint sprigs. The tea is best the day it's made, but the syrup, refrigerated, keeps for weeks.

Variation: For a stouter version of Minted Iced Tea, lace the tea with a healthy splash of bourbon.

Old-style iced teas didn't use mint flavoring, but it's a popular addition today, and, in the opinion of Jim Mattox, a Texas politico, it is an essential ingredient. When we had dinner with Mattox a few years ago at an upscale Dallas restaurant, we all ordered iced tea, but the drink arrived at the table without the garnish. The waiter explained that they hadn't been able to get any from their suppliers. Mattox was so confounded that he went into the kitchen, escorted the chef and staff out the back door, and showed them where they should be growing mint in the alley.

Hot Dr Pepper

The Dr Pepper company developed the idea for this hot beverage decades ago as a way of boosting sales of its product during the winter. Some of the original advertisements for the heated drink are displayed in the wonderfully wacky Dr Pepper Museum in Waco, Texas, located in the firm's first bottling plant.

12 OUNCES DR PEPPER
2 LEMON SLICES

Serves 2

Pour the Dr Pepper into a saucepan. Heat until the liquid is hot and bubbly, precisely 170° F, according to serious "Peppers." Place a lemon slice in the bottom of each of two mugs. Pour the Dr Pepper into the mugs, and serve immediately.

CHARLES ALDERTON, A WACO PHARMACIST, CONCOCTED DR PEPPER IN 1885, MAKING IT THE OLDEST OF ALL THE MAJOR SOFT DRINKS IN THE UNITED STATES. ALDERTON, WHO WORKED AT MORRISON'S OLD CORNER DRUG, NAMED HIS INVENTION FOR THE FATHER OF HIS BOSS'S FLAME, HOPING WITHOUT SUCCESS TO WIN FAVOR FOR MR. MORRISON. THE REAL DR PEPPER NEVER SUSPECTED HE WOULD BE IMMORTALIZED ON THE LABEL OF THE COUNTRY'S THIRD-BEST-SELLING SODA.

Central Texas Barbecue Sauce

Most of the old-time barbecue joints of central Texas don't serve a regular sauce for their meat, but that doesn't mean you can't get something red on the side. The drink of choice is Big Red, another Waco contribution to the world of soda pop.

1 PLATE OF BARBECUE, PREFERABLY BRISKET
   AND LINKS
1 BIG RED

Serves 2

 Trade bites of barbecue and sips of Big Red, mixing the flavors in the mouth.

Griver C. Thompson and Robert H. Roark invented Big Red in 1937 as a way to beat the summer heat in Waco, a goal reflected in their name for the beverage, Sun Tang Soda. While playing golf in the early 1960s, the owner of the San Antonio bottling plant asked the caddy to get him a couple of Sun Tangs. The caddy yelled out for two "big reds," inspiring a new name.

Mexican Hot Chocolate

Frothier than most versions, and cinnamon-scented, Mexican hot chocolate is just the ticket when a "blue norther" strikes.

1½ OUNCES MEXICAN CHOCOLATE, SUCH AS
  IBARRA
1¼ CUPS MILK
¼ CUP WHIPPING CREAM
WHIPPED CREAM, OPTIONAL
CANELA (MEXICAN CINNAMON) STICKS, FOR
  GARNISH

Serves 2

 Chop the chocolate, and place it in a blender. In a small, heavy pan, bring the milk and whip- ping cream just to a boil. Add them immediately to the blender, and whip until the chocolate is thoroughly blended and the mixture is frothy. Pour the hot chocolate into cups, top with whipped cream, if you like, and garnish with canela sticks.

Note: If you can't locate Mexican chocolate, substitute the same quantity of semisweet chocolate along with a pinch of ground canela or cinnamon.

Early Texas cookbooks usually contained a number of recipes for homemade wines and cordials and frequently called for wine and spirits in recipes. One way of making vinegar, for example, was with three quarts each of whiskey and molasses, seven and a half gallons of hot water, and three-quarters of a pint of yeast.

Galveston and Houston had an early edge on fancy alcoholic drinks because their ports gave them access to items such as ice and lemons. In the middle of the nineteenth century, Galveston's Tremont Hotel offered concoctions called deacon, moral suasion, vox populi, stone wall, poor man's punch, and cock tail. They all cost a quarter apiece.

Clarendon Cooler

A Methodist minister established the West Texas town of Clarendon in 1878 as a "sobriety settlement," where Panhandle cowboys could escape the boozy excesses of the boomtowns nearby. Ranchers and their hands quickly dubbed the burg "Saint's Roost." This lemon cooler, naturally, is as dry as the town.

1 CUP SUGAR
1 CUP WATER
2 CUPS FRESH LEMON JUICE (FROM ABOUT 9 TO 10 LEMONS)
1 QUART WATER
ICE CUBES
LEMON SLICES, FOR GARNISH

Makes about ½ gallon

Boil the sugar and water together in a small pan until the sugar dissolves and the liquid is clear. Pour the syrup into a pitcher, and add the lemon juice and about three-fourths of the water. Taste, and add more water if you like, keeping in mind that the ice will dilute the lemonade.

To serve, place a handful of ice cubes in each person's glass, pour the lemonade over, and garnish with lemon slices.

Booze was the downfall of Texas's most famous gunfighter, John Wesley Hardin. He spent much of his life in jail for killing a sheriff in a barroom duel, and then got shot in the back of the head himself while having a drink in El Paso's Acme Saloon.

Margarita

Everyone except the Baptist Church claims credit for the invention of the margarita. The most plausible contender is "Pancho" Morales, a Juárez, Mexico, bartender during World War II who later moved to El Paso. He says a gringo woman wandered into his bar on July 4, 1942, and ordered a "magnolia," a gin cocktail. Pancho didn't know the drink, so he made up a Mexican substitute based on tequila and called it a "margarita," the Spanish word for daisy. Most other accounts of the origin say the drink is named for a beloved woman; if so, she must have been a little on the tart side to inspire the salty-sour punch of the cocktail.

SALT, OPTIONAL
LIME WEDGE
1½ OUNCES HIGH-QUALITY GOLD TEQUILA
1 OUNCE TRIPLE SEC OR COINTREAU
1 OUNCE FRESH LIME JUICE

Serves 1

Place a thin layer of salt on a saucer. Rub the rim of an 8-ounce glass with the lime wedge, and immediately dip the rim in the salt. Set the glass aside. (Omit this step if you prefer your margaritas *sin sal*, "without salt.")

Pour the tequila, triple sec, and lime juice into a cocktail shaker or lidded jar, add several pieces of cracked ice, and shake to blend. Strain into the prepared glass, and serve.

> INDIANS IN MEXICO MADE A FERMENTED DRINK CALLED PULQUE FROM THE AGAVE PLANT LONG BEFORE CORTÉS AND HIS TROOPS CONQUERED THE LAND. THE SPANISH DISTILLED THIS LIQUOR TO PRODUCE MEZCAL. TEQUILA IS A REFINED VERSION OF MEZCAL, MUCH AS COGNAC IS A SUPERIOR TYPE OF BRANDY. MEXICANS STILL MAKE ALL THREE AGAVE PRODUCTS, BUT ONLY TEQUILA IS EXPORTED.

Grande Gold Margarita

Regular margaritas bite back, but this blend of premium ingredients is deceptively tame and mellow.

SALT, OPTIONAL
2 LEMON WEDGES
3 OUNCES PREMIUM GOLD TEQUILA, SUCH AS HERRADURA GOLD OR CUERVO 1800
2 OUNCES GRAND MARNIER
2 OUNCES FRESH LEMON JUICE

Serves 2

Place a thin layer of salt on a saucer. Rub the rims of two 8-ounce glasses with the lemon wedges, and immediately dip the rims in the salt. Set the glasses aside. (Omit this step if you prefer your margaritas *sin sal*, "without salt.")

Pour the tequila, Grand Marnier, and lemon juice into a cocktail shaker or lidded jar, add several pieces of cracked ice, and shake to blend. Strain into the prepared glasses, and serve.

Early Mexican settlers in Texas made pulque and mezcal just like their neighbors to the south. When they saw a maguey (as they call agave) about to bloom, they collected the aguamiel, or sweet sap, and fermented it in bags made of goat-, pig-, or sheepskin. The more patient distilled this pulque into mezcal.

The Mexican government imposes strict standards on anything labeled "tequila." It must be made from a blue agave—a special variety of the plant—and one that has been harvested in a small region near the town of Tequila, which is about forty miles from Guadalajara. Distilled cane sugar is permitted in the liquor, but the agave content has to be at least 51 percent, and it ranges as high as 100 percent in the top brands.

Bloody Maria

Maria is lustier than her cousin Mary, but she's just as much of a morning person.

1 32-OUNCE BOTTLE TOMATO JUICE

8 OUNCES GOLD TEQUILA

⅓ CUP FRESH LIME JUICE

⅓ CUP CHOPPED CILANTRO

1 TO 2 FRESH JALAPEÑOS, CHOPPED

BIG SPLASH OF WORCESTERSHIRE SAUCE

ICE CUBES

CELERY SALT OR SPICE ISLANDS BEAU MONDE
   SEASONING, OPTIONAL

SERRANOS OR SMALL PICKLED OKRA PODS,
   OPTIONAL

CELERY STICKS, OPTIONAL

Serves 6

Unless you have a blender bigger than any we've ever come across, pour half of the tomato juice into a pitcher. Pour the other half into a blender, and toss in everything other than the celery salt. Blend briefly, until the ingredients are well combined. Stir the seasoned tomato juice into the juice in the pitcher, and add a couple of handfuls of ice cubes. Pour the drink into glasses, and shake a little celery salt over each Bloody Maria, if you like. If you want to impress your guests as the creative type, attach serrano chiles or small, whole pickled okra pods to celery sticks with a toothpick, and add one to each drink.

> José Maria Guadalupe de Cuervo produced one of the first tequilas in 1795, calling it "vino de mezcal." During the next century, the Sauza family emerged as his company's major competitor. These old operations, still known as Cuervo and Sauza, continue to dominate the market from their distilleries in the town of Tequila.

Pear-A-Noid

This drink is really out to sea. We picked up the idea on a chartered yacht cruise in the Caribbean.

1½ OUNCES GOLD TEQUILA
1½ OUNCES PEAR NECTAR
½ OUNCE FRESH LEMON JUICE
¼ OUNCE CRÈME DE CASSIS
1 SLICE UNPEELED PEAR, OPTIONAL, FOR GARNISH

Serves 1

Fill an 8-ounce glass halfway with cracked ice. Pour all of the liquid ingredients over the ice, and stir to blend. If you like, garnish the rim with the pear slice.

BLUE AGAVE PLANTS PRODUCE THE AGUAMIEL USED FOR TEQUILA ONLY WHEN THEY ARE READY TO BLOOM, AFTER EIGHT TO TEN YEARS OF GROWTH. THE WHOLE PLANT HAS TO BE UPROOTED AND TRIMMED OF ITS SPIKE-SHAPED LEAVES TO GET AT THE MATURE HEART, WHICH LOOKS LIKE AN OVERGROWN PINEAPPLE AND USUALLY WEIGHS WELL OVER ONE HUNDRED POUNDS.

Next thing you know, Texans will be raising geese for foie gras. Not only does the state produce French-style wines now, Texas also has its own bottled mineral water, the lightly carbonated Artesia. Rick Scoville started the company, as he says, to "kick Perrier in the derriere."

Sangrita y Tequila

In Mexico, tequila is often sipped straight and chased with an accompanying glass of spicy sangrita.

SANGRITA

1 CUP TOMATO JUICE

½ CUP FRESH ORANGE JUICE

2 TABLESPOONS FRESH LIME JUICE

1 TABLESPOON CHOPPED ONION

2 TEASPOONS WORCESTERSHIRE SAUCE

1 FRESH SERRANO OR ½ TO 1 JALAPEÑO,
  CHOPPED

SALT TO TASTE

HIGH-QUALITY TEQUILA

Makes about 1¾ cups of sangrita

Place all the sangrita ingredients in a blender, and purée them. Chill the mixture at least 1 hour. Pour the drink into the smallest glasses you own, and serve it alongside shots of high-quality tequila. Leftover sangrita, refrigerated, can be kept for at least a week.

The finest tequilas are meant for sipping alone, perhaps after dinner like a cognac. Our favorite brands are Herradura and El Tesoro, each made from 100 percent agave. Both companies produce tequila in the three major styles: *plata* (clear and pure, without barrel aging), *reposado* or oro (tinted gold from aging in wood up to a year), and *añejo* (aged in oak, usually for several years). As you might expect, *añejo* is the most complex and expensive of the three.

Mint Julep

The main body of Anglo pioneers in Texas came from Tennessee and Kentucky, where they had acquired a fondness for distilled "corn likker." The drink evolved into bourbon, an American original, but the frontier version was about as sipping-smooth as aged bath water. One of the easiest ways to swallow the homemade rotgut was with liberal doses of sugar and mint. A concoction of all three became a mint julep.

MINT SYRUP

1 CUP SUGAR
1 CUP WATER
½ CUP FRESH MINT LEAVES

2 OUNCES BOURBON OR SOUR-MASH WHISKEY
MINT SPRIGS, FOR GARNISH

Serves 1

Boil the syrup ingredients together in a small pan until the sugar dissolves and the liquid is clear. Set the syrup aside; it will steep as it cools. Strain it before using it. Refrigerated, the syrup keeps indefinitely.

Spoon 1 to 2 teaspoons, or more to taste, of the mint syrup into the bottom of an 8-ounce glass. Fill the glass halfway with cracked ice, and pour 2 ounces of bourbon over it. Stir gently to blend, and garnish with mint.

In the first half of the nineteenth century, if you wandered west of the corn likker frontier in East Texas, whiskey got really raw. It might be crude alcohol colored with coffee or even more primitive spirits fortified with hot peppers or tobacco. One whiskey maker, Snakehead Thompson, became famous for fermenting his brand in barrels containing a half-dozen rattlesnake heads.

Texas Manhattan

This is our favorite bourbon drink.

¼ CUP CRUSHED ICE
1¼ OUNCES DRY VERMOUTH
2 DASHES OF BITTERS
3 ICE CUBES
2½ OUNCES PRIME BOURBON OR SOUR-MASH
  WHISKEY
1 FRESH CHERRY

Place the crushed ice in a 4-ounce cocktail glass. Stir in the vermouth and bitters, and swirl the mixture around the glass with an absorbed look on your face.

After 5 to 10 seconds, swirl everything in the glass down the sink. Put 3 ice cubes in the glass, and fill it with the bourbon. Pop the cherry in your mouth with the satisfaction of a born bartender, and then sip away.

It's just possible that everything has been sliding downhill since 1789. That was the year the United States adopted the Constitution, elected George Washington the first president, and conceived bourbon. Elijah Craig made the initial batch of corn whiskey in the county of Bourbon, then a part of Virginia and now in Kentucky. He was a Baptist preacher. To compound the irony, the county is now dry.

Holiday 'Nog

While not as rich as some recipes, this eggnog will still clog your arteries quicker than a bucket of lard.

1½ CUPS SUGAR
2 TABLESPOONS CORNSTARCH
PINCH OF SALT
4 EGGS PLUS 4 YOLKS
7 CUPS WHOLE MILK
1 CUP WHIPPING CREAM
2 TEASPOONS VANILLA
ABOUT 1 CUP BOURBON, TO TASTE
ICE CUBES
GRATED NUTMEG, FOR GARNISH

Serves 10 to 12

In a heavy saucepan, stir together the sugar, cornstarch, and salt. Add the eggs, and beat or whisk to combine well. Pour in the milk and the cream, and place the pan over medium-low heat. Stir the mixture continuously as it thickens. Do not let it boil unless you want scrambled eggs. The custard base is ready when it coats a spoon thinly. (It will thicken a bit more when chilled.) Strain the mixture into a pitcher or bowl, and refrigerate it at least 2 hours, preferably overnight.

Stir in the vanilla and the bourbon. Pour the eggnog into a blender in batches, blending with a few cubes of ice until the mixture is frothy. Pour the eggnog into a punch bowl or individual cups, and top with generous sprinklings of nutmeg. Serve immediately.

The U.S. government regulates what can be labeled "bourbon" just as the Mexican government regulates what can be called "tequila." Even a solid sour-mash whiskey like Jack Daniel's can't use the term because the company's special charcoal-filtering process doesn't fit the traditional standards.

Marpeani

Texas has been fresh out of native olives for a few eons, so, naturally, folks developed other kinds of martinis.

CRACKED ICE
3½ OUNCES VODKA
½ OUNCE DRY VERMOUTH
2 TWISTS OF LEMON
4 COOKED BLACK-EYED PEAS, FOR GARNISH

Serves 2

Chill a pair of 3-ounce martini glasses until they are frosty. Fill a martini pitcher, or another small pitcher, halfway with cracked ice. Pour the vodka over the ice to "smoke." Add the vermouth, stir, and strain the drink into the glasses. Drop 2 black-eyed peas into each glass, and serve immediately.

FRANK X. TOLBERT, THE DALLAS COLUMNIST AND CHILIHEAD, LIKED FARKLEBERRIES IN HIS MARTINIS, WHICH HE CALLED FARKLETINIS. USUALLY FARKLEBERRY PLANTS ARE SHRUBS, BUT IN THE PINEY WOODS OF EAST TEXAS THEY REACH THE SIZE OF TREES. MOST PEOPLE, WITH THE NOTABLE EXCEPTION OF TOLBERT, THINK THE DRY BERRIES SHOULD BE LEFT TO THE BIRDS.

The most famous saloon in Texas history was Judge Roy Bean's Jersey Lilly, in the tiny town of Langtry. In the late nineteenth century, Bean, who was justice of the peace, dispensed "the Law West of the Pecos" from his barroom, where he shamelessly badgered lawyers, defendants, jurors, and spectators to buy drinks during trials.

Ramos Gin Fizz

This version of a gin fizz originated either on the Mexican border, perhaps in Laredo, or in New Orleans. It's still popular in both places and made in almost identical ways.

2 OUNCES GIN
½ CUP CRUSHED ICE
2 TABLESPOONS CREAM
2 TABLESPOONS FRESH LIME JUICE
1 EGG WHITE
2 TEASPOONS POWDERED SUGAR
½ TEASPOON ORANGE-FLOWER WATER

Serves 1

 Put the ingredients into a blender, and mix well. Pour into a tall glass, and serve with a straw.

One of Houston's first principal structures was a saloon covered with canvas, built in 1837. The city loved its liquor in those early years, and the grog shops quickly went upscale. Within a decade, according to one thorough historian, Houston's most sumptuous businesses were bars, often splendidly furnished establishments full of patrons all day.

Brownsville Border Buttermilk

The Brownsville Convention and Visitors Bureau uses a version of this cooling drink to welcome groups of visitors to the Mexican border.

6 OUNCES FROZEN LEMONADE CONCENTRATE
4 TO 6 OUNCES RUM
ICE CUBES

Serves 6

Put the lemonade concentrate and the rum into a blender. Add ice cubes to fill the blender, and blend until the mixture is slushy. Pour it into cocktail glasses, and serve.

Hill Country Peach Fuzzies

A few of these on a summer day, and you'll feel as ripe and fuzzy as the peaches you're peeling.

2 RIPE MEDIUM PEACHES, PEELED AND PITTED
6 OUNCES FRESH ORANGE JUICE
6 OUNCES VODKA
2 OUNCES PEACH BRANDY
8 ICE CUBES

Serves 4

Put all the ingredients into a blender. Blend until the mixture is slushy. Pour it into tall glasses, and serve.

Sangria Suprema

*On his 1973 album, **Viva Terlingua**, Jerry Jeff Walker told the world, "I love that sangria wine just like I love old friends of mine." Sangria makes a rousing party punch, especially this top-drawer rendition.*

I BOTTLE DECENT RED WINE
JUICE OF 3 ORANGES
1 UNPEELED ORANGE, SLICED
JUICE OF 2 LIMES
1 SLICE UNPEELED LIME
1½ CUPS TRIPLE SEC, OR 1 CUP TRIPLE SEC
   PLUS ½ CUP LIME LIQUEUR
½ CUP BRANDY, PREFERABLY APRICOT
2 CUPS CLUB SODA
ICE

Serves 10 to 12

In a punch bowl, mix together the wine, juices and fruit, and liqueurs. Just before serving time, add the club soda and ice. A block or ring of ice will last longer than cubes. Stir the sangria, and serve it in cups or glasses.

> The Junior League of Dallas was leading the city to sophistication as early as 1935, when its *Cook Book* discussed the etiquette of serving wine with meals.

TEXAS BEER

German immigrants began coming to Texas in large numbers in the 1840s, and beer wasn't far behind. When Charles Nimitz—grandfather of Admiral Chester Nimitz—opened his frontier hotel in Fredericksburg, he thought it only natural for the establishment to have its own brewery as well as its own bakery. Residents of the town undoubtedly appreciated the idea every bit as much as did Horace Greeley, Robert E. Lee, and other famous Nimitz Hotel guests.

Scholz's Garden, the grand old Austin watering hole, has been serving beer since it opened as a German private club in 1866. About the same time, in San Antonio, the City Brewery built a small plant that became the headquarters for Pearl Beer in 1885. Under the leadership of Otto Koehler, Pearl purchased its formula from a brewery in Bremen, Germany, that called its product "Perle," after the pearl-like bubbles that rise in a glass when the beer is poured.

German and Czech farmers around the small town of Shiner started another Old World brewery in 1909. To make the kind of beer they wanted, the founders secured the services of Kosmos Spoetzl, a Bavarian whose family had a recipe dating back several generations. To this day, the Spoetzl Brewery makes its Shiner and Shiner Bock beers with the same formula, performing most tasks by hand and using one of the smallest commercial brew kettles in the country.

Both Pearl and Shiner survived Prohibition, when many other breweries died, by changing temporarily to other products. After Otto Koehler's death, his wife Emma guided Pearl through the tough times until that night in 1933, just 15 minutes after the repeal of Prohibition, when more than one hundred trucks and twenty-five boxcars loaded with beer rolled out of the plant down a San Antonio street full of cheering people.

Within the next decade, the Lone Star Brewery joined Pearl in San Antonio, setting up business in the landmark building that now serves as the San Antonio Museum of Art. That rounded out the trio of major local beers Texans enjoy today, but it wasn't the last nod to German brewing influence in the state. In recent years, the Dallas Brewing Company, a new microbrewery, began releasing a series of barley-malt beers made under the traditional German Purity Law, established in 1516. The German brewing heritage is still strong in Texas after 150 years, and it's likely to thrive at least that much longer.

> The outlaw Sam Bass earned a good reputation in Texas because of his unfailing generosity. When he robbed stagecoaches, Bass allowed passengers to keep one dollar apiece for their dinners, and he always treated any new acquaintance to a drink.

TEXAS WINE

Texans have made wine since frontier days, but they have always had trouble getting respect for their efforts. One visitor in the nineteenth century complained that the local handcrafted wild-grape wines were "sour enough to pucker up the mouth of a cannon." More recently, when the state's modern wine industry started production, unappreciative outsiders labeled the results "Chateau Bubba."

The derision probably reflected some truth in the past, but it obscures just as much reality. The same Spanish priests who introduced vineyards in California also cultivated grapes in Texas by the eighteenth century. We don't know anything about the quality of the mission wines, but it's evident that some later

European settlers, particularly Czechs and Germans, were accomplished home vintners. They developed ways of making decent wine from native mustang grapes, and they passed their techniques along for several generations up to the present.

The same lowly Texas wild grapes they used actually saved the French wine industry around the turn of the century. When an epidemic of a plant louse called phylloxera attacked vineyards everywhere, T. V. Munson of Denison, Texas, found a solution by grafting French vines onto disease-resistant local rootstock. Munson is still a hero in both Bordeaux and the Napa Valley.

By the beginning of Prohibition in 1920, there were at least sixteen commercial wineries in Texas. Only Val Verde in Del Rio reopened later, and it remained a lonely operation until the 1970s, when the national wine boom inspired a revival of production in the state.

The first bottles from the new wineries may have been more appropriate for Communion than dinner, but they improved quickly. At the San Francisco Fair and Wine Competition in 1986, of the 1,955 entries, Texas's Llano Estacado 1984 Chardonnay won one of the eleven double gold medals awarded, and the Pheasant Ridge 1983 Cabernet Sauvignon took one of the fifty-four gold medals. Both of these wineries continue to make some superlative selections, along with some lesser ones, and so do Fall Creek, Sainte Genevieve, Sister Creek, Moyer, Messina Hof, Slaughter Leftwich, Grape Creek, and a growing number of other producers. "Chateau Bubba" has become "Chateau Beaucoup."

Y'ALL·COME·BACK
DESSERTS

*O*f the world's four great cuisines—French, Chinese, Italian, and Texan—only the last-named requires a single knife and fork.

Jerry Flemmons, *Plowboys, Cowboys and Slanted Pigs*

*S*ome fancy Texas restaurants today will give you new silverware for dessert, but traditionally you licked the gravy from your fork and dug it immediately into a piece of pie. More like a consummation than a separate course, dessert was the diner's dénouement and the cook's curtain call. You didn't question whether it was wanted or needed, only what was available. From the beginning, Texans embraced an immense range of sweets. All the early cookbooks in the state devoted half their pages to desserts, offering complete chapters on subjects such as puddings, pastry, confectionery, ices, custards, brandied fruits, and fancy dishes, the last covering everything from meringue to macaroons. More recent cooks honed their specialties but never lost the sugar lust. In a nation known for its sweet tooth, Texans still take the cake.

Good-'n'-Gooey Peach Cobbler

When it's peach-picking time in Texas, a fresh-fruit cobbler is easily the most popular dessert around. Don't confuse the dish with the flaky-crust pies that some people call cobblers. A real Texas peach cobbler has an abundance of juicy fruit and a sweet, biscuit-like batter topping that's crunchy on the surface and doughy inside.

FILLING

12 TO 14 (ABOUT 3½ POUNDS) RIPE MEDIUM
    PEACHES, PEELED AND SLICED
¼ CUP SUGAR
1 TABLESPOON FRESH LEMON JUICE
2 TEASPOONS CINNAMON
¾ TEASPOON POWDERED GINGER
¾ TEASPOON VANILLA

BATTER

½ CUP UNSALTED BUTTER
1¼ CUPS ALL-PURPOSE FLOUR
1 CUP SUGAR
2 TEASPOONS BAKING POWDER
1 CUP MILK

VANILLA ICE CREAM OR WHIPPED CREAM,
    OPTIONAL

Makes a 9-by-13-inch cobbler

Spanish settlers brought peaches to Texas in the sixteenth century, when they planted trees at their missions. Today, the state is one of the leading peach producers in the country, harvesting about twenty million pounds of fruit annually.

Preheat the oven to 350° F.

In a bowl, mix together all the filling ingredients. Set the filling aside to draw out the juices. Cobbler filling should be a bit juicier than that of most pies.

While the filling sits, melt the butter in a 9-by-13-inch baking dish, either in the oven or on the stove. In another bowl, make the batter: Stir together the flour, sugar, and baking powder, and add the milk. Mix until lightly blended. Spoon the mixture evenly over the melted butter. Don't stir it—that would preclude the development of crunchy edges. Pour the peach filling evenly over the batter.

Bake 45 minutes. As the cobbler cooks, the batter will ooze up and around the fruit, creating a moist, golden brown crust.

Serve the cobbler warm. If you're a certified hedonist, top it with vanilla ice cream or whipped cream.

Variation: A strawberry-and-rhubarb filling also makes a great cobbler. In place of the peach filling, combine 1½ pounds rhubarb (cut in 1-inch chunks), 2½ to 3 pints strawberries (halved), ¾ to 1 cup sugar, 2 teaspoons ground anise seeds, 1 tablespoon fresh lemon juice, and the zest and juice of 1 medium orange.

Apple-Pecan Strudel

With a name that is German for "whirlpool," strudel should resemble just that, with ring upon ring of paper-thin pastry enveloping a fragrant fruit filling. You can buy strudels at many bakeries, particularly in central Texas, but even if you have that opportunity, it's fun to fix your own on special occasions. This is an updated version of a turn-of-the-century Tex-Czech recipe.

DOUGH (ENOUGH FOR 2 STRUDELS)
¼ CUP UNSALTED BUTTER
½ CUP HOT WATER
1 EGG
1 TABLESPOON CIDER VINEGAR, PREFERABLY
  UNREFINED
2½ CUPS ALL-PURPOSE FLOUR
¼ TEASPOON SALT

FILLING
8 CUPS PEELED, THIN-SLICED TART APPLES
  (ABOUT 6 APPLES)
½ CUP UNSALTED BUTTER, MELTED
1 CUP CHOPPED PECANS, TOASTED
1 CUP RAISINS
1 CUP GRAHAM CRACKER OR VANILLA WAFER
  CRUMBS
½ CUP DARK BROWN SUGAR
½ CUP SUGAR
2 TABLESPOONS MINCED CRYSTALLIZED GINGER
2 TEASPOONS GROUND CINNAMON
½ TEASPOON SALT

* * *

3 TABLESPOONS UNSALTED BUTTER
1 TABLESPOON SUGAR

Serves 12

Make the dough: Place the butter in a bowl, and pour the hot water over it, stirring to melt the butter. Add the egg and the vinegar, and mix in well. Add 2 cups of the flour and the salt, and stir until a sticky dough forms. Sprinkle the remaining ½ cup flour on a pastry board, and knead the dough on it for about 5 minutes, until the extra flour is incorporated and the dough is smooth and shiny.

Divide the dough in half, flattening both portions into 4- or 5-inch rounds. Refrigerate or freeze one round for later use. The amount of remaining dough may not look like enough to encase the filling, but it will. Cover it, and let it sit in a warm place. Some cooks put it in a bowl set in a second bowl of warm water; others use a barely warmed skillet. Allowed to rest, the dough becomes soft and pliable.

While the dough is resting, make the filling: Toss the apples with the butter in a large bowl. Add the remaining filling ingredients, and mix well.

Get ready to stretch the dough: Clear a table, and cover it with a thin smooth-surfaced dish towel. Sprinkle the towel with flour. (The towel eventually helps support the paper-thin dough.) Plan to work quickly once you get going. Center the dough on the towel, and pat it out as thin as you can by hand. Then put your hands under the dough, and start stretching it out from the center. Some people prefer to use their fingertips for this; others use their knuckles. We start with our fingertips, switching to the knuckles when the dough is thinner and can tear more easily.

To pull the dough evenly, you'll need either to turn the towel around periodically or to make your way around the table, whichever is easier. As the dough gets successively broader and thinner, you'll be able to tell where it still needs stretching by looking at it— if it's translucent, it's thin enough. Try to avoid tearing the dough, as it is difficult to patch. The edges will be thicker, but you can pull them thin or trim them off. You should end up with something resembling a rectangle at least 18 by 24 inches.

Preheat the oven to 400° F. Grease a baking sheet.

Melt the remaining 3 tablespoons of butter. Brush the dough, still resting on the towel, with about 2 tablespoons of it. Cover the dough completely with a single layer of the filling. Using the towel for support, begin rolling up one of the rectangle's longer sides jelly roll–style. If you ended up with tears in the dough concentrated in any one area, try to roll the strudel so that they will be hidden within it. Roll the strudel up snug, but don't make it extra tight, because it needs some room to expand while baking. Pinch it closed as you go to help hold in the juices.

When the strudel is rolled up completely, use the towel to transfer it from the table to the baking sheet positioned nearby. Form the strudel into a horseshoe to fit on the sheet. Brush it with the remaining tablespoon of melted butter, and sprinkle it with the sugar.

Bake the strudel for 15 minutes. Reduce the heat to 350° F, and continue baking for an additional 25 to 30 minutes, until the pastry is lightly browned and just crisp. Let the strudel rest for at least 20 minutes before you cut it.

Serve the strudel warm in thick slices.

TEXAS HORTICULTURISTS CALL BAXTER AND CAROL ADAMS THE ADAM AND EVE OF THE STATE'S APPLE INDUSTRY. THEY LEFT HOUSTON BEFORE THE FALL OF THE TEMPLE OF PETROLEUM, AS BAXTER PUTS IT, TO LAUNCH LOVE CREEK ORCHARDS ON A TWO-THOUSAND-ACRE HILL-COUNTRY RANCH. THEIR DWARF APPLE TREES PRODUCE PESTICIDE-FREE FRUIT WITH UP TO 40 PERCENT MORE SUGAR THAN APPLES FROM COLDER CLIMES. SEE "MAIL-ORDER SOURCES" (PAGE 554) FOR ORDERING INFORMATION.

TECHNIQUE TIP

The process of stretching the dough isn't as difficult as some books make it out to be, but it does require patience. For both the dough and the filling, thinness is essential. It makes the pastry light and flaky and the filling dense and juicy. If you don't want to deal with the dough, you can substitute store-bought phyllo pastry, though the texture will differ a bit. Follow the package directions for its preparation and layering, substituting graham-cracker or vanilla-wafer crumbs for the bread crumbs or corn flakes called for between layers.

Perfect Pecan Pie

Now a national favorite, pecan pie developed out of an old Southern dessert, molasses pie, when corn syrup became widely available at the beginning of the twentieth century. Perhaps Texan or Louisianan in origin, it spread rapidly throughout the pecan-growing states in the South and then followed the supermarkets to other areas. This recipe is influenced by John Thorne, editor of the wonderful **Simple Cooking** *newsletter and a former Texas resident, who came up with the method for making the filling so lusciously dense.*

1 CUP DARK BROWN SUGAR
⅔ CUP CANE SYRUP, PREFERABLY, OR ⅓ CUP
   LIGHT CORN SYRUP AND ⅓ CUP UNSULPHURED
   DARK MOLASSES
¼ CUP UNSALTED BUTTER
3 TABLESPOONS BOURBON
½ TEASPOON VANILLA
½ TEASPOON SALT
4 EGGS
2 TO 3 TABLESPOONS HALF-AND-HALF
2 GENEROUS CUPS PECAN PIECES
UNBAKED SINGLE FLAKY PIE CRUST (PAGE 513)
WHOLE PECAN HALVES

Makes a 9-inch pie

Preheat the oven to 350° F.

In a large, heavy saucepan, melt the brown sugar, syrup, and butter together with the bourbon, vanilla, and salt. Continue heating the mixture to the boiling point, stirring frequently. Boil for 1 minute, stirring constantly. Remove the pan from the heat, and let the mixture cool.

In a bowl, beat the eggs with the half-and-half until they are light and frothy. Add the mixture to the cooled syrup, beating until the mixture is well incorporated. Stir in the pecan pieces. Pour the filling into the pie shell. Top with a layer of pecan halves. Bake the pie 45 to 50 minutes, or until a toothpick inserted into the center comes out clean.

Serve the pie warm or at room temperature.

TECHNIQUE TIP

Although pecans can be found year-round, you can save money by purchasing large quantities in the late fall, shortly after harvest. If you store unshelled nuts in a cool, dry place, they will keep for up to a year. Shelled nuts last just as long when they are refrigerated or frozen.

Spanish explorer Cabeza de Vaca learned more than he wanted to know about pecans. During the six years he roamed Texas after his shipwreck on the coast, his Indian captors took him with them for their annual two-month sojourn on the "river of nuts," the Guadalupe, where they lived mainly on pecans. Cabeza de Vaca didn't think much of the nut, but then he never had it in a pie.

Flaky Pie Crust

Butter tastes the best, and lard makes it flake. That's the simple, if awful, truth about pie crust. You can substitute vegetable shortening for some of the lard, as we do here, without losing the lightness, but if you get more modern than that, you will be the only flaky thing in the dining room.

¼ CUP LARD, CHILLED
¼ CUP UNSALTED BUTTER, CHILLED
¼ CUP VEGETABLE SHORTENING, PREFERABLY CRISCO, CHILLED
2 CUPS SOFT-WHEAT FLOUR SUCH AS WHITE LILY, PREFERABLY, OR ALL-PURPOSE FLOUR
1 TEASPOON SALT
5 TO 7 TABLESPOONS ICE WATER

Makes a 9-inch two-crust pie

Using a food processor, a bowl with a pastry blender, or your fingers, cut the lard, butter, and vegetable shortening into the flour and salt. Whatever method you choose, be careful not to overwork the dough, which would reduce flakiness. Add the water a few tablespoons at a time, until the dough just holds together. Divide the dough into two mounds, wrap them in plastic, and refrigerate them at least 30 minutes (or wrap one mound for the freezer, if you don't plan to use it in the next couple of days).

If the pie crust is to be baked, preheat the oven to 400° F.

On a floured board or pastry cloth, roll out the dough in a circle a couple of inches larger than the pie pan. To avoid stretching the dough excessively, roll it from the center outwards, lifting the rolling pin after each stroke rather than rolling back over the dough in the opposite direction. Loosen the dough, drape it around the rolling pin, and center the crust over the pan, dropping it gently into place.

If you're making a one-crust pie, crimp the edges decoratively. If your pie is to have two crusts, roll out the second mound of dough, too.

For a single prebaked crust, prick the dough in several spots. Cover the pie shell with foil, and weight the foil with dried beans or pie weights. Bake the crust for 10 minutes, and then lower the temperature to 350° F and bake for an additional 15 minutes, or follow the directions in your pie recipe.

Peanut Butter Pie

Texas's other major nut also makes a great pie. You find two versions around the state, one baked and syrupy and this creamy style, which we fix with less sweetening than some people use.

FILLING

1 CUP WHIPPING CREAM

8 OUNCES CREAM CHEESE, AT ROOM TEMPERATURE

1¼ CUPS CREAMY PEANUT BUTTER

1 TABLESPOON VANILLA

1 CUP POWDERED SUGAR

9-INCH GRAHAM CRACKER PIE CRUST (PAGE 515)

¼ TO ⅓ CUP CHOPPED PEANUTS, PREFERABLY HONEY-ROASTED

Makes a 9-inch pie

 Whip the cream in a bowl until it is stiff, and set it aside. In another bowl, beat together the cream cheese, peanut butter, vanilla, and powdered sugar. Fold in the whipped cream, blending well. Spoon the filling into the graham cracker crust, and sprinkle the peanuts over the top. Refrigerate the pie, covered, at least 2 hours, or overnight. It will keep well for several days.

ACTUALLY, PEANUTS ARE NOT A NUT AT ALL, BUT A LEGUME, MORE CLOSELY RELATED TO PEAS AND BEANS THAN TO HICKORIES AND PECANS. IN SOME PARTS OF THE WORLD, PEANUTS ARE A MAJOR FOOD CROP, OF GREAT IMPORTANCE IN THE NATIVE DIET.

Graham Cracker Pie Crust

1¼ CUPS GRAHAM CRACKER CRUMBS (FROM
   ABOUT 16 CRACKERS)
2 TABLESPOONS SUGAR
5 TABLESPOONS UNSALTED BUTTER, MELTED

Makes a 9-inch pie crust

Preheat the oven to 350° F.
   In a bowl, stir together the graham cracker crumbs and sugar. Pour in the butter, and stir to combine.
   Pat the mixture into the bottom and up the sides of a 9-inch pie pan. Bake the crust for 10 minutes, until it is lightly set. Let it cool before filling it.

Terlingua is famed for its chili cook-offs, but they weren't always the only game in town.
   Steve Fromholz, a Texas musician, once sponsored the lesser-known Cookie Chill-off. Entries were limited to no-bake pies, cakes, and refrigerator cookies. The rules stipulated that the panel of judges had to include a kid with a sweet tooth and the local store's beer-guzzling goat.

Sweet Potato Pie

The annual East Texas Yamboree in Gilmer wouldn't be worth a local subway token without the yam pie competition. Annie Belle Collier, who has been involved in the festival nearly fifty years, says the contest got a little weird at one point when freestyle rules led to pies containing everything from grapes to grain alcohol. These days, the competition is back to purism, which means the judges wouldn't get to taste this delectable version, spiked with a little bourbon and spiced with praline.

UNBAKED SINGLE FLAKY PIE CRUST
   (PAGE 513)

PRALINE
½ CUP CHOPPED PECANS
4 TABLESPOONS DARK BROWN SUGAR
2 TABLESPOONS UNSALTED BUTTER

FILLING
2½ CUPS (ABOUT 3 MEDIUM) MASHED BAKED
   SWEET POTATOES
½ CUP DARK BROWN SUGAR
3 EGGS
¼ CUP UNSALTED BUTTER
¼ CUP MILK
2 TABLESPOONS VANILLA
1 TABLESPOON CANE SYRUP OR DARK CORN
   SYRUP
1 TABLESPOON BOURBON
½ TEASPOON SALT
½ TEASPOON GROUND CINNAMON
½ TEASPOON GROUND ALLSPICE
¼ TEASPOON GROUND NUTMEG

PECAN HALVES

Makes a 9-inch pie

Preheat the oven to 400° F. Place the pie shell in the freezer while you prepare the praline.

In a food processor, or in a bowl with a pastry blender, blend together the pecans, brown sugar, and butter. Remove the pie crust from the freezer, and spread the bottom of it with the praline. Bake for 12 minutes.

Combine all the filling ingredients in a mixing bowl, and beat them together with a mixer until they are smooth and light. Pour the filling into the warm praline-filled crust. Arrange the pecan halves decoratively around the pie's edge. Reduce the oven temperature to 350° F. Bake the pie for 45 minutes, until the filling is set and slightly puffed. The top will sink back down when the pie cools.

Serve the pie warm or at room temperature.

Apple Pie with Cheddar Crust

Many Americans like a slice of cheddar cheese on apple pie. Never shy on such a subject, some Texans just bake it in.

CRUST

3 CUPS SOFT-WHEAT FLOUR SUCH AS WHITE
  LILY, PREFERABLY, OR ALL-PURPOSE FLOUR
2 TABLESPOONS SUGAR
1 TEASPOON SALT
¾ CUP (3 OUNCES) GRATED SHARP CHEDDAR
  CHEESE, CHILLED
¼ CUP UNSALTED BUTTER, CHILLED
¼ CUP LARD, CHILLED
¼ CUP VEGETABLE SHORTENING, PREFERABLY
  CRISCO, CHILLED
5 TO 7 TABLESPOONS ICE WATER

FILLING

6 CUPS PEELED AND SLICED TART BAKING
  APPLES (ABOUT 4), SUCH AS ROME OR
  JONATHAN
⅓ TO ½ CUP DARK BROWN SUGAR
2 TABLESPOONS APPLE CIDER
2 TABLESPOONS ALL-PURPOSE FLOUR
1 TEASPOON GROUND CINNAMON
1 TEASPOON ANISE SEEDS, GROUND
½ TEASPOON GROUND NUTMEG
1 TO 2 TABLESPOONS FRESH LEMON JUICE

*Makes a 10-inch pie or
a 9-inch deep-dish pie*

For the crust, combine the flour with the sugar and salt in a food processor. Scatter the cheese over the flour. Cut the butter, lard, and shortening into small pieces, and add them. Process briefly, until a crumbly meal forms. (Alternatively, combine the ingredients in a bowl with a pastry blender.) Pour in the smaller amount of water, and process or blend until the dough holds together, adding the extra water if needed. Divide the dough into two balls. Wrap these in plastic, and refrigerate them for at least 30 minutes and as long as 24 hours.

Preheat the oven to 400° F.

Combine the apples with the smaller amount of brown sugar, adding the rest if they taste overly tart. Mix in the remaining ingredients.

Roll out both balls of refrigerated dough on a floured surface. Place one in the bottom of whichever size pie pan you're using, add the filling, and

You'll know you're in Medina, Texas, when you come across a 20-foot-high stone sculpture of an apple in the city park. If you visit during the summer, you'll be able to enjoy the International Apple Festival, when you can crunch into the honored fruit in everything from pies to pizzas.

top with the second crust. Crimp the edges, and prick a few holes in the top to allow the steam to escape. Bake the pie for 50 to 55 minutes, until the crust seems well set and lightly browned. Check it after 25 to 30 min-utes, covering the edges with foil if they appear to be browning too rapidly.

Serve the pie warm or at room tem-perature.

Buttermilk Pie

Tangy buttermilk pie evolved as a makeshift dessert when the cellar and cupboards were bare of fruit. Contemporary cooks make it for the distinctive taste, which is enhanced with a splash of fresh lemon juice.

1 CUP SUGAR
3 EGGS
3 TABLESPOONS ALL-PURPOSE FLOUR
1½ CUPS BUTTERMILK
¼ CUP UNSALTED BUTTER
2 TABLESPOONS FRESH LEMON JUICE
2 TEASPOONS LEMON ZEST
¾ TEASPOON VANILLA
SINGLE FLAKY PIE CRUST (PAGE 513), PRE-
    BAKED 5 TO 6 MINUTES AT 400° F
GROUND NUTMEG

Makes a 9-inch pie

Preheat the oven to 350° F.
Beat together the sugar and eggs until they are well blended and the mixture is light yel-low in color. Add the flour, and mix it in briefly. Add the buttermilk, butter, lemon juice and zest, and vanilla. Mix well.

Pour the filling into the prepared pie shell. Top the pie with a generous sprinkling of nutmeg, and bake it for 30 to 35 minutes, until the filling is well set.

Serve the pie warm or at room tem-perature.

Texas A&M once provided Franklin Delano Roosevelt with fifty special orange chiffon pies for the president's whistle-stop campaign. FDR must have liked the newfangled icebox dessert, because the following year he approved a $2 million appropria-tion for the university, a yield of $40,000 per pie.

Coconut Cream Pie

Coconut and custard are a combo no Texan can resist. This coconut cream pie isn't as sweet as some, but you can add a couple of extra tablespoons of sugar if you want more kick.

6 TABLESPOONS SUGAR

3 TABLESPOONS CORNSTARCH

½ TEASPOON SALT

1 13½-OUNCE CAN COCONUT MILK

4 EGGS, SEPARATED

1 TEASPOON VANILLA

½ TEASPOON ALMOND EXTRACT

1½ CUPS SHREDDED COCONUT

SINGLE FLAKY PIE CRUST, PREBAKED (PAGE 513)

Makes a 9-inch pie

Stir together the sugar, cornstarch, and salt in a heavy saucepan. Add the coconut milk, stirring to avoid lumps, and then add the egg yolks (reserve two egg whites, saving the other two for another recipe). Warm the mixture over medium-low heat, stirring up continuously from the bottom until the mixture is somewhat thickened. Expect this process to take 10 to 12 minutes; don't rush it or boil the mixture. The finished custard should still be runny but should cling thinly to the back of a spoon.

Remove the mixture from the heat, and stir in the vanilla, almond extract, and coconut. Beat the two reserved egg whites in a bowl, preferably copper, until they are stiff. Fold the egg whites into the custard. Pour the mixture into the pie crust, and bake the pie 30 to 35 minutes, until the filling is puffed and lightly set.

Let the pie cool for at least 30 minutes. It will deflate somewhat as it cools.

Serve the pie warm, or refrigerate it to serve chilled.

Dallas's home-style but uptown Highland Park Cafeteria sells a lot of "millionaire pie," a chilled confection of crushed pineapple, pecans, cream cheese, and whipped cream.

Big Thicket Coconut Cake

This cake is similar to one that Margaret McLean Ayres served during her 60 years as hostess of the old Bragg Hotel in the Big Thicket country of southeast Texas.

Not all cakes can be cut down in size successfully, but we've halved this recipe with excellent results.

CAKE

2½ CUPS CAKE FLOUR, SIFTED
2 TEASPOONS BAKING POWDER
¼ TEASPOON SALT
2 CUPS SUGAR
1 CUP UNSALTED BUTTER, AT ROOM TEMPERA-
   TURE
1 CUP COCONUT MILK (SEE TECHNIQUE TIP,
   PAGE 521)
5 EGG WHITES
1 TEASPOON VANILLA

GLAZE

2 EGG WHITES
1½ CUPS SUGAR
2 CUPS MILK OR ANY REMAINING COCONUT
   MILK TOPPED OFF WITH REGULAR MILK
3 CUPS SHREDDED COCONUT
1 TEASPOON VANILLA

*Makes a four-layer cake,
serving 10 to 12*

Preheat the oven to 375° F. Grease and flour four 8- or 9-inch round cake pans. Add waxed paper or parchment cut in circles to fit the pans, and grease and flour the paper.

Sift together the flour, baking pow-der, and salt in a small bowl, and set the bowl aside. In a mixing bowl, cream together the sugar and butter. Add the sifted dry ingredients in batches, alternating with the coconut milk, and then beat with a mixer.

Beat the egg whites in another bowl, preferably copper, until they are very foamy. Gently fold them with the vanilla into the batter by hand.

Divide the batter equally among the four prepared pans. Bake the layers for 20 to 23 minutes, or until a tooth-pick inserted in the center comes out clean.

Allow the layers to stand in their pans for about 5 minutes. Then run a knife around their edges, invert them, and remove them from the pans. Finish cooling the layers on cake racks. With a fork or small skewer, poke a few holes in the top of each one.

Make the glaze: In a heavy, high-sided saucepan, combine the egg whites and sugar. Place the pan over medium heat, and add the milk, stir-ring frequently to prevent sticking. Bring the mixture to a boil. Keep a close watch during this process, and reduce the heat a bit if the mixture threatens to spill over the sides of the pan. Sprinkle in all but ⅓ cup of the coconut, and allow the mixture to boil about 5 minutes more, or until the glaze thickens just a bit. The glaze will be thinner than most cake frostings. Remove it from the heat, and add the vanilla.

To assemble the cake, place one layer on a decorative serving plate. Spoon about one-fourth of the glaze over the top of the cake layer. Repeat with the remaining layers and glaze, sprinkling the remaining ⅓ cup of coconut over the cake's top.

The cake is best made a few hours ahead so that the glaze can ooze through the layers. Because it is so moist, the cake keeps, covered, for several days.

Texans ate some unusual cakes in the past. More than one cookbook presented a Soup-to-Nuts Cake that called for canned tomato soup and pecans. The Watermelon Cake had an outer white layer serving as the rind and an inner layer dyed red and sprinkled with raisins playing the role of seeds. Raisins were also the prominent feature in the Bug Cake.

TECHNIQUE TIP

In the oldest Texas cookbooks, coconut dessert recipes called for grated coconut and coconut milk made from the fresh fruit. References to coconut milk disappeared quickly, however, probably because of the effort required to prepare it. Water, milk, or a combination of the two became the easy substitute. Now you can get canned coconut milk—not to be confused with cream of coconut—and it's worth seeking out. Look for it in Asian food markets or regular supermarkets in areas with Asian communities.

German Chocolate Cake

This cake is so popular in Texas, we assumed for years that it had roots in the state's German population. It turns out the name comes from the mild dark chocolate made originally by a company called German's, later acquired by Baker's, which was then absorbed into the General Foods conglomerate. In 1957 a Dallas newspaper printed a recipe for a chocolate cake that suggested using Baker's German's Sweet Chocolate. Regional sales zoomed, and General Foods began promoting "German Chocolate Cake" nationally.

CAKE

4 OUNCES BAKER'S GERMAN'S SWEET
  CHOCOLATE
½ CUP WATER
1¾ CUPS CAKE FLOUR, SIFTED
1 TEASPOON BAKING SODA
¼ TEASPOON SALT
2 CUPS SUGAR
1 CUP UNSALTED BUTTER, AT ROOM TEMPERA-
  TURE
4 EGGS, SEPARATED
1½ TEASPOONS VANILLA
1 CUP BUTTERMILK

COCONUT-PECAN FROSTING

1½ CUPS EVAPORATED MILK
1⅓ CUPS SUGAR
¾ CUP UNSALTED BUTTER
4 EGG YOLKS, LIGHTLY BEATEN
2 TEASPOONS VANILLA
PINCH OF SALT
2 CUPS SHREDDED COCONUT
1¾ CUPS CHOPPED PECANS, TOASTED

*Makes a three-layer cake,
serving 10 to 12*

Preheat the oven to 350° F. Grease and flour three 9-inch round cake pans. Add waxed paper or parchment cut in circles to fit the pans, and grease and flour the paper.

Melt together the chocolate and water over low heat in a small saucepan. Keep the mixture warm.

Sift together the flour, baking soda, and salt in a small bowl, and set the bowl aside.

Chocolate hasn't played a large role in Texas history, but it did have a bit part once in the war for independence. Along with opium and champagne, chocolate was one of Santa Anna's many indulgences, which together may have undermined his preparedness at the Battle of San Jacinto.

With a mixer, cream together the sugar and butter. Add the egg yolks, then the chocolate and the vanilla, beating well after each addition. Mix in the sifted dry ingredients in batches, alternating with the buttermilk, and combine well.

Beat the egg whites in another bowl, preferably copper, until stiff peaks form. Fold the whites gently into the batter by hand. Divide the batter equally among the three prepared pans. Bake for 30 to 32 minutes, or until a toothpick inserted in the center comes out clean.

Allow the layers to stand in their pans for about 5 minutes. Run a knife around their edges, invert them onto cake racks, and remove them from the pans. Let them cool.

While the layers cool, prepare the frosting. Combine the milk, sugar,

The Texas A&M University food service invented cake mixes before they became a commercial product, as a way of expediting the baking process for all the cakes served to the student body.

butter, egg yolks, vanilla, and salt in a large, heavy saucepan. Cook over medium-low heat, stirring constantly, until the mixture is slightly thickened, about 12 to 14 minutes. Remove the pan from the heat, and stir in the coconut and pecans. Continue stirring the frosting until it stiffens enough to spread thickly.

To assemble the cake, place one layer on a decorative serving plate. Spread one third of the frosting over the top of the cake layer. Repeat with the remaining layers and frosting. The cake is best the day it's made, but because it's quite moist, it keeps another day or two tightly covered.

Cake recipes far outnumber all others in early Texas cookbooks. Some were simple, such as the pound cake recipes that called for a pound of each ingredient, and the 1-2-3-4 cakes that required one cup of this, two cups of that, and so forth. Other recipes were less orthodox. Some used pinto beans, Dr Pepper, sausage, and even sauerkraut.

The Driskill's 1886 Room Chocolate Sheet Cake

Over the years, Texas legislators have probably done more business in the bar and dining room of Austin's Driskill Hotel than in the domed capitol down the street. Many solons sealed deals over this dark fudgy cake in the 1886 Room, the former restaurant named after the hotel's founding date. The recipe for the one-layer sheet or "sheath" cake is the cherished favorite of the Heritage Society of Austin, which first published it in the **Austin Heritage Cook Book**.

CAKE

1 CUP UNSALTED BUTTER
⅔ CUP WATER
½ HEAPING CUP COCOA
2 CUPS ALL-PURPOSE FLOUR, SIFTED
2 CUPS SUGAR
1 TEASPOON SALT
2 EGGS, BEATEN LIGHTLY
1 CUP BUTTERMILK
2 TEASPOONS VANILLA
1 HEAPING TEASPOON BAKING SODA

ICING

½ CUP UNSALTED BUTTER
3 HEAPING TABLESPOONS COCOA
3 TO 4 TABLESPOONS HALF-AND-HALF
2 CUPS POWDERED SUGAR
1 CUP CHOPPED PECANS, TOASTED
1 TEASPOON VANILLA

Makes a 9-by-13-inch sheet cake

 Preheat the oven to 350° F. Grease and flour a 9-by-13-inch cake pan.

Melt the butter in a large, heavy saucepan over medium heat. Remove the pan from the heat. Add the water and cocoa, stirring well. Sift together the flour, sugar, and salt, and stir them into the chocolate mixture. In a large bowl, combine the eggs, buttermilk, vanilla, and baking soda, add the chocolate mixture, and mix well.

Spoon the cake batter into the prepared pan, and bake 30 minutes, or until a toothpick inserted in the center comes out clean.

While the cake is baking, make the

> Traditional Texas weddings often featured two cakes. The bride's cake was always white and often as light as an angel food, and the groom's was usually a dark and dense chocolate.

icing: Melt the butter with the cocoa in a heavy saucepan over medium heat. Add the half-and-half, and heat it through. Mix in the remaining ingredients, blend well, and remove the pan from the heat. Pour the icing over the cake in its pan while both are still warm.

Serve the cake warm or at room temperature. The cake is moist enough to keep for up to 2 days, if it is covered and refrigerated.

Fig Spice Cake
with Buttermilk Glaze

When mockingbirds didn't get the wild figs in Texas, the succulent fruit often ended up in a rich cake. This version erupts with sugar and spice, fruit, and nuts, all topped with a buttermilk glaze.

CAKE

6 OUNCES DRIED FIGS
3¾ CUPS CAKE FLOUR, SIFTED
2 TEASPOONS GROUND CINNAMON
2 TEASPOONS BAKING POWDER
1 TEASPOON BAKING SODA
1 TEASPOON SALT
1 TEASPOON GROUND NUTMEG
1 TEASPOON GROUND ALLSPICE
½ TEASPOON GROUND CLOVES
1 CUP UNSALTED BUTTER, AT ROOM TEMPERATURE
1 CUP DARK BROWN SUGAR
2 EGGS
1½ TABLESPOONS VANILLA
¼ CUP CANE SYRUP OR UNSULPHURED DARK MOLASSES
¾ CUP BUTTERMILK
1 CUP PECAN PIECES, TOASTED

BUTTERMILK GLAZE

¼ CUP BUTTERMILK
¼ CUP UNSALTED BUTTER
3 TABLESPOONS DARK BROWN SUGAR
1 TEASPOON CANE SYRUP OR UNSULPHURED DARK MOLASSES
¼ TEASPOON BAKING SODA
½ TEASPOON VANILLA

Makes a 10-inch tube cake

 Preheat the oven to 350° F. Grease and lightly flour a 10-inch Bundt or other tube pan.

Poach the figs about 15 minutes in water that covers them by ½ inch.

Pour off the figs' cooking liquid, and measure it. Add water or discard liquid as needed to end up with ⅓ cup. Reserve the liquid.

Chop the figs fine, and set them aside as well.

Sift the flour with the cinnamon, baking powder, baking soda, salt, nutmeg, allspice, and cloves.

Place the butter in a large mixing bowl, and beat it with an electric mixer until it is creamy. Add the sugar, and beat until the mixture is light and fluffy. Beat in the eggs one at a time, and then the vanilla.

Pour the fig liquid and cane syrup into the buttermilk. Add the liquids to the butter mixture in thirds, alternating with the dry ingredients. Continue beating the batter until all the ingredients are well incorporated. Fold in the pecans and figs.

Spoon the batter into the prepared pan. Bake 50 minutes, or until a toothpick inserted in the center comes out clean. Cool the cake in the pan for 10 to 15 minutes, and then invert it onto a baking rack. When the cake is cool, transfer it to a serving platter.

Make the glaze: Mix all the ingredients except the vanilla in a heavy saucepan (choose a large one—the mixture will increase in volume). Bring the glaze to a boil over medium-high heat, reduce the heat, and allow the glaze to simmer for about 5 minutes. Remove the pan from the heat, and stir in the vanilla.

Pour the warm glaze over the cake slowly, or spoon it over individual slices at serving time. The glazed cake is best the day it's made, but it can be frozen for up to a month.

Helen Corbitt created a big hit in the 1950s by frosting cubes of white butter cake, rolling them in coconut, and calling them "snowballs." For many years, you couldn't have a debutante party or afternoon tea in Texas without them.

The World's Best Fruitcake

The first cookbook known to have been published in Texas offered seven different recipes for fruitcake. The options have only proliferated since then, but making the right choice among them is simpler than ever. The finest fruitcake in the world, we're convinced, is made from an old German recipe developed originally by August Weidmann and his partner, Tom McElwee, bakers in Corsicana, Texas.

1 TELEPHONE
1 CREDIT CARD

Makes a 1⅞-, 2⅞-, or whopping 4⅞- pound cake

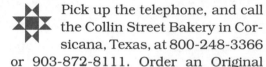 Pick up the telephone, and call the Collin Street Bakery in Corsicana, Texas, at 800-248-3366 or 903-872-8111. Order an Original DeLuxe Fruitcake. The friendly folks on the other end will have it at your door almost as fast as you can make an inferior version.

Variation: When your cake arrives, open the tin, douse the cake with ½ cup or more of brandy, rum, or bourbon, replace the cover, and let the cake mellow several days. Outstanding.

The Ringling Brothers Circus inspired the mail-order business at the Collin Street Bakery, by asking for a supply of fruitcakes for its troupe during a European tour. Now the bakery gets so many foreign orders—one came addressed simply to Fruitcake, USA—the cakes account for 4 percent of all surface packages shipped overseas from the United States during the busy holiday period. Ross Perot, never inclined to do anything on a small scale, once ordered 7,600 Original DeLuxes. A dozen or so end up at the White House each Christmas, even though Mr. Perot didn't.

The Collin Street Bakery consumes 2 percent of the world's annual pecan crop. Most of the nuts go into the bakery's fruitcakes, in which they constitute almost a third of the weight. The bakery chooses small native pecans with a high oil content and superior taste for the batter, and larger, more glamorous hybrids for decorating the top.

Pineapple-Ginger Upside-Down Cake

A cakewalk favorite, a good pineapple upside-down cake could be a major money-maker at a church social. The idea of adding ginger to the ingredients comes from a cookbook published by the Church of the Annunciation in the town of West to commemorate its hundredth anniversary in 1974.

TOPPING

6 TABLESPOONS UNSALTED BUTTER
¾ CUP DARK BROWN SUGAR
1½ TEASPOONS POWDERED GINGER
1 SMALL FRESH PINEAPPLE, PEELED, CORED,
    CUT IN ROUNDS, AND DRAINED
¼ CUP PECAN HALVES
6 TO 10 CHERRIES, OPTIONAL

CAKE

1½ CUPS CAKE FLOUR, SIFTED
¾ TEASPOON BAKING POWDER
¼ TEASPOON BAKING SODA
¼ TEASPOON SALT
⅔ CUP SUGAR
½ CUP UNSALTED BUTTER, AT ROOM TEMPERA-
    TURE
3 EGG YOLKS
1 TEASPOON VANILLA
½ CUP SOUR CREAM

Makes a 10-inch cake

Preheat the oven to 350° F.

Make the topping: In a 10-inch cast-iron skillet, melt the butter over medium heat. Stir in the brown sugar and ginger, and remove the pan from the heat. Arrange as many pineapple slices in the skillet as can be attractively positioned. Tuck the pecans and optional cherries in between. Set the skillet aside.

Make the batter: Sift together the flour, baking powder and soda, and salt. Set the mixture aside.

With a mixer, cream together the sugar and butter. Add the egg yolks, one by one, and then the vanilla, beating well after each addition. Mix in the sifted dry ingredients in thirds, alternating with the sour cream, and combine the ingredients well. The batter will be somewhat stiff.

Spoon the batter over the topping in the skillet, smoothing the top. Bake for 40 to 45 minutes, until the cake is golden brown and a toothpick inserted in the center comes out clean. Run a knife around the cake's sides, and invert it onto a serving plate. Allow it to cool at least 15 minutes before serving.

Serve the cake warm or at room temperature.

Angel Food Cake Borracha

Texans use angel food as a base for numerous dessert preparations. This is a sassy "drunken" variation of the angelic classic.

CAKE

14 EGG WHITES (FROM LARGE EGGS)
1¼ TEASPOONS CREAM OF TARTAR
½ TEASPOON SALT
1¾ CUPS SUGAR
1¼ CUPS CAKE FLOUR, SIFTED
1 TEASPOON VANILLA
½ TEASPOON ALMOND EXTRACT
1 TEASPOON LEMON JUICE

SAUCE

JUICE OF 6 ORANGES (ABOUT 2 CUPS)
ZEST OF 1 ORANGE
1 CUP SUGAR
¼ CUP BOURBON
¼ CUP DARK RUM
2 TABLESPOONS TRIPLE SEC OR OTHER ORANGE-FLAVORED LIQUEUR
JUICE AND ZEST OF 1 LEMON
1 CANELA (MEXICAN CINNAMON) STICK OR CINNAMON STICK

Makes a 10-inch tube cake

Preheat the oven to 325° F. In a glass or metal bowl (plastic holds grease, the enemy of angel food) beat the egg whites, cream of tartar, and salt with a mixer until soft peaks form. Gradually beat in 1 cup of the sugar. Continue beating until the egg whites form stiff peaks.

Sift together the flour and remaining sugar three times. Quickly fold the dry ingredients into the egg whites, about ¼ cup at a time. Gently fold in the vanilla, almond extract, and lemon juice.

Pour the batter into an ungreased 10-inch tube pan with a removable bottom. Run a knife through the batter to eliminate air bubbles. Smooth the top of the batter. Bake the cake until it is pale brown and springy to the touch, about 50 to 55 minutes. There are likely to be some cracks in the surface, but you shouldn't have any gaping canyons.

If your tube pan doesn't have metal feet, invert it over a wine or soft drink bottle, or maybe a longneck (beer bottle). Cool the cake upside down for at least 1 hour. This allows its structure to set without collapsing. Turn the cake back right side up, and loosen it by running a knife around its edges. Remove the pan's sides first, and then dislodge the cake from the pan's center section. Transfer the cake to a serving plate, and poke a good number of holes in it with an ice pick or skewer.

While the cake cools, make the sauce: Combine all the sauce ingredients in a medium saucepan. Simmer over medium heat 10 minutes, stirring occasionally to dissolve the sugar. Remove the pan from the heat.

Remove the canela or cinnamon stick from the sauce, and discard it. Spoon the sauce slowly over the cake. The fruit zest should be distributed evenly over the top. Let the cake sit at least 1 hour before serving.

Serve the cake at room temperature. Tightly covered, it will keep for a couple of days.

Variations: If you prefer your angel food sober, try one of these preparations. For a peppermint angel food cake, crush 10 to 12 hard peppermint candies, and fold the pieces in with the flour and sugar. Reduce the vanilla extract by 1 teaspoon, and replace the almond extract with an equal quantity of peppermint extract.

Other possibilities include topping a plain cake with fresh strawberries, spoonfuls of boiled custard, or whipped cream mixed with chopped Heath bars.

African-Americans started cakewalks as a party contest. The fanciest walker or dancer won a cake. Churches adopted the idea as a fundraiser, usually restraining some of the exuberance by making their cakewalks more like musical chairs.

TECHNIQUE TIPS

These suggestions apply to any angel food cake recipe:

Even a speck of egg yolk in your whites can make it impossible to beat the eggs to the necessary volume. Break each egg into a smaller bowl first, so that if some yolk does slip in with your white, only that egg is lost, rather than the whole bowl.

Egg whites increase most in volume if beaten in a copper bowl at room temperature on a low-humidity day.

Superfine (not powdered) sugar dissolves best into the fluff of egg whites. Make your own by grinding granulated sugar in a food processor using the metal chopping blade.

If you want to make angel food with any frequency, invest in a "folder," a spatula that makes it easier to combine the beaten whites with the dry ingredients.

At high altitudes, make your usual minor recipe adjustments, and beat the egg whites only until soft peaks form.

Gingerbread with Citrus Sauce

Gingerbread is a quick alternative to most homemade cakes and will bring just as many accolades from your family and friends. The addition of white pepper heightens the spicy taste. This recipe calls for a citrus topping, but you can use a sauce made from any fruit that's in season.

CAKE

1½ CUPS ALL-PURPOSE FLOUR, SIFTED
2 TEASPOONS POWDERED GINGER
1 TEASPOON GROUND CINNAMON
1 TEASPOON BAKING SODA
½ TEASPOON SALT
½ TEASPOON WHITE PEPPER
½ CUP UNSALTED BUTTER, AT ROOM TEMPERATURE
½ CUP DARK BROWN SUGAR
2 EGGS
½ CUP UNSULPHURED DARK MOLASSES
⅔ CUP BUTTERMILK

CITRUS SAUCE

¼ CUP SUGAR
1 TABLESPOON CORNSTARCH
DASH OF SALT
JUICE OF 1 GRAPEFRUIT, PREFERABLY A TEXAS RUBY-RED
JUICE OF 2 ORANGES
2 TEASPOONS UNSALTED BUTTER

Makes an 8-inch square cake

Preheat the oven to 325° F. Grease an 8-inch square pan.

Sift together the flour, ginger, cinnamon, soda, salt, and white pepper. In a bowl, beat the butter with an electric mixer until it is creamy. Add the sugar, and beat well until the mixture is light and fluffy. Add the eggs, one at a time, and the molasses, beating well after each addition. Add the dry ingredients and buttermilk alternately in thirds, continuing to beat as they are added.

Pour the batter into the prepared pan. Bake the cake 40 to 45 minutes,

The sweet, thin-skinned ruby-red grapefruits of the Lower Rio Grande Valley developed out of a natural mutation. A worker picked a few one day along with many other grapefruits but couldn't identify the tree. The next harvest, a year later, the grower found the special fruit on a single branch of one tree. With a much more plentiful supply today, you can get a whole branchful delivered to your door (see "Mail-Order Sources," pages 553–554).

or until a toothpick inserted in the center comes out clean.

While the gingerbread is baking, make the citrus sauce: Combine the sugar, cornstarch, and salt in a small, heavy saucepan. Stir in the fruit juices slowly, mixing well to avoid lumps. Cook over medium heat, stir-ring often, until the mixture is thick-ened. Add the butter, and keep the sauce warm.

Serve the gingerbread warm, accom-panied by the warm sauce. The gin-gerbread will keep for a couple of days tightly wrapped, but it's best the day it's made.

Poteet Strawberry Shortcake

Henry and Ida Fischer Mumme, the founders of Poteet, started their town on the way to becoming the Strawberry Capital of Texas when they planted a few rows of the fruit in their kitchen garden. You can sample the luscious local berry in dozens of dishes and drinks each spring at the Poteet Strawberry Festival, where we got the inspiration for this shortcake recipe.

CAKE

2 CUPS CAKE FLOUR, SIFTED

1 TABLESPOON BAKING POWDER

½ TEASPOON SALT

1½ CUPS SUGAR

¾ CUP UNSALTED BUTTER, AT ROOM TEMPERA-
    TURE

3 EGGS, SEPARATED

¾ CUP WATER

¼ CUP CRUSHED FRESH RIPE STRAWBERRIES

1 TEASPOON ALMOND EXTRACT

TOPPING

1 CUP WHIPPING CREAM

⅓ CUP POWDERED SUGAR

2 PINTS FRESH RIPE STRAWBERRIES, SLICED

Serves 8 to 10

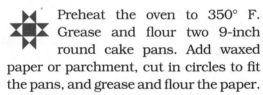 Preheat the oven to 350° F. Grease and flour two 9-inch round cake pans. Add waxed paper or parchment, cut in circles to fit the pans, and grease and flour the paper.

Sift together the flour, baking pow-der, and salt. With a mixer, cream to-gether the sugar and butter until the

YOU WON'T MISS POTEET IF YOU'RE DRIVING SOUTH OF SAN ANTONIO ON HIGHWAY 16. THE TOWN'S 130-FOOT WATER TOWER IS PAINTED TO RESEMBLE A GIANT STRAWBERRY.

mixture is light and fluffy. Add the egg yolks one at a time, beating well after each addition. Combine the water, strawberries, and almond extract. Add them to the butter mixture in thirds, alternating with the dry ingredients. Continue beating the batter until all the ingredients are well incorporated.

In another bowl, preferably copper, beat the egg whites until they are stiff. Fold them into the batter. Pour the batter into the prepared pans, and bake 20 minutes, or until a toothpick inserted in the center comes out clean.

Cool the layers in their pans for about 5 minutes, run a knife around the edges, and invert the pans over cake racks. Remove the pans, and allow the layers to cool.

Prepare the fruit topping while the cake cools: Whip the cream in a mixer with 1 tablespoon of the sugar. Refrigerate the cream until you are ready to use it.

Combine the strawberries with the remaining sugar, a tablespoon at a time, until they are as sweet as you like them.

Transfer one cake layer to a serving plate. Top it with half the berries, and spread half the whipped cream over them. Repeat with the remaining ingredients.

Serve the cake immediately.

Generations of Texans have sweetened desserts with Imperial sugar. The Imperial Sugar Company, founded in 1843, is the oldest business in the state that is still in its original location. The site, now the town of Sugar Land, used to be vast fields of sugar cane. A turn-of-the-century owner named the company after New York's Imperial Hotel, a symbol for quality at the time.

Peach-Ginger Crisp

Second cousins to cobblers, crisps come with similar fruit fillings, but their crusts are crunchier, often because of the addition of oatmeal or nuts.

TOPPING

¾ CUP PECANS, TOASTED
1 CUP OATMEAL
1 DOZEN GINGERSNAPS
⅓ CUP DARK BROWN SUGAR
¾ TEASPOON SALT
½ CUP PLUS 3 TABLESPOONS UNSALTED
  BUTTER
¼ CUP CHOPPED CRYSTALLIZED GINGER

FILLING

3½ TO 4 POUNDS FRESH RIPE PEACHES
2 TABLESPOONS FRESH LEMON JUICE
⅓ TO ½ CUP DARK BROWN SUGAR
1 EGG YOLK
2 TABLESPOONS ALL-PURPOSE FLOUR
2 GINGERSNAPS, CRUSHED

Serves 8

 Preheat the oven to 375° F. Grease a 9-by-13-inch pan or baking dish.

In a food processor, combine the pecans, oatmeal, and gingersnaps, and process until they are coarsely chopped. Add the brown sugar, salt, and butter, and process until the mixture resembles coarse meal. The mixture should remain a bit chunky. Set it aside.

Peel and pit the peaches, and slice them into a bowl. Mix them with the lemon juice to prevent discoloration. Stir in ⅛ cup of the brown sugar, taste, and add more if needed. Add the crystallized ginger, flour, crushed gingersnaps, and egg yolk, mixing lightly.

Spoon the fruit into the prepared pan. Cover it with the topping, spreading evenly. Bake until the topping is crunchy and a deep, rich brown.

Serve the crisp warm.

Like other pioneers, Sam Houston loved rice pudding, at least most of the time. One day at the home of prominent friends, he was jawing his way through dinner when the hostess brought out a steaming bowl of the dessert, just out of the oven. Wrapped up in his rhetoric but eager for the treat, Houston took a big bite of the pudding and promptly spat it out on the table. Trying to put the best light on his bad manners and burnt tongue, he reflected gallantly, "A lot of durn fools would have swallowed that."

Capirotada

The most common bread pudding in Texas comes from the New Orleans tradition, which involves a liberal use of eggs and cream. This version hails from the opposite, western side of the state, and gets its richness from butter and cheese.

½ CUP RAISINS

1 CUP BRANDY

10 TO 12 SLICES WHITE BREAD

½ CUP CHOPPED PECANS, TOASTED

1 CUP (4 OUNCES) GRATED MILD CHEDDAR OR MONTEREY JACK CHEESE

2 CUPS SUGAR

3½ CUPS HOT WATER

3 TABLESPOONS UNSALTED BUTTER

2 TEASPOONS VANILLA

1 TEASPOON GROUND CANELA (MEXICAN CINNAMON) OR CINNAMON

½ TEASPOON NUTMEG

PINCH OF CLOVES

WHIPPED CREAM, OPTIONAL, FOR GARNISH

Serves 8

Place the raisins in a small bowl, and pour the brandy over them. Set them aside to soften. Preheat the oven to 350° F. Butter a 9-by-13-inch baking dish.

Tear or slice the bread into bite-size pieces. Transfer it to the baking dish. Add the pecans and the cheese to the bread, mixing both in lightly. Scatter the raisins over the top, including any brandy not absorbed by the fruit.

Pour the sugar into a large, heavy saucepan. Warm it over medium-high heat, until the sugar melts and turns a deep golden brown, about 8 to 10 minutes. Stir the sugar occasionally to assure even melting. Pour the water into the molten sugar (stand back from the pan as you do so, because steam will rise as the water hits the sugar). The mixture will partially solidify. Continue cooking until the mixture becomes liquid again, stirring occasionally. Add the butter, vanilla, and spices to the syrup.

Ladle the caramel syrup carefully over the bread. The syrup should be about level with the top of the bread. If any bread pieces aren't coated, push them into the syrup.

Bake 20 to 25 minutes until the syrup is absorbed and the cheese has melted into the pudding.

Serve this pudding hot, topped with whipped cream, if you like.

Nanny's Boiled Custard

A Texas favorite for more than a century, boiled custard is never boiled, but it is cooked on top of the stove, distinguishing it from thicker baked custards like flan. Boiled custard can be eaten plain in a bowl with a spoon, ladled over angel food cake, or poured over strawberries, peaches, or mangoes.

This simple yet delicious version comes from the late Mary Helen Smith of Bonham, who got it from her mother, Nanny.

3 EGGS
1 CUP SUGAR
1 QUART WHOLE MILK
1 TABLESPOON VANILLA

In a double boiler or large, heavy pan, beat together the eggs and sugar. Whisk in the milk. Heat the mixture over medium-low heat, stirring constantly. Unless you want scrambled eggs, do not boil the custard. The custard is ready when it coats the spoon; this takes at least 20 minutes. Stir in the vanilla, and cook about 2 minutes more. The custard should remain thin compared to most puddings.

Serve boiled custard warm or chilled.

Variation: Boiled custard makes a great base for vanilla ice cream. Just freeze it according to the directions that come with your ice-cream maker.

Ruth Bauer, a Texas artist, fondly recalls her Aunt Mary Helen's boiled custard from childhood family reunions, where it was part of a feast that always included fried catfish from the stockpond on the family ranch, quail hunted nearby and wrapped in bacon, and a smoked turkey or ham. On the side, they had biscuits, jellies, sweet pickles, pear relish, watermelon pickles, and vegetables such as sliced tomatoes, raw green onions, fried okra, black-eyed peas, and green beans seasoned liberally with bacon and black pepper. The boiled custard topped vanilla ice cream and angel food cake. Pitchers of sweetened iced tea washed it all down.

Banana Pudding

This perennial barbecue dessert soared in popularity after Nabisco adapted it as a way to encourage sales of vanilla wafer cookies, which came on the market in 1945. Now 'Nilla Wafers and 'nana pudding are inseparable companions.

1 CUP PLUS 3 TABLESPOONS SUGAR

2 TABLESPOONS CORNSTARCH

PINCH OF SALT

6 EGGS, SEPARATED

2½ CUPS WHOLE MILK, HEATED

2 TEASPOONS VANILLA

1 12-OUNCE BOX VANILLA WAFERS

5 TO 6 BANANAS

⅛ TEASPOON CREAM OF TARTAR

Serves 8 to 10

In the top of a double boiler, stir together 1 cup of the sugar, the cornstarch, and the salt. Mix in the egg yolks, and place the pan over its simmering water bath. Pour in the warm milk, stirring constantly. Continue to stir frequently as the pudding cooks. It will gradually thicken, usually in about 15 to 20 minutes, but don't rush it. The eggs need to poach and thicken slowly, not scramble. When the pudding coats a spoon and slides off it slowly, it is done. Remove the pan from the water bath, and stir in the vanilla.

Preheat the oven to 350° F.

While the pudding cools a bit, arrange a layer of vanilla wafers at the bottom of a 9-by-13-inch baking dish.

Slice the bananas thin, and arrange half of them over the cookies. Spoon half of the pudding over the banana slices. Repeat with more cookies, the remaining banana slices, and the rest of the pudding. Tuck more cookies around the sides of the dish as well. We normally use only about two-thirds of the box of cookies, but some people manage more.

Beat the egg whites in a large bowl, preferably copper. When they become frothy, add the cream of tartar and salt. Gradually beat in the remaining 3 tablespoons of sugar, and continue beating until the whites form stiff peaks.

Crown the assembled pudding with the meringue, heaping it high in the center. Bake the pudding for 15 to 18 minutes, or until the meringue is firm and golden brown. Let it cool at room temperature 30 minutes before serving (refrigerate the pudding if you plan to hold it longer than that). Leftovers can be kept for another day, though the bananas will darken.

Variation: Eliminate the bananas, and substitute sherry or almond extract for the vanilla. Layer the pudding with

2 to 3 cups of coarsely crumbled macaroon cookies instead of vanilla wafers. Sprinkle the top with toasted almond slices before piling on the meringue and baking according to the recipe.

Pecan Praline Cheesecake

They don't make it quite like this in New York.

CRUST
1 CUP MINCED PECANS, TOASTED
¾ CUP GRAHAM CRACKER CRUMBS
¼ CUP DARK BROWN SUGAR
¼ CUP UNSALTED BUTTER, MELTED

FILLING
1 POUND CREAM CHEESE, AT ROOM TEMPERATURE
3 EGGS
¼ CUP SUGAR
1¼ CUPS CHOPPED PRALINES, HOMEMADE (PAGE 104) OR STORE-BOUGHT (ABOUT 3 TO 4 2-INCH PRALINES)
2 TEASPOONS MINCED ORANGE ZEST
½ CUP SOUR CREAM

CARAMEL SAUCE
2 TEASPOONS UNSALTED BUTTER
½ CUP DARK BROWN SUGAR
2 TABLESPOONS WATER
½ TO ¾ CUP MILK, WARMED
½ TEASPOON VANILLA

Makes a 9-inch cheesecake

 Preheat the oven to 325° F. Grease a 9-inch springform pan.

Make the crust: In a small bowl, mix together the pecans, graham cracker crumbs, and brown sugar. Pour in the butter, and stir to combine. Press the warm mixture into the prepared pan, packing it evenly around the bottom. Bake until the crust is set, about 10

> IN THE EAST TEXAS TOWN OF NEW YORK (POPULATION 12), LYN DUNSAVAGE MAKES "NEW YORK, TEXAS" CHEESECAKES THAT ARE GOOD ENOUGH TO BE MARKETED AS FAR AWAY AS MANHATTAN. GIVE HER STAFF A CALL (SEE "MAIL-ORDER SOURCES," PAGE 552) TO GET ONE DELIVERED TO YOUR DOOR.

minutes. Allow the crust to cool. It can be made a day ahead, if you wish.

Raise the oven temperature to 350° F.

Make the filling: Using a mixer, beat the cream cheese in a large bowl until it is light and fluffy. Add the eggs and then the sugar, continuing to beat until everything is well incorporated. Mix in the chopped pralines and the orange zest. Pour the filling into the prepared crust, and bake for 55 to 60 minutes, until the center is just firm.

Take the cheesecake out of the oven, and let it sit for 10 minutes. Raise the oven temperature to 425° F. Spread the sour cream gently and evenly over the top of the cheesecake. Bake the cheesecake an additional 5 minutes, until the sour cream bubbles at the edges. Cool the cheesecake completely on a rack. Run a knife between the cake and the sides of the pan to loosen it. Cover the cake, and refrigerate it until it is well chilled, at least 3 to 4 hours (the cake can be made a day ahead of serving).

Make the caramel sauce: Melt the butter in a heavy saucepan. Add the brown sugar and water, and cook over medium heat until the mixture reaches the soft-ball stage, 234° to 240° F. Remove the pan from the heat, and let the mixture cool a couple of minutes. Stir in the amount of milk necessary to achieve the sauce consistency you prefer, add the vanilla, and mix well. The sauce can be kept warm over a hot-water bath, or made ahead and rewarmed at serving time.

Serve the cheesecake topped with warm caramel sauce.

Shortly before his death, Texas's first native-born governor, James Stephen Hogg, said, "I want no monument of stone or marble, but plant at my head a pecan tree." His daughter Ima became the grand dame of the state in the mid-twentieth century, but, contrary to legend, Governor Hogg never had another daughter named Ura.

Molasses Spice Cookies

*According to Vera Flach in **A Yankee in German-America**, her family made so many molasses cookies for Christmas that they frequently showed up for birthdays in April. Texas cookbooks abound with different versions, but these may be the tastiest, inspired by Dan M. Woods's winning recipe from a Sanger-Harris department store cookie contest in the late 1970s. Generations of kids have called molasses cookies "earthquake" cookies because of their crackled surfaces.*

1 CUP DARK BROWN SUGAR
¾ CUP UNSALTED BUTTER
1 EGG
¼ CUP UNSULPHURED DARK MOLASSES
2 CUPS ALL-PURPOSE FLOUR
2 TEASPOONS BAKING SODA
1 TEASPOON GROUND CINNAMON
1 TEASPOON GROUND CLOVES
1 TEASPOON POWDERED GINGER
1 TEASPOON NUTMEG
¾ TEASPOON SALT
SUGAR

Makes 3 to 3½ dozen cookies

Preheat the oven to 350° F.

Cream together the brown sugar and butter with a mixer or in a food processor. Add the egg and molasses, and mix until everything is thoroughly combined. Sprinkle in the flour, baking soda, spices, and salt, and mix again. The dough will be soft.

Pour a few tablespoons of sugar onto a saucer. Roll the dough into small balls, about ¾ inch in diameter. Roll each ball in the sugar, and place the balls 1½ inches apart on ungreased baking sheets. Bake the cookies for about 10 minutes. Do not overbake: they should stay soft and chewy. Cool the cookies for about 5 minutes, and then transfer them to absorbent paper to finish cooling. They keep for five to seven days, covered.

> Sanger-Harris opened its doors in Dallas in 1872 as Sanger Brothers, predating Neiman Marcus by a quarter of a century. The department store gained some national recognition on the televison show "Dallas," as the place where Pam Ewing worked.

Heather's Triple Chocolate Toffee Brownies

These brownies helped get our daughter Heather through college in Denton, Texas. They pack enough energy for any final exam you'll ever take.

2 OUNCES (2 SQUARES) UNSWEETENED CHOCOLATE

½ CUP UNSALTED BUTTER

1¼ CUPS SUGAR

1 TEASPOON VANILLA

2 EGGS, LIGHTLY BEATEN

½ CUP ALL-PURPOSE FLOUR

1 TABLESPOON PLUS 1 TEASPOON COCOA

¼ TEASPOON SALT

2 1.4-OUNCE HEATH BARS, CHOPPED

½ CUP CHOPPED PECANS, TOASTED, OPTIONAL

*Makes 8 to 16 brownies
(depending on how big you like them)*

 Preheat the oven to 350° F. Butter an 8-inch square baking pan.

In a heavy saucepan, melt the unsweetened chocolate with the butter over low heat. Remove the pan from the heat, and stir in the sugar and vanilla to cool the chocolate slightly. Add the eggs, beating well by hand. Sprinkle in the flour, cocoa, salt, chopped Heath bars, and, if you like, the pecans. Stir to combine everything, but do not overmix.

Pour the batter into the prepared pan, and bake for 23 to 25 minutes. The brownies should remain a little "smooshy" in the center. Let them cool for at least 15 minutes before cutting and serving.

San Antonio, Fort Worth, San Angelo, Abilene, Waco, Austin, and Wichita Falls all have over five hundred acres of pecan trees within their city limits.

Watermelon Su-perb

Good watermelons are so naturally sweet that the fruit was once considered a source for refined sugar. One company even built an experimental processing plant about a hundred years ago. For a much smaller investment, this dessert draws out the sweetness just as well.

FRUIT

1 WATERMELON

1 CANTALOUPE, OGAN MELON, OR OTHER
   ORANGE-FLESHED MELON

1 HONEYDEW MELON, CANARY MELON, OR
   OTHER GREEN-FLESHED MELON

SAUCE

1 CUP GINGER ALE

½ TO ¾ CUP APRICOT JAM OR PRESERVES

JUICE OF 2 LIMES

FRESH MINT, FOR GARNISH

Serves 10 to 15

So that the watermelon will sit steadily, cut a very thin slice off its least attractive side. Lay the watermelon on this cut side, then slice about ¼ to ½ of the melon off the top. Set the piece aside.

With a melon baller, scoop out as much of the watermelon meat as possible. (If you don't have a melon baller, cut the meat into uniform bite-size chunks.) Discard as many seeds as is practical. Spoon the balls into a large bowl. Scrape out the remaining watermelon meat, and reserve it for another use. Pour all the accumulated juice into the bowl with the watermelon balls.

Cut the other melons in half, scrape out their seeds, and scoop out balls of their meat as well. Add these to the watermelon in the bowl, and lightly toss everything together.

In a small bowl, stir together the ginger ale, jam or preserves, and lime juice. If the melons are not especially sweet, add the greater amount of jam to the sauce. Pour the sauce over the melon balls, mixing gently.

Trim the top cut edge of the watermelon shell to a smooth finish. Or you

---

TECHNIQUE TIP

Although the only sure way to get a ripe watermelon is to buy it cut, the exterior of a whole melon yields some clues: for example, the melon's pale side—which was its underside in the field—should have a creamy rather than a greenish hue. Uncut melons can be kept in a cool, dark place for about a week. Covered and refrigerated, cut slices stay good for several days.

might zigzag it or otherwise shape it decoratively. Refrigerate the melon balls and shell as long as several hours, until you are ready to serve the dessert.

Shortly before serving, spoon the melon balls into the watermelon shell, piling them attractively above the melon's rim. Garnish with mint.

Save the leftover watermelon shell to turn into Watermelon Pickles (page 402).

Texas usually leads all other states in watermelon production and maybe in consumption as well. Before refrigeration was common, entrepreneurs opened watermelon parlors during the season in empty storefronts around the state, selling iced slices to go. Sure beats a Slurpee.

"When one has tasted watermelons one knows what angels eat."—*Mark Twain*

Poached Apricots

This is a honey of a way to serve summer apricots.

3 CUPS WATER
½ CUP HONEY
1 TABLESPOON MINCED FRESH MINT
1 TEASPOON ANISE SEEDS, GROUND
½ TEASPOON VANILLA
1½ POUNDS FIRM BUT RIPE APRICOTS (ABOUT 14 TO 16 APRICOTS), HALVED AND PITTED

Serves 6

Combine the water, honey, mint, anise, and vanilla in a heavy saucepan. Bring the mixture to a boil over high heat, stirring if needed to dissolve the honey. Add the apricots, and reduce the heat to a simmer. Cook the apricots until they are tender, 5 to 10 minutes.

Increase the heat to high, and reduce the poaching liquid to 1 cup, which will take about 20 minutes. Refrigerate the apricots, covered, for at least 2 hours and as long as 24 hours.

Serve the apricots chilled, with plenty of the tasty syrup.

Figs with Goat Cheese

An easy but elegant way to finish a special meal, these figs take only a few minutes to prepare.

6 OUNCES FRESH GOAT CHEESE
8 PLUMP WHOLE FIGS
MINT SPRIGS, FOR GARNISH

Serves 4

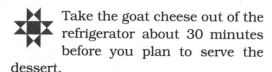 Take the goat cheese out of the refrigerator about 30 minutes before you plan to serve the dessert.

Slice each fig vertically as if to quarter it, but stop short of slicing all the way through the bottom. Pull the quarters back slightly to reveal each fig's center.

Divide the goat cheese into eight equal portions, and place one in the center of each fig.

Serve the figs on small plates garnished with mint sprigs.

Honey sweetens plenty of Texas desserts, and its production is a popular cottage industry in the state. Ann Richards even installed a gubernatorial beehive among the asparagus and asters in the Governor's Mansion garden. One wag claimed that she gargled the honey before sweet-talking legislators.

Paula Lambert's Mozzarella Company makes some of the country's best goat cheeses. The pint-size factory in downtown Dallas produces additive- and preservative-free cheeses with tastes as big as the Lone Star state. If you lack a local source for Mozzarella Company cheese, you can order directly (see "Mail-Order Sources," page 552).

Mission Oranges with Zest

This recipe originated in the Lower Rio Grande Valley, which produces oranges with skins mottled by spring winds. These oranges taste better than they look, but any kind of oranges work in this light, refreshing dessert.

4 MEDIUM ORANGES, PREFERABLY SEEDLESS
ZEST OF 2 ORANGES
¾ CUP SUGAR
¾ CUP WATER
**1 TABLESPOON TRIPLE SEC OR OTHER
ORANGE-FLAVORED LIQUEUR**
JUICE OF 1 LIME
CHOPPED PECANS, FOR GARNISH

Serves 4 to 6

Peel the oranges, and slice each into about four rounds. Arrange the oranges in a shallow serving dish.

Place the orange zest in a small, heavy pan with the sugar and water, and bring the mixture to a boil. Reduce the heat, and simmer the zest in the sugar syrup for about 15 minutes, stirring occasionally. Remove the pan from the heat, and stir in the triple sec and the lime juice.

Pour the syrup and zest over the oranges. Refrigerate the oranges for at least 1 hour. Just before serving, sprinkle the oranges with the chopped pecans.

The town of Mission now hosts a Tourist Fest in the early winter, when the "snowbirds" (visitors from the North) descend on the Rio Grande Valley, but the Citrus Fiesta a couple of months later is much more fun. Begun in 1932, the event features a costume show where the clothes have to be completely covered with local agricultural products, anything from orange skins to onion skins.

Red-Hot Apples

Nothing reminds us of childhood as much as red-hot apples, still a first-class comfort food. This version is based on one in a 1969 San Angelo cookbook, Lucille Hopkins's **Texas Cookbook: Finger Lickin' Fixins.**

4 TART APPLES, SUCH AS GRANNY SMITH
2 CUPS WATER
1¼ CUPS CINNAMON RED-HOT CANDIES
JUICE AND ZEST OF 1 LEMON
½ TEASPOON GROUND CINNAMON
½ TEASPOON GROUND CLOVES
½ TEASPOON GROUND NUTMEG

Serves 4 to 6

Peel, core, and quarter the apples. Combine them with the remaining ingredients in a saucepan, and bring to a boil. Reduce the heat, and simmer for 15 to 20 minutes, until the liquid is thickened and the apples are tender when pierced with a fork. Cool the apples in the syrup for at least 30 minutes.

Serve the apples at room temperature or chilled.

Maury Maverick, the San Antonio mayor who started the city's famed Riverwalk, failed to be reelected shortly before World War II because he provided public meeting space to a group of poorly paid pecan pickers. His political enemies made it an issue because the meeting organizer was a leader of the state Communist Party.

Butter Pecan Ice Cream

A food authority once claimed that Texans consume almost all the butter pecan ice cream made in the country. If you try this recipe, you'll understand why.

¼ CUP UNSALTED BUTTER
1 CUP CHOPPED PECANS
5 EGG YOLKS
1 PINT HALF-AND-HALF
1 CUP WHIPPING CREAM
¾ CUP SUGAR
1 TABLESPOON VANILLA

Makes about 1 quart

Melt the butter in a small skillet over medium heat. Add the pecans, and cook until the nuts are coated with the butter and lightly crisped.

Strain the excess butter into the top of a double boiler. Add the egg yolks, half-and-half, whipping cream, sugar, and vanilla. Set the pan over its water bath.

Warm the custard mixture over medium-low heat, whisking until the mixture is well blended. Continue heating, frequently stirring up from the bottom, until the mixture thickens. (Make sure it does not come to a boil; the egg yolks should poach, not scramble.) This process takes about 15 minutes. Remove the pan from the heat and pour the custard through a strainer into a bowl. Chill it thoroughly.

Transfer the custard to an ice-cream maker, and process it according to the manufacturer's directions. After churning, stir in the pecans, and place the ice cream in the freezer until serving time.

This ice cream is best eaten within several days.

TEXAS RANKS THIRD AMONG STATES IN THE PRODUCTION OF COMMERCIAL ICE CREAM. BLUE BELL, A CREAMERY IN BRENHAM, HAS LED THE WAY SINCE 1911, WINNING ACCOLADES FROM *TIME* AND *SPORTS ILLUSTRATED* AS THE BEST IN THE BUSINESS ANYWHERE.

If there's no time to make your own ice cream, you can still get some real Texas flavor. Start with store-bought vanilla ice cream and top it with Life-Enriching Fig Preserves (page 394), Calico Jalapeño Jam (page 395), or Candied Pecans (page 479).

Iced Sunshine

This makes a bright but cooling finish to a spicy meal. Fruit and liquor ices, or sorbets, became trendy in restaurants during the 1980s. Exactly the same thing happened a century earlier in Texas home kitchens.

4 CUPS PINK GRAPEFRUIT JUICE (FROM ABOUT 5 LARGE GRAPEFRUIT, PREFERABLY RUBY RED)
¾ CUP TEQUILA, PREFERABLY SILVER
½ TO ¾ CUP SUGAR
SPLASH OF GRENADINE, OPTIONAL

Makes about 1 quart sorbet

 In a medium bowl, stir together all the ingredients, mixing until the sugar dissolves.

Transfer the mixture to an ice-cream maker, and freeze it according to the manufacturer's directions.

Grapefruit got its name because the fruit grows in clusters like grapes. Grapefruit wasn't well known in the United States until the Depression, when citrus fruits came free with food stamps. Even then, welfare agencies reported, many people remained suspicious, saying they had boiled their grapefruit for hours and it was still too tough to eat.

Peanut Patties

Homemade candies, like pecan pie, got a big boost from the development of corn syrup early in this century. Cane sugar tends to crystallize, especially in heat and humidity, which makes it difficult to use for candies. Corn syrup alleviated the problem and, as a bonus, provided the proper texture for peanut patties, Texas's favorite roadside snack.

3 CUPS SUGAR
3 CUPS RAW PEANUTS
1 CUP LIGHT CORN SYRUP
½ CUP WATER
½ CUP UNSALTED BUTTER
1 TABLESPOON VANILLA
¼ TEASPOON SALT
A FEW DROPS RED FOOD COLORING

Makes a bunch

Lay a large piece of waxed paper on a dishtowel on a counter.

In a heavy saucepan, combine the sugar, peanuts, corn syrup, and water. Stirring constantly over medium heat, cook the mixture to the high end of the soft-ball stage, 240° F.

Remove the pan from the heat, and stir in the remaining ingredients, adding enough food coloring to get a vibrant red shade. Stir the mixture frequently for approximately 20 minutes, or until it cools to about 125° F. The mixture will become very thick and creamy opaque, and the peanuts will be suspended.

Immediately spoon out the mixture in patties, the larger the better. Let the patties sit for at least 1 hour before eating them. Their texture should be chewy like nougat rather than creamy like praline. Wrap them individually for storage. They'll keep a week.

Goodart makes the original peanut patty, which is sold in gas stations, convenience stores, and cafes throughout Texas. Lammes, in Austin, created another popular snack, "Texas Chewie" Pecan Pralines, which D. T. Lamme used to make to order in 25-pound batches at the Red Front Candy Shop. Newer, but destined for distinction, is the jalapeño pecan brittle from Windmill Candy. Both Lammes and Windmill will ship to your door (see "Mail-Order Sources," page 552).

Candied Grapefruit Peel

Candied grapefruit peel adds sunny perk to the Christmas season. For many Texans, it's as essential as an egg at Easter.

PEELS FROM 3 GRAPEFRUIT, IN LARGE PIECES

SYRUP
2 CUPS SUGAR
1 CUP WATER
¼ CUP LIGHT CORN SYRUP

SUGAR

Makes about 3 cups

Place the grapefruit peels in a saucepan, and cover them with water. Bring to a boil over medium-high heat, then reduce the heat to a simmer. Cook for 20 to 25 minutes, or until the peels are soft. Drain the peels, and remove the bitter white pith with a paring knife, leaving just the skin. Slice the peel into thin strips.

In a heavy saucepan, bring the syrup ingredients to a boil over high heat. Reduce the heat to a simmer, and add the strips of peel. Cook the strips until they become translucent, about 40 to 55 minutes, depending on their thickness.

Remove the strips with a slotted spoon, and drain them. Sprinkle a thick layer of sugar onto a large plate. Spoon the peel strips onto the sugar, and toss them with a fork to coat them evenly. Transfer the strips to a large sheet of waxed paper, and allow them to dry, which takes about 1 to 2 hours.

Serve the peel, or store it, covered, at room temperature. It will keep at least 2 weeks. Pint or half-pint jars packed with candied peel make pretty little holiday gifts.

Mail-Order Sources

*T*he following companies represent only a fraction of the businesses that make and sell products useful in Texas home cooking. The recent explosion of firms in the specialty food market makes it impossible to cover everybody. This list ranges broadly in scope, addressing most needs, but it includes only well-established companies that we've personally found superior.

Sources with Extensive Product Lines

El Paso Chile Company
909 Texas Avenue
El Paso, Texas 79901
915-544-3434
Brochure
American Express, MasterCard, Visa
Chiles, chili fixings, chips, condiments,
salsas, sauces

D.L. Jardine's
Post Office Box 18868
Austin, Texas 78760
800-544-1880; 512-295-4600
Catalog
MasterCard, Visa
Chili fixings, chips, condiments, dressings,
jams and jellies, nuts, salad dressings,
salsas, sauces

K-Paul's Louisiana Mail Order
Post Office Box 23342
New Orleans, Louisiana 70183
800-457-2857; 504-731-3590
Catalog
American Express, MasterCard, Visa
Minimum credit card order, $15
Condiments, cookware, sauces, smoked
meats, spices

Specialized Sources

BARBECUE AND OUTDOOR COOKING EQUIPMENT AND SUPPLIES

Pitt's and Spitt's
14221 Eastex Freeway
Houston, Texas 77032
800-521-2947; 713-987-3474
Brochure
American Express, Discover, MasterCard, Visa

CAKES AND CHEESECAKES

Collin Street Bakery
401 West Seventh
Corsicana, Texas 75110
800-248-3366; 903-872-8111
Brochure
American Express, Discover, MasterCard, Visa

New York, Texas Cheesecake, Inc.
Route 2, Box 220
LaRue/New York, Texas 75770
800-225-6982; 903-675-2281
Catalog
American Express, MasterCard, Visa

CANDIES

Lammes Candies
Post Office Box 1885
Austin, Texas 78767
800-252-1885; 512-835-6794
Brochure
Discover, MasterCard, Visa

Peanut Butter Warehouse Pantry
100 Twentieth Street
Galveston, Texas 77550
800-845-5949; 409-762-6308
Brochure
American Express, MasterCard, Visa
Minimum credit card order, $15

Windmill Candy, Inc.
6310 Genoa, Suite C
Lubbock, Texas 79424
800-955-6501
Brochure
MasterCard, Visa
Minimum credit card order, $10

CHEESE

Mozzarella Company
2944 Elm Street
Dallas, Texas 75226
800-798-2954; 214-741-4072
Brochure
MasterCard, Visa

CHILES

Don Alfonso Brand
Macondo Corporation
Post Office Box 201988
Austin, Texas 78720-1988
800-456-6100; 512-335-2370
Catalog
MasterCard, Visa

Stonewall Chili Pepper Company
Post Office Box 241
Highway 290
Stonewall, Texas 78671
800-232-2995; 512-644-2667
Catalog
MasterCard, Visa
Minimum credit card order, $20

COFFEE AND TEA

La Crème
6211 Denton Drive
Dallas, Texas 75235
214-352-8090
Brochure
MasterCard, Visa
Minimum mail order, 1 pound

CORNMEAL AND FLOUR

Adams Milling Company
Route 6, Box 148A
Napier Field Station
Dolthan, Alabama 36303
205-983-4233
Price list
No credit cards; checks accepted

Arrowhead Mills
Post Office Box 2059
Hereford, Texas 79045
800-749-0730; 806-364-0730
Catalog
MasterCard, Visa
Minimum credit card order, $5

San Antonio River Mill
Post Office Box 18627
San Antonio, Texas 78218-0627
800-627-6455; 210-662-9732
Catalog
American Express, Discover, MasterCard,
Visa

White Lily Foods Company
Post Office Box 871
Knoxville, Tennessee 37901
615-546-5511
Brochure
Prepaid orders only

CRAWFISH

Caddo Creek Crawfish
Post Office Box 8
Frankston, Texas 75763
903-876-4123
Prepaid orders only

FRUITS AND VEGETABLES

Frank Lewis' Alamo Fruit
100 North Tower Road
Alamo, Texas 78516
800-477-4773; 210-787-5971
Catalog
American Express, Discover, MasterCard,
Visa

Love Creek Orchards
Post Office Box 1401
Medina, Texas 78055
210-589-2588
Brochure
Discover, MasterCard, Visa

S. M. Jacobson Citrus
1505 Doherty
Mission, Texas 78572
210-585-1712
Brochure
Prepaid orders only

GIFT BASKETS

Capitol of Texas Provision Company
6701 Burnet Road
Austin, Texas 78757
800-375-2198; 512-451-2198
Brochure
American Express, MasterCard, Visa

JAMS, JELLIES, AND PRESERVES

Das Peach Haus/Fischer and Wieser
Route 3, Box 118
Fredericksburg, Texas 78624-9301
800-369-9257; 210-997-7194
Order form
American Express, MasterCard, Visa

Faye's Texas Naturals
Post Office Box 116
Goliad, Texas 77963
800-231-3293; 512-645-3136
Brochure
No credit cards; checks accepted
Minimum mail order, two jars

New Canaan Farms
Post Office Box 386
Dripping Springs, Texas 78620
800-727-5267
Brochure
MasterCard, Visa

MEAT AND GAME

B3R Country Meats
Post Office Box 374
Childress, Texas 79201
817-937-3668
Brochure
American Express, MasterCard, Visa
Natural beef

The Native Game Company
Post Office Box 1046
Spearfish, South Dakota 57783
800-952-6321; 605-642-2601
Brochure
MasterCard, Visa
$10 surcharge on orders under $75

Southwest Texas Quail Farm
Post Office Box 159
La Pryor, Texas 78872
210-365-4354
Price list
Prepaid orders only

Texas Wild Game Cooperative
Post Office Box 530
Ingram, Texas 78025
800-962-4263
Brochure
MasterCard, Visa

NUTS

The Peanut Hut
Box 314
Highway 6 West
Gorman, Texas 76454
817-734-2776
Catalog
MasterCard, Visa

San Saba Pecan Inc.
2803 West Wallace
San Saba, Texas 76877
800-683-2101; 915-372-5727
Brochure
MasterCard, Visa

SALSAS, SAUCES, AND OTHER CONDIMENTS

Brazos Country Foods
700 South Bryan Street
Bryan, Texas 77803
409-775-1611
Brochure
American Express, MasterCard, Visa

Cafe Serranos Salsas
1608 West Sixth Street, Suite 200
Austin, Texas 78703
800-285-5002; 512-322-9900
Brochure
American Express, MasterCard, Visa

Fredericksburg Herb Farm
Post Office Drawer 9271
Fredericksburg, Texas 78624-0927
800-259-4372; 210-997-8615
Catalog ($2, refundable with first order)
American Express, Discover, MasterCard,
Visa
Minimum credit card order, $15

La Martinique Salad Dressings
Luzianne Blue Plate Foods
640 Magazine Street
New Orleans, Louisiana 70130
800-535-1961; 504-524-6131
Prepaid orders only

McIlhenny Company
Tabasco Country Store
Avery Island, Louisiana 70513
800-634-9599; 318-365-8173
Catalog
American Express, MasterCard, Visa

Ro-Tel Tomatoes and Green Chilies
Knapp-Sherrill Company
Post Office Drawer E
Donna, Texas 78537
210-464-7843
Brochure
MasterCard, Visa

Tastes of the Southwest
Post Office Box 131731
Tyler, Texas 75713
903-597-0546
Catalog
Prepaid orders only

Texafrance
Post Office Box 162462
Austin, Texas 78716
512-339-9412
Brochure
Prepaid orders only

Travis County Farmers' Market
6701 Burnet Road
Austin, Texas 78757
512-454-1002
Brochure
MasterCard, Visa
Minimum credit card order, $25

SMOKED MEAT, FISH, AND POULTRY

Greenberg Smoked Turkeys
Post Office Box 4818
Tyler, Texas 75702
903-595-0725
Brochure
MasterCard, Visa

Guadalupe Smoked Meat Company
1299 Greune Road
Boerne, Texas 78130
800-880-0416; 210-629-6121
Catalog
American Express, Discover, MasterCard, Visa

Kreuz Market
208 South Commerce Street
Lockhart, Texas 78644
512-398-2361
Call for price information
Prepaid orders only

Hans Mueller Sausage
2459 Southwell
Dallas, Texas 75229
800-777-2793; 214-241-2793
Catalog
American Express, MasterCard, Visa

New Braunfels Smokehouse
Post Office Box 31159
New Braunfels, Texas 78131
800-537-6932; 210-625-7316
Catalog
American Express, MasterCard, Visa

Pickwick Catfish Farm
Highway 57
Counce, Tennessee 38326
901-689-3805
Price list
MasterCard, Visa

Pietsch's
Post Office Box 192
Yoakum, Texas 77995
800-456-8204; 800-999-6997; 512-293-3541
Catalog
American Express, Discover, MasterCard, Visa

Ranch House Mesquite-Smoked Meats
303 San Saba Avenue
Menard, Texas 76859
800-749-6329; 915-396-4536
Catalog
American Express, Discover, MasterCard, Visa

Acknowledgments

Cookbooks are much more fun than broths because they can't be spoiled by too many cooks. You just gather a gang and play with food. At least we did.

One of our best times was a four-day barbecue blow out with PJ and Wayne Whitworth. We cooked and ate a good fifteen hours a day, relieving the inevitable stress with an array of medicinal fluids. Lots of people stopped by, then and at other times, to bend their backs—or elbows, at least—with us. Ed Reid brought the cabrito and his bewildered wife, Ellen Bradbury, who had only thought she knew her husband before then. Bob and Lisa Wade told tales tall and sometimes—probably by accident—true. Gayther Gonzales stayed too sober to sing, but Susie's spirit danced anyway. Rob Coffland and Mary Kahlenberg added their good taste to the crowd, and so did Frances and Gene Poteet, Dorothy and Tommy Hicks, Cindy and Jim Turner, Terry Melton, Herbie Mann, Cindy Graves, and Susan Curtis. Finally, by the end of that summer, even John Loehr, the aging pig farmer, hobbled in with the support of the spry Sally Martin to claim a plate and proclaim his point of view.

Many other people shared skills and insights. Most of those who furnished recipe expertise are acknowledged where their contributions appear, but we want to extend special thanks to Mrs. Lyndon B. Johnson, Dick and Susanna Clark, Shirley and Richard Jones, Irene Martínez Garcia, Karen Erxleben Weiner, Lois Gilder, Ruth Bauer, Carol Haugh Brejot, Gloria Bledsoe Goodman, Jason Griffin, Jayne Bridges, Kay Morse, Betty Alters, and Julie Brueggeman. Lula Mae Austin, who probably never needed a recipe in her life, allowed us to peer over her shoulder in the kitchen. Years before, Betty Shannon assisted in a similar way.

W. Park Kerr, Paula Lambert, Nancy Gerlach, Kathy Reeves, Dr. Jimmy Keeton, John Richard, Paula Garcia Jones, and Art Pacheco aided us with product information, and Seva Dubuar was a particularly invaluable and informed advisor about meat. Bruce Shaw, publisher, and Dan Rosenberg, editor, spent hours on the phone counseling us on a range of issues concerning the book. Linda Ziedrich ably oversaw the editing of the manuscript. Diana Clark helped with everything except the writing, providing support, contacts, and ideas that were essential to the project.

Other than Diana and Seva, our most important allies were other authors, notably the ones who penned the Texas cookbooks and other resource works listed in the bibliography. We thank them all, but especially the ones below who gave us permission to use their recipes and words:

Red Caldwell. Ol' Red's Barbecue Sauce from *Pit, Pot, and Skillet.* Copyright © 1990 by Don D. Caldwell.

Heritage Society of Austin. The Driskill's 1886 Room Chocolate Sheet Cake from *Austin Heritage Cook Book.* Copyright © 1982 by the Heritage Society of Austin. Permission granted by Elaine V. Mayo.

International Chili Society. Wick Fowler's Lazy-Way Chili and C.V. Wood's World's Championship Chili. Permission granted by Jim West.

W. Park and Norma Kerr. Kerr Family Masa Biscuits and W. Park Kerr's Chicken-Fried Steak from *The El Paso Chile Company's Texas Border Cookbook.* Copyright © 1992 by W. Park Kerr, Norma Kerr, and Michael McLaughlin. Permission granted by W. Park Kerr.

Ninfa Laurenzo. Ninfa's Green Sauce, Ninfa's Fajitas, Chicken a la Fajitas, and Ninfa's Marinated Onions. Recipes copyright © by the Rio Star Corporation for Ninfa's Mexican Restaurants. Permission granted by Richard P. Holgin.

Rosalea Murphy. Steak Dunigan from *The Pink Adobe Cookbook.* Copyright © 1988 by Rosalea Murphy.

Sam Pendergrast. Sam Pendergrast's Old-Time Texas Restaurant Chili from *Zen Chili: The Real Terlingua and Other Boondoggles,* third edition in progress. Copyright © by Sam Pendergrast (Post Office Box 2431, Abilene, Texas 79601).

Jani Schofield. Hot Pants Chili, Hornadillo Chili, and Mind-Expanding Therapeutic Chili Verde from *Allegani Jani's Cookbook.* Copyright © by Jani Schofield.

John Thorne. Buffalo Breath Chili from *Just Another Bowl of Texas Red.* Copyright © 1985 by John Thorne (Post Office Box 88, Steuben, Maine 04680).

Frank X. Tolbert. Frank Tolbert's Original Bowl of Red from *A Bowl of Red.* Copyright © 1953 by Frank X. Tolbert. Permission granted by the Tolbert family.

Texas Cookbooks

This is far from a complete compilation of Texas cookbooks. We looked at many more in libraries around the state, and almost certainly missed scores of others that never made it to those shelves. This is simply the short list of books that had an impact on ours. If you want to have a look for yourself, the best single collection is at the Barker Texas History Center at the University of Texas in Austin.

We're grateful to each of these authors for their contributions to our thinking, cooking, and eating pleasure. All of them are wonderful dinner companions.

Austin Woman's Club. *Treasure Pots.* Austin: 1940.

Barbour, Judy. *Cowboy Chow.* Bay City, Tex.: 1988.

Benell, Julie. *Julie Benell's Favorite Recipes; Plus Low Fat, Low Cholesterol Recipes.* Dallas: 1966.

Bennack, Nick. *Tastes of Deep South Texas.* Missoula: 1990.

Blue Lake–Deerhaven Cookbook Committee. *A Texas Hill Country Cookbook.* Marble Falls, Tex.: 1976.

Brittin, Phil, and Joseph Daniel. *Texas on the Halfshell.* New York: 1982.

Bueno, David. *Tex-Mex Food: All You Need to Know.* San Antonio: 1978.

Business Woman's Circle of the Presbyterian Auxiliary. *Presbyterian Philathea Cookbook.* Gonzales, Tex.: 1924.

Caldwell, Red. *Pit, Pot, and Skillet.* San Antonio: 1990.

Chitwood, Ida. *Mrs. Ida Chitwood's Choice Recipes, Food Charts and Reducing Methods.* Fort Worth: 1927.

Clark, Morton Gill. *The Wide, Wide World of Texas Cooking.* New York: 1970.

Coleman, Arthur, and Bobbie Coleman. *The Texas Cookbook.* New York: 1949.

Corbitt, Helen. *Helen Corbitt's Cookbook.* Boston: 1957.

———. *Helen Corbitt's Potluck.* Boston: 1962.

Dallas County Home Demonstration Clubs. *Favorite Dallas County Recipes.* Dallas: 1950.

Davenport, Mary, ed. *The Club Woman's Cook Book.* Tyler, Tex.: 1928.

Davis, Emma, and Anna Leigh. *The Texas "Four Hundred" Cookbook: Four Hundred Recipes Tested and Proven to a Point Beyond Failure.* Dallas: 1909.

Dillow, Louise B., and Deenie B. Carver. *Mrs. Blackwell's Heart-of-Texas Cookbook: A Tasty Memoir of the Depression.* San Antonio: 1980.

Diocese of West, Texas, Church of the Annunciation. *Cookbook, 1874–1974.* West, Tex.: 1974.

Dybala, Barbara, and Helen Macik. *Generation to Generation: Czech Foods, Customs, and Traditions, Texas Style.* West, Tex.: 1980.

Eckhardt, Linda West. *The Only Texas Cookbook.* Houston: 1981.

Ex-Students' Association of the University of Texas. *Cook 'em Horns.* Austin: 1981.

Fearing, Dean. *The Mansion on Turtle Creek Cook Book.* New York: 1987.

———. *Southwest Cuisine.* New York: 1990.

The Ladies Association of the First Presbyterian Church, eds. *The First Texas Cookbook.* Houston: 1883; reprint, Austin: 1970.

Gardner, Russell M., and Chris Farkas. *Texas Celebrity Cookbook.* Fort Worth: 1984.

Garza, Lucy. *South Texas Mexican Cookbook.* Austin: 1982.

Gebhardt's Mexican Cookery for American Homes. San Antonio: 1936.

Griffith, Dotty. *Wild About Chili.* New York: 1985.

Guild of the Dallas County Heritage Society. *Through Our Kitchen Door.* Dallas: 1978.

Hein, Peg. *Tastes and Tales from Texas.* Austin: 1984.

Heritage Society of Austin. *Austin Heritage Cook Book.* Austin: 1982.

Higginbotham, Family of Hattie and Rufus. *This Little Higgy Stayed Home.* Dallas: 1989.

———. *This Little Higgy Went to Market.* Dallas: 1966.

Hopkins, Lucille. *Texas Cookbook: Finger Lickin' Fixins.* San Angelo, Tex.: 1969.

Hughes, Mike. *The Broken Arrow Ranch Cookbook.* Austin: 1985.

Imperial Sugar Company. *One Hundred Twenty-five Years Ago.* Sugar Land, Tex.: 1968.

Jetton, Walter, and Arthur Whitman. *Walter Jetton's LBJ Barbecue Cookbook.* New York: 1965.

Junior League of Dallas. *Cook Book.* Dallas: 1935.

———. *The Dallas Junior League Cookbook.* Dallas: 1976.

———. *From Texas Tables.* Dallas: 1961.

————. *South of the Fork*. Dallas: 1987.

Junior League of El Paso. *Seasoned with Sun*. El Paso: 1974.

Junior League of Houston. *Houston Junior League Cookbook*. Houston: 1968.

Junior League of San Antonio. *Flavors*. San Antonio: 1978.

Junior Service League of Longview. *The Bounty of East Texas*. Longview, Tex.: 1977.

Kerr, W. Park, and Norma Kerr. *The El Paso Chile Company's Texas Border Cookbook*. New York: 1992.

Koock, Mary Faulk. *The Texas Cookbook*. Boston: 1965.

Kute Kooking Klub. *K.K.K. Cookbook*. Honey Grove, Tex.: 1894.

Ladies' Aid Society of the Hempstead Baptist Church. *A Bunch of "Daisies" Recipes*. Hempstead, Tex.: 1918.

Miller, Rita, ed. *Fresh from the Garden: Time Honored Recipes from the Readers of* Texas Gardener. Waco, Tex.: 1986.

Morehead, Judith, and Richard Morehead. *The New Texas Wild Game Cookbook*. Austin: 1985.

Peabody, Elizabeth, ed. *State Fair of Texas Prize Winning Recipes*. Dallas: 1987.

Public School Auxiliary of Fredericksburg. *Fredericksburg Home Kitchen Cookbook*. Fredericksburg, Tex.: 1921.

Randall, Jo, and Kit Scott, eds. *Square House Museum Cookbook*. Panhandle, Tex.: 1973.

Ross, Larry. *Nanny's Texas Table: Texas Country Cooking at the Houghton Ranch*. New York: 1987.

San Antonio Junior Forum. *Celebrate San Antonio*. San Antonio: 1986.

Seale, Bobby. *Barbeque'n with Bobby*. Berkeley: 1988.

Smith, Edna M., ed. *Aggies, Moms, and Apple Pie*. College Station, Tex.: 1987.

Smith, Joanne. *Texas Highways Cookbook*. Austin: 1986.

Sophienburg Museum. *Guten Appetit*. New Braunfels, Tex.: 1978.

Thornton, Mrs. Paul F., and Mrs. I. V. Davis. *Our Home Cook Book*. Austin: 1891.

Trahey, Jane, ed. *A Taste of Texas*. New York: 1949.

Wagner, Candy, and Sandra Marquez. *Cooking Texas Style*. Austin: 1983.

Other Books of Interest

These authors and books also contributed in a special way to this project. Some we have quoted and cited in other chapters, and some we have used with nary a mention before now. Again, we're grateful for the help.

Adams, Ramon. *Come an' Get It: The Story of the Old Cowboy Cook*. Norman, Okla.: 1952.

Albright, Dawn. *Texas Festivals*. El Campo, Tex.: 1991.

Anderson, John Q., ed. *Tales of Frontier Texas*. Dallas: 1966.

Andrews, Jean. *Peppers: The Domesticated Capsicums*. Austin: 1984.

Ash, John, and Sid Goldstein. *American Game Cooking*. Reading, Mass.: 1991.

Bainbridge, John. *The Super-Americans*. New York: 1961.

Beranbaum, Rose Levy. *The Cake Bible*. New York: 1988.

Bolt, Richard. *Forty Years Behind the Lid*. Guthrie, Okla.: 1974.

Bridges, Bill. *The Great American Chili Book*. New York: 1981.

Carbia, Maria A. de. *Mexico Through My Kitchen Window*. Boston: 1961.

Cartwright, Gary. "I Am The Greatest Cook in the World." *Texas Monthly* (February 1983).

Chariton, Wallace O. *This Dog'll Hunt*. Plano, Tex.: 1989.

Cooper, Joe E. *With or Without Beans*. Dallas: 1952.

Dale, E. E. "Cowboy Cookery." *The Hereford Journal*, Kansas City, January 1, 1946.

De León, Arnoldo. *The Tejano Community, 1836–1900*. Albuquerque, N. Mex.: 1982.

DeWitt, Dave, and Nancy Gerlach. *The Whole Chile Pepper Book*. Boston: 1990.

Dobie, J. Frank. *The Longhorns*. New York: 1941.

Duval, John C. *The Adventures of Big-Foot Wallace*. 1870; reprint, Lincoln, Nebr.: 1966.

———. *Early Times in Texas*. 1892; reprint, Austin, 1967.

Egerton, John. *Southern Food*. New York: 1987.

Everett, Donald E. *San Antonio: The Flavor of Its Past, 1845–1898*. San Antonio: 1975.

Fehrenbach, T. R. *Lone Star: A History of Texas and the Texans*. New York: 1968.

Flach, Vera. *A Yankee in German-America*. San Antonio: 1973.

Flemmons, Jerry. *Plowboys, Cowboys and Slanted Pigs*. Fort Worth: 1984.

Fox, Margaret S., and John Bear. *Morning Food*. Berkeley: 1990.

Frantz, Joe B. *Texas: A Bicentennial History*. New York: 1976.

Fuermann, George. *Reluctant Empire*. New York: 1957.

Glenn, Camille. *The Heritage of Southern Cooking*. New York: 1986.

Graham, Don. *Cowboys and Cadillacs: How Hollywood Looks at Texas*. Austin: 1983.

Greer, Anne Lindsay. *Cuisine of the American Southwest*. New York: 1983.

Hammett, Samuel Adams. *Piney Woods Tavern; Or, Sam Slick in Texas*. Philadelphia: 1858.

Hanle, Zack. "The New Texas Cuisine—Chef Stephan Pyles." *Bon Appétit* (September 1986).

Herbst, Sharon Tyler. *Food Lover's Companion*. New York: 1990.

Hogan, William Ransom. *The Texas Republic: A Social and Economic History*. Norman, Okla.: 1946.

Johnson, Ronald. *The American Table: A Celebration of the Glories of American Regional Cooking*. New York: 1984.

Jones, Evan. *American Food: The Gastronomic Story*. New York: 1981.

Landry, Wanda A. *Boardin' in the Thicket*. Denton, Tex.: 1990.

Lang, George. *Lang's Compendium of Culinary Nonsense and Trivia*. New York: 1980.

Linck, Ernestine Sewell, and Joyce Gibson Roach. *Eats: A Folk History of Texas Food*. Fort Worth: 1989.

McGee, Harold. *On Food and Cooking: The Science and Lore of the Kitchen*. New York: 1984.

Miller, Joni. *True Grits: The Southern Foods Mail-Order Catalog*. New York: 1990.

Miller, Mark. *Coyote Cafe*. Berkeley: 1989.

National Council of Negro Women. *The Black Family Reunion Cookbook*. Memphis: 1991.

Neal, Bill. *Biscuits, Spoonbread, and Sweet Potato Pie*. New York: 1990.

Pryor, Cactus. *Inside Texas*. Bryan, Tex.: 1982.

Ramsdell, Charles. *San Antonio*. Austin: 1959.

Rombauer, Irma S., and Marion Rombauer Becker. *Joy of Cooking*. New York: 1964.

Root, Waverley. *Food*. New York: 1980.

Root, Waverley, and Richard de Rochemont. *Eating in America: A History*. New York: 1976.

Schlesinger, Chris, and John Willoughby. *The Thrill of the Grill*. New York: 1990.

Sitton, Thad, and Lincoln King, eds. *The Loblolly Book II*. Austin: 1986.

Smith, H. Allen. *The Great Chili Confrontation*. New York: 1969.

Sweet, Alexander Edwin, and John Armory Knox. *On a Mexican Mustang Through Texas*. London: 1905.

———. *Sketches from "Texas Siftings."* New York: 1882.

Thorne, John. *Just Another Bowl of Texas Red*. Boston: 1985.

Tolbert, Frank X. *A Bowl of Red*. Dallas: 1953.

———. *Tolbert's Texas*. New York: 1983.

Velazquez de Leon, Josefina. *Mexican Cook Book*. 1956.

Villas, James. *American Taste*. New York: 1982.

West, Richard. "Our Lady of the Taco." *Texas Monthly* (January 1986).

White, Owen P. *Lead and Likker*. New York: 1926.

Wicker, Tom. "Lyndon 'n' Ludwig." *Texas Monthly* (January 1986).

People and Places Index

McMahan, Jacqueline
Higuera, 158
McMurray, Fred, 124
McMurtry, Larry, 32, 147
Madisonville Sidewalk
Cattlemen's Association
Celebration,
Madisonville, 176
Madisonville, Texas, 176
Mallard, Mary Jane, 314
Mann, Herbie, 557
Mann, Pamela, 430
Manor, Texas, 371
Mansion on Turtle Creek,
Dallas, 42, 211, 232,
350
Manual for Army Cooks, 128
Marfa, Texas, 60, 61
Martin, Sally, 557
Martin's Kum-Bak. *See*
Dirty's
Martínez, Mike, 66
Martínez, Narciso, 63
Mason, John Landis, 414
Mattox, Jim, 485
Maverick, Albert and Jane
Maury, 456
Maverick, Maury, 456, 546
Maverick, Samuel Augustus,
456
Maxim's, Houston, 152, 247
Medina, Texas, 517
Melton, Terry, 557
Menard, Texas, 424
Meredith, Don, 450, 451
Meridian, Texas, 52
Messina Hof Wine Cellars,
Bryan, 397, 503
Mexican and Mexican-
American influences, 3,
24, 34, 59–104, 191,
216, 222, 276, 280,
371, 422, 423, 426,
455, 488, 490, 491,
494, 498
Midland, Texas, 121, 176
Miller, Mark, 264
Mission, Texas, 545
Mi Tierra, San Antonio, 61
Morales, "Pancho," 490

Morehead, Judith and
Richard, 232, 250
Morgan, Emily, 61–2
Morning Food (Fox and
Bear), 436
Morse, Kay, 557
Moyer, Harriet, 87
Moyer Champagne
Company, New
Braunfels, 503
Mozzarella Company,
Dallas, 544, 552
*Mrs. Blackwell's Heart of
Texas Cookbook* (Dillow
and Carver), 144
*Mrs. Ida Chitwood's Choice
Recipes, Food Charts
and Reducing Methods*
(Chitwood), 465
Mumme, Henry and Ida
Fischer, 532
Munson, T. V., 503
Murphy, Rosalea, 169, 558

Nacogdoches, Texas, 52
National Championship
Barbecue Cookoff,
Meridian, 52
National Polka Festival,
Ennis, 446
Native Game Company,
554
Neiman Marcus, 75, 291,
305, 451, 540
New Braunfels, Texas, 73,
179
New Braunfels Smokehouse,
New Braunfels, 555
New Canaan Farms,
Dripping Springs, 258,
468, 554
*New Texas Wild Game Cook-
book, The* (Moreheads),
232, 250
New York, Texas, 538
New York, Texas
Cheesecake, Inc., New
York, 538, 552

Nimitz, Charles and
Chester, 501
Ninfa's, Houston, 74, 88,
460, 558
Noom, Peter, 181
Noonday, Texas, 354
North Dallas Forty (Gent),
471

O

O'Daniel, "Pappy," 28, 323,
328
Odessa, Texas, 63, 121, 176
O'Grady, Alice, 2
Old Borunda Cafe, Marfa,
60, 61, 65
*On a Mexican Mustang
through Texas* (Sweet
and Knox), 22, 190, 267
Only Texas Cookbook; The
(Eckhardt), 324
Orange, Texas, 269
Original Mexican
Restaurant, San
Antonio, 94
Our Home Cook Book
(Thornton and Davis),
212, 483
Oysterfest, Fulton, 269

P

Pace, David, 78
Pace Foods, San Antonio, 78
Pacheco, Art, 557
Paris, Texas, 1, 340, 370
Peabody, Elizabeth, 399
Peanut Butter Warehouse
Pantry, Galveston, 552
Peanut Hut, Gorman, 555
Pearl Beer, 501–2
Pecan Festival and Venison
Chili Cook-off, San
Saba, 438
Pecos, Texas, 308, 309
Pecos Bill, 225
Pendergrast, Sam, 125, 127,
558
Perot, Ross, 527

Recipe Index